Inside

CIA's

Private

World

Inside CIA's

Private World

Declassified Articles from the Agency's

Internal Journal, 1955–1992

Selected and edited by
H. Bradford Westerfield

Yale University Press

New Haven and London

A version of chapter 17 appeared under the title "Improving Intelligence Analysis: Some Insights on Data, Concepts, and Management in the Intelligence Community," by Richards J. Heuer, Jr., in *The Bureaucrat,* Winter 1979–80.

A version of chapter 26 appeared under the title "Squaring the Circle: Dealing with Intelligence Policy Breakdown," by L. Keith Gardiner, in *Intelligence and National Security,* vol. 6, no. 1, published by Frank Cass & Co. Ltd, 1991.

Published with assistance from the foundation established in memory of Philip Hamilton McMillan of the Class of 1894, Yale College.

Designed by James J. Johnson and set in Caledonia Roman by The Composing Room of Michigan, Inc., Grand Rapids, Michigan.
Printed in the United States of America by Edwards Brothers, Inc., Ann Arbor, Michigan.

Library of Congress Cataloging-in-Publication Data

Inside CIA's private world : declassified articles from the agency's internal journal, 1955–1992 / edited by H. Bradford Westerfield.
    p.   cm.
  Includes bibliographical references and index.
  ISBN 0-300-06026-2

  1. Intelligence service—United States. 2. United States. Central Intelligence Agency. I. Westerfield, H. Bradford, 1928– .
JK468.I6I56 1995
327.12'0973—dc20   94-49082

A catalogue record for this book is available from the British Library.

The paper in this book meets the guidelines for permanence and durability of the Committee on Production Guidelines for Book Longevity of the Council on Library Resources.

10 9 8 7 6 5 4 3 2 1

Contents

Introduction   vii

I. **Imagery Intelligence Collection (Imint)**
  1. DC Power and Cooling Towers   3
  2. The Unidentifieds   8

II. **Overt Human Intelligence Collection (Overt Humint)**
  3. The Interpreter as an Agent   29
  4. Obstacle Course for Attachés   35
  5. Soviet Reality Sans Potemkin   41

III. **Clandestine Human Intelligence Collection (Clandestine Humint)**
  6. Techniques of Domestic Intelligence Collection   51
  7. The Elicitation Interview   63
  8. Psychology of Treason   70
  9. The Practice of a Prophet   83
  10. Catch-as-Catch-Can Operations   93

IV. **Humint and Its Consumers**
  11. The Collector's Role in Evaluation   99
  12. The Reports Officer: Issues of Quality   108
  13. Clandestinity and Current Intelligence   118
  14. The Not-So-Secret War, or How State-CIA Squabbling Hurts U.S. Intelligence   185
  15. Assessing DDO Human Source Reporting   194

V. The Analysis Function

16. What Basic Intelligence Seeks to Do — 207
17. Do You Really Need More Information? — 218
18. Basic Psychology for Intelligence Analysts — 232
19. The Hazards of Single-Outcome Forecasting — 238
20. Bayes' Theorem for Intelligence Analysis — 255
21. The Sino-Soviet Border Dispute: A Comparison of the Conventional and Bayesian Methods for Intelligence Warning — 264
22. FACTIONS and Policon: New Ways to Analyze Politics — 274
23. Scientific and Technical Intelligence Analysis — 293
24. Economic Intelligence in CIA — 305

VI. Analysis and Its Consumers

25. Cognitive Biases: Problems in Hindsight Analysis — 333
26. Dealing with Intelligence-Policy Disconnects — 344
27. New Links Between Intelligence and Policy — 357
28. UNCTAD V: Intelligence Support at a Major International Economic Conference — 366

VII. Counterespionage

29. Nosenko: Five Paths to Judgment — 379
30. Defense Against Communist Interrogation Organizations — 415
31. Observations on the Double Agent — 437
32. The Case of Major X — 450

APPENDIX A: The Next Most Valuable Articles — 479

APPENDIX B: Abbreviations, Acronyms, and Definitions — 481

Acknowledgments — 483

Index — 485

Introduction

Early in the Cold War, the U.S. Central Intelligence Agency launched an internal journal called *Studies in Intelligence,* to promote a sense of professional identity, enhance proficiency, and build knowledge of intelligence cumulatively from the shared insights of its practitioners. For nearly four decades these articles have been classified "Secret" and sequestered from the American public. Now, as part of its post–Cold War "openness" campaign, CIA is declassifying and releasing most of this material. In this time of reappraisal of American international relations after the fall of the Soviet Union, it is fitting that the public be able to inspect what CIA's insiders have been telling each other all these years about the kinds of work they do.

CIA took shape in the late 1940s and early 1950s, principally through a gradual reassembly of parts of America's World War II Office of Strategic Services.[1] OSS itself had been created near the onset of the war to supplement the traditional military intelligence services of the Army and Navy and the internal security work of the Federal Bureau of Investigation. During and after the war the military intelligence services continued to operate worldwide, and the FBI's jurisdiction included Latin America. OSS achieved prominence in operations that assisted underground resistance movements in German-occupied Europe and some Japanese-occupied parts of China and Southeast Asia; and quietly it distinguished itself in intelligence research and analysis performed in the United States and abroad. But in the brief period between

---

1. The most comprehensive history of CIA is John Ranelagh, *The Agency: The Rise and Decline of the CIA,* rev. ed. (New York: Simon & Schuster, 1987), but its treatment of the years after 1977 is less reliable. An even more perceptive history, in my judgment, is Thomas Powers, *The Man Who Kept the Secrets: Richard Helms and the CIA* (New York: Knopf, 1979), but it ends in 1977. The subsequent years can be pieced together, unsatisfactorily, from Stansfield Turner, *Secrecy and Democracy: The CIA in Transition* (Boston: Houghton Mifflin, 1985); Bob Woodward, *Veil: The Secret Wars of the CIA, 1981–1987* (New York: Simon & Schuster, 1987); and Mark Perry, *Eclipse: The Last Days of the CIA* (New York: Morrow, 1992). The best survey of intelligence activities is Abram N. Shulsky and Gary J. Schmitt, *Silent Warfare: Understanding the World of Intelligence,* rev. ed. (Washington, D.C.: Brassey's [U.S.], 1993). The best critiques, from the right and the moderate left, respectively, are Angelo Codevilla, *Informing Statecraft: Intelligence for a New Century* (New York: Free Press, 1992); and Loch K. Johnson, *America's Secret Power: The CIA in a Democratic Society* (New York: Oxford University Press, 1989).

the end of World War II and the onset of the Cold War, these capabilities were judged dispensable (partly as potential infringements upon the jurisdictions of the FBI and the military services—and supposedly even upon civil liberties); so OSS was dismantled along with nearly all the other new wartime agencies. Yet pieces survived, scattered here and there, long enough to be available for reassembly and expansion as the Cold War gathered momentum.

An initial preoccupation was prevention of surprise attack. A lesson drawn from the debacle of Pearl Harbor was that information in the hands of the separate armed services and the State Department needed to be drawn together and analyzed centrally and timely forecasts made that would be useful to policymakers. Thus at first what was commonly supposed to be central about the new Central Intelligence Agency was its role in this analysis and forecasting function (and not just about surprise attack). The legacy of OSS had included some analysis work. The emerging Cold War, however, also reactivated the remnants of the other OSS capabilities: covert action, paramilitary operations, espionage, and counterespionage. And as these gradually came together at CIA in a directorate called Plans (later, more frankly, Operations), they came to overshadow CIA's Directorate for Intelligence (meaning "analysis"). Partly as a consequence, the latter was less effective than its precursors had hoped in integrating national security forecasts from the key departments and agencies in ways useful for policymakers.

Except inside the United States, where counterespionage remained mostly under FBI control, CIA's responsibilities for operations and analyses did become worldwide, including Latin America, ceded to CIA by the FBI. But for most parts of the world, the U.S. military services and the State Department also had responsibilities bearing autonomously on intelligence. And control of the collection tool that was usually much more important than espionage, namely, signals intelligence (*sigint:* making and breaking codes, as well as performing and preventing electronic interceptions), was mostly consolidated away from the individual military services not into CIA but into a majestically independent and hypersecretive new National Security Agency (NSA). (CIA works on some sigint technologies and operations.)

CIA thus emerged from the boom of the first Cold War decade not central with regard to intelligence collection, not very central with regard to intelligence analysis (depending on the particular subjects and CIA's "chemistry" with particular administrations), but truly central with regard to covert action (secret propaganda and political intrigue) and paramilitary operations. Indeed, in these functions CIA became hyperactive around the world for about a decade before the American public (as distinct from the publics of many other countries) began to be widely conscious of it. And that eventual awareness came mainly from CIA's failure to overthrow Fidel Castro at the Bay of Pigs in 1961. Not until another decade later were CIA's covert actions and covert wars generally treated as "scandalous" in U.S. public discourse—chiefly as part of the anti-interventionist reaction to the Vietnam War. Then, by 1975, it was small comfort for CIA to be able to plead, in essence, that even if its operators might have been too gung-ho about Vietnam, at least its analysts had been presciently defeatist.

Actually, had the extent of CIA covert action been revealed in its "glory days"—1948–68—the American public probably would not have been scandalized. Those were years of national consensus for the Cold War against communists at home and abroad, a passion leading even to McCarthyism. From the later perspective of the mid-1970s, however, the revelations seemed horror stories, and the "firestorm" of criticism (as CIA insiders called it) soon reduced the agency's covert action and paramilitary capabilities to embers. Earlier, in the 1960s, whatever espionage CIA had managed to mount against the Soviet bloc had been hobbled by the extreme suspiciousness of its own counterintelligence chief, James Angleton. In reaction, in 1974, a virtual internal coup at CIA removed him and soon diminished CIA counterintelligence. Whether CIA espionage would then rebound was unclear. For a while, at least, without much covert action, counterintelligence, or espionage the agency might have to depend on making its *analysis* function more useful in the eyes of policymakers. Some analysts began to crusade for that, but traditionalists damned it as "politicization."[2]

There was one other foothold for CIA: in *techint* (technical means of collection). To be sure, this niche was small in sigint, but large in what was coming to be called *imint* (imagery intelligence). Imint had formerly been known as *photo-reconnaissance,* and its role had expanded enormously since the early 1960s. Photo-reconnaissance, mostly from planes, became *overhead reconnaissance,* mostly from satellites, and *photos* became *imagery,* collected by radar and infra-red and other sensor devices. CIA itself had had the good fortune to be the pioneer in this area during the early 1950s, when the Air Force would not bother itself to develop powered gliders for reconnaissance—the "toys" that became, under CIA auspices, the famous U-2 spy planes—and the special skills to interpret the photos. When in the 1960s the U-2s were

2. About all the Cold War years, for convenient, knowledgeable approximations of the changing relative expenditures for covert action and paramilitary operations, vis-à-vis other expenditures in CIA and in the intelligence agencies as a group (omitting *tactical* intelligence of the military services), see Johnson, *America's Secret Power,* p. 103; and Bruce D. Berkowitz and Allan E. Goodman, *Strategic Intelligence for American National Security* (Princeton, N.J.: Princeton University Press, 1989), pp. 143–144.

largely superseded by other, less delicate spy planes, and especially by satellites, the Air Force took back the imint lead; but CIA managed to hold on to a significant role in technology and imagery interpretation.

Satellite reconnaissance became a rather widely understood function, though the Air Force component, the National Reconnaissance Office (NRO), was ritualistically not named. By contrast, the signals intelligence agency, the National Security Agency, was openly acknowledged, but NSA's independence from CIA helped keep its functions essentially immune from public notice or understanding.

Thus, in summary, both before and after the mid-1970s firestorm, CIA was a "full-service intelligence agency." It had a share (major or at least substantial) in analysis, collection in the forms of techint (here, chiefly, imint) and *humint* (human-source intelligence, espionage), counterintelligence (here counter-espionage), covert action, and paramilitary capabilities. But the firestorm and anti-Angletonism drastically shifted the internal balance at CIA. Covert action and paramilitary operations—and, to a degree, counterespionage—had been primary, with imint burgeoning and analysis and espionage precarious. Afterward, by the late 1970s, imint was still growing, but counterespionage, covert action, and paramilitary operations were being diminished, and there was more room for analysis and espionage.

However, Ronald Reagan won the 1980 election, in a pendulum swing that was in part a reaction against the way the Vietnam debacle had led to supposedly excessive noninterventionism during and after the firestorm years, when the United States had "lost" Iran and Nicaragua and endured setbacks elsewhere. Reagan appointed to head CIA his friend William Casey, himself an elderly throwback to the swashbuckling "glory days"—all the way, indeed, to the OSS aid to underground resistance forces in German-occupied Europe. Casey was now determined (and won appropriations) to rebuild almost all parts of CIA, a new boom for the agency. Thus analysis and espionage were expanded, and imint rocketed onward, now linked somewhat more with sigint as dual-use satellites improved. Most startling, as the stories began to leak out, were Casey's efforts to stir the embers of covert action and paramilitary operations into the blaze of covert wars in (at least) Afghanistan, Nicaragua, Angola, and Cambodia. In addition, coups d'état were fomented unsuccessfully in Libya, and massive multilateral covert assistance was given to Saddam Hussein's Iraq in its war of reciprocal attrition against the Ayatollah Khomeini's Iran, as well as substantial nonlethal aid to the Polish underground against Russia and communism. Most of the Reagan-Casey interventions became open secrets within a few years, and only the one in Nicaragua encountered much objection from the American public—the United States was "standing tall" once more. But inside CIA, many survivors of the 1970s firestorm were worried that the congressional pendulum would later swing again the other way. Casey avoided much of this internal dissent. Sometimes he used Defense Department units, and he rehired on temporary contracts many CIA operations veterans who had been let go. They were often attached now to jerry-built structures outside of (or on the fringes of) CIA itself, notably Oliver North's enterprises based in the National Security Council staff at the White House. But this edifice proved precarious for aiding the Contra opposition to the government of Nicaragua. The structure finally crashed in the Iran-Contra scandal, autumn 1986 to summer 1987. Coincidentally, Casey died, and soon the Cold War ended. The covert action and paramilitary part of the intelligence boom in the 1980s was over.

CIA could have reverted to the situation in the late 1970s: imint strong, analysis and espionage advancing, covert action and (especially) paramilitary operations declining steeply, and counterespionage barely creeping forward. Even Casey had been slow to rebuild counterespionage; it might have gotten in the way of his activism. Actually, however, the end of the Cold War and the end of the George Bush administration have brought a more general retrenchment at CIA and the other intelligence agencies. Priorities are uncertain, and the extent of cutbacks is ultimately unsettled. There exists a wider range of options than heretofore—and greater openness in discussing them.

This period of reevaluation is an appropriate time for the public to learn how CIA officers among themselves have for many years been discussing their functions and professional aspirations. "Professional" is the right word, at least for many of the insiders. They have not been consumed by the subcultural rivalries that I have set forth as a context for this book. Many of them want to believe that intelligence (comprising its various branches) is a distinct and worthy profession, of service to the public, with techniques and ethics that can be studied and taught in ways analogous to those of the more established professions. Thus, CIA does applied research on intelligence methodology, and it has acculturation programs, official historians, a library covering many centuries of intelligence activities, visiting scholars and scholarly conferences, a journal and monographs, and other professional apparatus. In house, a lot of this dates back to the agency's early days. Since 1975 CIA's own think tank for the intelligence profession, the Center for the Study of Intelligence, has promoted these functions.

There is also an external dimension, fostered since the firestorm—an effort to encourage outside professionals and institutions to study, teach, and write about intelligence. Of course, this is partly a matter of public relations. But in the eyes of many insiders—and numerous intelligence veterans outside who find time to devote to this work—there is much more to it. Goals include enhancing proficiency of service, promoting professional recognition, and surviving firestorms, the ends of wars, and even a new wave of isolationism.

Professions can outlast agencies.

One embodiment of the would-be professionalism is CIA's in-house journal, *Studies in Intelligence*. From the selection of articles presented here, readers can now improve their own judgments about how much has been accomplished at CIA toward professionalization.

World War II drew young Sherman Kent to OSS from Yale University, where he was teaching European history. Except for the brief postwar interval, Kent's service with OSS and CIA lasted most of his professional life, until the middle of the Vietnam War (1967). Usually he was near the top—and for sixteen years he was at the top—of the most prestigious analysis unit, the Board of National Estimates, responsible during the peak Cold War years for coordinating principal analytical judgments on national security affairs across key governmental departments and agencies. Yet the attributes of a professional historian remained part of Kent's personal identity at CIA, prefiguring his aspiration to achieve for the intelligence world the pride and respect that come from building a truly professional identity, or a set of professional identities.

The head of the agency during the 1950s, Allen Dulles, had a similar desire. For example, he and Kent each wrote books about intelligence, Kent's reaching further than Dulles's in an effort to generate theories about it. (Dulles popularized the homey expression "tradecraft" to denote the principles and practices of secret operations.) A somewhat ruminative habit of mind contributed in part to Dulles's moving the agency several miles away from Washington to a rustic new "campus." That attitude also allowed Kent's analysts (more royalist than the king) to idealize their own objectivity and want to keep policymakers at arm's length.

In 1955 Kent was a proud leader, and he heralded to his colleagues how far they had come since 1941, when "intelligence was to us . . . nothing in itself, [lacking] the attributes of a profession or a discipline or a calling. Today things are quite different":

> We are at strength . . . we are not novices . . . we have . . . a career to be followed to retirement. . . . We have orderly and standardized ways of doing things. . . . We have developed a host of new and powerful overt and covert techniques. . . . Most important of all, we have within us a feeling of common enterprise, and a good sense of mission.
>
> With these assets, material and experiential, intelligence is more than an occupation, more than a livelihood, more than just another phase of government work. Intelligence has become, in our own recent memory, an exacting,

highly skilled profession, and an honorable one. Before you can enter this profession you must prove yourself possessed of native talent and you must bring to it some fairly rigorous pre-training. Our profession like older ones has its own rigid entrance requirements and, like others, offers areas of general competence and areas of very intense specialization. People work at it until they are numb, because they love it, because it is their life, and because the rewards are the rewards of professional accomplishment.

Yet something was still lacking, and Kent the scholar was troubled:

> Intelligence today is not merely a profession, but like most professions it has taken on the aspects of a discipline: it has developed a recognized methodology; it has developed a vocabulary; it has developed a body of theory and doctrine; it has elaborate and refined techniques. It now has a large professional following. What it lacks is a literature. From my point of view this is a matter of greatest importance.
>
> As long as this discipline lacks a literature, its method, its vocabulary, its body of doctrine, and even its fundamental theory run the risk of never reaching full maturity. . . . What I am talking about is a literature dedicated to the analysis of our many-sided calling, and produced by its most knowledgeable devotees. The sort of literature I am talking about is of the nature of house organ literature, but much more. You might call it the institutional mind and memory of our discipline . . . the permanent recording of our new ideas and experiences . . . [steps] towards making our findings cumulative [so that the] point is reached where an individual mind, capable of using the stock, can in a day encompass the accumulated wisdom of man-decades of reflection and action. . . . Where would . . . chemistry or medicine or economics . . . be if no one aspired to the honor of publishing an original thought or concept or discovery in the trade journals of his profession? . . . In our calling we do not do enough . . . systematic professional literature.[3]

Kent wanted this literature to deal with (1) "first principles," that is, "missions" and "methods"; (2) rigorous definition of terms—otherwise "we are likely to find ourselves talking at cross purposes"; (3) "an elevated debate," leading to synthesis, which would become "an intellectual platform upon which [new debates] can start . . . solid . . . durable enough . . . so that no one need get back in the bushes and earth to examine its foundations. This is the way . . . the Western World has achieved . . . knowledge"; and (4) "such things as new techniques and methods, the history of significant intelligence problems and accomplishments, the nature of intelligence services of other countries, and so on."

---

3. This quotation and those that follow are from Kent's article, "The Need for an Intelligence Literature," *Studies in Intelligence,* vol. 1, no. 1 (Sept. 1955), pp. 1–8.

Orchestration for implementation of Kent's clarion call was well arranged in advance. A group of senior CIA officers convened by the director of training had begun the work twelve months before. Kent's appeal itself emerged as the lead article in the first issue of *Studies in Intelligence,* in September 1955, with the editors affirming in their first sentence, "We agree with the basic ideas set forth by Mr. Kent. . . . *Studies in Intelligence* is a first modest attempt to meet these needs."[4]

Kent's goals were so lofty that to call this in-house professional journal a "modest attempt" was candid, not just decorous. But the usefulness of *Studies in Intelligence* has continued ever since 1955, and the journal has been published quarterly with scarcely a break. Each issue contains several articles, each averaging about a dozen pages, and often a number of book reviews. In rare instances, articles of around one hundred pages have appeared, sometimes in appendixes to the regular issues. In order to encourage relatively forthright expression and participation—which Kent wanted, within the confines of this unconventional profession—each issue of the journal was classified "Secret" as a whole and included a considerable number of articles individually classified "Secret," sometimes with additional restriction on access by foreigners or by persons under temporary contract to the agency. Other articles have carried the lower classification "Confidential." Many have been individually unrestricted, but these articles, bound together with the "Confidential" and "Secret" items, have also been inaccessible to outsiders. Further, the tables of contents and indexes have also been marked "Secret."

Outsiders knowledgeable about intelligence matters had long been aware of the existence of *Studies in Intelligence.* In the early 1990s, CIA came to see that releasing most of this material would further its institutional interests. Indeed, the agency wanted these disclosures to have the special visibility that could come from publication by a major university press. Discussions were initiated with Yale.

But outsiders would obviously need to be on guard against even an appearance of being co-opted by CIA. The problem was not about the articles that actually would be released—sometimes with deletions (*redactions,* in officialese) of names, words, phrases, or whole sentences—but about those that would be reviewed but withheld. Would CIA be manipulating the process? All the many hundreds of pages of released articles, whether or not they were published by Yale, were to be deposited at the National Archives. People would be able to compare them there and verify the judgments that the Press would

---

4. Editors of *Studies in Intelligence,* "The Current Program for an Intelligence Literature," *Studies in Intelligence,* vol. 1, no. 1 (Sept. 1955), pp. 14, 12.

be making in selecting its set. And the size and location of the redacted passages would be conspicuous, allowing free speculation. But what about the articles that CIA was going to withhold? Would selective releasing give an appearance of co-optation or disinformation by the agency?

This was also a concern of people at CIA who were promoting the idea of publication. Their pride in the new image of openness and in the intrinsic quality of their colleagues' writings would be damaged if the declassification and review process were to appear rigged.

It was at this point that I became seriously involved in the project. I was vetted for temporary access to the "Secret" level of classified materials and then spent three full days leafing through all the original volumes of the journal (1955–92). For the ongoing declassification, my goal was to request priority review for every article that met my standards for possible Yale publication but had not already been declassified and released to Yale. (The standards are explained below.)

My list eventually contained sixty-four articles, and CIA proceeded within a short period to declassify forty-seven of them (sometimes, of course, with redactions). Many of these articles are now in this book, among the "Confidential" and "Secret" items, together with articles released without my special request.

The other seventeen of my sixty-four were withheld. By the time the review process is complete, a good many more articles will no doubt be withheld, articles that did not particularly interest me for this project. There were about half a dozen that did but which I did not waste time requesting because they were bound to be withheld and probably should be; they dealt with exceptionally sensitive sources and methods.

Nonetheless, among the original sixty-four I deliberately sought the release of many articles that would test CIA's openness, and generally I felt rewarded by the outcomes. For example, I got the particular article I most wanted (William R. Johnson, "Clandestinity and Current Intelligence"), even though this item boldly defies important conventional notions about CIA that exist both inside and outside the agency, and even though another department of government also had to give it clearance. Much that I requested even about sources and methods of human-source intelligence (humint) and counter-espionage was approved. Also released were some items about imagery intelligence (imint). However, the journal had never had an article on signals intelligence (sigint); the National Security Agency controls most sigint and is hypersecretive about it. Students of intelligence need to keep this crucial omission in mind when they read almost anything published about the hush-hush world.

Regrettably, what CIA has also omitted from its journal over the years is covert political action—the U.S. intelligence function that is unique to CIA and has received the most outside attention. Yet *Studies in Intelligence* almost ignores it, except for occasional reviews of outsiders' books about it. And the one or two articles that did appear and that I requested were refused declassification. The point is not that *Studies in Intelligence* is an organ only of the Directorate for Intelligence, that is, of CIA's analysts; their work is indeed overrepresented, I would say. But the journal also includes material from the Directorate for Science and Technology (on imint) and from the Directorate for Operations (on espionage and counterespionage). There is even a fair amount from the Directorate for Operations on paramilitary activity, though the best such item was understandably withheld. What is lacking is coverage of covert political action, including covert propaganda. It cannot be that practitioners of this tradecraft lack writing skills, for they have produced a stream of memoirs. But they do not write about the subject for *Studies in Intelligence,* or at least their articles have not been accepted for publication there.

That said, I perceive no other way in which *Studies in Intelligence,* in its original in-house form, has systematically distorted CIA's role. Nor has the declassification process distorted what the journal in fact contains. (Probably the degree of reliance upon "liaison" collaborations with foreign intelligence services is underplayed, but it does crop up often.) So the burden for any residual distortions rests squarely on me. The reader needs to know what my selection criteria were.

First, I have excluded from this volume pieces on intelligence history before the Cold War. This criterion shuts out a large part of *Studies in Intelligence.* Many of the authors clearly have vocational interest in the history of their profession, and they concentrated on the eighteenth and early nineteenth centuries in Europe and America and on the world wars. For quality alone, many of these articles merit publication. Generally they had not been individually classified "Confidential" or "Secret"; only the author's name (clue to affiliation) was sometimes concealed. Excluding these articles from the present volume is simply a matter of contemporary relevance. From the Cold War period, two or three historical items have not been included because they are too long, although they would qualify admirably on all other grounds.

Second, with one or two exceptions, items published accessibly elsewhere are excluded, no matter how high their quality. Most of these articles had been reprinted in *Studies in Intelligence* to bring to its inside readers' attention significant items from outside that they might not otherwise have noticed. Much the same can be said for the journal's book review policy. I had hoped that reviews by insiders would enlighten knowledgeable outsiders, even at this late date. But such reviews turned out to be now of little interest; so reviews are also excluded from this collection.

Third, the controlling criterion for the volume as a whole is which articles (pertinent of the era since the end of World War II) contribute the most additional knowledge about intelligence activities to what has by this time become fairly widely available through nonfiction publications. Thus, knowledgeable outsiders interested in the subject could learn new things from what CIA is now disclosing, not just a rehearsal of familiar ideas. I myself have learned from each of the articles in this book, though I do not, of course, always fully agree with them.

What, then, are my own qualifications to verify the essential fairness of the declassification and to apply the stated selection criteria? The first is personal autonomy: I have never been, even briefly, in the employ of any part of the intelligence community of this or any other country—neither directly nor, so far as I know, indirectly. Nor have I knowingly engaged in intelligence activities of any kind for governmental or nongovernmental organizations.

Does that "inexperience," on the other hand, raise questions about my competence in these matters? I am a political scientist; my field, since the end of World War II, has been the conduct and control of American foreign relations. In my writing and teaching I have always, more than most scholars, recognized the importance of the covert dimension and have incorporated what I could find in the public domain. When the massive exposés occurred in the 1970s and CIA and its veterans started to offer insights and information, I began to network carefully and to read very thoroughly about intelligence since World War II. I have developed confidence that I know what is in the public domain in nonfiction and what nearly all the debates are, including those about classification and declassification. That is why I feel that I am competent to make the selections for this volume, using the stipulated criteria, even though I have no hands-on intelligence experience.

In the end, I chose thirty-two articles. They are reprinted almost exactly as released. All CIA redactions have been left conspicuous, though not always exactly proportional to the original ones. The only silent editorial corrections concern obvious misspellings and lapses of grammar and punctuation. In a few instances an emendation has been made to clarify an obscure phrase; such changes are shown in brackets. Consistency in citation form throughout the book and in other matters of form within each article has been sought.

How should the articles be arranged? What thread might tie them together? I concluded that it would be appropriate to adapt the structuring principle now standard in the United States, that an "intelligence cycle" links the practitioners' activities. Raw information gets collected, analyzed, and disseminated—made available to be acted upon. Complications arise from the different ways information can be collected; the ways (commonly called "processing") it can be made more usable by the analysts or, bypassing them, usable by those who make or execute policy; the secretiveness of all this activity and the ways ("counterintelligence") one guards it from adversary interference; the ways one may take advantage of the secretiveness for the further implementation of certain policies ("covert action"); and the ways that these diverse functions are supervised and coordinated.

Thus in its simplest form the conventional cycle is collection → processing → analysis → dissemination → policy making → implementation → outcomes → more collection. Here the cycle goes around again. Counterintelligence is in the cycle everywhere; it is not a distinct stage of it. And policy making and implementation may often not pay attention to the intelligence activities or products at all; but if they do, one way can be through covert action, so that is where this function would, perhaps sporadically, fit into the cycle.

The adaptation I make in this cycle to accommodate the articles actually selected and to maintain logic and readability is to present (1) articles relating to imint collection; (2 and 3) articles on humint, differentiated on the basis of how open the collection activity is—"overt humint" and "clandestine humint"; (4) articles on the complex interface between humint and "consumers" (usually analysts who incorporate humint in reaching conclusions for transmission to policymakers, but often also some policymakers who prefer to size up the humint directly themselves); (5) articles on some aspect of the analysis function; (6) articles on the relation between that function and its consumers, ordinarily the policymakers and the implementers but now increasingly Congress and the wider public; and (7) articles on counterintelligence (here counterespionage), which suffuses the whole cycle.

These seven rubrics merit further explication. (Comments on individual articles are reserved for the headnotes that precede each article.) The first set of articles, on imint, presents no special problems. Remember that essentially imint's partner, sigint, is NSA's province.

In the second set—on humint, or espionage—there may be some question about my differentiating "overt humint" and "clandestine humint." One can choose to define only the clandestine as humint at all; collection activities by human beings in the open would then be assigned to a separate category, open-source collection (*osint*), like subscriptions to periodicals. One article deals in part with open-source documents collection, but I have located it with the analysis function because such bookworming is in practice institutionally associated mainly with analysis. Physically active reconnoitering by people seems to me to fit better with humint, even when in the open. The articles in this set show how it is done by interpreters for international delegations, by military attachés on excursions, and by foreign residents shopping local markets to learn about the local economy. These people are not just filling a diplomatic pouch with local newspapers. They are keeping their eyes and ears open while remaining in full view of any onlookers.

Such vigilance shades into the clandestine through "elicitation," a concept discussed in the third set of articles, on clandestine humint. Here the tasking (assignment of mission) is more focused and deliberate, the initial concealment of intelligence-collection intentions much more careful. One elicits information, draws it out as in ordinary conversation, from a source who does not realize that this is happening. Elicitation may be a collection end in itself or part of a process of spotting, assessing, and recruiting somewhat more witting continuous sources, even agents or intermediaries. Those so recruited can be foreigners or one's fellow citizens who have access to particular foreigners. The set of articles on clandestine humint starts with that. Other articles dissect elicitation strategies and tactics, probe the motivations of people willing to switch over from an adversary's side, exemplify some American ingenuity in agent-running, and provide a lengthy case study of Russian agent-running in Sweden. There is much to be learned, I believe, from each of these articles—even in a field as written about as espionage methods.

In the fourth set, on humint and its consumers, two articles deal with collectors doing a lot of (preliminary) analysis themselves, much more than the conventional literature acknowledges. The next three articles boldly explore from different perspectives what consumer-mindedness has been doing to American humint. Has the distinctive secretiveness of espionage been withering away at CIA? Is the reason a *modus vivendi* symbiosis, in which the State Department's Foreign Service lets CIA's Clandestine Service preoccupy itself with routine reporting (quasi-journalism), which the Foreign Service itself could, should, but would rather not do? Do CIA's analysts encourage this convenient flow, being skeptical of waiting for the rarities, truly clandestine revelations? Does everyone rely on liaison with foreign services to provide most of the really clandestine humint that gets into the system at all? And does everyone rely most of all on techint (at CIA this is chiefly imint, unless sigint relations with NSA happen to be good at a particular time)? Could one not characterize most U.S. humint-collection operations officers abroad as mere "intelligence attachés"? These are heady, critical questions, cutting deeply into the U.S. intelligence community and especially relevant now. It is fashionable to say that CIA ought to emphasize American humint (truly clandestine humint?), in the amorphous post–Cold War world, as being cost-effective and to CIA's comparative advantage vis-à-vis other U.S. intelligence agencies. Think again about the practicability of such dreams after you have read these three articles.

Studies in Intelligence, I have noted, gives disproportionate space to articles about analysis (perhaps the disproportion arises in the range of articles initially submitted). I have reached for the ones that seemed to have the most to add now to the outside literature. That means, for example, that there is no article on strategic surprise. Though often very good indeed, such articles and books have reached a saturation point. Instead, the fifth set, on analysis, begins with a thoughtful account of how and why CIA builds the files of its own reference facilities, what it calls "basic intelligence." This article, mentioned before, gives attention to open-source documents collection, along with much else that lacks glamour but deserves to be recognized as probably indispensable to analysis. How large, in fact, need such data banks be? A companion article is entitled "Do You Really Need More Information?" Together, they follow neatly upon the preceding three articles, which question whether American espionage has been turning itself into daily journalism (at best, investigative journalism) to help fill these and other governmental library files and classified dailies.

Next in this set is a veteran analyst's shrewd rendition of the bureaucratic survival lore of his part of CIA, followed by a compact statement of a principal theme of those who have been trying to change much of that ethos since the late 1970s. The next three articles are rather novel for CIA, in that they urge that analyses be based on frontier social science. Old-timers at CIA are unlikely to find the appeals persuasive. But those being newly recruited out of American Ph.D. programs may well bring this social-science orientation into the agency (for better or worse). The set ends with two insightful expositions of the special problems that arise for analysis work in the fields of science and technology and of economics. The latter has particular relevance today, and it is unsettling to the intelligence community.

The would-be reformers of CIA analysis usually want to enhance its usefulness to the policymakers and the implementers, perhaps also to Congress and the wider public. Traditionalists fear this "politicization," but they are accused, in rebuttal, of in-house institutional conformism. This debate boiled into the open in the 1991 Senate confirmation hearings on Robert Gates as head of CIA. But the media did not understand what was going on, largely because Gates would not venture to acknowledge that he had been a leader of those who feared politicization less than insular conformism. Bush's reelection defeat deprived Gates of his chance to try to manage both fronts, which remain volatile. The sixth set of articles, on analyst and consumer relations, deals first with how cognitive biases distort perceptions of analysts' usefulness, then with those relations as a whole, and then with recent efforts at amelioration. The last in this set is an article I was particularly pleased to have declassified. It is a detailed case study of analysts and humint operatives as back-up for U.S. negotiators at the very scene of an ongoing international economic conference. The episode took place in 1979, and there are many redactions. This is nevertheless a remarkable prefiguring of the real world of post–Cold War intelligence.

Counterintelligence (understood to include preventive security measures) belongs everywhere in an intelligence world, though how much and in what forms are hotly disputed. Unfortunately, *Studies in Intelligence* does not contribute much that is still new to that general debate. Four articles, however, add valuable particulars to the mosaic of what outsiders have come to know about counterespionage.

The star item in this seventh set of articles is about Yuriy Nosenko and James Angleton. Of the thousands of pages written about this cataclysm in CIA counterintelligence, these thirty pages are the best I know. Until and unless credible accounts emerge from the former Soviet Union, this version of the case seems likely to stand.

Three methods articles conclude the volume. The first is a remarkably detailed manual for American case officers and their agents on how to resist interrogation if caught. It bears some comparison with Nosenko's resistance to American pressures. Also it fits with a 1961 article that demonstrates fully (as disclosures in the 1970s finally indicated; hence that article's exclusion here) that CIA was eagerly studying the use of "truth drugs" in interrogation.[5] The second article is an insightful overview of double agents, and the last is a memoir and case study by a CIA veteran who early in his career found himself being what would at least loosely be called a double agent.

Besides the thirty-two articles included in this book, there are another twenty-five of such high quality that they came very close to being selected. Some readers may wish to seek them out through the National Archives. These articles are listed in appendix A, annotated wherever the title is not self-explanatory. (They include two on the ethics of humint, a question that *Studies in Intelligence* addresses periodically.) Also, CIA itself is publishing an index to every article ever published in *Studies in Intelligence* that either was initially unclassified or was later declassified during the review process of recent years.

Can *Studies in Intelligence* survive the publicity that will attend the declassification and unrestricted publication of these articles? Even if current issues of the quarterly remain classified, as is the plan, prospective authors will have to ponder some possibility of early release and may guard their words more carefully. Note, however, that authors' names are sometimes redacted, or a pen name may have been used originally and remains on the article as released. Thus CIA says that several of the authors' names given in this volume are the

---

5. George Bimmerle, "'Truth' Drugs in Interrogation," *Studies in Intelligence*, vol. 5, no. 2 (Spring 1961), pp. A1–A9.

original pen names, and I cannot always be sure which ones. For future releases, assurances of anonymity upon the author's request might be helpful. The grounds would not be limited to institutional reasons of personnel security. In contrast, some authors might welcome a wholly open journal, like some of the high-quality publications of the American armed forces.[6] CIA's present compromise is to publish two editions of *Studies in Intelligence*. One is the standard in-house quarterly, combining classified and unclassified articles; the other is an annual volume, available to anyone, containing the unclassified articles from the past year.

This compromise seems to me sensible, though it does not—indeed, cannot, with the precedent of declassification—do away with a possibly chilling impact upon some authors. What if their initially classified writings were released some time in the future, even though not so soon as in the annual volume? In the long run, I think it best to minimize the chill—best for the interested public and for CIA and its internal communications. I suggest that declassification review be regularly delayed for at least ten years, perhaps even longer. Otherwise, *Studies in Intelligence* might cease to be significantly different from good outside journals like the *International Journal of Intelligence and Counterintelligence* and *Intelligence and National Security*. The public would never get, even years later, the on-the-job, authentic insights of practitioners writing mainly for each other in a forum of mutual education about their mysterious calling. These special qualities are worth waiting quite a while for. Note that a ten-year rule would have excluded only one-quarter of this book.

Each outside journal depends heavily on articles submitted by veterans of the intelligence community. Even in retirement, they have to submit their writings for CIA's security review, but perhaps their perspective has widened. Nevertheless, a special kind of authenticity comes from writing about job-related matters to one's co-workers and from being currently engaged in them. That is what *Studies in Intelligence* has had for its readers. I like to think that this volume, therefore, has it too. Care should be taken to maintain that distinctive quality for future generations and thereby cautiously help Sherman Kent's initial call for intelligence professionalism to resonate outside CIA as well as within.

6. See *Airpower Journal*, *Parameters: U.S. Army War College Quarterly*, and *Proceedings: United States Naval Institute*.

I.

Imagery Intelligence Collection (Imint)

1.

An imagery intelligence (imint) expert here uses a case study to show how his very valuable specialty typically requires not just arduous, costly, high-tech "picture-taking" but also an elaborate fusion with other means of intelligence collection and analysis.

DC Power and Cooling Towers

HENRY RUBENSTEIN

In October, 1962, the tensions of the Cuban missile crisis were increasing with each U-2 photograph and with each fresh bit of intelligence from Cuba. At the same time, the last big series of the 65 Soviet nuclear weapons tests which had started on 1 August 1962 was being conducted on and over the mountains of Semipalatinsk and the ice of Novaya Zemlya. Nikita Sergeyevich Khrushchev's moves were under intense scrutiny. We knew the number of ICBMs available to him. Compared to U.S. capabilities, his were wanting. Consequently the CIA position was that he was bluffing.

There was, however, little doubt that the USSR had thermonuclear (TN) warheads. These dated back to the Soviet nuclear detonation on 12 August 1953, the Soviets' fourth, of a device designated JOE 4 by the U.S. Although Soviet propaganda built up this accomplishment as implying a great military threat, the Russians had no TN warhead suitable for ICBM delivery until at least 1957–58, and that probably was deployed no earlier than 1960. By the end of the tests on Christmas Day, 1962, there was ample evidence that a number of well-designed families of Soviet TN devices and weapons were available to the Soviets. Early in 1963 they signed the Test Ban Treaty, and their testing program went underground. The big question became, "What of the future?"

The Requirement

Two key materials upon which a TN weapon program is based are tritium and lithium. We had quite a bit of qualitative information on Soviet lithium technology including its isotope, lithium-6, but almost none on tritium, a hydrogen isotope usually produced by exposing lithium-6 to neutrons in a nuclear reactor. We needed quantitative information on Soviet production, raw mate-

Henry Rubenstein, "DC Power and Cooling Towers," *Studies in Intelligence*, vol. 16, no. 3 (Fall 1972), pp. 81–86. Originally classified "Secret."

rials, and patterns of use as well as future applications and trends. This also meant pinning down the laboratories, plants, processes, personalities, and organizations involved. Of special importance was the amount of electric power and other utilities available to the production plants we thought might be involved.

Hunt for the Lithium Plants

A great deal of good analysis had been done with respect to the Soviet lithium problem long before the author's arrival on the scene, and there was a general consensus that the isotope separation process the Soviets were using was similar to the one which the U.S. Atomic Energy Commission had set up at the Y-12 plant at Oak Ridge, Tennessee. That process consists of using direct current to make a liquid mercury alloy (called an amalgam) with lithium metal enriched in the lithium-isotope. The amalgam is then brought in contact with a water solution of lithium hydroxide having a natural isotopic ratio of 12.5 parts lithium-7 to one part lithium-6. The lithium-6, having a greater affinity for the amalgam, gradually replaces the lithium-7. As a result, a more highly enriched lithium in a number of forms can then be obtained by treating the mixture with water. The process has one characteristic which it shares with other isotope separations—the amount of heat it emits is approximately equal to the electric power input. Each plant under study had a large supply of direct current and of steam, and except for Nizhnyaya Tura, a ventilation system suitable for handling large amounts of mercury safely by Soviet standards. U-2 photography helped to provide us with two candidate production-scale plants for lithium isotope separation by the amalgam process. The first was in the remotely situated Area 1 of the Nizhnyaya Tura Atomic Energy (AE) Complex near Sverdlovsk, in the Urals. The other was in the AE Complex along the northeastern outskirts of Novosibirsk in Siberia. The Novosibirsk plant was directly along the main line of the Trans-Siberian Railroad.

By the middle of 1963 Jack Lundin, Bob Vasey and I had quite a few new questions seeking answers. Jack had succeeded in getting the classification of some of the U-2 photographs downgraded, and descended upon John G[o]ogin and some of the other Union Carbide people at the Y-12 plant. After a long but stimulating session, including a tour of the amalgam plant, then on standby status, we had a much better feel for the lithium amalgam process.

Both Area 1 at Nizhnyaya Tura and the Novosibirsk plant are part of AE nuclear complexes which are functionally and organizationally correct for lithium-6 separation plants. Moreover, the necessary administrative and technical support is present, and operation in an AE complex permits use of existing security facilities as well as the health, safety, and other functions peculiar to AE operations.

Area 1 has two connected buildings which could adequately contain an isotope separation process and a supporting chemical or ore processing operation. The west building because of the height of its probable bay area would contain the isotope separation process. We noted a strong resemblance between this building (22) and a U.S. electromagnetic separation building at Y-12. Since several articles pertinent to electromagnetic separation of lithium had been published by the Soviets, it was considered quite possible that the Soviets used this expensive process in the early 1950s to prepare small amounts of lithium for use in development of nuclear devices.

We estimated that electric power available at Area 1 was limited to 2 and 3 MW, judging by the relatively small size of a probable rectifier building situated between the 50- to 100-MW capacity substation and building 22. Since 2 to 3 MW would be sufficient to support a production of only modest size, we concluded that an additional 16-MW DC of motor generator capacity might be obtained from within the lower sections of building 22. A 40-MW cooling tower which was available was more than adequate to dissipate the byproduct (heat) from decomposition of the amalgam. The tower's location, however—a quarter of a mile from building 22—was not consistent with good plant layout, although it could have been used. Moreover, we had never been able to detect the steaming which normally comes from operating cooling towers. Nevertheless, there was cooling water available for pumping from the Tura River 1 to 1¼ nautical miles from the site, or from the Nizhhe-Turinskiy Pond within 3 nautical miles. According to John G[o]ogin, water from a nearby lake is often used at Y-12 for cooling without steaming towers. The general lack of steam and vapor from the postulated process buildings also continued to bother us.

The ventilation system appeared to be very diversified—a factor we had considered inconsistent if the facility was actually planned for the amalgam process we believed existed at Novosibirsk. Once again, however, the visit to Oak Ridge paid off by reminding us that perfectly satisfactory ventilation can be obtained by blowing the air contaminated by mercury vapor out through a hole in one end of the building while clean air is drawn in through an opening in the other end wall. In summary, therefore, we concluded that Area 1 of Nizhnyaya Tura was quite possibly an amalgam process plant rated at 16- to 18-MW DC, where production-scale operations might have started between 1951 and 1955.

We believed that a portion of the Novosibirsk AE Complex between the uranium metal plant and thermal power plant contained the separation facility. U-2 coverage, supplemented by collateral photography, enabled us to conclude that this was probably a lithium isotope separation facility. It appeared to fulfill the requirement that power input should approximately equal the heat rejected: 42 Mwe (Megawatts electric) of AC and DC electricity plus 25 Mwt (Megawatts thermal) of hot steam, balanced against two 35 Mwt cooling towers. This was supported by the large amount of energy available per square foot of roof space (about 0.5 kw/ft^2) in buildings 15 and 16, which was of the same magnitude as that in Soviet gaseous diffusion plants. Production was believed to have started between August 1957 and April 1959, with about 31 megawatts of DC power.

Although the Novosibirsk facility is almost classic in pattern, we have yet to confirm its function. We have kept our eyes open for other locations possibly associated with lithium production. One such possibility is a uranium gaseous diffusion building belonging to the AE program, which would meet the requirements of organization, security and personnel. Adequate ventilation, power and many cooling towers are available.

The Analysis

Converting our megawatts of direct current power to kilograms of weapon-grade lithium-6 was quite a task. It was possible only with support from the Office of Reports and Research (later the Office of Economic Research) on the supply of mercury, and of lithium minerals and concentrates available to the Soviets domestically and from Communist China. The evidence showed that the Chinese had supplied half of the Soviet requirements, and it indicated that without such Chinese assistance or some new sources, the Soviet lithium-6 program was limited by available ore supplies. In light of this conclusion, and some use patterns we observed, we estimated that there was only a 15 percent diversion of concentrates from TN weapons.

Important assistance was provided by AFTAC and by Y-12 so that we could make logical deductions about the percentage of lithium-6 available to the Soviets that could be considered of weapon grade. This varied with time as shown by debris analysis and by the mention in collateral reports of highly enriched samples with lithium-6 contents. These mentioned samples of 91.7 percent being used in physics, and 92.5 percent in chemical experiments; as available for sale in the form of metal and chemicals at 95 percent; and in a piece of analytical apparatus at 99.8 percent. In August 1960 a sample was bought from the Soviets which assayed 92.16 percent. This also contained mercury in a quantity that could only be explained by contact with that metal during exchange processing.

John Jennings of SOVMAT (now FORMAT) helped us to set up and operate a sampling program to keep watch for items in the Soviet economy that would be likely to contain lithium amalgam process tailings. In June of 1964, he turned up several packing cases of a Soviet diuretic medicine called "Urodan," labelled as having been manufactured on 11 February 1964. This variety of medicine had been chosen with the assistance of the Agency Medical Staff as being likely to contain lithium. Analysis indicated 3.08 percent lithium-6 (or a depletion of 58.5 percent from the normal content of 7.42 percent), which matched Y-12's suggestions fairly well. We concluded that this tailings assay was the most probable value to have been used throughout the Soviet program.

It was necessary to use some somewhat unorthodox techniques in order to get a true grasp of the large range of much of our basic data. This resulted in carrying three separate calculations, the probable value, and the probable maximum and minimum values. The final results of our analyses were published with a spread of plus or minus 62.5 percent, which was an order of magnitude higher than most engineers like to see or report on. Nevertheless, these results have had some utility for making estimates of the number of TN weapons available to the USSR.

Tritium

Tritium, which is vital to advanced and compact nuclear weapons, has continued to be an enigma, although AFTAC has been able to detect its use in the weapons program by the Soviets. Soviet scientific writings on matters related to the subject of tritium production technology have been traceable to U.S. experience or practice. U-2 photography has not provided us with direct answers on processing techniques and production quantities. Except for very small quantities that can be made by strong isotopic neutron sources or in accelerators, production of tritium requires a nuclear reactor. The Soviet reactors possessing sufficient reactivity to handle any tritium production, and which also were available (prior to 1954) at the right time to have contributed to the Soviet program, are the TVR heavy water reactor in Moscow, the IR isotope reactor suspected to be at Kyshtym, and the plutonium production reactors at Kyshtym. The TVR could have yielded enough for R&D only starting in 1949 or early 1950. The IR at Kyshtym could have contributed about 20 grams and the production reactors at that site could have contributed about 2100 more grams if operated for maximum tritium production, which was considered unlikely.

Calculations for tritium production were made by assuming that 10 percent of plutonium-equivalent was diverted to tritium and consequently the result was based on fairly good numbers. Fortunately, this result agreed with the maximum requirement for tritium derived from OSI's estimate of the Soviet nuclear weapon stockpile. Despite our problems in obtaining hard data on tritium, we thus had been on the right track.

2.

Here CIA's most prominent imint specialist, who later wrote the best book about the Cuban missile crisis, *Eyeball to Eyeball* (parts of which had originally appeared in *Studies in Intelligence*), uses relatively nonsensitive cases to alert his readers to the painstaking craft of photo interpretation, emphasizing (as in article 1) how much it depends on multidisciplinary sourcing (including amateurs) and even on serendipity.

The Unidentifieds

DINO A. BRUGIONI

No matter how well-trained and experienced a photographic interpreter may be, there are frequent occasions when he simply cannot identify some object, installation, or activity, and when initial research efforts by collateral support personnel fail to provide an answer. In such cases the target is labeled as an "Unidentified." The problem of identifying the "unidentifieds" is the subject of this article.

Photographic interpretation has become highly complicated since World War II. Only a modest number of military or industrial targets had to be considered in the previous era, and interpretation was based on an equally limited number of "indicators" and "signatures." In the language of photographic interpretation, a feature or pattern of features suggesting the presence or the function of a target or activity is called an indicator, and a unique combination or pattern of indicators which permits positive identification is called a signature. Storage sites for weapons, for instance, may have many indicators in common such as security fences and well-spaced, revetted storage buildings, but a building with a specific type of roof and ventilators may be the signature that confirms identification of chemical warfare storage.

In today's world, the scope of the interpreter's responsibility has expanded to include practically all the land surface of the globe, and the number of indicators and signatures to be remembered is far greater than any one individual can possibly master.

Photographic coverage has increased because few land areas in our day are without some relationship to modern weaponry. Deserts and remote islands are missile, nuclear, and chemical warfare proving grounds. Arctic wastelands

Dino A. Brugioni, "The Unidentifieds," *Studies in Intelligence*, vol. 13, no. 3 (Summer 1969), pp. 1–20. Originally classified "Secret" and "No Foreign Dissem[ination]."

are frontiers for electronics defenses. Farmlands and forests are missile deployment areas. Airfields are constructed in remote areas. Submarines and warships are found in isolated anchorages. Canyons and heavily eroded or strip-mined areas are ideal for rocket, missile, and jet-engine testing, and mountains are tunneled for weapons storage or testing of nuclear devices.

The number of indicators and signatures to be remembered has also greatly increased because of the introduction of new weapons systems in this age of atomic fission, electronics devices, jet engines, and missiles. Our problems in this respect are further complicated by the increased scope of photographic coverage. When scanning photography, an interpreter is not only searching for new targets; he is also concerned with discovering any unusual object, installation, or activity at known complexes which may be related to a new weapons system or which may otherwise attract attention as an item of potential interest to intelligence. Sifting the unusual from the usual, however, becomes a highly complicated task when the interpreter is dealing with a part of the world with which he is unfamiliar. The process of interpretation depends in part on immediate recognition of cultural features peculiar to the locality under consideration. Cultural features are manmade changes to the natural environment such as cultivated areas, houses, roads, industrial establishments, religious structures, and cemeteries. An analyst who was born and raised in rural America immediately recognizes a barn, a silo, or a windmill on an Iowa farmstead. His parameters for Iowa (and the United States in general) are well-established, and he wastes no time on well-known cultural features that have no bearing on his mission. The same analyst, however, might spend hours trying to identify fishnets drying on poles in Thailand because they resemble antenna arrays at certain electronics sites in the west, even though drying fishnets are as common in Thailand as windmills in Iowa. This is simply to state the obvious fact that cultural patterns vary greatly in different parts of the world, and parameters that apply to one culture often do not apply to another. A domed building in a remote area of the western world is at once suspect as a radar site, but a domed building in an area inhabited by Moslems is usually a mosque. Radars are often built on hilltops, but in the Orient a hilltop structure is often a Buddhist shrine.

Through his training and from experience, the photographic interpreter has catalogued in his memory and reference files hundreds of patterns of signatures that relate to specific weapons systems. Many signatures consist of geometric patterns such as circles, triangles, ellipsoids, squares, trapezoids, or cones, and some are combinations of several patterns such as a type of surface-to-air missile site which appears on photography to be a Star of David within a circle.

A large and growing body of literature is available on the theory and technique of pattern recognition, but no study is known to this author dealing with the photographic interpreter's mental processes of categorizing and retrieving pattern information.

Because of the many complexities of photographic interpretation, the profession has become highly specialized. Individuals concentrate on specific weapons systems, activities, and cultural features of limited portions of the earth's surface and become highly trained and experienced experts in limited fields. They are, in turn, supported by equally specialized and experienced collateral research personnel. Now and then, however, even the most experienced interpreter has no choice but to report on some subject, installation, or activity as "unidentified."

Any unidentified image that provides the slightest evidence of being significant from an intelligence standpoint becomes the subject of research in depth. The photograph is circulated for study by a variety of specialists, and the film is subjected to intensive technical analysis by laboratory and photogrammetric technicians. In almost all cases an identification is eventually made. Some turn out to be highly significant. Many others are found to be innocuous and of no interest to intelligence—except that the files gain another "pattern" which may be of help to others in the future.

In many cases, a target long unidentified by the professionals and their supporting personnel is finally identified by a person who has some special knowledge gained from travel, from residence in a foreign country, or perhaps from an interest in some esoteric branch of the arts or sciences. Most of the people making up the intelligence community qualify in some of these respects as amateur interpreters of the "unidentifieds," and any individual who can solve an identification problem is urged to pass the word through appropriate channels. The professional welcomes assistance from any amateur when confronted by an unidentified object.

The rest of this article is devoted to discussions and illustrations of selected cases of unidentified objects or installations which were deemed significant enough to justify study in depth. All of these cases were solved, mostly by persevering research and the application of scientific techniques, but in at least one case the solution came from a person with special knowledge gained from travel. As it happened, identification in these cases resulted in little that was of interest to intelligence. In other instances, however, the same techniques have also resulted in highly significant (and often highly classified) identifications.

When scanning aerial photography, the watchword could well be "expect the unexpected." Atmospherics, soil conditions, mechanical performance phenomena, aberrations, sun angles, winds, time of exposure, image acquisition materials, and other factors often provide information over and above that normally expected in the design characteristics of the system. This phenomenon has been labeled the "serendipity effect" by the Director, NPIC.

Modern transportation and communications have resulted in cultural exchanges leaving unusual imprints even in the remotest parts of the world. Every so often photographic interpreters are surprised by finding something which appears out of place. Recently, while scanning photography of East Germany an interpreter was surprised to see Indian teepees, a covered wagon, and the gate of a western cavalry fort. The photo interpreter rechecked his location, since this was obviously a movie set. Despite the initial disbelief that the East Germans were making western-type films, supporting collateral researchers provided information that the German Film Corporation, an East German government monopoly, does in fact produce western films.

The first aerial photography of Tibet presented many enigmas. None was more baffling than structures that appeared to be guard posts situated on roads or trails at the tops of hills or on mountain passes. These structures were usually flanked by mounds or ridges, and at first it was assumed that these were military strong points with attendant bunkers and protective revetments. A second guess was that the structures were toll collection booths. Neither theory held up when questions were raised as to why the posts were in such remote areas and why they were exposed to the worst of the Himalayan weather.

Research into Tibetan culture eventually paid off in the case of the Himalayan "guard posts," and a ground photograph of one of the structures, shown on Figure 1, was found in a travel book. The posts turned out to be religious shrines, each containing an image of Chenresik, the god who protects travelers. In keeping with local religious practice, a Tibetan traveler approaching a hill or pass appeals for divine protection by picking up a stone in the valley and carrying it to the shrine. There the traveler makes the proper invocation to Chenresik and deposits the stone before the shrine. Over the years large piles of stones have accumulated at the shrines along heavily traveled routes, accounting for the military appearance of the posts on aerial photography.

To a photographic interpreter, circular excavations seen from above are suspect as gun positions. If several excavations form a circular pattern, an antiaircraft role may be indicated. Linear arrays of excavations suggest a ground defense system. In arid parts of the Middle East, however, care must be taken to avoid interpreting a line of excavations as a row of foxholes or gun positions since it may be evidence of a centuries-old yet ingenious system for tapping underground water called a *qanat*. Such a system consists of an underground conduit which brings water from a water-bearing bed or earth stratum (aquifer) in the highlands to the surface at a lower level where the water is used in households and for irrigation. Shafts are in a line at regular intervals, and the conduit is excavated from the bottom of one shaft to the next, the spoil being dumped on the surface around the top of the shaft. Seen on aerial photography, as on Figure 2, a series of parallel *qanats* resembles a defense-in-depth series of

Figure 1. This shrine to Chenresik, god of travelers, resembles a military strongpoint on overhead photography.

fortifications. The inset on Figure 2 shows a ground view of the spoil around the tops of a line of *qanat* shafts.

Identifying the function of an installation during initial stages of construction is often difficult. Clearings, ground scarring, excavations, and foundations seldom provide enough indicators. The signature enabling identification is often slow in emerging, and in some cases a known signature does not develop, even though familiar indicators may be present. Periodic coverage of the target, perseverance, and attention to detail often provide an answer.

Cuba has been and is searched continually for new installations, and special vigil is maintained to detect the construction of electronics installations which could monitor missile activity at Cape Kennedy or military activity in the United States. A large, circular installation observed under construction in Cuba in 1964 attracted immediate and continuing interest because a circular scar usually connotes the construction of a direction finder. Reported initially as an "unidentified," the progress of its construction was followed closely.

Figure 2. These long lines of excavations seen in Iran could be defense positions in depth, but in parts of the Middle East they are evidence of underground water conduit systems known as *qanats*.

Figure 3A. The circular configuration of the unidentified installation in Cuba suggested that an electronics installation was under construction.

Figure 3B. Subsequent coverage revealed that the installation is a cattle feeding station.

Suspicion that it would become an electronics installation was heightened when holes were dug (for antenna masts?) at regular intervals within the circle as seen on Figure 3A. This theory received a setback when trees were planted in the holes. Weeks passed into months, when suddenly animals appeared within the enclosure (Figure 3B). The unidentified installation was simply a cattle feeding station.

Modern architecture with its dramatic departures from conventional design often plagues interpreters in their attempt to make identification. A case in point occurred in Cuba when four odd structures were constructed atop the highest elevations of the Sierra Maestra mountains. As seen on an aerial photograph (Figure 4), these structures resembled large parabolic dish antennas. A missile or satellite space tracking role was postulated, but the necessary powerplant or electrical transmission lines for such an installation could not be detected, and this facility was carried as unidentified for more than a year. Suspicion that it was a military installation was heightened when a helicopter was observed at the site. Great was the surprise, therefore, when the Cubans, in a September 1963 issue of the periodical *Bohemia,* unveiled the installation as Castro's Museum of the Revolution (see inset on Figure 4). Because of lack of water at the hilltop location, the roofs of the buildings had been designed by the "revolutionary" architect to trap rainwater and channel it to storage tanks.

An area where physical, cultural, and historical coherence exists presents the fewest difficulties, once the parameters for the area have been established. By the same token, areas where there is extreme physical contrast, where cultures conflict, or where a wide variety of religions is practiced, present greater difficulties, and the search must be especially thorough and intense. China, a vast area undergoing cultural and technological revolution, is unique, as are the problems it presents to interpreters.

In the immediate environs of Peking and in several other Chinese cities, large circular areas, each containing a tall tower, began to appear in the early 1960s. This was of considerable concern to intelligence because it could mean that the Chinese were deploying a sophisticated microwave communications system. On one aerial photograph, however, a white circular "glob" was discerned near the tower, as shown on Figure 5. Photographic enhancement techniques, detailed analysis, and a ground photograph (see inset, Figure 5) from a newly acquired Chinese book, *Peking Under Construction,* revealed the facilities to be parachute towers.

Photographic interpreters in the Washington area have an advantage over those in the field because a large variety of libraries, both governmental and private, are available for research purposes. Also, a large number of foreign service personnel, experts on countless facts about foreign lands, are available for consultation and often provide the solution for unidentified problems. For

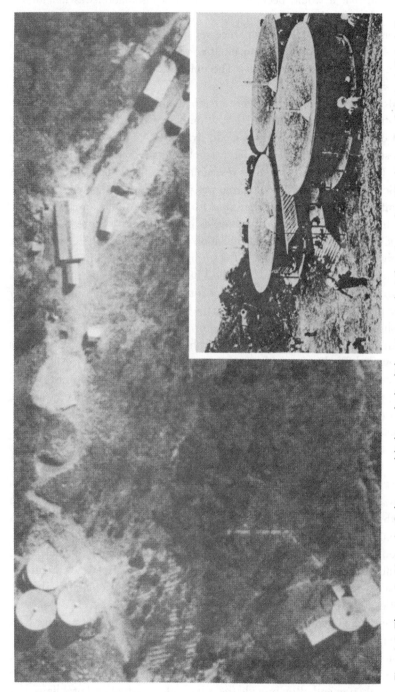

Figure 4. These structures in Cuba resembled parabolic dish antennas, but they turned out to be roofs of Castro's Revolution Museum, shown in the inset.

Figure 5. This unidentified tower in a circle could have been a Chinese electronics facility, but detailed analysis supported by a picture (inset) from a Chinese publication led to identification as a parachute tower.

Figure 6. The triangles seen on this photograph of a Chinese island puzzled interpreters but were quickly identified by a long-time resident in the Far East as fishnets drying in the sun, as shown in the inset.

instance, one such officer who had lived in China solved the problem of identifying the triangular patterns (see Figure 6) seen throughout an island off the southern coast of China. The long-time resident of the Orient easily recognized the triangles as fishnets drying in the sun.

Whenever new activity is observed at a deactivated military installation, the normal surmise is that the installation is being restored for a military role. In the early 1960s, construction of buildings was observed at four abandoned airfields in the vicinity of Canton, China. These buildings, which appeared to be for storage purposes, were constructed on the runways, as shown on Figure 7. A detailed search revealed no military activity. Nevertheless, the airfields were kept under close surveillance, and research in open source materials at various repositories was maintained. Eventually, a book published in China and entitled *Peoples Communes* provided the answer. The supposed storage buildings were hogpens, and the installations were hog communes.

The world of the average Asian ends at the horizon. Except for an occasional short trip or a rare pilgrimage, his interests are centered in the village or town where he lives. Life follows a routine of stereotyped activities, mostly concerned with his quest for a livelihood. These activities are reflected in cultural patterns visible on aerial photography, and there is a similarity in the patterns of villages, towns, and cultivated areas throughout large portions of the earth's surface. When a new pattern emerges, it is studied in depth. Such was the case when white, paddle-shaped pads were observed in a small area south of the Plain of Jars in Laos. This pattern, shown on Figure 8, has not been seen anywhere else. The function of these pads has not yet been confirmed, but people who have been in the area have suggested they are pits of wet lime used by natives to catch birds. Allegedly, "Judas" Birds are placed in cages on or near the pads to call their wild friends. Birds landing on the pads become mired in the mortar-like lime, and a native then appears to catch the trapped birds. Another version is that nets are suspended over the white pads. birds are enticed with food and "Judas" birds to come under the net. At appropriate times, the nets are dropped and the birds captured.

The use of military equipment for civilian purposes at times complicates identification. For instance, Quonset huts were originally associated exclusively with the military, but since World War II the huts have been put to a wide variety of civilian uses, both at home and abroad. Many are still used for military purposes, however, and the criteria for determining which are used by the military are based on factors such as location, number, arrangement, and upkeep of the huts and the existence of security measures. One such Quonset installation in the USSR, shown on Figure 9, met all the criteria for identification of a military installation. The huts are laid out neatly in military fashion and are surrounded by "security" fencing. Research, however, revealed it to be a poultry farm.

Figure 7. Construction on the runways of four inactive airfields near Canton, China, was suspect as renewed military activity, but pictures from a Chinese publication (see insets) showed the airfields are now "hog communes."

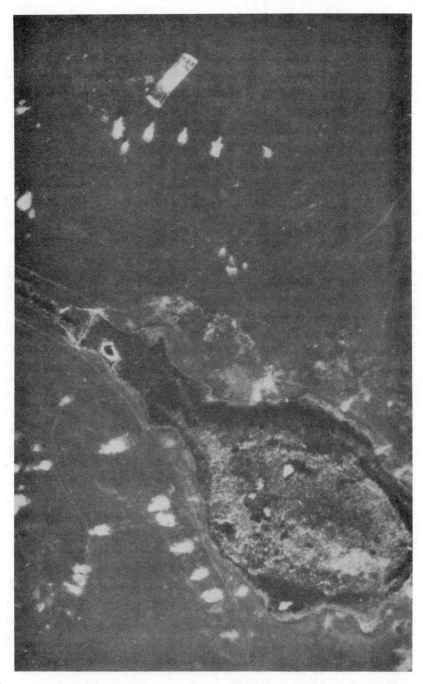

Figure 8. These white pads observed near the Plain of Jars in Laos are unique, and identification is still in doubt. There is reason to believe that they are pits of wet lime used to trap wild birds.

Figure 9. This fence-secured area consists of Quonset huts arranged in a military fashion, but it is actually a poultry farm.

Tents are like Quonset huts in that they are firmly associated with the military but are also used for a variety of nonmilitary purposes. This creates a problem in the Middle East where military tents have been used in recent years in refugee and immigrant camps. Many of the refugee tent camps are laid out in a haphazard fashion, but those built under UN auspices have been planned to insure proper spacing for sanitary and logistical purposes, and they bear a striking resemblance to military tent caps. One such camp [which] without collateral information would probably be identified on photography as a military installation is shown on Figure 10.

The large people's communes in China which combine industry, agriculture, education, and military affairs are relatively easy to identify. The smaller communes in the Communist Far East, however, are a different story. Some 20 small complexes built in North Korea since the Korean War give every appearance of being military installations, such as the one shown on Figure 11. They consist of barracks-like buildings, shops, and vehicle sheds, but other facilities normally found at a military installation such as firing ranges, parade grounds, and training areas are missing. These installations were carried as unidentified until a North Korean book, *Facts About Korea,* provided a photograph of a small North Korean commune. The identification then became positive that their role was agricultural rather than military.

As has been mentioned, the existence of security measures is an indicator of a military installation, and security measures discernible on aerial photography normally are items such as fences, walls, guard posts, and strong points. In certain parts of the world, however, photographic interpreters are presented with the problem of distinguishing between military and civilian security practices. In western China, for instance, most of the farmsteads, villages, and towns are walled for protection from marauders and wild animals, and fenced enclosures for animals are often found on the open plains. Much experience and study are needed by an interpreter before he can distinguish civilian from military security patterns. For a time, certain installations in the loess country

Figure 10. Tents erected in orderly rows are normally associated with a military installation; however, the tent camp shown here is a UN refugee camp in the Middle East.

Figure 11. This small North Korean installation was thought to be associated with the military until research revealed it to be an agricultural commune.

THRESHED GRAIN

Figure 12. Groups of cave dwellings in the loess country of western China present an illusory appearance when seen on overhead photography, as shown on the inset. Whenever a natural vertical slope is unavailable, rectangular excavations are made in flat surfaces, and the cave homes are then dug into the sides of the pits.

of western China presented an interpretation problem because their foundations apparently were being built within walled enclosures. Research eventually revealed that the people of the loess country often live in cave dwellings such as are shown on Figure 12, and overhead photography of groups of such dwellings (see the inset on Figure 12) often presents deceptive or illusory imagery to the viewer.

All the foregoing examples of installations or activities initially reported as unidentified, and hundreds more, have been catalogued by photographic interpretation organizations, and many have been or will be incorporated in photographic interpretation keys dealing either with regions or with specific objects, installations, weapons systems, and activities. Such "keys" are basic manuals used by photographic interpreters and are designed both to fulfill training needs and to serve as quick reference tools. A solved U/I should never pose a problem in the future.

Because of the growing importance and scope of photographic interpretation in the national and international intelligence program, all personnel who serve in overseas posts are urged to photograph where possible and report objects and installations that could be confusing to interpreters of aerial photography. Also, those who scan and review foreign literature are urged to keep the problem of the "unidentifieds" in mind and to call the attention of photographic interpreter organizations to illustrations and articles that might help solve interpretation problems and further reduce the list of unidentifieds.

II.

Overt Human Intelligence Collection (Overt Humint)

3.

It may be obvious and time-honored, as this knowledgeable author says, that language interpreters are used for intelligence collection (and presumably also for some disinformation), yet the literature has neglected this practice. Here is an introduction to the tradecraft.

The Interpreter as an Agent

FRANCIS AGNOR

The rather obvious time-honored practice of using interpreters assigned to international exchange delegations as intelligence agents (or, conversely, of getting intelligence personnel assigned as interpreters) has both advantages and disadvantages. If the interpreter makes the most of his intelligence mission, however, and observes some common-sense rules of behavior, there can be a net advantage both in the direct yield of information from such an assignment and in the improvement of an asset in the person of the interpreter. The advantage in immediate information is likely to be limited; the improvement of personal assets can be considerable.

In discussing these advantages we shall assume that the interpreter can be given adequate intelligence training and briefing (or that the intelligence officer is competent as an interpreter, and not compromised). We shall ignore the technical aspects of the interpreter's art and the occupational diseases, nervous indigestion and undernourishment, contracted in his attempts to gulp food while translating banquet conversations. We shall examine his domestic and foreign assignments separately: the advantages and disadvantages of assignment at home and abroad often coincide, but there are also important differences.

Gains on Home Ground

Let us look first at the domestic assignment, where the interpreter is on his own native soil, attached to a group of foreign visitors or delegates. As the communications link between the visitors and their strange surroundings, he possesses a strong psychological advantage in his available option to confine himself strictly to the business portions of the trip, leaving the visitors to fend

Francis Agnor, "The Interpreter as an Agent," *Studies in Intelligence,* vol. 4, no. 1 (Winter 1960), pp. 21–27. Originally classified "Secret."

for themselves in their spare time. Even if they have their own interpreter along, there are a number of matters—shopping, local customs, the availability of services—in which it would be convenient for them to have his help.

Recognizing their dependence on his cooperation for the smooth progress of their visit, they will usually do their best to establish, if not a cordial friendship, at least a good working relationship. A great deal depends on the interpreter himself, of course, but normal friendly overtures on his part will usually be met at least halfway by the visitors. Just by being relaxed and perhaps willing to do a small extra favor here and there, he can become accepted as an indispensable member of their family group. An excellent way to break down reserve and promote a free exchange of ideas is to invite the group to his home. (It does *not* pay for him to be so obliging that he becomes a valet, and it is advisable to establish this principle early in the game.)

Continued friendly gestures are likely to result in time in the establishment of a genuine rapport, with its attendant benefits. If the interpreter is knowledgeable in the field of the official discussions which he is interpreting, he can clarify in private discussions with the visitors some of the ambiguous or contradictory statements made during the official talks. Without appearing too curious or asking too many questions of intelligence purport (he should be particularly circumspect at the outset of a trip, when his bona fides is subject to greatest suspicion), he will sometimes be able to get definitive statements in private which are lacking in the confusion and interruptions of official discussions. It is here that he may bring to bear his training or natural bent for elicitation, whether for official purposes or for his own education.

At the same time the interpreter himself is the target of numerous questions which reveal both intelligence and personal interests on the part of his charges. Their intelligence questions may indicate gaps in their own service's information, and their personal ones are more broadly useful in showing the preconceived picture of this country that the visitors have brought with them. Although they often realize that their questions betray a lack of sophistication, they are willing to sacrifice dignity to satisfy their burning curiosity. Honest, natural answers, despite the apparent rudeness of some of the questions ("How much do you make?" "How much are you in debt?"), strengthen the interpreter's position and may lead to even more revealing questions. If the visitors are from a controlled society the very opportunity to put certain kinds of questions is a luxury they cannot afford at home. And when one of them is alone with the interpreter he often shows eagerness to ask questions of a kind not brought up in group discussions.

In all these discussions the interpreter is gaining knowledge which no academic training can give him. First, he is given a glimpse of his own country through the warped glass of foreign misconceptions and propaganda. The image will not be fully that which hostile propagandists have sought to fix, but it will show where they have succeeded and where they have failed. Second, he learns how to get ideas across to these representatives of another culture, learns where he must explain at length and where he can make a telling point in just a few words. Finally, as a sort of synthesis of his experience, he can arrive at some conclusions concerning the visitors' inner thought processes, often quite alien to his own.

In addition to gaining these insights, the interpreter makes what may prove to be useful contacts in future assignments. How potentially useful depends on the spirit in which he parts company with the visitors, but anything short of outright hostility is likely to make them of some value.

Drawbacks and Limitations

The chief disadvantages of domestic assignment for the agent-interpreter lie in the shallowness of his cover. Visitors from Communist countries, in particular, start with a strong presumption that any interpreter is at least working hand in glove with local intelligence or security groups if he is not actually a member of one. The barrier thus imposed in the initial stages of a trip may break down as rapport is established, but there always remains a lurking suspicion that the interpreter is not what he seems, and the visitors are always on guard against the slightest hint of prying or propaganda. Furthermore, they collect a large file of biographic information on him in the course of their association, material which is certainly delivered to their own security forces. Matching this up with some earlier trace they may have of him may blow his organizational connections.

Another limiting factor is that foreign delegations, particularly from Bloc countries, are drawn from the elite and so are not typical of the peoples they represent. The impressions the interpreter receives concerning their beliefs and feelings may not be applicable to their countrymen at home. Though the delegation members may not be as orthodox abroad as on their home ground, where conformity is obligatory, they have a more compelling stake in the regime than the average citizen.

The last disadvantage to be noted depends in large part on the capabilities and limitations of the interpreter himself. It lies in the difficulty of retaining facts and figures in one's head while performing the complicated task of translation. It is possible to store in one's mind only a limited number of figures before the whole delicate structure of memory disintegrates into a jumble of confused statistics which are of no use to anyone. While it is permissible to take notes during long speeches where it is obviously impossible to remember everything said between pauses, this device is not appropriate for short conversations. If the interpreter is caught frantically scribbling notes immediately after a visitor has casually let drop the annual production of some electronic gadget, his usefulness to intelligence has largely evaporated. Furthermore, he has pinpointed an area of intelligence interest. A dash to the toilet after some particularly significant slip on the part of a visitor can sometimes provide privacy for note taking, but too frequent use of this dodge excites embarrassing commiseration or, more often, suspicion.

On the Opponent's Home Field

The foreign assignment differs in many respects from the domestic. On the profit side, in addition to getting the same positive intelligence take as the domestic interpreter, the interpreter abroad can be an observer, reporting on things which have nothing to do with his linguistic job. If he has had proper training, such observations can be quite valuable. Furthermore, he can acquire a feeling for the country and a sense of what intelligence activities can be undertaken and what cannot. He may, for example, attempt photography in areas on the borderline of legitimacy just to test reaction, or take a stroll before going to bed in order to check surveillance patterns. If he is an area specialist, the trip provides an education which no amount of book learning could give. He confirms certain of his preconceptions while discarding others, and he returns with a far more solid grasp on his specialty than he had previously. The confidence thus gained from first-hand experience is a very valuable asset if he is to be involved in operations against the country in the future.

On the negative side we find all the disadvantages noted in the domestic assignment: the interpreter accompanying a delegation abroad is, if anything, under sharper scrutiny as a probable agent, and should be prepared for a more or less clandestine search of his baggage; his memory is still strained to hold on to useful data; his official foreign contacts are the most loyal stalwarts of the regime; his digestion deteriorates. In addition, he finds himself a prisoner of his cover profession. Whereas the foreign delegation's dependence on him during his domestic assignment led to enlightening discussions, his own party's need for his help, not only on official matters but on everything that requires communication during every waking hour, now obliges him to spend *all* of his time with his own countrymen. He becomes a communications machine, unable to introduce any of his own ideas or queries into the conversations. Contacts are pretty well limited to those which the hosts have thoughtfully provided for about eighteen out of every twenty-four hours, and a delegation of six-foot Americans accompanied by watchful hosts is not the sort of group which a dissident member of a closed society is likely to approach in order to unload his true feelings about the regime.

Finally, even the diffident admissions of ignorance implicit in questions put to the interpreter on his own home ground are lacking when he goes abroad. Particularly in Communist countries the officials he contacts need to show that they have not been contaminated by his ideology; each tries to out-party-line the rest, less as an effort (usually counter-productive) to influence the visiting delegation than as a demonstration of his own orthodoxy for the benefit of his comrades. This compulsion precludes any serious discussion about either the hosts' or the visitors' country. During such exhibitions of chest-beating the interpreter is put on his mettle to hold his temper and restrain himself from active participation in the conversation.

Criteria and Other Considerations

From the foregoing we may conclude that the principal intelligence value of the domestic assignment lies in the psychological field—exploration of mental attitudes, blind spots, thought processes, strength and weakness of beliefs—whereas the value of the foreign assignment derives from first-hand experience in the country and from the collection of observable operational and positive intelligence. It is perhaps unnecessary to warn that the interpreter *cannot* fulfill the classic agent roles of recruiting spy nets, agitating for revolution, or personally stealing the master war plans. He will pay his way by less dramatic acts.

Here are some of the factors that should be taken into consideration in recruiting an interpreter for an intelligence mission or utilizing an existing intelligence asset in interpreter capacity. First, it must be borne in mind that almost any interpreter will be the target of intense scrutiny by the opposition, particularly in Bloc countries. The prevailing political climate today, however, is such that the interpreter's official position as part of a delegation protects him from arbitrary arrest, except perhaps in Communist China. The rest of the Bloc is so committed to East-West exchanges that it would not jeopardize the program for one rather insignificant intelligence fish.

Second, the interpreter should not be the only briefed member of the delegation going abroad. As we have shown, the interpreter has his hands full with his official duties and has little opportunity for taking notes. The official delegate, however, has good opportunities and excellent cover for taking notes. In addition, being presumably an expert in the field of the discussions, he can recognize significant material better than the interpreter.

Third, the size of the delegation is an extremely important factor affecting the usefulness of both domestic and foreign interpreter assignments. A delegation of more than six or seven people imposes such a burden on the interpreter that he has no time for an intelligence mission. He is kept continually busy rounding up strays, making travel reservations, getting people settled in hotels, and generally playing nursemaid. The best possible delegation would consist of one very lazy man who neither demanded nor rejected the presence of the interpreter.

Finally, the itinerary itself must be considered. On domestic assignments the most important thing is a relaxed schedule which will give the visitors enough spare time to observe their surroundings and ask questions about non-official matters. On the foreign assignment perhaps the most important consideration is the previous accessibility of the areas to be visited. If the area is completely off the beaten track or had previously been closed to foreigners, there is excellent reason to employ a trained observer as interpreter. Even the standard tourist trips, however, may provide useful information if the interpreter is alert.

This paper has been oriented primarily towards the interpreter-agent question as it obtains in visits to or from the Soviet Bloc, but many of the same factors are valid for neutralist or uncommitted areas. With the steady increase in cultural and professional exchanges among most countries of the world, opportunities for placing interpreters have also expanded. The expansion is not only making more experience and training available but is affording better cover for interpreters with intelligence objectives. Perhaps more of them should be given such objectives, despite the drawbacks we have noted.

4.

No one has ever doubted that military attachés at diplomatic missions are "licensed spies" (licensed by both sides). How, then, from a counterintelligence standpoint, are their gleanings to be kept limited? And, from the collection standpoint, how are the restrictive devices to be overcome? Here is some of the tradecraft, from the experience of a U.S. air attaché in the USSR in the late 1950s.

Obstacle Course for Attachés

THOMAS W. WOLFE

It may be useful, now that it seems possible the Soviet Union may one of these days agree to admit nuclear inspection teams to its territory, to review the kinds of obstacles it regularly strews in the path of other legitimate trained foreign observers, the military attachés. As Soviet officials have already given voice to their suspicion that any nuclear inspectors will be bent on spying, so they have taken the attitude, in their obsession with secrecy, that the attachés are spies when they exhibit an interest in matters which in most other countries lie open in the public domain. Hence, although as a bow to international usage they accept the military attachés of foreign diplomatic missions, they severely circumscribe their opportunities to travel and make observations—a traditional attaché activity since the system came into being during the Napoleonic era.

Soviet measures to limit the observations of military attachés fall into two categories. First, there are express legal proscriptions on attaché movement and activities—off-limits areas, travel registration, prohibitions on photography, etc. Second, there is a large body of unannounced restraints—administrative, psychological, and physical—which take up where the legal obstacles leave off. It is this second category of obstructive techniques over and above the formal restrictions which I shall illustrate from my own experience in Russia as American Air Attaché from October 1956 to October 1958.

Manipulating transportation. This is one of the most common methods of interference through administrative measures after an attaché has obtained formal permission to travel. For example, you have made reservations for a flight in daytime from Moscow to Baku, but at the last minute you find that your

Thomas W. Wolfe, "Obstacle Course for Attachés," *Studies in Intelligence*, vol. 4, no. 3 (Summer 1960), pp. 71–77. Originally classified "Official Use Only."

seat has been switched to a night plane. If you announce your intention of waiting for the first available daytime flight, you are informed that all day flights are sold out "for the indefinite future." The same thing happens on trains. Sometimes the schedules are altered to keep you from passing points of interest in daylight. I have been on trains which for no apparent reason pulled into a siding and waited until dark, to the bewilderment of Russian fellow-passengers and even some members of the crew. Similarly, civil air flights have altered their routes or skipped scheduled stops in perfectly good weather for no other reason than to deny us observation of some inconveniently located installation.

Compartment companions. Rarely are attachés able to secure a compartment to themselves on a Soviet train, no matter how far in advance they book transportation. The Soviet citizens who turn up to share a compartment are in most cases readily identifiable as security agents. They keep the attaché under constant scrutiny during waking hours and occasionally can be found going through his belongings in the middle of the night. An auxiliary practice is that of splitting up foreign travellers: even American husbands (including myself) have on occasion been obliged to spend the night in one compartment and their wives in another with male Russian companions. This sort of thing naturally does nothing to endear the watchdogs of Soviet security to members of the attaché corps, and run-ins with them have been frequent. After one such skirmish with a particularly obnoxious security type in the Caucasus, I was called a "hooligan" and other uncomplimentary names in the Soviet press, a publicity measure which serves to put psychological pressure on the attachés as well as to foster among the Soviet populace the desired attitude of suspicious vigilance toward foreigners.

Timely interruption technique. Even if an attaché and his friends or family have managed to secure a train compartment without Soviet company, their privacy is seldom respected for long. Whenever the train approaches the industrial section of a city, for example, the car attendants suddenly find it necessary to tidy up your compartment. If the door happens to be locked they let themselves in with a pass key, so great is their urge to look after your comfort. The window always seems to need the most attention, and they swipe away at it with a dust-rag, effectually blocking the view, until you have passed through the factory district.

If this routine cannot be stretched out long enough, there is a variation which I encountered once while travelling through a large industrial city on the Volga. Factories were strung out for several miles on the outskirts of the city, among them a big aircraft plant. It stood alongside the tracks, offering about the same view you get from a train of the Martin plant in Baltimore, except that the Soviet plant was boxed in by a high board fence. On this occasion I found the view spoiled not only by the fence and the customary activity of the car attendant. Making doubly sure that I would have no chance to observe this particular stretch of industrial scenery, the attendant rubbed the window down with a greasy rag.

Frosted window routine. On train trips in winter, nature often cooperates with the Soviet authorities by frosting over the windows of your car. When nature fails to do the trick, however, there is usually someone around to lend a hand, as I found once when boarding a train in Rostov. It was a clear, cold day and every window in the train was completely free of frost and ice, with one exception. The window of my compartment, in the middle of a car, had been sprayed on the outside until it was covered with a quarter-inch glaze of ice. When I attempted to chip some of the ice away, I was immediately stopped by a detail of militiamen. "You are violating Soviet regulations," they said. "You might scratch the glass."

Helpful hostess. When attachés board an airplane for a trip in the Soviet Union, word is passed along to the crew that foreigners are aboard. The hostess then makes it her business to distract the attention of the foreign traveller at moments when he might observe installations of military or industrial significance. A favorite technique when an airplane is taking off or approaching an airport is for the hostess to lean over your seat with an offering of reading material. Somehow she usually manages to hold a magazine in front of your face so you can't see out the window. If you wave the solicitous girl away at such a moment you are of course being rude and unappreciative.

Smoke screen. When the Soviets are particularly anxious to conceal some installation from foreign eyes, they may use this standard military device. It takes a certain amount of preparation and good communications to time a smoke screen to go up just as an attaché drives down the highway or passes on the train, but they usually pull it off without a hitch. This technique, however, has the disadvantage of calling attention to the very object they wish to hide. On one train trip in central Russia an airfield we passed at a distance of three or four miles was ringed with upwards of 50 smoke generators belching away. "What's going on over there?" I asked one of the Russians who had been assigned to keep an eye on me during this journey. "It looks as though that airfield is on fire." I got a blank stare in return. "Airfield? Fire? I don't see anything," said the Russian, as though he could persuade me thus that there was nothing in sight but the natural Russian landscape.

Highway escort. When attachés undertake an automobile trip in the Soviet Union, they are accompanied by several cars of plain-clothes security agents. These keep shifting the order of their line-up along the highway to preserve the fiction that there is no surveillance of foreigners; but since auto traffic on most out-of-town roads in the Soviet Union is very light, the pretense is bound to wear thin as the same "protective" cavalcade of Pobedas and Zims rolls along behind you hour after hour. When you stop by the roadside to stretch your legs, the cavalcade pulls up a hundred yards or so away. For some reason, the security personnel always make a minute inspection of your stopping place after you have moved on. Perhaps they imagine that attachés may plant nefarious devices or hide messages to conspirators along the highways.

Roadside reception committees. Should an auto trip take you through a region in which military or industrial installations are located, the motor escort is usually deemed inadequate to keep a proper curb on your curiosity, and the local militia and troops from the nearest military base are turned out en masse. They stand guard at every intersection to prevent you from turning off the designated route. Along some stretches of road they are posted at 10-yard intervals to keep you from making an "unauthorized" stop, thus often calling attention, like the smoke screen, to the very installation you are supposed not to observe. Running the gauntlet of such reception committees is generally bothersome, however, especially when they bar access to the only decent roads in the vicinity and require you to detour along rutted backcountry wagon trails to get to your destination. Frequently the only satisfaction on attaché gets from such a trip is the knowledge that the Soviets have tied up an inordinate amount of manpower to control his itinerary.

Phoney militiaman routine. Around cities it is not always feasible to have a guard posted at every corner when attachés happen to be in town, and a portable militiaman must be improvised. The militia are the uniformed police, whom you are legally required to obey when they flag your car down and tell you to turn around. Not so the security agent in plain clothes unless he shows his credentials, a revelation which security operatives are loath to make. To get around this difficulty, each auto-load of security men has in its kit a militia uniform which one of the operatives may put on as occasion demands. The car speeds ahead, the phoney militiaman jumps out still buttoning up his jacket, and you are hailed to a stop. This technique more or less effectively confines attaché sightseeing in the environs of a Soviet city to churches, cemeteries, and other approved cultural attractions.

Frequent interceptions on a drive about a large city may produce the curious result that you keep encountering the same phoney militiaman at widely separated points. Once in Leningrad an agent with a torn shoulder strap on his militiaman's uniform flagged us down several times in the same afternoon. As the crowd of onlookers would gather around we would ask him, each time a bit more caustically: "So it's you again. Haven't you got that strap fixed yet? Bozhe moi! you sure are setting a sloppy example for all the genuine militiamen in Leningrad!" His wrathful frustration was a pleasure to behold, for no one wants less than a security agent to become the butt of attention in front of a crowd of fellow-citizens: his next assignment might involve checking up on one of those same citizens.

"Road under Repair" routine. The pretense that a bridge is out or that a particular stretch of road is under repair is often used to keep motoring attachés from reaching a destination the authorities do not want to declare formally out of bounds. On one occasion, when some travellers were told by local Soviet officials that they could not proceed to the town of Pskov because a bridge en route "had been washed out in a storm,' they insisted on going ahead anyway. They had not got very far along the road when a truck full of soldiers sped past. A few minutes later they came to a small wooden bridge in time to see the soldiers beginning to take it apart plank by plank.

Kerosene in the crankcase. When other devices fail to discourage attachés from an undesirable motoring itinerary, there is always the alternative of a little midnight attention to their automobile. Cars which had passed a searching inspection before the start of a trip sometimes used to develop peculiar ailments after having been parked overnight in the courtyard of a Soviet hotel. I had a brand-new automobile, mileage still under 3,000, break down with burned-out engine bearings on a trip in southern Russia. Kerosene in the crankcase—hardly the work of a mere prankster—turned out to be the cause.

Indignant citizen act. The attitude of ordinary Soviet citizens toward foreigners is generally a combination of curiosity and friendliness. Deliberately hostile behavior is quite out of character, for ordinary citizens are aware that they can get into trouble by unsanctioned demonstrations of ill will. It is an obvious artifice, therefore, when planted agitators attempt to incite a crowd of Soviet citizens against attaché travellers. I recall a typical instance wherein two attachés were set upon while visiting the historic Kremlin of the city of Kazan.

The Kremlin, sitting on high ground, affords a distant view of the city's industrial suburbs. Apparently the Soviet authorities thought it best to deny this view to foreign attachés, but since the Kremlin was open to the public they had no plausible excuse for barring admittance. Professional agitators were therefore called into action to create a scene. They collected a crowd, ranted at the travellers, and threatened to shoot them if they did not leave the premises at once. When the agitators were asked to show their credentials, they claimed to be "indignant citizens" who did not have to identify themselves. This tactic usually proves effective, for attachés cannot afford to become involved in altercations with Soviet citizens, however strong the provocation, lest they be officially accused of violating Soviet order. As on many similar occasions, the attachés in this case were harried off the streets and obliged to take refuge in their hotel room until time to catch the next train out of town.

The foregoing provides a sample of the harassments and petty subterfuges by which Soviet authorities prevent military attachés travelling in nominally open areas from making the most commonplace observations, observations of a kind which Soviet representatives in Western countries are perfectly free to make without hindrance. It seems reasonable to expect that nuclear inspectors, if they are admitted, will be faced with the frustration of these and similar obstructive contrivances.

5.

CIA's analysts have been criticized particularly for their decades-long overestimation of Soviet economic strength (whether or not they also misjudged Soviet military strength). Nor in that era were the analysts (even less the collectors) much interested in having CIA humint directed at general Soviet economic conditions. The analysts trusted themselves to massage the Soviets' own statistical data, however dubious that may appear in retrospect.

Here, one of the analysts shows how she found an opportunity during four months in Russia in 1967 to get behind the Potemkin-village facade and live some of the onerous life of an ordinary Muscovite. Social scientists would call this "participant observation." Her conclusions seem farsightedly critical of other analysts. The *Studies in Intelligence* editor at the time implicitly endorsed her methodology as "logical but little used." Sadly, it remained so.

Notice that in this instance the person knew that the Soviets had been informed in advance that she was a CIA analyst. But any resulting surveillance problems for her would probably not have been greater than for other U.S. officials in Moscow at the time. They would all have to assume that the Soviets would be suspicious of them.

Soviet Reality Sans Potemkin

GERTRUDE SCHROEDER

Statements about the size and growth of the Soviet economy in relation to that of the United States have long occupied an important place in intelligence estimates of the USSR's capabilities. So also have statements about the comparative levels of living in the two countries and how they are changing over time. CIA's current estimates are that the Soviet gross national product is somewhat less than half of U.S. GNP and that per capita consumption is about one-third.

Consumption Analysis

In presenting these deceptively neat figures the economic analyst goes on to say that they undoubtedly overstate the relative position of the USSR because the calculations cannot allow adequately for the superior quality of U.S. products and the much greater variety and assortment of products available

Gertrude Schroeder, "Soviet Reality Sans Potemkin," *Studies in Intelligence,* vol. 12, no. 2 (Spring 1968), pp. 43–51. Originally classified "Confidential" and "No Foreign Dissem[ination]."

here. These qualitative factors are particularly important in comparing levels of living in the two countries. For the purpose of this comparison the economic analyst first assembles data on consumer expenditures, product by product, for the United States in dollars and for the USSR in rubles. He must then convert the figures to a common currency unit by calculating ruble-dollar ratios for these products on the basis of their prices in the two countries. This later is an extremely difficult and laborious process, for the analyst must try to match the individual products as closely as possible and include as many as he can.

In the latest set of consumption comparisons[1] CIA concluded that with respect to food, clothing, and personal services the allowance made for the quality factor had been more or less adequate. We had equated apples with apples and bread with bread, and we had compared Soviet prices for items of clothing with the prices of the cheapest counterparts in a Sears Roebuck catalogue. We decided that a haircut was a haircut in either country. With respect to consumer durables like refrigerators, radios, and automobiles, however, we concluded that the best matchings we could make still did not take sufficient account of the superior quality and durability of the U.S. product. To make some allowance for this factor we raised the ruble-dollar price ratios for these products by an arbitrary 20 percent. And we said that even this adjustment was probably not enough and that in addition there was no way at all to allow for the much greater variety and assortment of goods available to consumers in the United States, not to mention such extras as paper bags, plastic wrapping, and attractive, well-lighted stores. Besides doing our best to quantify the comparative lot of consumers in the two countries, our estimates also talk about the shoddy goods in Soviet stores, about queues, about the poor quality of personal services to be found everywhere.

From all this I had formed a mental picture of what everyday life for the average Russian was probably like. But I was eager to see for myself, and when the chance to do so finally arose I was determined to do my utmost to check on these preconceptions and acquire the best possible basis for the judgments that I as an economic intelligence analyst must make all the time.

An Attaché Goes Native

The opportunity for a first-hand look was a four-month (June–September 1967) assignment as assistant to the economic counselor in the American embassy in Moscow. I was given the diplomatic title of Attaché, and the Soviet Ministry of Foreign Affairs was informed that I was a research analyst in CIA on temporary assignment with the Department of State to help out the hard-

1. CIA/RR ER 66-6. *US and USSR: Comparisons of Size and Use of Gross National Product, 1955–64*, March 1966. Secret.

pressed economics section of the embassy during the summer. My main task was to read the daily press and the economic journals and write despatches on significant items. Aside from doing a good job for the embassy the principal objective of my TDY was to learn as much as I could about the daily life of the ordinary Russian and obtain some insights into the workings of the Soviet economic system.

I became aware very quickly that extraordinary measures of one kind or another would be needed to accomplish this objective. Going about Moscow in embassy cars, participating in the busy diplomatic social life, and walking the streets in my typically American summer clothes would net me little more than the superficial impressions that a tourist gets. I tried this way of doing things and found it pleasant but unprofitable: going about as someone quite obviously foreign, I got the usual treatment accorded foreigners. People were friendly and polite; they insisted that I go to the head of any line I might be standing in. It was evident that they wanted to make a good impression; they wanted me to see the good side of Soviet society. As much as possible I would be shown Potemkin villages and the people who lived in them.

Clearly, I had to break out of this impasse. I needed to shed my obvious foreignness and "go native." I needed to participate to the maximum in the daily life of Moscow as ostensibly a Soviet citizen, so as to experience and systematically observe the Soviet scene without eliciting the Potemkin-village behavior. But I also had to take care not to do anything that could create a problem for the embassy. I believe that I succeeded in both respects: that is, I created no problems for the embassy, and to a considerable extent I managed to become just one more Muscovite going about his business.

To go native one needs first of all to look and dress more or less like a Russian, or at least someone from one of the other republics. I managed to take on the drab appearance of the average Soviet woman by wearing a tacky outfit consisting of gray-green skirt, nondescript tan blouse, much-worn brown loafers, and of course head scarf. I shed my stockings; Russian women don't wear them in the summer, and American-type nylons are scarcely to be found anywhere. Since I had brought along only one such outfit, I looked more and more "native" as the weeks passed.

In addition to the appearance of a native, one needs a high degree of fluency in the language. This I had, thanks to several years of visiting the language laboratory and countless hours of practice. In the process I had somehow acquired a Baltic accent, for to my surprise Russians often took me for an Estonian. Finally, going native entails a willingness to do things the hard way, i.e., the Soviet way. Being taken for a foreigner in Moscow is much more pleasant than being taken for an Estonian. Having an embassy car pick one up after the ballet is nothing like fighting one's way onto a Moscow bus!

Attired in my sloppy and deteriorating outfit and equipped with the required language skills plus a willingness to rough it for the sake of learning something, I spent almost all of my free time in Moscow wandering about the city. I rode subways, buses, trolleys, trams, and suburban commuter trains; I acted the would-be purchaser in dozens of bakeries, gastronoms (grocery stores), food stores, meat stores, fish stores, furniture stores, book stores, department stores, clothing stores, and gift stores. Ditto for collective farm markets and yarmarkas (miniature shopping centers), savings banks and stolovayas ("greasy spoons"). I wandered through parks and railroad stations, visited churches and even the crematory. I walked about the street in all parts of the city at various times of day and evening; I went on city sightseeing tours with Russians. In all these activities I systematically observed the people and their behavior, listened to their conversations, and talked with them as one does in casual, everyday contacts.

To the extent possible I did the same thing in other cities I visited—Leningrad, Kiev, Tbilisi, Yerevan, Baku, Vladimir, and Novosibirsk. Except for Novosibirsk, however, I could spend only a day or two in these cities. My conclusions therefore relate for the most part to things I observed in Moscow.

Shopping Pleasures

What are things like for the average urbanite in the USSR? From what I myself experienced I concluded that everyday life is hard and very, very frustrating. One of the worst aspects is the uncertainty about almost everything. Take the matter of getting your groceries bought. In the first place, you nearly always have to stand in a queue. I stood in scores of them just to find out why the queue was there and what it was like to stand in one. I would listen to the gripes: "What puny little tomatoes! And 40 kopecks a kilogram! My God, how is a person to get along?" "Don't give me that one. Can't you see it's rotten?" "No cabbage, huh? There was some yesterday, why not today?"

These were the complaints at a street stall on October Square near my apartment. There were several such stalls near this square which I inspected almost daily. You never knew whether a given stall would be operating, and you could never be sure what would be for sale. Tomatoes and eggs today, maybe. Tomorrow it might be only green apples. Several times there was a barrel of pickled fish. Once there were plaster statuettes! Another time a truckload of melons was dumped on the sidewalk, and a long line quickly formed to buy them.

Across from the embassy one day a 30-person line formed to buy shoddy-looking black briefcases. In Sokolniki Park I stood for a while in a block-long line of would-be purchasers of nylon shopping bags imported from Yugoslavia and selling for 3 rubles 50 kopecks (about $4) each. People grumbled about the price but bought the bags anyway. At 2 pm on a Tuesday 18 persons were standing in a line at a counter where sausages were sold; apparently some rarely available delicacy had appeared. Once on a Saturday afternoon I saw a half-block line in front of a small dingy bakery near the Kazan railroad station. Why? Having spent the preceding two hours pushing my way through the mobs in three railroad stations that I wanted to inspect, I was too tired to want to find out. Maybe there were sweet rolls for sale that day: although bread was always available, I once visited five bakeries within walking distance of October Square in search of a sweet roll.

I made it a practice to visit a gastronom near the embassy at different times during the day and on different days of the week. One could never be sure of finding even the most staple of foods there. Frequently there was no fresh meat, and if there was it was pretty poor quality by American standards. Rarely were there any vegetables except tomatoes (in season) and cabbage, and sometimes there were none at all. There was usually a sign "No potatoes." On street cars and trolleys women carrying loaded string bags would greet each other, "Ah, potatoes! Where did you get them? How much did you have to pay?" or "Where did you find that melon?"

On Wednesday about 5:30 I walked into a large gastronom on the Arbat. The place was bedlam—packed with a pushing, shoving crowd of women shoppers, each trying mightily to buy a thing or two. I decided to take on the process of trying to buy tea and a can of fish. I pushed my way through the mob in the dimly lit store in the general direction of the counter where tea was sold. The particular queue for tea was hard to locate in the crowd, but I finally stationed myself at its end after having inadvertently gotten into its middle and been rudely pushed aside and chewed out by the woman in back of me. In due course, I got up to the counter.

The clerk was standing with her back to the customers, talking angrily with a fellow clerk. I waited, and people back of me started grousing. Finally, she turned around and glared at me. I asked does she have a small package of tea and how much is it? "What kind?" I hesitated. "Well, don't you know what you want? Can't you see all these people are waiting? Make up your mind!" I pointed to a stack of boxes of tea, and she said, "All right, 60 kopecks."

But that was only the first queue. Next I had to fight my way through the line for the particular cashier that served the tea department in order to pay 60 kopecks and get a ticket. Then I had to return through the original queue to hand the ticket to the surly clerk and get my tea. Ditto for the purchase of a can of fish. In dire need of a cup of coffee after all this, I made my way to a coffee bar in a far corner, only to find it hopelessly mobbed. It was nearly 7 o'clock as I left the store, physically and nervously exhausted.

In my wanderings in and out of stores of all kinds I was particularly struck by the miniscule amount of variety and assortment in the goods available to Soviet purchasers. Shelves and showcases were usually half empty. Where a woman in the United States or Western Europe can choose from 20 to 30 kinds of shoes in her favorite store, a Soviet woman can choose from perhaps five or six kinds in all the stores selling shoes in Moscow. Although book stores, in contrast, were chuck full of books, opera librettos were not to be found even in music stores, and the Russian classics (Pushkin, Tolstoy, Gogol) were as scarce as hen's teeth. One can do much better for these at Kamkin's in Washington, D.C.

Social Graces

With difficulties and frustrations such as those to put up with every day, one can understand why the Russians treat one another (but not foreigners) so very rudely. If you adhere to our custom of keeping to the right when walking on the sidewalk, you merely get pushed aside and glared at. Subway crowds at rush hours are frequently violent; they shove you hard through the turnstile, race pell-mell down the corridors, and push you onto the train with a brute force that I had never experienced even in the crowded subways of New York and London. If you can't keep up with the mob, say just pause to read a directional sign, they start yelling at you.

Similar experiences are to be had on buses, which always seem to be packed to twice their capacity. Once I had been pushed (literally!) onto a bus and pressed against a pole near the door with such force that I could neither stand up straight nor move. The bus stopped. "Are you getting off?" asked a large middle-aged woman near me. No, said I. "You're not! Then why are you here? Can't you see you're in everyone's way? You're blocking the door. Move!" I felt myself become one with the pole as she and others pushed past me and out the door.

And then there is the experience of getting dinner in one of the better Moscow restaurants. (Incidentally, there are fewer than a dozen good ones in this city of six and a half million; the rest are *really* greasy spoons or worse. And one or two of the good ones are frequently closed for repair.) There are always queues in front of the restaurants at dinner hours. The doorkeeper locks the door after letting each diner in, and those left outside bang on the door and shout at him. When we were let in ahead of everyone else, having had the embassy reserve a table, I would always be astonished to see many empty tables.

Just as I had heard, it does nearly always take three hours to get through dinner. The waiters are a seeming eternity between successive operations.

Signaling to them will get you nowhere. You can see that they are not busy; they merely lean against the wall and talk to one another. Often there seems to be some kind of argument going on. Once in the hotel restaurant in Tbilisi while waiting to be seated I listened in great embarrassment to the manageress reading the riot act to a waitress. "Why are you sulking? Stop acting like a child. You know it's not *kulturniy* to behave this way in public. If you want to be naughty, do it at home!" The indifferent attitude of clerks and waiters is not surprising; they have no real incentive to behave otherwise. Their salaries are little above the legal minimum wage (now 60 rubles a month), and the bonus system is such that they can't add much over 5 rubles a month to this no matter what they do. Tipping is rare.

Even getting a little recreation is full of difficulties for the ordinary Russian. One Sunday morning, dressed in my native attire, I went to the park "Exhibitions of the Achievements of the National Economy." The entrance fee was 30 kopecks. The crowd got larger and more vociferous the nearer I got to the gate. What was the problem? I soon found out: only two cashiers' cages were open that day to accommodate the huge crowd. I pushed my way through, trying to locate the end of the queue. There seemed to be several, and people argued loudly about which was first and who was or was not ahead of whom.

Near the cashier's cage stood a man whose job apparently was to supervise the queues and mete out justice. After a half hour of being pushed about and scolded for allegedly crashing some line, I decided I had had it. I pushed ahead and clutched at the sleeve of this supervisor, amid a barrage of verbal abuse from those around. "What are you doing here?" said he. "The queue is over there! This is no way to act." I assumed a helpless and confused air and said in halting Russian, "I am an American. I don't know where the right line is or how things are done here. I only want to get into the park." Presto, in seconds I had bought my ticket and was in!

In Novosibirsk I talked with a young girl, who said to me, "There is so much here that is disgusting. Our papers are always telling us how great things are. Tell me, did you see anything interesting in our stores here in Novosibirsk, anything you wanted to buy?" No, I said. "Of course not! There's nothing here, nothing! Do you know that there are no women's shoes in this city and there haven't been for a long time? Once in a while some will come in and then there is such a melee as you can't possibly imagine! And the prices! A pair costs 30 rubles, and the things wear out in a few months. Why? And all of us have to work so hard." I myself saw no women's shoes in the stores I visited, and the bareness of the shelves was indeed startling. Of the two so-called department stores in the downtown section of this city of over a million, one was closed for repair, and the one that was open resembled a small store that had just had a close-out sale.

Daily life has a dull sameness. After a while everything seems to look alike and the people seem bored and preoccupied. In Moscow they walk about with a frown. And in Novosibirsk a young psychiatrist said to me, "What have I to look forward to? Only to getting married, maybe, and living out my days in this place. It's so boring!" "Why don't you try to get to Moscow to do research, perhaps?" I say. "To Moscow! Why, that's quite impossible. You have to have connections, and I don't." "But you could work toward it." "No, it's no use, none at all. You just don't understand. Connections mean everything here."

New Perspective

In summary, I went to the USSR with a set of notions about what to expect that I had formed over the years from reading and research on the Soviet economy. I also had a collection of judgment factors, partly intuitive and partly derived from this same research and reading, that I applied in drawing conclusions and speculating about probable future developments in the Soviet economy. My four months of living in the country itself, however, greatly altered these preconceptions and modified the implicit judgment factors in many respects. No amount of reading about the Soviet economy in Washington could substitute for the summer in Moscow as I spent it.

As a result of this experience I think that our measurements of the position of Soviet consumers in relation to those of the United States (and Western Europe) favor the USSR to a much greater extent than I had thought. The ruble-dollar ratios are far too low for most consumer goods. Cabbages are *not* cabbages in both countries. The cotton dress worn by the average Soviet woman is *not* equivalent to the cheapest one in a Sears catalogue; the latter is of better quality and more stylish. The arbitrary 20 percent adjustment that was made in some of the ratios is clearly too little. The difference in variety and assortment of goods available in the two countries is enormous—far greater than I had thought. Queues and spot shortages were far more in evidence than I expected. Shoddy goods were shoddier. And I obtained a totally new impression of the behavior of ordinary Soviet people toward one another.

III.

Clandestine Human Intelligence Collection (Clandestine Humint)

6.

More than is generally perceived, CIA collects inside the United States much of its clandestine and semi-clandestine humint about foreign countries. This is not just a process of Americans' spontaneously volunteering information to their government. Often they (and aliens) need to be induced to do so by methods that include a large part of clandestine espionage tradecraft (though not the full range, this article contends, not the coercive end of that spectrum). The article (obviously based on personal familiarity) is extraordinarily frank in depicting some of the techniques of spotting, assessing, recruiting, tasking, reporting, sometimes using "cut-outs" (intermediaries), sometimes providing compensation, and more. Most of this is about CIA contacting U.S. businesspeople and aliens. But academics may be startled at some of the precise tactics described as being used to penetrate universities, at least in the 1950s.

Techniques of Domestic Intelligence Collection

ANTHONY F. CZAJKOWSKI

The process of getting intelligence information out of people is normally associated with overseas operations, but it was demonstrated during World War II that this clandestine activity can usefully be supplemented by collection in the analyst's own back yard. Potential sources of intelligence within the United States are myriad. U.S. concerns have been active in various parts of the world for many decades and their records often contain information which a clandestine agent would have little hope of obtaining, especially in war-time. Representatives of industrial plants travel continually and compile expert reports and evaluations on foreign economic and financial affairs. The current increase in East-West contacts has sent thousands of U.S. citizens as travellers to countries of the Soviet Bloc. Scientists and academicians attend international meetings and conferences, where they meet and exchange information with opposite numbers from all parts of the world. Refugees from the Soviet Union and its satellite nations continue to enter the United States for permanent residence.

For more than ten years the Contact Division of CIA's Office of Operations, with its network of field offices throughout the country, has been tapping this vast potential of information on behalf of the intelligence community. Since

Anthony F. Czajkowski, "Techniques of Domestic Intelligence Collection," *Studies in Intelligence,* vol. 3, no. 1 (Winter 1959), pp. 69–83. Originally classified "Confidential."

1948 over forty thousand individuals and companies have supplied information ranging into every field of intelligence. Through this collection operation the community has at its disposal the expert analysis and commentary of the most knowledgeable people in the academic, scientific, professional and industrial fields.

Getting information from these individuals calls for techniques different from those employed in clandestine collection. The contact specialist, as the domestic field collector is known, has no control over his Source. The Source provides the information voluntarily, with no hint of pressure or threat, because he has been convinced that he can be of singular assistance to the U.S. Government; but mere waving of the flag does not automatically trigger the cornucopia of intelligence plenty. U.S. citizens, as a rule, know little of intelligence organizations and intelligence needs. A visit to a businessman by a government representative arouses instinctive fear that the company books are about to be examined for tax purposes, that an anti-trust suit is pending, or that an investigation is being conducted against a friend. Academicians and missionaries are apprehensive that their cooperation with U.S. intelligence will become known and hinder their future activity in a foreign area. The alien, wise to the ways of intelligence and security services, distrusts the contact officer (credentials are easily forged, he claims) or fears for the safety of relatives still living behind the Curtain.

To convert the hesitant businessman or fearful alien into a cooperative Source, the contact officer must have a wide diversity of skills. He must be a salesman, selling his prospect on the importance of the intelligence function; he must be an intelligence officer, knowing the needs and the gaps in the community's information; he must play the practical psychologist, handling dissimilar personalities with dexterity; and finally he becomes a skilled reporter, putting the Source's information into a concise and readable intelligence report.

Locating and Contacting the New Source

Since the contact officer cannot hope to approach all the commercial, banking, educational, and scientific institutions, as well as all the aliens, in his area, he must learn to select from among his possible sources. He obtains leads from trade journals and directories, from established sources, from Agency headquarters, and from other government agencies. Matching these leads against his knowledge of current intelligence requirements, he tries to pinpoint those individuals and companies in his area which have the best potential for filling the requirements.

Once he decides or is directed by his field chief to "open up" a new company, institution, or individual, his first step is to brief himself on the company and if possible on the individual he is to contact. At the same time he reviews intelligence requirements in the prospective contact's field, making preliminary exploration of its potential for his purposes. He will offer no pretensions to expertise in the Source's field of specialty, but will be able to win confidence and rapport by recognizing the Source's professional interests and understanding his terminology. He cannot walk in cold on a new Source and hope to establish the proper rapport for a continuing contact.

No security clearance is required for initial contact with a U.S. citizen. The existence of the Central Intelligence organization and its general purposes are public knowledge, and no classified information is discussed in the initial interview. Contact with an alien, on the other hand, must first be cleared with the FBI as a matter of internal security.

In approaching a new company or institution, the contact officer always goes to the top man, to the president, the chairman of the board, or whoever determines broad policy for the company. Once cooperation is obtained at the highest level, it is assured at all subordinate levels. The president will not ordinarily have the information intelligence is seeking, but he will designate the official in the company who does have it and who will be the future contact. If a subordinate is contacted first, experience has shown, an embarrassing situation can arise when the president inquires why his company is being "penetrated" by the U.S. Government.

To interview the executive an appointment is of course necessary, and executives have secretaries whose function it is to keep unwelcome visitors away and screen phone calls to the "boss." The secretary wants to know who is calling and why. The contact officer gives her his name and identifies himself as a representative of the federal Government who wishes to speak to her boss on a confidential matter. Few secretaries dare to block such a call except in companies which have frequent contact with government agencies. The persistently inquisitive secretary is told that the caller will explain his purpose fully to the boss.

Once he has been put through to the executive, the contact officer identifies himself more fully by revealing his association with U.S. intelligence or, if pressed, with CIA. He outlines briefly why he desires a personal interview. Most individuals, when first approached, associate a government official with one of the enforcement agencies, and the contact man therefore seeks an early appointment.

The First Interview

Since the contact officer's objective is to convert the prospect into a continuing and cooperative Source, he must take especial care to make the best initial impression. Temperaments and social customs vary in different parts of the country, and the officer must comport himself according to the Source's taste. Whereas a ten-gallon hat and a string tie may be acceptable in Texas or in Arizona, they cause raised eyebrows in Boston and New York. It has become axiomatic that the contact man should dress as conservatively as the most conservative of his contacts for that day. Religious or fraternal pins are better not worn. In calling on a missionary or religious source discussion of religion is avoided. The intelligence officer cannot allow himself the liberty of drawing racial, color, or religious lines.

When, promptly at the time of his appointment, the contact officer arrives and is ushered into the Source's office, he immediately shows his credentials and underscores his association with CIA to emphasize that he does not represent the FBI or any other federal agency. The Source is naturally curious about the visit, and may even have been troubled since the first phone call. The officer tries to put him at ease immediately. The approach will vary, depending on circumstance, on the personality of the Source, and even on the area. In the North and [East], and to some extent on the West Coast, the typical Source is a busy man who has sandwiched this appointment into a tight schedule. The contact officer must talk fast and convincingly, in a business-like manner, to win his cooperation. In the South and the Midwest a certain amount of pleasantry or chit-chat may be in order before getting down to the issue at hand.

Whatever approach he uses, the contact man must accomplish three things during his initial visit—explain the intelligence mission, assess the potential of the company for his purposes, and show the Source how he or his company can be of assistance to the cause of national security.

Private citizens have varying amounts of knowledge about intelligence, and the first task is to orient the Source on Central Intelligence purposes and its place in the federal Government. The contact officer brings out the Director's advisory function to the National Security Council headed by the President, stressing how necessary it is for policy makers to be well informed on conditions and events throughout the world. He also explains that he represents all the intelligence agencies in the Government, so that needless duplication in visits by other intelligence representatives can be avoided. The Source can contribute to the welfare of the country, he says, by making available whatever information on foreign plants, research and development, or other matters he may possess or acquire.

The assessment of the company's potential then follows naturally. The Source is usually willing to cooperate but may fail to see how any information he has will be of value to the intelligence effort. The contact man then introduces questions on the company's foreign branches or affiliates, the extent of its foreign business, and the degree to which the home office is kept aware of conditions in areas in which the company operates.

At this point the Source may become apprehensive that any information he provides may boomerang against his interests, through punitive action by another federal agency, through revelation of proprietary information to a competitor, or through embarrassment in his future dealings with foreign companies or governments. The contact man convincingly reassures him that a guiding principle of all relations with informants is Source protection. The name of the Source is never connected with his information. Nor is data provided by a Source ever turned over to another federal agency for any regulatory or punitive action. Information given by the Source is circulated only in intelligence channels within the United States, and the Source need not have any apprehension that his name or his information will get into unauthorized hands. His cooperation with intelligence, as well as the information provided by him, is kept classified.

Conversely, the Source is requested to treat the contact as classified and not to reveal to anyone the purpose of the visit. It is pointed out that the need for security is mutual. Further, since this confidential contact may be followed by other visits in which classified requirements may be used, biographic information on the Source for security assessment is requested. Ordinarily, if the contact officer has laid the proper basis for a continuing contact with the Source, whether the top executive or one of his subordinates, he has no difficulty in securing biographic data.

The officer cannot rely on his memory to retain the information divulged during the interview. He inquires whether the Source has any objection to note-taking—an inquiry which is generally academic, for it adds to the Source's feeling that he is doing something important if his words are taken down. On biographic and technical data note-taking is naturally a matter of course.

The length of the first interview is governed by the time available to the Source and the contact officer's estimate of the Source's intelligence potential. The experienced contact man can assess the company's potential in a short time, and if his assessment is negative he arranges for a graceful exit as soon as possible. If he believes that the company does have access to useful information, he explores the possibilities as completely as time and circumstance allow. In this case, the length of interview must be gauged by the Source's attitude and his appointment book. It sometimes happens, on the other hand, that the Source has time on his hands and relishes having the ear of a government representative into which to pour all his ideas on what he thinks is "wrong with Washington." Here the contact officer politely steers the conversation to the purpose of his visit, creating the impression that he himself is a busy man.

The first interview is terminated with the understanding that the officer will probably return to explore the company's information further. If a return is actually contemplated, he leaves a personal card which bears his name, his field office's post-office box number, and his (unlisted) office telephone number. The name of the Agency does not appear on this card. About a week or ten days later he writes the Source to thank him for his cooperation, mentioning that he is looking forward to another visit. The letter serves to remind the Source of intelligence interests and gives him again the officer's name and phone number, should he have misplaced the calling-card.

After the initial interview the contact officer must estimate the future usefulness of the Source and his company. Should he follow up or not? If after consultation with his field office chief he decides that the company has insufficient potential to warrant further expenditure of time and effort, he sends a complete account of his visit, plus the biographic data he has obtained on the Source, to Division Headquarters, with a notation that further contact is not contemplated. A copy is of course retained in the field office, for the guidance of other contact officers who may some day obtain a lead on the same company. If, on the other hand, he decides that the company and the Source can and will supply intelligence information of value, he submits to Headquarters not only an account of his visit but also a request for security clearance on the individuals with whom he will be dealing. The secretary, if she is witting to the intelligence contact, may also have to be cleared.

Continuing Contact

How often the contact officer calls on a company depends on several factors—the amount and type of information it has available, its distance from his field office, his own work-load, the Source's own preferences and schedule. If the contact officer has determined that a company has information periodically, he makes it a point to pay it several visits a year, even though each visit may not produce intelligence. An ideal Source is one who has been "trained" to such a point that he will telephone when he has information of interest or when a company official has returned from a trip abroad. But the contact man is well aware that a company official thinks in terms of his own daily business needs and tends to forget intelligence needs. Like the salesman, the contact specialist must periodically revive interest in his product.

Subsequent visits to a company are relatively easy to handle. In a large company the contact officer utilizes as principal Source the person designated by the president, but also continually attempts to become acquainted with the head of every department in which foreign intelligence may be found. This intelligence may take the form of reports from managers of overseas branches or affiliates, contracts or negotiations with foreign companies or countries, or interviews with returning officials. Travellers abroad are an important font of intelligence, and the officer tries to arrange for regular immediate notification when such travel takes place.

When the contact officer learns that a cleared company official is about to travel on company business abroad, he is faced with the often difficult question of whether to brief him, that is, to instruct him beforehand in specific intelligence interests in the areas to be visited. The decision to brief, involving security and psychological hazards, is an infrequent one. Sometimes the business traveller is outraged at an attempt to recruit him as a "spy." But if the officer has worked with a Source for some time, considers him reliable, and is confident that he will not interpret the briefing as a mandate to engage in cloak-and-dagger activity, then he requests the entire intelligence community, through his headquarters channels, to provide questions for which the Source may be able to obtain answers. If he decides that a specific outlining of intelligence gaps is not desirable, he reminds the prospective traveller of the general needs of the community and suggests that whatever is of interest to him as a specialist in his field will be of interest to intelligence as well. In either case the Source must be discreet enough—and not all business travellers have been—to avoid advertising abroad that he is out to get "inside dope for CIA."

After the traveller has returned, the contact officer seeks an interview as soon as mutually convenient. If there was a briefing, the same questions may be used in debriefing. If the Source was not specifically primed with requirements for the trip, community requirements may be obtained for the debriefing. Formal requirements, however, are only guides to the interview rather than limitations on it. The contact officer tries to get as much detail as possible on all items of interest the Source may have encountered. Since a detailed interview takes time and the returned traveller is generally preoccupied with business matters that have piled up during his absence, a copy of the trip report which he must usually write for his company may by helpful. This report, however, will deal exclusively with his company's business, and interviews will still be necessary to explore any other subjects or areas on which the Source may be competent to report.

Mechanical aids are occasionally used to expedite the interview process. Although the modern businessman is well acquainted with the tape recorder or dictaphone and generally has no objection to their use, the contact man makes it a point to get advance permission for them. Some Sources, suggesting that an outline of the type of information desired be left with them, offer to dictate the answers as time permits into a tape recorder. Under this procedure the Source must be reminded to specify which questions he is answering and to spell out proper names.

Intelligence collected is not limited to the spoken and written word, but often includes maps, flow charts, photographs, graphics, floor plans, etc. These items are of most use to intelligence analysts when they are obtained for permanent retention, preferably in the original copy; but the Source usually has only a few copies and may balk at providing any for retention. Here the persuasiveness of the contact man must again prove itself. If he cannot talk the Source out of a copy, he tries at least to obtain the item on loan for 30 days so he can send it to Washington for reproduction.

Intelligence collection is essentially a one-way street, with the Sources giving and the collector receiving, but occasionally a Source requests reciprocity. The contact officer does have such unclassified items as the FBI's daily report on foreign broadcasts and translations of Soviet scientific abstracts at his disposal for distribution to selected Sources, and this *quid pro quo* helps to cement a cordial relationship. A greater strain on the relationship with a firm occurs when the Source requests specific information in return. A company may be opening a new branch overseas and desire information as to whether its proposed indigenous branch manager is proCommunist or unreliable in some other way. Or a firm may request assistance in arranging for the immigration of a skilled worker. Such requests are especially embarrassing when they come from a company which has been thoroughly cooperative and which may itself have provided covert support to the Agency. The contact man extricates himself from such situations by referring the requester whenever possible to the appropriate federal agency. If that does not work, he agrees to take the matter up with his Washington headquarters and throws on Washington the blame for inability to comply with the company's request.

The many foreign specialists who visit U.S. firms and institutions also have information of intelligence interest. These, however, the collector cannot talk to directly; intelligence policy forbids interviewing aliens in the United States on temporary visits. If time and occasion permit, the contact officer enlists the aid of an established Source within the firm visited to act as a cut-out or middleman. He briefs the cut-out on intelligence interests and encourages him to intertwine intelligence questions into his conversations with the visitor. The cut-out is also in a good position to assess the visitor's technical competence and personal idiosyncrasies. Interviewing through a cut-out, even more than interviewing through an interpreter, is less satisfactory than a direct encounter, but is preferable to creating an impression that visitors are invited to the United States only for intelligence exploitation.

University Exploitation

Thus far we have dealt almost exclusively with commercial or industrial firms as sources of intelligence. Other fruitful Sources are found in universities, research institutes and hospitals, pharmaceutical houses, etc. The contact officer often finds that he must approach these Sources somewhat differently than he approaches industrial ones. In the industrial firm he deals with Sources as officials of the company. In universities and similar institutions he deals with professors and researchers as individuals.

The basic approach is nevertheless the same. The president of the university is the initial point of contact; the contacter needs his blessing for the exploitation of university personnel and records. Lesser officials and faculty members also tend to be more cooperative when they know that the president is aware of the intelligence collection activity and approves of it. The deans of the schools, the dean of students, and department chairmen are worth cultivating, for most of the day-to-day activity of the university filters through their offices. They can, for instance, provide information on special research projects, foreign travel of faculty members, visiting foreign scholars, foreign graduate students, and other points of intelligence interest.

But the best Source is usually the individual professor who has just travelled abroad, attended an international conference, or entertained a foreign visitor. Like the businessman, the professor must be convinced that his information will receive the highest degree of protection.

The contact officer finds it rewarding to consult a *Who's Who* or some other reference work to obtain personal data and to determine the Source's professional stature and specific field of research interest. The Source is usually flattered that his professional competence is known to a layman. At the same time the officer must not pretend to knowledge he does not have on a technical subject, for such a sham is easily and quickly detected by the Source. Every man, and especially a professor, likes to talk about his work; and the interviewer's manifested interest in learning more about a subject of which he knows little usually kindles the academic spark. As a novice in the subject, the contact officer has ample excuse to ask for explanation and detail on each point made, even though the information may appear elementary to the Source. The officer must, however, take especial care to record faithfully this kind of data, for technical information has little value unless it is accurate. This may require another visit to the Source to verify the accuracy of the officer's report after he has finished writing it.

A problem the contact officer may encounter in his visits to a university is the lack of privacy. Few universities have individual offices for all members of the faculty. Doubling-up is frequent, and in some schools general faculty rooms or departmental offices are used in common. The officer makes every effort to arrange a meeting in private, soliciting the aid of the professor himself in trying to find a private spot. Even a quiet corner of the cafeteria or a meeting in the officer's automobile is preferable to one in a room where the interview can be overheard by other individuals. The professor is usually impressed by the officer's insistence on a secure meeting, and the confidential nature of the relationship is thus underlined.

The Alien

Getting information from the alien involves techniques vastly different from those used in dealing with U.S. citizens. For collection purposes an alien is defined as a recent arrival for permanent residence in this country, as opposed to the visitor or foreign student. In practice, alien Sources have been refugees from eastern Europe, with a small sprinkling of immigrants from the Far East. Initially the displaced persons of World War II, driven or escaping from lands occupied by the German military forces, were exploited for their knowledge of areas which were under Communist rule after 1945. The influx of Hungarians after the events of October 1956 presented another golden opportunity to collect current intelligence on an inaccessible area. More recently the increased travel between the Soviet Bloc and the United States and the greater emigration of Satellite nationals to visit or rejoin relatives here have given impetus to the alien exploitation program.

Because techniques in contacting and exploiting aliens are so different from those used in dealing with industrial or academic Sources, alien specialists with language ability and particular adaptability and perseverance have been assigned to field offices where alien concentrations are greatest. Adaptability is needed because of the varied types of alien with whom the contact officer must deal, ranging from a former minister in an exiled government to the janitor in a munitions factory. Perseverance is required to spend the time and effort needed to track an alien as he moves from one address to another. The interviews must usually be conducted in the evening or on weekends, since the alien in most cases cannot be interviewed at his place of employment.

In addition to the difficulty of locating the alien, and the odd hours involved, the contact officer faces the much greater problem of eliciting the cooperation of the Source. The greatest barrier is the alien's suspicion. He is likely to have lived by his wits almost continually since 1938, and to have been interrogated and reinterrogated by various intelligence and security services, not always in friendly fashion; his instinctive reaction is to have nothing to do with an intelligence agent. A second barrier is the language, for few aliens speak enough English to carry on a detailed interview. The contact officer's language ability may overcome this handicap, but he should be aware of the danger that a native fluency may cause the Source to suspect him as the agent of a foreign security service. Frequently the alien has greater trust and confidence in a contact man whose crude working knowledge of the foreign language betrays him as obviously American. If there is no mutual language in which to converse an interpreter must be obtained. Field offices maintain lists of cleared Sources who can act as interpreters, but here again the alien may doubt the *bona fides* of the interpreter. He may trust the contact man but be suspicious of his co-national.

The contact officer tries to make an appointment with the alien, by telephone if any, or by letter. Often, though, he must knock on the door without previous appointment, hoping that his prospect is at home. The scene that greets him when he enters the alien's home is that of the entire family arrayed behind the man of the house, who, they fear, is in trouble. He realizes that he cannot possibly speak to the alien in private, for any attempt to lead him away from the family group confirms their suspicion that something is wrong. He is forced to present the purpose of his trip to the entire family in an effort to allay their fears. Most aliens are quick to grasp the needs of an intelligence service but they must still convince themselves that their caller is actually a representative of the U.S. and not a foreign intelligence service. The officer tells them that if they have any doubt about the authenticity of his credentials they should call the local office of the FBI. He stresses very emphatically, however, that he is not an FBI agent, but represents an intelligence organization interested only in foreign intelligence.

Once the hard shell of suspicion and distrust is pierced, the alien becomes a most cooperative source. He is flattered that the U.S. Government has sought him out and pleased that he can contribute to the fight against Communism. He is useful both in supplying information from his own knowledge and experience and in giving leads on co-nationals who may have additional information. Aliens also correspond and send packages to relatives abroad and the correspondence may be of intelligence interest, but the contact officer must first overcome their fear that harm may come to a relative if they reveal too much.

The officer is very often the federal Government's only contact with the alien, who therefore tends to look to him as a general father confessor, employment counsellor, psychiatrist and sounding board for pet ideas or pet peeves. His immigration and citizenship problems, obstacles to the immigration of his relatives, or his dissatisfaction with his employment he presents to the contact man for solution, since in his mind an intelligence service is above the laws and regulations established for ordinary citizens. The contact officer is careful not to make any commitments, referring the alien to the appropriate federal agency. He must also take care not to involve himself in the politics of ethnic groups, for most of them are split into hostile camps.

The matter of payment sometimes arises here. The vast majority of alien Sources are happy to make available whatever information they have as a contribution to their new country. Occasionally, however, having spent a considerable amount of time in preparing a detailed and important report, an alien may express a desire for compensation. The contact officer must obtain an evaluation from Headquarters before he can make such compensation; and even with Headquarters' approval he is treading on dangerous ground, for there is an effective grapevine within the nationality groups, and his future request for cooperation from others may be met with similar demands for payment. In general, an occasional lunch or dinner should constitute the extent of financial outlay on an alien.

o   o   o

This discussion of domestic collection techniques has of necessity been cast in terms of averages and stereotypes. Every contact specialist in the field could point out many exceptions to the generalizations here drawn and show the peculiarities of dealing with Sources in his own area. The techniques which have been developed remain individual and flexible, varying with three variable factors, the collector, the Source, and the material to be collected. Each collector applies those personal techniques, gained through experience, which are called for in a given situation to extract the greatest amount of raw intelligence from his Source; but his methods are likely to fall roughly into the patterns outlined above.

7.

Elicitation is a core technique of espionage (though a rather "soft" one). Here, a practitioner details the tactics used in a spotting operation that was targeted at friendly-country scientists. They were regarded as prospectives for possible recruitment as U.S. intelligence sources. In the post–Cold War world, this is likely to occur often.

The Elicitation Interview

GEORGE G. BULL

Not so long ago, during a tour of duty in West Germany, the author spent a good deal of time engaged in elicitation in the scientific sphere. What follows is intended to illustrate some of the features of this form of the art, the object of which, of course, is to obtain information without giving the subject the feeling that he is being interrogated. Elicitation, that is to say, like a lot of other tradecraft techniques, has its Scylla and Charybdis. On one hand, the cautious seeker risks concealing his purpose in such general questions or remarks that he evokes nothing of value. On the other hand, if the questions are excessively direct, the contact may quickly suspect he is being interrogated for intelligence purposes and bring the interview to an abrupt and unpleasant end.

The writer, who has a scientific background, was provided with solid but not impenetrable cover. My task was to interview West German scientists in order to determine the nature and extent of their contacts behind the Iron Curtain, without, however, disclosing an intelligence association. If the person contacted appeared to have agent potential, he would subsequently be approached for assessment and recruitment by another individual without embarrassing my ostensible employer. It soon became clear to me that success in elicitation depends on the solution of several practical problems:

1. Devising an ostensible reason for talking to the potential source;
2. Locating the potential source;
3. Positively identifying him as the potential source;
4. Maintaining cover during the actual elicitation;
5. Keeping the potential source on the topics of intelligence interest.

In the course of an elicitation, I often found myself attempting to solve simultaneously problems 3, 4, and 5, while being subjected to cross-elicitation,

George G. Bull, "The Elicitation Interview," *Studies in Intelligence*, vol. 14, no. 2 (Fall 1970), pp. 115–22. Originally classified "Secret."

or sometimes a blunt interrogation of a friendly but occasionally hostile nature.

The Reason for the Interview

Finding an ostensible reason for an interview was sometimes easy. Frequently, publications were readily available associating the individual with one of the countries in which we were interested. For a prominent person, a *Who's Who* type publication often showed that he had been born, had studied, or worked in such a country. Sometimes the potential source had written about it or had received some sort of public recognition there, such as a medal or an honorary membership in a learned society.

Potential sources among the less prominent were sometimes listed in catalogs of specialists or translators of various languages. Sometimes college and university publications listed background items on faculty, students, and alumni of foreign origin. I found that saying I had seen my contact's name in such publications always seemed to allay suspicion or hostility, at least momentarily.

After deciding that a particular individual might be worth talking to, I would institute certain checks in an attempt to make sure he was not working for the opposition, or otherwise questionable, and therefore best left alone. Frequently the information that turned up was not derogatory, but instead furnished or reinforced a good excuse for an interview and helped to make it more friendly and fruitful that it otherwise could have turned out.

Although my cover gave me considerable latitude, the questions I asked nevertheless had to be consistent with a particular position in the U.S. government. In such a situation one does not have the latitude of the free-lance writer, something a contacting officer would do well not to claim to be unless very well back-stopped or already a well-known writer.

Interviewers sought [supposedly] for the purpose of finding someone to do translations present other potential difficulties. The interviewer must be sure the material he talks about has not been translated already. He must provide the material and pay for it promptly. Word about "lots of interviews and no translation jobs" can quickly get around. Even where payment has been prompt, the specialists can become very suspicious, especially if newspapers have carried the story of a blown operation that had started with the "doing translations" approach to the agent involved. A mother in Gelsenkirchen said to me firmly, "My son does not want to do translations for the Americans." And there was the Offenbach school teacher, listed in a catalog of Russian translators, who bluntly asked, "Is this for intelligence, or really to do translations?"

If the potential source is very prominent, there will be special problems in eliciting information. He may have a tight schedule on a given day, and not be amenable to any questions other than those immediately related to the stated reason for the meeting. The man who has pleasant relations with individuals behind the Iron Curtain presents another kind of problem, because often he is very fearful of losing his friends or causing trouble for them, if it gets out that he has had friendly meetings with an American official. Such people tend to be cautious and curt, or unavailable for an interview. Sometimes this fear only arises after the person has agreed to receive the interviewer. Thus one of my meetings started with the contact saying, "Mr. Bull, I had hoped you were not going to come." In another situation of this kind, the subject knew I had had a tedious journey to his home near the Lüneburg Heide. He reluctantly received me, but the interview was so stilted and concern for Russian friends was so frequently expressed that the meeting was soon over by mutual consent.

Sometimes the interviewer is fortunate enough to be able to make an approach under the auspices of a mutual friend, who has suggested the name of the target person as someone who should be seen. If the person is not too busy and receives the interviewer, the circumstances can be particularly favorable. Such a source is usually ready to talk freely, and the operative does not have to engage in subtle combat with any fixed idea that he has come to talk about some particular topic of no real interest whatever.

This use of a mutual friend is usually safe if one's role is limited to spotting, and ultimate recruitment is done by someone else. If the interviewer follows up later with an attempted recruitment, however, he of course blows his cover. He will probably alienate the mutual acquaintance, and perhaps lead the potential source to believe that this mutual friend has a relationship to intelligence which in fact he does not have.

If the information that the potential source has contacts in the Soviet Bloc has been obtained through a letter intercept program, one's ingenuity will be strained to the limit to think up a reason for an interview. Such intercept programs may disclose old friendships between an available person and one in the Soviet Union. A third person (such as the hopeful elicitor) is not expected to know about such a relationship and is likely to be told, as was the writer (not under his cover but fortunately under alias), "I had not heard from Sonya for many years. When I heard she was alive I wrote to her. Your people read my letter and sent you to see me."

Finding the Potential Source

Often the information that identifies the person as of possible value is old. He or she may have moved. In such a case the interviewer can find himself the target of an interrogation or elicitation operation by some friendly and helpful person who seems to demand as a price for the target's new address a complete life history of the hopeful interviewer and a detailed explanation of the planned business with the target person. How these questions are answered is very important. Such a person, say a neighbor, may well be in touch with the target before the contacting officer. Thus when finally located, the potential source may say he has no information and refuse to be interviewed.

If the interviewer is a stranger to the locality, he will probably find it useful to visit the city hall, where a directory of the inhabitants can normally be found. In Germany it is called the *Einwohnermeldamt*. It will furnish addresses gratis, or for a small fee, and usually no questions asked. In the city it is better not to ask directions from a policeman walking along the street. Find one tied down by traffic point duty. In one such case in Bayreuth the writer found himself in the clutches of a friendly officer just going off duty who insisted that we go together to the local precinct station where there was adequate information. On arrival at the precinct station there followed a long conference to the general effect that Herr A. would be a much better man to do translations than Herr B., whom I had hoped to locate in a certain hard-to-find street.

Identifying the Prospect

In many nations there is a name equivalent to John Smith in frequency of occurrence. The contacting officer's headquarters naturally wants to be certain whether such and such John Smith is the one on whom they already have information, or instead is really a new John Smith about whom they wish to build up a file. The way to avoid this kind of coincidence is to determine dates and places of birth.

In the case of prominent people, this information is usually available in *Who's Who* type almanacs, and the question of identity can easily be disposed of even before an interview is sought. In the case of not-so-prominent people, good luck and/or skill in elicitation is the only answer.

Research in the city hall can reduce the need for elicitation from the prospect. Registry cards in foreign countries often have the date and place of birth on them. When the operative asks for the address of a person, the registry clerk may just hand him the official card for a minute to copy the address. Other identifying data can be remembered until one is outside and has a chance to write that down also. Sometimes the functionary will not be averse to conversation. On one occasion I asked if the person I was tracing had come to Bad Ems from such and such a place. (The place name had been picked out of thin air.) By sheer good luck the official was only too glad to correct me with a flood of desirable information.

If the interview is under way and the identifying data has yet to be obtained, the contacting officer faces a major challenge. It is easy to induce a person to talk about his work and interests, but he may not wish to disclose his place of origin, because of a local prejudice against outsiders, or fear that the interviewer may have a prejudice against people from his area. Here again, however, the desire to contradict a wrong statement with correct information can often be easily aroused. The interviewer can sometimes do this by saying something like, "You have been quite successful here, I suppose you were born here." Or, if the interviewer speaks the language of the prospect fluently, he can try the accent ploy. "Your accent seems a little different from that of the people I know from around here. Did you grow up here?" If one can get the prospect on the subject of travel and vacations, the birthplace data can often be obtained. If the interviewer suspects his subject is from a certain area it is easy to say he once visited the area, found it charming and then ask if subject has been there. (The interviewer had better be telling the truth about having been there!) The subject of vacation travel can often be used to determine birthplace, sometimes the specific place or at least the general area. People usually like to talk about their vacations and it is natural to ask how they picked the place and whether they came from the area in question originally.

Date of birth is more difficult to obtain. Many people are very clever about concealing this detail even from their intimate friends. Unless one can identify oneself as a representative of the Pension Bureau, the Census Bureau, or some such governmental office, which might involve showing credentials, one cannot politely ask a stranger's age, at least in most of Western society. (Greece is perhaps an exception.) This is particularly true if the interview has been sought on the pretext of discussing the man's work on some technical topic, or a long-standing political problem like Franco-German relations. Sometimes events in science or politics can be cited by the interviewer in such a way as to make the subject respond in a helpful manner. The interviewer can say, for instance, if atomic energy is being discussed, something along these lines: "Yes, I was only 24 and just out of college when the Hiroshima bomb was exploded." Hopefully the subject will volunteer a similar statistic in his life. Other events covering a limited span of time, like the ownership of a crystal radio set or a certain style of clothing, can be used, as well as specific political or other events, such as Lindbergh's flight. Wars or war service can sometimes be used as the basis of a rather challenging assertion that can flatter the prospect's vanity so he or she will boastfully produce information about age. This was successful in producing the age of a not-so-young-looking man in Lübeck to whom the writer said: "I suppose you were too young to have been in World War I?" Luckily the answer came back, "I served three years and I am now 72." This, of course, demanded an immediate and automatic response. "You certainly don't look it!" In such cases the target personality may reply, "Yes, I was 72 last August 4th." If not, the interviewer may be able to say something about his father having turned 72 on such and such a date, and hopefully the target will volunteer his birth date.

Keeping the Source on the Desired Topics While Maintaining One's Cover

This can be a vexing problem. Often the meeting has been requested on the pretext of discussing a topic very different from the real one of interest to the contacting officer. In such cases, the elicitor's pay dirt is often to be found in the digressions that take place. Thus, I found it hard not to appear upset when the subject said cheerfully, "Well, Mr. Bull, you did not come here to hear about my travels in Russia and my friends there. Now about the electric motor my institute here in Karlsruhe is developing . . ."

Some authorities hold that elicitation is easier in a group than in a face-to-face interview, but this writer disagrees. In my experience individuals are much more cautious in their statements when in a group than in a face-to-face interview. In a group situation, the potential source often acts as if he feels that he must not spend too much time in dialogue with a particular person lest he be thought rude to the others present.

In certain unplanned situations where the writer's wife was present, it appeared desirable to try to elicit certain possibly useful information. The source would just begin a topic, drop a gem or two, and then turn to the writer's wife, saying: "This cannot be very interesting to you. How are you enjoying your stay here in Germany?"

One of the most annoying obstacles to keeping the source talking about the desired subject may be his desire to talk about his contacts in the interviewer's own country. The writer, trying to elicit information about the Soviet Union, found it very difficult to keep a distinguished professor of mechanical engineering in Aachen from telling him in great detail about his trips to the United States and the good time he had had at a professional meeting in Philadelphia.

It is obvious that the interviewer in an elicitation situation must always keep in mind the stated purpose of the meeting and not become too intent on getting pay dirt from the digressions. Elicitation targets are often likely to be persons of above average or superior intelligence. Like most people, they are wary in talking to a stranger who has asked to meet them. Too much interest in the digressions can easily make the whole interview go completely sour, resulting in hostility on the part of the source who suspects that he is being used. It was an unhappy moment for the writer, who became too interested in the adventures and information potential of a certain Volga German woman whom he had approached in her now home at Saarbrücken on the subject of doing translations, when she suddenly asked, "Why are you so interested in me as an individual instead of talking about translations?"

The need for precautions to prevent the interview from blowing up in this manner is essential even if the elicitor is working only as a spotter, and protects his cover by turning over subsequent recruitment approaches to a different individual. The spotter will often want to re-interview some subjects. Sometimes more information is desired by the [agency] before a case officer contacts the prospect. For cover purposes, the contacting officer must re-interview some people. He must be careful not to become known as the man who "saw lots of people only once and some of them were approached by an intelligence recruiter."

It is axiomatic that a successful elicitation interview obtains information on which a case officer can open negotiations and take over the contact. It is also desirable that the interviewer stay on a friendly basis with the subject. He can go back to visit him in an atmosphere of developing friendship. Such subsequent visits can obtain useful information even if no recruitment has been carried out, attempted, or even planned.

Far different from the episodes recounted above was a successful elicitation in which the writer built up rapport, obtained useful information, and turned it over to his superiors. Some months later, he was asked to see this distinguished professor of theoretical physics at Hannover again, and obtain certain information about his planned attendance at some meetings where there would be a large Soviet delegation. During a pleasant luncheon in an atmosphere of increased cordiality, the professor asked the writer if he knew a certain person from the city where the writer was stationed. Recognizing the alias of a colleague, I offered a suitable denial. The professor then lowered his voice and said, "He called on me recently. I don't think I want to have anything to do with him, for I think he is connected with intelligence."

8.

A search for prospective agents who will be useful against their own country's regime often includes "walk-ins," who have come on their own seeking various kinds of attention. All recruitment of agents requires an elaborate assessment process that CIA has tried to systematize in various ways. One is to employ psychiatrists to devise a set of personality profiles. Here is a relatively recent summation of this work, written by one of the psychiatrists. The focus is Cold War, but the assessment approach is adaptable enough to outlast that context.

Psychology of Treason

WILHELM MARBES

The Agency definition of a defector is an individual who has committed treason, a person who first accepted identification with a regime and then betrayed his allegiance to cooperate with a hostile foreign intelligence service. Thus the word is used here differently than in the media. The Agency recruits every year sources and access agents who are not really committing treason, individuals cooperating against a third nation, for example. The emphasis here is on the hard core defector, the individual who has committed an act of treason.

Because I am a psychiatrist, this paper reflects a psychiatric bias. A sociologist, a political scientist, a historian would present a different view. But additionally my being a psychiatrist has certain clinical implications. I wish to allay any misconception implying that defectors are crazy, or that a person has to be crazy to become a defector. Quite to the contrary, the percentage of mental disorders of the psychotic type or of seriously neurotically impaired individuals among defectors is less than one would expect to find in an ordinary population of the same size. Psychotics and neurotics rarely enter the kinds of work that would make them attractive, as defectors, to the Agency. Though it might take different forms in other societies, a certain amount of screening goes on. Even without a psychiatrist or psychologist involved, there would be commanding officers and physicians or teachers weeding out individuals who were obviously mentally or emotionally unsuitable to receive information of a national security interest. When we find amongst our defector population people who do suffer from psychotic or neurotic difficulties, their disorders are usually of a very late and/or insidious onset. Even disorders such as alcoholism appear less fre-

Wilhelm Marbes, "Psychology of Treason," *Studies in Intelligence*, vol. 30, no. 2 (Summer 1986), pp. 1–11. Originally classified "Secret."

quently among defectors than among the population at large. Overall, severe clinical psychopathology is not usually a major factor among defectors.

Nonetheless, one of the early great defectors to the Agency was discovered not long after his defection to be clinically psychotic. This was a terrible embarrassment to the Agency. It was decided shortly thereafter that before the Agency gave its stamp of approval, each defector, in addition to having his bona fides established and passing a polygraph examination, would have also a complete medical examination, including a psychiatric evaluation. After we had interviewed many defectors we were asked to create a profile of a typical defector. I think the original requesters had something in mind akin to the profile of a skyjacker. This paper evolved out of the search for that profile. I begin by acknowledging defeat. We never found one single profile that would describe them all. After a dozen years of searching we were convinced that this was a futile task. If anything, what we did discover were parallel mutually exclusive pathways toward eventual acts of defection. So this is, in fact, a paper of generalizations, describing clusters of characteristics which fit most defectors.

Despair

That said, I will begin with the one statement (aside from something as obvious as they all defected) which does describe all defectors: nobody ever defected because he was happy. While a defector might look happy at the moment, exhilarated at having executed a dramatic escape, or having pulled off a personal coup, or even after considerable contemplation having finally resolved his dilemma with a deliberate decision, the act was first put in motion by despair. Defection, at least on the part of people who are willing and/or driven to commit treason, is an act of strong feelings. Often it is an act of desperation. It is the act of a person who feels compelled to do it out of dissatisfaction, disillusionment, depression, and defeat. In our experience defection is a response to an acute overwhelming life crisis or to an accumulation of crises or disappointments; the individual finally feels forced to act. We use the word unhappy in the widest sense—someone unhappy because he was passed over for promotion, someone desperate because the auditors were arriving on Monday.

What are defectors unhappy about? This runs an enormous gamut of feelings and circumstances in life. Contrary to what you might believe, ideology would rank very low on the list of motivations. The reasons are much more likely to be personal, the stuff of soap operas, the ordinary unhappiness of everyday life. It is more likely to be intimate than ideological—marital problems, mistress problems, wrong sexual preference problems, drinking problems, gambling problems, money problems, career problems. Ideology seldom, certainly seldom alone, causes a defection. Almost never Leninism or communist ideology. The ideological exceptions in our experience were much more likely to be those of nationalism or of religion. But even those ideological defections seem to have been historically and geographically limited. The nationalistic defectors for the most part have been Lithuanians, Latvians, and Poles. We are still waiting for Ukranian nationalist defectors. We have had quite a number of defectors with Ukrainian surnames, but when you talk with these individuals they make it plain that they do not think of themselves as Ukrainians. They think of themselves as Muscovites because that's where they were born and raised. Or another fellow thought of himself as a Siberian because that's where he was brought up. The religious issue seems to be almost totally confined to the Poles.

Defection should not be viewed as a problem of communism, but as a human problem with security and political consequences. We have had serious defections from our side and the defectors who have gone from our side to the other were a mirror image of what I describe. The difference was in style. Most of the defectors who come our way include in their plans the option of leaving their original country and resettling in America. Most of the American defectors chose to remain in this country, to work in place for the opposition, to take the money, but then retire in place.

The psychological underpinnings of defection transcend not only ideological but also cultural lines. One of our first important Chinese mainland defectors spoke no English, making it necessary to use a Chinese interpreter. The interpreter dutifully approached me before the interview to learn what sorts of questions I was going to ask. After being informed he was very apologetic. "Doctor, I'm afraid you're wasting your time," he said. He had already met this young man—a very traditional Chinese, unlikely to say anything critical about his parents. The Chinese accept their parents totally and unequivocally. The Chinese are not raised to think about their parents in a critical way. Eventually I asked this defector about his family background. And he began a very excited response: "You know, I'm glad somebody asked me that. Because you know but for the character of my mother, I don't think I'd have been here."

Defections, then, are seen as reactions to the vicissitudes of life playing upon an already existing character structure. I have designed a rough equation to describe this: $I \times C = D$. "I" stands for the individual psychology, times "C" stands for the circumstances of life, equals "D" the act of defection. I have drawn this model to make a simple mathematical analogy. There are many combinations or variables by which you can arrive at 48. The extremes are 48 times 1 and 1 times 48. There is a relationship between the magnitude of the crisis or circumstances that precipitates a defection and the underlying character structure or life history of the individual who is being impinged upon. As you can imagine from this equation, the more overwhelming the crisis, the fewer distortions in the individual psychology and the life history required. If someone is making "progress" in his personal life he is seldom motivated to defect. Not only did defectors need an inclination or vulnerability to defect, many of them had to be moved by external circumstances.

An example of an overwhelming crisis: There was a Soviet couple in Buenos Aires, illegals without any diplomatic protection. They were caught and found themselves in the hands of the Argentine service. The Argentines quickly determined that they had rolled up the whole net, so this Soviet couple was of little or no further interest to them. But we were very interested in larger issues, such as how they were selected, how they were trained, how they were dispatched. The Argentine authorities gave us access to this Soviet couple. We told them that they had a choice to make. They could remain in the hands of the Argentines or they could elect to come to the United States, be debriefed by American intelligence, and then resettled in the United States, an offer they could hardly refuse. They elected to come with us. We debriefed them. We interviewed them. They were psychiatrically evaluated and from the psychiatric point of view, looked and sounded less like two defectors than any two people we had ever interviewed. Not surprisingly, they quickly redefected.

At the other extreme, we have seen people defect simply because they were miffed, passed over, disregarded, humiliated. They defected to seek vengeance, to strike back. Between these two extremes we see an enormous range of human possibilities. We have had people defect for such base reasons as attempting to avoid legitimate pursuit by the ordinary justice of their own countries. One was an embezzler. The auditors were coming on Monday. He knew he had information of interest to American intelligence so he came rushing to make a deal. We have had people defect to us who imagined themselves to be under suspicion. They were frightened, perhaps feeling guilty, or suspicious of the intentions of their colleagues.

Many crises are related to age and circumstances. For example, a "Dear John" letter to a 21-year-old border guard could result in his defection because it comes when a young man is still forming his sense of identity and sexual acceptance. Not getting a promotion would probably have a less severe effect on him because many alternative career paths remained open. A 51-year-old executive might be much more overwhelmed by being passed over because of a lack of options at that time of his life.

Some defections are so deliberately dangerous as to risk life and limb. These are desperate attempts: escapes from immediate physical dangers, or flights from depression. Some defections have followed suicide attempts. Others were hardly more than suicide equivalents, the acts of individuals who had nothing more to live for and were desperately seeking a relief from the agony of despair as much as a wild hope for a second chance in a new life. Obviously the potential for redefection would be high in such individuals if their fantasized hopes could not be adequately realized in their new lives.

Runners and Fighters

What about the motivations of the people who defect in fact versus the motivations and/or character of those who remain defectors-in-place? When we began our study, it was commonly believed that there were enormous differences between the characters of these apparent two groups of individuals. Our work convinced us that this was not really the case. One could posit the data pool as a bell curve.

At one extreme you might find individuals who seemed destined to defect in fact, versus on the other extreme individuals who were destined to be defectors-in-place. What do the people on the extremes look like? (Remember that those at either extreme are just a very small proportion of the total.) The classic defector-in-fact is usually a frightened individual whose motivation is shallow, who is seeking an escape. His life history usually contains a series of mini-defections. Whenever this individual has seen a crisis approaching he has attempted to escape or flee. He is not given to confrontations. Faced with a crisis, he runs.

On the other end of the scale there is a small group of people with very different life histories. They usually have been oppositional people all of their lives: fighters, counterattackers. Early in the course of their life histories, when they saw a crisis coming, they attacked. More often than not they were defeated, but survived. So they modified their technique, first by "sideswiping," letting the crisis seemingly roll by and, as it comes abreast, swiping at it. By the time they modify their technique to "backstabbing," they are ripe for us. In fact more often than not we do not recruit these people; they are volunteers. They seek us out. They are looking for opportunities once again to counterattack. These are the individuals who are much more motivated by getting even. They are seeking vengeance and justification.

Between these two extremes fit the overwhelming majority of defectors. The most important thing to know about them was what determined whether they worked in place or defected in fact. We discovered that there were three main factors.

The most important factor was the actual logistic circumstances of the original defection or attempted contact. Could the person turn around and go back if he wanted to? Obviously if somebody jumps out of the third floor window of the Soviet Embassy there is no point in attempting to turn him around. But there are many cases in which individuals walk in with rather

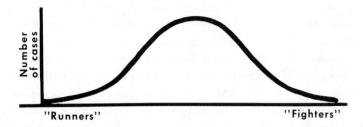

uncertain logistic circumstances. When I first came to the Agency the rule of thumb was see if the defector carried a package. If it was a suitcase full of laundry, he was quickly [defined as a defector-in-fact and (unfortunately) was accepted as such]. If he was carrying a briefcase filled with documents and photographs, he was a "live one," a likely defector-in-place. We were probably shooting ourselves in the foot because human circumstances are more complicated than that.

Which leads us to the second factor, the way in which this defector was dealt with by the first American contact. If his defection was accepted and he was converted into a defector-in-fact, for all practical purposes, it was very difficult several days later to turn him around, both logistically and psychologically. But if he was dealt with from the first by an individual who immediately sought to reassure his practical concerns about getting back safely, and if he was quickly turned around, very often we had ourselves a recruitment or an in-place asset. Turnarounds were the result of an aggressive officer pressing the opportunity to convince the defector to remain working in-place.

The third factor, a rather distant third, was the individual psychology of the particular defector. In most cases the first two factors turned out to be overwhelming because only at the extremes were the psychological variables that important.

Prominent in the psychology of many defectors is the mechanism of projection, the casting out of devils. The individual preserves his emotional virginity and deflects guilt, blame, and responsibility. Whatever the actual source of his difficulties, the defector perceives them as arising outside of himself rather than from within and so preserves his grandiose view of his immediate self.

A British historian archly noted that a man is never so dangerous as when he can identify a private grievance with a matter of principle. Defection usually has a significant personal meaning in the context of patterns and expectations implicit in the earlier life history. Sometimes the act of defection seems to be a replaying of an earlier life crisis, especially in cases where there was in the life history a parental abandonment by separation, divorce, or death.

Few of us are actually as self-contained or independent as we imagine. The human condition is one of interdependency. Most of us have dependency needs without apologies, and inherent in most relationships are the reciprocal obligations implied on the part of both parties to meet the needs of the other. An unwritten social compact exists in all societies involving all the parties, individuals, and organizations. Many defections arise out of situations in which the individual feels that the regime reneged on its part of this implicit compact. The ties of reciprocal obligation are broken and often the individual will respond to this perceived betrayal with a treason of his own.

The defectors the Agency deals with usually are quite pragmatic, street-wise, cynical people who seldom really accepted the ideology of the system. They understood the corruption of the system the way a surf rider knows waves. They used the system to their individual advantage. Only when the system failed their pursuits or when the system turned upon them did they suddenly become excited about the problems of communism. Scattered throughout the world must be many ordinary refugees who left for ideological reasons. But the kinds of people whom the Agency defines as defectors were not the downtrodden of the earth, because if they were they would have never obtained access to the kind of information that they traded or sold to us. Their defections may have been made psychologically easier for them simply because they were never committed to the official ideology. Even individuals who are not ideologists may express their personal discontent in political terms. This is especially likely to be the case if the person has been conditioned to explain himself this way or if he thinks picturing himself as politically motivated will convince a listener of his sincerity. Also ideological arguments tend to be high sounding and apt to be less embarrassing than a confession of base motives or humiliating personal indiscretions. One seldom chooses to play the fool.

Loyalty

I will now address the individual psychological factor in our equation and the factors underlying the development of an individual defector psychology. Since we are discussing treason we might stop and ask, "Where does loyalty come from anyway? Why is anybody ever loyal to anything?" There may be some genetic exceptions, but almost everyone is born with a capacity for loyalty. But this capacity has to be engaged and engendered in early life. Most of us learn about loyalty in the family. It has its origins in the mother-child relationship and in the natural process of growth and maturation. This sense of mutual warmth, obligation, response, and reciprocity expands to include the larger family, the neighborhood, friends, schoolmates, teammates, our colors, our flag, our country. We have to look at the special circumstances which might interfere with this normal development. Increasingly, studies are suggesting that there may be some individuals born with a diminished capacity for experiencing love, warmth, and hence loyalty.

There are individuals born in unusual geographical circumstances, such that there might be an attachment to mother and family but no sense of an attachment or affiliation to any larger field. I think of a young man who was the son of an Italian-Jewish mother and a Coptic Christian Egyptian father. This young man was born in Alexandria, Egypt. His parents separated and were divorced. He moved with his mother to an ethnically divided community. I don't think this young man had any geographical sense of identity whatsoever.

The vagaries of geopolitical history are such that defectors may not feel loyalty to a nation but only to a tribe or an ethnic group or to a people. Frequently the nation in which they had been raised or the nation in whose service they found themselves may have played a role in the fracture of the original identity of that tribe or the turf of that tribe or ethnic group. The identification may be only cultural. I am reminded of the Bloc defector who told me that his loyalty was to Mozart.

But even assuming that someone was born intact and that his geographical circumstances were tolerable, an individual still needs a home, a warm, receptive, understanding, and encouraging family. Many defectors were born into chaotic families divided or broken or shattered, often with its parts scattered, what is colloquially referred to as a broken home. The opportunity to form a sense of affiliation was absent in their childhood. They grew up without the proverbial ties that bind. My classic anecdote about this involves a man who had served as a double agent for many years. When his time came he had to be dragged out of place because he loved the life, which in itself is unusual. His mother and father had hated each other for as long as he could remember, so much so that they didn't sleep in the same bed and would undress on opposite sides of the room with a curtain or screen between them. The ever empathic psychiatrist attempted to commiserate with the defector about his terrible childhood. The defector responded, "Oh no, doctor, it was wonderful. You see with my father I would pretend to be on his side against my mother. And with my mother I would pretend to be on her side against my father. And both of them were wonderful to me." He spent his whole childhood playing both ends against the middle. It would be difficult to invent a better childhood training ground for a lifelong history of duplicity. Indeed, after he was dragged out of place and we attempted to resettle him, he was never to be as happy again as he had been as a defector-in-place playing every day so well the game that he learned to play with such skill and joy as a child.

The capacity for splitting and shifting loyalties, once incorporated into the personality of the developing child, remains present even if unconscious throughout life, a latent mechanism which can be quickly reactivated and drawn upon later.

So defectors often come from broken homes or distorted family backgrounds. But not always. This is a point at which there are parallel but mutually exclusive pathways toward defection. Obviously any defector is in opposition to his regime. But that doesn't mean that every defector is necessarily a rebel. Some defectors in their oppositional behavior are playing out in their adult lives the unresolved conflict of the adolescent striking back at his parents. Only now the regime has taken the place of the parent. An obvious instance of an immature individual striking back at a parent could be seen in a young Soviet defector, who smiling from ear to ear said, "I hope what I did doesn't kill my father." He claimed that his father was a colonel in the KGB. He imagined that his defection would put a crimp in his father's career. Not surprisingly the family history revealed that this young man hated his father. Obviously what we were seeing was the playing out of a family romance on the international stage. Such immature rebellious defectors often demonstrate an opposition and immaturity in many aspects of their adult behavior and so they are frequently difficult individuals to deal with under any circumstances.

But we also see defectors who are not rebels, individuals who are obviously identified with the values of their parents, products of warm, receptive, understanding, and encouraging families which were secretly dissident against the regime. The family history might have included some defeat at the hands of the regime with the defector now imagining himself the loyal avenger of the family. In his defection he is picking up the family's fallen banner of honor and shafting the regime with it. He is striking back not only in his own name, not just out of his own disappointment, but further emboldened, further strengthened by the emotional support he imagines from the family. He fantasizes that his parents would secretly applaud his actions. In some cases the support is even more obvious. Some potential defectors have confided their wistful, tentative intentions to their families and were immediately and wholeheartedly encouraged to act.

A defector's father was a pioneer of the communist regime. He had fought in his youth against the oppressions of a prior dictatorship. The defector had grown up amongst the elite of that communist society, the son of an important and well-regarded man. Yet, and this was very close to being an ideological defection, he was dissatisfied with the society and disillusioned with its prospects. He discussed his feelings with his father: "You look at your life and see how bad things were and how much better they are now . . . you told me how much better things could be and I see that they are never going to be that way." And the father told his son, "I understand you and from your vantage point you're right." The young man felt that his father had given him implicit psychological permission to defect. So a defection can arise out of a warm and close family. Defectors who come from families with close ties are usually more mature and more stable individuals. They are usually easier to manage as agents and likely to resettle more smoothly in their new lives.

Traits

In examining the individual factors I use words which in another context could be psychiatric diagnoses. While some defectors met such criteria, most did not. But I wish to emphasize that now I use these terms not as psychiatric diagnoses but as adjectives only because defectors often exhibit behaviors, traits, vulnerabilities, and proclivities which are best described by such words. Frequently it is a combination of these traits and proclivities which interact and culminate in the individual decision to defect.

We have observed a triad of three frequently recurring traits in defections. The first of these is immaturity or impulsivity. In particular these people exhibit a lack of tolerance for frustration and/or an inability to defer gratification. The conduct of such individuals is often emotion ridden. They display a consequent impairment in the regulation of their conduct. They act before they think or they over-react. Example: the young man who gets a "Dear John" letter and goes over the wall. Or the pilot who is the teacher's pet of the squadron commander. When the squadron commander is suddenly replaced by a severe disciplinarian the young man doesn't even wait for the change to sort out. He takes his plane over the border at the next turn. I would include in impulse disorders the individual who cannot control his gambling or his expenditures. Occasionally we will see a defector who is so grossly immature or so obviously disordered in terms of his impulse control that the clinical diagnosis is justified. More often we are dealing with an individual in whom we see only indicators.

The second trait of this triad is sociopathy. These individuals demonstrate problems with conscience or morals. They seldom hesitate to violate the rights of others to serve their own ends. A lay definition might be a chronic "son-of-a-bitch." There are two basic types of sociopaths. The less common variant would be the "hit and run" sociopath, the common criminal. Such people usually turn up in courts as defendants and they frequently wind up in jail. You read about them in the newspapers because they tend to do very exciting and dramatic things. The much more common variant is the "smile and suck" sociopath, the hustler and the confidence man, the con artist. They frequently turn up in court also, but are just as likely to be lawyers, judges, jurists; unfortunately they are sometimes psychiatrists, physicians, and case officers as well. Their depredations are in the long run probably more damaging than those of their "hit and run" colleagues but are usually less obviously dramatic. Often their acts are betrayals of a trust or a confidence. Although these people are an enormous problem, many of them never leave a discernible trail. Sociopaths are frequently referred to as people with "moth-eaten or swiss cheese" consciences. With some of these people what falls through the hole is a sense of loyalty to their country.

The third trait in this triad is narcissism. This is difficult to describe to a lay audience, especially in our society where self-reliance, initiative, confidence, self-assertiveness, and competitiveness are so emphasized as positive attributes. But narcissism is more than just self-love. It is a pathologic self-absorption, a preoccupation with the self at the expense of all else. Such individuals often possess a grandiose sense of their own importance. They exaggerate their accomplishments. They make unrealistic demands upon the attentions and affections of others, yet they are unable to reciprocate. Thus they are seen as exploitative. Their interpersonal relationships are fraught with disappointments. Often they alienate others and so defeat themselves. Such individuals are grievance accumulators. They go through life perceiving themselves as the unjust victims of jealous or incompetent but powerful rivals. Often a defector in [whom] this trait is prominent was the special child of the family, the mother's obvious favorite. The family banner was handed down to him at an early age. Special things were expected. The obvious narcissist is totally unaware of his arrogance. These individuals almost never have any sense of humor about themselves. They are terribly defensive, sensitive to any slight. Often they verge on the paranoid. When their exaggerated ambitions for pre-eminence are thwarted they may become assassins or defectors as an attempted cheap shot into at least the footnotes of history where they all along believed that they belonged. Consider Lee Harvey Oswald, first a defector, then a redefector, ultimately an assassin. His mother referred to herself as "a mother in history."

Narcissistic individuals frequently possess a sense of special entitlements in terms of how other people will regard them and behave toward them, special exemptions from some of the ordinary anticipated rules of human conduct. The exemptions possibly include loyalty to one's country. I make an analogy to a dark star or black hole. Their self-absorption is so enormous that everything goes in. No light, no love, no warmth, no understanding ever comes back out.

In rare cases grandiosity can take a magnanimous form as in the martyr complex. The individual imagines that he has been selected by God or History to Advance Science or Save Humanity. Often this is the attempt of a desperate defeated individual, many times betrayed by his own lights, now finally seeking to identify with an intellectualized formless ideal which cannot betray him in a human sense. At this level of sublime aspiration even in the event of failure the word defeat would not apply.

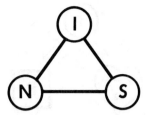

I originally described the individual psychology and the circumstances of life as independent variables. In real life, of course, they are not. In real life the individual plays a very large role in creating his circumstances. What if the individual has problems with the control of impulses or problems with sociopathic tendencies? Add problems with narcissism. How easily such problems become the mother of mischief. I will cite a complicated example illustrating this point. I was called upon to interview a young Soviet immediately following his defection because he had made a genuine suicide attempt. I asked him to tell me about himself. He told me that he was "the first male child born in my village following the end of the Great Patriotic War." He went on to explain that most of the men who had left that village to fight in the war had never returned. Imagine what it meant to the survivors living in that village about the continuity of life to see the first male child born amongst them following the end of such a horrible war. He grew up as a special child in that village. The men and the women of the village would bribe him with shares of their anticipated winnings if he would just stand behind them while they gambled. He was obviously a kind of ambulatory totem in the village. His defection was one of those cases of the auditors coming on Monday. They would find an enormous discrepancy in the operational funds which had been placed in his trust. Anyone care to venture [a guess] as to what happened to the money? Yes, he gambled it away. For some reason he was certain that he was born lucky.

In summary, imagine a triangular diagram with the individual at the apex and the family and the regime forming the two points at the bases. Each leg of the triangle represents an emotional tie that binds each part in a reciprocal affiliation susceptible to fracture. The child that is welcomed, raised with understanding, love, and encouragement can be expected to respond to this love and warmth with a reciprocal love and loyalty. The family members are loyal citizens of their regime and serve its interests. The regime recognizes their contributions with rewards, responsibilities, and opportunities. The state provides the child with the possibilities to fulfill his potential. This child responds by becoming a loyal citizen of his country. But that's only in the best of all possible worlds. In the real world there are many other possibilities. Imagine

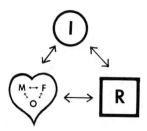

the consequences of a break in any of these links. I have mentioned the divided family. I have described the case of a young man who hated his father. What about the case of a family secretly dissident against the regime? Or a family through no perceived fault of its own repressed by the regime? What about the delayed effects of such a history? A defector may tell us how years before his family was damaged by the regime; now years later he strikes back. But this individual had his life impacted upon even while his character and his attitudes were in formation. The proverbial twig was bent. He might have simply taken all of this in, lived with it, lived around it, apparently succeeding anyway, but now a crisis occurs in his own life. On top of this background it is too much. Now he must strike back against that regime.

◦   ◦   ◦

Life has its balances and its compensations for the adaptable, flexible, and well-balanced individual who can share the success of others. The more immature individual, the more narcissistic person, will be less able to accept a share of anybody else's success. With many defectors the problems are cumulative. Perceived insults, failures and humiliations are particular burdens upon character structures with a lessened capacity to accept these setbacks.

So in the end I can't give you any one profile. Life is simply too variable and complex. Individuals' backgrounds differ enormously. Each child brings into the world a different capacity with which to react to opportunities and vicissitudes. I am sure that there are many latent defectors who never defected simply because they avoided failure. Some broke out on top and managed to remain front runners. The Agency probably has had many potential defectors who retired with honors.

9.

In the early Cold War years, a Swedish naval warrant officer fitted a profile for recruitment by Soviet intelligence; he proceeded to serve Moscow "in-place" in Sweden, efficiently for a few years, until his Russian handler blundered. Writing a decade later, an intelligence historian at CIA, apparently privy to the Swedish counterintelligence interrogations, recounts the story with an eye particularly to tradecraft.

The Practice of a Prophet

INQUIRER

The public examination last year of the Lonsdale-Kroger-Houghton-Gee case of Soviet espionage in England[1] and its parallels with the Abel-Hayhanen case in the United States[2] bring to mind an earlier rather full public exposure of postwar Soviet espionage that was given a great deal of attention in the target country but is little remembered here—that of Ernst Hilding Andersson, whose skill, ingenuity, and devoted diligence gave the USSR a series of prize reports on Swedish naval defenses from 1949 to 1951.[3] This was not a KGB deep-cover operation like the other two, but run from official cover by one of the Soviet military intelligence services without any of the elaborate technical devices Abel and Lonsdale had at their disposal. It is notable, among other features, for the way Andersson's security practices, at first exceedingly loose, were gradually tightened up until, although they never approached the scrupulous care exercised by Colonel Abel, they were about on the level of Lonsdale's. But while the Russian handler Lonsdale was blown by the indiscretion of his agent Houghton, security-conscious agent Andersson was caught through the ineptitude of an ill-trained young case officer sent out from Moscow.

Inquirer, "The Practice of a Prophet," *Studies in Intelligence*, vol. 6, no. 4 (Fall 1962), pp. A29–A41. Originally unclassified.

1. See John Bulloch and Henry Miller's *Spy Ring*, reviewed in *Intelligence Articles* V/4, and Arthur Tietjen's *Soviet Spy Ring*, reviewed in *Intelligence Articles*, VI/2.

2. See W. W. Rocafort's "Colonel Abel's Assistant" in *Intelligence Articles*, III/4.

3. The story of this case is told in Curt Falkenstam's *Röd Spion* (Stockholm, 1951). English-language summaries are included in Francis Noel-Baker's *The Spy Web* (London, 1954) and John Baker White's *Pattern for Conquest* (London, 1956). All of these accounts lack some of the details that an intelligence officer finds intriguing.

The Prophet Molded

Ernst Hilding was one of eight Andersson children supported on the proceeds of a too small truck garden at Strängnäs, not so far from the prosperity of metropolitan Stockholm as to be spared rude contrasts with their own poverty. Moreover, his father was crippled early on by rheumatism, so that the boy had to leave school when he was eleven and go to work in the neighboring farmers' fields. He did heavier work for longer hours than he had the strength for. He was an intelligent, oversensitive, and therefore lonely lad, something of an outsider even with his own family. His mother, who it was gossiped had Communist leanings, took in sewing to help ends meet. One of his sisters contracted tuberculosis. Another fell prey to some disease, probably syphilis, that incapacitated her mentally.

When Ernst was seventeen he went to Stockholm and got a job as delivery boy, living with a sister. As soon as he turned eighteen he joined the Navy—on impulse, he said, but knowing that he would not only be better off financially but have a chance to broaden his intellectual horizons. He began to study voraciously. For five and a half years he took night courses in technical subjects, specializing in electrical engineering. Still all his energies were not engaged, and when he found some fellow-sailors whose economic and social philosophy seemed to fall in with his own emergent ideas and these introduced him to others of their persuasion in the city, he joined them in the Swedish section of the Communist Youth International, his first taste of real comradeship. For two years, until sea duty took him away, he helped prepare and propagate their illegal newspaper *Torpeden*.

In 1933, at 24, he married a domestic maid. His wife appreciated his kindness and admired his industry and intellect, but she did not understand his ideas or share his interests. They came to live amicably but distantly together. Nevertheless, sixteen years later when she could afford to quit work, they had a son.

In 1934 Andersson was graduated as a chief machinist. Still he studied, especially electrical engineering but also a variety of unrelated subjects from artillery fire control to foreign languages. In 1950, 41 years old, he was certified as an electrical engineer. He was now what we would call a warrant officer. He had found life in the service satisfying—good treatment, plenty of opportunities, a promising future. Although he had no money to throw away, he was better off than most enlisted men. He had no gripes against any of his associates or any group of people. It pleased him to do a good job, and he did it earnestly.

But as the Soviet-American cold war came to constitute the mainspring of world affairs he was convinced that the future welfare of the Swedish people—and the rest of mankind—lay in "learning from the Russians" and that the main threat to Sweden came from the United States. He believed it inevitable that the Americans would sooner or later try to take over Swedish bases for an attack on the USSR, setting off World War III, and this thought horrified him; when it came to that he would much rather have the Russians occupy them as a preventive measure. He made no particular secret of these ideas, which, along with his passion for study, earned him among his fellows the nickname of "The Prophet." In these circles he was also sometimes branded Communist; but there was little informal contact, as in most navies, between NCO and officer ranks, and his officers thought highly of his abilities and his devotion to duty. He could be trusted in whatever work you gave him.

The Spy Matriculates

In the fall of 1946 Andersson was stationed, as he had been during most of his service, at the Skeppsholmen naval base, an island in the channel that cuts Stockholm in two. One evening at the home of his friend Sixten Rogeby, one of the men who had introduced him to Communism eighteen years before, he met Konstantin Vinogradov, then First Secretary of the Soviet embassy in Stockholm, who honored him by asking him to dinner at his home. At Vinogradov's there were just a few other guests, but food, drink, and hospitality such as only a Russian can lay on. Amid the general conversation there were enough references to Andersson's job and to the quality of the Swedish fleet that he knew to what proposal he was being led. He had his answer ready now, two years before the question was to be asked.

Andersson accepted a second invitation to dine with Vinogradov one evening before Christmas, but it turned out he couldn't make it. No matter; on New Year's Eve the diplomat showed up unannounced at the sailor's west side apartment near the Traneberg bridge, bearing a gift of several bottles in honor of the occasion, and they made another dinner date for January. This time Vinogradov, introducing the only other guest, Tass representative Viktor Anissimov, announced that he was leaving the Stockholm post; and to complete the unacknowledged handing-over ceremony Anissimov invited Andersson to dinner at his apartment.

That dinner was the first of many meetings and the beginning of a close relationship that flourished for three years and a half. At first the two friends simply got together at one or the other's apartment; but it occurred to Andersson—as well, presumably, as to Anissimov—that it wouldn't be a good idea for a Swedish warrant officer to be seen going around with a Soviet representative, so they agreed to meet most of the time outside the city proper, where they might be recognized, in suburbs and outlying towns like Huddinge, Tullinge, Stäket, and Hägernäs. They would go for walks and bicycle rides and eat in restaurants or picnic in the country. After almost a year of this Anissimov once brought a camera along and took several pictures of his friend. Later he got Andersson to bring him his identity documents and a list of his naval service assignments, honors, and achievements. Still no demands, no talk of espionage, but in anticipation Andersson grew more reticent among his fellows about his political views and stopped his open Communist associations. He had never joined the Party proper.

Another year, and finally, at the end of November 1949, the Tass man asked if Andersson would be willing to provide some information on the Swedish fleet. The spy presumptive had had moments of doubt that year after his son was born: if he were caught and jailed for the rest of his life the baby might have as rough a childhood as he himself had had. But he had thought the problem through and decided that such sentimental, personal considerations had no weight beside the larger issues. Now he assented without hesitation. His handler then wrote down three questions: the names of the warships stationed at Skeppsholmen and the battle-readiness of each; future plans for reassigning or remodeling any of these ships; and the composition and command organization of the Swedish coastal fleet. He offered no guidance on how to get this information; the means were left to Andersson's initiative.

The first two questions, about his own base, presented no great problem. Stationed as he was on the destroyer *Romulus*, he knew most of the answers already, and he could fill in the rest by discreet and indirect questioning, often by saying something wrong and letting a colleague show his superiority by correcting him. He even included several of the small minesweepers attached to the base in his report. But on the coastal fleet he had little first-hand information. Nevertheless, by dint of diligent research and questioning, he learned the names of all the ships in it and could make some observations on their divisional subordination. Before the end of December he wrote out his report in pencil on board the *Romulus* and took it with some pride to Anissimov's apartment. Anissimov barely glanced at it, set a date for a meeting in January, and told him he'd better go.

In January the Tass man began by expressing his dissatisfaction with the report; it didn't include data on *all* the minesweepers! Andersson, hurt, resolved never again to put himself in a position to get such a reprimand; and he never did. The rest of this meeting and others for the next five months were devoted to tightening up security procedures and training in them. Reports were to be done in invisible ink, a sodium sulphate solution. All meetings were to be at 8 p.m.; the day would be signaled by disguised chalkings on a wall or building, "T" for Monday, "W" for Tuesday, etc. If a meeting ever failed, it would be tried again exactly two weeks later at the Karolinska Hospital. Against the possibility that Anissimov might have to send a substitute handler, Andersson should make himself recognizable by carrying a briefcase, lock side out, in his right hand, with a roll of paper sticking up out of it. For mutual recognition there were four key words that should be used in the opening sentences, two on each side, of a self-introductory conversation. The left hand in pants pocket would be a danger sign.

Busy Days

In May Andersson learned that he was to be transferred to the icebreaker *Ymer*, which was sailing south on 10 June for an overhaul at the Karlskrona naval base. A meeting with Anissimov had already been set for 27 May, and here Anissimov presented him with a written request for a repeat of the report he had made in December; it seemed the Russians wanted this updated semi-annually. Andersson wished he had saved his notes for the first one, and after that he did. In addition, this time, he was asked for full details about security arrangements at Skeppsholmen, including shelters, stores, and supply depots, together with a sketch covering all installations. He would now have less than two weeks to complete the assignment. When he told the Russian about the *Ymer* he was given as a subsequent assignment the job of reporting much the same things about Karlskrona as he was doing for Skeppsholmen, but with more sketches and covering additional subjects such as communications facilities and foreign representatives or visitors at the base. He got 400 kronor (about $100) for expenses; no receipt required, but he would have to account for it when he submitted his report.

He continued to have trouble with the coastal fleet in preparing his second report, but he did a smashing good job of the required Skeppsholmen sketch-map. He bought an ordinary streetcar map of the island, enlarged it, sketched the three dozen or so important buildings in to scale, and keyed these by numbers to an attached description of each. Most of them he had been familiar with before, but he made it a point to visit a typical bomb shelter and note things like the locations of its entrances, the thickness of its roof, and its resistance to gas. He copied the map and his eight-page report in invisible ink, and on the day before the *Ymer* sailed he went to a bicycle stand on St. Erik's Terrace, found Anissimov's bicycle, as agreed, parked there, and put the apparently blank papers in its tool case.

The *Ymer* was docked in Karlskrona for over three months, until 14 September. Plenty of time for observations and questions, which security-wise were easier than at Skeppsholmen: it was natural to be curious when you hadn't visited a place for three years. But Andersson didn't therefore take it easy. He used his lunch hours to wander about the base, refreshing his memory, observing changes, and taking mental notes, and his longer periods of free time were spent in excursions in the area, notably to prominences on the mainland and islands in the archipelago surrounding the base. He would study maps and hydrographic charts, try to figure out the logical places for military installations, and then go verify his guesses. He usually went in civvies on his bicycle, having given out among his acquaintances that he was fond of picking berries and mushrooms.

He would keep all his observations in his head until he got back to his quarters and could sketch them; there was too much danger that someone might become suspicious and set the police on him. Twice, in fact, he was accosted. Once an MP sergeant asked him what he was doing there. He said he was looking for the personnel office, trying to get on as an engineer in Karlskrona; and the sergeant, though he still looked suspicious, let him go. Another time, when he was examining defense erections on one of the islands, a man came up and asked him why. Andersson, who had just had a couple of bottles of beer, said "I'm spying for the Russians." The man stared and shook his head and went away.

He found hanging on plywood in the Karlskrona base's electrical shop, where he frequently went on business, a big map of the dock and base area, as well as part of the city, with numbers keying some 800 installations to a legend and flags indicating the location of all ships being worked on. He persuaded the electricians, since, he said, his comrades on the *Ymer* were having an awful time finding their way around the base, to lend it to him as a guide for the icebreaker's crew. He hung it up on deck and then, choosing times when the crew were all busy elsewhere and keeping a sharp lookout, he copied it in four sections as the basis for his report. In the two months it took him to complete it, he tripled the number of original notations with additional observed detail. He hid his sketches and notes in an old pair of field boots. He went over the notes again and again, memorizing and compressing, until there were only three or four cramped pages, mostly figures, besides what he had in his head.

Two or three British destroyers called at Karlskrona that summer of 1950. Andersson observed them closely and succeeded in getting aboard one of them and talking to the crew. He asked them what they thought about the world situation, the next war, and the Russians and what the British were doing in the Baltic.

Back in Stockholm in mid-September, he worked far into the night for many nights expanding his report and putting it into secret writing. He had previously agreed to meet with Anissimov during the third week of that month on a not yet specified day at 8 p.m. in Örby, a suburb on the south of the city containing a small forest. Now he put a red chalk mark on a building near the Tass office to indicate the day. He traveled to the rendezvous by bus, Anissimov by taxi, and the two walked into the woods, where Andersson handed over his 20-page report with map and sketches and his expense account. He told the

Russian about the risks he had run in copying the big map of the base and suggested that he could have avoided these if he had been sure of being able to make a satisfactory photograph of it. As personal chitchat he mentioned that his baby had just got over a serious attack of bronchitis, and the hospital bill was terrific. Anissimov promptly lent him 400 kronor, which he later gratefully repaid. they decided that Stäket, fifteen miles northwest on the way to Enköping, would be the best place for future meetings, and they set a date for the next one. Then they rode back to town together.

New Skills and Voyages

They rode to Stäket on the same train but ignored each other until they had walked from the station out into the countryside. Anissimov said he would be leaving Stockholm sometime before the spring of 1951, so at some future prearranged meeting it would be his successor that would appear, to be recognized by the prescribed procedures. Andersson for his part reported that in December the *Ymer* would be sailing up the Norrland coast on ice-breaking missions, and he would be the ship's chief electrician. He was therefore given, in addition to the semiannual Skeppsholmen report to prepare before he left, written requirements for information on Norrland coastal fortifications, ports, and likely landing areas near important centers and military installations. But more generally he was to observe and report anything that might be of intelligence interest; his judgment was now trusted.

Most of the five- or six-hour meeting, however, was devoted to photography. Anissimov had brought along a small Exacta for Andersson to practice with under his direction. He gave him 1200 kronor to buy one like it and presented him with two handbooks, one in German and one in English, on document photography. Since the *Ymer* would be gone five months, the next meeting, presumably with a new handler, was set for 4 June. The next day Andersson splurged on 2000 kronor worth of photo equipment, including a telescopic lens and materials for developing and printing his own pictures. He threw himself with characteristic energy into mastering the new art, both by practicing all its aspects and by research in the City Library.

Concurrently he was preparing his routine Skeppsholmen report, not hurriedly because he thought he had plenty of time. But suddenly the *Ymer* was ordered to leave a week earlier than planned, on 6 December, and he had to work frantically. He stayed up all night putting it into writing before the morning she was to sail, and barely a couple of hours ahead of departure time he rushed across town to Anissimov's apartment and handed it to him personally. He would never see him again.

On board the *Ymer* he let it be understood that he had won the camera in a lottery and had become engrossed in his new hobby. He enthusiastically took pictures of the ship, the crew, the scenery, sea gulls, everything that came by, and incidentally of coastal features for his report. With the captain's permission he set up a dark room in a lavatory in the sick bay. When the ship made an ice run up the Ångermanälven river as far as Gustavsvik he was able to photograph the defense establishment there. Aside from photographs and his own observations he picked up a good deal of incidental information. One day, for example, when an officer and two NCO's hitch-hiked a ride down the coast on the *Ymer,* they pointed out where work was being done on fortifications to which thirty-odd men would be assigned.

At the end of March 1951 the *Ymer* returned to a secret bunker in the Stockholm archipelago for refueling. Here the Exacta got six or seven good pictures showing its approaches, defenses, and the entrances to its rock tunnels. Moreover, Andersson took advantage of the fueling stop to strike up a conversation with some of the men stationed there and learned how many ships the bunker serviced, what thickness of rock lay over the tunnels, and what kind of fuel was stored in each of the various compartments.

For the first half of May, after the ice became workable in the northernmost tip of the Bothnian Gulf, the *Ymer* was stationed up in Luleå. Here the ship's NCO's were invited to dinner by the NCO's of the local airbase, F 21. Andersson was able to observe F 21's bunkers and defenses and took advantage of the friendly social conversation to learn the number and types of planes at the base and get some notion of their operational mission.

A few days before the icebreaker was to leave Luleå the officers and NCO's from F 21 and other airbases in the area were invited on an excursion up the river to Boden to tour the fortress there. Through Andersson's good offices the *Ymer*'s NCO's were included in this invitation, and he and two others went along. The party was taken on a guided tour of the fortress area and through one of the forts and given explanations of present and planned dispositions. Although he had had to leave his camera outside and could not make notes, Andersson was able by intense application to observe and memorize a mass of detail about anti-tank obstacles, the location of gun batteries, the caliber of guns, the power of the diesels, the construction of the armored turrets on the forts, tunnel entrances, camouflage devices, and many other features. He could even make an educated calculation of the strength with which the place was manned. As soon as he got back to his ship he wrote all these things down.

A New Regime

When the *Ymer* got back to Stockholm he bought three General Staff maps covering the Luleå and Boden area and used these as the basis for maps for his Norrland report, which filled twelve pages and was accompanied by three or four hundred photographs. He was so busy doing this, he later explained, that he completely forgot the 4 June meeting arranged with his handler; but one suspects that the repugnance he felt at being taken over from his admired friend Anissimov by a stranger may have interfered with his normally acute memory. At any rate he got a telephone call at home the next evening with "greetings from his friend" and agreed to arrangements for a meeting at the same time and place the following day.

The new handler, it turned out after the recognition ritual, was 26-year-old Nicolai P. Orlov, a clerk for the Soviet naval attaché. His head full of the precepts taught in the Operations Course he had just completed, he laid down some new procedures. These risky personal meetings would be the exception. If Andersson had a report to deliver, he could request by three vertical red chalk marks that Orlov's bicycle be left on St. Erik's Terrace, as Anissimov's had once been, to receive it. He could start by delivering the Norrland report this way. Alternatively he could hide a report under a certain rock in the woods around Frescati, on the northern outskirts, and signal by a horizontal white chalk mark that it was there. Orlov would use counterpart procedures for transmitting assignments and pay. Punctilious about the pay aspect, he asked if 700 kronor would do for the immediate future, which would be devoted to the semiannual Skeppsholmen report.

Andersson completed this routine assignment handily before the end of June and left the report in the bicycle tool case on St. Erik's Terrace. He didn't like this impersonal means of delivery as a regular practice, especially in such an open spot where he could easily be observed. He resolved to protest it, and he soon had a second reason to signal that he wanted a meeting with Orlov. He had been scheduled for transfer to the destroyer *Öland* that summer, but now two alternative possibilities opened up, a well-paid engineer assignment in the electrical section at Skeppsholmen or a course in radar which could lead to running a radar station. He was attracted by the engineer pay but decided that he could be more useful to his other employers if he took the radar training, and he wanted to tell Orlov about it.

They met in Stora Mossen out in Bromma, not far from where Andersson had used to live. They agreed that in the future Orlov would park his bicycle by the busy shops under the viaduct at Tegelbacken and Andersson would pick it up and ride it down to the Southern Hospital and leave it there; thus he could do his business with the tool kit at any opportune point along the way. Orlov approved his decision on the radar course and promised that he wouldn't suffer financially. A few days later he received an envelope containing 200 kronor.

Last Mission

It apparently hadn't occurred to Orlov that his ostensibly aimless wanderings on foot and bicycle didn't conform with the normal activities of Soviet embassy personnel, but it occurred to the Swedish security police, especially when he went out on bicycle and came back on foot or vice versa. His shabby vehicle, moreover, was distinguished by a flashy new tool kit. They began to follow him discreetly on these expeditions. On the evening of 11 September they saw him park the bicycle at Tegelbacken and go away, and they took the opportunity to search it. They found in the tool kit two sheets of blank paper rolled and tied with blue and gold string, each enclosing several 100-kronor notes, a total of 1200 kronor. They tied them up again and put them back and watched. The next morning they saw Andersson come and ride the bicycle away, leaving his own in its place. The tag on it identified him.

The paper around the money, Andersson found, contained instructions for him to go to Karlskrona and report what he could about a fleet of British submarines visiting there. He asked for emergency leave, saying he had to go to Nässjö on urgent personal business, and took the morning train on 13 September straight through to Karlskrona. He traveled in civvies but took his uniform, as well as his bicycle, along. He spent a day finding out as much as he could from friends, then went in uniform to the quay where the British ships were tied up and engaged the crews in conversation. In the afternoon, as a civilian, he succeeded in joining one party that was taken aboard a submarine and another that was shown around a delimited area of a sub tender. On the latter he told the guard he had been invited down below by one of the crew and so managed to gain admission to the restricted area also.

Returning to Stockholm, he prepared an eight-page report and on 20 September rode Orlov's bicycle from Tegelbacken to the Southern Hospital. The police, finding the eight blank sheets wrapped around the pump, succeeded in developing the writing and discovered that it conveyed information not only on the British submarines but on Swedish warships currently at Karlskrona, their armament and prospective missions, the strength of the coast artillery regiment there, and the disposition of the internal guard at the base.

Andersson was arrested the next morning on his way to work. At his trial he was calm, straightforward, and unhesitating in his testimony. He had acted, he said, only as a Swedish patriot should: "I wanted to do as much good as I could with as little harm as possible." "Harm?" asked the prosecutor. "Yes, harm for mankind, and in that I include also you who judge me here," he answered. And when an unperceptive lawyer asked him whether he had never tried to fake his reports, he was offended. "That would have defeated my purpose," he said. "I always tried to make correct reports."

He was sentenced to life imprisonment at hard labor, the latter a thing not strange to him.

10.

A veteran CIA case officer recounts the improvisatory ingenuity of his tradecraft during his salad days.

Catch-as-Catch-Can Operations

BENJAMIN F. ONATE

Once upon a time there was an American who had grown gray and venerable in the service of an international ideology. He served as theorist and right-hand advisor to the leader of that Movement in Highland, where the Movement was in opposition. Coincidentally, he had also served for some years as a contract agent of the Central Intelligence Agency.

I was a very inexperienced case officer but an old hand at moving about in Europe when I came to Highland to handle VUZYX,[1] as we shall call him, more than 20 years ago. He was based in the Highland capital, I in the commercial center, and to reduce the risk of his being noted in bad company, we met anywhere except in the capital.

There had been time, years before, to train VUZYX briefly domestically, and he was a joy to handle. Productive, careful, motivated—in his view, there was no great gap between the goals and ideals of the United States and those of the Movement, in which he sincerely believed. The gaps he found it difficult to bridge lay between his own view of the Movement, and those of its international leaders, who were prone to disregard his advice and his theories on occasion.

It came to pass, after he and I had been working together for about a year, that all of the leaders of the Movement were summoned to Metropolia, the capital of Lowland, for an international conference to sit at the feet of their Greatest International Leader. About a week before the conference, VUZYX came to my base for our regular meeting and informed me that he had been chosen to attend with *his* leader, and then accompany him on a European tour

Benjamin F. Onate, "Catch-as-Catch-Can Operations," "Studies in Intelligence, vol. 20, no. 4 (Winter 1976), pp. 27–29. Originally classified "Confidential."

1. If any country operations then or now used the digraph VU, I apologize; I don't mean it to point in any direction.

which would last a good two weeks before he would be able to report again. Did CIA want any immediate coverage in Metropolia while he was there?

Overnight, before he left town again, I got a fast turndown from Headquarters, noting that after all they had plenty of assets in Lowland. So VUZYX and I arranged for a next meeting immediately after his return, and he went back to the capital.

The next day, of course, Headquarters changed its mind; VUZYX was, after all, just about our best penetration of the Movement and one of the few if not the only one who might be thoroughly objective about the views of the Great International Leader.

There *was* a minor problem or two:

1. VUZYX had no idea I was coming.
2. I had no idea where he would be staying in Metropolia.
3. I had no plausible cover for approaching him in Metropolia.

This was something we had not prearranged, and which was not set forth in any Standard Operating Procedure either of us had had in tradecraft training.

So the answer was improvisation.

I had his telephone number, rarely used because of the sensitivity of the operation; I, in fact, had never called him. But I called, identified *myself* by *his pseudonym*[2] in case he didn't recognize my voice, and informed him I now had the information on the life insurance he had asked me about; would he be available next week so I could call on him?

He played up beautifully; No, he would be accompanying his leader on a visit to Metropolia in midweek.

Ah, in the latter part of the week I might be in Metropolia myself; might I ask where he would be staying?

But of course, at the Hotel Splendide.

So far, so good; he now was alerted to the fact that I would try to meet him in Metropolia, and that Headquarters obviously had changed its mind. And I knew where he would be staying.

Now, Lowland was a friendly country, and its intelligence services cooperated with ours, but took a dim view of poaching. Inasmuch as Lowland and the United States differed somewhat in their evaluation of the Movement, it didn't seem advisable to cut them in on VUZYX. I had, however, spent a great deal of my former life in Lowland, and had many friends in Metropolia whom I might logically visit, ostensibly on a combined R&R and shopping tour. The Lowland authorities were probably aware that I was with CIA, but unless I made some

---

2. He never used his pseudo except in signing contracts, expense accounts, and similar Agency business. I didn't use mine, because he didn't know it, whereas the *nom de guerre* under which he knew me served me in several operations and, if intercepted, might have aroused suspicion.

egregious blunder, I should be able to contact VUZYX without arousing their suspicions.

And so, on the day the conference began, I too reached Metropolia, a day behind VUZYX, and called him at the Splendide. The leader himself (gulp!) answered the phone and passed it to VUZYX. (I later learned that they were in fact seated side by side on one of the beds with a batch of documents spread out around them, planning strategy for the conference.) Once again, Operation Improvise.

This time, still using VUZYX's pseudo, I was a salesman calling from Flinflan's (not notional) Bookstore; the books he wanted could not be obtained until the day of his departure, but we would be glad to send them to him at the airport if he would give us his flight number and departure time.

After that, I was free to shop and visit friends until departure time except for two chores: a) I booked passage on the same flight; and b) I went to Flinflan's in the course of my shopping, picked out a couple of books and had them wrapped up, and took them to a messenger service for delivery to VUZYX at the airport.

On departure day, I checked through the gate at the airport without difficulty into the waiting lounge, where VUZYX was already seated next to his leader, ostentatiously reading a *Saturday Evening Post*. I turned to the newsstand, bought the same issue myself, let him see it under my arm, and headed for the men's room.

VUZYX followed me and without saying a word or exchanging a glance we took adjoining urinals. When the room was briefly clear of third parties, we exchanged our magazines, then walked back out separately at a respectable interval, sat down, and boarded the plane when the flight was called. I got off at the first stop and returned to Highland; VUZYX went on to Midland and other countries with his leader.

In his *Saturday Evening Post* I found a carbon of a complete account he had typed for his leader detailing the proceedings of the Movement's closed sessions, together with some worthwhile remarks and statements made by the various international leaders. I ultimately received indications from Headquarters that VUZYX's report was not only faster but more comprehensive than what we received through Lowland assets.

Critique: VUZYX and I had played the whole thing by ear. What mistakes did we make, and what risks did we encounter or overlook?

1. When VUZYX first told me he was going to Metropolia, I should have obtained all the details and set up contingency arrangements to pick up his report then and there, without waiting for Headquarters' "final" decision. Then it would have taken one simple signal of some kind, rather than the two dicey phone calls, to alert him to the airport contact.

2. Failing a contingency plan, the first risk lay in assuming that VUZYX could also fly by the seat of his pants and would understand and respond correctly to my improvisations. This is something one can rely on infallibly only in Leslie Charteris' *Saint* stories or *Mission Impossible.* Fortunately VUZYX turned out to be a first-class improvisor.

3. I thought I had been as careful as possible about the Metropolia telephone call; I walked aimlessly around Metropolia for some time without spotting a tail; then I used one of those glass telephone booths where nobody can get within earshot without being seen. But I had no grounds for assuming that VUZYX would have had any opportunity during his trip to be in touch with Flinflan's Bookstore. That could have tripped him up if he had to explain the phone call.

4. When I myself went to Flinflan's, I picked out a couple of books *I* was interested in, not necessarily a couple that would interest VUZYX, and they were books that came right off the shelf; no need for Flinflan to have hunted them down. After all, I was paying for the books myself. I should, of course, have picked some hard-to-find book that VUZYX would enjoy (and put it on the expense account).

In the end, however, it all worked, and the moral appears to be that you *can* improvise and get away with it as long as you (a) have a good partner, and (b) think three or four times about every possible pitfall and pratfall. VUZYX himself subsequently had the only sour evaluation when he brought me the books: "If you had to saddle me with these dumb books, couldn't you have picked smaller ones?"

IV.

Humint and Its Consumers

11.

The author, evidently a humint operations officer, explains and advocates a major role for collectors in preliminary analysis. Written in 1961, the argument apparently had to be made in rather elementary form, even though directed to the audience of insiders. Observe that the next article, almost a quarter century later, was freer to take most of these basics for granted. Outside the agency, they still are little understood.

The Collector's Role in Evaluation

BRUCE L. PECHAN

Ever since the establishment of a defined and ordered central intelligence program, the community has performed one of its fundamental functions on the basis of a fiction. This fiction has by now come to be accepted as fact in some circles, and there is a dangerous chance that ultimately it could be universally accepted. I refer to the notion that the collector of information is not qualified or authorized, much less obligated, to participate in the evaluation of the reports he transmits. If this idea in its full implication is ever accepted by the collector, it will do great harm not only to our evaluative and estimative performance but to our performance in clandestine collection as well.

The official fiction makes Evaluation a ritual which only analysts are ordained the high priests to perform. Clandestine collectors, with their often impressive qualifications, may subject an item to a thorough process which bears all the earmarks of evaluation, but this is not officially accepted as Evaluation and may not be designated by that term. Recipients of clandestine reports are protected against any such misconception by the solemn warning, "This is unevaluated information."

This pre-emption of the word "evaluation" to denote a particular step in what is a composite process has left us floundering for terms to apply to other steps. For the field collector's judgment as to the probability that a report is true we must use the synonym "appraisal" in order to preserve the analytic monopoly on Evaluation. The collector's judgment as to the significance of an item of information must be designated vaguely "comments" to avoid the implication that he has some evaluative responsibility.

Bruce L. Pechan, "The Collector's Role in Evaluation," *Studies in Intelligence*, vol. 5, no. 3 (Summer 1961), pp. 37–47. Originally classified "Secret."

The tortured circumlocutions that must thus be employed in referring to the collector's role in evaluation are unbecoming in a profession in which search for objective truth and precision in the use of language are cardinal principles; but the official fiction has more serious consequences than these semantic ones. The best of our collectors, ignoring the codified absurdities, have for years been offering their own evaluations as appropriate, unconcerned by what name they are called. But some collectors have been honestly confused by the hazy language describing their evaluative functions, and some have accepted literally the dictum that the collector has no responsibility in the evaluation of an item's significance. When this happens, the quality of collection and reporting inevitably suffers and valuable judgments are lost.

There is a tendency in some quarters to regard collection as a technical process and collectors as mere technicians. But a technique that employs human agents rather than black boxes requires considerably more than technical skill. It is the purpose of this paper to examine the duties of the clandestine collector in connection with evaluation in order to clarify his natural and proper role in making the judgments of which evaluation consists. The discussion will be confined to evaluation done for the benefit of estimators and policy makers, not touching the slightly different characteristics of the same process undertaken for the purpose of guiding collectors in the pursuit of further information. Although addressed specifically to the role of the covert collector, much that follows will apply equally to that of the overt collector.

Determination of Probability

Evaluation, as the term is used in the intelligence world, consists of determinations on two matters—the truth or probability of facts reported, and their significance if true. Evidence about probability is of two kinds. One kind of evidence lies in the origin and acquisition of the report, i.e., the reliability, capability, access to information, etc., of the source, and the circumstances surrounding his acquisition of the information. The second kind has to do with the information itself—the amount of confirmatory or contradictory information already in hand, or in the absence of direct confirmation or contradiction, the internal logic of the new information in its relation to what is already known.

The collector is held responsible for providing the first, external kind of evidence—an evaluation (officially labeled such) of his source's reliability, and an account of the circumstances surrounding the acquisition of the information. These two elements of external evidence are to be used by the analyst as factors in determining the degree of probability that the information is true. In providing them the collector has discharged his major assigned responsibility in the evaluative process, and he is not regarded as having thereby engaged in evaluation of the information itself. To see whether this is a realistic view let us look more closely at the nature of these two elements.

Source. The one accepted evaluative judgment of the collector, his source evaluation, is generally considered to be independent of the particular information reported. Source reliability is regarded as a relatively stable factor, and a C source has to prove his reliability over a considerable period to be advanced to a B rating. Once he achieves this, he is not deprived of it unless his reliability shows a decrease over another considerable period. This is a convenient practice and serves reasonably well for most of our clandestine sources, but in any given instance it may be invalid. A source who is reliable in one field may be less reliable in another, whether for lack of competence, lack of access, or lack of will to be reliable. The collector who smugly rests on his source's B rating is flirting with disaster; there is always the possibility that the B rating may not apply in the instance at hand.

This means that the collector must be constantly alert to possible shifts in his source's reliability, brought about by variations in the source's access to information or in his motivation or by lack of competence to report intelligently on a new subject. These can be detected only by regular analysis and *evaluation of the significance* of the information being received in terms of the source's capability and access and especially of his motivation. This analysis may be only a matter of form in the case of a staunch anti-Communist ██████████ reporting the movements of Communist organizers, but it can be an endlessly complex job when a ███████████ socialist is reporting on ██████████ ████ political undercurrents.

Circumstances. In the simplest of situations, that in which the source is reporting on something of which he has direct participating knowledge (such as a plot in which he is one of the leading conspirators), the source evaluation bears directly on the probable truth of the information. But when the source is reporting information he acquired second hand, the source evaluation can bear only on the credibility of his account of how he got the information; and the circumstances of its acquisition here gain importance as the only valid external evidence bearing directly on the probability of its being true.

An account of the circumstances of acquisition is expected of clandestine collectors for each individual report. Many agent operations have a standard pattern in which agents of fairly stable reliability report regularly in one or two sectors and their mode of acquisition remains unchanged in any important particular over a long period of time. But if a situation being reported on grows tense or if security conditions for the source become more stringent, this comfortable stability diminishes; the circumstances surrounding acquisition become of increasing importance and tend to vary appreciably from report to report. This is particularly true of political reporting on an area in crisis where the source may have to acquire his information in a variety of ways. In such situations the factors of acquisition pertinent to a determination of truth are often closely related to the *significance of the information.* To get at these factors the collector must analyze the information itself and work back from that point to draw out his source to best advantage.

In sum, the collector must for his own purposes evaluate the information he receives if he is to perform with discrimination his tasks of evaluating the source and reporting acquisition data. He thus has a head start toward fulfilling his third assigned function in the evaluative process, that of "appraising" factual probability. For this purpose, however, before he can make a judgment of validity, he needs additionally a respectable store of knowledge on the subject to which the new information pertains. We shall return to this point shortly.

Determination of Significance

In evaluating the significance of a report there are at least four elements to be determined. The first is whether it has relevance to an established requirement. The second is its meaning in terms of the requirement, in other words its place and contribution in the fulfillment of the requirement. The third is its relative weight, impact, or importance. And the fourth is the timeliness of the information, with particular reference to the timing of events predictable therefrom.

A study of the extended implications of these several elements shows some significant characteristics of the evaluation function. First, evaluation is an exercise of human judgment, under the best of circumstances subject to human limitations and human error. Any single evaluation may be wholly accurate, but the sum total of all our evaluations will fall short of perfection. Second, it is a transitory judgment, rarely if ever a fixed and stable truth. It is subject to change with changes in the facts themselves or with the acquisition of new information. Third, it is an organic process comprising a number of successive steps, and though each of these may be complete in its own terms no one of them is the whole of evaluation. Some of these steps occur very early in the official life of an item of information. Let us then look at them more closely, and determine who it is that logically takes each of them.

In denying responsibility to the collector for evaluation we have overlooked entirely that he is de facto authorized to exercise evaluative judgment regarding relevance, importance, and timeliness, and that these judgments of his are often final and irrevocable. His right to kill a report for lack of relevance is uncontested. To cut down marginal reporting he is given lively encouragement even to kill information of limited relevance or importance. And because of his frontline location in the collection process, he must judge both timeliness and importance in deciding whether to send a report by pouch or by one of several orders of cable precedence. Whether his judgments are good or bad, the actions based on them are definitive: once a report is destroyed in the field it is beyond our reach to recall and reconsider. Or once pouched as having limited timeliness or importance, the delay in its transmission is an unchangeable fact.

These judgments, however, are not Evaluation with a capital E, which is apparently thought to require a study in depth of relevance, importance, and factual probability for which the collector is not qualified. Let us then examine the prerequisites for such a study.

Capabilities of the Collector

The qualifications needed to be capable of evaluation in depth may be summed up in two categories: ability as a thinking man to reach sensible conclusions, and command of a pertinent body of knowledge on which to base them. With purely personal capabilities there is no reason to suppose that the collector is less generously endowed than the analyst; there is nothing in the analytic function that increases or in the collecting that decreases the native ability of the naked man to think. It is held in some quarters, however, that the practice of the different functions enhances the ability of the one and detracts from that of the other to apply his logical capacity to the function of evaluation in depth, that analysis contributes to and collection detracts from the conditioning of the mental equipment for evaluation.

This effect is said to be produced in two ways. First, since the analyst must evaluate regularly as part of his job, his equipment for evaluation becomes more and more highly trained, whereas the collector, who by definition does not evaluate as a necessary part of his job, lets his equipment, however naturally great and highly trained when he starts out, become rusty from disuse. I have already shown that evaluation of the significance of information is a necessary adjunct to a collector's proper performance of his assigned evaluative responsibilities. I shall deal further with this point in a moment.

The second argument is that the influence of contact with his sources and his personal interest in the success of his operations render the collector undependable as a maker of objective judgments. I will concede that bias may be introduced into his thinking by his identification with sources and operations, but I believe the danger is often overstated. First of all, the possibility of such bias is accepted by collectors themselves, and the seasoned collector builds up a healthy skepticism to minimize it. Second, since his personal interests are bound up in the success of his operations, the experienced collector realizes that overselling his product may reflect badly on himself and so cultivates a counteracting tendency to undersell.

Admitting that bias, while not inevitable, remains a possibility in the collector's evaluative judgments, we should note that it is not peculiar to the collector. The analyst too may, and sometimes does, exhibit bias toward a point of view and interpret new facts in such a way as to make them support a preconceived conclusion. Pearl Harbor and a number of more recent strategic surprises bear memorable witness to the possibility that analysts may reject or downgrade evidence not in accord with their preconceptions. And since bias is a human failing that afflicts all of us to some degree, the best way to ensure objectivity in evaluation is to take into account the judgments of all those in a position to render valid opinions.

Is the collector in such a position? Theoretically, only a person with access to all related knowledge can render the definitive evaluation of a new fact. The analyst most nearly meets this condition: in addition to his own knowledge of the area or subject matter he can call on a vast organized store of related facts from all available sources. But he does not approach an allness in this store, and on some areas and subjects it is pitifully thin. So if it were true that evaluation is not Evaluation unless it is based on the entirety of data we should have no Evaluations whatever. Actually, we seldom need all the facts to make a valid evaluative judgment. Of the hundred thousand facts about a country we may have stored up in machine records, ranging from the makeup of the party of the opposition in 1897 to the number of aluminum teeth worn by the current labor minister, we may find that only sixteen are of any use in determining the significance of a new item. The workaday analyst quickly learns to confine his consideration of data on hand to those of substantial pertinence. Otherwise he would turn out precious few evaluations.

Given that the analyst must evaluate on the basis of incomplete data, what kind of data is he most likely to lack? On many countries and subjects his store of organized and usable information grows sparse as we approach the immediate now, because of the inescapable lags in acquisition, transmission, organization, and assimilation of up-to-the-minute facts. In a rapidly changing situation he usually lacks the facts most essential for a valid evaluation of new information. That this is recognized by analysts themselves is shown in a recent review of clandestine reporting on a certain area: ". . . During a critical situation . . . field interpretations of the significance and probability of the information reported are needed by the customers to a greatly increased extent." This plea lacks any official standing as a directive for collectors to evaluate, but it remains a direct and realistic expression of need by one set of analysts aware of the limitations placed on their own judgments by circumstances.

The field collector, and I speak here of both the overt and the covert collector, is best situated to acquire what the analyst most keenly lacks: current information on the area in which he works. He it is who can immerse himself wholly in the life of the area, have daily contact with broad segments of its people and its thought, and develop a capacity for judgment which under some circumstances is beyond the capability of the distant analyst. The 1956 uprising in Hungary was unforeseen in our national estimates not because we lacked excellent analysts working on the area or knowledge of the history of Hungary or information on the economic situation, but primarily because we had no qualified body of observers present on the scene to report the things that could be experienced and interpreted only by being there.

It is argued that the collector can fill this gap by furnishing the analyst that evidence on which he himself would base an evaluative judgment were he called on to make one. But this is impractical in many cases. There are often too many small details, some too elusive to capture in a written report, too closely bound up with the physical presence of the collector in the area. Many of the indicators simply do not speak to the analyst in his remote office with the same ring they have for the collector experiencing them in the field.

The collector is not only thus uniquely qualified under certain circumstances to evaluate new information, he *must* evaluate if he is to produce good reports. We have already discussed the importance of evaluating the significance of information as an adjunct to the task of evaluating the source and providing useful acquisition data. Evaluative judgments are required also in getting the maximum of information from agents and informants. The skilled collector in the field, overt or covert, far from being a mere technician, is a whole intelligence community in miniature. When he debriefs an agent he runs through the entire intelligence cycle, sometimes several times over. As an agent makes a report, the collector evaluates it as to relevance. If it is relevant, he hastily evaluates its significance as nearly as he can and uses it to formulate new requirements. These he immediately puts to the agent in the form he judges most likely to draw out additional facts and related information which the agent may have overlooked, not realized he knew, or intended not to reveal. By this means the collector often greatly increases the substantive value of his report.

The important thing here is that the collector is limited by his capacity to judge significance. When he reaches the limit of the body of particular facts and broad general knowledge at his command and therefore of his ability to analyze the new facts in relation to them, he must content himself with accepting whatever the agent offers and sending it on for others to work on. It is axiomatic that, other things being equal, a collector who is well grounded in a subject is a better collector in that subject than one who is not. He can instantly analyze, evaluate, and extemporize his own requirements, short-circuiting by days or weeks the process of getting further guidance from the analyst. The mental operations of analysis and evaluation, by whatever terms they are designated, are inextricably involved in this short-circuiting, and it is clear that the skilled collector must have an evaluative technique well polished by use.

Limitations on the Collector

Limitations there certainly are on the qualifications of the individual field collector to evaluate. Being only one person, he cannot become expert in all subjects on which he may collect information, and his judgment about the significance of many items he reports is therefore of little or no value. On geographic areas other than the one in which he is working he can have at best only a limited up-to-date knowledge; hence, while he may be able to evaluate political news meaningfully in terms of its local impact, he may have little to offer with respect to its impact abroad. For these reasons, each collector should take stock of the limitations of his knowledge and not attempt to go beyond their bounds.

Although in some situations the collector may have all the data available to the analyst and more, he can never be sure that this is so. The analyst usually has, and in every instance may have, pertinent other-source information not available to the collector. Further, by virtue of the nature of his job, the collector is usually inhibited from indulging in the depth and thoroughness of deliberation expected of the analyst. Hence no evaluation by the collector, however accurate and thorough it may prove to be, can properly be regarded as more than tentative until it has been reviewed and confirmed by the analyst.

Finally, full cognizance should be taken of the fact that the primary job of the collector is to collect, and in this job analysis and evaluation are means to the end. It would be foolish for the collector to waste his time writing evaluations of every item he collects. He should make evaluative comments only when he believes he has something to offer that the analyst can probably not supply.

Recognition of these limitations should keep the collector's evaluations of the significance of information within workable limits. At the same time, to ensure to the community that his judgments, which at times are irreplaceable, are not lost, as well as to enable him to enhance his own collection technique, it should be clearly acknowledged to the collector that he has a responsibility to make evaluations. It should be a part of his indoctrination to accept that responsibility and understand its limitations, of his training to learn how to carry it out, and of his performance to act his logical part in the evaluative process with skill and discrimination. Improvement in reporting will not be the least of the resulting benefits.

By the same token the analyst should be aware of the worth and of the limitations of field evaluation, as well as of his own. He should not act arbitrarily in discounting collector opinion, but give it the weight it deserves; he should never simply discard it because it does not agree with his own beliefs. Differences of opinion should be carefully examined, documented, and in important cases referred back to the collector for further consideration. Such a procedure may be cumbersome, but reliable evaluations cannot be arrived at by denying the collector's responsibility to express his opinion or by ignoring it once expressed.

12. The preliminary-analysis activity in humint operations came to rest particularly with "reports officers." They also became involved in tasking. In this article a career reports officer, writing from personal experience, discusses problems of the craft.

The Reports Officer: Issues of Quality

W. J. McKEE

Within CIA's Directorate of Operations, the reports officers constitute the substantive corps which follows intelligence developments in Headquarters and in the field and provides collection guidance, targeting advice, and specific requirements for activities of the Directorate designed to collect information. Reports officers evaluate and disseminate information the Directorate acquires, provide substantive support to Directorate components, and serve as principal intermediaries between collectors and consumers. Their central purpose is to maintain standards of value and objectivity in the Directorate's information product.

Much about the activity of reports officers is controversial: their judgments, how important these judgments are, who should perform their different functions, how much freedom of decision and authority they should have. The differences of opinion apply in part to policies of administration or personnel, differences that may be reflected in varied practices among divisions of the Directorate of Operations. For purposes of general discussion, what matters is less who does the tasks than what issues their performance raises and what contribution their performance makes to accomplishing the overall intelligence mission.

These are issues that arise in the context of collecting intelligence clandestinely, and they all belong under general headings of quality promotion and quality control. They usually involve finding the least damaging of compromises between competing values and interests; absolutes of right and wrong are the exception. I intend to outline here some of the issues in the context where they occur and to express some opinions on how the different values may be balanced. Because the subject is judgmental throughout, the opinions are

W. J. McKee, "The Reports Officer: Issues of Quality," *Studies in Intelligence*, vol. 27, no. 1 (Spring 1983), pp. 11–18. Originally classified "Secret" and "Noforn." For definitions, see appendix B.

necessarily in some measure personal and may not be shared by others of similar working background and experience.

It is best to start in the middle, because the issues all interrelate, and there is hardly a beginning or end to them. The middle, in this context, is reports dissemination.

Although the Operations Directorate has repeatedly tried to codify its interests and its wisdom, the officer who must decide whether to publish a report finds that the rules are of limited help. They advise him to publish information from clandestine sources if it will be useful, not to jeopardize sources and methods, not to mislead the reader with false information or false confirmation of other reporting. They cannot provide advice on what to do with a particular report that probably has both strengths and weaknesses.

In my early days as a field reports officer in ▓▓▓▓▓▓▓▓▓▓ , a report was delivered recounting in a few sentences ▓▓▓▓▓▓▓▓▓▓▓▓▓▓▓▓ positive comments to a small group of political associates about a recent policy decision in Washington. ▓▓▓▓▓▓▓▓▓ had made the same comments in a public speech. My chief thought it was important we could confirm, through clandestine coverage, that ▓▓▓▓▓▓▓▓ was saying the same thing in private that he was saying in public. I thought the report would only be valuable ▓▓▓▓▓▓▓▓ was saying something different in private. The report was disseminated.

The questions we faced had to do with judging in what sense the information was already known, to what extent our secret access to ▓▓▓▓▓▓▓ political friends added authority to US understanding of ▓▓▓▓▓▓ attitude, to what extent US policy-level officers wanted and needed such reporting, and—in my view a key point—whether our reinforcing the public record on a matter of sensitivity between ▓▓▓▓▓ and Washington might skew US perception and judgment. The main issue as I saw it was objectivity. The main issue as my chief saw it was fulfilling the mission of a foreign intelligence office to report any policy-level information it received.

As I think about it now, I cannot believe the decision was as important as it seemed at the time, but if my memory has reproduced the facts accurately, I would now opt for disseminating the little report with comments drawing attention to ▓▓▓▓▓▓▓ public statement and noting the extent to which ▓▓▓▓▓▓▓▓ might be expected to confide—or not confide—in the friends he was talking to. That procedure would have made the information available while underscoring our uncertainty about its significance.

If experience applies, my solution will provoke strong dissent from one side or another, for there is no single correct answer, and the issues that arise connect with values that are emotional as well as intellectual. The emotions can be simple, personal, and apolitical. Consider the operations officer who has overcome months of operational frustration and finally has produced some information. Should we publish his report only for the sake of his morale? I have given in to such arguments as these when the balance of judgment wavered.

Objectivity

The question of objectivity is all-pervasive. For those, including reports officers, who are engaged in the collection process, imaginative immersion in the foreign milieu is essential for understanding and pursuing the substantive issues, and the operations officer may be unable to develop and maintain the loyal cooperation of his reporting sources if he does not sympathize with their feelings. But to include the effects of this immersion or sympathy in the reporting can mislead the reader, whether it influences the selection of the reports or the way they are worded. Bias—from whatever cause it derives—must be recognized, identified, given a due place, not passed on without notice to the hurried and possibly unsuspecting reader.

Let us go back to the summer of 1982, when a report might state that Andropov was in line for the Soviet leadership and favored a more cooperative relationship with the West. The usefulness of that report would hang in large part on its provenance and its target. The report would probably deserve publication only if it could be shown to belong in a specified context, as an indication of a Soviet propaganda line to a particular government or political party in the West, of rumors circulating in specified Soviet circles, or, possibly, as the direct and honest impression of someone who had known Andropov. The source's reliability, competence, and attitude—and, probably, the attitude and purpose of his informants—would determine the way in which the report might be judged useful within any of these categories. Only the Operations Directorate would be in a position to know the details of operational origin. So the published report must include an objective and perceptive statement to guide the reader.

But one man's objectivity and truth may not be another's. The operations officer who got the report might believe intensely that his Soviet source was candid and reliable, while readers expert in Soviet affairs but knowing nothing of the source might assume that the information was sheer propaganda. Perhaps one who reviewed all the operational and substantive evidence together might conclude that the report was a genuine account of a genuine rumor, no more, but also no less. Its value, and the need for its publication, would then depend on whether the fact that such a rumor was circulating in the USSR was already known at the time.

The examples may help to make clearer why one issue involves another.

Strung together, the interrelated questions are formidable: to publish or to withhold publication; to filter, and how much, the emotions and perceptions that accompany collection; to promote quality or to promote quantity of reporting; to emphasize speed or emphasize accuracy; to explain origins or forgo explanations for the sake of security; to encourage use of information for policy purposes or to protect sources at the expense of use; to emphasize initiative and imagination in the collection process or to emphasize discipline and system.

Quality Versus Quantity

No one intentionally publishes poor reporting. Information that is unreliable, poorly authenticated, inaccurate in fact or sloppy in presentation does little service to policy or analysis and may mislead it. The customer is rarely in a position to make needed corrections. Although intelligence officers all know this, the pressures of working reality can lead to reports with any of these weaknesses being published. Correcting defects before publication, for instance, can be difficult.

When flawed information arrives at a field collection office, the office may decide to go back to the source and question him again or task him with research or interviews he should undertake. The source may then fail to produce further information, or the communication with him may be too slow to get answers while the information matters to US policy. Field and Headquarters offices will then employ what ingenuity they can to overcome the difficulties, engaging other field offices and other sources in the effort, perhaps recruiting help from information collectors in other US agencies or friendly foreign intelligence services, and perhaps drawing on factual background that suggests a plausible way to read a distorted story.

When, as often, none of the procedures produces definitive results, the report may be discarded as too confusing to be useful, or the report may be published to let readers know that such a story exists. If the report is published, explanations can be included calling attention to the weaknesses in the account and to other information, perhaps contradictory information, that pertains to judging it. Such a report is a product of quality even when its content is less than satisfactory, for its published version reflects the efforts that went to improving it, and it will mislead no attentive reader.

Each of these activities demands perseverance, patience, and skill. Pressures of time, other work, or the mechanics of distribution can lead to the omission of vital explanations in publishing a defective report. The more that offices are oriented toward quantitative production, the easier and more likely such errors become.

But some quantity is also essential. Collecting offices that have been reporting high level information may lose their access and reach an impasse. They may fail, for practical reasons of operational difficulty, to get back to the levels of information US policy most needs, and they may then produce little or no intelligence reporting. The offices may then decide to collect information that is of lesser significance but that is more readily available, judging that information of this kind, in the absence of better reporting, may give clues to important policy.

In the course of moving toward greater productivity, offices may go so far as to set production quotas for themselves, hoping to stimulate the operations officers to greater effort and more visible results. The effect of this well-intended strategy can be unfortunate. For even when the intelligence product is not directly misleading, it competes for attention in overflowing in-boxes, and quantities of mediocre reports may result in a poor reputation that affects the reception of a good report in the same series. In situations like these, someone has to point the needle of collection and dissemination back toward selectivity.

Speed Versus Accuracy

I suppose that any large organization, even such an active and positive-minded entity as the Directorate of Operations, includes pockets of inertia, psychologies which are disconnected to any outside reality and which disregard any need for haste or policy imperatives. One of the correctives is to emphasize the mechanisms of rapid communication. This corrective, with its commitment to speed, carries danger as well as merits. The pressures for fast dissemination of intelligence often conflict with the need to assure optimum accuracy.

In view of the emotions that sometimes flare over decisions on this subject, perhaps I should tell a story against myself. Some years ago advance word was brought to me conveying the gist of new information from a sensitive operation. The information, which was initially available only in oral form, pertained directly to negotiations a US Cabinet member was conducting that day. After getting the necessary senior approval, I picked up the secure telephone and arranged for the information to be relayed to the Cabinet member's executive assistant, explaining that a more complete account was not yet available. The Cabinet member's answer came back to me: he did not want the information orally; he wanted it in writing and he wanted it right. The rest of the story was now on its way, and I succeeded, with difficulty, in getting a full written account to the Cabinet member within about three hours. The Cabinet member then expressed his thorough annoyance at top Agency levels; he thought we should not have notified him until we knew precisely what we had to report.

Whatever the rights and wrongs of that incident, it illustrates a dilemma of information handlers. On the one hand, the mechanisms of communication are designed to meet a true perception: information is useless if it arrives too late. On the other hand, a misleading message may be worse than none. Even a subsequent correction may never catch up with all those in whose minds the original message has stuck.

In matters of timeliness I believe there can be no general rule. There is information which has little use until it has been worked over in detail, organized, collated, edited, and corrected after re-questioning the source. Reporting like this, from defector sources, for instance, can be of high value, leading perhaps to reorientation of whole US defense programs, and a delay in its processing may be exactly what is needed to assure its adequacy. At the other extreme, some kinds of terrorist reporting require the most immediate action, to assure, for instance, an ambassador's security. And there are all other kinds of reporting in between, each requiring judgment of what kind of contribution it can make, how serious are its flaws, what action can be taken to correct the flaws and how quickly, and in conclusion, when the line is drawn and the report is published, what advice and warnings shall it carry to the reader. The danger is in confusing categories, imagining that urgent information can be pondered over or that important but doubtful information must be hurried through without extra efforts to get it right. There is no substitute for informed, balanced judgment of each separate case.

Security Versus Use

Losing a source means losing the ability to continue a line of reporting, and if the loss occurs through revelation of US Government information, it may also constitute, from the perspective of the Operations Directorate, a breach of faith with its source. The negative effects extend from relations with that source to the attitudes of prospective sources and hence to other reporting. Protecting sources comes as high as any value in the Directorate's focus.

The whole effort of clandestine collection takes place, on the other hand, to serve customers by providing information that is useful and can be used. The information must be distributed to outside readers, and it must include adequate indications of its origin. To use it, the customer may wish to make some aspect of it public, to draw on it in talking with foreign officials, or to paraphrase it rather precisely in a formal demarche to a foreign government. All these actions, starting with the dissemination of the report, endanger in some degree the security of the source.

These contrary interests cannot always be reconciled, and the attempt to reconcile them may and often does produce a compromise that does not fully satisfy the requirements either of security or of use. The report may be distributed to a restricted number of readers, leaving out those who have an interest less than primary. The Directorate may not feel free to provide the background about the origin of a report that an analyst or policy officer believes he needs to know. Or the Directorate may have to insist that the wording of a demarche be blurred with vague language when precision would be more effective.

The Directorate has devised a variety of ways and words for protecting the source while getting the information to those US officials who most require it, and including in the report the background explanations that the readers need. The Directorate also permits and encourages the individual initiative of its officers in finding new ways and new language when standard methods will not meet the case. For this is a dynamic process, involving new problems constantly.

Authentication is a central issue here, because it is the authentication which gives authority and credibility to intelligence reporting and defines its message. Authentication means a truthful description of the source's access and an honest judgment of his reliability. The more controversial or political the report or the more complex its origin, the more important are this description and judgment. The reader must know what kind of information is before him, what foreign purposes or biases it may reflect. But it is precisely those reports that pertain to matters of current interest or controversy that are most likely to become public without authorization, that is, to leak. Often in just those reports where there is the greatest danger to source security, there is the greatest need to explain origins and to identify ulterior motives.

Directorate officers must exercise all their ingenuity to find ways out of these impasses, to assure that those customers who most need the information receive it in a form they will find meaningful and not misleading, yet to assure reasonable protection to the source.

System Versus Initiative

The objectives and priorities of intelligence collection in the Directorate of Operations must be systematized for the orderly, responsible employment of clandestine resources. Formal definitions of intelligence needs are set annually and assigned to the field stations in priorities that balance the importance of the task against the capacities of each station. Parallel to this written guidance are oral instructions, including changes in collection priorities, to assure that the service maintains a centralized discipline and responds to policy-level judgments.

Supplementing, supporting, and feeding this general guidance is a whole range of activity involving systematic reviews of the information product, identifying strengths to be supported and weaknesses to be corrected, information needs that should be met, and follow-up actions that individual reports require. The activity involves a dialogue between those, largely outside the Directorate, who know in detail what information is needed and missing and those who know what priorities have been set and what collection possibilities exist within the Directorate. From initiatives originating both inside and outside the Directorate, collection guidance is developed that steers collection toward real and specific needs.

Differences of judgment and interest arise in two connections: the extent to which the Directorate should be responsive to customers' definitions of their information needs, and the extent to which the Directorate should pursue ad hoc requirements on the initiative of its own officers.

The Directorate of Operations is a service organization which normally seeks to respond to customers, and customers often find that the Directorate is the US collector most easily moved and most readily responsive to their requirements. But the Operations Directorate must not only manage its resources with system and selectivity; it must also take into account the disadvantageous aspects of its collection methods. Its access is never universal, its operations often involve time delays, and insofar as its operations are clandestine, they carry risks. Clandestine collection against unfriendly countries endangers the sources and may endanger officers of the Directorate, while collection against friendly countries, if it becomes known, may damage US relations with those countries. So the Directorate's perception of a proposed collection project may not be identical with the customer's view of it. The Directorate tries to set a rather high threshold among the requirements that are proposed to it, to assure that its clandestine activity concentrates where that kind of collection is most important. So it must decide case by case whether to respond to particular requests and, if so, in what measure. Even when it rejects a requirement for collection, it may try to serve the customer by helping to find pragmatic, nonclandestine means to meet the needs.

In many types of collection, the working requirements are developed to a large extent within the Directorate. This happens in different ways. Specialists who have been concerned with reviewing the information product against other available information may become expert in defining information needs for clandestine collection, translating questions on what the future will bring into questions that sources can answer factually, and wording these questions for specific sources. Field offices may become exceptionally well informed on developments in the country where they are placed and may be the first to identify new trends and new questions.

I have heard officers in analytic and policy components express concern over whether a service organization, especially a collector of clandestine information that may be engaged in efforts of clandestine influence as well, should be free to analyze and judge information or to formulate requirements. They have feared that the clandestine service might lead the whole government into following a wild conjecture or a blind presupposition that the service finds fragments of fact to support.

In practice, activities of analysis and judgment, of initiative and imagination, must be balanced constantly within the Directorate through central guidance and systematic review. In this respect the Directorate is normally self-correcting. But individual thought enters into every step of collection.

The topic of technology transfer has received top-level attention. Analysts have defined the factual questions, staffs within the Directorate have instructed the field collectors what kinds of information they should collect and should not collect. But for years before this central guidance was prepared, one of the European field offices was producing evidence that made the case. As happens often, the initial intelligence reporting preceded the policy interest and helped arouse it. Even now, after all the definitions and requirements have been set, field offices may find and report unanticipated information that will lead to revising the analytic judgments and the requirements' guidance. Collection offices must respond to centralized advice, but they must also remain independently intelligent and alert.

And somehow the focus must be kept objective. I mentioned the difficulty of keeping reporting dispassionate when the officers who are producing it become engaged—must become engaged—imaginatively and in some measure emotionally in the foreign milieu. If they fail to develop and maintain this engagement, they will be unable to function effectively as vital nerve ends of government awareness. Yet system, discipline, objectivity must also prevail.

Perspective

This account applies to aspects of the intelligence collection effort which are not always clearly represented in distinct office functions or a separate career. My approach is from the perspective of the reports officer, because my personal experience has been within that role. In reality, the issues raised here concern officers with other titles as well, and all of these concerns come together in some degree or form in the management of the Directorate.

Planning operations, recruiting agents, and maintaining collection mechanisms are the primary activities in the Directorate of Operations; no collection can take place without them. These activities are so complex, so difficult, and so interesting that they often absorb the full attention of those who are responsible for them. It has not been uncommon in the Directorate that a concern with the product of these activities has been perceived as an extra virtue, not an unconditionally required element of the process.

A balance to this strong and essentially necessary weight on operations is needed if the product is to serve its purposes. I have intended the present sketch of issues involved in promoting the usefulness of the product to suggest both what is at stake in these decisions and how complex they are. First, they matter. Decisions of what information to collect and disseminate, how to explain the origin of information while protecting the security of sources, how to balance the different time factors, to whose attention the information should be brought—these decisions often determine whether or not the information makes a difference to policy and analysis. That is, they determine whether the collection effort has served its purpose.

And they demand full attention. Each decision is separate to its case and involves a complex of facts, surmises, principles, judgments, and conflicts. Officers who are engaged with these issues need to develop a perspective that serves as a tool to their resolution. It must be a perspective in which discipline and independence of thought are balanced, in which reason and objectivity predominate.

13.

This remarkable article and the next two were introduced on p. xix. William Johnson is an exceptionally trenchant, forthright veteran who has written the best American handbook on counterespionage, *Thwarting Enemies at Home and Abroad: How to Be a Counterintelligence Officer.* His article below was considered by the editor of *Studies in Intelligence* to be so controversial that the editor introduced it with much more than the usual caption: "This study, prepared at [CIA's] Center for the Study of Intelligence, presents the personal point of view of an experienced and thoughtful DDO officer, recently retired after 28 years of service. It is the kind of argument seldom put to paper, but often heard orally in places where Agency shop is talked. Some will agree heartily with the author's conclusions; others will reject them vigorously. But most who read the monograph will find it engaging and lively, full of challenging comments on the state of our Agency today." That was 1976; many would consider it still broadly applicable for the 1990s.

The "editor" referred to in some of the endnotes and asterisked footnotes is CIA's original *Studies in Intelligence* editor.

Clandestinity and Current Intelligence

WILLIAM R. JOHNSON

This paper has one main theme, that the production of current intelligence and the conduct of espionage are incompatible.

The argument will be that our present plight was caused by our inability, or at least our failure, to maintain the clandestinity of our clandestine operations, and that this failure resulted in large part from the corruption of our espionage disciplines by those of journalism. I do not mean that commercial journalists themselves have corrupted the process, or that the printings of commercial and academic journals have damaged the discipline of espionage. I mean rather that the techniques employed by journalists and the journals to gather and report information have been appropriated by our clandestine service and have seriously degraded our emphasis on the real technique of espionage.

I shall not argue that current intelligence should not be produced, and I shall not argue that espionage should not be conducted, for as a relatively old hand in the spy business I have had a personal need for the one and a devout commitment to the other. But I shall try to demonstrate that efforts to combine the two activities in the same organization have caused and continue to cause the transformation of espionage into something non-clandestine. This is not

William R. Johnson, "Clandestinity and Current Intelligence," *Studies in Intelligence*, vol. 20, no. 3 (Fall 1976), pp. 15–69. Originally classified "Secret" and "No Foreign Dissem[ination]."

because espionage does not on occasion produce information that is current, but because such information cannot be produced continuously, by espionage, in the volume that consumers of information on current events require. When espionage tries to compete with journalism, it changes its character, can no longer be itself, and cannot do its proper job of providing the raw material needed for truly significant intelligence production.

The conclusions reached at the end of this paper do not include recommendations for specific organizational change. Research for this paper has required perusal of too many specific recommendations by too many Commissions, Task Forces, Select Committees, and Professors of Government, all vain of effect, to let this commentator hope that specific organizational recommendations from any quarter will have any immediate impact on the superstructure or the infrastructure of the nation's machinery for supporting the conduct of foreign affairs with intelligence.

But perhaps this paper may serve as a catalyst in a changing mental chemistry of officialdom. Such chemistry would seek to alter the frame of mind of executives, managers, analysts, estimators, and operators toward two forms of activity:

Current reporting. It would be recognized broadly that current information, whether political, economic, or military, and whether related to an immediate crisis or a continuing situation of routine concern, is a perishable, high-volume commodity. To satisfy a continuously changing customer demand, it must be collected and processed into intelligence continuously and rapidly. Its sources are primarily overt, and their exploitation requires a strong, open apparatus among overt agencies of the government.

Espionage. An activity illegal under foreign law, it provides, when efficiently planned and executed, the material of finished strategic intelligence. Because its planning and execution require foresight and phased preparation, it cannot produce volume without degenerating into the mere purchase of easily acquireable information at low risk, i.e., without competing with the overt collectors at the expense of its own discipline.

The chemistry I seek might also dissolve whatever congenital lesions and historically conditioned thought patterns cause the syndrome of what is later called in this paper "candoism." It might help alter the pattern of our Service's present knee-jerk reaction to every stimulus from the other organs of government, including those which happen to be sheltered and paid within the same Agency, and of compulsively devising ways to interact with those other organs in ways not related to our basic mission. It might give us a maturity, a confidence, a feeling of security that would permit us to cease competing outside our own proper territory and to steady down to a real performance. We might then afford an understanding of those other organs of government (and of the Agency) that would permit more effective cooperation and interaction.

The argument of this paper may appear to put aside rather arbitrarily other notorious causes of our present dilapidation, so belabored in the press, in the legislature, and in our own troubled discussions inside the shop:

The overtness of paramilitary and psychological warfare operations. Harry Rositzke handles this rather succinctly: "The broad assortment of propaganda, political, and paramilitary operations was assigned to the secret intelligence service in order to hide their official sponsorship. . . . 'Plausible denial' . . . was even then a hollow phrase, for it was impossible to deny operations that were exposed. . . . What was always an uneasy pairing became in time a self-defeating amalgam of disparate missions, and the damage not only to the reputation of the CIA but to the conduct of secret intelligence became progressively more serious."[1]

The corrosion of intelligence analysis and reporting by political action. A foreign commentator's summary of this painful subject is as good as any of our own: "Individuals who work for an organization that displays a strong commitment to a policy or outlook will be tempted to send back news which shows that they are on the right side, and to ignore or underplay uncomfortable facts so as not to risk unpopularity with their colleagues and superiors. In these circumstances, it is not always possible to distinguish between what is seen and what is regarded as expedient to see. . . . If the intelligence service is dominated by a group of powerful decision makers, it will become the prisoner of these decision makers' images, dogmas, and preconceptions. Instead of challenging these dogmas and correcting these images when they clash with its objective findings, the intelligence service will be no more than a rubber stamp of these preconceptions."[2] The writer is speaking of Israel's failure to anticipate the Egyptian attack at Yom Kippur in 1973, but how many examples can we not think of in our own experience, from the Ardennes Offensive of 1944 to the collapse of the Vietnamese army in 1975, in which our intelligence was corrupted by one or more of the factors listed above? And who now will deny that nowhere is there a stronger "commitment to a policy or outlook" than by a Service that is actively supporting a political faction, movement, or government with funds, advice, equipment, paramilitary resources and propaganda?

The bureaucratic stultification that accompanies bigness and power. The *bigness* has not much afflicted the espionage elements of the Service, but these

---

1. "America's Secret Operations: A Perspective," *Foreign Affairs*, LIII/2 (January 1975), 341–344.

2. Avi Shlaim. "Failures in National Intelligence Estimates: The Case of the Yom Kippur War," *World Politics*, XXVIII/3 (April 1976), 348–380.

have been afflicted by the bigness of the covert action elements, which grew like Jack's beanstalk in the early fifties, and of the agency overall, which is sometimes attributed (by Lt. Gen. Daniel O. Graham, for example)[3] to the Director's community-coordination position and sometimes, conversely, to the Director's failure to coordinate and consequent need to expand competitively. The *power*, says our former colleague, Tom Braden, "was too easy to bring to bear—on the State Department, on other government agencies, on the patriotic businessmen of New York, and on the foundations whose directorships they occupied. The Agency's power overwhelmed the Congress, the press and therefore, the people."[4]

In the argument that follows we shall not be able to avoid considering the destructive forces just listed, for they are closely related to the incompatibility of current collection and espionage. All are products of the same history.

History: How OSS Won the War

Dr. Ray S. Cline, who headed the first current intelligence production office in the Coordinator of Information's Research and Analysis Branch, and went on for 30 years to serve in such positions as Deputy Director for Intelligence, Chief of two of the Clandestine Service's larger stations ███████████████████ and Director of State's Bureau of Intelligence and Research (INR), remarks that current intelligence is always a saleable commodity.[5] That is certainly true at the present time, for most officials in Washington keep abreast. They read *Time* and *Newsweek*, the *New York Times* and the *Washington Post*, sometimes the *Economist* and the *Wall Street Journal*, occasionally, if able, the *Neue Zuericher Zeitung* or *Le Monde*. Those in foreign affairs read the daily and weekly summaries published by CIA's Office of Current Intelligence (OCI). The President and a handful of other officials read, from OCI, the *President's Daily Brief*, familiarly called the PDB.[6] Let us look briefly at the origins and evolution of the PDB, starting with General Donovan and OSS.

---

3. *U.S. Intelligence at the Crossroads, USSI Report 76-1* (United States Strategic Institute, Washington, 1976), 11*f.*

4. Tom Braden, "What's Wrong With the CIA?" *Saturday Review*, 5 April 1975, 2. Roger Hilsman ("Intelligence Through the Eyes of a Policy Maker," *Surveillance and Espionage in a Free Society*, Richard H. Blum, ed., New York, Washington, London, 1972, 171*f*) attributes the power of CIA to nine sources: size of staff, ability and talent of personnel, money, control of information, secrecy, patriotic appeal, political leverage, speed of communications, and (for many years) the family relationship of the Director with the Secretary of State.

5. Seminar, 15 July 1976, Center for the Study of Intelligence. A draft of Dr. Cline's *Secrets, Spies, and Scholars* (Acropolis Press, Washington, D.C., 1976) was used at this seminar several months prior to publication.

6. Center for the Study of Intelligence, *CIA Intelligence Support for Foreign and National Security Policy Making* (January 1976): "Broad spectrum reporting from CIA is conveyed principally through the *National Intelligence Daily* and *Bulletin* and by the *President's Daily Brief*."

Since one cannot talk about intelligence without talking about government, and about government without talking about bureaucracy, the history of government, and of intelligence, is largely an account of the internal, often internecine politics of bureaucracy.[7] General William Joseph Donovan was a patriot who worked within the bureaucracy to help get the war won, starting with British help before the United States was formally in it. At many points his colleagues in government found his actions disruptive and expansionist, that is, in conflict with their own. On 8 April 1941, General Sherman Miles, then G-2 of the Army, wrote to Chief of Staff General George C. Marshall:

> In great confidence O.N.I. tells me that there is considerable reason to believe that there is a movement on foot, fostered by Col. Donovan, to establish a super agency controlling *all* intelligence. This would mean that such an agency, no doubt under Col. Donovan, would collect, collate and possibly even evaluate all military intelligence which we now gather from foreign countries. From the point of view of the War Department, such a move would appear to be very disadvantageous, if not calamitous.[8]

State's reaction to Donovan was expressed by Breckinridge Long, an Assistant Secretary:

> Bill Donovan—"Wild Bill" is head of the C.I.O. [sic]—Coordinator of Information. He has been a thorn in the side of a number of the regular agencies of the Government for some time—including the side of the Department of State—and more particularly recently in [Sumner] Welles'. He is into everybody's business—knows no bounds of jurisdiction—tries to fill the shoes of each agency charged with responsibility for a war activity. He has had almost unlimited money and has a regular army at work and agents all over the world. He does many things under the *nom de guerre* of "Information."[9]

Because one of the benign ways to promote one's purposes within a bureaucracy is to get close access to the Top Man and then keep his interest so that the access, and the influence it provides, continue, it was important to Donovan, the man with the new idea, a Republican who had been close to President Hoover but knew Franklin Roosevelt only through the President's Republican Secretary of the Navy, Frank Knox, to keep as close to the President as possible.

7. See Anthony Downs, *Inside Bureaucracy*, a Rand Corporation Research Study (Little, Brown, Boston, 1967).

8. Thomas Francis Troy, *Donovan and the CIA*, Intelligence Institute, OTR, CIA, 1975, I, 55. Troy's footnote cites "Memo, Miles to Marshall on 'Coordinator for the three Intelligence Agencies of the Government,' April 8, 1941. Records of the Army Staff, Army Intelligence Decimal File, Records Group 319 (Wash. Nat'l Records Center, Suitland, Md.)."

9. Breckinridge Long, *The War Diaries of Breckinridge Long: Selections from the Years 1939–1944*, ed. Fred L. Israel (U. of Nebraska Press, Lincoln, 1966), 257. Cited by Thomas F. Troy, "Donovan's Original Marching Orders," *Studies in Intelligence*, XVII/2.

Being a restless man, he did this kind of constructive apple-polishing in various ways, but he did not neglect to establish, where possible, a sense of personal ownership, a kind of paternalism in the mind of the President for the organization that Donovan had created and was struggling to expand against the rival bureaucracies of War, Navy, State, Treasury, FBI, and others. That is, he tried to make the President feel that his elite, strategic, special Office functioned to serve the President personally. And one of the ways he did this was to send frequent intelligence memoranda directly to Roosevelt under a personal letter. These reports did not much resemble a PDB vintage 1976, for Donovan had never become what his original title dubbed him, "Coordinator" of information. The State, Navy, War, and Treasury Departments and the FBI had kept their independence; and Donovan's Research and Analysis Branch (R & A) never became what we would now call a national-level evaluative or estimative shop. Donovan's memoranda served a purpose for him, however; they gave the President glimpses of personalities and events that provided a feeling of texture lacking from the well staffed and researched, but usually turgid reports and recommendations that came to him through his cabinet officers. By August 1941, Donovan had begun to send the President frequent, almost daily reports on a variety of subjects, some the result of research by R & A, some raw from the field, all calculated to interest and amuse as well as to instruct.[10]

Toward the end of the war, the memoranda contained a fair amount of name-dropping, which after all is a function of the specificity essential to sound reporting and also happened to suit the taste of his reader:

> Alexander Constantin von Neurath, German Consul at Lugano, has just returned from a meeting with Field Marshal Albert Kesselring, Commander of German Army Group "C" Italy; Rudolph Rahn, German Ambassador to the Mussolini regime in North Italy; and Obergruppenfuehrer and General der Waffen SS Karl Wolff, the Higher SS and Police leader in Italy and chief of Himmler's personal staff. . . .
>
> On Wednesday, September 27, I saw the King. He gave me a warm welcome and spent an hour with me chatting about the present situation. He told me . . . that Winston Churchill sent a sizzling telegram to Tito telling him in effect . . .[11]

10. For an account of the beginning of this process several months before Pearl Harbor see Troy, *Donovan and the CIA*, Chapter V, "The First Six Months." Three batches of Donovan's memoranda to the President have been published under low classification in *Studies in Intelligence:* the "Sunrise Reports" on negotiations for the German surrender in Italy (VII/2 [Spring 1963], OFFICIAL USE ONLY); the "Boston Series" (IX/1 [Winter 1965], CONFIDENTIAL); and a sampling of the "Peter to Tito Series" chronicling the secret diplomacy (IX/2 [Spring 1965], CONFIDENTIAL).

11. *Studies in Intelligence*, IX/2, 53. Report of meetings held by Mr. Bernard Yarrow in London with King Peter and Prime Minister Subasic.

Occasionally, General Donovan's personality came through as a luridness of style that would not be permitted by today's editors:

> Sincerely regret that you cannot at this time see Wood's material as it stands without condensation and abridgement. In some 400 pages . . . a picture of imminent doom and final downfall is presented. Into a tormented General headquarters and a half-dead Foreign Office stream the lamentations of a score of diplomatic posts. . . . The period of secret service under Canaris and diplomacy under the champagne salesman is drawing to an end. . . . Ribbentrop has beat a retreat to Fuschl . . . that old fox, Horthy, playing the role of a 1944 Petain. . . . In Sofia cagy Bulgarians are playing all kinds of tricks on Beckerle and going off to Turkey on pleasure trips. . . . The final death-bed contortions of a putrefied Nazi diplomacy. . . .[12]

These examples show that during the war Donovan set the precedent of a Service Chief building, expanding, and protecting his organization by providing a flow of interesting *current* information to the Chief Executive, although current intelligence was not the main mission of his Research and Analysis Branch. Donovan had originally envisaged this mission as of longer range. Ludwell Lee Montague, a senior analyst in and later chief of R & A, records that the General, believing

> that the President should be better informed than the State, War and Navy Departments, acting separately, could possibly inform him, . . . assembled a group of eminent scholars, men knowledgeable of foreign affairs and practiced in the techniques of research and analysis in a way that regular Army, Navy, and Foreign Service officers could not be . . . [to] assemble all of the information in possession of the Government, not only in the State, War, and Navy Departments, but also in the Library of Congress and other places, and . . . prepare for the President a fully informed and thoughtful analysis of interest to him. . . . The analyses actually produced by this R & A Branch were not estimates. They were academic studies, descriptive rather than estimative, more like an NIS than NIE.[13]

But Donovan knew the market value of current information, and so at the beginning a small group of R & A analysts, under Ray Cline, produced it.

---

12. *Studies in Intelligence,* IX/1, 89. A report in April 1945, commenting on material from "George Wood," an alias for one of Allen Dulles' wartime "crown jewels" who was subsequently identified as Fritz Kolbe, an official in the German Foreign Ministry. This "George Wood" is not to be confused with the late Sam Edison Woods (1892–1952), who was U.S. Consul General in Zurich during Dulles' tenure in Bern and had been collecting intelligence from well-placed German sources since 1937, when he was Commercial Attaché, in Berlin. [See Barton Whaley, *Codeword BARBAROSSA* (MIT Press, Cambridge, 1973), 37f *et passim.*] Woods, interned in Germany for five months after Pearl Harbor, was formally assigned to OSS on 20 January 1944.

13. "The Origins of National Intelligence Estimating," *Studies in Intelligence,* XVI/2.

Donovan was by no means the only provider, official or unofficial, of this combination of instruction and entertainment that Franklin Roosevelt relished, but he had an advantage over his rivals: he had an organization oriented, unlike the War Department's Military Intelligence Division, the Office of Naval Intelligence, or State, toward the Presidency rather than toward a departmental customer; at the same time, it was large enough to outrange such unofficial competitors as Vincent Astor and John Franklin Carter.[14]

For an organization like OSS that had been created to serve a President who had been in office for 13 years and for a man like Donovan who had created it, the death of FDR was a change of environment. Harry S Truman was a different kind of boss, and he used his intelligence service in a different way. He wrote that

> On becoming President, I found that the needed intelligence information was not coordinated at any one place. Reports came across my desk on the same subject at different times from the various departments, and these reports often conflicted. . . . A President has to know what is going on all around the world in order to be ready to act when action is needed. The President must have all the facts that may affect the foreign policy or the military policy. . . . Under the new intelligence arrangement [OSS abolished, CIG established, first under R. Adm. Sidney W. Souers, then under Lt. Gen. Hoyt S. Vandenberg] I now began to receive a daily digest and a summary of the information obtained abroad. . . . Here, at last, a coordinated method had been worked out, a practical way of keeping the President informed as to what was known and what was going on. The Director of the Central Intelligence Agency, as the Central Intelligence Group was renamed in 1947, became, usually, my first caller of the day. . . . I brought Admiral Souers to the White House in the new capacity of Special Assistant to the President for Intelligence. Thus he, too, sat in with me every morning when the Director of Central Intelligence came with the daily digest. . . .[15]

Thus Donovan's spicy memoranda evolved into a Daily Digest, and as with a daily newspaper, the production of the digest required a continuous gathering of information from all available sources. The pressures familiar in a

14. One competitor of whom Donovan was apparently unaware until after the war was Colonel Jean Valentin Grombach, whose espionage organization was truly clandestine in its administration and communications, though its collection mechanism was uncontrolled and its sources essentially unreliable. The history of the Grombach organization has not yet been compiled from the mass of data on hand. Nor have the various conspiratorial and clandestine activities been chronicled of one of Grombach's patrons, Adolph Augustus Berle, Jr. The selection of Berle's papers published by his widow (*Navigating the Rapids, 1916–1971,* ed. Beatrice Bishop Berle and Travis Beal Jacobs, Harcourt Brace Jovanovich, New York, 1973) sheds no light. For Berle's comment on Donovan see: 403, 412, 417.

15. *Memoirs, Volume II: Years of Trial and Hope* (New York, 1956), 55–58. I have transposed sentence order, retaining the logic.

newspaper—deadlines, space to fill, continuity of stories—began here, and as we shall see, eventually were passed on to the Agency's clandestine collection element.

CIG/CIA and the Sales Department

The new CIA, activated from the Central Intelligence Group (CIG) in September 1947, was a little like the Baltimore Orioles when they were first admitted to the American League. All the old minor league enthusiasm was there, but the competition was suddenly very, very big, not in the intelligence business, but in the government business. To change the metaphor, the new agency's position was like that of a corporation suddenly given the opportunity to expand. Three decades later, sitting in the headquarters of what is now justly called a diversified conglomerate,[16] we have difficulty remembering what it was like to be so poor and so small. But in 1947, needing to expand its capital, the company had first to expand its market, and this meant modifying its product to compete with that of other corporations. The obvious product for which Truman had registered a demand when he called in February 1946 for a daily digest, was current events, and clearly a Sales Department was needed to market the product, especially since

> . . . the State Department had challenged CIG on the issue of access to the President. Truman had requested that CIG provide him with a daily intelligence summary from the Army, Navy and State Departments. However, Secretary of State Byrnes asserted his Department's prerogative in providing the President with foreign policy analyses. While CIG did its summary, the State Department continued to prepare its own daily digest. Truman received both.[17]

The Sales Department began modestly in CIG as the Central Reports Staff, and was originally manned by people contributed somewhat reluctantly from the payrolls of State and the military services. By July 1946, the daily digest had been replaced by the more extensive and formal Daily and Weekly Summaries, and this prestigious journalistic mechanism could be used as the base from which to expand into that area so heavily contested among the various services, national strategic intelligence.[18] Using the Central Reports Staff as a nucleus,

16. Peter Szanton and Graham Allison, "Intelligence: Seizing the Opportunity," *Foreign Policy*, no. 22 (Spring 1976), 85f.

17. Anne Karalekas, *History of the Central Intelligence Agency: Supplementary Detailed Staff Reports on Foreign and Military Intelligence, Book IV, Final Report of the Select Committee to Study Governmental Operations with Respect to Intelligence Activities*, United States Senate, 94th Congress, 2nd Session, Report No. 94-755 (Government Printing Office, 1976). This is Book IV of the *Church Committee Report*.

18. Eugene C. Worman, Jr., *History of the Office of Current Intelligence* (Five-volume

DCI Vandenberg established the Office of Research and Evaluation in July 1946, and although it hardly produced what these days would be called finished national estimates, it had no significant competitors elsewhere in the government.

In an expanding XEROX or IBM, the Sales Department has considerable influence on the Departments of Planning, Engineering and Production. Since our concern is with the Clandestine Service, we may ask what influence the Central Reports Staff, which later evolved into the Office of Current Intelligence, had in these early days on the activities of the Office of Strategic Operations (OSO), which later evolved, along with a mutant called OPC, into the present Directorate of Operations.

The old Clandestine Service had nearly ceased to exist in the great rush to demobilize after World War II. When OSS was disbanded by Executive Order 9621, dated 20 September 1945 and effective 1 November, the two classically clandestine branches, Secret Intelligence (SI) and Counterespionage (X-2), kept skeleton *apparati* functioning. SI had espionage stations in the Near East and North Africa, in Germany and Austria, in China, and a handful of men in Southeast Asia, all grouped under a "Strategic Services Unit (SSU)" in the War Department. X-2 had offices in these stations and representations in several European capitals, where R & A, under State, provided real estate. Strength had been reduced from more than 9,000 to less than 3,000 and was still shrinking when the Secretary of War ordered SSU abolished by 30 June 1946. Abolition was avoided on 2 April by transferring SSU to the Central Intelligence Group (CIG), where the Research and Analysis Branch had already been rescued from the State Department.[19]

This was a period of transition with no assurance of eventual survival, in which some veterans of the old espionage (SI) and counterespionage (X-2) elements of OSS, with a few retreads from the disbanded paramilitary (SO) and propaganda (MO) branches, kept running operations and kept maintaining files. X-2 had 400,000 dossiers, mostly on Nazi and Fascist personalities, and these were invaluable for mounting postwar operations.

The SI and X-2 veterans also redirected the espionage and counterespionage effort against the new enemy, welcoming as a charter the recommen-

---

unpublished typescript, 1972, sent to Archives on termination of OCI). See also Elwood G. Dreyer, *The Office of Current Intelligence: A Study of its Functions and Organization,* School of Intelligence and World Affairs, Training Manual Number 5, CIA Office of Training, May 1970. SECRET.

19. Arthur B. Darling, "Origins of Central Intelligence," *Studies in Intelligence,* VIII/3, 88. This article, like others of Professor Darling in the *Studies,* is condensed from a portion of *The Central Intelligence Agency: An Instrument of Government, to 1950,* 12 volumes (CIA Historical Staff, 1953).

dation of an interdepartmental committee chaired by Colonel Fortier in February and March 1946 that SSU, subordinated to CIG, "concentrate on the current activities of the Soviet Union and its Satellites."[20] And to make their emerging new Service secure against the new enemy, they performed a thorough internal housecleaning.

At this time, the Service [OSO] was not sure that it was, wanted to be, or should be part of the corporation that was forming. Professor Darling records that

> Colonel [Donald H.] Galloway [Assistant Director for Strategic Operations, i.e., Chief of Clandestine Operations of the time] admonished his subordinates in OSO that they were to reduce to the minimum their associations with people from State, War, and the Navy and handle this minimum through a Control Officer. They were to carry on nothing but official business with other offices of CIG. Vandenberg, Wright, and Galloway wanted OSO to be as free as possible from connections which might expose its affairs. They believed that its operations should be kept apart from the observation and influence of the departmental chiefs of intelligence in the ARB; these were different from other "services of common concern" to the departments. OSO had to keep in touch with agencies which used its product, and it was authorized on October 25 to receive requests for information or action from those agencies through its Control Officer.[21]

Strategic Espionage

At some point the office of *Strategic* Operations (OSO) came to be called the Office of *Special* Operations,° possibly because of discomfort at the association with the Office of Strategic Services, possibly because "Special Operations" is a bland designator, a cover term, one that could be applied to some of the political action operations (such as the Italian elections) that OSO, before the advent of OPC, did conduct on a modest scale. Whatever the reason, OSO still believed that its activities should be considered "strategic." Implicit in the concept of strategy is a notion of planning, foresight, preparation. In warfare, it means largely the positioning of reserves, and so it is in espionage. Implicit in the concept of strategic espionage is the notion of strategic coverage, the positioning of agents in advance of their commitment to stealing secret information.

20. *Ibid.*, 69f. [Lawrence R. Houston recalls that at least the Cairo OSS had been "redirected" against Soviet activities and intentions in the Balkans as early as the spring of 1945.—HBW]

21. *Ibid.*, 87f. [I have found ARB to be unidentifiable at this late date. William R. Johnson believes it may have been a misprint for IAB, Intelligence Advisory Board to the DCI.—HBW]

°[Houston believes the name was changed when SI and X-2 were merged—possibly in the spring of 1946.—Ed.]

Writing in 1948, Sherman Kent, himself a veteran of Research and Analysis rather than of the SI or X-2 branches, expressed the concept of strategic espionage coverage in terms of what he called the "surveillance force":

> The surveillance force in a strategic intelligence operation is supposed, in the first instance, to watch actual, fancied, or potential ill-wishers or enemies of the United States and report on their activities. In the second instance, the surveillance force is supposed to procure a less dramatic sort of information which is calculated to forward the success of our own policies. In certain aspects of both lines of work the surveillance force must work clandestinely. Or to put it another way: a surveillance force which was not equipped to work clandestinely could not deliver on a small but extremely important part of its task. *Generally speaking, it could not deliver information which another country regarded as a secret of state.* Many such secrets can be apprehended only by fancy methods which are themselves secrets of state. Thus a certain important fraction of the knowledge which intelligence must produce is collected through highly developed secret techniques.[22]

In this very seminal book, Dr. Kent discussed all the difficulties of communication between a strategic collection apparatus and the analysts and policy makers to whom it exists to provide information. He gave special attention to what he calls "the segregation of the clandestine force" which is "dictated by the need for secrecy." We shall discuss this problem later in this paper, and we shall later give attention to requirements and feedback, a problem that is particularly acute in the collection of current information.

It was this problem of communication between the clandestine apparatus and the analysts that caused Colonel Galloway, the clandestine chief at the time, to inquire in August 1946 about getting evaluations of OSO reports from the Office of Reports and Evaluation (ORE), which was then less than a month old. He was told that "ORE had neither the personnel nor the working files . . . [while] the Reports Staff was . . . equipped only for current intelligence and attempting to synthesize departmental estimates." An evaluation mechanism was finally put into operation about ten months later,[23] but OSO viewed it as a support facility rather than a guidance channel, i.e., a device to assist in validating agents rather than planning future production. And the greatest reticence was maintained toward ORE regarding the identity and *modus operandi* of agents.

---

22. *Strategic Intelligence for American World Policy* (Princeton, 1966), 166. (Emphasis added.) This is the second edition; 1st ed. was published 1949. For Dr. Kent's thinking on production of strategic intelligence after a further 25 years of experience, see *The Law and Custom of the National Intelligence Estimate*, 1975, released in Donald P. Steury, ed., *Sherman Kent and the Board of National Estimates: Collected Essays* (Washington, D.C.: CIA, 1994), 43–115.

23. Darling, "With Vandenberg as DCI," *Studies in Intelligence*, XII/1, 75.

No prestige was attached within OSO to the importance of the ultimate customer. Doubtless a case officer would be pleased to hear that the gist of one of his reports had been read by Harry Truman at breakfast, but normally he would not expect to be told of this; what the case officer wanted to know was whether his agent was lying to him, was not performing diligently, was being deceived by a sub-source. The last thing a case officer, or his desk, would think of would be to consult a customer about the value of an operation.

The Central Reports Staff and other components of ORE had not yet even come to be regarded as The Other Side of the House, for the average OSO officer did not feel that any one House with one roof existed, except OSO itself. Recipients of reports existed, to be sure, outside that door guarded by the Control Officer, and OSO sincerely wanted to know whether the reports it sent out were judged by the recipients to be accurate. *Accuracy* was the criterion, not relevance or importance, for OSO saw its task as the management and control of agents. OSO was obsessed with the *reliability* of agents, and saw accuracy as a factor of reliability.

Now the grading system of the time (which had been taken over rather mechanically, I believe, from military procedures for evaluating reconnaissance and interrogation reports),[24] was designed to give the evaluator the minimum amount of information that would identify or describe a source and to require the user to evaluate reports on the basis of their relative plausibility in the context of all reports from all other sources on the subject. Evaluation of agents (what is now called "authentication") was strictly the job of the agent handler and his helpers, including sometimes a specialized "Reports Officer."[25]

Names of the Games in OSO

We see from the foregoing that the barrier between OSO with its espionage and counterespionage apparatus constructed on the principle of strategic coverage, and the analysts of ORE, was a real one. It was bothersome to both sides, though for different reasons. We may possibly understand the barrier better if we recollect the OSO working definitions of the period. What were (to OSO) the meanings of the words given to the activities with which OSO was charged—espionage and counterespionage? And what were the relationships of these activities to such related concepts as counterintelligence and security?

---

24. For a lucid and characteristic expression of the military intelligence officer's view of espionage, see Major General Sir Kenneth Strong, *Men of Intelligence* (Cassell, London, 1970). For the American view, as held before COI and OSS were born, see Shipley Thomas, *S-2 in Action* (The Military Service Publishing Company, Harrisburg, Pa., 1940).

25. Bruce L. Pechan, "The Collector's Role in Evaluation," *Studies in Intelligence*, V/3, 37–47. [Reprinted here, pp. 99–107.]

These definitions are crucial not only for what the words mean, but for what they do not mean:

— *Espionage* is the theft of information in contravention of another nation's laws by a person known as an "agent." This act of theft may be direct, as in the secret copying of a classified document, or indirect, as in the hiding of an eavesdropping device, or merely oral, but it is done by an agent and it breaks either a foreign law or the internal regulation of an alien organization. Espionage is *not* the confidential purchase of information where mere embarrassment, rather than illegality, is risked. It is *not* the flattery, bribery, or coercion of a person to influence his actions within *legal* limits. It is not "a scuttling, violence-prone business . . . incompatible with democracy,"[26] but rather a silent, surreptitious, violence-shunning business serving the nation.

— *Counterespionage* is that branch of espionage of which the target is an alien organization which uses conspiratorial methods, whether as part of a foreign government or of some non-national or international group,[27] and whether against the United States or against another entity. Counterespionage is, therefore, *also* the theft of information by [one's] agent, who will in this circumstance usually be called a double agent or a penetration, depending on [the] status [(agent or officer) he holds] in the enemy apparatus.[28]

These are the two branches of espionage, the two disciplines of clandestinity. Note their relationship to other activities associated with the spy business:

— *Counterintelligence* is a name given to a congeries of techniques, one of which is counterespionage. Its other techniques are mainly various types of investigation and detection. They all have as their objective the frustration of

26. Rod Macleish, Editorial Page, *Washington Post*, 2 February 1976.

27. E.g., the Curiel Apparatus, the Tupamaros, the Palestine Liberation Organization, the Black Septembrists, the Irish Republican Army, and in former years the Irgun Zvai Leumi and the NTS.

28. The overt literature of double agent operations in World War II is richer than that referring to counterespionage and deception during later periods of history. See the after-action report on British double agent operations (assisted by OSS' X-2), declassified and published as John Cecil Masterman's *The Double-Cross System in the War of 1939 to 1945* (New Haven and London, 1972). An exhaustive review, classified SECRET, appears in *Studies in Intelligence*, XVIII/1, by "A. V. Knobelspiesse," the pseudonym of one of our experts in the discipline. The reader with a decrypting bent may discover the origin of the name of OSS' counterespionage branch in the title of Masterman's book: our cousins normally referred to double agents as "XX agents." The board which cleared information for provocative passage ("build-up" or "smoke") was called the "Twenty Committee." So close was OSS to the British at the beginning that the CE service was named X-2 from one of the cousins' bits of inhouse whimsy.

the *active* efforts of alien conspiratorial organizations to acquire secret or sensitive information belonging to our government.[29]
— Note that counterintelligence is *not* security.
— Note that counterespionage is *not* security.
— *Security* is a dimension of clandestinity in espionage, counterespionage, counterintelligence, adultery, and poker. It is to these activities what style is to a writer, an athlete, or a musician, but it is not itself a work, a game, or a performance. Its purpose is prophylactic: it excludes toxic and infectious organisms and conserves the vital fluids.
— *Physical security* keeps out burglars and helps prevent accidental or absent-minded loss of information.
— *Operational security* is a function of all clandestine action and a function of the command channel within that action. Responsibility for operational security can be delegated to a specialized element only at the risk of the collapse of all the disciplines of clandestinity.

Today these definitions, particularly the distinction between counterintelligence and security, are blurred. In the decades that have passed since the absorption of OSO into the Plans Directorate (which was an event simultaneous with the establishment of the Office of Current Intelligence) a process of bureaucratic dialectic worked itself out with ironical results for all the conflicting factions. Among the operations officers of this period of history were many whose personal inclinations, tastes, ambitions, and wartime conditioning led them to prefer those courses of action leading to the extension of the practice of espionage to include as many forms of information gathering as possible. Many of these officers came from the disciplines of combat intelligence—prisoner interrogation, censorship, military liaison, field order of battle; many had backgrounds in analysis of voluminous information; many, like General Donovan before them, saw production of reports in quantity as a way of gaining recognition within the organization, and for the organization within the government. Together, they comprised what might be called the production [faction].

Mingled with this faction were many operations officers whose personalities and backgrounds were in a different tradition of intelligence. Rather

29. In the Office of Training's program for the Operations Directorate, many subjects are taught with varying emphasis at various times in response to the changing, and generally diminishing, demand of the desks and branches. Some of these subjects which are thought of as belonging to the CI disciplines are Basic Investigative Techniques, Surveillance Techniques (physical and technical), CI Detection, Collation and Analysis ("Notebooking"), Operational Use of the Polygraph, Penetration of Liaison, Double Agentry and Provocation, and Deception. Subjects often given the CI label, but more properly elements of operational security, are Control of Fabrication, Security Assessment, Damage Reporting, and Operational Testing of Agents.

alien to the American drive for quick success (the touchdown pass compared with the intricate checkmating combination) and big numbers, whether of things, people, or reports, this tradition was one of secrecy in espionage and of long-range coverage of strategic or potentially strategic targets.

One should not suppose that there was more or less ambition in the very able men and women who comprised the two factions. Ambition was in abundance, but it was of two very different kinds. And so a synthesis occurred: the faction that wished, from whatever ambitions for self and service, to extend the practice of espionage to all forms of information gathering, in order to have *production,* colluded with its basic rival, the faction that wished to keep operations centrally controlled and as clandestine as possible and to contrive strategic *coverage.* The result of the compromise gave the secrecy faction a staff authority (embodied some time after the Korean War ended in the Counterintelligence Staff) to police the clandestine professionalism of the entire Service, including its political action and propaganda efforts. The production faction thus got operational security out of the realm of command responsibility and delegated it to the Staff, to which inspection chores could be assigned and bucks passed. The verbal formula which consecrated this event was to say that counterintelligence consisted of:

> Two matching halves, security and counterespionage. Security consists basically of establishing passive or static defenses against all hostile and concealed acts regardless of who carries them out. Counterespionage requires the identification of a specific adversary, a knowledge of the specific operations that he is conducting, and a countering of those operations through concentrating and manipulating them so that their thrust is turned back against the aggressor.[30]

The eventual principal beneficiary of this process was current production, and the eventual loser was strategic coverage, for the intrinsically strategic and intrinsically clandestine practice of aggressive counterespionage now is associated, and therefore identified, with those routine but somewhat tiresome, somewhat inefficient practices that ensure security of operations. The two became associated, identified, in the minds of case officers, branch chiefs, certain division chiefs, and certain chiefs of the Service (including in each category those officers whose interest was in covert action rather than intel-

---

30. The organizational arrangements that effected these changes were more complex than is here indicated. Readers are invited to recall or to research in our historical material the reorganization of the Plans Directorate's original Staffs A and C, under James J. Angleton and William K. Harvey, respectively, into the Counter Intelligence and Foreign Intelligence Staff. The quotation is from A. C. Wasemiller, "The Anatomy of Counterintelligence," *Studies in Intelligence,* XIII/1, 10. See also Austin B. Matshulak, "Coordination and Cooperation in Counterintelligence," *Studies,* XIII/2, 25–36. The *Church Committee Report, op. cit.,* Book I, includes a chapter on Counterintelligence which takes its definition and much of its other terminology from Wasemiller.

ligence) because they were bureaucratically associated and identified in a single staff, the Counterintelligence (CI) Staff.

The result was that, as choices of management developed between sound tradecraft and expediency, expediency prevailed. Lapses of tradecraft could be glossed over ("That's not my job; I'm not a CI man"); policing of compromises could be delegated (REQUEST TDY OF EXPERIENCED CI OFFICER TO CONDUCT DAMAGE ASSESSMENT); the conduct of complex operations against a hostile (or friendly) intelligence service could be avoided ("Too time-consuming; produces few dissems"); the collation of information on hostile and friendly services could be reduced; and the maintenance of unilateral investigative facilities, which also produce no dissems, could be cut back in the budget.

But, at the period of which we speak, this evolution had not yet occurred. True counterespionage was still a viable concept. OSO was not bureaucratically or functionally close enough to ORE (renamed the Office of Research and Reports in 1950; ORR) to recognize a conflict between the real demands of espionage and the reportorial needs of current intelligence. Such criticism of the production of descriptive and narrative commentary on current events as was heard came mainly from those engaged in predictive and estimative analysis, and from senior critics who shared the view that current intelligence was the proper purview of the Department of State. Among these was William H. Jackson, who had participated with Allen Dulles in the so-called Dulles-Jackson-Correa Survey a year and a half earlier.

A version of OCI's difficulties within ORR, which reflects the point of view of ORR and OCI deponents, is given by Miss Anne Karalekas, a historian employed by the Senate's Select Committee, chaired by Frank Church, which investigated the Agency in some detail:

> Completely contrary to its intended functions, ORE had developed into a current intelligence producer. The Dulles-Jackson-Correa Survey had sharply criticized CIA's duplication of current intelligence produced by other Departments, principally State. *After his appointment as Deputy Director of Central Intelligence, Jackson intended that CIA would completely abandon its current political intelligence function.* State's Office of Intelligence Research would have its choice of personnel not taken into ONE and ORR, and any former ORE staff members not chosen would leave.
>
> In spite of Jackson's intention, all former ORE personnel stayed on. Those who did not join State, ONE, or ORR were first reassigned the task of publication of the Daily. Subsequently, they joined with the small COMINT (communications intelligence) unit which had been established in 1948 to handle raw COMINT data from the Army. The group was renamed the Office of Current Intelligence (OCI) on January 12, 1951. Drawing on COMINT and State Department information, OCI began producing the Current Intelligence Bulletin

which replaced the Daily. As of January 1951, this was to be its only function—collating data for the daily CIA publication.

Internal demands soon developed for the Agency to engage in current political research. Immediately following the disbandment of CIA's current political intelligence functions, the Agency's clandestine components insisted on CIA-originated research support. They feared that the security of their operations would be jeopardized by having to rely on the State Department. As a result of their requests, OCI developed into an independent political research organization. *Although OCI began by providing research support only to the Agency's clandestine components, it gradually extended its intelligence function to service the requests of other Departments.* Thus the personnel which Jackson never intended to rehire and the organization which was not to exist had survived and reacquired its previous function.[31]

This would appear to credit the Clandestine Service with having interceded to protect an endangered species, the Current Intelligence Analyst, from extinction. Actually, if witting intervention can be said to have occurred, it was for selfish and defensive reasons: OSO wanted operational intelligence to use in mounting and maintaining strategic agent operations, and it wanted help in validating its agents, nothing more.

Looking back from the bicentennial anniversary of the death of Nathan Hale,[32] we can see that in our own time the relationship between the practitioners of espionage and the analysts of current intelligence developed in four stages:

— the stage of segregation, wherein the Clandestine Service mounted and maintained operations to cover potential and actual targets and engaged in collection of information for strategic intelligence by penetrating those targets with spies, while OCI struggled within the departmental bureaucracy to establish its reputation as the best producer of current commentary;

— the stage of alliance, wherein the Service and the current information analysts sought to exploit each other for nonmutual goals; the analysts seeking to increase volume of reportage from the Service (among other sources), the Service seeking support from OCI in the form of operational intelligence and evaluation of agent reliability;

— the stage of symbiosis, in which the Service was coopted as a main originator of parts, components and fuel for the current intelligence sales product and

31. Karalekas, *op. cit.*, 22. (Emphasis added.)

32. "An agent dispatched on what turned out to be a useless errand, caught because of insufficient preparation and only elementary attention to cover, immediately and unceremoniously executed, and buried in a forgotten grave. . . ." Streeter Bass, "Nathan Hale's Mission," *Studies in Intelligence,* XVII/4. Mr. Bass's judgment of this early casualty in the Service is worth our thought: "Hale is what he is in the American pantheon not because of what he did, but because of why he did it."

in which day-to-day management of the Service was dominated by current information requirements;

— a final stage of syngenesis, which, to quote Webster, is "reproduction in which two parents take part . . . according to a . . . theory that the germ of the offspring is derived from both parents, not from either alone," though parents may be spaniel and terrier, elephant and ape.

Here we are considering the earlier part of the second stage, when the elephant OCI and gorilla OSO were groping in a darkened cage for some contact with each other. Years were to go by as the weight of the elephant gradually bore onto the hairy shoulders of the Clandestine Service, and as late as February 1952 "the impression in OSO (presumably of OSO representatives on OCI's Intelligence Staff) was that not many field personnel . . . knew of OCI's mission to brief the President and high policy makers."[33]

The creation of the Intelligence Staff of the Office of Current Intelligence in 1951 was a major step toward the assignment of a tasking function to OCI, the process of tailoring the Service's collection to fit OCI's sales requirements. It had representation from both OSO and OPC and embodied a change from Galloway's concept of a Control Officer who had acted as a one-way mirror between OSO and the outside and thus had given the Service freedom to proceed with installing operations for strategic coverage without the hindrance or distraction of daily pressures to provide information of transitory relevance. Another change during the Korean War was the establishment at some overseas stations of the first "Strategic Division" of the Intelligence Directorate, which for the first time brought OCI analysts under the same roof as the OSO operators and permitted, though it did not exactly encourage, both groups to study one another's language.[34]

Elephants and Apes

These days, when ecumenism is the fashion and soft target collection a respectable activity, it may be a little hard to recall how thick was the barrier of language and thought between the OCI chaps in Q-Building and the OSO people along the Reflecting Pool. Our memories may be assisted by considering the basic difference between the types of people who sat in the two places, a difference that still exists for observation. The good analyst in OCI and the good case officer in a DDO Field Station are both pretty bright, pretty honest,

33. Worman, *op. cit.*, 151.
34. *Ibid.*, Chapter I.

pretty diligent, but they have different habits. Give an OCI analyst a paper with sentences of information on it and he will immediately do three things:

— check it for accuracy;
— evaluate its place in the context of his own knowledge of its subject matter;
— try to exploit it for production of a finished report or study.[35]

Now if you give the same paper to a field case officer, he will also do three things, but they are different things. He will:

— examine it to identify its source;
— attempt to learn or guess the author's motive for promulgating it;
— grope for a way of using it to influence somebody, usually a prospective agent.

In other words, the analyst's habit is to react *ad causam,* the case officer's *ad hominem.* The analyst thinks about subject matter and its relevance to events, the operator about people and their motives.

They are two different breeds, elephants and gorillas. One might be led by this metaphor to think that by bringing the two breeds too close together, by making them interdependent, by possibly crossbreeding them, one might corrupt both. The analyst might come to rely on a specialized source for information to collage with that from a mélange of sources and come eventually either to lose objectivity toward his other sources and to be lazy in exploiting them, or lose patience with the special source for its biases, its fragmentary nature, its slowness to respond, and dismiss the special source from his calculations. Meanwhile, the case officer, finding a ready market for information on current matters that is easy and safe to procure, might tend to put his time on agents that are not secret, i.e., not special, and to cater to the analyst's hunger for a volume of accurate, but not necessarily secret, information.

This, however, anticipates a later argument. In any event, because of the differences of habit and thought between analysts and operators, the process of

---

35. What an analyst should be, and sometimes is, was described by Captain Richard Bates, USN, Commandant of the Defense Intelligence School, at a conference in February 1976 on training of Science and Technology analysts. According to a participant, R. C. Schreckengost of CIA's Office of Training, ". . . Captain Bates described the good analyst as one who: works well under uncertainty; works well with fragmentary information; is able to perceive deception; does not expect foreign developments to parallel those of the United States in terms of design electives; recalls when the point of diminishing returns has been reached in analysis; knows how to convey accurately the amount of uncertainty in his analysis; knows how to communicate effectively with others both in and out of the intelligence community; is aware of the sources, forms, flaws, and other factors relating to data processing; and has an ability to work well in situations in which the necessary information to solve a problem may be obscured by a great deal of noise."

acculturation that went on in the Intelligence Staff of OCI, Washington, and between DDI's "Strategic Divisions" overseas and the stations that sheltered them was slow, but the fact that, in Korea, there was another war on raised the temperature of the acculturation process and speeded the chemical reactions within it. And there were other wartime effects that were adverse to all kinds of coordination. More money, new components, more people, and the atmosphere excitingly reminiscent of World War II all encouraged uncoordinated initiative in Indians, chiefs, and squaws. The intelligence production directorate was distracted by interdepartmental quarrels and frictions with and among State, the Pentagon, and NSA, especially over access to and exploitation of sensitive technical intelligence.[36]

OPC was operating its own independent corporation with a budget expanding toward $200 million and a staff complement of about 2,700, its own system of cryptic reference, its own communications, and its own charter, which forbade it to coordinate more than absolutely necessary with any other component.[37] The DCI, General Walter Bedell Smith, reported unhappily to the National Security Council on 23 April 1952 that

> The presently projected scope of these [psywar and paramilitary] activities has, during the past three years, produced a threefold increase in the clandestine operations of this Agency and will require next year a budget three times larger than that required for our intelligence activities. . . .[38]

OSO, the espionage and counterespionage service, was not expanding appreciably, but its operating climate was affected by several current events like the Berlin Blockade, the Haganah-Irgun insurgency, the bloodbath in what had been British India, and the Korean War.

In this atmosphere, the Sales Department's voracity for the raw materials of production grew. OCI, by its own lights and in accordance with what it saw as its mission, was always searching for new information and for ways of speeding its circulation. In the words of OCI's historian, Mr. Eugene C. Worman, Jr., this

> . . . search for new information and for ways of speeding its circulation involved OCI in intensive dealings with other offices in CIA during 1952. One of the most active of these relationships was with the Office of Special Operations (OSO) of the Clandestine Services, which not only was a source of information but a collector which *could service requirements generated by OCI.* . . .

By February 1952, OCI had collected enough statistics on OSO reporting to

36. Worman, *op. cit.* A version of ORE/ORR's troubles is given by Karalekas, *op. cit.*, 20*ff.*

37. Gerald E. Miller, *History of the Office of Policy Coordination*, DDO Registry, CS HP 228. Intro. and summary chapters reprinted w/o footnotes in *Studies in Intelligence*, XVII/2-S. (CIA/IUO.)

38. Ludwell Lee Montague, "The Psychological Strategy Board," *Studies in Intelligence*, XVII/2-S, 19. (CIA/IUO.)

undertake an effort to make that reporting more useful. Noting that OCI had destroyed over half of OSO's pouched reports because of their late arrival, Paul Eckel, Chief, Publications Board, suggested that OSO establish some sort of screening panel to review incoming reports and to send pertinent information to OCI by special preliminary dissemination. He also suggested that OSO divisions in Washington as well as station chiefs abroad be briefed regarding OCI's requirements. He urged that the latter be instructed to send important information to Washington by cable.[39]

Now what did it mean to a station chief to be told to cable important information? Most station chiefs were accustomed to send a number of cables, and in those days of less sophisticated communications most station chiefs kept cables in the category of what they already considered important information, meaning operational matters requiring rapid servicing by the desk. Most important *intelligence*—the stuff that OSO disseminated—took some time to acquire, was often bulky, and went home by pouch, preceded by a cable announcing its acquisition and explaining the circumstances.

Let us take an example. As this was being written, several of us recalled in another context, but still with a sense of awe, the time just before the OPC-OSO merger when our Service acquired a comprehensive plan, issued under very high classification by a major Soviet command, for the deployment and dispersion of ground forces in the event of nuclear combat in Europe. Many cables were exchanged discussing the manner in which the agent (who years later was executed in line of duty, i.e., for treason) had acquired, copied, and delivered the document. This document was *pouched* to Headquarters for customers other than OCI. It was considered to be strategic espionage, of a kind no station expected to acquire every day and which could be valued in savings to the U.S. Government at roughly the cost of a weapons system.

It was this kind of intelligence that stations thought they were in business to acquire by having properly established a strategic espionage apparatus. The principal case officer handling the agent worked at the operation full-time, or quite a lot more than full-time, and he kept himself extremely well informed on current intelligence on the Soviet Union, on the country, and on the city in which he was working. To require him to report on these matters would have been to impair is efficiency and that of the station.

For the field station, the order to cable current information amounted to a new definition of important information. That information and intelligence which was previously considered important by the stations was of little interest to this strange new consumer with his deadlines and publication schedules— he wanted information that had hitherto been regarded as perishable and

39. Worman, *op. cit.* (Emphasis added.)

trivial. But what he wanted, apparently, could be acquired by a moderate (or at least initially moderate) amount of moonlighting at the station.

Some stations found that the one or two local journalists whom they had been using to provide operational intelligence for planning purposes, or to act as spotters, could be used as sources for the cables of OCI. Elsewhere, Reports Officers were put to work, if they were already on hand, or requisitioned from Headquarters to be put to work, picking station brains for items of reportable current information, or conducting semi-clandestine contact with agents who could be converted to providing their own instant political analysis. Some station chiefs began devoting their own time to composing periodic commentaries in competition with those of the Embassy Political Sections and Ambassadors. The practice of relinquishing soft political information to State began to fall into disuse.

And where was the harm, an espionage officer might well ask himself, so long as the OSO corporation was not forced into merger with OCI as it had just been forced to merge with OPC?

The Merger

The merger of which we speak so often was a critical event in the history of the Service with very important results. The Church Committee's version is partly correct:

> The merger did not result in the dominance of one group over another; it resulted in the maximum development of clandestine operations [i.e., covert action] over clandestine collection [i.e., espionage]. For people in the field, rewards came more quickly through visible operational accomplishments than through the silent, long-term development of agents required for clandestine collection. In the words of one former high-ranking DDP official, "Collection is the hardest thing of all; it's much easier to plant an article in local newspapers."[40]

After the merger, most OSO officers were looking for allies to help fend off the human wave of OPC. Any alliance that might help keep a few slots commissioned and a few dollars authorized for spy-running could not be all bad. OCI looked like a promising ally.

There was also an element of vanity. Most station chiefs felt in their hearts that they really knew quite a lot about local affairs in their area, that they could hold their own in any conversation with a political section foreign service

---

40. Senate Select Committee to Study Governmental Operations with Respect to Intelligence, *Activities, Foreign and Military Intelligence: Final Report of the Select Committee*, Book I, 108.

officer or an OCI analyst, on the real power structure of a cabinet or the real significance of an irredentist movement, or the real workings of a local Communist party. Recognition of this expertise was pleasing, even to a man who knew clearly that his primary job was to recruit and exploit agents to steal information in the Soviet military command, the Hungarian Embassy, the Office of the New China News Agency, etc.

It is not astonishing that over the first two years of the DDP, a number of station chiefs adjusted comfortably to the role of resident expert, nor that in the next two decades this role has evolved into that of pundit, so that a committee of top CIA managers, writing 20 years later in a time of great trouble, can note without normative intonation that

> . . . from time to time CS Station Chiefs—often at the request or even direction of policy-level consumers—send back interpretive assessments of events in their country. These are circulated in Washington as the views of the senior U.S. intelligence officer on the scene, no more and no less.[41]

These on-the-scene appraisals, now rubricked ███████████, are the logical and unforeseen result of that instruction in 1952 that station chiefs "send important information to Washington by cable." The element of vanity, combined with the theory that a senior Clandestine Service officer ought to be equally adept at "one or several of the broad fields of intelligence: espionage, counterespionage, overt procurement, [and] analysis,"[42] resulted in some awkwardness. The cabled current information and current analysis often bypasses OCI and goes instantly to the consumer at State or the White House, and when, as has occurred, the Station Chief's analysis of a situation is at variance with that of OCI, the bonds of affection between OCI and the Service become strained. A research group on intelligence support for policy recently found an instance where a

> . . . State Department official remarked that CIA *analysis* was first rate. The analysis he referred to turned out to be a situation report from a Chief of Station.[43]

Given the strength of personality of most Chiefs of Station, their influence on the young, their authority over reporting and support elements in the field,

41. "The Directorate of Operations," *Taylor Report, Annex F,* named for a committee chaired by Deputy Comptroller J. H. Taylor. Annex F was prepared by a sub-committee chaired by W. W. Wells, then chief of the European Division of the Operations Directorate. (October 1975.)

42. Gordon M. Stewart, "What is a Generalist?" *Studies in Intelligence,* II/3, 3. Stewart was Director of Personnel when he wrote this piece. Himself a generalist, he was twice chief of ███████████ Station, Inspector General, and member of the Board of National Estimates.

43. Center for the Study of Intelligence, *CIA Intelligence Support for Foreign and National Security Policy Making,* 65.

their prestige among other officials of a Mission, the devotion of a COS's attention to current political commentary of the journalistic kind can influence the Service only in the direction of journalism.

Similar dynamics at Headquarters helped develop the journalistic pattern:

> Back home, a system was eventually developed whereby OCI did receive preliminary disseminations of Clandestine Service reports—and sometimes even raw cables in urgent cases—which enabled OCI to publish its evaluations even before other offices received their copies of the original reports. After some time, preliminary TDCS reports[44] became standard fare, and the delayed reports virtually disappeared from OCI's daily mail. . . . In November 1952, in an effort to obtain the maximum benefit from Clandestine Services reporting, representatives of the Office of the DDI and Frederick Voight of OCI met with representatives of the Clandestine Services to review material received by the latter but not disseminated in intelligence reports. Though agreeing in most cases with the decisions that had been made, the representatives of the Intelligence Directorate suggested that OCI personnel scan the information daily in search of items useful not only to OCI but also to OSI and ORR. The Clandestine Services agreed, and this activity began on 14 November.[45]

This is a point at which to record disagreement with the historical judgment of the Church Committee, which, in my opinion, is influenced by testimony from officers of the Intelligence Directorate who do not know their facts. The Committee has it that

> . . . within the Agency the DDP was a Directorate apart. As the number of covert action projects increased, elaborate requirements for secrecy developed around operational activities. The DDP's self-imposed security requirements left it exempt from many of the Agency's procedures of accountability. Internally, *the DDP became a highly compartmented structure*, where information was limited to small groups of individuals based primarily on a "need to know" principle.[46]

It may appear to some of our younger analysts unfamiliar with history that the DDP *became* a highly compartmented structure. Actually the Service, in its OSO manifestation, had once been compartmented from the rest of the Agency, but in the years here discussed (1952–1962), it steadily became less so. From the point of view of the espionage specialist, the Committee's next paragraph is about 173 degrees off course:

> The norms and position of the Clandestine Service had important repercussions on the execution of the CIA's intelligence mission in the 1953 to 1962

44. TDCS: Telegraphic Dissemination of the Clandestine Services. Now called TDFIR, Telegraphically Disseminated Foreign Intelligence Report.

45. Worman, *op. cit.*, 151.

46. *Church Committee Report,* Book I, 112.

period. Theoretically, the data collected by the DDP field officers should have served as a major source for DDI analysis. However, strict compartmentation prevented open contact between DDP personnel and DDI analysts. Despite efforts in the Directorates, the lack of real interchange and interdependence persisted.[47]

It would be more accurate to say that "efforts in the 1960s to break down the barriers between the Directorates" resulted in a degree of "interchange and interdependence" that had an effect on the discipline of espionage similar to the effect of whiskey on the American Indian.

Ironically the trade for OCI's getting current reporting from what had so recently been OSO was the provision of OCI's product to what had been OPC. Mr. Worman records that

> . . . a two-way flow developed . . . on 17 November 1952. . . . DDP transmitted to OCI a list of priority interests of the Political and Psychological Warfare Staff with a request that OCI attempt to publish as much information as possible in its Current Intelligence Digest on those subjects or otherwise notify the Staff of its existence.[48]

Mr. Worman cites this as an example of mutual benefit between DDP and DDI, but he fails to distinguish between the still very distinct OSO and OPC elements of the new DDP. OSO veterans of the time still saw the benefit to their Service as extremely limited. Information in the *Current Intelligence Digest* was, of course, immensely useful to the Paramilitary and Psychological Warfare Staff for programming radio broadcasts (especially Radio Free Europe), preparing material for release in the printed media, and for other non-clandestine activities. For espionage operations it was only marginally useful as background operational intelligence, a supplement to the vernacular press, reports from surveillance, the coffeehouse grapevine, etc. The espionage officer continued to view the contact with OCI as a means of getting evaluation of his agents' reports. Gradually, however, the OCI point of view, that the contact was for purposes of levying requirements on the Service, began to prevail.

Speed + Volume = Production

In any event, the procedure by which OCI screened reports from the Clandestine Service evolved so strongly that nobody could doubt the biological success of the CIA Sales Department in the ecology of Washington. Seven

---

47. *Ibid.*

48. Worman, *op. cit.*, 153. So strong was the animosity between the two factions that OSO officers normally wrote among themselves of Political and Psychological Warfare (PP) as "pee-pee."

years after OCI's first formal liaison with the Service, an institution was born which put CIA on top of a heap whose tactical crest had been an objective for years of the Pentagon, the Department of State, the Joint Chiefs of Staff, and the National Security Council itself. This was the Intelligence Watch Officers Group, often incorrectly called the Watch Office, or better, the IWOG. There were communications centers and war rooms of some kind in all of the organizations just named, and it was OCI's proper dream, under authority granted to the DDI, to form, manage, control, and staff an Intelligence Watch Officers Group. The difficulties, as Mr. Worman records, lay mainly in the nature of competition, both inside the Intelligence Directorate and outside, where State, NSA, the Military, and the DDI all competed for jurisdiction over exploitation of sensitive technical intelligence. But one difficulty also lay in the reporting from the Clandestine Service, especially the cabled reports that OCI was now receiving.

To see how the formation of the Watch Officers Group altered the climate of the Operations Directorate, we must step back a bit and look at the traditional methods of disseminating incoming information from the field. Our average station chief, accustomed to continuous correspondence with his home desk on the details of his operations, naturally mixed operational information with the intelligence his operations produced. He did not consider this a difficulty, but from OCI's point of view it was a difficulty. Thus, looking back from an Office of Training vantage point in 1970, a critic who had participated in the IWOG process could say:

> From its beginnings, the Clandestine Service had had a serious problem in moving information rapidly from field station to consumer. The problem was rooted not only in human fallibility but in the very nature of clandestinity. The identities of sources must be zealously protected, yet the reader must be given an adequate idea of their access, qualifications, and reliability. To make possible the discharge of these obligations, cabled intelligence was often interlarded with operational and semioperational information requiring thorough sifting by the Headquarters desk. In the matter of presentation, Headquarters reports officers sat in judgment on the field collector—interpreting, rewriting, converting what was merely a "cable" into something that could properly be called a "report." If they sometimes overdid the interpretation, annotation, and editing, that was an inescapable hazard of the system. All this took time.
>
> For some years it was thought that the only alternative to this method was that of the Foreign Service, whose field reports went directly to Washington consumers without prior review by the Department of State. This alternative was considered impracticable for the Clandestine Service, primarily because a Headquarters review was deemed essential on security grounds and also because field stations, knowing their cables would be rewritten, often did not attempt to turn out a finished product. At its worst, this practice developed into

a vicious circle; sloppiness in the field provoked fussiness at Headquarters, and vice versa. *At its best, it enabled the field to concentrate on operating without editorial distraction.*[49]

The "very nature of clandestinity," it would seem, made the processing of current information difficult—that is, difficult when done in bulk, and bulk is what OCI's mission called for. For the "very nature" of *current intelligence* was and is journalistic. The objective of all the watch offices and indications centers and global war rooms in Washington was and is to process *all the news that's fit* for analysts and leaders to know, and the chief competitor was/is the *New York Times*.

The divergence of view and habit between the Office of Current Intelligence and such other components of the Intelligence Directorate as (at various times) the Office of National Estimates, the Office of Political Research, the Office of Economic Research, and the Office of Strategic Research, was analogous to the divergence between, say, an international news service like Associated Press and a Department of International Relations at a University. It was natural that analysts in OCI who competed daily with, for example, Victor Zorza on the USSR and Joseph Alsop on China should think of the Clandestine Service stations ████████████ as natural competitors of the U.P., A.P. and N.Y.T. bureau chiefs in those places. And it was natural for the analysts not only to solicit a greater volume of information but also to seek to improve the processing system so that OCI could equal or surpass the reporting, rewriting, editing, and publishing machinery of the news services.

The solution to the problem of operational information in cables was to move the desk-editing function to the field. The device was one that looks obvious and rational, if one ignores misgivings within the Clandestine Service at both Headquarters and Field levels. This device was the INTEL Format Cable.

There was nothing particularly mysterious or complicated about the "INTEL format cable." INTEL format was nothing more than a standard format which separated operational data from intelligence and which contained mandatory entries in sequence: the country the report dealt with; the date of the information; the subject; the place and date the information was acquired; the field report symbol and report number; the source authentication statement; the text of the message; and finally a record of the field dissemination given the report. At the top and bottom of the intelligence portion it was necessary to insert classification and controls. These required entries ensured that all essential elements enabling Headquarters to pass rapid judgment on the information

---

49. George H. Montminny, "Rapid Transit in Clandestine Intelligence," *Studies in Intelligence*, XIV/1, 36. (Emphasis added.)

would always be present. It guaranteed that cabled intelligence would be received in Headquarters in something approximating disseminable form.

In a short time, the station-to-consumer span was reduced from days to hours—an average of thirty-six hours. This was better, but still not good enough. Fortunately, the state of the communications art improved, but there were still unacceptable delays—about eighteen hours' time—in the action divisions while specialists edited, checked references, added Headquarters' comments, and sometimes rewrote the whole report.

The INTEL format, instituted in October 1957, was the first major breakthrough in the search for speed and paved the way for a serious attack on the problem of too much time between case officer and consumer.[50]

As late as 1959 a senior Requirements Officer could deplore the habit of seeing the field operator as an all-purpose collector and refuse[ing] to believe that he can't undertake such easy tasks as collecting publications, clipping the press, etc. . . . The demands for this kind of thing are greatest in times of crisis, when analysts and policy-makers expect the covert operator to turn himself into a news association. . . . More elevated chiefs . . . often generate the greatest confusions by expecting and encouraging their particular collectors to range the spectrum of conditions and events. The result is wasteful competition, duplication, and superficial coverage. Policy-makers have even greater expectations. Anachronistically and conflictingly in this age of science, their naive faith in the collector as seer and soothsayer is the last refuge of the belief in magic. . . . The clandestine collector . . . , though often extremely well informed, is a methods specialist, not a subject specialist.[51]

But once a beginning had been made to get the CS officers in the field into the business of news production, the way was open for what OCI thought of as "a serious attack on the problem of too much time between case officer and consumer." One prong of the attack was the Watch Officer:

On March 1, 1959, a proposal was approved for the establishment of a team of intelligence Watch Officers who would work around the clock and would be responsible for the immediate processing and the fastest possible dissemination of the more urgent intelligence cables. Initially, this group would consist of a Chief, an intelligence and administrative assistant and six Watch Officers, and would act only during *non-duty* hours. The hope was expressed that after a period of trial the hours might be extended and the unit might be able to handle an increasing number of intelligence cables. The original proposal recommended that the Intelligence Watch (IW) should handle cables bearing the precedence IMMEDIATE and PRIORITY, and, where time permitted, selected routine cables.[52]

50. *Ibid.*, 37.
51. Lowell M. Dunleigh, "Spy at Your Service, Sir," *Studies in Intelligence,* III/2, 81–93.
52. Montminny, *op. cit.*, 37.

There were misgivings at the working level of the Service, of course. George H. Montminny—a pen name for a DDP officer who assisted in setting up the INTEL Format Cables system and later was involved in training people for it—records that

> . . . there was an understandable reluctance on the part of the [DDP's] area Divisions to accept the principle that a group of officers, centrally located and not attached to a specific Division, could master the intricacies of reporting from all corners of the globe. But the Deputy Director of Plans had approved the establishment of the Intelligence Watch, and all concerned realized that the need for speed was paramount even if in the early stages the quality of the product might suffer.[53]

One must add that the concern on the part of the methods specialists in the Service's Area Divisions was not limited to the quality of the product or the global qualifications of the Watch Officers; there was also concern to maintain proper control of operations through continuous communications between Headquarters and Field, unmonitored and unedited by processors of information.

But the DDP, then Richard M. Bissell, Jr., had approved, and so the pressure on clandestine officers to produce timely prose in volume became an institution of the Service, while the manufacture of INTEL Format Cables in the field became a required skill for case officers, and the function of Reports Officer became a more prestigious specialty. Montminny says:

> The centralization of Washington dissemination of cabled field intelligence in a small group of officers who could not be experts on every country required a further improvement in the caliber of field reporting. The Office of Training included solid blocks of reports instruction in operational courses, and a new course in Intelligence Reporting, Reports and Requirements was established. To date (early 1970) there have been more than 80 runnings of this latter course, and more than 600 persons have been trained in it.[54]

On 2 May 1960, the Intelligence Watch Officers Group (IWOG) assumed total responsibility for screening all cables received in INTEL format, and as of 1970 was disseminating four of five intelligence cables received, thus enabling the CS Reports Officers "to devote more time and attention to professional guidance of field collection efforts."[55] In other words, Reports Officers, especially at Headquarters, became Requirements Officers, with predominant attention to serving the Watch Officer system, which put predominant emphasis on what Mr. Montminny calls in the title of his piece "Rapid Transit in Clandestine Intelligence."

53. *Ibid.*, 38.
54. *Ibid.*, 38.
55. *Ibid.*, 40.

Meanwhile, the old *Memorandum to the President,* which had been invented by Donovan, institutionalized by Harry Truman as the *Daily Digest,* expanded by OCI for President Eisenhower into the *Central Intelligence Bulletin,* "did not suit President Kennedy's style." So at about the same time that IWOG, together with a parallel and more senior CIA Operations Center under OCI, was becoming corporeal, OCI initiated publication of the *President's Daily Brief* (PDB). It was

> . . . a new publication different in style, classification, format, and length but not different in fundamental concept—a medium whereby we present to the President in the tersest possible form what he should know about the play of the world for that day, particularly as it impinges on U.S. national security interests. This publication became the President's own, leaving the Bulletin to serve readers at the next level down.[56]

OCI's Operations Center became the senior watch office in town,[57] with a facsimile transmission circuit to the Situation Room at the White House. The ascendency of CIA's Sales Department over its competitors in other Departments and Agencies is indicated by the fact that the Situation Room at the White House was and is staffed by officers seconded from CIA's Operations Center. To ensure that nobody ever again forgets "OCI's mission to brief the President and high policy makers,"[58] a tour of the White House Situation Room is now included in OTR's Advanced Intelligence Seminar, which is an ecumenical course given to officers from all Directorates.

Now so far we have been talking mostly about Washington, where the Headquarters of the Service still strives to respond to its stations overseas and to direct those stations in ways moderately in consonance with the tradition of clandestinity. What is the effect of the Sales Department on the people actually doing the work abroad? We can lead into this question with a war story.

The Case of John Smith

The time is early 1974, the place Saigon. We have just learned in time for the Station Morning Staff Meeting that the evening before, down the street in the Palace, various GVN leaders held a meeting where they discussed impend-

---

56. James P. Hanrahan, "Intelligence for the Policy Chiefs," *Studies in Intelligence,* XI/1, 6. This article is substantially the text of a paper read by Mr. Hanrahan to the Intelligence Methods Conference in London in September 1966.

57. There are six major watch offices in the Washington area: CIA, NSA, DIA, JCS/J-B, State Department's Bureau of Intelligence and Research (INR), and the White House. These are connected by a secure telephone conferencing net called the National Operations and Intelligence Watch Officers Net (NOIWON). See United States Intelligence Board, *Handbook of Operating Procedures for the Reporting of Critical Information* (USIB-D-30.6/7, 15 April 1967).

58. Quoted earlier [note 33] from Worman's *History of OCI.*

ing transfers of corps commanders, the impact of increased petrol costs on the military budget, the status of the American supplementary aid bill, and certain other, more frivolous, matters. Immediately after the Station Staff Meeting, the chief of the Saigon Base calls in the chief of the Base's Internal Branch and asks for details of the Palace meeting.[59] Within minutes a half-dozen case officers reach for their telephones, call politicians and military officers, make appointments. Within hours the case officers are back from their interviews tapping at typewriters. Before Saigon's day is over, their efforts have been consolidated by the Station Reports Office, and when Washington's day begins, the Office of Current Intelligence has the poop minus the frivolous matters. Everybody is pleased, or seems so.

But the next morning, a young case officer of the Communist Operations Branch comes to see the Base Chief and requests transfer to the Internal Branch.

"Why?"

"I need a promotion."

"But you are now working on Priority A, the enemy, John. You speak French and Vietnamese. You have become expert on the structure and personalities of VC MR IV.[60] You're physically brave and diligent. You're in line for promotion. Why in the name of Christ, Buddha and all our Ancestors, not to mention the Constitution of the United States, do you want to spend your time interviewing a bunch of politicians?"

"Because what counts toward promotion are dissems and recruitments. One, dissems; two, recruitments. In VC ops I may get out two dissems a month, and maybe make one recruitment before my tour is over."

"I hope so. We need another one."

"But in Internal Branch I can produce four or five dissems a week and recruit a new agent every time the Palace or the JCS has a reshuffle. All I have to do is hustle a little and get your approval to offer dough, get a POA[61] and all that. Mind you, I like VC operations; I know why they are important; I can hack it in them as well as the next guy; but I have a family to feed; Linda is pregnant; the kids have to be put through school."

---

59. Station Headquarters was in the Embassy; Saigon Base was in a nearby building, and the Base Chief attended the daily morning staff meetings of the Chief of Station. The Base had three branches: Internal, which covered the host country political and military target; External, which covered the Soviet Bloc target; and the Communist Operations Branch, which covered the Lao Dong Party (VC) unilaterally and handled liaison with the Vietnamese Services.

60. "VC MR IV": Viet Cong Military Region Four, the element responsible under COSVN (the DRV/VC forward command post) for espionage, sabotage, guerrilla warfare, and support of regular North Vietnamese Army Operations in the Capital District of Saigon, Cholon and Gia Dinh.

61. POA: Provisional Operational Approval from CI Staff.

"I'm beginning to see your point."

"I know that in my Fitness Report you will praise my work against the hard target, but I have it on good authority that the Promotion Boards compare *numbers* of recruitments and *numbers* of dissems. I'm afraid the distinction between a penetration of the Lao Dong Party or the Armed Reconnaissance Section of the VC MR IV *An Ninh*[62] and an Assemblyman who likes our money may not be recognized, especially when everybody in Washington reads the stuff from the Assemblyman, while you'll P & L[63] my penetration if I get him. I'll have to spend most of my time arranging commo with him to get the one P & L report a month that will have very small readership among future members of my Promotion Board."

Since what is written above is fact, not fiction, and since were are using fact to illustrate a situation, the result of the foregoing conversation—how the Base Chief handled his personnel problem—can be suppressed. But we cannot suppress the general problem. Inspirational leadership or tight-shippery may solve John Smith's problem after a fashion and for a while, but given the pressures the supervisor is under to keep that volume of soft-target reporting in the flexowriter, it is more likely that Smith will indeed wind up in the Internal Operations Branch. Certainly so long as the Sales Department of our diversified conglomerate sets the tone for the whole organization, a well-staffed Internal Operations Branch will continue to exist wherever the operating climate is not so hostile as to preclude it.

In areas where the operating climate is hostile, the so-called Denied Areas, our stations contribute a quantity of reporting to each Mission's product of current information. They are occasionally required by Headquarters to comment on Kremlinological evanescences (what is your assessment of Przybyszewski's absence from the podium on International Women's Day?); but, according to officers who are serving or have recently served in the Curtain Posts directed by the Soviet Europe Division, the desks protect them from this kind of pressure more than station chiefs elsewhere are protected. On the other hand, Curtain officers normally carry a huge cover load, maybe 80 percent of their normal 60 to 75 hour week, and this involves them in reporting of non-clandestinely acquired information. The device still used is that of *relinquishment*, which is discussed later in this paper. The real job of our Curtain officers, of course, is maintaining and supporting communication with agents,

62. Mission of *An Ninh* ("Security"): VC Law Enforcement/Assassination. The 316th *An Ninh unit,* formed about this time, was chartered to "eliminate American Tyrants."

63. P&L: "Prescribed and Limited." See *DDO Instruction,* DOL 70-11, 18 October 1974, CONFIDENTIAL. Such penetrations were automatically given P&L handling to protect the identity of the source and the safety of the case officer.

and if truly clandestine operations are still conducted anywhere in our Service, it is in SE Division.[64]

The fact that true clandestine operations are conducted precisely in those stations where the accomplices in journalism—friendly government officials, cooperative American businessmen, refugee camps, police and intelligence liaison counterparts, and venal politicians—are *not* accessible demonstrates one of the main points of this paper.

A Review

We have seen that by the time of the first Presidential flaps—Eisenhower's U-2 and Kennedy's Bay of Pigs—the relationship between the conductors of espionage and the analysts of current events had evolved from a state of symbiosis into a condition approaching syngenesis. We have sketched the causes of this, which can be summarized:

— Expanding competitively in the departmental milieu, the Agency built up production of current intelligence partly in order to fulfill its role as a *presidential* instrument and partly to establish its position as a *central* agency dominant over the intelligence producing organs of the departments;

— OCI, expanding competitively within the Intelligence Directorate and among the departments, sought ways to exploit the Agency's overseas facilities to increase the volume of raw materials for its processing plant and to establish a company-controlled subsidiary source of those raw materials, independent of departmental competitors;

— OSO and its successor faction in the Plans Directorate, competing defensively against OPC and its successor faction, sought to exploit the Intelligence Directorate for support of espionage operations. Initially this took the form of soliciting operational intelligence for planning and of evaluation of reports for authentication of agents. Later, it became an effort to create a dependence of OCI on raw material that a *modified* espionage mechanism could produce.

Such were the causes. Since causes in history often, if not usually, result in effects not desired or anticipated by history's participants, we may ask whether the present situation is agreeable or beneficial to the participants.

— Does the analyst of current information need what he is now getting from the Clandestine Service?

64. Nothing in this paragraph, however, should be construed as reflecting the author's endorsement of SE Division's recent performance in the field of counterespionage or counterintelligence.

— Does the Clandestine Service need the advice, support or guidance of analysts of current information? If so, what kind?

— If either of the foregoing is answered, "yes," under what conditions is the answer true? After what assumptions or presumptions?

Economic Intelligence: No and Yes

For some of the answers to these questions, let us move away from the Office of Current Intelligence and look elsewhere. Economic intelligence is one kind in which current information predominates, much as it does in political intelligence; often the two kinds are so interdependent that the same item is competed for and consumed in both the economic and political bureaus, which remain separate according to the immutable laws of bureaucracy.

About a year after our young Smith made the importunation recorded earlier, Leo Cherne of the President's Foreign Intelligence [Advisory] Board (PFIAB) made a ten-day trip through Western Europe interviewing the U.S. officials involved or involvable in economic intelligence—Chiefs of Mission, Economic Ministers/Counselors, Treasury Attachés, and DDO Station officers—"to discuss economic intelligence, to learn more about the means involved in assembling such intelligence, to observe the relationships among those directly involved in that process and between them and their colleagues in the embassies, and to ascertain how well directed are our economic intelligence efforts."[65] Mr. Cherne asked people in the missions whether the economic reporting of the CIA Stations was worth anything. He got two answers.

The response from the Foreign Service Officers in Economic Sections, the Treasury people, and the senior diplomats was "No":

> By and large, missions do not think of the CIA station as an integral part of the process of economic analysis and reporting. The tendency is [to] view CIA efforts as detached, often irrelevant, sometimes irritating, occasionally embarrassing and, in the best of cases, mildly helpful. More than one ambassador and several senior Economic Section officials are of the opinion that there is no real need for any major restructuring of intelligence resources for the pursuit of economic intelligence—that the problem is one of too much data rather than too little, and that the vast preponderance of desired information is already available. Indeed, the proposition was forcefully advanced that intelligence in the traditional sense (which is understood to mean "clandestine") has little to contribute in the economic area. . . .

65. "European Trip Report, 17–27 March 1975, Paris, Bonn, Rome, Zurich, Bern, Brussels, London," to the President's Foreign Intelligence Advisory Board, 18 April 1975. Copy #40, SECRET. This report is only 20 pages long, so page numbers are not cited for quotations. I have altered the sequence without modifying the logic.

Clandestine collection of economic intelligence targeted against the host country is authorized in limited degree ▆▆▆▆▆▆▆▆▆▆ . The mission's Economic Section personnel in these embassies acknowledge only marginal value to the results of these clandestine efforts as they relate to an understanding of the economic situation in the host country; they also assert that *only a limitation in the resources of their Economic Section prevents the obtaining of similar information through normal channels.* Where a small contribution by the Clandestine Service is conceded, it is assessed as between 5 and no more than 15 percent of the totality of mission economic reporting; yet, in no instance was an acknowledgement made of any essentiality to the information produced through clandestine sources. *It is a bedrock belief on the part of Economic Section personnel that virtually any information of significance regarding host countries in Western Europe is obtainable without resort to clandestine methods.* At the extreme, one well-informed, experienced economist, having a long association with the intelligence community, denied that he *has ever, over a 15-year period, seen any economic intelligence produced by the Clandestine Service that was of more than marginal interest—that at best it was titillating.*

You will recognize this as partly the traditional State attitude toward the spooks, and you will see further examples of it in an examination of political intelligence in a later section of this paper. Mr. Cherne observes that some of the animus of State's view of the Service is engendered by interdepartmental rivalry:

This view by the mission staff is almost certainly derived from the fact that station activity overseas (as distinguished from intelligence community functioning in Washington) is almost entirely concerned with clandestine collection. Station personnel perceive themselves—but, more importantly, are perceived by others in the mission—in precisely that context. There is not the leavening such as exists in the United States where clandestine activity is only one of a variety of sources, which include as predominant inputs serious research, determined professional effort, and important academic substance. Where in contrast the work is essentially illicit, as in the case abroad, it cannot be surprising that attitudes among those not directly involved in that work reflect suspicion and hostility. Also, it would be remarkable if the critical attention which has been focused on intelligence activities in the United States during recent months has not made a further negative contribution to the attitude of mission personnel toward clandestine operations and intelligence officers. . . .

There were a few embassy/CIA station relationships that clearly reflect tension which is not merely an outgrowth of the perception that clandestine intelligence activity has little relevance to economic analysis; it is reflective of a deeper sense of suspicion that manifests itself in a "we-they" syndrome. . . . There is a great concern for the disruptive potential of CIA personnel interfering with contacts and sources that Economic Section officials would use. In some instances where this has occurred, mutual embarrassment of varying orders of significance has resulted. Further, a point was made regarding the "clubbiness" of Treasury personnel—U.S. and foreign—who prefer to deal only with their professional counterparts.

But the answer Mr. Cherne got from our people in the DDO Stations was "Yes":

> Contrasting sharply with the view of Economic Section officers, who see little or no need for clandestine collection of information against Western European countries, CIA station personnel firmly believe they can make valuable contributions. That conviction matches and is in turn reinforced by high ratings which the CIA (DDO) accords to the present, constrained efforts of stations. It is important to note, however, that these assessments of worth are given to collectors by other collectors and only infrequently do they reflect comments of policy makers. There is no comparable rating mechanism to establish the consumer's sense of worth.

What a curious and dramatic situation! Six of our Stations and one of our Bases had made a point of telling the important visitor that "the primary orientation of CIA personnel remains the Soviet Union, the People's Republic of China and other Communist entities, [and] even in the embassies where host government targeting is authorized, a preponderance of resources is devoted to these targets." The stations and base were at least as sensitive as Mr. Cherne to the indifference, disapproval, or hostility of the overt Foreign Service and Treasury collectors toward their efforts; nevertheless, they pleaded to stay in the act of collecting nonsensitive economic information.

That the direction of their ambitions is non-clandestine is made clear in Mr. Cherne's report:

> There are a few locations in which mission personnel consider the efforts of the intelligence officer to be valuable. This appears to result from the fact that the intelligence officer is the nearly exclusive source of information in a lucrative area and, by virtue of long-established contacts and personal competence in the field, is able to produce useful assessments. In such cases the bulk of the officer's product is not obtained by resort to traditional clandestine methods; in other words, he functions almost as any similarly equipped Foreign Service Officer might. . . .
>
> Among the CIA station officers who believe they can make significant contributions are those who value themselves as informed economists with well-placed, essentially overt contacts rather than as clandestine operatives. . . .
>
> One CIA station officer discussed a different approach for using the Clandestine Service to collect economic intelligence—that of emphasizing "elicitations" from a wide range of contacts who are aware of the officer's competence in the economic field and on whom the officer may be able to call for the

fulfillment of specific data requests. This concept would concommitantly de-emphasize the recruitment of controlled agents. The extent to which this ap-proach has been implemented and its effectiveness in practice are unknown.

As we ponder this extraordinary statement we should remember that eco-nomic intelligence suddenly became fashionable after the Arabs raised the price of oil and nobody sent any gunboats to put them in their place. The Station Chiefs with whom Mr. Cherne talked in Europe may have had time a year earlier to read *Foreign Affairs* and to note that their former colleague William P. Bundy, editor of that magazine, had organized a five-article sympo-sium of "The Year of Economics"[66] with Germany's Minister of Finance Hel-mut Schmidt writing the lead piece. The former top authority in the commu-nity for requirements, USIB (the United States Intelligence Board), with which Mr. Bundy had been prominently associated,[67] assigned only five "Sub-stantive Objectives" to the community for Fiscal Year 1976. Number Five was to collect and produce intelligence on

> Major foreign economic developments and trends relevant to U.S. international policy decisions and negotiations, particularly those related to energy, raw ma-terials, food resources and to international trade arrangements.[68]

The nine Key Questions (numbered 60 through 68) composed by USIB to achieve this Substantive Objective do indeed offer opportunities for the proper use of spies, if we agree that proper spies are those who acquire significant information not obtainable except by theft. Number 61, for example, asks for *principal objectives* of France, Germany, Japan, the UK, Italy, Canada and Brazil—in negotiating multilateral trade arrangements. Numbers 62, 63 and 64 ask about *policies*. Number 67 asks for *plans* within European Community programs. Number 45, under the Substantive Objective No. 3 on potentially volatile situations, asks "what are the *plans* and actions of the Arab States for the political use of petrodollars?" To answer any of these questions fully, one might have to commit a theft, since most of the objectives, plans, and policies here considered may have some aspects that their formulators do not wish to share with the United States. One can imagine a role for a subverted secretary

66. "The Year of Economics," *Foreign Affairs,* LII/3 (April 1974). Five articles by Helmut Schmidt, Gerald A. Pollack, William Diebold, Jr., Bension Varon with Kenju Takeuchi, and Lyle P. Schertz. All deal mainly with oil except Schertz, whose subject is food.

67. See William P. Bundy, "The Guiding of Intelligence Collection," *Studies in Intelligence,* III/1, 37–53. This is the text of an address to an international conference in Melbourne which Mr. Bundy attended in his capacity as a member of the Board of National Estimates, on which he served from 7 September 1958 to 21 January 1961.

68. Director of Central Intelligence, Memorandum for the United States Intelligence Board, "Key Intelligence Questions for FY 1976" (USIB-D22.1/42, 27 August 1975), SECRET. Short Title: USIB KIQ 76.

at one point or an invisible microphone at another, and one can imagine that the agents used would be of long-range value, or potential value, on the principle of strategic coverage as distinguished from current production.

Indeed some of Mr. Cherne's DDO informants may have been thinking along these lines when "time and again the point was made of the impracticality of expecting the Clandestine Service to hatch an agent on demand." Perhaps our colleagues who thus "time and again" spoke up were thinking that the demand for economic information might be used as the vehicle for developing agents in banks or oil companies or legal firms to steal that occasional significant document or implant an eavesdropping device in that occasional secret conference where the man in the burnoose exchanges the big secret with the man with the monocle. And perhaps the agents thus recruited, trained, developed, and controlled may have a long-range function—*coverage* of potentially or recurrently difficult targets, as distinguished from voluminous, continuous *production* on easy targets.

But I do not think that is what my colleagues were thinking, for to think so is to be ready to practice relinquishment, and relinquishment is an obsolete practice.[69]

Relinquishment

Relinquishment was the name given years ago to a device used partly to save time, partly to curry favor with our [cover-job] colleagues—those genuine ████████ Officers in the ███████ Sections we inhabited—and partly to make sure that the government got all the information that came along whether by accident or design. To practice relinquishment required no great skill: if, for example, you had conducted a rendezvous with an agent whom you controlled within the Foreign Office and who gave you the latest results of his secret maneuverings with, say, the Albanian Minister, and he incidentally told you that his ambassador in Ottawa had proposed a cultural exchange with the Canadians, you walked down the hall to the FSO who was keeping track of such matters as cultural exchange and gave him the Canadian story. If he did not already have it, he could report it as his own acquisition, or he could make a note of it and use it for background later. You had "relinquished" it to State, and could get on with your own report on the Albanian story and the operational implications for the development of your agent, through whom you hoped to recruit the Albanian.

69. The practice was still current in 1964, or at least was accepted as doctrine. See Theodore H. Tenniswood, "The Coordination of Collection," *Studies in Intelligence*, VIII/2, 50: "Overt collection by CIA station personnel as a by-product of their official cover duties or of their clandestine operational activities, often reported through embassy channels. . . ."

But the practice of relinquishment is not heavily in use now, except by the tiny number of our Service's officers in stations where ████████ ████████████████ the work is operational. Mr. Cherne's unnamed informant in Western Europe clearly was not planning to reduce the workload of his reports officers when he proposed more elicitation at the expense of de-emphasizing espionage.

A slightly cynical but pertinent way of commenting on the remarks of the anonymous DDO officer who would "de-emphasize the recruitment of controlled agents" is to cite Anthony Downs's observation that

> Bureaus threatened with drastic shrinkage or extinction because of the curtailment of their original social functions will energetically seek to develop new functions that will enable them to survive with as little shrinkage as possible.[70]

As Mr. Cherne points out elsewhere in his report, the impact on the morale of DDO officers abroad of the press and legislative campaign against the Agency had been deep, serious, and of long-lasting character.[71] In part, his unnamed DDO informant was probably groping for a way to keep busy and maintain the T/O in a circumstance where the news from home indicated that total abolition of himself and his unit was conceivable. In part, he was reacting to stress in the manner of Henry James's little dressmaker, Amanda Pynsent, who "threw herself into little jobs, as a fugitive takes to by-paths, and clipped and cut, and stitched and basted, as if she were running a race with hysterica."[72] But most importantly he was acting in the venerable DDP-DDO tradition of "Cando-ism." When a wheel turns up from Washington with a requirement, whether to bodyguard a VIP, solve the nation's narcotics problem, provide a secure communications channel from Ambassador X to the Honorable Y, suppress skyjacking, stop gold smuggling, interdict Cuban shipping, prevent earthquakes, or lose a war, the Service seldom says, "No Can Do." The Church Committee rightly says of "the (traditional) way people within the DDP, the DDI, and the DDA perceived the Agency's primary mission, the way policy makers regarded its contribution to the process of government," that

70. *Op. cit.* (footnote 7), 264.

71. Cf. Daniel O. Graham, *op. cit.* Writing some months after his retirement as Director of DIA, General Graham says, "The morale problem is serious. Men and women, civilian and military, who have proudly devoted a large part of their lives to the intelligence profession, are faced with a barrage of accusations against themselves and their superiors which paint them as fools, if not agents of utter wickedness. The intelligence 'heroes' on the current scene are those who break their oaths and for profit, ego, or even vengeance, vilify their embattled former colleagues. Disillusionment, frustration and bitterness are common among intelligence professionals. The morale problem is worst at CIA, which has borne the brunt of the flagellations by Congress and the media."

72. Henry James, *The Princess Casamassima* (Thomas Y. Crowell Apollo Edition, New York, 1976), 17. A novel about terrorism, anarchism, and civilization, first published in 1886.

covert action was at the core of this perception. The importance of covert action to the internal and external evaluation of the Agency was in large part derived from the fact that *only the CIA* could and did perform this function. . . . Political action, sabotage, support to democratic governments, counterintelligence—all this the Clandestine Service could provide.[73]

It has been our devout presumption that the DDO can do anything any other bureau may try better than that bureau, and few are the bureaus that have not experienced our benevolent intervention, whether it required diverting our resources from espionage to some other job or not.

On balance we must conclude that Mr. Cherne's unnamed DDO officer was conditioned by the same stimuli as John Smith. Otherwise why think of, much less audibly suggest, "emphasizing elicitations" while "de-emphasize[ing] the recruitment of controlled agents"? Overt reports "elicited" from economic sources do, after all, come in larger volume than stolen documents or traitorous oral revelations; they are simpler to evaluate, require no special handling, and can be acquired without the bother of countersurveilled meetings, dead drops, SRAC,[74] cut-outs, and all the paraphernalia necessary to protect spies.

In the face of diametrically opposed views on the feasibility and viability of using espionage to procure economic information, Mr. Cherne reserves final judgment, suggesting that the intelligence community, together with two nonmembers (as he sees them) of that community, namely State and Treasury, "should determine whether covert collection in Western Europe has a proper role in the field of economic intelligence, and, if so, specifically what that role should be." We should mark well a distinction that Mr. Cherne does not here make, the distinction between *covert collection* and *espionage*, since it is necessary to the logic of this paper that we not confuse the kind of elicitation earlier mentioned with espionage. If we assert that distinction, the question raised by Mr. Cherne's paper is whether to use the management and labor time of the Clandestine Service in activity peripheral to espionage. Clearly Mr. Cherne's conclusions regarding espionage as a producer of economic intelligence would be adverse.

Incidentally, while Mr. Cherne was conducting his interviews in Europe, the Murphy Commission in Washington was reaching the same conclusion, and in the report delivered to the President on 27 June 1975 said:

Unlike military intelligence, which frequently requires enormous investments in data gathering, most economic issues do not depend *upon secret information.*

73. *Church Committee Report,* Book I, 111.
74. SRAC: "Short Range Agent Communication," a term usually applied to several kinds of radio.

The key to their understanding lies in highly competent analysis of readily procurable data. Commendably, CIA has greatly strengthened its capability for economic analysis in recent years. But—with some exceptions—this is not a field in which CIA or the intelligence community generally has a strong comparative advantage.[75]

And so one answer, the economic, to the question whether the analyst of current information needs clandestine sources remains "No," our DDO colleagues ███████████████████████████ to the contrary notwithstanding.

Returning to the larger subject of political intelligence, we find still tabled the question, do the analysts need current political reporting from the Clandestine Service? If the answer to this turns out also to be negative, we shall be faced with an obvious recommendation: let political collection, the current variety of it, be left to the overt collectors in our missions abroad. This would affect the functions of at least two bureaus—the Department of State as well as the Central Intelligence Agency—and of at least two services—State's Foreign Service as well as CIA's Clandestine Service. And so, before asking whether our own OCI really needs our semi-journalistic endeavor, let us get clear what State's view of the question is, and what the Foreign Service is.

How the Hippopotami Answer

One of State's thinkers who has recorded his views is Charles W. Yost, a Career Ambassador who had forty-one years' service when he retired in 1971 to write his book.[76] He finds that although "'intelligence'—that is, information—is extremely important . . . most significant current 'intelligence' is published in the daily, weekly, or monthly press."[77] He notes that "much proficient and useful political contact and reporting is . . . done by the Central Intelligence Agency. . . ."

> But the fact is that nine-tenths of the really valuable contacts they have maintained and information they have collected could have been handled as well by State Department political officers if the embassies had been properly staffed

75. Commission on the Organization of the Government for the Conduct of Foreign Policy, established by Public Law 92-353 of 13 July 1972. Chairman Robert D. Murphy. This Commission employed a very large number of staff researchers and consultants, some of whose separate reports are quoted elsewhere in this paper. The report is published by the Government Printing Office under a letter from Mr. Murphy dated 27 June 1975. Hereafter *Murphy Commission Report*.

76. *The Conduct and Misconduct of Foreign Affairs* (Random House, New York, 1973). For a review reflecting the Clandestine Service point of view as of time of publication, see Walter Pforzheimer, *Studies in Intelligence*, XVII/2, 82.

77. *Ibid.*, 158. Ambassador Yost's final judgment on the Agency is adverse, though he was always a sensible, understanding, and friendly colleague in the many embassies (among them Bangkok, Prague, Vienna, Athens, Vientiane, Paris, and Rabat) ███████████████

for that purpose. In addition, this could have been done without the stigma and risks that attach to a covert operation and which reflect on the embassy sheltering such operations. There remains the 10 percent or so of desirable political intelligence which cannot be collected by overt means, but this could either be garnered by vastly smaller covert stations than now exist or could be dispensed with altogether without great loss.[78]

Ambassador Yost would agree with Messrs. Szanton and Allison that "Foreign Service reports from posts abroad—not considered intelligence in the usual sense—are probably the largest and often the most important source of information on foreign political and economic developments"[79] and with Miss Karalekas's observation that even before the Clandestine Service began producing current intelligence in volume, that is, "between 1946 and 1949, CIG and later CIA received almost all its current information from State . . ." rather than from the other departments or bureaus.[80] And much agreement with this view is on record from other diplomats. In 1973, for example, a panel convoked by the Murphy Commission interviewed four senior officials of the Department on "Intelligence and Information for Policy and Operations."[81] Roger P. Davies, whose Bureau within State worries about India, Iran, the Arabs, the Israeli[s], and all other lands and peoples from Dacca to Athens, opined that "the greater part of information available to country operators in the Department as well as to other agencies of government is derived from Foreign Service reporting from posts abroad."[82]

This statement was in only quantitative disagreement with INR Director Ray S. Cline's estimate that "about 40 percent of what I call intelligence—that is, evaluated information being reported to the highest levels of our government in all agencies including the White House—is based on economic and political reporting from the embassies abroad, from the Foreign Service. . . ." Both agreed that "it is a very vital input and we are very anxious that it be used well and in a sophisticated fashion."[83] The proportion of FSO reporting that "goes into the intelligence process," as estimated by the Murphy Commission's William J. Barnds, is only 20–25 percent, but Barnds notes that

---

78. *Ibid.,* 159.

79. *Op. cit.,* 188.

80. *Op. cit.,* 15.

81. Murphy Commission, "Minutes of Meeting Convened 17 September 1973," chairman William S. Mailliard. Present for the Commission were 18 persons, including Senator Mike Mansfield; panelists from Department of State were Ray S. Cline, Director, Bureau of Intelligence and Research; Roger P. Davies, Deputy Assistant Secretary of State, Bureau of East Asia and Pacific Affairs; and Samuel Fry, Director, Operations Center, Executive Secretariat. A copy of the minutes was made available to the Center for the Study of Intelligence.

82. *Ibid.,* 19.

83. *Ibid.,* 13. Percentages on this subject are somewhat like those used by weather forecasters to tell us how much rain will fall.

Another major source of information comes from the reports of civilian officials of U.S. government agencies including CIA stations abroad. The most important of these are the reports of the Foreign Service Officers in embassies and consulates, but also included are the reports from U.S. AID missions, attachés from the Treasury, Labor, and Agricultural Departments, and USIS personnel. The cables and dispatches of Foreign Service Officers, containing as they do the results of conversations with local government officials as well as background studies, probably are the most important sources of political information available.[84]

And the Church Committee says:

The Department of State and the American Foreign Service are the chief producers and consumers of political and economic intelligence in the United States Government. . . . The Foreign Service competes with the Clandestine Service in the production of human source intelligence, but operates openly and does not pay its sources. . . .

The reporting of the Foreign Service, together with that of the military attaché system, based on firsthand observation and especially on official dealings with governments, makes up the most useful element of our foreign intelligence information. Clandestine and technical sources provide supplementary information, the relative importance of which varies with the nature and accessibility of the information sought.[85]

The Church Committee gives high marks to the Foreign Service's reporting, and quotes a CIA survey to support them:

Surveys carried out by the Director of Central Intelligence make clear the importance of Foreign Service reporting in the production of national intelligence. In these surveys analysts are asked which collection sources had most often made a key contribution to the *National Intelligence Bulletin* and national intelligence memoranda and reports. The ranking reflects intelligence inputs regarded by the analysts as so essential that basic conclusions and findings could not have been reached without them. The State Department's collection inputs have consistently led the ratings.[86]

There seems to be a consensus that leans toward Mr. Yost's judgment that the use of spies to procure current information on political and economic subjects is a paltry endeavor, if only because the significant bulk of such information is obtained by

84. William J. Barnds, "Intelligence and Policy Making in an Institutional Context," *Murphy Commission Report,* Appendix U, 25.

85. *Church Committee Report,* Book I, 306.

86. *Ibid.,* 315, footnoted "Key Sources of Selected CIA Publications. Annual Survey done by Directorate of Intelligence of CIA (1975)."

— overt officials openly interviewing foreign persons abroad, or

— research of foreign overtly published and broadcast information.

The answer for political intelligence, as for economic, to the question whether the analyst of current information needs clandestine sources, as given by consumers outside the Central Intelligence Agency, is "No."

FSOs: The Shy Élite

Earlier we noted a difference of species between the clandestine operator and the analyst, between the gorilla and the elephant. In the jungle of foreign operations there is also a third species, like a hippopotamus, called the Foreign Service Officer, the FSO. Between the FSO and the intelligence officer, whether collector or analyst, there appear to be qualitative and functional differences which may be ecologically necessary to the functioning of all three species. The analyst Theodore H. Tenniswood, writing in 1964, says:

> The Foreign Service does not wish its officers, and most of the individual FSOs do not wish themselves, to be looked upon as "intelligence officers."[87]

And the official definition of the Foreign Service in the *United States Government Manual* stresses diplomatic activity, i.e., the conduct of relations and the forming of policy rather than the reporting function:

> To a great extent the future of our country depends on the relations we have with other countries, and those *relations are conducted* principally by the United States Foreign Service. Our representatives at 129 Embassies, 9 Missions, 73 Consulates General, 44 Consulates, 1 Special Office, and 13 Consular Agencies throughout the world *report* to the State Department on the multitude of foreign developments which have bearing on the welfare and security of the American people. These trained representatives provide the President and the Secretary of State with much of the raw material from which foreign policy is made and with the *recommendations* which help shape it.[88]

This is a rather élitist concept. John W. Huizenga notes for the Murphy Commission that:

> The FSO does not, and does not like to, think of himself as an intelligence collector. Part of his problem is imagery and semantics: he does not mind reporting "information," but he does not think of it as "intelligence," though in fact it is. Also, some missions tend to emphasize reporting on operational

87. Tenniswood, *op. cit.,* 50.

88. *U.S. Government Manual, 1974–75,* Office of the Federal Register, National Archives and Records Service, General Services Administration (GPO, 1975).

diplomacy and neglect in-depth study of forces behind the politics and policies of their host countries.[89]

And John Ensor Harr, writing for the same body, calls the FSO Corps "the permanent and high-status core group of personnel in U.S. foreign affairs."

It is a system identified with professional groups in the public service, and the profession in this case is conventional diplomacy, consisting of reporting, negotiating, and representing U.S. interests abroad generally. The style is that of the humanist rather than the scientist, the investigative journalist rather than the scholar, and the teacher rather than the manager.[90]

The Department's own task force, established in 1970 under the Deputy Under Secretary of State for Administration (William B. Macomber, Jr.) to "design a modernization program," says:

The Foreign Service is a closed, hierarchical professional corps devoted to assisting in the formulation and implementation of the foreign policy of the United States. . . .

The Foreign Service is a carefully selected professional service whose cohesion and discipline are essential to maintaining continuity and professional competence in the conduct of U.S. foreign policy. . . . However, these qualities and the mission of the Foreign Service make inevitable a significant degree of insularity. . . .

These conditions of the profession engender a clan mentality, a sense of detachment from the physical environment of the moment and from the community of ordinary Americans as a whole.[91]

Here is an Inside-Outside mentality not unlike that found in Clandestine Service personnel by Tom Braden,[92] but there is a great difference—the Candoism of CIA's Clandestine Service is not characteristic of the Foreign Service.

Looked at historically, U.S. foreign policy is a continuum. Present positions are the product of a long chain of historical events, identification of interests and previous policy decisions. Only rarely does a Foreign Service officer encounter

89. John W. Huizenga, "Comments on 'Intelligence and Policy Making in an Institutional Context,'" *Murphy Commission Report*, Appendix U, 43.

90. John Enser Harr, "Organizational Change in U.S. Foreign Affairs: 1945–1975," *Murphy Commission Report*, Appendix O, ("Making Organizational Changes Effective: Case Analyses of Attempted Reforms in Foreign Affairs"), chap. 1. See also Harr's *The Professional Diplomat* (Princeton University, 1969).

91. *Diplomacy for the 70s: A Program of Management Reform for the Department of State.* Department of State 143. Released December 1970 under a letter of the Deputy Under Secretary of State for Administration William B. Macomber, Jr.; p. iii. Hereafter *Macomber Report.*

92. *Vide supra* [note 4].

an absolutely new situation. This fact of professional life has an important influence on the Foreign Service officer's mentality. It causes him to approach a current issue with a heavy sense of responsibility. He knows that there are no ideal solutions, that good men have gone over the ground before and that existing policy represents a synthesis of interests and objectives which was presumed to be valid once and may still be. These same factors also encourage a tendency toward inertia. . . . He tends to be reserved toward the outside expert who enjoys the luxury of not having to deal with the real-life consequences of his misjudgments.[93]

This is very judicious language, summarized elsewhere in terms of the indefinable term "creativity":

In its investigation of the mores, values, procedures, and system of rewards in the Department and the Foreign Service, the Task Force found that all of these acted as barriers to creativity. We found that the value system of the Service respected precedent and conformity to standards above all else and that this led to resistance against innovation. We also found that the Foreign Service's notion of itself as a kind of élite corps, while it has been of value in the maintenance of high professional standards, has also produced a tendency toward insularity which leads to resistance to ideas from the outside.[94]

Candoism and Creativity

Candoism and Creativity are not the same thing, of course, for much of our Service's Candoism is merely reactive, but there is an element of assertiveness or aggressiveness common to both. Task Force VII of the Macomber Group, which examined "creativity" in the Department,

. . . concluded from its investigation of the top leadership . . . that while these leaders have favored creativity in principle, their record in fostering a climate for creativity has been poor. . . . The intellectual atrophy . . . during the fifties was a compound of presidential dissatisfaction, political reaction, Departmental conservatism, bureaucratic proliferation. . . . New ideas to cope with the Sino-Soviet dispute and the end of monolithic Communism, the fast-emerging nuclear economies, and the diplomacy of guerrilla war . . . were greeted by conservative dismay in an organization fearful of change.[95]

If we hold the concepts of Candoism and Creativity as lenses in either hand and view CIA's Clandestine Service and State's Foreign Service in stereovision, we see that both are élitist, but only one is competitive. Indeed, part of the Foreign Service's élitism is a sort of militant noncompetitiveness. Morton H. Halperin sees it in just such terms:

93. *Macomber Report,* 381f.
94. *Ibid.,* 293.
95. *Ibid.,* 292. Task Force VII's full report, "Stimulation of Creativity," occupies 291–341.

Career Foreign Service officers view their enterprise as an élite organization composed of generalists, and they resist the introduction into the department of novel functions and of experts who might be needed to perform those functions. . . . State has continued to resist the transfer to it of such agencies as USIA and AID and in so doing has demonstrated that organizations may oppose expansion instead of seeking it. . . .

Many Foreign Service officers resisted the policy ordained in the letter from President Kennedy to ambassadors instructing them that they would have operational control over all programs in their bailiwick, including at least some of those of the Central Intelligence Agency. These officers feared that control over such programs might prove to be embarrassing and would prevent them from focusing on the important functions of reporting and negotiation.[96]

When the Church Committee looked at the Department of State's behavior in regard to the distribution of resources between representation and reporting, it was startled to find:

. . . no evidence of any correlation between the importance attached by the intelligence community to the Foreign Service collection operation and the application of resources in men and money to that operation. Indeed, political and economic reporting positions abroad have been steadily reduced for some years. In one major European country crucial to America's security there is only one Foreign Service political reporting officer located outside the capital due to such cutbacks. The Ambassador said that if he had additional resources, the first move would be to reestablish political reporting officers in the several consulates in the country. The Ambassador explained that by law the Foreign Service must carry out a number of consular functions and that with ever-tightening resources the political reporting function has been squeezed out. The Committee determined, however, that the CIA has sufficient resources to consider a major new clandestine collection program in that same country.[97]

And yet, despite the fact that "CIA, with its 'operational funds' and even the Military Attachés have a much greater degree of funding and flexibility . . . [and] there is no separate fund to facilitate overt collection of political and economic information," nevertheless, "the Department has been unwilling to press the Congress for more funding. . . . As a result, the largest, most important, and least risky source of political and economic intelligence for the United States Government is neglected in the Federal budget and severely underfunded."[98]

Like State's own Macomber Group, the Church Committee found not much efficiency, not much competitiveness, and not much initiative in the way

96. *Bureaucratic Politics and Foreign Policy* (Brookings Institution, Washington, 1974), 37.
97. *Church Committee Report,* Book I, 316.
98. *Ibid.,* 316f.

State and the Foreign Service went about their business of being an élite service:

> . . . the Department itself seems to have made little effort to direct the Foreign Service collection effort in a systematic way. The Department itself levies no overall requirements. Most regional bureau Assistant Secretaries send periodic letters to field posts indicating subjects of priority interest and these letters are supplemented by "official-informal" communications from the Country Director (desk officer). In addition the Department participates in the development of inter-agency intelligence requirement lists, and those lists are transmitted to the embassies and consulates abroad. The Department believes that these procedures suffice, and does not favor the development of a more elaborate requirement mechanism for the Foreign Service.
>
> The Department has made no significant effort to train junior Foreign Service Officers in the techniques of political reporting. The record is somewhat better for economic reporting. A recent report of the Department's Inspector General concluded that the Department has generally been remiss in setting and maintaining professional standards through systematic training, assignment, and promotion policies.[99]

The cause of this, of course, lies in the earlier-noted conviction of Foreign Service Officers that they are diplomats first, reporters and commentators second, collectors of information last. Indeed this circumstance is institutionized in the way the State Department and Foreign Service are organized. One of the hippopotami, the analyst Stanley E. Smigel, recorded this fact in 1958:

> In the Department, the principal collection arm, the Foreign Service, lies outside the intelligence organization. Instructions to the Foreign Service are drafted by the Intelligence Bureau, but, with small exception, these instructions must receive the approval and clearance of other bureaus before transmission. On the other hand, the approval of the Intelligence Bureau, again with small exception, is not required on instructions to the Foreign Service drafted by other bureaus. In contrast to the clear-cut responsibility the service attaché has to his headquarters intelligence unit, the foreign service officer has responsibility to the Department as a whole and has indirect responsibility at best to the Intelligence Bureau.[100]

Mr. Halperin is a little more specific:

> Career Foreign Service officers view the regional bureaus of the State Department—those dealing with Europe, East Asia, the Near East and South

---

99. *Ibid.,* 317.

100. "Some Views on the Theory and the Practice of Intelligence Collection, "*Studies in Intelligence,* II/2, 40.

Asia, Africa and Latin America—as the heart of the State Department operations. They believe that the Assistant Secretaries for these regions should be career officials and should have flexibility in managing relations with the relevant countries. They resist the growth of functional bureaus such as those dealing with economics and political-military affairs, in part because such bureaus tend to be dominated by civil servants or in-and-outers rather than by Foreign Service officers.[101]

And he goes on to make the significant point that the bureaucratic competitiveness that we have found lacking in the Department and Foreign Service toward other bureaus exists internally:

> To the extent that they differ over missions, career diplomatic officials contest the relative priority to be given to different geographic areas. Sub-groups within the department do not rally around particular kinds of missions, as in the case of the CIA, so much as they take sides over the relative attention to be given to improving relations with different parts of the world or, in the case of potential enemies, effectively opposing them. There is a West European group, Soviet group, an "Arabist" group, and groups concerned primarily with African and Latin American affairs. Internal controversy consist of disputes among these groups over particular policy issues.

A Paradox

Now we started this reconnaissance of the Foggy Bottom sector because we had been told that the main collectors of current political and economic information were the FSOs and that the main consumer was the Department. Having established that the gentlemen of the Foreign Service and the Department of State, who are the main collectors and consumers of current political and economic information, have a low regard for the "clandestine" product, we expected to be able to raise the question whether collection of all current information should not be left to the overt agencies. We expected to be able to say, as years ago we used to say among ourselves, "Let the FSOs do it; it's their job."

But what we discovered was a paradox:

— State's Foreign Service, militantly non-competitive, using slender resources and few people, produces the bulk of *used* current information as a rather casual and reluctant chore, secondary in importance and inferior in prestige to its primary task of Representing the Nation Abroad.

— CIA's Clandestine Service, militantly competitive, expending comparatively vast wealth, employing the Guild's vast mechanism of safe houses, disguised

101. *Op. cit.*, 38.

modes of transport, cross-connecting switchboards, instantaneous multi-channel radio, locally suborned police and military support, produces a very modest amount of little-used, basically overt information with great enthusiasm.

Sometimes, to be sure, the flow from the DDO offices abroad is more than a trickle, and in fairness it should be recorded that not all the analysts of State scorn such reporting. In June 1976, for example, we had occasion to interview candidly and informally a member of State's Bureau of Intelligence and Research who had been spending a proportion of his time on the political situation in ███████ , and whose anonymity we here protect. Asked whether INR could dispense with the reporting from the Clandestine Service, he said emphatically that if it had not been for the reporting from the Service's station ███████ in the first four months of 1976, the U.S. Government would not have known what was going on during that period in that place, which was of tender concern to our diplomatic, military, and intelligence establishment. Asked whether the Political Section of the ███████ Embassy could not have produced adequate information if tasked, he said that the present configuration of that Embassy is such that all current political information is produced by the Clandestine Service Station. Asked whether, as Ambassador Yost had suggested, the Embassy could be staffed with FSOs to do the job and could then perform without using clandestine or semi-clandestine methods, he said he presumed so, although he did not possess operational information on the Station's sources and could not judge which might be true penetrations and which merely friendly contacts.

Following this conversation up informally, we then talked with fellow officers of the Service who are familiar with the operational details as well as the production of ███████████ political sources during the period of concern. Without conducting a statistical analysis of all reporting (some 300 to 400 reports) in combination with a detailed review of the personal dossiers and operational files of the sources, we can give only an estimate of the degree of clandestinity employed in that particular exercise in current intelligence collection. That estimate is that perhaps one percent of the reports disseminated came from agents who:

— were really agents, i.e., who deliberately and secretly broke ███████ law to provide information, and
— had unique access, not duplicable by a non-clandestine agent.

Now some of this information came from liaison. And the history of our Service, from its first feeble squirming in the arms of its old British aunt, has been dominated in many ways by liaison. Indeed, we have created whole national services, internal and external, from one end of the world to the other, trained them, vetted them, funded them, in order to be able to conduct liaison in their countries, and to get them to do work that we, though expending vast sums in training and subsidy of operations, thought we were too small or too poor to handle ourselves.

The Sun Never Sets On Liaison

████████████████████████████ in nearly every capital that is friendly host to an American Embassy, and in some that are not so friendly, the Stations of the Operations Directorate spend a little or a lot or sometimes all of their effort consulting and consorting with officials ("counterparts") of the intelligence, security, and police organizations ("host services") of the local government, and often with the intelligence services of other foreign governments who have stations in the same countries. The result of this activity is a volume of dispatches and cables to CIA Headquarters, often repeated laterally to other stations and so-called field customers, that comprises a very large proportion of all information arriving there. Most of this material is classified SECRET, since the arrangements for exchange between our Service and the foreigners require the protection by each party of the other fellow's sources, and most of it is captioned NOT RELEASABLE TO FOREIGN NATIONALS ("NOFORN") in order to avoid duplication and false confirmation in the complex of exchange relationships that spreads like a Vietnamese extended family around the globe, as well as to let each service choose its own friends.

Our critical competitors in the Foreign Service, aware of our penchant for liaison, usually approve of it. Thus, John Franklin Campbell, who left the Foreign Service after nine years and has devoted some effort to recording his best thoughts on reform, recommends:

> . . . development, by State and CIA, of more specific and limited guidelines regarding the functions of intelligence officers in the field; it should be the *presumption*—unless a specific exception is granted for a particular country— that Foreign Service embassy officers handle traditional diplomatic reporting on the internal politics and economics of the country to which they are assigned, while CIA staff cover specific security-related targets and do so, wherever possible, *in overt, cooperative liaison with the host country security services.* [102]

In terms of local, current, political information, this point of view is understandable. Despite many patient explanations by espionage officers to diplo-

---

102. *The Foreign Affairs Fudge Factory* (New York and London, Basic Books, 1971), 162. (Emphasis added.)

mats at home and abroad, no Foreign Service Officer ever seems to grasp the possibility that an intelligence service working in France might be more concerned with operations against Germany, Vietnam, or the Soviet Union than with information on France itself. State lumps the Soviet Union and its East European protectorates together into one of five geographical Bureaus (Africa, East Asia/Pacific, Latin America, Near East/South Asia, and Europe). The USSR is one of nine offices in the Bureau for Europe, while in the Bureau of Intelligence and Research there are five geographical areas, one of which is called "Office of Research and Analysis for Europe and the Soviet Union." State organizes its desk structure in terms of its Foreign Service *representations* in specific areas abroad,[103] whereas CIA's Clandestine Service organizes its desk structure in terms of global intelligence *targets*. The Clandestine Service therefore has a major Area Division (roughly analogous to one of State's Regional Bureaus) called "Soviet and East European," which gives operational direction to virtually every station, though its own stations behind the Curtain are tiny compared with those in less denied areas. The principle influences operations throughout [the] desk and station structure of the Service: the element called "China Operations," less than a Division,, more than a Branch, gives direction to ▮▮▮▮▮▮▮▮ and other stations as well as to ▮▮▮▮▮▮▮▮ If there is an ▮▮▮▮ Embassy in ▮▮▮▮ the Station in ▮▮▮▮▮ is not bewildered to receive operational direction originating on the ▮▮▮▮ desk. In fact, if the chap in ▮▮▮▮▮ happens to believe in strategic espionage, he may welcome an opportunity to mount or assist an operation against a target far removed from the current events ▮▮▮▮▮▮▮▮ especially if it involves unilateral clandestine effort and not just negotiation with local liaison counterparts.

A separate essay could be written on the psychology of liaison and its effects on clandestinity. Quarrels have occurred, sometimes developing into locally famous feuds, between espionage operators who favored use of liaison relationships primarily to develop controlled penetrations of host services and those who used liaison to acquire maximum production and refrained from any insidious or secret act that might, if detected, impair the atmosphere of mutual affection, respect, or dependence that counterparts on both sides always profess. Famous flaps, like the compromise a decade and a half ago of an attempted false-flag penetration by our Service of the ▮▮▮▮▮▮▮▮▮▮▮▮▮ or, the eventually detected, but initially successful, penetration of ▮▮▮▮▮▮▮ are used as evidence to bolster arguments on both sides of the controversy.

The controversy, of course, is a manifestation of the larger problem we have

---

103. V. Department of State, *Telephone Directory Autumn 1975*.

been discussing in this paper, the effect of anti-clandestine or semi-clandestine or non-clandestine collection for production in volume on the ability of the Clandestine Service to conduct espionage for strategic coverage. In these terms, much liaison activity, despite the secret agreements that underlie it, is a form of journalism. The situation in ███████ is a pertinent example, for much of the production in that situation that our friend in State/INR liked so much was from present or former ███████ liaison counterparts of our officers in ███████ , whom these officers simply interviewed on an overt basis.

And so in one case, at least, we have the DDO's essentially overt political *information* being valued and appreciated by a non-CIA producer of political *intelligence*. In this case, according to the explicit opinion of the consumer in INR, the reporting function of the diplomats had been deliberately and organizationally neglected by the State Department command structure in favor of exploiting the local capacity of the Clandestine Service to produce volume at a cost charged to other than the Department's budget.

Let us take another case. Perhaps the greatest volume of political information ever transmitted from a foreign post was that to which our John Smith wanted so ambitiously to contribute, namely what was sent from the DDO's station in Saigon before that city had its name forcibly changed to honor a terrorist saint. Curious to learn the real value of this material to the analysts at home, we used the occasion of a seminar to solicit the opinion of several old hands in the analytic, estimative, and spy trades, including that of an OCI analyst who had worked with the material at home and was familiar with the collection mechanism in Saigon from numerous visits. (Although he did not request it, we afford him anonymity here.) He believed that "in most instances, the DDO product from Vietnam added little to what we already knew," and went on to generalize:

> From my standpoint, this question is being asked of the Agency: How much do we *need* in terms of a clandestine mechanism to provide us with any kind of intelligence to meet the needs of the U.S.?[104]

Combined, the views of our CIA/OCI analyst and our State/INR analyst put the semi-clandestine reporting of the Clandestine Service in a strange light. A State producer likes the raw material from our station in ███████ because he is not getting enough from the Embassy, while a CIA man finds the stuff from the Saigon Station (that on the changing or unchanging political situation in South Vietnam; he did not see the material from VC penetration) irrelevant and prolix. To be sure, other analysts probably found the reporting on the political situation in Vietnam more useful. Nonetheless, there does not appear

104. Seminar, 22 October 1975. Center for the Study of Intelligence. Notes taken by Nancy Ocque.

to be any general endorsement of its value in producing current intelligence. Certainly, there is no justification for continuance of the semi-clandestine task by the Service, but the general problem of requirements and feedback is raised. We must examine this in relation both to current intelligence and to strategic espionage.

Current Requirements & Current Feedback

The necessity for a close relationship between the analyst and the collector of current information is seldom argued. That a continuous dialogue is necessary, for example, between the Foreign News Editor of the *New York Times* and his foreign correspondent goes without saying, for how else is the reporter overseas to know what the paper wants to print at any moment, or what slant he should give to his stories? That continuous dialogue is desirable between Order of Battle analysts at Arlington Hall and Defense Attachés doing reconnaissance and observation in, say, Poland also goes without saying, for this kind of current collection requires continuous reference to maps and running lists and continuous posting of discrete items from the field. That intercourse should occur between the analysts in State and the Political Officers in embassies brooks no argument, for the trick at both ends of the line is to be as well informed in as rapid a manner as possible, and this is helped by a lot of discussion back and forth and sideways. In other words, communication between producer and collector of current information from labile sources is to be encouraged by such devices as the Human Resources Committee's (HRC) Current Intelligence Reporting List (CIRL), which is addressed to "country teams."[105] Its explicit purposes are to:

— provide collectors with a community-approved selective list of important issue- or event-oriented questions believed to be answerable by human sources;

— provide the post with a tool that could assist in the development of coordinated collection or reporting; and

— increase the dialogue and understanding between collector and analysts (or users) through demonstrated responsiveness to previous reporting and indications of reporting efforts which would be most useful.

In his Letter of Instruction to the HRC, DCI Colby commanded that:

Our national human resource objectives should emphasize maximum development of overt information-gathering capabilities. Clandestine and technical

105. See, for example, USIB, HRC, *Current Intelligence Reporting List. Southeast Asia and Pacific* (CIRL-SEA/PL-76) February-June 1976 (SECRET).

resources should be applied only when the required information is of considerable importance and is not obtainable by improved overt collection.[106]

The LOI also enjoins the Committee to:

Seek ways to further improve informal, but controlled, substantive dialogue between community production analysts and field collectors.

I leave it to others to seek examples of "informal, but controlled, substantive dialogue" while recalling an address in the Dome, possibly in early 1973, by the newly appointed Deputy Director of Operations in which Mr. Colby applied the term "journalism" to a trend which he foresaw and approved in his newly renamed Directorate. I should be lax in my development of the argument of this paper if I did not point out that the distinction between the obvious necessity for intercourse between analysts and overt collectors of information and the requirements process necessary to strategic intelligence or espionage is one that former Director Colby did not emphasize.

Although present writing is not yet far enough removed from Mr. Colby's directorship to afford historical objectivity, it is clear that he was adhering to the precepts of his original predecessor, General Donovan, in promoting the Service as the Government's best competitor with the *New York Times* as well as the outfit that could do whatever odd, non-intelligence chores needed doing to implement policy around the world. Those of us who insist on the distinction between the Clandestine Service and the "intelligence service" nevertheless, nay consequently, take small comfort from his assertion in early 1976 that "although the costs of the past year were high, . . . they will be exceeded by the value of this strengthening of what was already the best intelligence service in the world."[107] The distinction upon which we insist requires distinguishing ruthlessly between strategic espionage and the "journalism" that Bill Colby espoused while still Chief of the Clandestine Service.

Strategic R & FB

In 1948, when one of the wisest of the elephants wrote the first book on *Strategic Intelligence for American World Policy,* intelligence had not yet become a major industry. Dr. Kent's precepts on the problem of requirements and feedback may, by the spareness of their language, sound naive to present ears:

106. DCI, "Letter of Instruction to Acting Chairman, USIB Human Resources Committee," Attachment. USIB-D-80, 2/3. 13 November 1975 (SECRET).
107. William Egan Colby, "After Investigating U.S. Intelligence," *New York Times,* 26 February 1976.

. . . Now if the man on the other end of the wire has formerly been a worker in the home office, if he has a feel for home office functioning and personally knows the home staff, and if he is on his toes, he will do it with efficient good grace. He will grasp the instructions (which can be given in office shorthand) and will act pretty much as an overseas projection of the home staff. But if he has not served in the home office, and instead has gone to his foreign post improperly briefed on home problems, then there may be difficulties.[108]

But though the language now seems archaically pure on comparison with the jargon that is used today to describe problems of requirements and feed-back,[109] the essence of the problem, the barrier of communication between estimator and collector, has not been changed by the growth of the industry.

The essence has not changed, but the shape of the problem has changed. Kent could write almost 30 years ago that:

> there are some cases on record where clandestine intelligence has exploited a difficult and less remunerative source while it has neglected to exploit an easy and more remunerative one. . . .[110]

But if the case of John Smith, sketched earlier, and the case of Leo Cherne's anonymous informant in Europe are typical outside of our Curtain stations, the present tendency would appear to be the reverse of that deplored by Dr. Kent in 1948; the tendency now is for case officers to exploit easy sources in prefer-ence to hard ones because they are rewarded for volume, not quality, for production, not coverage, for journalism, not espionage. And this despite a DCI Directive to USIB/HRC, which says:

> . . . We need, particularly, gains in the interrelationships between *overt and clandestine* and technical and human sources. We must establish *more direct links* between our human collectors and our technical collectors.[111]

108. Kent, *op. cit.*, 165. Not actually the first book, but the first in the U.S. Historians may consult Maximilian Ronge, *Kriegs-und Industriesponiage* (Vienna, 1925) by the Chief of the Austrian Imperial Military Intelligence through World War I. This work, having been banned and destroyed by the Germans after the Anschluss of 1938, is rare. General Ronge, the officer who detected, confronted, and succeeded Redl, was a pioneering genius of the arts of espionage, counterespionage and estimative intelligence. Until his death in 1954, at the age of 92, he was also a great trainer of young men.

109. Cf. George Bush, "Guiding Principles of the Intelligence Community" (Memorandum NFIB-D22.1/49 to the National Foreign Intelligence Board Principals, 13 May 1976, UNCLASSI-FIED): "Continuing attention will be given to improving the interface between national and tactical intelligence capabilities, seeking to capitalize on the potentiality of inputs to national intelligence needs from tactical resources in peacetime and the capabilities of national resources to provide intelligence of import to both peacetime force readiness and wartime operations."

110. *Op. cit.*, 168.

111. DCI, *Perspectives for Intelligence 1976–1981*, USIB/IRAC-D-22.1/44 (October 1975, SECRET NOFORN).

A glance at any one of a hundred charts of the so-called intelligence cycle that are prepared for briefing, training, and study by committees and task forces set up to reorganize the government will provide a typical picture of the present maze of "interrelationships," including those between "overt and clandestine and technical and human sources." If we restrict our present glancings to the cycle of collection of current information and production of current intelligence, we find that on the diplomatic side the producers in INR and the Regional Bureaus are also consumers, not only from the Foreign Service but also from CIA's Clandestine Service, which disseminates directly via Distribution B of *Foreign Intelligence Reports* (FIRDB) and from CIA's OCI. OCI itself, a producer, consumes the Foreign Service reporting directly, the production of the State Bureaus, and the Clandestine Service reporting. But among its suppliers, only with the Clandestine Service does OCI have direct two-way communication.

In view of this relationship, which OCI views as a family affair, it is not astonishing that when OCI is dissatisfied with DDO collection of current information, it seeks to alter the relationship rather than to abolish it. The Director of OCI recently conjectured a bit on the future and offered the possibility that:

> Congress will generate directives placing much more emphasis on analytical capabilities than has been true in the past, . . . [OCI] will be required to have more analytic experience physically located in the field, either PCS or TDY [on permanent or temporary assignment]. Further, assuming reduced personnel ceiling, it is evident that we will need multidisciplinary, i.e., ops/analysis cadres located in our overseas stations. The logical conclusion of this is that in tomorrow's world, the clandestine collection function will be of less importance than the analysis function. . . . Without doubt, relative priorities to be established in the future will stress collection of political and economic intelligence, often overt in nature. . . .[112]

By thus placing the analysts at points in or just above the mine shafts, OCI would acquire even better control of the company's own ore. Mr. Parmenter added that what he had said

> . . . does not mean that there will not be a continued critical need for clandestine [sic] collection, especially in those areas which impact on American multinational corporations. . . .

and drew a further conclusion:

112. William Parmenter, quoted in Notes of Interview by Fellows of the Center for the Study of Intelligence, 17 December 1975.

The above clearly points out the fact that there will have to be much more cross-training of DDI and DDO officers as there will be situations where knowledge of both operations and analysis will be a critical factor.

"Cross-training," "multidisciplinary cadres in overseas stations," "relative priorities stressing collection of political and economic intelligence, often overt in nature." Well, before we get back to talking about espionage and strategic intelligence, we can note one point that stands out clearly: between collectors of *current* information and producers of *current* intelligence there has to be a symbiotic if not syngenetic relationship. But it hardly needs to be reiterated that such a relationship fosters *current* production, not strategic coverage. It therefore fosters collection of information, as Mr. Parmenter has it, that is often overt in nature. Far more often overt than clandestine.

For Sherman Kent in 1948 there was a problem in the production of *strategic* intelligence caused by a barrier that, as we have seen, now has been largely demolished—that barrier caused by the natural laws of clandestinity that are sometimes labeled "operational security":

> . . . the major methodological problem of the collection stage of the intelligence process . . . begins with the segregation of the clandestine force. This segregation is dictated by the need for secrecy. An absolute minimum of people must know anything about the operation, and the greatest amount of caution and dissimulation must attend its every move. But unless this clandestine force watches sharply, it can become its own worst enemy. For if it allows the mechanisms of security to cut it off from some of the most significant links of guidance, it destroys its own reason for existence.[113]

Obviously, for Dr. Kent as for us, the producer of strategic intelligence must enjoy a relationship with the collector of the information that is the raw material of strategic intelligence, and the collector, to work rationally and efficiently, must receive guidance from the producer. But symbiosis, let alone syngenesis, is not required. Despite those charts of the intelligence cycle that are presented by the foot, yard, and mile whenever the subject of requirements and feedback is raised, the problem can be formulated in a series of four simple questions, two for the espionage case officer and two for the analyst.

The Simple Questions

—For the espionage case officer:

1. How can I know where and when to mount an operation?
2. How can I know how to manipulate my operation to satisfy a given requirement?

113. *Op. cit.*, 166f.

—For the analyst:

1. How can I know the relevance of an espionage report?
2. How can I best communicate my requirements to the espionage case officer?

These questions seem ingenuous in the context of the papers and charts on the intelligence cycle that we noted above, but if we concentrate on strategic intelligence and the task of espionage for strategic intelligence, including that occasional and unusual item of espionage that is both strategic and current, the only question of significance is the first. The other three are mechanical; their answers depend on devices of communication that can be contrived and modified once an operation has been installed. For the reader whom we have categorized as elephant, that is, the officer whose experience has lain with processing the information rather than with manipulating the human beings who steal it, this answer may seem insufficient. But it is not within the scope of this paper to recapitulate all of OTR's courses in clandestine tradecraft, much less the on-job training still given by operations officers in our stations. The gorillas among the readers of this paper, however much they may have been beguiled, like Leo Cherne's informant in Europe, into competition with the Foreign Service and with the journalists, will require no examples.

Let us now summarize the argument of this paper in a series of propositions and a series of conclusions in order to speculate on what would happen if the conclusions were somehow translated into organizational and procedural changes:

Propositions

1. Current information, whether political, economic, or military, and whether related to an immediate crisis or a continuing situation of routine concern, is a perishable, high-volume commodity. It must be collected and processed into finished intelligence continuously and rapidly to satisfy a continuously changing consumer demand.
2. Strategic information (the material produced by strategic espionage), whether political, economic, military, scientific, or "counter"-intelligence, is far less perishable. Its collection, by clandestine or technical means, must serve a processing function comprising basically collation and research.
3. The task of a Clandestine Service is espionage (and "counter"-espionage). It employs secret agents to perform acts that break foreign laws.
4. Secret agents with illegal functions require time, careful planning, and ingenuity to install and maintain. Espionage is therefore suited to the collection of strategic information and unsuited to collection of current information.
5. The overt agencies are suited to collection of current information. These are

the Foreign Service, the Defense Attachés, the overseas representatives of Treasury, Commerce, Agriculture, USIA, USAID, and the commercial journalists.

6. Management, whether "by Objective" or otherwise, includes reward for performance. The objectives of current collection differ radically from those of strategic collection. Specifically, the one rewards volume and speed, the other prescient, long-term coverage. Therefore, the two kinds of collection cannot both be effectively managed within the same organization.

Conclusions

A. There should be a requirement-feedback mechanism between the Clandestine Service and the producers of finished *strategic* intelligence, especially those of CIA's own Intelligence Directorate, which produce other than current reporting.

B. There should be *no* requirement-feedback mechanism between the Clandestine Service and the producers of current intelligence, including such policy-level consumers as the Regional Bureaus and senior officials of the Department of State and their counterparts in the staffs of the National Security Council, and including OCI.

C. There should be a requirement-feedback mechanism between the *overt* agencies (named above) and the producers of *current* intelligence, including policy level consumers such as the Regional Bureaus and senior officials of the Department of State, and, of course, OCI.

What Would Happen?

There is an apparently ineluctable drift of affairs that bears the Agency along with other organizations of government in a determined direction. The Agency drifts ineluctably because it is an organization of government, and the Clandestine Service is steadily altered, bent out of its original shape, and bent away from its earlier direction because it is part of the Agency. What would happen if this drift could be arrested, if the conclusions set forth above could somehow be translated into organizational and procedural realities? What would happen:

— to current intelligence?
— to strategic intelligence?
— to related endeavors such as diplomacy, covert political action, and military combat?

What would happen to current intelligence if we of the Clandestine Service emulated the Foreign Service of the Department of State in a different kind of élitism, asserting that we are not the omniversatile sergeants of the government, but specialists, élite because elected to a high calling? What if we merely provide, as best we can contrive and as best we can plan, selective, long-range, judiciously anticipated, laboriously installed *coverage* of targets through penetration by controlled, secret agents? And what if we refuse to compete in the collection of any kind of information that could be collected by other means?

One of the things that would happen is that the Clandestine Service would become again primarily a *consumer* of current intelligence. The Service would be serviced by the analysts, whose support would assist the Service in installing the kind of secret human machinery that would produce stolen information of real use in keeping that intelligence cycle a-spinning throughout the community.

Another thing that might happen (and this would require translation of our conclusions into organizational and procedural change at the Department of State) is that the Foreign Service could expand its reporting and expand its overseas complement, to supply the market. Indeed, for several years there has been a movement within the diplomatic corps to increase and redirect Foreign Service reporting, a movement based on the realization that the market has long been saturated. The so-called Prince Study, completed for the Murphy Commission in March 1975, makes a number of recommendations for redirection of reporting toward greater analytical content, changing of analytical and editorial procedures, and training of FSOs.[114] In 1973 a Secretary of State had written:

> Over the last four years I have been struck . . . by the sheer volume of information which flows into the State Department, contrasted with the paucity of good analytic material. . . . Mere reportage of events which have already taken place and about which in many cases we can do little is not sufficient. For that reporting to be useful to me, I require not only information on what is happening, but your most thoughtful and careful analysis of why it is happening, what it means for U.S. policy, and the directions in which you see events going.[115]

And on 16 June 1976 he made a similar point to a group of CIA officers in the Dome:

> Kissinger's central substantive point was that the government's greatest intelligence need is in the area of predicting, discussing, and ruminating about future developments, rather than current developments. Fifty percent of foreign policy problems will usually cure themselves. This 50 percent is usually

114. William D. Coplin, Michael K. O'Leary, Robert F. Rich, *et al.*, "Toward Improvement of Foreign Service Field Reporting," *Murphy Commission Report,* Appendix E.

115. Henry A. Kissinger, "Reporting from the Field" (Departmental Notice), U.S. Department of State, 7 November 1973.

included in current reporting, along with other, more meaty issues. The government, in general, is usually working on the wrong 50 percent of the problems.

Still, State must by necessity concentrate on immediate day-to-day problems. The Agency must help by telling State what it should be looking for in the future "even five-ten years" out. Will Europe be unified? What will Chinese policy do? What can the U.S. realistically achieve in various areas of the world in a defined period?[116]

In fact, this movement has lately been operating throughout the community, as can be inferred from such planning documents as the Director's *Perspectives*. The one put out by USIB over Mr. Colby's signature in October 1975, says:

Human-source collection capabilities will remain an important part of the collection process. Mechanisms are being devised at the national intelligence level, as well as the diplomatic mission level abroad, to improve the management, coordination, and exploitation of human-source capabilities. This trend must be pursued energetically. There is considerable potential for improved reporting from overt personnel of both intelligence and non-intelligence agencies abroad. Contributions of such agencies as State, Defense, Treasury, USAID, USIA, Agriculture, and Commerce can be enhanced substantially by more effective approaches to information gathering and in the reporting aspects of their activities.[117]

If the overt reporting of all the overt agencies, and of the overt elements of CIA such as FBIS and the Domestic Collection Division, is to evolve into greater "effectiveness," the withdrawal of the Clandestine Service from competition will probably accelerate the evolution.

Something else that would happen inevitably and beneficially would be the provision of occasional but critical current information from a well-placed agent whose access to it would be all his own. Sometimes it occurs now, as we saw at the time of the ████████ war, that an agent with unique access to critical information provides a report that goes swiftly to OCI and to the decision makers, but so great is the present volume of soft-target reporting from the Service that such reports are likely to be disregarded or rejected because the analyst cannot distinguish the significant clandestine item. In the ████████ War ████████ an agent report gave accurate warning of the impending ████████ offensive, but was disregarded by the analysts,[118] and therefore by the decision makers.

116. Remarks at CIA on 15 June 1976 (from unofficial notes). [The discrepancy between the dates in the note and in the text is unresolved.—ED.]

117. DCI, *Perspectives 1976–1981*.

118. From an official, reliable, tested, well-placed source with proven access to the information.

And what would happen to the Office of Current Intelligence itself? Well, it would lose control of a small percentage of the raw material it processes into its daily, weekly and occasional products, namely that raw material that comes from the company's own mine. But there is no reason it could not establish some supervisorship over the other rich mines abroad. The precedent of the mis-named "Strategic Divisions," those Intelligence Directorate representations of long ago at overseas posts, exists, though one has heard the complaint that those offices were coopted by Chiefs of Station for purposes not directly serving OCI's interests. Then let them be reestablished and given status where they belong, in the Foreign Service's Political Sections. Let OCI, which uses overtly collected, field-evaluated information, the bulk from the Foreign Service, strike a bargain with the Department, undermanned and underfunded as it is. And let these OCI units abroad be independent of the Clandestine Service, which in turn will be independent of them. Let there be the same relationship between whatever forces OCI can deploy abroad and the DDO stations as there is between those stations and the intercept units of the Foreign Broadcast Information Service, friendly but correct, above all non-competitive.

Finally, what would happen to our case officers abroad who have been producing current information by non-clandestine, if sometimes discreet, interview of liaison counterparts, politicians, friendly business men, American expatriates, etc.? They would simply suddenly find themselves in a world where the objectives by which they were managed were defined in terms of the sensitivity, potential value, and present worth of agents recruited to spend a lifetime stealing information or performing illegal tasks in support of a program of such theft. Not in terms of the number or length of reports submitted from the largest possible number of encrypted contacts. Morale would rise. Professionalism would improve. We would again be doing strategic espionage.

Could Management Cope?

If for a while we are to use the paraphernalia of MBO, the Objectives that we assign for quantitative evaluation against performance will have to be described in terms of coverage rather than production. This should pose no great problem since many, especially in the Soviet Bloc target area, are already so described (Recruit two members of the Soviet Trade Mission and one KGB officer in coming Fiscal Year; induce defection of Polish, Hungarian, Czech Chief of Mission, or GRU *Rezident* if he has studied in Frunze Military Academy, etc., etc.). These are bureaucratic formulae, no more or less useful than others of their ilk. The point is that management, of which our Service has no perceptible shortage, can enlist whatever devices are needed to do research, to conduct futurology, to codify operational intelligence, in short to *plan* strategic coverage. If the objective—where and when to mount an operation—is defined by a planning process, management, that most available of all resources, can devise the tactics of communication between the producers of strategic intelligence and the collectors of strategic information.

Another result of the change here envisaged would be the revival of that branch of espionage called counterespionage.[119] Oddly (for it seems odd in these days of assault from press and the legislature) many of our critics grasp the central value and significance of counterespionage. Herbert Scoville, Jr., for example, is one of those former officials of the evaluative side of the Agency, in this case of the Scientific and Technical Directorate, who has turned his concern for the Agency's present plight into articulate prose. In the title of a recent article he asks, "Is Espionage Necessary for our Security?" On balance, he answers his own question negatively, but he gives special place to counterespionage, which for him is those "covert human operations abroad" which are a sub-category of counterintelligence. After assessing espionage—"recruiting agents in foreign nations, encouraging the defection of knowledgeable individuals, audiosurveillance, and other techniques,"[120] he finds it largely inadequate, though sometimes potentially valuable, for military development and deployment, military intentions, and political affairs, except in some Third World situations. He finds it inappropriate for economic matters and for political affairs in sophisticated areas. "In sum, espionage would appear to have limited but nevertheless critical potential as a source of intelligence information."[121] On the other hand,

> Counterintelligence is very different, very arcane, but nevertheless very important. Not only must we continue to detect and counter the continuing very extensive operations of the KGB, the Soviet secret intelligence organization, but we must also now deal with the new and rapidly growing threats from terrorism by unstable individuals and dissident groups. . . . There can be little doubt that covert human operations abroad—all that goes into counterespionage—remain a vital technique . . . in the world of today . . . it is hard to avoid the conclusion that effective counterintelligence, in turn largely covert, is

119. Nomenclature used here is that attributed to OSO before the merger. "That branch of espionage of which the target is an alien organization which uses conspiratorial methods, etc."

120. *Foreign Affairs*, LIV/3 (April 1976), 483. Dr. Scoville headed the Office of Scientific Intelligence from 1955 to 1961 and was Assistant Director for Research until 1963, when he went to the Arms Control and Disarmament Agency for six years as Assistant Director. There his preoccupation was with Nuclear Weapons and Advanced Technology (one of the Agency's Bureaus) and with intelligence support to the Strategic Arms Limitation Talks (SALT). Thus his experience has been in exploiting information from all sources rather than with collection from clandestine sources.

121. *Ibid.*, 495.

essential to our true security—indeed that it may in itself justify the continuance of a major covert foreign intelligence organization in some form.[122]

Dr. Scoville's mention of the KGB reminds us that the foremost practitioners of strategic coverage are the clandestine services of the Soviet Union. Few present-day commentators remember, or ever knew, that during the period of the USSR's greatest crisis, when the armies were struggling in Stalingrad and Leningrad to halt the German invasion, illegal agents under false Spanish identities were being dispatched from Moscow via China to Mexico, and the *rezidentura* in Mexico City was conducting strategic espionage in the United States. The battles on the steppes ended while the Soviet espionage service was stealing the secret of the uranium bomb from the Manhattan Project. That was coverage, unmodified by Crisis Management.

But to think with Dr. Scoville that counterintelligence is "different" and "arcane" is to make a mistake that should be left to persons outside the Service to make. For us, remembering our nomenclature, counterespionage should simply be part of our regular work.

Beg, Borrow, Buy? No, Steal

It takes, however, very little exegesis to achieve the perception that what Dr. Scoville is advocating is clandestinity, that what he is asserting is that the only intelligence of value produced by "covert" means is that which is produced by *clandestine* means. Or to revert to earlier language, that the job of our Service is not to beg, borrow, or buy information, but to steal secrets. It is heartening to note that the Senate Select Church Committee, which devoted enormous effort, talent, and expense to examining the Service because of acts and events largely peripheral to the Service's main work, grasped the essence of clandestinity and the intrinsic connection between clandestinity and the specialized form of espionage that is called by the Committee counterintelligence, and by us counterespionage:

> . . . a discipline of great importance, for the rock-bottom obligation of an intelligence service is to defend the country; meeting this obligation is the very *raison d'être* of counterintelligence. The discipline also represents the most secret of secret intelligence activities—the heart of the onion.[123]

---

122. *Ibid.*, 493*ff*. Dr. Scoville does not neglect to point out that "the defectors and agents that have produced the best positive intelligence in many areas have also come from foreign intelligence services—for example, Penkovsky."

123. *Church Committee Report,* Book I, 171.

The author of this eloquent passage obviously has his heart, if not his onion, in the right place, and we are pleased that his evident ignorance of the origin of his metaphor lets us reinforce his point. The origin: Henrik Ibsen, *Peer Gynt,* Act V, Scene 5.

> (Peer is peeling the onion.) There's a most surprising lot of layers! Are we never coming to the kernel? (Pulls all that is left to pieces.) There is not one! To the innermost bit it is nothing but layers, smaller and smaller. Nature's a joker! (Throws the bits away from him.)

The heart of the onion, the essence of clandestinity, has no existence of its own. It is the principle of onionhood, layers of clandestinity to the innermost bit, where the layers end. It is not only "a discipline of great importance"; it is the essential discipline.

Finally, what would happen to the diplomats, the soldiers, the propagandists, the guerrilla fighters, the influence applicators? As for the Foreign Service, it might find a union with our Office of Current Intelligence beneficial. Since the average FSO spends about 60 percent of his time writing reports, though he thinks of this chore as a kind of sideline, he might welcome some professional help from the overt shop in CIA. The Bureau of Intelligence and Research, manned now largely by FSOs who ache to get into a more representational job, might find helpful an alliance with professional producers, professional requirements people, professional analysts. The decision makers, or policy makers, or contributors to policy in the Regional Bureaus might benefit from having an unabashed analytical element down the hall, ready to accept responsibility for judgments made and estimates recorded. The soldiers, who sometimes alone among us keep their mind on the Soviet nuclear submarines, the ICBMs, and perhaps on other unmentionable weapons that may destroy us in the time it takes you to read a line on this page—these professional and utterly essential guardians might feel more assured that somebody was putting all his effort, undistracted and not greedy for recognition, on Soviet *intentions.*

As for the political action people, the media planters and the grey radio broadcasters, and the corrupters of venal politicians, let them make their accommodation wherever it suits. Their work is not clandestine, and their relation to conductors of espionage is not important. Let the Security Council find a place for them somewhere removed from the conduct of espionage.

14.

Like William Johnson, Hugh Tovar combines outspokenness with vast experience in CIA's Directorate of Operations. Here he focuses on the State Department/CIA interface. Both articles had to be cleared by State as well as by CIA; the arguments the writers make are bureaucratically very sensitive.

The Not-So-Secret War, or How State-CIA Squabbling Hurts U.S. Intelligence

B. HUGH TOVAR

The 1978 upheaval in Iran, unforeseen and unpredicted, sparked a succession of postmortems on the performance of U.S. intelligence. Had it failed? If so, why? The answers—developed by scholars, journalists, legislators, and diplomats—hit the policymakers hard and for the most part let intelligence off rather lightly.

As it should be? Maybe so. Iran was a special case. But the policymakers who failed to heed what intelligence told them should not shoulder all the blame. Some critics have made this clear, citing the Iran mission's neglect of contacts with the religious and other elements opposed to the Shah. And yet they skirt a more fundamental issue, one that in almost all U.S. missions impacts sharply on performance and professionalism—namely, working relations between local State Department and Central Intelligence Agency representatives. This *secret war* has been going full blast for over thirty years, at great cost. Iran may indeed have been an exception to the rule. Missions under fire usually pull together. But more than one intelligence failure can be traced to the inability of those two major agencies of government to collaborate effectively.

As a matter of fact, the *secret war* is not so very secret. Ask any State Department officer at the junior or middle levels for his opinion of CIA. The response, depending on one's bias, will gladden the heart—or shatter composure. Visceral, it will surely be. The same question put to senior levels may evoke a different reaction. ("Some of my best friends are CIA men.") A wider

B. Hugh Tovar, "The Not-So-Secret War, or How State-CIA Squabbling Hurts U.S. Intelligence," *Studies in Intelligence,* vol. 25, no. 1 (Spring 1981), pp. 43–49. Originally classified "Secret" and "Noforn." For definitions, see appendix B.

range of experience overseas and in the Washington bureaucracy generally adds a Parkinsonian acceptance of life as it is. The senior diplomat is mellower, no longer threatened, but he can still tell a few horror stories—and if coaxed, probably will. CIA people likewise have plenty to say on the subject. Where the Foreign Service Officer is less inhibited about talking to outsiders, his CIA counterpart is more likely to brood privately or in-house over his grievances, real or imagined. Paranoia on both sides, though, is rather evenly matched.

If this sounds absurd, it is. It is also a grinding reality in the daily lives of men and women who are paid to think constructively about other things. And it is a serious aspect of the Agency's cover problem at a time when even the comparative security of diplomatic status offers no guarantee of immunity against outrage. Curiously enough, what was originally a forced marriage has evolved after thirty-odd years into a symbiotic relationship from which there is no escape. If State would like to live without CIA, the Agency certainly cannot live without State. The State Department recognizes this, and knows that it cannot let CIA out of its grip. By CIA, of course, we mean only the Directorate of Operations, which is in effect the Agency's foreign service.

Let's face it, espionage is not an appealing art form. If the traditional concepts of diplomacy clash with certain present day realities, this matters little to the newly fledged FSO. Reading other people's mail is not something he likes to do. Add to that CIA's notoriety of recent years, and it is very small wonder that the FSO shies away from contact and its risk of contamination.

Behind this, there is the issue of jurisdiction and authority. Before World War II, the State Department was unchallenged in foreign affairs. Today the field is crowded, and jurisdictional boundaries grow fuzzier every day, though at least in theory State is still preeminent. Its writ runs to everything not specifically delegated by law or by the President to someone else. But those delegations have bourgeoned with each passing year, and the State Department sees its traditional role threatened daily. In its relations with other elements of the federal bureaucracy, State's role is now essentially that of watchdog, to ensure that the *action* agencies operate in a manner consistent with U.S. foreign policy interests—in other words, stay in line and out of the newspapers.

To energetic and ambitious bureaucrats the watchdog often looks like a dog in the manger. Resistance is natural and State Department frustration mounts accordingly. Overseas, however, where even the large missions are closely knit families compared to the Washington arena, the ambassador stands supreme, his authority strengthened by the actions of a succession of presidents. But it is not absolute. He has his hands full, coordinating and controlling the bureaucratic pot-pourri that manages to get itself involved overseas. Gray areas abound. If the ambassador is assertive and strong, he will generally get his way.

Against this backdrop, CIA emerges in State Department eyes essentially as a usurper, intruding on a once private preserve. It is always in the way. Why, asks the FSO who sees his section invaded and his rank on the diplomatic list lowered, do there have to be so damned many of them? The problem is aggravated by CIA's preference for assignment to the so-called substantive sections of the embassy, which carry more prestige among host country officials and offer better access to people of interest. Almost any CIA officer would prefer the title of *political officer* than that of *general services assistant.*

But there are limits. Among foreign representations at a given capital, American embassies are generally the largest. People are used to seeing them big and overstaffed. The posts in key capitals are mammoth. Yet an embassy political or economic section can hold only so many people without looking outlandish. FSOs are understandably griped at CIA for what they see as its excessive presence, and at the State Department for acceding to such bureaucratic rapine.

There is also deep conviction in the FSO's belief that CIA operatives not only raid territory that has been traditionally a State preserve, but steal embassy sources, upstage the embassy's reporting and generally try to make the embassy look silly. Add to that a widespread view that CIA often muddies the local waters, finds crises where none exist and then wants more CIA people to cope with them.

Finally, there is the issue of money. The FSO view: CIA has unlimited amounts; the embassy is penurious. CIA's largesse enables its officers to entertain lavishly, while their FSO counterparts pay out of their own pockets and therefore cannot compete. CIA, they think, can then go on to bribe or buy the assets it needs to do its bidding.

If reality is distorted here—as indeed it is—there is enough fact to give credence to individual legends that are always current in Foreign Service circles. This is essentially the way things are seen and believed among junior and middle level FSOs. If their seniors have outlived these particular anxieties, they too have their worries, which at times reach monumental proportions. One is a feeling that they cannot trust CIA, that they cannot take what they are told at face value. This applies to ambassadors and key embassy officers who of necessity work very closely with Agency representatives. They fear CIA's use of its independent lines of communication, its access to the White House and top echelons of other agencies. They note and often envy the more effective direction and more expeditious support the local station may receive from its headquarters. There is a deep-seated fear that CIA can and does read the embassy's communications, and finally a gut feeling, rarely voiced but nonetheless real, that CIA has an overseas security role and "investigates" its State counterparts. If the latter suspicion has its origins in the paranoia of the McCarthy era, it was certainly given a major fillip by the revelations of CIA's domestic security role in the early seventies.

The sword cuts both ways, obviously, and CIA people counter these charges with some of their own. If State wishes CIA would go away, it should talk to the Congress which set the Agency up, and to the president who saddles it with tasks that Congress never dreamed of. If State is the custodian of U.S. foreign policy and the watchdog vis-à-vis other meddling agencies including CIA, that does not mean State has a monopoly of ideas or a *liberum veto* on anything it thinks impinges on *policy*. If intelligence collection and covert action are instruments of policy—as they unquestionably are—it would be exciting to see State play a *positive* role in planning and directing their exploitation. If CIA seems hyperactive, State in turn strikes CIA people as massively committed to non-action, to borrow a phrase, and blind to trouble until hit in the face with it.

The size issue clearly has its Parkinsonian aspect, but often derives from decisions only partly controllable by CIA; i.e., the assignment by higher authority of tasks which ipso facto call for more people. CIA is known to have difficulty saying *no* to the White House. On the other hand, there has to be a rational balance in any embassy component used for cover. The problem is one for State and CIA to negotiate in Washington, and CIA people in general owe it to State to be more understanding of the latter's concerns. Better distribution of Agency staffers would help, as would also a genuine commitment to the performance of cover work. On the latter point, tough resistance comes from both sides. CIA people object to wasting any more time than necessary doing work they may see as unproductive, and State is loath to allow the camel's nose further into the tent.

The territorial imperative thus complicates everybody's life. If certain sectors of a host country government such as the foreign office have traditionally been State's preserve, there is no law that says so. And there are times when a foreign office offers intelligence opportunities beyond the embassy's interest or ability to exploit. In the realm of politics, embassies would like CIA to keep its cotton-picking hands off everything but the local communist party. The same applies to labor, academic, professional and other circles. Common sense usually prevails, and the operational pie is divided on rational lines, but only after much bureaucratic blood has passed through the scuppers. Both State and CIA, for different reasons, need the widest possible range of contacts, and these should not be restricted by preconceived notions of prerogative. In most countries there is more than enough work to go around, and the perils of being out of touch with and failing to report on the emerging movers and shakers was illustrated forcibly in Iran.

Another facet of CIA methodology that irritates and occasionally infuriates ambassadors and their political counselors ties into the Agency's hunger for analysis of events. Say things get hot in Country X. The crowds are in the streets and columns of smoke are sighted in the suburbs. Quick as a whistle, analysts at Langley—and at State, Defense and the Executive Office Building as well—are clamoring for interpretation. An alert embassy that knows its business will pour out a steady flow of information and analysis aimed at keeping Washington off its back. Some, however, do not. Others do, but only after being prodded repeatedly by Washington. CIA Headquarters will usually ask its station chief to send in his own appraisal of the situation, and if he is properly plugged into the local scene, his views are likely to be cogent. The point is that Washington wants, and frequently has great difficulty getting, independent slants on the meaning and thrust of events. Embassy analytic reporting as a rule reflects the ambassador's overall viewpoint, and dissent within the mission is submerged. If the station chief's appraisal differs from the ambassador's, he must incorporate the latter's position in his own message. That usually keeps things on an even keel, though not always. Tension may also develop when the station includes comments—i.e., interpretations—in the body of its factual intelligence reporting to give perspective to the information itself. Embassies instinctively resent this as one more encroachment on what they deem their proper function. CIA officers chafe at what they consider State's lack of a sense of urgency. The mob has to be moving on the presidential palace or swarming over the embassy wall before some political counselors see fit to flash a *sitrep* back to Washington. Conversely, State officers take a dim view of the Agency's proclivity for reporting today's secrets when the same secrets may be on the wire services tomorrow. They also dislike going out on a limb to forecast the denouement of a bourgeoning upheaval. The CIA station, however, is more attuned to the consequences of getting caught flat-footed by the unexpected crisis, especially in an era when crisis-management is Washington's favorite indoor sport. Successful station chiefs are likely to be of a mind with an astute former British ambassador, who once fixed the writer with his beady eye and said, "I am *paid* to predict!"

An easy way out of this clash of mind and will would be for the State Department to recognize that it too is in the intelligence business. The Office of Intelligence and Research within the Department, though very competent, is an anomaly—a component inherited from the war-time Office of Strategic Services, and most FSOs will do anything to avoid assignment there. They see intelligence and the art of diplomacy as basically incompatible. Representation and negotiation are the prime functions of the American diplomat, and reporting—which is what political and economic officers spend the greater portion of their careers doing—is considered only a by-product. This refusal to recognize reporting as an important intelligence function makes little sense, but it remains an article of faith in the Foreign Service.

Security, or the lack of it, is another CIA gripe. It is bad enough to cope with institutional flaws that make State cover so transparent that local employees of an embassy can identify an Agency employee even before he reports for duty. It is worse to have [one's] cover blown by Foreign Service people in casual conversation among themselves or with outsiders—unfortunately a common occurrence, but not surprising in an environment where spotting the spook is still a common parlor game. Part of this stems from genuine uncertainty as to how FSOs should talk and act in relation to CIA. And CIA itself offers them little or no guidance on the question.

The State Department's Foreign Service Institute now gives a four-day course in intelligence and national security which, though useful to the people who take it, is not likely to approach the intelligence-related issues which FSOs encounter overseas. Nor will CIA make a serious effort to bridge the gap. In the field, the ambassador and his deputy will be told whatever they want to know about the CIA station's operations and interests; the rest of the mission, including officers who deal regularly with CIA on specific matters, remains largely in the dark. Junior and middle grade FSOs who badly need some perspective and understanding of what CIA is all about, and who might be more cooperative if they had it, are left to pick up what they can and imagine the rest.

It would be wrong to assume that all problems can simply be talked out. The overstuffed mission and the encyclopedic diplomatic list are a pain in everybody's neck. Misconceptions die hard. Both State and CIA are guilty of loading the list with people who have no business being there. The presence of CIA officers under State cover does not, as widely touted, hurt the State officer's promotion prospects. Nor do CIA personnel get promoted more rapidly than the latter. In the long run a Foreign Service career offers much greater material reward.

Money and the uses thereof will always be a source of contention. CIA is not rolling in money, and Agency officers overseas do not spend it as if it were going out of style. State uses its money differently, concentrating on representation at the senior level of its missions, with obvious emphasis on the ambassador. CIA concentrates its spending in directions that are or should be operationally productive. Stations are rarely in a position to splurge, although there have been some egregious departures from that norm in years past. Almost all ambassadors and chiefs of station who do their jobs effectively, especially at large posts, have to reach into their own pockets to cope with unreimbursed representational expenses.

The problem of trust noted earlier, the uncertainty as to what CIA is really doing, is subjective and resists easy solution. Even close friendships between State and CIA personnel, evolving over years of parallel career development and professional collaboration, fail to quell suspicions derived from ancient specters. The State Department's urge to regain control of its communications, one of many wild horses unleashed by the Macomber Report of 1971, reflects that nagging feeling that its telegrams are not private. The feeling is ill-founded. CIA does not read embassy messages. Nor are station chiefs looking for ways to circumvent the ambassador. The latter is recognized as The Boss; his authority is understood and respected, and station chiefs spend a major portion of their working lives trying to satisfy his needs. Once, years ago, Robert Kennedy asked Director John McCone what instruction CIA gave its station chiefs on how to deal with ambassadors. McCone's instant response was, "Genuflect!"

In turn, ambassadorial attitudes toward CIA's presence in their missions vary greatly—from consuming interest on the one hand, to utter boredom or barely concealed distaste on the other. The ambassador naturally sets the tone for the mission as a whole. The station chief too can affect it significantly, depending on his personal competence, his presence and his common sense. From time to time a less than felicitous combination emerges, and the results can be unpleasant for everyone. In other missions there is bliss among the seniors and open warfare at the working levels. Fortunately, from the extreme where people are barely civil to each other and backbiting replaces cooperation, we can point to the other where station and embassy meld their respective capabilities and perform superbly as an integral unit. The explanation is leadership, not always in plentiful supply.

And so after thirty years of struggle among people said to rank with the government's best and brightest, the war continues. Officially, of course, people are working on the problem, as the bureaucrats like to put it. Each side professes to understand the other's needs and concerns. Both sides are in effect willing to settle for the status quo as the alternative to really closing with the issues that divide and irritate. There is a certain detachment on the part of the negotiators, whose daily chores devolve on the minutiae of State/CIA administration at the Washington end. Curiously, the latter are rarely drawn from the ranks of those who have the greater stake in the proceedings. On the State side, liaison with CIA on the mundane aspects of cover, slotting, grades, titles and finance has traditionally been conducted by the Department's own administrators, most of them Washington-based people in civil service status. FSOs whose careers are overseas and who have fought the good fight for years with CIA in the field avoid such jobs. So too on the CIA side: the Agency's Directorate of Operations officers view assignment to cover liaison [liaison about cover] as utter disaster, the end of a career.

Jobs no one else wants often prove satisfying to those who are thrust into them. Thus over the years State/CIA liaison has settled into a comfortable groove where the motto is *don't make waves*—a few, okay, but don't overdo it. Advice most often given is try to solve the problem in the field. The field, naturally, prefers to see them resolved in Washington. And the last thing Washington wants is to have to seek arbitration. If in a given overseas mission the embassy and station are at odds over, say, local political reporting and the operational activity that produces it, and *if* there is an attempt at the Washington end to resolve the issue, the odds are that the decision—assuming it attains that exalted status—will reach each party from its respective head office, and as likely as not will be open to divergent interpretations. For one thing, the State Department does not like to tell an ambassador what to do, particularly in a hassle with CIA. CIA in turn is adept at working out what it tells itself is an understanding with State, then telling the station chief to work out the details with the ambassador. Everybody is then back on square one. Strangely enough, this often proves effective—a tribute to the common sense of ambassadors and their deputies, and to the survival instincts of the abler chiefs of station. Sometimes it works very badly, and important tasks remain undone with potentially disastrous consequences.

The appointment of former Ambassador Frank Carlucci as Deputy Director of Central Intelligence in 1978 stands out as perhaps the most constructive single move in the history of State/CIA relations. His credentials were obviously of the best, and there was every reason to hope that thenceforth things would improve. It is no derogation from his performance to say that they have not.[1] They are simply beyond one man's ability to rectify. Among the issues, the most malleable are those that impinge directly on operations. The others—and they encompass most aspects of the cover problem—are rooted in the unreconcilable administrative barriers between State and CIA. The only way out is through elimination of the barriers.

Some years ago a proposal aimed in that direction was submitted to the Murphy Commission on Governmental Reorganization. It called for a *unified personnel system* for the foreign affairs agencies, designed to eliminate rivalries and provide a mechanism to support all non-military overseas operations. In effect, the channels through which the State Department, the Central Intelligence Agency, the International Communications [United States Information] Agency and the Agency for International Development now recruit, train and deploy their junior offices would be replaced by a single body. It would be controlled not by the administrators but jointly by the operating elements of the respective agencies in order to ensure an effective response to the needs of

---

1. The author retired in mid-1978 and may not be aware of changes since that time.

the professional services with their unique overseas orientation. The recruits would enter the government through a common pipeline, and receive the same basic training and indoctrination. They would in due course choose their own career tracks and be guided into them, with possibilities for future rotation and cross-fertilization of experience and ideas. The intelligence track would be one facet of the larger whole, and with ingenuity it could be made at least as secure as the existing system.

Now legislation would almost certainly be necessary for such a violent assault on the feudal rights of the bureaucratic establishment. If the Murphy Commission in its wisdom ever looked seriously at the proposal, nothing emerged to reflect its interest. When circulated in select precincts of both State and CIA, the idea provoked surprising endorsement from individual FSOs, but a negative reaction from the majority. CIA people took a dim view of it. The known devil is always preferable.

Today the same pattern would doubtless prevail. CIA is still traumatized by its experiences of the past five years, and resistant to any change. The State Department, comfortable after passage of the new Foreign Service Act and well protected by its union, the American Foreign Service Association, would see little to gain. The skirmishes of the *secret war* are thus fated to continue at least awhile longer.

15.

In this article, the Directorate of Operations pats itself on the back for finding that its consumers do indeed like what they get. Johnson's contention (later echoed in part by Tovar) that this symbiosis may not really be healthy for either the humint collectors or the consumers is simply ignored. Thus do hegemonic bureaucratic ideologies hold sway, for good or ill.

Assessing DDO Human Source Reporting

FENTON BABCOCK

Sherman Kent's call for close and continuing contact between intelligence producers and consumers came in the CIA's formative years. It is appropriate to sound it again as centralized management of the intelligence community takes on new form and importance and new life. In recent years, the Directorate of Operations (DO) has been making a particularly conscious effort to get closer to the people who use its products as it seeks to produce better intelligence, on a wider variety of subjects, with fewer resources. The DO has gotten direct payoff from this development; hundreds of consumers and users of DO reporting have found benefit in responding to the DO's techniques for getting their evaluative feedback; and closer communication has brought some problems and solutions that could well have relevance at the intelligence community level.

This is a record of producer-consumer contacts that have settled into a well-defined relationship that is, in Sherman Kent's terms, both proper and effective. As a result, progress has been made toward the goal of producing valuable reporting from economical exploitation of resources. Much remains to be done, however, in relating collection results to resources in a systematic way. Human source reporting does not defy centralized management; it simply requires that the development of systems for this purpose proceed with extra care and attention to the human and security factors involved. This applies to the collection and production of HUMINT as well as the assessment of its effect, impact, and value. The DO record of improvement in its evaluation system is one of careful pioneering. It has involved:

a. increasing the field collector's responsibility for pre-selection of intelligence information according to its projected value;

Fenton Babcock, "Assessing DDO Human Source Reporting," *Studies in Intelligence*, vol. 22, no. 3 (Fall 1978), pp. 51–57. Originally classified "Secret."

b. shifting emphasis in the headquarters reports officer's role from that of intelligence processor to that of quality control specialist responsible for providing reliable value readings and projections to the field; and

c. developing communication with consumers and users so as to increase the regularity, scope, and depth of evaluative feedback for collection guidance, resource allocation, and budgetary purposes.

Value Assessment in the Field

Historically and typically, the DO reports evaluation process begins in the field with the quality control applied by the individual case officer overseas, or the Domestic Collection Division (DCD) intelligence officer in the United States, under the supervision of their chiefs. The important task of the field collector has already been well described in terms of fundamental responsibility and technique by Bruce L. Pechan in "The Collector's Role in Evaluation."[1] In brief, the case officer must provide up-to-date evaluation of his source's reliability, and as collector he is also responsible for giving a current account of changeable circumstances surrounding the acquisition of the information being reported. In addition to these evaluative inputs, the field collector must also apply his judgment on the relevance, importance, and timeliness of the information obtained. If he kills his own draft report, his judgment is usually final, and his right to do so is virtually uncontested. Indeed, he is enjoined not to process information that he confidently judges to be marginal.

In recent years there has been fairly steady increase in the percentage of the DO's overseas field reports that are received in cable form for dissemination. Much of that reporting is held briefly (at the field's request) for special review by the controlling area division, but it arrives in finished form designed for consumer use in response to expressed requirements. Headquarters evaluation may result in stopping dissemination or adding commentary which is clearly labelled as such and differentiated from any field comment or source comment the report may contain. Field comment rarely addresses the basic value of the information reported, for that is implicit in the finished form of the report. Determination of the value of a disseminated report is properly left to headquarters, where a good basis for comparison with other information exists and direct reading from Washington consumers can be obtained. Intelligence information of a largely tactical nature is frequently passed by the field collector to the U.S. mission directly concerned without formal dissemination. In those cases, the local consumers of such "actionable intelligence," on narcotics for example, are obviously most accessible to the field collector for his evaluation purposes.

1. *Studies*, V/3, 37–47. [Reprinted here, pp. 99–107.]

Field evaluation as a basic responsibility is similar in the case of DCD's domestic voluntary collection.[2] Only a small percentage of DCD's reporting is processed in cable form, but it is nevertheless prepared by the field intelligence officers in finished form, ready, in their judgment, for dissemination in response to legitimate need. Again, the individual collector is acting as initial evaluator and is expected to equip himself constantly through the reading of available collection guidance, standing and spot requirements, and collateral material such as finished intelligence.

In recent years, the DO has been pushing and improving its training courses on reporting for both clandestine and DCD collection officers in order to sharpen not only their processing capabilities but also their evaluative skills and judgment. There has been direct payoff in terms of quality control exercised by the field collector on his own and his responsiveness to the headquarters quality control measures described below. The best evidence of this is the substantial decline recorded in the Directorate's total volume of reporting over the past few years and the assessed general increase in quality relative to the total number of reports produced. What makes this assessment possible is the advent of truly systematic collection of consumer feedback by a Directorate-level evaluation staff.

Value Assessment in the Headquarters Divisions

Evaluative comment to the field collector is routinely made by the operating area divisions on nearly all clandestine reports that are published. DCD similarly sends comments to the domestic field offices concerned on most of the reports they produce. In both cases the comment made and the grade given each report are supposed to be, and often are, directly reflective of consumer evaluation obtained by the headquarters reports or desk officers. In general, such contacts are limited to obtaining timely feedback on current reporting. Most such comment is obtained by telephone, but often the desk-level officers consult directly with one or more analyst consumers of the report. Consistency in this desk contact procedure is spotty, however, and increasingly so as it extends to the analyst consumers outside the CIA headquarters building and to the users at the policy and program level.

The grades given to DO reports by headquarters are weighted to reward quality and discourage reporting that is of minor value. In 1974 the criteria for grading reports were standardized throughout the Directorate. By 1978, however, it had become clear that the area divisions were applying the "stan-

---

2. The term "domestic voluntary collection" is introduced here as a substitute for the misleading expression "overt collection," as applied to the Domestic Collection Division of the DO.

dardized" grades with different degrees of strictness, while DCD had developed its own quite different set of grades. In general, grade Category V, for reports that "contribute substantially to an identified national intelligence need," has been overused. In part, this is because the next lower grade available under the existing system is Category I, for reports that "fall near the lower limit of acceptability." The result has been inflated use of the V grade. This, combined with the differing standards of application among the divisions, prevents use of grading results for central management purposes.

Within the various divisions, the grading of reports has generally served its original purpose of improving quality relative to quantity. Judicious use by the divisions of the higher grades, on the whole, has contributed to this pattern of improvement; the grade X (10) is applied to reports making a "major contribution to a national level need," and XX (20) to a report that is "outstanding in its significance to the well-being of the U.S." It is on the assignment of these higher grades that consumer influence often is brought directly to bear. The biweekly grading sessions on China reporting, for example, are regularly attended by NFAC analysts who comment specifically on the grades being assigned.

Value Assessment at the Directorate Level

Complementing and following up on this *ad hoc* communication with consumers of the Directorate's human source reporting is the systematic process carried out by the Evaluation Group, a direct staff element of the Deputy Director for Operations. This group makes regular, personal contact with a cross-section of key consumers and users of the DO reporting throughout the intelligence community and beyond. The immediate Washington customers for both the DO's foreign clandestine and DCD collection products range from specialized analysts in NFAC, State/INR, and DIA to departmental policy action officers. The ultimate users of the DO's intelligence information are the policymakers of the Cabinet and the National Security Council, the heads of U.S. missions and military commands, and the U.S. military R & D project managers throughout the country.

The 500 key Washington consumers and users who are interviewed quarterly by members of the Evaluation Group have been remarkably responsive to this evaluation effort, many of them recognizing that regular, active and responsible participation in the process pays them direct dividends. In anticipation of the Evaluation Group's direct periodic contact, many of the analyst consumers and policy-level users not only read the DO reporting with a somewhat different perspective, but many save up specific comment in mental or written note form. In the interviews they are called upon to react to monthly computer listings of the reports by title. In this way, memory of a certain report often serves as an initial indicator of effect.

The interview becomes successful, however, only when the customer spells out his actual use, or non-use, of an individual report or the reports in an identifiable stream. When circumstances call for it, he or she will be asked to explain as exactly as possible how a certain report affected the writing of an item of finished intelligence or a U.S. policy action, or how it may have frustrated the customer, or failed to meet requirements. In the interviewing, the Evaluation Group contact specialists have been successful in getting a mix of candidly critical and complimentary feedback because of the personal, substantive nature of the dialogues they sustain with the customers. Thorough preparation for the interviews is made through prior reading of all the reports being evaluated along with the pertinent operational messages, plus other agency reporting, finished intelligence on the subjects being pursued, and open-source information that bears on them. The subjects covered in interviews are: the "hard targets" (USSR, PRC, Eastern Europe, Cuba, North Korea, Indochina); some 50 non-Communist world countries; and international functional topics, including economics, nuclear proliferation, terrorism, and narcotics.

Significant comments on individual reports, critical or complimentary, are passed on to the collecting divisions to complement the results of their own earlier *ad hoc* contact with some of the same customers on some of the reports. Usually, the source of a particularly candid comment made to the Evaluation Group officer on a report, or a collection effort, is not revealed to the division. The retrospective evaluation obtained by the Evaluation Group is frequently passed on farther by the operating desks and reports officers to the collector in the field. The independent character of the Evaluation Group's feedback from customers often complements very effectively the earlier feedback obtained by the division at the time of a report's dissemination. In a significant number of instances the value of a report will have risen or fallen substantially since it was assessed by a consumer on a current basis.

It is the continuum of feedback and its cumulative weight that contribute so effectively to desk-level or field decisions on reward or termination of a reporting source and to their review of progress and direction in individual collection operations. The customers appreciate this pattern of discreet and effective use of their comments, and many have come to feel personally involved in an evaluation process that they like and respect. They and their supervisors judge their time to be well spent in responding to requests for current evaluation, and they value and use the privileged channel to the Deputy for Operations and his collection managers that the Evaluation Group provides.

The results of the Evaluation Group's interviews have other uses after they are compiled and synthesized in narrative form every six months. Combined with statistics prepared by the Group, the customer commentary provides the DDO with a semi-annual independent evaluation of the Directorate's foreign intelligence production. The DDO uses portions of this material frequently in responding to oversight inquiries, and a significant portion of it feeds into the human source collection part of the CIA's annual budget presentation. The narratives are sent to the collecting divisions, which use them in overall collection guidance and send specific extracts to the field stations concerned.

A Careful Approach to Quantification of Value

The feedback achieved through personal contact with consumers and users of DO reporting stands in sharp contrast to the unsuccessful use of cover sheet questionnaires in the past, which were designed to bring a degree of quantification to the evaluation process. Quantification of the unquantifiable in human source reporting is not now being attempted by the DO. The use of cover sheet questionnaires on approximately one-third of the clandestine reports disseminated came to an end in the mid-1970's. By then, many analyst consumers had been turned off by that mechanistic technique for obtaining evaluation, and the unreliable results had fallen into disuse within the DO. The Domestic Collection Division still uses such forms for some of its Science and Technology reporting but mainly for obtaining follow-up requirements and direct collection guidance, as opposed to evaluation.

The Evaluation Group's system of direct, personal contact with customers has, however, been used in a measured approach to value quantification. In 1976 the Evaluation Group's personalized approach brought consumer identification of certain streams of DO reporting that pointed toward dollar value impact among the ultimate users of the intelligence information in the U.S. military R & D community. From DIA and the service command intelligence staffs, the trail led to many U.S. military sub-commands, their foreign intelligence officers, and on to individual R & D project managers in a variety of military and civilian installations and institutions throughout the country. Tracing the reporting through its use in finished intelligence proved to be no problem, for the same warm response was encountered among the ultimate users of the DO human source information as had been the case in the Washington community of customers. Most quickly came to recognize that the DO needed to include in its budget preparation and resource allocation processes what *evidence* it could of actual effect, impact, and value in its reporting product. The tangible benefit feedback thus obtained by the Evaluation Group over the past two years has identified utility gains associated with certain disseminated information, including beneficial redirection of some U.S. funds in very large amounts and some actual dollar savings. In many cases, the evidence of impact has included information on certain U.S. military vulnerabilities and capabilities that carried an obligation for the Evaluation Group to give it the most careful protection.

A few examples will indicate the scope and magnitude of human source report impact that have been certified under the Evaluation Group's tangible benefit feedback program. In the course of several years, DO reports provided information on Soviet electronics countermeasure capabilities and tactics that transformed the U.S. perception of that threat and led to very extensive beneficial change in certain U.S. equipment and troop training procedures. In other instances, the DO's human source reporting has combined critically with the results of technical collection, often providing the confidence factor required by analysts before publishing their findings in vital areas of research and development. This has been the case in many fields including naval weaponry, electronic warfare, aircraft, and missiles. In most cases, very large amounts of R & D funds have been involved, with the cumulative total related directly to DO intelligence information running into billions of dollars. Specific correlation between this human source reporting and dollar value impact has not been pressed by the Evaluation Group in most instances during its personal contacts throughout the U.S. military R & D community. This is because the direct nature of the impact has been so readily certified by nearly all of the key customers involved, and because of methodological difficulties that are encountered in moving the last mile toward quantification of value.[3]

Conscious of the fundamental difficulty in quantifying the value of human source reporting, the Evaluation Group has moved carefully in extending its effort in this regard beyond the tangible benefit feedback program. At one extreme the Group highlights for the DDO many instances of reporting where intangible benefit of considerable significance has been identified by policy users. A good example here is frequent reporting on bilateral or multilateral negotiations involving the United States. Cabinet-level officials have been quick to certify direct, heavy impact of DO intelligence upon negotiations they have conducted, particularly in the field of international economics. Similar hard evidence of impact, however intangible, has been readily forthcoming with regard to nuclear proliferation. Here, policy users have several times been able to trace for us the connection between the DO intelligence they received—often a combination of clandestine and DCD reporting—and successful U.S. diplomatic demarches made to foreign governments.

3. Max S. Oldham, "A Value for Information," *Studies*, XII/2, 29.

At the other end of the Evaluation Group's quantification spectrum lie the tentative steps taken so far toward possible scalar valuation of the Directorate's human source reporting. So far, this has involved learning about the efforts made under professional guidance at the Department of Health, Education, and Welfare, for example, in placing numerical values on the intangible results of some of its programs.[4]

The Evaluation Group's contact specialists have undertaken some systematic use of specific value criteria in their interviews on an experimental basis. This has been done with a view to bringing outside methodological expertise to bear in analyzing the results, for possible use in moving toward limited quantification where it is feasible. The Evaluation Group's approach to the quantification of value in its human source reporting has been one of alert carefulness, and the appropriateness of this approach has been confirmed by the experience of other collection managers in the intelligence community.

Along with its narrative accounts of key customer feedback in synthesized form, and the certifiable evidence of impact and benefit noted above, the Evaluation Group's comprehensive semi-annual production reviews have included various statistical arrays designed to give the DDO semi-quantitative evaluation of the DO reporting product. These have included recorded use of reports in finished intelligence; responsiveness to Key Intelligence Questions; and responsiveness to those national-level information needs identified in the course of FOCUS reviews (carried out by the National Intelligence Officers and the DCI's Human Resources Committee), which have been accepted by the DO as suitable for clandestine collection and levied as requirements on the field. In addition, the Evaluation Group has tracked reporting responsiveness to portions of DCID 1/2 and some of the draft National Intelligence Topics, on an experimental basis.

Relevance at the Intelligence Community Level

Many of the Evaluation Group's regular contacts have sought to use it as a channel for levying requirements and giving collection guidance. Although generally discouraged by the interviewers, this type of customer feedback is recorded by the Group when it is evaluative in nature. Most of the consumer analysts know well that other, regular channels exist for requirements and guidance, but a dismaying number simply don't know exactly what those channels are or how to use them. A substantial number of customers have felt frustrated in their use of regular, formal channels over the years, and have overloaded the informal channels that exist or stopped using either effectively.

4. See "Effectiveness Assessment in Government," by Lynn P. Madden (Management Sciences Training Center, U.S. Civil Service Commission).

The Evaluation Group's experience over several years has shown, for example, that the present system of communication between some U.S. military end-users and CIA's collectors of human source intelligence is not adequate. In many instances, the fact that certain human source information, if collected within a certain time frame, could have tremendous impact on very high-cost U.S. military programs has just not found its way through the existing communication circuit. That circuit contains various filters that serve the good purpose of preventing tasking overload, but they are counterproductive when they stop the kind of directional feedback cited above from reaching critical points. The present system for U.S. military tasking of human source collection lacks a reliable, centralized tuning capability. Clear beneficial results have come from careful correlation between HUMINT collection effort and ultimate potential yield in this realm of very large U.S. military payoff; but they have often stemmed only from special task force approaches or crusades carried out by individual users.

This tasking-type feedback on relative priority among customers' needs for information from human source collection has made up an integral part of the semi-annual production reviews prepared by the Evaluation Group for the DDO. For the division reports officer, who may upon occasion get too close to the intelligence information he is processing, and the operations officer who may get overly bound up in his particular collection effort, this type of directional feedback from key customers can be very useful. This is particularly true, of course, where all-source comparison by the customers brings out undesirable duplication of collection effort and helps to identify those areas of intelligence need where human source collection can contribute best, if not uniquely.

Reliability in consumer and end-user feedback on the effect, impact, and relative value of intelligence information depends much upon the nature of the relationship between the collector and these customers. If it is a proper relationship, both systematic and personalized, then built-in dangers such as human error and bias can be dealt with professionally.[5] Statistical support to evaluation and the goal of quantification can, as a result, be kept on the right perspective. With the array of techniques now in use, and direct customer participation steadily adding scope and depth to evaluation, the DO can proceed with some confidence in matching its shrinking resources to the increasing demands of our time.

Could other intelligence agencies and the community as a whole benefit from the DO's experience? Several agencies have been interested enough to

5. See Richards J. Heuer, Jr., "Cognitive Biases: Problems in Hindsight Analysis," *Studies*, XXII/2. [Reprinted here, pp. 333–343.]

request detailed briefings on the DO system, and a community seminar is being organized on the problem of quantification in assessing human source reporting.

As the DO has found, close consumer contact, with evidence of results obtained therefrom, is the best way to make intelligence consumers and users clear on both the potentialities and the limitations of human source collection, as compared to other forms. Good, regular communication on through to the field, by extension, has also helped many customers better assess, sort out, and articulate their intelligence needs and priorities. Such, then, can be the mutually beneficial results of the proper, effective relationship between intelligence and its users that Sherman Kent called for some thirty years ago.

V.

The Analysis Function

16.

Here are the nuts and bolts of some CIA in-house reference services (which nowadays would be largely computerized).

What Basic Intelligence Seeks to Do

JOSEPH W. MARTIN

This paper seeks to open a discussion of basic intelligence doctrine: that is, of the objectives this type of intelligence should aim at and of the standards by which effective performance in it should be judged. This kind of discussion—which, I believe, was one of the things *Studies in Intelligence* was originally founded for—is not likely to end in full agreement but, as experience with other types of intelligence has shown, does offer the prospect of reducing the area of disagreement and making the product more sophisticated and more useful to the consumer.

The files of *Studies in Intelligence* to date show a near absence of papers taking this approach to the subject, though there have been a number of good factual surveys of particular basic intelligence programs. The omission is probably due to the topic's being widely considered lacking in interest rather than lacking in importance. "Basic intelligence" is denominated one of the three main categories of intelligence in Sherman Kent's *Strategic Intelligence* (i.e., the "basic descriptive element" along with "current reporting" and "estimates of the speculative evaluative element"), and the community's principal basic intelligence program, the National Intelligence Survey, has in the past year or so undergone extensive examination and review—the most recent of a number of such comprehensive reviews. Considerable attention has also been given to the statutory basis of the NIS and to its administrative aspects.

The present paper is not concerned with matters of statutory authority or administration but with intelligence doctrine. Since it seeks to open a dialogue on this subject, it begins necessarily on an elementary level and states somewhat dogmatically a number of definitions and main propositions as a basis for discussion. The value of the effort will depend very considerably on its success

Joseph W. Martin, "What Basic Intelligence Seeks to Do," *Studies in Intelligence,* vol. 14, no. 2 (Fall 1970), pp. 103–113. Originally classified "Confidential."

in stimulating expressions of informed opinion from other concerned persons—those concerned as consumers perhaps more than those concerned as producers.

Part of the difficulty the "basic descriptive element" has always labored under may be a simple matter of nomenclature. To some ears, the term "basic intelligence" sounds so elementary as to be quite without interest; to others, it tends to have the slightly moralistic connotations of "essential" and to offend by its seeming pretentiousness. But the concept itself is simple enough and should be non-controversial. It is perhaps better to start with the concept of "the reference document," a concept which rightly puts the emphasis less on the information itself than on a user's need for the information. Reasons for including any given set of data in a reference document are essentially pragmatic: (1) it is information likely to be needed by many persons for many purposes ("central" information might be a more accurate term than "basic"); and (2) it is information capable of being so organized that it can be turned to readily. Essentially the reference document is a money-saver because, human memory being what it is, the alternative to one reference work serving many people is often a series of *ad hoc* documents each serving a half-dozen or so.

A modern industrial civilization could not operate without a wide variety of reference documents—with forms and contents varying widely according to the special concerns of their intended users. *The Morning Telegraph*, the racing man's Bible, is very different from *The Wall Street Transcript*, a weekly compilation of financial evaluations from various informed sources—and only a person specialized in both horse racing and corporate finance could come close to determining which is really "better." The continuing financial solvency of each publication is, however, a rough indication that each is satisfying a valid consumer need.

The subject of special concern to the US intelligence community— international affairs—is no less complicated than horse racing or corporate finance, and is considerably more difficult to deal with in an official reference document. One difficulty is that the subject of international affairs is less sharply separable from the rest of the universe and, partly because of this, the prospective readership much harder to envisage and define. The man who turns to *The Morning Telegraph* or *The Wall Street Transcript* may be presumed by the producer to be already knowledgeable about horse racing or corporate finance and reasonably clear on what he is looking for.

Not so with the man who turns to a government reference document for information on South Ruritania or East Parastatia. This presumed reader may be either an expert on East Parastatian affairs who wishes to check the exact age of its ruling general and the relative standing of its three most important export commodities or, at the other extreme, a US general's briefing officer who is not quite sure just where East Parastatia is but who within the next hour must give his boss a fill-in about an attempt still in progress to assassinate the Parastatian dictator and seize the government. Or, less dramatically, the reader may be a civilian or military official about to proceed to a new assignment in East Parastatia—or possibly at the capital of its bitter rival, West Parastatia. Some of these various readers may be presumed to have ready access to such non-government reference books as the World Almanac, the Statesman's Yearbook or the Encyclopaedia Britannica. Each reader, moreover, will naturally want to find the Parastatian information important to him with a minimum of dilution or delay caused by the presence of the other reader's Parastatian data.

A second difficulty for the reference work on international affairs is more serious. A good non-governmental work like the Statesman's Yearbook will meet most needs for purely factual non-classified data about any given country. But legitimate government needs also include military and political data which are normally classified and, more difficult still, go beyond mere hard factual data to involve judgments and evaluations of complex situations from the standpoint of US security interests. More important than just the size of East Parastatia's armed forces or the nature of their equipment are their loyalties to the ruling dictator, their relations with the traditional political parties or the labor unions and their prevailing orientation toward Moscow or Washington. Questions such as these go beyond the capabilities of a privately produced reference work and indeed tax those of the government as a whole. In really critical or fluid situations they are in part the subjects of national estimates, and even in relatively routine situations there is an evident advantage for the US official in being able to turn to a reference document which is coordinated national intelligence.

Criteria of Excellence

What, then, is excellence in a reference document? I would like to propose three main criteria: systematic in its fundamental organization, clear and precise in its detailed presentation, realistic in what it seeks to include. Thus blandly put, these criteria probably attract little dissent; controversy arises when their implications are more extensively explored. All three criteria rest on the premise that the essential problem of the reference document is not recondite research but effective communication.

A reference document needs to be systematically organized primarily in the sense that it is part of a system; that its producers have recognized that their task is not just to manufacture a product but to provide a continuing service. The reader consulting a reference work naturally needs assurance of its validity but, second only to this, he needs to find the desired information quickly and, if possible, be given a little guidance on where to find further data on the same subject. And—a point often overlooked—he is also helped by some prior assurance that the reference work will be there to consult. Meeting these varied needs for a wide variety of readers necessarily requires a considerable degree of standardization in the way a reference work is organized internally; it also requires the external organization that will ensure the work's remaining in print and being adequately disseminated. It is these characteristics of organization, not just the nature of the contents, which establish the reference work as a distinct genus.

The importance of system for a reference document is easy to underestimate or even ridicule, since no standard plan of organization is ever likely to fit a particular case precisely. At any given moment, moreover, there is also certain to be a more exciting way to tell the story than the way the reference document does it. Most of us can remember from our college days at least one lecture in which the speaker held his audience spellbound by starting with a very minor detail and skipping around in a seemingly chaotic fashion, yet covering by the end of the hour all relevant aspects of the subject with a vividness and memorability absent from more conventional presentations. But however successful as an occasional teaching technique, such a way of organizing information is no model for a reference document. Here the readers must be presumed to be seeking plain information and not entertainment, and a substantial proportion of them to be seeking not the total picture but specific facts or judgments about some part of it.

Another and more topical kind of illustration may also be pertinent. During the course of any given year, the Washington visits of foreign chiefs of state and the corresponding trips of US dignitaries abroad are likely to produce a number of excellent intelligence memoranda on the countries concerned—memos which, along with the very current matter addressed to the immediate occasion, also contain much sound basic intelligence often more attractively stated than that in a standard reference work. Yet a memo of this sort, no matter how perceptively its basic intelligence is presented, is no real substitute for a standard reference document on the country, since (a) it will probably go out of print soon after its original dissemination and (b) having been originally designed for one particular occasion, it is unlikely to be ideally organized for a number of quite different purposes at later points in time. The general nature and influence of one of the country's opposition parties may, for example, be given very glancing attention in a "backgrounder" on its president's visit to Washington, but this may be just the subject on which a subsequent reader would want a quick evaluation.

"Systematically organized" of course includes having the data appear in a pattern that most people consulting the document will find compatible with their own particular interests in turning to it. For works on international affairs the most useful initial category is generally agreed to be countries—rather than economic commodities or weapons or diseases—but there seems to be no firm rule on the order of categories within a given country. Uniformity in treating widely different countries is neither necessary nor desirable, but the reader does have a right to expect a certain standardization among reference documents in the same series and a plain indication in the table of contents of the pattern being followed in that book, an indication couched in terms immediately familiar to him. The complaint has more than once been made regarding the NIS General Survey, for example, that "manpower" as a sub-section of "sociology" is a somewhat forbidding category to confront a man who wants to find out in a hurry how powerful the country's trade unions are and whether they have any extensive record of Communist infiltration.

The second criterion of excellence—clarity and precision in the more detailed presentation of data—is of course always accepted in principle, but frequently with insufficient appreciation of what must be done to meet it adequately. It is too often forgotten that the primary task of intelligence is to get a fact or judgment from the inside of a specialist's brain to the inside of a layman's, not simply to state it in words which a fellow specialist can certify as not irrelevant and not untrue.

The user's needs are positive; whether he is novice or old hand on the country, it will do him little good to encounter either bland generalities or esoteric allusions. The novice will not be much helped by a delicate reference to declining Communist influence in East Parastatia based on the tacit assumption that "everybody knows" there was a pro-Communist regime there in the late 1950s. The old hand can only be exasperated by being told that the country experienced trade and payments difficulties in the mid-1960s, when he is trying to check on how serious these difficulties were and whether the critical year was 1964 or 1966. To convey the needed information effectively to two such different readers requires a kind of flexibility and imagination which not all analysts have. The producer of reference works, moreover, should write in the expectation of his product's remaining usable not merely for a week or two but perhaps for several years, and he must do his job without the psychological boost which people often receive from dealing in headline material ("It's happening right *now*"). Furthermore, the complexity of his subjects gives him no valid license to be ponderous and murky in his treatment of them; it creates rather a special need for his language to be crisp and clear.

The third (and most easily misunderstood) criterion of excellence in a reference document is how realistic it is in what it seeks to include. The critical questions to be asked are really two—though many people stop with the first, which simply inquires what are the central facts and judgments about a country which a US official might want to know before taking action. The corollary question—necessary but often overlooked—is to inquire which of these facts and judgments can be effectively communicated through this particular reference work, given its agreed size, processing time, revision schedule and the like.

Since the canon of relevant intelligence for the senior US official obviously includes much current reporting and estimative material, there is a natural tendency to stretch reference works to take in much of these categories also. I see no absolute objection in principle to doing this, but at least two powerful limitations in practice. One is mechanical and almost inescapable: unless organized like a newspaper throughout, a reference work cannot hope to stay abreast of the news ticker. Everyone accepts this fact intellectually, but the dream dies hard of having a single document which will provide all the answers for, say, the rushed and harried briefing officer suddenly confronted with the attempted coup in East Parastatia. A reference work on the country which is only three weeks old will naturally be more convenient for him than one three years old, but it will in itself provide no guarantee of accuracy, since the events he is chiefly concerned with are probably those of the past three days or three hours. In a world of unlimited intelligence resources one might seek to ease his difficulties by decreeing that every reference book in the series be updated every three months, but a more realistic approach is to insist that each work be so arranged as to make its relevant information quickly accessible to the uninitiated reader and, if possible, provide him with leads to more detailed and current publications on the subject.

The other limitation derives from a reference work's need for a certain detachment and perspective such as is extremely hard to attain regarding particular events still in progress or judgments still in controversy. By and large, it is probably more useful for the reference document to avoid very recent detail and to confine itself to those judgments which have become generally accepted in the intelligence community—what is sometimes pejoratively described as "the conventional wisdom." It seems to me important, however, for the reference work to make sure that these evaluations are within the conventions of the present, not the past; to insist that its successive editions do not simply go on repeating the evaluations of, say, the Stalin era in tone if not in explicit statement.

Just which central facts and received judgments can be efficiently included in a given reference document must probably remain a matter of informed human judgment, at least till machinery for obtaining meaningful consumer responses becomes more highly developed than at present. Nor is it really an economical use of limited resources to try and determine revision schedules just by formula, i.e., strictly by elapsed time since the last edition. For reference works consisting almost entirely of statistical resumes and lists of officeholders, this can be a quite valid method; most statistics are issued on an annual basis, and life expectancy tables apply to government officials as to anyone else. But for more complicated reference works concerned with basic evaluations of larger political, economic and social entities, the strict elapsed-time formula is likely to prove crude and inefficient. It is actual events, not the mere removal of leaves from the calendar, which causes such reference works to go out of date. One country of course changes more rapidly than another, and the same country may change more rapidly in one decade than in another. To cite a somewhat extreme example, an NIS General Survey on Cuba produced in late 1958 (i.e., just before Castro) would have been more out of date in its basic evaluations by mid-1960 than one produced at the same time on the Netherlands would have been by mid-1970.

Naturally, every user prefers a recently published reference work to an old one, just as he prefers his car to be this year's model and his office to be one with a fine view from the window—and the prestige of having such preferences gratified may in certain circumstances have a validity of its own. But, to continue the analogy, it is not realistic planning to equate such gratification with economy of transportation or the most efficient way of conducting the office's business.

The Question of Importance

At this point it may be asked: granted that these are indeed the proper standards of excellence in a reference work, why is having excellent reference works a matter of any importance? I believe there are at least three reasons why.

The first reason might be considered budgetary, in that it concerns the most efficient use of limited resources. To state the principle figuratively: it is of course well recognized that the very best rifles for big game hunting are still handmade (and these, besides their greater precision of operation, are also an addition to the user's social prestige), but for most workaday uses of weaponry, the world long ago learned that the unromantic assembly-line product would do. In terms of intelligence production in a period of growing budgetary austerity, the question may well arise as to how many of the needs for background memos might not be met by a standard reference work and a few updating paragraphs rather than by a whole new handmade product. (I am speaking, of course, only about *ad hoc intelligence* memos—not, for example, about the necessarily custom-made paper on what policy lines to pursue toward General X's dictatorship in East Parastatia, but of an intelligence memo describing the general status of East Parastatia after 18 months of the General's rule.) By no means all needs for background information can be met by supplemented reference documents, but with the rising competitive demand for research which really breaks new ground, the question of how many is likely to be asked with growing insistence.

The second reason I would cite for reference works' importance is the evident fact that many places—notably military commands—are so situated as to be denied ready access to most basic evaluative material except through reference documents. This point needs no elaboration here.

The third reason is in some respects parallel to the second. As some intelligence needs are too remote in space to be met by the more precise intelligence media of current reporting, formal estimates and *ad hoc* evaluations, so other needs are too remote in time—or perhaps too uncertain to predict safely. One must assume that other situations may arise like those arising a decade or so ago in Cuba and the Belgian Congo, where a country of relatively low intelligence interest suddenly became a hot spot when powerful figures there courted Soviet assistance. Even if the estimative process adequately foresees 90 percent of these situations, there remains the tenth case which still requires insurance.

One mechanism for such insurance is producing contingency intelligence—which in any given instance looks no different from any other reference document. The term applies simply to the reason for the intelligence being produced: to make sure that the US Government has available beforehand a modicum of central information about every part of the world and, beyond this bare factual minimum, organized evaluative material on any country which, by reason of formal sovereignty, possesses the option exercised by Congolese and Cuban leaders when they called in Soviet advisers.

Basic intelligence performs this insurance role, it may be noted, simply by seeing to it that its reference material for day-to-day use is prepared on a suitably inclusive basis. (It does not, for example, try to foresee the special kind of intelligence that might be called for by the unexpected descent of a satellite in a remote part of the globe.) But the operative word for the contingency consideration is "inclusive." One cannot say, in scheduling the production of country surveys: "For most countries, yes; but surely the President of newly-independent Contracolonia will never be so misguided as to risk Soviet intervention. Let us, instead, use our basic intelligence resources on a country more people have heard of and are interested in right now." To act on this principle is to cancel the insurance policy.

Improving the Product

A further question remains: can one find specific means—not just sterner editing—of making the US Government reference document on international affairs a more efficient mechanism?

I think one can—though I am also aware of some of the difficulties inherent in the nature of basic intelligence. For example, the structure and format of an encyclopaedia cannot be changed as readily as a daily newspaper's can, for issuances of an encyclopaedia are not replaced the next day but are expected to remain in use for a matter of years. I also recognize that improvements in government programs involve administrative problems and affect related programs also; excluding administrative problems from this paper does not mean that I am unaware of them. Some possible lines of improvement, such as more extensive use of consumer surveys and of the resources of automatic data processing, I leave to be discussed by those more knowledgeable in these specialized fields. But there are two particular lines on which I would like to initiate discussion here.

The first amounts to urging a more critical look at the present intelligence-producing needs of the government, in the light of the massive research effort mounted by US universities and affiliated research institutes on the non-European world over the past two decades. The intelligence community has already reacted to this effort in part. Few would now consider it necessary for the main aspects of even a small and remote country—and the long-standing forces that work against basic US interests there—to be thrust uninvited on the policy-maker's attention in a current intelligence memo rather than kept ready for him on call in a standard reference document. The scope of what is considered necessary for embodiment in formal classified "basic intelligence" has likewise been much reduced. The NIS program, which in the late 1940s set out to cover some 50 different aspects, each in a detailed section, of every country in the world, has formally dropped over half of these detailed sections and now concentrates on a General Survey, covering in a single integrated volume the principal aspects of each country as these are considered to relate to US security interests. But I would still wonder how fully the intelligence community has recognized its activities as essentially supplementary to the larger American effort—public and private—and conceded that more of its own attention should center on facilitating, by various means, the government official's access to these other sources of information.

The principle of "supplementary and facilitative" provides no magic formula in itself but does suggest a way of using limited government resources to maximum advantage. For some parts of the intelligence effort the problem seems to be largely one of suitable awareness and, in the broad sense, translation. In the field of reference documents, one might assume the government task to be that of producing a set of nationally coordinated country surveys providing contingency coverage on each of the sovereign states of the world and seeking to outline the US relationship to that state; beyond this, the burden of proof would lie on those maintaining that the US Government needed to undertake the additional research task itself. This need would be easy to establish on subjects like the armed forces and the intelligence systems of hostile powers, where the importance is obvious and the significant data classified and hard to get. As easy to determine on the other side would be the case of the economic and social affairs of Western Europe, where the US is well served by a wealth of open sources. In between are a great number of other cases where the decision might seem far from open-and-shut. These might include sociological research on minor African countries, where the data are not classified but sometimes hard to get and the subject often of little interest to nongovernment publishing enterprises; transportation research in which military or other government requirements may be markedly different from those of the economic world; even possibly some political research on subjects so controversial that the value of the end product for government use would be enhanced by its being officially sanctioned.

The second line of improvement for the reference document lies in constantly remembering that its critical problem is effective communication—reaching the reader's mind, not merely the page in front of his eyes. The mechanical costs of graphics are of course far higher than for ordinary print, and it is easy to dream up photomontages or three-color work which merely decorate the text. But it is necessary to remember also that graphics are a bargain for the US taxpayer when they significantly shorten the time a senior official takes to absorb needed information—though the cost accounting system for measuring this has not yet been invented. There is also some reason to believe that many consumers would prefer a more fanned-out, outline type of presenting basic data (with frequent use of standardized tables) to the solid paragraphs of intelligence prose that are prevalent now. But converting all existing presentation to such a new format is something else again. Aside from a genuine (but often exaggerated) danger of distortion if one tries to make the story too simple or too exciting in the process of increasing its communicability, there is also a writing problem for reference works produced by nonprofessional writers. Not every analyst has the writing skill and intellectual flexibility for this task of translation.

More immediately, there are a few simple things that can be done to meet some of the user's legitimate desires for speed and convenience. Detailed indexing takes a great deal of a producer's time, but it can also save a great deal of a reader's time. There is also help for the hurried reader in a generous use of headings and subheadings, so worded as to aim at the reader's interests and not just the writer's—and adequately picked up in the table of contents.

Many may disagree with these suggestions on communication, as indeed with a number of other propositions advanced here. But, as indicated at the outset, the purpose of this paper is not to pass judgments but to initiate discussion and set up a frame of reference in which such discussion can meaningfully take place. Those who are particularly in a position to forward the discussion are, of course, not the producers but the users of reference documents—those who in the past may have simply put a tick in a box on a questionnaire without stopping to explain what, specifically, they used the document for or what they hoped to find there and didn't. I trust that some of them may be moved to respond now.

17.

Acting as a gadfly, a prominent CIA analyst uses methods of cognitive psychology to press for a more "conceptually driven" paradigm of how to do analysis. He argues against the traditional "data-driven" method and for a model-building/model-testing process. (Such a process might also be less complacent about data reservoirs swelling daily with a sophisticated journalism that only calls itself humint.)

Do You Really Need More Information?

RICHARDS J. HEUER, JR.

The difficulties associated with intelligence analysis are often attributed to the inadequacy of available information. Thus the intelligence community has invested heavily in improved collection systems while analysts lament the comparatively small sums devoted to enhancing analytical resources, improving analytical methods, or gaining better understanding of the cognitive processes involved in making analytical judgments.

This article challenges the often implicit assumption that lack of information is the principal obstacle to accurate intelligence estimates. It describes psychological experiments that examine the relationship between amount of information, accuracy of estimates based on this information, and analysts' confidence in their estimates. In order to interpret the disturbing but not surprising findings from these experiments, it identifies four different types of information and discusses their relative value in contributing to the accuracy of analytical judgments. It also distinguishes analysis whose results are driven by the data from analysis that is driven by the conceptual framework employed to interpret the data. Finally, it outlines a strategy for improving intelligence analysis.

The key findings from the relevant psychological experiments are:

- Once an experienced analyst has the minimum information necessary to make an informed judgment, obtaining additional information generally does not improve the accuracy of his estimates. Additional information does, however, lead the analyst to become more confident in his judgment, to the point of overconfidence.
- Experienced analysts have an imperfect understanding of what information

Richards J. Heuer, Jr., "Do You Really Need More Information?" *Studies in Intelligence*, vol. 23, no. 1 (Spring 1979), pp. 15–25. Originally unclassified.

they actually use in making judgments. They are unaware of the extent to which their judgments are determined by a few dominant factors, rather than by the systematic integration of all available information. Analysts use much less of the available information than they think they do.

As will be noted in further detail below, these experimental findings should not necessarily be accepted at face value. There are, for example, circumstances when additional information does contribute to more accurate analysis. There are also circumstances when additional information—particularly contradictory information—decreases rather than increases an analyst's confidence in his judgment. But the experiments highlight important relationships between the amount of information an analyst has available, judgmental accuracy, and analyst confidence. An understanding of these relationships has implications for both the management and conduct of intelligence analysis. Such an understanding suggests analytical procedures and management initiatives that may indeed contribute to more accurate analytical judgments. It also suggests that resources needed to attain a better understanding of the entire analytical process might profitably be diverted from some of the more massive and costly collection programs.

Betting on the Horses

Intelligence analysts have much in common with doctors diagnosing illness, psychologists identifying behavioral traits, stockbrokers predicting stock market performance, college admissions officers estimating future academic performance, weather forecasters, and horserace handicappers. All accumulate and interpret a large volume of information to make judgments about the future. All are playing an "information game," and all have been the subject of psychological research to determine how this game gets played.

Experts in these and similar professions analyze a finite number of identifiable and classifiable kinds of information to make judgments or estimates that can subsequently be checked for accuracy. The stock market analyst, for example, commonly works with information relating to price/earnings ratios, profit margins, earnings per share, market volume, and resistance and support levels. By controlling the information made available to a number of experts and then checking the accuracy of judgments based on this information, it has been possible to conduct experiments concerning how people use information to arrive at analytical judgments.

In one experiment,[1] eight experienced horserace handicappers were shown a list of 88 variables found on a typical past-performance chart—for

---

1. Paul Slovic, "Behavioral Problems of Adhering to a Decision Policy," Mimeo, 1973.

example, weight to be carried; percentage of races in which horse finished first, second, or third during the previous year; jockey's record; number of days since horse's last race. Each handicapper was asked to identify, first, what he considered to be the five most important items of information—those he would wish to use to handicap a race if he were limited to only five items of information per horse. Each was then asked to select the 10, 20, and 40 most important variables he would use if limited to those levels of information.

The handicappers were at this point given true data (sterilized so that horses and actual races could not be identified) for 40 past races and were asked to rank the top five horses in each race in order of expected finish. Each handicapper was given the data in increments of the 5, 10, 20 and 40 variables he had judged to be most useful. Thus, he predicted each race four times— once with each of the four different levels of information. For each prediction, each handicapper assigned a value from 0 to 100 percent to indicate his degree of confidence in the accuracy of his prediction.

When the handicappers' predictions were compared with the actual outcomes of these 40 races, it was clear that average accuracy of predictions remained the same regardless of how much information the handicappers had available. Three of the handicappers actually showed less accuracy as the amount of information increased, two improved their accuracy, and three were unchanged. All, however, expressed steadily increasing confidence in their judgments as more information was received. This relationship between amount of information, accuracy of the handicappers' prediction of the first place winners, and the handicappers' confidence in their predictions is shown graphically in Figure 1. Note that with only five items of information, the handicappers' confidence was well calibrated with their accuracy, but that as additional information was received, they became overconfident.

The same relationship between amount of information, accuracy, and analyst confidence has been confirmed by similar experiments in other fields, especially clinical psychology.[2] In one experiment, a psychological case file was divided into four sections representing successive chronological periods in the life of a relatively normal individual. Thirty-two psychologists with varying levels of experience were asked to make judgments on the basis of this information. After reading each section of the case file, the psychologists answered 25 questions (for which there were known answers) about the personality of the subject of the file. As in other experiments, increasing information resulted in a strong increase in confidence but a negligible increase in accuracy.[3]

2. For a list of references, see Lewis R. Goldberg, "Simple Models or Simple Processes? Some Research on Clinical Judgments," *American Psychologist*, 23 (1968), p. 484.

3. Stuart Oskamp, "Overconfidence in Case-Study Judgments," *Journal of Consulting Psychology*, 29 (1965), pp. 261–265.

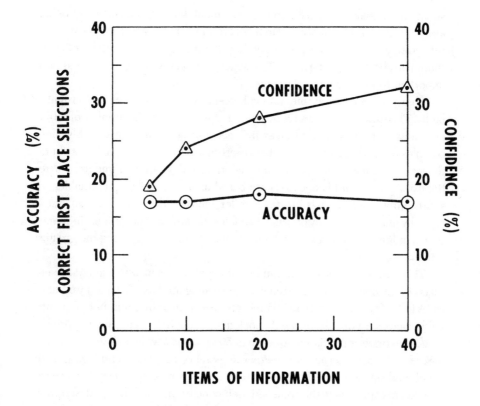

ITEMS OF INFORMATION

A series of experiments to examine the mental processes of medical doctors diagnosing illness found little relationship between thoroughness of data collection and accuracy of diagnosis. Medical students whose self-described research strategy stressed thorough collection of information (as opposed to formation and testing of hypotheses) were significantly below average in the accuracy of their diagnoses. It seems that the explicit formulation of hypotheses directs a more efficient and effective search for information.[4]

Modeling Expert Judgment

Another significant question concerns the extent to which analysts possess an accurate understanding of their own mental processes. How good is our insight into how we actually weigh evidence in making judgments? For each

4. Arthur S. Elstein *et al.*, *Medical Problem Solving: An Analysis of Clinical Reasoning* (Harvard University Press, Cambridge, Mass., and London, 1978), pp. 270 and 295.

situation we analyze, we have an implicit "mental model" consisting of beliefs and assumptions about which variables are most important and how they are related to each other. If we have good insight into our own mental model, we should be able to describe accurately which variables we have considered most important in making our judgments.

There is strong experimental evidence, however, that such self-insight is faulty. The expert perceives his own judgmental process, the number of different kinds of information he takes into account, as being considerably more complex than is in fact the case. He overestimates the importance he attributes to factors that have only a minor impact on his judgment, and underestimates the extent to which his decisions are based on a very few major variables. In short, our mental models are far simpler than we think, and the analyst is typically unaware not only of which variables *should* have the greatest influence on his judgments, but also of which variables actually are having the greatest influence.

This has been shown by a number of experiments in which analysts were asked to make quantitative estimates concerning a relatively large number of cases in their area of expertise, with each case defined by a number of quantifiable factors. In one experiment, stock market analysts were asked to predict long-term price appreciation for each of 50 securities, with each security being described in such terms as price/earnings ratio, corporate earnings growth trend, and dividend yield.[5] After completing this task, the analysts were instructed to explain how they reached their conclusions, including a description of how much weight they attached to each of the variables. They were told to be sufficiently explicit so that another person going through the same information could apply the same judgmental rules and arrive at the same conclusions.

In order to compare the analyst's verbal rationalization with the judgmental policy reflected in his actual decisions, multiple regression analysis or some similar statistical procedure can be used to develop a mathematical model of how each analyst actually weighed and combined information on the relevant variables.[6] There have been at least eight studies of this type in diverse fields,[7] including one involving prediction of future socioeconomic growth of underdeveloped nations.[8] The mathematical model based on the analyst's actual

5. Paul Slovic, Dan Fleissner, and W. Scott Bauman, "Analyzing the Use of Information in Investment Decision Making: A Methodological Proposal," *The Journal of Business*, 45 (1972), pp. 283–301.

6. For a discussion of the methodology, see Slovic, Fleissner, and Bauman, *loc. cit.*

7. For a list of references, see Paul Slovic and Sarah Lichtenstein, "Comparison of Bayesian and Regression Approaches to the Study of Information Processing in Judgment," *Organizational Behavior and Human Performance*, 6 (1971), p. 684.

8. David A. Summers, J. Dale Taliaferro, and Donna J. Fletcher, "Subjective vs. Objective Description of Judgment Policy," *Psychonomic Science*, 18 (1970), pp. 249–250.

decisions is invariably a better predictor of that analyst's past and future decisions than his own verbal description of how he makes his judgments.

Although the existence of this phenomenon has been amply demonstrated in many experiments, its causes are not well understood. The literature on these experiments contains only the following speculative explanation:

> Possibly our feeling that we can take into account a host of different factors comes about because although we remember that at some time or other we have attended to each of the different factors, we fail to notice that it is seldom more than one or two that we consider at any one time.[9]

How Can This Happen to Smart People Like Us?

In order to evaluate the relevance and significance of these experimental findings in the context of our own experience as intelligence analysts, it is necessary to distinguish four types of additional information that an analyst might receive:

1. *Additional detail about variables already included in our analysis.* Much raw intelligence reporting falls into this category. We would not expect such supplementary information to affect the over-all accuracy of our judgment, and it is readily understandable that further detail which is consistent with previous information increases our confidence. Analyses for which considerable depth of detail is available to support the conclusions tend to be more persuasive to their authors as well as to their readers.

2. *Information on additional variables.* Such information permits the analyst to take into account other factors that may affect the situation. This is the kind of additional information used in the horserace handicapper experiment. Other experiments have employed some combination of additional variables and additional detail on the same variables. The finding that our judgments are based on a very few critical variables rather than on the entire spectrum of evidence helps to explain why information on additional variables does not normally improve predictive accuracy. Occasionally, in situations when there are known gaps in our understanding, a single report concerning some new and previously unconsidered factor—for example, an authoritative report on some policy initiative or planned coup d'état—will have a major impact on our judgments. Such a report would fall into either of the next two categories of new information.

9. R. N. Shepard, "On Subjectively Optimum Selection Among Multiattribute Alternatives," in M. W. Shelly II and G. L. Bryan, eds., *Human Judgments and Optimality* (Wiley, New York, 1964), p. 266.

3. *Information concerning the level or value attributed to variables already included in the analysis.* An example of such information would be the horserace handicapper learning that a horse he thought would carry 110 pounds will actually carry only 106. Current intelligence reporting tends to deal with this kind of information—for example, the analyst learning that coup planning was far more advanced than he had anticipated. New facts clearly affect the accuracy of our judgments when they deal with changes in variables that are critical to our estimates. Our confidence in judgments based on such information is influenced by our confidence in the accuracy of the information, as well as by the amount of information.

4. *Information concerning which variables are most important and how they relate to each other.* Knowledge and assumptions concerning which variables are most important and how they are interrelated comprise our mental model that tells us *how* to analyze the data we receive. Explicit investigation of such relationships is one factor that distinguishes systematic research from current intelligence reporting and raw intelligence. In the context of the horserace handicapper experiment, for example, handicappers had to select which variables to include in their analysis. Is weight carried by a horse more, or less, important than several other variables that affect a horse's performance? Any information that affects this judgment affects how the handicapper analyzes the available data, that is, it affects his mental model. Events in Iran in late 1978 have probably had a permanent impact on the mental models not only of the Iran analysts, but of analysts dealing with internal politics in any of the Muslim countries. As a consequence of Iranian developments, analysts will consciously or subconsciously pay more attention and attribute increased importance to conservative religious opposition movements throughout the Muslim world.

The accuracy of our judgment depends upon both the accuracy of our mental model (the fourth type of information discussed above) and the accuracy of the values attributed to the key variables in the model (the third type of information discussed above). Additional detail on the variables in our model and information on other variables that do not in fact have a significant influence on our judgment (the first and second types of information) have a negligible impact on accuracy, but form the bulk of the raw material we work with. These kinds of information increase confidence because our conclusions seem to be supported by such a large body of data.

Important characteristics of the mental models analysts use vary substantially according to the type of intelligence problem faced. In particular, information is accorded a different role in different types of problems. In analyzing the readiness of a military division, for example, there are certain rules or procedures to be followed. The totality of these procedures comprises our mental model that influences our perception of the overhead photography of the unit and guides our judgment concerning what information is important and how this information should be analyzed to arrive at judgments concerning readiness. Most elements of the mental model can be made explicit so that other analysts may be taught to understand and follow the same analytical procedures and arrive at the same or very similar results. There is broad though not necessarily universal agreement on what the best model is. There are relatively objective standards for judging the quality of analysis, for the conclusions follow logically from the application of the agreed upon model to the available data.

Most important in the context of this discussion is that the accuracy of the estimate depends primarily upon the accuracy and completeness of the available data. If one makes the reasonable assumption that the analytical model is correct, and the further assumption that the analyst properly applies this model to the data, then the accuracy of the analytical judgment depends entirely upon the accuracy and completeness of the data. Because the analytical results are so heavily determined by the data, this may be called *data-driven analysis.*

At the opposite end of this spectrum is *conceptually driven analysis.* For example, in most political analysis the questions to be answered do not have neat boundaries and there are many unknowns. The number of potentially relevant variables, and the diverse and imperfectly understood relationships between these variables, involve the analyst in enormous complexity and uncertainty. There is little tested theory to inform the analyst concerning which of the myriad pieces of information are most important, and how they should be combined to arrive at estimative judgments. In the absence of any agreed upon analytical schema, the analyst is left to his own devices. He interprets information with the aid of mental models which are largely implicit rather than explicit. The assumptions he is making concerning political forces and processes in the subject country may not be apparent even to the analyst himself. Such models are not representative of an analytical consensus. Other analysts examining the same data may well reach different conclusions, or reach the same conclusions for different reasons. This analysis is conceptually driven because the outcome depends at least as much upon the conceptual framework employed to analyze the data as it does upon the data itself.

Not all military analysis is data-driven, and not all political analysis is concept-driven. In citing military and political analysis as the opposite ends of this spectrum, we are making a broad generalization that permits many exceptions. In comparing economic and political analysis, we note that economic models are usually more explicit, and that they represent a consensus of at least broad factions within the discipline.

In the light of this distinction between data-driven and conceptually driven analysis, it is instructive to look at the function of the analyst responsible for current intelligence, especially current political intelligence as distinct from longer-term research. His daily work is driven by the incoming reporting from overseas which he must interpret for dissemination to consumers, but this is not what is meant by data-driven analysis. The current intelligence analyst must provide immediate interpretation of the latest, often unexpected events. Apart from his store of background information, he may have no data other than the initial, usually incomplete report. Under these circumstances, his interpretation is based upon his implicit mental model of how and why events normally transpire in the country for which he is responsible. The accuracy of his judgment depends almost exclusively upon the accuracy of his mental model, for he has virtually no other basis for judgment.

If the accuracy of our mental model is the key to accurate judgment, it is necessary to consider how this mental model gets tested against reality and how it can be changed so that we can improve the accuracy of our judgment. There are two reasons that make it hard to change one's mental model. The first relates to the nature of human perception and information processing. The second concerns the difficulty, in many fields, of learning what truly is the best model.

Partly because of the nature of human perception and information processing, beliefs of all types tend to resist change. This is especially true of the implicit assumptions and "self-evident truths" that play an important role in determining our mental models.[10] Information that is consistent with our existing mindset is perceived and processed easily. However, since our mind strives instinctively for consistency, information that is inconsistent with our existing mental image tends to be overlooked, perceived in a distorted manner, or rationalized to fit existing assumptions and beliefs.[11] Thus, new information tends to be perceived and interpreted in a way that reinforces existing beliefs.

A second difficulty in revising our mental models arises because of the nature of the learning process. Learning to make better judgments through experience assumes systematic feedback concerning the accuracy of previous judgments and an ability to link the accuracy of a judgment with the particular

---

10. We are often surprised to learn that what are to us self-evident truths are by no means self-evident to others, or that self-evident truth at one point in time may be commonly regarded as naive assumption 10 years later.

11. We are, of course, referring to subconscious processes; no analyst is consciously going to distort information that does not fit his preconceived beliefs. Important aspects of the perception and processing of new information occur prior to and independently of any conscious direction, and the tendencies described here are largely the result of these subconscious or preconscious processes.

configuration of variables that promoted an analyst to make the judgment. In practice, however, we get little systematic feedback, and even when we know a predicted event has occurred or failed to occur, we typically do not know for certain whether this happened for the reasons we had foreseen. Thus, an analyst's personal experience may be a poor guide to revision of his mental model.[12]

Improving Intelligence Analysis

To the intelligence policy maker seeking an improved intelligence product, our findings offer a reminder that this can be achieved by improving analysis as well as by improving collection. There are, of course, many traditional ways to seek to improve analysis—language and area training, revising employee selection and retention criteria, manipulating incentives, improving management, and increasing the number of analysts. Any of these measures may play an important role, but we ought not to overlook the self-evident fact that intelligence analysis is principally a cognitive process. If we are to penetrate to the heart and soul of the problem of improving analysis, we must somehow penetrate and affect the mental processes of the individuals who do the analysis. The findings in this article suggest a central strategy for pursuing that goal: this strategy is to focus on improving the mental models employed by the analyst to interpret his data. While this will be very difficult to achieve, it is so critical to effective intelligence analysis that even small improvement could have large benefits.

There are a number of concrete actions to implement this strategy of improving mental models that can be undertaken by individual analysts and middle managers as well as by organizational policy makers. All involve confronting the analyst with alternative ways of thinking. The objective is to identify the most fundamental analytical assumptions, then to make these assumptions explicit so that they may be critiqued and re-evaluated.

The basic responsibility for proper analysis rests, of course, with the individual analyst. To guide his information search and analysis, the analyst should first seek to identify and examine alternative models or conceptual frameworks for interpreting the already available information. Because people have very limited capacity for simultaneously considering multiple hypotheses, the alternatives should be written down and evidence compared against them in a

---

12. A similar point has been made in rebutting the belief in the accumulated wisdom of the classroom teacher. "It is actually very difficult for teachers to profit from experience. They almost never learn about their long-term successes or failures, and their short-term effects are not easily traced to the practices from which they presumably arose." B. F. Skinner, *The Technology of Teaching* (Appleton-Century-Crofts, New York, 1968), pp. 112–113.

systematic manner. This permits the analyst to focus on the degree to which the evidence is diagnostic in helping him select the best among competing models, rather than simply the degree to which it supports or undermines his own previous belief. This helps overcome the tendency to ignore the possibility that evidence consistent with one's own belief is equally consistent with other hypotheses. The analyst must, from time to time, attempt to suspend his own beliefs and develop alternative viewpoints, to determine if some alternative— when given a fair chance—might not be as compelling as one's own previous view. Systematic development of an alternative scenario generally increases the perceived likelihood of that scenario.

The analyst should then try to disprove, rather than prove, each of the alternatives. He or she should try to rebut rather than confirm hypotheses, and actively seek information that permits this rather than review passively information flowing through the in box. It is especially important for the analyst to seek information that, if found, would disprove rather than bolster his own arguments. One key to identifying the kinds of information that are potentially most valuable is for the analyst to ask himself what it is that could make him change his mind. Adoption of this simple tactic would do much to avoid intelligence surprises.

Management can play a role by fostering research on the mental models of analysts. Since these models serve as a "screen" or "lens" through which we perceive foreign developments, research to identify the impact of our mental models on our analysis may contribute as much to accurate estimates as research focused more directly on the foreign areas themselves. When the mental models are identified, further research is in order to test the assumptions of these models. To what extent can one determine, empirically, what are the key variables and how these variables relate to each other in determining an estimated outcome?

Management should insist on far more frequent and systematic retrospective evaluation of analytical performance. One ought not generalize from any single instance of a correct or incorrect estimate, but a series of related judgments that are, or are not, borne out by subsequent events can be very diagnostic in revealing the accuracy or inaccuracy of our mental model. Obtaining systematic feedback on the accuracy of our past judgments is frequently difficult or impossible, especially in the political analysis field.

Political estimates are normally couched in vague and imprecise terms (to say that something "could" happen conveys no information that can be disproven by subsequent events) and are normally conditional upon other developments. Even in retrospect, there are no objective criteria for evaluating the accuracy of most political estimates as they are presently written. In the economic and military fields, however, where estimates are frequently concerned with numerical quantities, systematic feedback on analytical performance is feasible. Retrospective evaluation should be standard procedure in those fields where estimates are routinely updated at periodic intervals. It should be strongly encouraged in all areas as long as it can be accomplished as part of an objective search for improved understanding, rather than to identify scape-goats or assess blame. This requirement suggests that retrospective evaluation ought to be done within the organizational unit and perhaps by the same analysts that prepared the initial evaluation, even if this results in some loss of objectivity.

The pre-publication review and approval process is another point at which management can impact on the quality of analysis. Such review generally considers whether a draft publication is properly focused to meet the perceived need for that publication. Are the key judgments properly highlighted for the consumer who scans but does not read in depth? Are the conclusions well supported? Is the draft well written? Review procedures should also explicitly examine the mental model employed by the analyst in searching for and exam-ining his evidence. What assumptions has the analyst made that are not dis-cussed in the draft itself, but that underlie his principal judgments? What alternative hypotheses have been considered but rejected? What could cause the analyst to change his mind? These kinds of questions should be a part of the review process. Management should also consider the advisability of assigning another analyst to play the role of devil's advocate.

One common weakness in the pre-publication review process is that an analyst's immediate colleagues and supervisor are likely to share a common mindset, hence these are the individuals least likely to raise fundamental issues challenging the validity of the analysis. Peer review by analysts handling other countries or issues and with no specialized knowledge of the subject under review may be the best way to identify assumptions and alternative explana-tions. Such non-specialist review has in the past been a formal part of the review process, but it is not now common practice.

At the policy making level, CIA directors since 1973 have been moving the agency in directions that ensure CIA analysts are increasingly exposed to alter-native mental models. The realities of bureaucratic life still produce pressures for conformity, but efforts are made to ensure that competing views have the opportunity to surface. There is less formal inter-agency coordination than there used to be, and increased use of informal coordination aimed more at surfacing areas of disagreement and the reasons therefor than at enforcing consensus.

Sharply increased publication of CIA analyses in unclassified form has stimulated challenge and peer review by knowledgeable analysts in academia and industry. The public debate that followed publication of several CIA oil estimates in 1977 is the most noteworthy case in point. Such debate can only sharpen the perception and judgment of the participating CIA analysts. The 1976 Team A–Team B experiment in competitive analysis of the strategic balance with the Soviet Union, on the other hand, was a miscarriage. Confrontation of alternative mental models is a critical element of the analytical process, but this confrontation must take place in an environment that promotes attitude change rather than hardening of positions.

The most recent development has been the formal establishment in December 1978 of the Review Panel within the National Foreign Assessment Center. The panel, which presently consists of three senior officials from the State Department, the military and academia, is designed to bring outside perspectives to bear on the review of major analytical products.

Conclusion

The function of intelligence is frequently described by analogy to a mosaic. Intelligence services collect small pieces of information which, when put together like a mosaic or a jigsaw puzzle, eventually enable us to see a clear picture of reality. The analogy suggests that accurate estimates depend primarily upon having all the pieces, that is, upon accurate and relatively complete information. It is important to collect and store the small pieces of information, as these are the raw material from which the picture is made; we never know when it will be possible to fit a piece into the puzzle. Much of the rationale for large, technical collection systems is rooted in this mosaic analogy.

The mosaic theory of intelligence is an oversimplification that has distorted perception of the analytical process for many years. It is properly applied only to what has been described as data-driven analysis. A broader theory of intelligence encompassing conceptually driven as well as data-driven analysis ought to be based on insights from cognitive psychology. Such insights suggest that the picture formed by the so-called mosaic is not a picture of reality, but only our self-constructed mental image of a reality we can never perceive directly. We form the picture first, and only then do we fit in the pieces. Accurate estimates depend at least as much upon the mental model we use in forming that picture as upon the accuracy and completeness of the information itself.

The mosaic theory of intelligence has focused attention on collection, the gathering together of as many pieces as possible for the analyst to work with. A more psychologically oriented view would direct our concern to problems of analysis, and especially to the importance of mental models that determine what we collect and how we perceive and interpret the collected data. To the extent that this is the more appropriate guide to comprehending the analytical process, there are important implications for the management of intelligence resources. There seem to be inherent practical and theoretical limits on how much can be gained by efforts to improve collection, but an open and fertile field for imaginative efforts to improve analysis.

18.

Wherever its data come from or its estimate/prediction reports go, analysis is internally a bureaucratic, not just a cognitive, process. There is a game to be played, for survival and for advancement. Here's how—in the words of a seasoned practitioner, who displays a lighthearted mood about the ambient culture.

Basic Psychology for Intelligence Analysts

CHARLES D. CREMEANS

When Allen Dulles chose to have the words "For ye shall know the truth and the truth shall make you free" carved in white marble at the entrance to the Headquarters building he was giving expression to an article of faith in the intelligence profession. We must believe that knowledge of the truth sustains and supports our government or we couldn't justify what we are doing.

Working intelligence officers know, however, that it isn't always as easy as it sounds. What is the truth? How much evidence do you have to have? how selected? how organized? how presented? how evaluated before we have the truth that will make our country free?—and free from what? We all know that good and true men disagree on these matters, as on the evidence on any given subject of intelligence concern. We also know that from time to time, every intelligence officer worth his salt wakes up with a shock to realize that he has been misreading the evidence on some familiar topic. This can happen because he has gone along with the common wisdom, accepted unexamined assumptions, or just plain gotten into a rut. It can also happen if preoccupation with success or mere survival in the intelligence culture become more important than intelligence itself.

The sensitive intelligence officer becomes aware from time to time of the effect on our finished product of the interaction of personalities and institutions within the intelligence community. We are, after all, human beings; we have deadlines to meet; we tend to favor our own conclusions over those of others; and we all know that a little salesmanship here and there, a little blarney, a measure of cajolery, and some basic psychology can often get a paper agreed to and on its way to the White House, while without such inputs it might

Charles D. Cremeans, "Basic Psychology for Intelligence Analysts," *Studies in Intelligence*, vol. 15, no. 1 (Winter 1971), pp. 109–114. Originally classified "Confidential."

languish and spoil under the heavy hands of some well meaning but less subtle colleagues.

The object of this paper is to look at some of the ways in which we get our work done, ways that depend more on human psychology than on cold reason. The purpose in mind is not to collect a bag of tricks, a primer of intelligence-manship, but to focus a spotlight on one aspect of our craft which is usually ignored. The purpose in doing this is not to suggest that an end be put to this kind of thing. God forbid that we stop being human, that we coldly reject, as being unsuited to our profession, such phenomena as the well-known eloquence of the distinguished dean of photointerpreters. But we should be aware of ourselves as we really are and not be misled into thinking all our peccadilloes foster the rapid and certain discovery of the truth.

We may start with a look at some of the oft quoted laws of intelligence.[1] The most famous of these is Platt's Law, which reads, as set down by its discoverer: "Whether or not the necessary explanatory details and pet phrases of an intelligence paper appear in the paper as finally published, depends entirely upon whether the number of higher groups which successively review the paper is even or odd respectively."[2] In the Office of National Estimates this is sometimes rendered: "If the Staff writes it long, the Board wants it short—and vice versa."

Another famous principle is that of Excessive Approval. Every intelligence Indian—i.e., drafter—knows that when the review board or panel, or whatever the higher echelon is, responds to a request for comments with unstinted praise, there comes a point at which the drafter feels a sense of foreboding. It usually means that his paper is about to be torn to shreds.

All veterans of intelligence coordination are familiar with the law of Emphasis by Place. This law is often referred to in this manner: "I suggest that the item referred to at the end of the paragraph—or section, or paper—be brought up to the beginning in order to give it greater emphasis." It is equally often cited by urging that an item that appears at the beginning be put at the end "in order to give it greater emphasis." Adjudication on this matter usually depends on whether the Chairman wants to argue about whether emphasis is bestowed by early or late reference or whether he thinks the time is suitable for a throwaway concession in the hope that the gesture can be collected on at a later time.

Most notorious of the laws of intelligence is Murphy's Law: "When something can be misunderstood, it will be." The archives contain no record of

---

1. We do not propose to set down all the "laws of intelligence," but only those commonly cited or applied in the production of intelligence. Kent's Law, for instance—"Any coup d'état I have heard of isn't going to happen"—is a profound truth but not within the scope of this paper.

2. *Studies*, XIII/4, 89–90.

Murphy. He may have been an honorable and well-intentioned man, but, sad to say, his law is more often than not cited by someone whose opinion of his boss is that he can and will read only one sentence at a time. The result of this assumption is that all the supporting calculations and data must be stuffed into the sentence in question, making it incomprehensible [to] the most intelligent reader, and probably to the boss for whose benefit the re-writing is being proposed.

A quick look at these laws of intelligence shows that they really are techniques of persuasion rather than laws the knowledge of which enables one to understand the behavior of phenomena in the real world. In fact it is in the realm of persuasion—of others, as well, sometimes, as of ourselves—that psychology most often obtrudes into intelligence.

Almost every intelligence analyst learns that if he wants to play it safe, or if he just doesn't know what is going to happen, an easy way out may be found through the Continuation of Present Trends formula. Unless he runs into really bad luck, an intelligence analyst of modest competence can usually go through a career with good marks simply by summarizing the evidence, and then pronouncing thus: "present trends are likely to continue." When this gets boring or too conspicuous, the More and More formula is often called into use. "King Hussein will find it more and more difficult to maintain control . . . ," or he "will find it increasingly difficult. . . ." This gets to be a problem when he has been finding it more and more, as well as increasingly, difficult for years and years and still hangs on. Then it becomes increasingly difficult for the analyst. The point is not that he should be ashamed of himself for being unable to find an answer to King Hussein's future in all that mass of paper that flows across his desk but that it should be quite clear to himself and to his readers that the evidence doesn't provide the basis for much of a judgment—which, of course, he should go on looking for despite the inadequacies of information and insight.

Perhaps the fundamental relationship among intelligence officers is that between the expert and the nonexpert. The former, of course, being the person who is supposed to know—although he doesn't necessarily really know all about Patagonia just because he is on the desk—and the latter being the person who reviews, edits, revises, or just approves his work. We are talking, of course, about the Indian and the chief in the intelligence analysis tribal culture. In real life the expert is usually comparatively young and the nonexpert or supervisor, comparatively old. The supervisor was probably an expert once but has to cover too wide a field, has too much administrative responsibility, or is too tired to be anything but a "generalist."

Actually, both the specialist and the supervisor have essential jobs to do, but the relationship is inherently a difficult one and, as a consequence, the ingenuity of man (read "intelligence officers") rises to the challenge with formulae that make life easier—sometimes for one, sometimes for both parties. For the expert the neatest solution is to know so much, to calculate so well the requirements and the quirks of the supervisor as well as the supervisor's supervisor, and to translate this into such a good end-product that the boss can only sigh and sign off. Unfortunately, not every supervisor knows when he is getting a perfect draft, and so even the best of the experts resort to certain stratagems to make their lives tolerable.

One approach, very often overdone, is that of laying on the expertise with a trowel: "Well, you know, sir, unless you have lived with the Khmers as I have it is quite impossible to understand their reaction to the current situation." Another frequently used ploy is that of drowning your opponent, or boss, with facts. One famous "expert," who did know as much about the Arabs as anyone in town, insisted on going into the fine points of tribal differences, whatever the issue at hand, until in the end he had only to open his mouth to provoke groans and numerous visits to the washroom. In the first case, by taking the line that only experts can understand, and in the second, by becoming irrelevant, the expert weakens his position and indeed emphasizes the need for the intervention of a nonexpert, preferably one with good sense and judgment.

For his part the nonexpert (or no longer expert) supervisor can fall into equally dangerous traps if he tries too hard to compensate for his inadequacies. One of the most common dodges of the one-upped supervisor is the counterexpertise play: "Well, I don't know anything about the Khmers; I'll be the first to acknowledge it; but I remember a situation very like this Southeast Asia thing we are discussing which took place some time back when I was in Central America, and I can tell you. . . ."

The old timing game, of course, is played by both sides in this contest of generations. How often has the drafter of a paper come rushing into a senior's office, saying, breathlessly, "Hope you can read this right away, sir. I spent all weekend on it and it's got to go to the DD this afternoon. Incidentally, the girls have started typing, so I hope you won't have too many suggestions." Of course, there have been a few times when a supervisor has stopped a staff man in the hall, saying, "By the way, I had lunch with the DD and he asked about that paper you gave me to look at. I thought I had better give it to him right away. Sorry I didn't have time to consult with you about it, particularly as I rewrote the last section and put it at the beginning."

Well, we're not all perfect, and this sort of thing goes on partly because in many cases things would not get done if it didn't. The point here seems to be that the better a man the expert is and the better a man the supervisor is, the less the need for stratagems. So, if you're an expert, get a good supervisor, and if you're a supervisor. . . .

There are, of course, a good many pitfalls that specialists and nonspecialists together can get into. One of the worst, both from the point of view of the people involved and of the whole intelligence community, is a syndrome best represented by the famed "numbers game." The problem usually arises when there is a strongly felt need on the part of the top users of intelligence for a degree of precision which the evidence, or, indeed, often the subject, does not permit. When the top policy makers ask, for example, "How many Russians are there in Cuba anyway? Just give us your best guess," the people down the line ought to be very cautious, we all know now, about giving them a figure at all unless there is a certain minimum evidentiary basis for it. The consequence, of course, can be finding ourselves unable to change figures even when our intelligence improves, because of the difficulty of explaining how we got the original figures on the books anyway. All this adds up to one of the most important rules for the intelligence officer: Don't fool yourself into thinking that if higher authority demands it, it makes sense to put out something that is basically unsound.

The intelligence officer's working life is not spent only at his desk or in consultation with his supervisor. There is the group: the meeting, the committee, the task force, the discussion, the debriefing—all standard situations in the intelligence culture. These intelligence groups' experiences might not seem to some to be as dramatic as what we are told goes on at the Esalen Institute in California where people grope, in the company of others, for self-understanding, but they can be pretty real and earnest. They probably produce as much self-realization and as much bloodshed as similar competitive situations anywhere. On any good workday one will find as wide a variety of successful personal styles on display in intelligence groups, as in a Madison Avenue idea session, in a back boardroom, or an academic committee.

Every experienced participant in group intelligence knows the country boy who talks of the inner mysteries of Soviet space technology with just enough of a southern drawl to add a human touch. There is the blustering Devil's advocate who specializes in outlandish and unanswerable propositions. There is the man with a cause who specializes in stripping the flesh off the proponents of a rival school of analysis. There is the specialist in the scathing personal attack at the right moment. (My favorite, and one done in good humor, is an instance where [a criticized sentence] in a draft paper was conceded by the author to have been "ambivalent." "Sir," said the critic, "you do yourself too much credit. An ambivalent sentence has two meanings. Yours has none at all.")

Along with the bad guys, and the bores, the sycophants, and the fools—intelligence officers may be carefully screened, but no foolproof battery of tests has yet been devised—there are, naturally, a fair proportion of good guys of all sorts. Here, as elsewhere, the observer of the intelligence culture must conclude that the fact that intelligence people are people is all to the good, as well as being unavoidable. Furthermore, it does not obscure or change the fact that, whatever the style, the ability to produce sound intelligence is the payoff in the end.

There is still another situation in which intelligence officers interact and which gives rise to its share of specialized behavior patterns. I refer to the joys of coordination, particularly of that highest form of agony known as interagency coordination. Getting things done within an agency, as amply suggested above, is complex enough, but in an interagency situation, where the boss can't resolve the disputes, a very specialized form of interaction takes place. How it all works, I shan't pretend that I understand, though there are a few clues. When the Navy representative says, "Can't you please mention submarines in this section?" his colleagues are inclined to go along if it won't mess up the paper too much and if he can be expected to be agreeable when their turn comes. Perhaps the most time-honored and symbolic device of the interagency coordination process is the convention of bestowing "The Order of the Lion" on a representative who has done his duty and manfully presented his superior's case to an unreceptive audience. (The idea is that he can go back home and tell the boss that he fought like a lion but that the other agencies wouldn't have it.)

Nowhere else is the art of the trade-off so highly developed. Nowhere else is such skill applied to the artful suggestion of a different form of words to say what is already in the text in order to save the face of a colleague who can neither withdraw nor make his proposal specific. The worst burden for coordinators is the colleague who insists that he, or his boss, doesn't like something but doesn't know why or what he wants to do about it. The greatest problem, of course, is the intervention of departmental interest, or policy commitment, into the discussion of an intelligence judgment. Most representatives realize that this is a high crime—or at least that it stultifies the process—but all tend to be sympathetic with the colleague who they know has to go back to a boss who doesn't know or care about the distinction between intelligence and policy. The miracle is that interagency coordination of intelligence works as well as it does, that the people who do it get along, and that the end product is almost always sound intelligence.

What is there to conclude from all this? That we are people, like other people, and that our personalities, our instinctive drives, and our subconscious minds get deeply involved in the process of "knowing the truth"? I believe so, and I believe it is essential that we acknowledge and take account of this while doing our best to create as much as possible of that marvelous stuff, objective intelligence, which is what Allen Dulles probably had in mind when he selected that quote from the Bible.

19.

Ever since the late 1970s, reformers in the Directorate of Intelligence, where analysis is principally done, have been advocating major changes in the culture there. One goal is to wean analysts and consumers alike from their penchant for single-outcome predictions, and orient them toward probabilistic ones instead. Here is a good example of the reformers' advocacy, reinforced by important case studies.

The Hazards of Single-Outcome Forecasting

WILLIS C. ARMSTRONG
WILLIAM LEONHART
WILLIAM J. MCCAFFREY
HERBERT C. ROTHENBERG

"In this report we have attempted to determine the causes, in instances when the intelligence community did not adequately anticipate significant events on the world scene, and to identify measures which might improve performance in the future." So began a report from the Senior Review Panel to the Director of Central Intelligence and Deputy Director of Central Intelligence. The panel was responding to a request for a study "on the quality of intelligence judgments preceding significant historical failures over the last twenty years or so."

In the report, dated 16 December 1983, the Senior Review Panel dealt with cases the DCI and DDCI nominated for review and added others "which have also had major consequences for US interests." The panel prepared twelve case studies:

Case	Critical Date
The Likelihood of North Vietnam Intervention in South Vietnam	1945–1965
The Likelihood of All-Out Soviet Support of Hanoi	1950–1965
Cuba	1957
Sino-Soviet Split	1959
First Chinese Nuclear Test	1964
The Soviet ALFA-Class Submarine	1969
Libya	1969

Willis C. Armstrong, William Leonhart, William J. McCaffrey, and Herbert C. Rothenberg, "The Hazards of Single-Outcome Forecasting," *Studies in Intelligence*, vol. 28, no. 3 (Fall 1984), pp. 57–70. Originally classified "Secret."

	Critical Date
The OPEC Price Increase of December 1973	1973
Ethiopia	1973
Afghanistan	1978
Iran	1978
Nicaragua—The Nature of Somoza's Opposition	1978

What follow are selections from the panel's report and five of the twelve case studies.

Methodology

Our method of approach in general was to concentrate on community and Central Intelligence Agency publications—including typescripts and periodical articles—in the two or three years preceding the critical or transforming outcome. The retrieval effort varied widely, from a few years back to over twenty-five, and depending on the publications record, from less than a hundred items for each to more than four hundred. For each of our case studies, we attempted:

a. To determine the main lines of the analytical and estimative judgments of the period.

b. To examine the extent to which these judgments were supplemented by the use of alternative hypotheses, speculative analyses going beyond developments strongly supported by the evidence, or conjectures about lesser probabilities than favored outcome forecasts.

c. To judge whether more speculative approaches might have proved in the end more realistic and succeeded in alerting the policy community earlier to outcome potentials largely ignored at the time.

Findings

Both community processes and CIA analytical quality have significantly improved in the last two or three years. No one we think can fairly read the record of these case studies without reflecting on recent qualitative improvements in the system. NIEs/SNIEs of the present period are simply better written, better presented, more timely, and more relevant to policymaker needs. Recent CIA assessments provide better coverage, are analytically more thorough, have frequently superior estimative quality. We much doubt, for example, that practice today would overlook—for several years before and after—overseas developments of a significance to US interests similar to those in Libya in 1969, Ethiopia in 1974, Afghanistan and Nicaragua in 1978.

The one area in which we think contemporary production has not much improved is length of papers. Apart from technical studies, where special considerations apply, too many estimates remain too long for useful communication between the intelligence and the policy communities.

The strength of performance in the cases we have examined lay in the promptness, extent, and variety of current intelligence production. The main weaknesses were in analytical integration and estimative projections. These conclusions seem to us valid for each of the cases we have studied. But we do not think that all of them should be considered "historical failures."

a. Vietnam remains controversial, and it may be some years yet before history has a verdict on intelligence performance,[1] as on other kinds of performance there. As we read the record, intelligence publications were throughout generally careful, realistic, and thorough. There were occasional errors of fact and interpretation, as in the use and utility of Sihanoukville. There was more of a tendency to overestimate the effectiveness of our initiatives than to underestimate those of our opponents. There were few—too few—broadly ranging strategic analyses. But on the two key issues we were asked to examine—North Vietnamese intervention in the South and all-out Soviet support to Hanoi— our conclusions are that the policy community and the executive agencies had an adequate, if diffuse, body of intelligence available and that there is little basis to conclude that either constituted a strategic surprise.

b. Similarly, on Cuba and the significance of Castro a year or two before he took power and on Nicaragua and the nature of the opposition to Somoza, the argument can be made that the exercise of community processes was belated, that early Agency assessments remained ambiguous longer than was desirable, and that there was too little speculation in the period when evidence was thin. But there seems to us no persuasive conclusion of failure. From 1957 on in the case of Cuba and from 1978 [in the case of] Nicaragua, community and CIA assessments clearly documented and projected the orientation of the main players and the probable and actual outcomes.

c. And on the first Chinese nuclear test, occurring in 1964, the community scored a successful prediction—albeit for a number of very wrong reasons.

d. The other cases seem to us clearly a set of faulty intelligence judgments. In most, last-minute or early retrospective analyses soon corrected the record, but there were significant failures to assess the direction of events and the

---

1. See US Intelligence and Vietnam, special issue of Studies in Intelligence, XXVIII/5. (SE-CRET/NOFORN.)

strengths of competitive forces; to estimate goals, directions, and the velocity of events; and to anticipate probable outcomes early enough to alert policymakers to emerging new situations.

In the estimates that failed, there were a number of recurrent common factors which, in retrospect, seem critical to the quality of the analysis. The most distinguishing characteristic of the failed estimates—the Sino-Soviet split, the development of the ALFA submarine, the Qadhafi takeover in Libya, the OPEC price increase, the revolutionary transformation of Ethiopia, the Soviet invasion of Afghanistan, or the destruction of the Shah's Iran—was that each involved historical discontinuity and, in the early stages, apparently unlikely outcomes.

The basic problem in each was to recognize qualitative change and to deal with situations in which trend continuity and precedent were of marginal, if not counterproductive, value. Analysts of the period clearly lacked a doctrine or a model for coping with improbable outcomes. Their difficulty was compounded in each case by reluctance to quantify their theories of probability or their margins of uncertainty. Findings such as "likely," "probable," "highly probable," "almost certainly," were subjective, idiosyncratic, ambiguous between intelligence producer and consumer, uncertain in interpretation from one reader to another, and unchallenged by a requirement to analyze or clarify subordinate and lesser probabilities.

Too many of the analyses were incident-oriented and episodic; too few addressed the processes that produced the incidents or speculated about underlying forces and trends. And in many of the cases, information sources were not sufficiently representative, were themselves prisoners of continuity assumptions, and were ultimately overtaken by sequels they failed to foresee.

In our view, however, the major factor in the failed estimates was overly cautious, overly conservative, single-outcome forecasting. Many of their judgments can be faulted in hindsight as clearly wrong. The case against them, however, is not so much retrospective error as contemporary inadequacy. For the most part, they rested on the prevailing wisdom of the time and were reinforced by professional assessments of the available evidence.

But in none of the flawed cases did contemporary analysts present or analyze, in their publications of record, alternative outcomes; speculate on possible developments suggested but not fully supported by "hard evidence"; or conjecture about lesser possibilities than their preferred most probable projections.

This addiction to single-outcome forecasting defied both estimative odds and much recorded history. It reinforced some of the worst analytical hazards—status quo bias and a prejudice toward continuity of previous trends, "playing it safe," mirror-imaging, and predispositions toward consensus intelligence. It was compounded by what the British call "perseveration" (a tendency for judgments made in the early stages of a developing situation to be allowed to affect later appraisals and an unreadiness to alter earlier views even when evidence requiring them to be revised becomes available) which narrowed collection requirements and froze their priorities to overtaken analytical frameworks. The practice invited failure.

A Few Observations

In our view, the central problems that emerge from our study are how to deal with inevitable uncertainty, how to manage concurrently both greater and lesser probabilities, and how to cope with discontinuity and apparently unlikely outcomes. Single-outcome forecasting is clearly less than an ideal approach to these problems.

To attack them, probably the most important requirement is to increase sensitivities on the part of middle-level managers and analysts alike that these are in fact real problems and that failure to deal adequately with them will be invitational to repeated failures, both in the substance of projections and in the timeliness of intelligence advice.

The world will stay a chancy and changeable place and the only rule is perhaps that there is an inevitability of uncertainty which we ignore at our peril. Information at best will always be in some part fragmentary, obsolete, and ambiguous. "Hard evidence" about the future will remain a contradiction in terms. Intelligence professionals can, and should, attempt to decrease uncertainty, the number of surprises, and the unexamined consequences of their interacting variables. They cannot hope to live in an environment immune to the contingent, the unexpected, and the unforeseen.

The need is for estimative resources and efforts that are highly flexible, that take into account the extraordinarily complex array of matters which determine future developments, that have a significant surge capacity, and that are addressed to contingent futures. Single-outcome forecasts poorly serve this requirement. They do not reduce uncertainty. They only increase the margins of surprise.

A number of your [DDI/DDCI] initiatives are obviously addressed to these issues: improved substantive leadership, more sophisticated training methodologies, heightened precision in collection targeting and techniques. We believe that substantial improvements have been made in the last several years.

To reduce and respect the claims of uncertainty and surprise, we think a few other substantive and procedural techniques merit consideration in the production of community estimates (and, for that matter, CIA assessments) concerned with probable outcomes. In most such analytical problems, there is an initial distinction between two categories of cases:

a. Those in which the likely outcome and the distribution of probabilities cannot be agreed.
b. Those in which there is consensus on the likely outcome, but differences on the degrees of probability to be attached to it and to conceivable but less likely developments.

The former seems to us the easier case. Where there is no agreement on the most likely line of development—if the estimate cannot be deferred for further collection and analysis—greater reliance on separate, adversarial, and competitive analyses would seem appropriate. The competing analyses, by whatever means derived, should go to the National Intelligence Council for its collegial consideration and advice on relative probabilities. Any subsequent publication should, of course, contain analyses of the competing outcomes.

For the other category of cases, perhaps the preponderance, where there is general agreement on likely outcomes, we think that, as a general rule, NIEs/SNIEs should include an "Alternative Outcomes" section. Its main purpose would be briefly to spell out lesser probabilities and other possible developments—not fully supported by the evidence but suggested by visible clues, fugitive data, or newly emerging trends or personalities.

For the technique to work, two further changes in NIE/SNIE format would be indicated:

a. Probabilities in both majority and minority cases should be quantified. We do not favor elaborate arithmetical calculations or definitions. We think some rough approximation—"slightly better than even," "two to one," "three to one," or possibly even "four to one"—would cover most human events and be sufficiently precise for clear communication between intelligence producers and consumers and among disparate policy readers. Apart from this added clarity, the value of the approach would be to emphasize the possible prospects for alternative outcomes and to provide improved guidance for the collection community.
b. A list of future indicators should invariably be included. Its aim should be to underline those contingent developments, decision points, and future policy crossroads which could affect the durability of the analysis, alter its major judgments, or influence the odds on outcomes.

•   •   •

In the past generation, many Western analysts have assumed that, as the era of colonialism has drawn to a close, major change, systemic revolutions, and radical transformations of society would be less frequent and progress toward democracy and peace more assured. Government change, palace revolutions, coups, etc., might occur but there would be fewer cases of historical discontinuity capable of fundamentally transforming political and social circumstances or abruptly altering power relationships. We think this a highly mistaken view. Over the next twenty years, the community may well confront analytical and estimative challenges, no less severe, and very possibly much more complex, difficult, and dangerous, than those reviewed in this study. The prospects for historical failures will be no less present, and we must prepare for them.

SELECTED CASE STUDIES

First Chinese Nuclear Test

Summary evaluation. Community estimates of early 1962 and mid-1963 relating to the Chinese nuclear program represented a comedy of errors, resulting in an intelligence success.

Drawing on limited information, in 1962 it was thought the Chinese could have produced enough material, by late 1961, to load an as yet undiscovered plutonium production reactor to produce enough material for a [plutonium]-based explosive by early 1963. By mid-1963 an installation at Pao-tou had been identified as a probable plutonium production reactor, capable of providing enough material for a test device, under ideal circumstances, by early 1964, although dates in late 1964 or 1965 were more likely.

An installation at Lanchou had been identified in airborne photography of 1959 as a uranium-235 (U-235) gaseous diffusion plant, but in 1963 it was estimated it probably could not enrich enough material for a test before 1966, although 1968 or 1969 was thought more likely.

When the test actually took place, on 16 October 1964, it was discovered that the device was based entirely on U-235; subsequently, it was determined that the facility at Pao-tou was not a plutonium production reactor at all, and the first use of plutonium in a test occurred in 1968, using material from a facility at Yu-men, which was not found until 1966.

Thus, while the timing of the first test was reasonably well anticipated, the anticipation was an accidental coincidence, based on incorrect analysis of limited data. It also was the result of inadequate appreciation of Chinese technical skills, innovativeness, and determination in pushing forward with the U-235 gaseous diffusion plant after the Soviet departure in 1960 left them with a partially completed facility. It represented a single-minded commitment to a preconceived notion of the Chinese approach.

The Chinese nuclear program. The Chinese nuclear program was established in the 1950s with major assistance from the Soviets, who provided scientific and technical training, and aided in the construction of uranium mining and processing plants, plutonium production reactors, a gaseous diffusion plant for U-235 enrichment, and weapons design. The Soviet departure in mid-1960 introduced delays in the Chinese program.

An Estimate of 25 April 1962, NIE 13-2-62, "Chinese Communist Advanced Weapons Capabilities," judged that enough uranium metal could have been produced by September 1961 for a single 200 megawatt load for an as yet undiscovered reactor. If full power operation had been achieved early in 1962, enough plutonium could be available about a year later for a single weapon test. All this assumed no delays and no difficulties. This was considered unlikely, and a first test would be delayed, perhaps by as much as several years. No evidence of construction of a plutonium production facility had been found by photographic coverage. A building at Lanchou, seen in airborne photography of 1959, was thought to be part of a gaseous diffusion plant, but the absence of electrical power and the belief that an additional building would be required to produce weapons grade U-235 led to the conclusion that an all-U-235 or composite device could not be tested before 1966.

New information, especially photographic, led to the judgment, in SNIE 13-2-63, "Communist China's Advanced Weapons Program" (24 July 1963), that the Chinese advanced weapons program was more ambitious than previously thought. Gaps in information were still substantial, but a probable plutonium production reactor had been found at Pao-tou. Plutonium from this reactor alone, it was believed, could lead to a device in early 1964 at the earliest, and late 1964 or 1965 with even normal difficulties. It was judged that there possibly were more plutonium production facilities than the one identified, however, and therefore the Chinese perhaps could achieve a first detonation of a plutonium-based device at any time. Electrical power serving the gaseous diffusion plant had been noted in photography of 28 March 1963, but it was judged that the Chinese probably could not produce weapons grade U-235 before 1966, and that 1968 or 1969 were more likely dates.

The nuclear test. A 26 August 1964 SNIE 13-4-64, "Chances of an Imminent Communist Chinese Nuclear Explosion," reviewed new photographic evidence and concluded that a suspect facility at Lop Nor was a nuclear test site which could be ready for use in about two months. The weight of evidence indicated, however, that the Chinese would not have enough material (plutonium) for a test in the next few months—on balance, not before the end of the year.

The Chinese tested an all-U-235 device on 16 October 1964. The source of the U-235 was unknown, but debris collected in an air sampling program was dissimilar to that produced by the Soviets since about 1955, hence probably was of Chinese origin. Airborne infrared collection in December 1964 confirmed that the Lanchou U-235 enrichment plant was in operation.

In 1967, a facility at Yu-men, found in satellite photography of 1966, was identified as a plutonium production reactor. The Pao-tou facility was determined to have other functions. The Yu-men reactor probably provided the material for the device detonated in the eighth Chinese test in 1968, the first based on plutonium.

The estimative problem. Information on the Chinese nuclear program was sparse, of uncertain validity, and infrequent provenance in the early 1960s. Photographic inputs were particularly scarce. The community accidentally predicted the timing of the first test fairly accurately. Although the prediction was based on misinterpretation, senior consumers had been alerted some two and a half years earlier that a detonation could take place as much as a year before its actual occurrence, but more likely at about the time of the event. The failure to predict the production and use of U-235 is traceable both to insufficient information and a lack of appreciation for Chinese technical skills, innovativeness, and determination, in the absence of Soviet help. In all, there was a preconception of the likely Chinese approach, and a failure to consider seriously alternative options.

The Soviet ALFA-Class Submarine

Significance. The Soviet ALFA-class submarine is a weapon system of impressive capabilities deriving from technological achievements which are, largely, well ahead of US levels. Although the decision to develop and build the ALFA dates back to 1956, and the first hull was seen under construction in 1967, it was not until the late 1970s that the intelligence community began to appreciate the nature of this new system and not until July 1979 that a fairly complete system description was published.

Summary evaluation. The intelligence community's performance was spotty. Although a CIA paper of 1971 had introduced the reasonable, although lesser, probability that the ALFA hull was titanium, there was no concerted effort until 1979 to explore the operational or strategic consequences, if that probability proved to be correct. Analytical efforts to combine and integrate work separately done on hull, propulsion, and guidance and control subsystems were belated. Neither on an individual agency level nor on a community level was a group established to carry out analysis, using all relevant disciplines, and technological parametric extrapolations of possible system performance.

In analytical performance, the Panel has been impressed by three points:

a. The high level of expertise of a number of technical analysts in the community, who had to deal with a very difficult intelligence problem.
b. The excellent quality of several of the analytic papers, which showed a high degree of technical sophistication and intelligence insight, as contrasted with the rather inadequate organizational or institutional approach to the problem.
c. The virtual absence of broad, speculative strategic analyses which would have attempted to examine ALFA-class developments in the context of their strategic implications. A conceptual framework is still to be developed which would place the new submarine technologies in the forefront of the Soviet effort to overtake or offset the US submarine force lead.

The community was almost completely surprised by the 41-plus knot speed attained by the ALFA-class submarine in March 1979, almost 10 years after the first ALFA was launched. While ALFA's deep-diving potential had long been suspected, its extraordinary high-speed maneuverability, an indication of a high degree of automation, was a further surprise. The Soviets not only "won" their 25-year high risk "race" to develop a truly advanced submarine by the 1980s—combining breakthroughs in hull metallurgy, nuclear propulsion systems, and probably advanced automation—but also managed to keep the US and the West from appreciating the magnitude and nature of their achievement until after the fact. However, once the extraordinary capabilities of the ALFA-class submarine were revealed in the March 1979 speed runs, the community came together promptly and very quickly arrived at a consensus on the principal technical characteristics of the boat.

The OPEC Price Increase of December 1973

The impact of the OPEC oil price increases of 1973 on all countries became the major international economic event of 1974, and persisted well into succeeding years. The OPEC price increase of 1979 dealt a crushing blow to the world economy. The subsequent recession, debt crises for LDCs, and rampant inflation were directly related to the OPEC action. To what extent was the action foreseen by the intelligence community?

During 1973 the intelligence community produced two estimates of the world oil situation: NIAM 3-73, of 11 May, entitled "International Petroleum Prospects," and NIE 1-1-73, of 5 December, entitled "The World Oil Crisis: Economic and Political Ramifications for Producers and Consumers." Both papers are carefully written, well documented, and statistically supported. Analysis of political and economic factors, such as Arab restraints on exports in the autumn of 1973, possible future political action, and the reaction of consumers and non-Arab producer countries is comprehensive and adequate. What is omitted from serious consideration is OPEC itself and its potential for collective action on the price front. Its political action in restraining production and exports is taken into account, but OPEC as an institution receives scant attention.

This view of OPEC as a relatively unimportant element in the world oil scene was identical with contemporary conventional wisdom in government and business. Astonishment was evident in Western circles in late December 1973 and early 1974 over the effectiveness of OPEC's collusive action in doubling prices. Naturally, prices in the non-OPEC world oil market went up along with OPEC's. Neither the OPEC potential for such action, nor its likelihood, was foreseen in the two estimates cited, nor in a steady flow of periodical CIA comments on the world oil scene during 1973.[2] Note was taken of the gradual rise in prices occurring as individual countries negotiated with oil companies, and the estimative work predicted a rise in prices, in large part because of rising world demand and restrictions on supply potential, but the prospect of an OPEC administered floor was not part of the picture. Explicit intelligence reports on many OPEC government actions always showed the Shah as the price hawk, and Yamani as the apparent dove.

Subsequent analytical work by the community included three products in early 1974: (1) a CIA publication (No. 7932/74) of 4 January 1974, entitled "International Oil Developments," (2) a CIA publication identically titled, dated 18 January 1974 (CIA No. 7934/74), and (3) an "Intelligence Report: The Future of OPEC as a Cartel," dated June 1974 (ERIR 74-15). The first two assess in brief but statistically well supported terms the effect of the 23 December 1973 OPEC price increases on the world economy. They appear to avoid drawing any firm conclusions about OPEC collusive action on prices, or about OPEC's potential as a regulator of price and supply. The third is a serious but rather serene study of OPEC. Conclusions were that OPEC would face a serious decline in demand and would be unable to pro rate production. Therefore, it was not a serious problem for the world. (Apparently, one analyst in the energy group had a different view which was well sustained by later developments, but written evidence has not been apparent.)

A major international event, with enduring consequences, was thus not visible in intelligence estimates in advance, and seems to have been somewhat

2. CIA did not analyze non-Soviet and non-Chinese oil developments on a systematic basis until late 1972, when a group of analysts was organized and began serious work, which has been continuing since that time. Special bulletins on a weekly basis characterized its efforts during 1973–74.

soft-pedaled in immediately subsequent analysis. Because the world market was tight in 1973, a price increase was logical, and rather easily absorbed by an active world economy. OPEC's real muscle was shown in 1979 when a colossal price increase began its destructive work on world economic activity.

Ethiopia

The 1974 Ethiopian revolution was a major event for Africa, for the strategy of the Horn, and for great power positioning in the Third World. It shattered the 55-year reign of Haile Selassie; transformed the most feudal and conservative society in Africa to perhaps the most radical and militant; it moved Ethiopia from a close associate of the US to a Soviet/Cuban surrogate.

It was not until 1977 that the community produced a steady focus on these outcomes. We have examined the analytic work of the period (1968–1977) to review estimative judgments as they matured. We have particularly focused on the 1973–1974 record—some 350 publications, including periodical items—to determine whether a more speculative approach, going beyond "hard evidence" but based on reported information and reasonable inferences, might have been more rewarding in alerting policymakers earlier to the revolution's potentials. Our conclusions follow.

The community and the national estimative process were not used during the critical early period. Agency estimative products—two in 1973 and one in 1974—partially filled the community gap.

a. At the beginning of 1973, the Emperor ruled supreme, an absolute, if not divine, monarch. By the end of 1974, he had been deposed, a broken and discredited man under house arrest; two civilian governments had fallen; an extremist military held power; an undefined "socialism" had been proclaimed as the revolution's philosophy; and a largely unknown Major Mengistu Hailemariam had surfaced as the strong man of a radical Marxist dictatorship.

b. The last community estimate was published five years before these events—SNIE 76.1-1-68: "The Outlook for Internal Security in Ethiopia," 11 April 1968. The next was a year after—IAM 2461-75, "Prospects for Ethiopia in the Next Year," 25 November 1975, followed by NIAM 7611-77, "The Ethiopian Revolution and Its Implications," 28 March 1977.

c. The 1968 SNIE was a very good paper which strongly influenced subsequent interpretations of Ethiopian events. It was heavily influenced by the prevailing notion that Haile Selassie could keep emerging problems in hand but that great uncertainty "which could be prolonged and violent" would follow his passage from the political scene. The estimate noted that: "The chief US interest in Ethiopia is the Kagnew Station communications facility in Eritrea," and predicted that: "After the Emperor's passing US ties with Ethiopia will probably loosen, even if a government generally favorable to the US takes office."

Current intelligence was on the whole timely, comprehensive, and relevant to Ethiopian developments and US interests. In 1973, the CIA published 24 finished intelligence reports, including periodical items, on Ethiopia; and, in 1974 as the revolution gathered force, some 330.

a. Very few events of the period were overlooked. In 1973 analysis chiefly concentrated on the Emperor's health and succession prospects, the search for oil, tribal problems, anti-government activity, Somalia, and Eritrea. In 1974, coverage was especially thorough on the quickening pace of civil and military unrest.

b. In hindsight, a few matters were missed. Among them: Major Mengistu, not identified as the key player until 19 November 1974 (a long shot had been taken on 15 October at Air Force Colonel Tessema Abaderash); some over-estimation of Generals Aman and Teferi as the first two heads of the Armed Forces Coordinating Committee (as in the Argentine and Egyptian takeovers, two nondescript generals preceded the strong man's entry); a commentary, sustained too long, attributing unwarranted influence to the Emperor's circle and Ethiopian conservatives generally. But, in general, current intelligence did a first-class job, covering the period well and occasionally supplying clues and speculative leads, which might have led to a different estimative line.

Estimative projections by the CIA were cautious, circumscribed, and con-strained to single-case forecasts. No alternative interpretations of the likeli-hood of a sustained and ultimately successful radical transformation of the state were published.

a. Throughout 1973–1974, the estimative focus did not widen much be-yond the range of the 1968 SNIE. An Office of National Estimates Memoran-dum, "Some Worrisome Developments in the Horn of Africa," 2 February 1973, discussing the Ogaden and the Crown Prince's health, concluded that: "It seems likely that a monarchy of some kind will survive, and the country will not fragment. There is little prospect for a military seizure of power unless the contest for the throne were to appear insoluble." An Office of Current Intel-ligence typescript, "Developments in Ethiopia," 30 March 1973, defined what it called "the worst case" as Somali intervention in a succession crisis through support of Ogaden and Eritrean insurgencies.

b. The succession question remained the major focus (17 of the 24 Ethio-pian reports in 1973). By early 1974 in the wake of mounting civil and military unrest, attention shifted to a perceived political struggle between "conserva-tives," supporting the monarchy and its institutions, and "moderates" seeking constitutional remedies for the country's increasingly serious problems. With few modifications this interpretive line held until after the deposition of the Emperor.

c. There were some clues and enough information in the current intelligence reporting of the time for a different line of speculation. But occasional insights—on military restiveness and indiscipline, on emerging "radical forces," and on urban and rural violence—were neither developed nor further explored. The interpretative line lingered on the contest between "conservatives and moderates," and the judgment that "the military moderates are still the most powerful force in Ethiopia" (NID 30 May 1974) went unchallenged until the Armed Forces Coordinating Committee—the Derg—publicly assumed power in September.

d. In its first analytic commentary on this outcome (and the only one published in 1974), "Ethiopia: The Unfinished Revolution"—Intelligence Memorandum 23 October—the CIA noted that the situation had not yet unfolded to the point "where the nature of the successor regime or the policies that will eventually take shape can be described with confidence." Its principal judgments were that (a) the moderates would stay reasonably united and retain control of the revolution at least in the short run, (b) radical elements might win concessions on some issues, (c) the coordinating committee would declare a republic headed by General Aman, (d) land reform would be the first major program, and (e) "Ethiopia will give stronger emphasis to nonalignment while trying to maintain good relations with Western countries, especially close economic and military ties with the US."

e. A year later, when the community regarded the problem in an Interagency Intelligence Memorandum, "Prospects for Ethiopia in the Next Year," 25 November 1975—a study largely devoted to tribal and international security problems in the Horn—it did not move much beyond the CIA's analysis of the preceding October. Another year and a half was needed before the community, in its next IIM, "The Ethiopian Revolution and Its Implications," 28 March 1977, concluded that Ethiopia, which had been "the centerpiece of US policy in the Horn of Africa," had been:

> transformed from a difficult, occasionally embarrassing, but relatively reliable client of the US into a radical socialist regime struggling to keep control of the country and looking to the USSR, Eastern Europe, Cuba, and China for help.

• • •

As in all revolutions, the Ethiopian analytic problem was to identify the main forces at work and their relative strengths; to estimate goals, directions, and pace; and to derive a sense of probable, and of alternative, outcomes. In retrospect, where hindsight is always close to 20/20, it is evident that analytics stayed too long with theories of the Emperor's authority; dwelt overmuch on "conservatives" and "moderates" as the main players; underestimated the radical forces and their aims; accepted too uncritically the stated desire of the revolutionaries for good relations with the US; overlooked the capacity of the Russians to alter their Somali and Ethiopian relationships. Above all, there was a failure to understand—or to allow for the possibility—that what was involved was not a coup nor a change of regime but a full-blown revolution which would, before it was spent, radicalize the armed forces, politicize an uneducated peasantry, replace the long dominance of the Christian Amharas with that of the Muslim Gallas, drastically redistribute wealth and power, and reverse the country's alliances.

Clearly, there were unusual analytic and estimative difficulties in the Ethiopian case:

a. Politically, the revolution moved slowly, at times imperceptibly, and often inconsistently through successive stages of apparent moderate reform and constitutional revision, expanding radical influence, and collegial military rule, to extremist dictatorship.

b. Operationally, and unlike the Libyan takeover which needed less than four hours, "the creeping coup" which deposed the Emperor took nine months from the Neghelle mutiny of January 1974. The monarchy was not abolished until eight months after the Emperor's arrest; "socialism" was not proclaimed as official dogma for a year, and another year was required before the outlines of its Ethiopian variant became reasonably clear; Kagnew was not closed until April 1977.

c. Throughout these processes, the Derg maintained extraordinary secrecy as to its membership, tactics, and goals. The military extremists who ran it were as effective in their security as they were adept in dissimulation and slicing salami slowly. And their aims had no precedent in Ethiopian history: The resolution was historical discontinuity run riot.

In the circumstances, it is not surprising that the analytic community took a long time to accumulate the "hard data" which the straight-line evidentiary method required to bring Ethiopian events into adequate focus. The basic criticism of estimative performance during the period is not so much its specific analytic conclusions—which by and large rested on assessments of Ethiopian history and the weight of information and evidence available at the time—but its neglect of alternative possibilities, its reluctance to speculate on lesser probabilities, and its general aversion to conjecturing beyond the known data. The system lacked a process or a model for dealing with very unlikely outcomes, and thus reinforced tendencies to ignore the apparent improbabilities, or to assume that they would not happen, or to decline to speculate about them. And, in consequence, judgments missed or trailed the pace of real events.

In the Ethiopian context of 1973–1974, a more speculative approach, resting less on evidence than on insight and imagination, might well have produced a more realistic view of the outcome; could have focused collection requirements and priorities more sharply on less apparent but in the end more meaningful targets; and would have alerted US policymakers much earlier to the possibility of the revolutionary changes chronicled for the first time in the 1977 IIM.

Afghanistan

An Intelligence Memorandum, "The Afghan Succession," dated 3 March 1978, a little over a month before the first pro-Soviet coup of 27 April 1978, failed to mention either the pro-Soviet Communist KHALQ party or the names of any of the new leaders who stormed into prominence so soon thereafter. A biographic Research Paper, "Leaders of the Democratic Republic of Afghanistan," published after the coup, indicated the revolution was the culmination of more than three decades of Communist activity.

From this time on, Afghanistan was the subject of a steady stream of community publications. Some, such as the Intelligence Assessment, "The Afghan Revolution After Six Months," were noteworthy in the cogency of their exposition of recent events and the alternative options and possible future trends. A 4 April 1979 memorandum, entitled "Reply to Questions on Afghanistan," discussed the extent of foreign involvement in Afghanistan, estimated that the prospects for rebel success were dim and concluded that the possibility of Soviet intervention could not be completely discounted. This paper reflected a community mindset which postulated that although the Soviets had the manifest capability to intervene, it would not be to their overall advantage to do so, and therefore that they would pursue alternative strategies.

Special Reports to the President in May and June of 1979 updated the situation in country and concluded the Soviets would not send in ground forces to restore order in the escalating rebellion. On 30 July another Special Report expressed doubt that Moscow could settle the Afghan imbroglio by diplomatic means. A memorandum dated 17 August 1979 prepared by the Office of Strategic Research, "Soviet Options and Forces for Military Intervention in Afghanistan," speculated that Soviet planners were approaching the decision point wherein they must withdraw, expand the advisory program, or commit Soviet combat units. The paper doubted that the Soviets would introduce combat units. A 31 August Special Report stated, "We do not exclude the use of limited Soviet combat units to insure the survival of the Kabul regime."

A 15 December 1979 memorandum stated that the Soviets had committed themselves to continued Marxist rule in Afghanistan. Spot Commentaries on 15 and 16 December stated the buildup of Soviet forces was accelerating. On 19 December an Alert Memorandum advised that the Soviets had introduced three airborne battalions into Afghanistan and concluded that this indicated that the Soviets had significantly changed the nature of their commitment. On 25 December 1979 a Spot Commentary stated that the Soviets had apparently completed their preparations for a major intervention in Afghanistan and that the cross-border movement had begun. On 26 December a memorandum analyzed the capabilities and limitations of the insurgents in light of the massive intervention of Soviet combat troops.

In hindsight, the intelligence community accurately estimated the advantages and disadvantages of intervention. The community held to a premise that the disadvantages of intervention outweighed the advantages and concluded therefore that the Soviets would act rationally in accordance with our perception of Soviet self-interest. As real as the penalties to the Soviets have proved to be, we failed to comprehend the imperatives of Soviet policy as they perceived them. We had a clear understanding of their capabilities, but we misjudged their intentions.

20.

Probabilism in some simple form may finally be digestible—but Bayesianism? It has seemed too far-out, too "social-sciencey." This article and the next (its case-study companion) were pioneer efforts to explore the intellectual possibilities, a quarter-century ago. Is a new generation from graduate schools ready for this kind of thing? (Should it be?)

Bayes' Theorem for Intelligence Analysis

JACK ZLOTNICK

The intelligence interest in probability theory stems from the probabilistic character of customary intelligence judgment. Intelligence analysis must usually be undertaken on the basis of incomplete evidence. Intelligence conclusions as therefore characteristically hedged by such words and phrases as "very likely," "possibly," "may," "better than even chance," and other qualifiers.

This manner of allowing for more than one possibility leaves intelligence open to the charge of acting the oracle whose prophecies seek to cover all contingencies. The apt reply to this charge is that intelligence would do poor service by overstating its knowledge. The very best that intelligence can do is to make the most of the evidence without making more of the evidence than it deserves. The best recourse is often to address the probabilities.

The professional focus on probabilities has led to some in-house research on possible intelligence applications of Bayes' Theorem. At the time of my participation in this research, I was an analyst in the Central Intelligence Agency, which sponsored the scholarship but took no position of its own on the issues under study. My personal views on these issues, as elaborated in the following pages, have no official character.

The Bayesian Approach

Bayes' Theorem in its odds-likelihood form served participants in our test program as their diagnostic rule for appraising new evidence. The odds-

Jack Zlotnick, "Bayes' Theorem for Intelligence Analysis," *Studies in Intelligence,* vol. 16, no. 2 (Spring 1972), pp. 43–52. Originally unclassified; it had been presented as a paper at the Conference on the Diagnostic Process, Ann Arbor, Michigan, 18 June 1970.

likelihood formulation of Bayes' Theorem is the equation

$$R = PL$$

R is the revised estimate of the odds favoring one hypothesis over another—the estimate of the odds after consideration of the latest item of evidence. P is the prior estimate of the odds—the odds before consideration of the latest item of evidence. There is no escaping some starting estimate of P. However, after the starting estimate was in hand, the participating analysts offered no judgments about P. It was a value carried forward in machine memory from previous analysis. R, the result of the mathematical processing, was what went back into machine memory to become the value of P used in consideration of the next item of evidence. The participating analysts offered judgments only about L, the likelihood ratio.

The likelihood ratio was the analyst's evaluation of the diagnosticity of an item of evidence. Evidence is diagnostic when the chances of its appearing are different if one hypothesis is true than if another hypothesis is true. Suppose intelligence is asked to estimate the comparative merits of two hypotheses— one of imminent war, the other of no imminent war. The estimate is to be expressed in terms of the odds favoring or disfavoring the war hypothesis. The latest evidence is deployment of foreign troops to a border area. Is the deployment deemed to be say two times more likely if the war hypothesis is true than if the no-war hypothesis is true? Then the evidence is certainly diagnostic. The value of L, a judgment of the analyst communicated to the machine processor, would in this case be the fraction $2/1$.

Three principal features of Bayesian method distinguish it from conventional intelligence analysis. The first is that the intelligence analyst is required to quantify judgments which he does not ordinarily express in numerical terms. This requirement to quantify probabilistic judgment is the feature that perhaps draws most of the critical fire against the Bayesian approach in intelligence analysis. A debating point of the critics is that analysts are bound to disagree in their opinions of the exact figure that should represent the diagnostic value of an item of evidence. The Bayesian rebuttal is that disagreement among analysts is just as much a characteristic of traditional method and is no less serious for being implicit rather than explicit in the analysis. The critic returns to the debate by observing that the typical analyst, being a verbal and not a mathematical man, finds it inordinately difficult to express his degree of belief to the precision implied by a numerical value. The partisan of Bayes, for his part, takes the position that people have been quantifying probabilistic judgments since the beginning of time—whenever they offered or accepted betting odds on the outcome of any doubtful issue.

The second distinguishing feature of Bayesian method is that the analyst does not take the available evidence as given and draw therefrom his conclusions about the relative merits of opposing hypotheses. He rather postulates, by turns, the truth of each hypothesis, addressing himself only to the likelihood that each item of evidence would appear, first under the assumption that one hypothesis is true and then under the assumption that another hypothesis is true. The analyst is under no ego-supporting need to hold to positions previously taken on the merits of the respective hypotheses; he does not feel called upon to reinforce his self-esteem by reaffirmation of opinions previously put on the record.

The third distinctive feature of Bayesian method is that the analyst makes his judgments about the bits and pieces of evidence. He does not sum up the evidence as he would have to do if he had to judge its meaning for final conclusions. The mathematics does the summing up, telling the analyst in effect: "If these are your readings of the individual items of evidence, then this is the conclusion that follows." The research findings of some Bayesian psychologists seem to show that people are generally better at appraising a single item of evidence than at drawing inferences from the body of evidence considered in the aggregate. If these are valid findings, then the Bayesian approach calls for the intelligence analyst to do what he can do best and to leave all the rest to the incorruptible logic of a dispassionate mathematics.

The Bayesian approach was not studied with any idea of its replacing other approaches in intelligence analysis. The responsibility of intelligence is to depict, as best it can, the current and prospective state of international affairs. The intelligence estimate is a closely-reasoned analysis of such important matters of interest as the top political leadership of a foreign country, evolving popular attitudes in that country, changing force structures in its military establishment, its levels of scientific achievement, and the hard choices it is making in allocation of resources to the guns and butter sectors of the economy. The intelligence estimate is sketched in all the lights and shadows of descriptive, narrative, and interpretive commentary. This task is not reducible to terse statement of the odds favoring one particular hypothesis over another.

There are, however, areas of intelligence analysis where Bayes' Theorem might well complement other approaches. One crucially important area is that of strategic warning—the analysis directed to uncovering any pattern of activity by a foreign power suggestive of a major and imminent threat to US security interests. The patterns of events leading to Pearl Harbor in 1941 and to the Communist invasion of South Korea in 1950 are cases in point. Strategic warning analysis focuses primarily on just the problem that Bayes' Theorem addresses—the odds favoring one hypothesis (say imminent attack) over another hypothesis (no imminent attack).

The Research Task

One way to test the usefulness of Bayes' Theorem for intelligence analysis is to replay intelligence history. This means going back to international crises of years past. It means assembly of the evidence which was available before the outcomes of the crises were known. It means reading the old intelligence estimates and other studies in order to find out how the analysts of the day interpreted the evidence. It means assignment of L values—likelihood ratios—that honestly reflect these analyst evaluations of the evidence at the time and not our present hindsight knowledge.

Another way to test Bayes' Theorem is on current inflows of evidence. The advantage of this kind of testing is that hindsight knowledge does not intrude; Bayes' Theorem is pitted fairly and squarely against the conventional modes of analysis. Offsetting this advantage for honest research, however, is a disabling disadvantage.

The disadvantage derives from the very nature of the hypotheses at interest in strategic warning. The alternative hypotheses are commonly of two types. One stipulates continuation of the status quo. The other stipulates sudden change from the status quo. Usually the situation today is pretty much what it is going to be a week from today. The status quo hypothesis, in other words, usually turns out to be the true one in strategic warning analysis. But the main test of strategic warning effectiveness is the capability to give forewarning of the sudden changes that occasionally do occur in the status quo. The intelligence interest in Bayes' Theorem is primarily in how well the Bayesian approach to strategic warning would meet this main test of performance in situations of general surprise, without chronic resort to cry-wolf false alarms. Unfortunately, intelligence research cannot be speeded up by focus on the particular current issues which will turn into occasions of intelligence surprise. If intelligence could pick out in advance the issues on which it was going to be surprised, it would by definition never be surprised, and it would have no interest in the possible contributions of Bayes' Theorem to improved analysis.

The outlook, then, is that many tests of Bayes' Theorem on current inflows of evidence will be needed to get the few interesting occasions that show Bayesian performance in circumstances of general intelligence surprise. And just a few interesting examples are not enough to make the case for or against the Bayesian approach, which may do better than conventional method sometimes and not as well other times. A large enough sample of interesting examples is needed to justify confident findings of comparative performance on the average.

The results of the testing so far have been interesting enough to make a good case for further testing of Bayes' Theorem in intelligence analysis. Among the interesting results has been an uncovering of problem areas that flank the path of intelligence analysis and that are not very easily outflanked.

The Life-Span of Evidence

One such problem area has been called nonstationarity. In situations of nonstationarity, that is, when hypotheses are being effectively altered by the passage of time, evidence will have a limited life-span. An intelligence hypothesis about current Soviet policy is not exactly the same hypothesis on 15 January that it is on 15 February. The date has changed, so the hypothesis is to a degree different; and evidence back in January which had a certain bearing on the hypothesis of what was then current Soviet policy does not have the same bearing on the hypothesis of what is current Soviet policy a month later.

Consider, for example, some evidence which was available to intelligence and to the public at large in the summer of 1962, before photographic confirmation was received of missiles in Cuba that could reach targets deep in the United States. Soviet leaders gave public assurances during this period that the expanding military aid to Cuba was for defensive purposes only. Now an analyst's appraisal of this kind of assurance will depend partly on how honorable or dishonorable he believes Communists to be. But whatever his views about the honor of Communists, he would certainly not consider any government's assurances to constitute a commitment for all eternity. Governments do make new decisions and reconsider old ones. This amounts to saying that the diagnostic value of evidence bearing on hypotheses about current government policy tends to erode over time. A mathematical logic for strategic warning analysis has to be attentive to this erosion. Perhaps the analyst can specify the expected rate of erosion when he first encounters an item of evidence. If he cannot or prefers not to, the Bayesian approach does not quite attain the mechanistic ideal that would require of the analyst only his one-time attention to each item of incoming evidence. The analyst instead finds himself looking back from time to time at his whole body of past evidence, to consider whether its diagnostic value, as recorded in machine memory, is still valid and not outdated.

Causal Evidence

Another problem area spotlighted in the testing is the occasional reversal in cause and effect relationship between hypotheses and data. The disease generates the symptoms of the disease, and so the physician can infer the disease from the symptoms. Similarly in his surveillance of the Soviet scene, the intelligence analyst in Washington can infer from Soviet actions a good deal about

Soviet policy. But the analyst also has his eye cocked for relevant data other than Soviet actions, data which have less a derivative than a causal relationship to Soviet policy. I draw again on the Cuban missile crisis of 1962 for my historical example.

On several occasions that year, President Kennedy publicly warned that the United States would take a grave view of strategic missile emplacements in Cuba. How would a Bayesian analyst evaluate President Kennedy's warnings for their relevance to opposing hypotheses about Soviet missile shipments to Cuba? If the analyst were a mechanical, uncritical Bayesian, he would say to himself: "President Kennedy is more likely to issue these statements if the hypothesis of imminent Soviet missile shipments to Cuba is true than if the hypothesis of no such missile shipments to Cuba is true. My L in the Bayesian equation $R = PL$ is greater than $1/1$, and so my mathematics works out to an increase in the odds favoring the missile hypothesis."

Well, the analyst in this case is surely not reasoning as President Kennedy reasoned. The President no doubt felt that the clear communication of American concern would either have no effect on Moscow or, hopefully, would dissuade the Soviet leadership from shipping strategic missiles to Cuba. He thought, in other words, that his statements would tend to reduce, not increase, the odds favoring the missile hypothesis.

The complication for the Bayesian analyst is the causal character of President Kennedy's statements. Soviet actions are direct derivatives of Soviet policy. President Kennedy's statements were not. They were important primarily for the chance that they would affect, not reflect, Soviet policy.

It can be shown that, in principle, Bayes' Theorem is as applicable to causal evidence as to derivative evidence. In practice, Bayes' Theorem often offers slippery ground to the analyst appraising causal evidence. In practice, the analyst does better by putting a little sand in his tracks. He gets better mental traction in this case by making a direct judgment about the impact of the causal evidence on the comparative merits of his hypotheses. He says to himself: "If the odds were even-money in favor of the missile hypothesis before receipt of the causal evidence, what would the odds be now after receipt of this evidence?" When the prior odds are even-money (that is, $1/1$), the revised odds equate to the likelihood ratio, according to the Bayesian equation $R = PL$. So, by making a direct judgment of revised odds following a stipulation of even-money prior odds, the analyst obtains an effective likelihood ratio to give the computer.

This is an approach which respects the mathematics of Bayes but does violence to the spirit of Bayes. One of the attractive features about Bayesian method in its pristine purity is that the analyst need address himself to the merits of the hypotheses only at the very beginning of his analysis. In principle, he does not thereafter reaffirm his first opinion, admit to a change in opinion, or criticize anybody else's opinion on the subject. He is supposed to make a judgment, instead, of quite another sort, a judgment about the evidence which postulates the truth of each hypothesis in turn, a judgment which does not involve him again in debate about the merits of each hypothesis. His encounters with causal evidence, however, often do not allow him to keep quite this detachment from the hypotheses. He finds himself addressing R, not L.

Catchall Hypotheses

Another problem area encountered in our research has been examined in Bayesian literature as the nonindependence issue. Nonindependence enters into analysis as a complicating feature when the likelihood ratio—the L value of an item of evidence—is affected by the previous pattern of evidence.

Nonindependence is an arcane subject to analysts who are new to probability mathematics, mainly perhaps because items of evidence which are independent if one hypothesis is assumed true can be nonindependent if another hypothesis is taken as true. Analysis is easier when items of evidence are independent (or to put it more properly, conditionally independent)—that is to say, when the likelihoods of their being received do depend on which hypothesis is assumed true but when these conditional likelihoods hold regardless of the previous pattern of evidence. Intelligence analysts have their way of reaching for conditional independence, whether or not they have ever heard of the nonindependence issue. They reach for a new hypothesis to do service for some hypothesis that no longer seems suitable as originally worded.

Such an unsuitable hypothesis could be the one postulating continuation of the status quo in the strategic warning problem. This catchall hypothesis can be divided into two or more subhypotheses (and it can be divided different ways into different sets of subhypotheses). For an illustrative example, take any case in history of a big power threatening its much smaller neighbor and finally invading the little country when threats alone did not avail.

Suppose the invasion is preceded by reports that the big power is moving its troops toward the border. Considered later in time from the vantage point of hindsight, the troop movements certainly would seem to be strong evidence, which ought to have tipped the odds substantially in favor of the invasion hypothesis. But the analyst of the day would probably find himself reflecting on at least two relevant subhypotheses of the no-invasion hypothesis. Subhypothesis A might be that the big power will not invade the little country but will apply very strong pressures—psychological, political, and other—just short of military invasion. Subhypothesis B might be that the big power will neither invade nor apply other extremes of pressure against the little country.

Now the analyst using Bayes' Theorem introduces an initial opinion about the hypotheses when he begins his analysis. He must similarly introduce an opinion about the subhypotheses if he comes to make them explicit elements in his analysis. By the time he receives the reports of troop movements, the previous evidence will have inclined him to the opinion that subhypothesis A—strong pressures against the little country—is the only reasonable interpretation of the no-invasion hypothesis. The events leading up to the troop movements (the grim warnings, the shrill propaganda, the military alerts) will constitute such virtual contradiction of subhypothesis B—no extremes of pressure—as to give it a near-zero probability. If this is the analyst's view, then the troop movements toward the border must seem almost as likely under the no-invasion hypothesis as under the invasion hypothesis. His L is just about $\frac{1}{1}$. His Bayesian approach has done virtually nothing to change his current odds.

This undiagnostic character of incoming evidence near the climax of international crises may seem novel to novices; it is familiar enough to experienced intelligence analysts. The more experienced they are, the more rueful they are likely to be in their recollections of evidence that was ambiguous to contemporaneous vision but became telling in retrospective inquiries.

False Evidence

Perhaps the most difficult problem area is the suspect character of some evidence. The intelligence analyst gets his information in accounts from sources of varying reliability. He does not know for sure which accounts to believe and which to disbelieve. So he has to appraise his evidence, not only for its bearing on the hypotheses, but also for its probability of being accurate. The estimated probability of accuracy will enter into the analysis and will affect final results.

Unfortunately, an analyst's opinion about a report's probable accuracy or inaccuracy will be influenced by his current opinion about the hypotheses. Does he find it hard to give credence to reports from Cuban refugees who claim to have seen objects resembling medium-range missiles near Havana? If he is skeptical, it may well be because he finds it hard to give credence to the hypothesis that the USSR will do anything so foolish as to ship such missiles to Cuba. So once again, we have a case of information not doing the work which critics later, in all the wisdom of hindsight, will say it should have done.

The Research Promise

My exposition of these problem areas is not meant to imply that they muddle only the Bayesian approach; they plague with fine impartiality all types of intelligence analysis—traditional method as well as Bayesian method, verbal logic as well as mathematical logic. Traditional method also must cope with the eroding diagnostic value of past evidence as it recedes into history. Traditional method also finds it harder to draw probabilistic conclusions about the state of the world from causal evidence than from derivative evidence. Traditional method also sometimes explains away evidence that can be explained away by a favored subhypothesis of a catchall hypothesis. Traditional method also has to contend with the implausibility of evidence that is not in character with the climate of prevailing opinion.

My purpose in expanding on the problem areas is to show that much of the difficulty in intelligence analysis is not the difficulty to which the Bayesian approach is addressed. The Bayesian approach seeks to insulate analysis from frailties of logic in aggregating the evidence. The working world of intelligence, however, is concerned not only about possible inconsistency in everyday thinking between the conclusion drawn from the body of evidence considered as a whole and the conclusion that should logically follow from judgments about the evidence considered item by item. Intelligence views with concern also the possibilities of mistaken judgments about individual items of evidence. The intelligence pragmatist is wistful about evidence which almost speaks for itself, evidence to which most people will attribute much the same probability values because the values can be documented by, say, actuarial statistics or other such extrinsic authority. The pragmatist feels that an increase in the amount of this kind of evidence would do more to help men reach sound conclusions than could any formal logic—Bayesian or other—for reasoning from uncertain propositions about the evidence.

Conceding this point, the Bayesian responds that intelligence must still do the best it can with what it has. In a word of fallible judgments about evidence, the Bayesian approach is not a path to perfection; it can be at best only a path to improvement. The promise of the research on Bayesian method is a mathematical logic to which intelligence can have recourse for substantiating or contradicting the verbalizations of the traditional analysis. When the different approaches lead to discrepant conclusions, intelligence should perhaps undertake to rethink, recalculate, and if possible reconcile. The research interest at this time should be to find out whether such a Bayesian cross-check on other reasoning would significantly improve the quality of analysis.

21.

This is a companion article to "Bayes' Theorem for Intelligence Analysis," by Jack Zlotnick (chapter 20).

The Sino-Soviet Border Dispute: A Comparison of the Conventional and Bayesian Methods for Intelligence Warning

CHARLES E. FISK

Problems of "indications analysis" or "intelligence warning" are essentially questions of how to assign probabilities to hypotheses of interest. For example, a problem of indications analysis occurred in August 1969 when two hypotheses arose; namely, the conjecture (H_1) that within the next month the USSR would attempt to destroy China's nascent nuclear capabilities, and the alternative hypothesis (H_2) that such an attack would not occur.

A method of indications analysis is a rule for eliciting probability judgments from intelligence analysts, and alternative methods for this purpose have been studied within the Agency since 1967.[1] The usual and most direct method is simply that of asking analysts to make either verbal or numerical probability judgments about hypotheses of interest. As an alternative to the conventional approach, the so-called Bayesian method does not require analysts to assign probabilities to the main hypotheses of interest; instead, analysts are asked to specify values for certain "conditional" probabilities, from which one can infer judgments about the main hypotheses.

It has been argued[2] that the Bayesian method is better than the conven-

Charles E. Fisk, "The Sino-Soviet Border Dispute: A Comparison of the Conventional and Bayesian Methods for Intelligence Warning," *Studies in Intelligence,* vol. 16, no. 2 (Spring 1972), pp. 53–62. Originally classified "Secret."

1. Two examples of these studies are "A Mathematical Model for Intelligence Warning" (Intelligence Report No. 1396 67, November 1967) and "Bayes' Theorem in the Korean War" (Intelligence Report No. 0605 68, July 1968). For references to various studies done outside the Agency, see *A Bibliography of Research on Behavioral Decision Processes,* by Ward Edwards (University of Michigan, Human Performance Center, Memorandum Report No. 7, January 1969).

2. A detailed exposition of this argument is offered by Ward Edwards *et al.,* in "Probabilistic Information Processing Systems: Design and Evaluation," *IEEE Transactions on Systems Science and Cybernetics,* vol. SSC-4, no. 3 (September 1968). Further expositions have been put forth by Jack Zlotnick in "A Theorem for Prediction," *Studies in Intelligence,* XI/4.

tional approach to problems of intelligence warning. This article will illustrate the two alternatives, and will then explain the results of an experiment that was designed to test the assertion of the Bayesian method's superiority.

The Conventional Method of Intelligence Warning

The conventional approach to intelligence warning begins when a set of hypotheses first comes under active scrutiny. For example, during August 1969 several intelligence officers warned that the USSR would probably launch a major attack against China within the next month. This warning spawned various hypotheses, two of which were (H_1) that the USSR would begin the offensive during September 1969, and (H_2) that there would be no attack.

For a large class of hypotheses, the problem of indications analysis remains essentially the same: certain Agency officials must first elicit from qualified analysts judgments about the hypotheses, and then must synthesize these judgments into a warning. The officials obviously cannot pore over every bit of evidence observed by each analyst, so analysts must focus and summarize their views.

Generally, then, the first step in the conventional method involves the gathering of either verbal or numerical probability estimates. On 30 August 1969, for example, each of six senior analysts from six Agency offices was asked to estimate the probability of the war hypothesis H_1. Their estimates—i.e., values for $P(H_1)$—appear in Table 1. As time passes, further estimates are elicited, and previous warnings are either amplified or damped on the basis of the new estimates. Clearly, then, a key question is how an official ought to elicit probabilities from analysts. The conventional approach suggests that an official

Table 1

Analyst	The Probability of H_1 on 30 August 1969°
A	.20
B	.85
C	.40
D	.25
E	.35
F	.20

°The symbol H_1 denotes the hypothesis that during September 1969, the USSR would launch a nuclear attack against China.

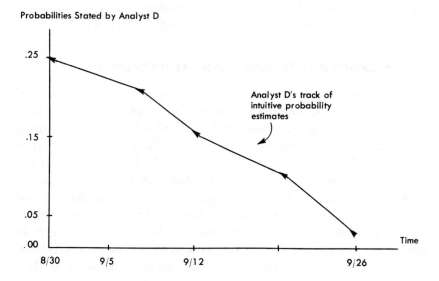

Figure 1.

should simply ask analysts to state the probabilities whenever the official wants to reconsider his warning.

As part of an experiment that was designed to compare the conventional method with an alternative system (the Bayesian) for eliciting probabilities, each of the six analysts mentioned above was asked on 5 September 1969 to re-estimate the probability that a Sino-Soviet war would erupt before 29 September. On 12 September the analysts were asked again, and so forth for each week in September. As a result of this process of questioning, each analyst produced an "intuitive" probability track such as the one shown in Figure 1. Each point on the illustrated track denotes the best probability judgment that Analyst D could offer after reading the all-source intelligence available to him.

On the basis of a considerable amount of research involving simulated questions of intelligence warning, however, Edwards,[3] Zlotnick,[4] and other proponents[5] of the Bayesian method for eliciting probabilities would argue that the sequence of estimates shown in Figure 1 was *not* the best sequence that Analyst D could have specified. They claim that an official who had asked "the

3. Edwards, *op. cit.*
4. Zlotnick, *op. cit.*
5. See the bibliography cited in [note 1].

right questions" could have obtained from Analyst D—and from each of the other analysts—a better sequence of probabilities. This alternative method of questioning will be explained in the following section.

The Bayesian Method of Intelligence Warning

There is no unique "Bayesian method": dozens of systems, each slightly different from its predecessors, have been proposed and tested on simulated problems of intelligence warning. Most of these systems, however, involve substantially similar steps. The steps taken in the Sino-Soviet Experiment to obtain from each of the six analysts a Bayesian track that could be compared with the analyst's intuitive track are as follows:

(a) On 30 August 1969 each of the six analysts was asked to estimate a value for $P(H_1)$, which at that time denoted the probability that the war hypothesis H_1 was true. This first step duplicated the first step in the conventional method discussed above, so each analyst's estimate for $P(H_1)$ appeared as in Table 1.

(b) In contrast to the conventional method, on 5 September the Bayesian approach did not require the analysts to re-estimate $P(H_1)$. Instead, each analyst was asked to list the major events whose occurrence during the previous week had influenced his opinion about the war hypothesis. For example, during the week Analyst D might have observed that no men in the Soviet reserve army had been called for active duty. This event of "no calls" could have been denoted by E_1. And, since Analyst D might have believed that a call-up during the previous week would precede the event of a Soviet attack in September, the event E_1 might have lowered his intuitive probability judgment concerning the chance of war. Similarly, E_2 might have denoted the event of no increases in Soviet propaganda against the Chinese, and so forth for other events that an analyst might have thought relevant to the war hypothesis H_1.

(c) A majority of the analysts listed virtually the same set of relevant events, although some analysts' views had been influenced by events that other analysts had not listed. From the separate lists, a master event list was compiled, such that the events E_1, E_2, . . . on the master list exhibited two properties; namely, (i) each event proposed by each analyst was reflected in the master list; and (ii) each master event was, roughly speaking, independent of each other master event.[6]

---

6. The notion of independence can be illustrated as follows: suppose that Analyst D has listed the event of "a high-level diplomatic probe by the USSR to ascertain probable US reactions to a Sino-Soviet war," while Analyst E has listed "a war-related contact between US and Soviet officials." These two events clearly refer to the same thing, so the master list would contain only one event referring to a diplomatic probe. In some cases, however, the two properties of inclusiveness and independence were difficult to achieve in compiling the master list.

(d) When the master list had been compiled on 5 September 1969, some of the analysts asserted that certain events suggested by other analysts had not actually occurred. Such differences over raw intelligence were recorded as each analyst estimated a probability of occurrence for each of the events E_1, E_2, . . . on the master list.

(e) In addition to specifying probabilities of occurrence, each analyst estimated various conditional probabilities on 5 September. For example, with respect to the event no reserve calls during E_1 of the previous week, Analyst D was asked to specify a value for $P(E_1|H_1)$, which denotes the probability that E_1 would have occurred, given the assumption that the war hypothesis (H_1) was true. Moreover, Analyst D was asked to estimate $P(E_1|H_2)$, the probability of E_1 on the assumption that the no-war hypothesis (H_2) was true. For each of the other events on the master list Analyst D specified a similar set of conditional probabilities, as did each of the other analysts.

(f) A modified version of Bayes' Theorem was then used on 5 September 1969 to calculate for each analyst a "revised" probability of war.[7] This probability was called an analyst's Bayesian estimate, and was plotted on the same graph as his intuitive probability. Thus for Analyst D in particular, on 5 September 1969 the two probability tracks shown in Figure 2 had been obtained—one track by the conventional method, and one by the Bayesian approach.

(g) On 12 September 1969 the Bayesian procedure outlined above was repeated, with the exception that the "prior" probabilities used in the revision process were the Bayesian probabilities of war that had been obtained on 5 September 1969. Thus after two weeks, a typical analyst's probability tracks appeared as in Figure 3.

(h) After the Bayesian procedure had been repeated at weekly intervals during September, the Bayesian tracks derived from conditional probabilities specified by Analysts A, B, and D appeared as in Figure 4. The Bayesian and intuitive tracks compiled for Analysts C, E, and F resembled the tracks shown for A and D, in the sense that for five of the six analysts, the Bayesian track always fell below the intuitive track.

A Criterion for Comparing Probability Estimates

A criterion for comparing methods of probability elicitation can be illustrated with reference to Figure 3. In retrospect, we know that the hypothesis H_1 was false: Russia did not attack China. Thus if an analyst's "probability tracks" had actually appeared as in Figure 3, then on 12 September 1969 an

---

7. This method of calculating revised probabilities is sometimes called a "roll-back" procedure. See *Applied Statistical Decision Theory*, by H. Raiffa and R. Schlaifer (Harvard Business School, Division of Research, 1961).

Probabilities Stated by Analyst D

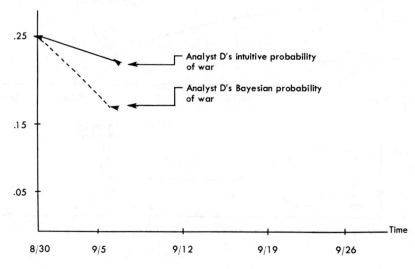

Figure 2.

Probabilities Stated by Analyst D

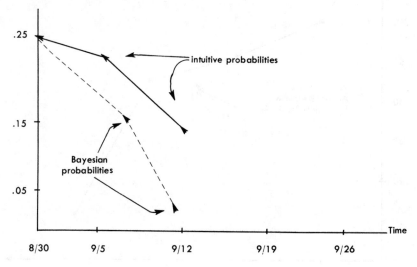

Figure 3.

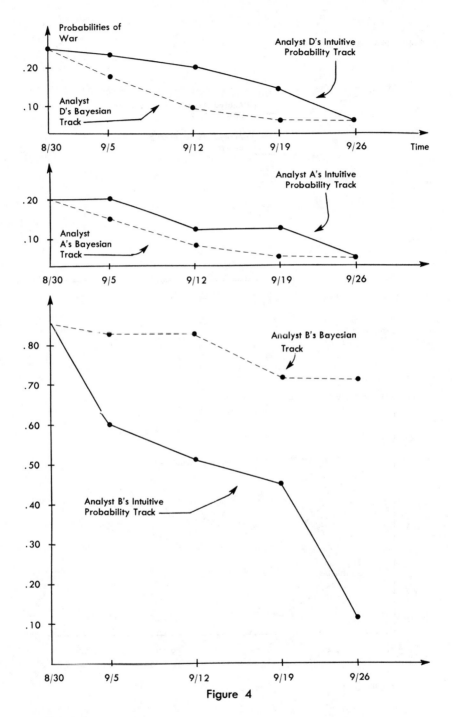

Figure 4

Figure 4.

official would have acted more wisely on the basis of the Bayesian sequence of estimates. In other words, if one had been forced to gamble according to either the Bayesian or the intuitive tracks shown in Figure 3, one would in retrospect have preferred the Bayesian sequence.

Of course, if Russia had attacked China, and if a typical analyst's probability tracks had appeared as in Figure 3, then one would have preferred to have acted according to the analyst's intuitive track. But according to the advocates of Bayesian analysis, such a preference for an intuitive track will seldom occur: if Russia had attacked, then—according to the Bayesian proponents—prior to the attack the Bayesian track for a typical analyst would have been above his intuitive track, such that in retrospect the Bayesian method would again have been preferred. As is evident in Figure 4, Analyst B proved to be an exception to this assertion: his Bayesian track always fell above his sequence of intuitive estimates.

This criterion of "retrospective superiority" has served as the basis for dozens of experiments[8] in which researchers have compared the Bayesian method with alternative techniques for eliciting probabilities, and in most cases the Bayesian approach has triumphed. But there is no firmly established analytical justification for the method. Bayes' Theorem is a mathematical truism, but there are no axioms from which one can infer that repeated applications of the theorem to conditional probabilities specified by analysts will yield superior intelligence warnings. Thus, in the fall of 1969, it was of considerable interest to review the Bayesian method's effectiveness in the context of the actual intelligence problem posed by the chance of a Sino-Soviet war.

The Sino-Soviet Experiment

As explained above, the six analysts met at weekly intervals during September 1969 in order to re-estimate the probability of the war hypothesis H_1, and to specify the conditional probability estimates that were processed according to the Bayesian method. In October 1969 (when the war hypothesis H_1 was known to have been false) the probability tracks derived from the two methods were compared as in Figure 4. The primary result was that for five of the six analysts, the Bayesian track had always been below the intuitive sequence of probabilities. Thus in retrospect, an official would have preferred to have acted according to the Bayesian estimates, rather than according to the analysts' best intuitive judgments concerning the war hypothesis.

8. See the references cited above [in notes 1 and 2].

An Evaluation of the Bayesian Method

Several results of general interest emerged from the Sino-Soviet experiment. First of all, when the experiment began the analysts differed widely in their views concerning the chance of a war; but the reasons for their differences were murky at best.

A typical argument between two analysts would arise when one would accuse the other of having ignored certain crucial facts in estimating the likelihood of war. The accused would then respond that he had indeed considered all relevant information, and that his estimate was based on facts that other analysts had overlooked. Such arguments were difficult to evaluate, since there was no record of who had considered what, or of how each analyst's probability estimate had evolved over time.

Once the Sino-Soviet experiment had begun, however, one could easily determine the relative importance that an analyst had assigned to any given event. For example, it was evident from Analyst B's conditional probability estimates that he had considered the event of Kosygin's visit in September 1969 to Peking as being irrelevant to the war hypothesis. In contrast, Analyst E had regarded the meeting as a profound indicator that war would not occur. The issue of whether Analyst B exercised good judgment in this respect remains an open question; but at least his assessment of the Peking trip had been recorded and could be evaluated.

Thus the Bayesian approach provided a kind of accounting system for intelligence analysis. If such a system were implemented for other questions of indications analysis, a significant class of disagreements among analysts might be resolved. And to the extent that such disagreements would persist, an official who must synthesize warnings on the basis of analysts' estimates could discern and evaluate causes for the disagreements.

A second contribution of the accounting system was the fact that after the system's inception, the analysts definitely did consider the same relevant events. In particular, Analyst E wrote the following review of the experiment.

> In the case of Office E, interchanges with other offices are usually on an unsystematic *ad hoc* basis. The Bayesian experiment afforded an opportunity to bring these interchanges into focus on a systematic basis. Its particular merit lies in the manner in which participants are led to identify the factors influencing their estimates and to present these for critical review by others approaching the question from varying angles. I would emphasize the value of focus, though perhaps no less valuable is the exposure of participants to lines of analysis—as one analyst noted—of which they are dimly if at all aware.

Similarly, Analyst C wrote:

The meeting was a useful forum for the interplay of ideas and the exchange of information which might otherwise not occur. Interchanges would take place in the absence of such a meeting; but they would be limited because of their bilateral nature (in most cases).

In summary, an improved system of accounting for analytical judgments is needed. Although it cannot be said categorically that the Bayesian method excels as a forecasting device, the Sino-Soviet experiment indicates that it might provide a means for such accounting.

22. Here is another (more recent) example of trendy social science intruding: is it animating? or intimidating? or dismissible? The author-advocate sees it as "both justified and inevitable." Time may tell.

FACTIONS and Policon:
New Ways to Analyze Politics

STANLEY A. FEDER

Two challenges facing every political analyst are the complexity of political phenomena and the sea of information flooding our inboxes. During the late 1970s and early 1980s a small group of academics began to make some headway against these problems. Two tools—social choice theories of politics and computers—have made this progress possible.

The theory of social choice focuses on the outcomes of processes by which groups make decisions. Applications of the theory rely on information about the relative strength of political actors, outcomes they want, or candidates they are backing. This is information [of] which most country specialists have a strong intuitive grasp. The theory uses concepts such as cost/benefit analysis and actors' orders of preference for the possible outcomes. The former is used to make inferences about how individuals will behave in making political choices, such as when voting; the latter, to make inferences about the positions a candidate should advocate in order to win the most votes. FACTIONS and Policon[1] are both based on parts of social choice theory that deal with individual behavior and the aggregation of individual preferences.

In contrast to the information requirements of traditional analysis, those of social choice theory are quite parsimonious. In addition, the relationships among political variables in social choice theory are described with much more precision than in classical political theory. In social choice theory political relationships are described mathematically; this makes the computer an appro-

Stanley A. Feder, "FACTIONS and Policon: New Ways to Analyze Politics," *Studies in Intelligence,* vol. 31, no. 1 (Spring 1987), pp. 41–57. Originally classified "Secret" and "Noforn." For definitions, see appendix B.

1. Policon is a method for political forecasting and analysis developed by Policon Corp. and used by the CIA under contract from 1982 until 1986. FACTIONS was developed internally by the Directorate of Science and Technology, Office of Research and Development, and is very similar to Policon.

priate tool for political analysis. Computerized social choice analysis of the interactions of dozens of political actors can be done with consistency and theoretical rigor in a fraction of a second. Analysts who learn FACTIONS or Policon will not only improve the quality of their analyses but should increase their output as well.

More specific and detailed forecasts. Since October 1982 teams of analysts and methodologists in the Intelligence Directorate and the National Intelligence Council's Analytic Group have used Policon to analyze scores of policy and instability issues in over 30 countries. This testing program has shown that the use of Policon helped avoid analytic traps and improved the quality of analyses by making it possible to forecast specific policy outcomes and the political dynamics leading to them.

For example, 60 percent of the Policon analyses done between October 1982 and October 1985 forecast specific outcomes. (The other 40 percent forecast general trends.) In contrast, only 33 percent of DI analyses published during the same period forecast specific outcomes. More than 60 percent of the Policon analyses also predicted the political dynamics leading to the outcomes. Political dynamics were included in less than 35 percent of the traditional finished intelligence pieces. Interestingly, forecasts done with traditional methods and with Policon were found to be accurate about 90 percent of the time. Thus, while traditional and Policon-based analyses both scored well in terms of forecast accuracy, Policon offered greater detail and less vagueness. Both traditional approaches and Policon often hit the target, but Policon analyses got the bull's-eye twice as often.

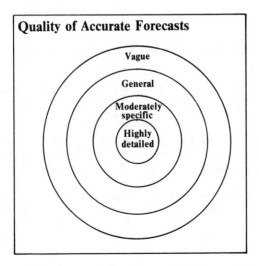

Quality of Accurate Forecasts

Vague

General

Moderately specific

Highly detailed

Beyond that, analysts have found that the use of Policon and FACTIONS makes it easy to analyze alternative scenarios systematically and in detail. Questions like "What if the leader of country X dies?" or "What if the Soviet Union intervenes?" can be answered quickly with FACTIONS or Policon, and in terms of policy outcomes and political processes. Also, both methods make it possible for analysts to test which of the assumptions they have to make will have a major impact on analytic conclusions.

An efficient way to structure political analysis. Like many approaches to political analysis, Policon and FACTIONS assume that once a political environment has been described, inferences can be made about how political actors will behave, how issues will be resolved, and what outcomes will occur. Unlike some approaches, however, Policon and FACTIONS assume that political behavior is purposeful, that individuals and groups compete with each other to obtain outcomes they desire, and that policy outcomes are the result of such competition. Thus, an analyst using Policon or FACTIONS describes a political environment in terms of issues, actors trying to influence the politics of those issues, and each actor's relative political clout and its policy priorities.

As a conceptual framework, these methods indicate what information is important and provide rules for organizing and analyzing political information and for forecasting. Policon and FACTIONS also provide guidance on how to

---

How the Policon model helps analysts avoid traps

Traps	Model's Benefit
Continuity expectations—the future will look like the past.	The model assumes policies or leadership are a product of estimable political forces, not a continuation of a trend.
Too few alternative outcomes considered.	Examines the possibility of each outcome favored by each actor of occurring.
Anchoring—new evidence yields unjustifiably small changes in an earlier estimate.	New evidence is processed systematically to produce a completely new analysis and forecast.
Causality—policies and orders are assumed to be carried out immediately and smoothly in other countries.	Highlights conflicts with ruling groups and between ruling groups and the bureaucracy and military.
Rationality—others are often expected to behave in ways consistent with our expectations.	Assumes behavior is a result of patterns of goals and capabilities, and as each actor sees them from his/her/its perspective.

break an intelligence problem down into a number of smaller questions. For example, analysts concerned about the potential for instability would examine issues over which a governing group would face strong opposition, such as leadership succession, the degree of fairness of elections, or the level of government subsidies on consumer items. A country's East-West orientation could be explored by examining pressures for a shift in trade patterns, a reduction of foreign basing rights, or support for wars of national liberation.

How and why FACTIONS and Policon work. At the heart of FACTIONS and Policon are two models. The first is a model that is used to forecast policy outcomes. This model is derived from what social choice theorists call the "spatial" theory of voting. Spatial models use locations in a coordinate system as an analogy to how close or far apart on an issue groups are politically (as in Table 1).

With FACTIONS and Policon, the coordinate system is unidimensional. This means that issues to be analyzed must be conceived of as having possible outcomes that can be ordered along a line. Some issues have multidimensional aspects; these cannot be analyzed with Policon. Our experience, however, has been that the outcomes of most issues can be portrayed in a single dimension.

[Table I includes] a spatial model of an issue the Office of European Analysis explored in 1983. The Italian Parliament had to decide how large a budget deficit to permit. The Policon analysis not only forecast the outcome with an error of less than one percent, it also correctly indicated that the Italian government would fall over the issue.

In the diagram [section of the table], possible outcomes are described in terms of the size of the debt each group wanted Italy to incur. An abbreviation of the name of each group is placed above the line corresponding to its position on the debt issue. The full names are spelled out in the list above the diagram.

In spatial models of voting, it has been shown theoretically and empirically that the outcome that wins is the one that can derive the most support from nearby groups—the median position in terms of votes or power resources. Policon and FACTIONS use voting as an analogy to other forms of political processes. With these methods, analysts' estimates of an actor's relative political, economic, or coercive resources are used to approximate the number of "votes" an actor controls.

FACTIONS and Policon also assume that an actor may not use all of its clout on issues that are not very important to it. The resources an actor will bring to bear on an issue are, therefore, assumed to be proportional to the importance of that issue to the actor.

The model also assumes that each actor can support or oppose any policy proposed, depending on how near to or far from the actor's desired outcome the proposed policy is. The amount of support an actor will give to a proposed

Table 1   The Italian Budget Deficit Issue

Actors

Ministry of Budget	BUD	Christian Democrats	CDM
Socialists	SOC	Communists	COM
Employers' Association	COC	Unions—Socialist	UNS
Unions—Communist	UNC	Unions—Christian Democrats	UND
Financial Press	FIN	Political Press	POL
Bank of Italy	BAN	Treasury Ministry	TRE
Pertini	PRE	Spadolini	SPA

Issue Diagram

What size deficit will the Italian Parliament permit?

```
BUD
CDM
COC
BAN
TRE                       UNS
PRE        POL            UND
SPA   FIN  COM            SOC   UNC

       |    |    |          |     |
  ┌────┴────┴────┴──────────┴─────┴────────┐
 50        60        70        80       90       100
trillion                                       trillion
  lira              F                             lira
 deficit            O                            deficit
                    R
                    E
                    C
                    A
                    S
                    T
```

---

policy depends on the "utility" of that policy for the actor. With FACTIONS and Policon, utility is inferred from a policy's position on an actor's list of possible outcomes ordered from most to least preferred. These preference orderings are derived from nearness to the actor's position in the spatial diagram of an issue.

To use FACTIONS or Policon, an analyst would take these steps:

- First, define the intelligence problem in terms of a set of policy or leadership choice issues. For each policy issue, identify the actors that will try to influence the outcome.
- Then diagram the issue by placing the groups that advocate opposing and most extreme positions at the opposite ends of a straight line.

- Next, indicate where on the line the policies advocated by the other groups lie. Take care to make the distances between the groups' positions represent the analyst's feel for how near to each other or how far apart groups' advocated policies were. For leadership choice questions, list each actor's order of preference among the possible candidates.
- Next, identify the strongest actor and arbitrarily assign that actor a value of 100. Assign proportional values to other actors based on judgment or gut feeling about their relative strength. Lastly, again use a 100-point scale to estimate how important the issue is to each actor.

Thus, analysts who use FACTIONS and Policon draw heavily on their judgments and impressions about political forces in the countries they follow. FACTIONS and Policon make it possible for the country specialists to make accurate forecasts based on their intuition and judgments. If an analyst is not sure about the strength or position of a group, or the salience of the issue, a range of values can be used to see at what point the values of these variables make a difference in the forecast outcome or patterns of cooperation and conflict.

In mathematical terms in the policy forecasting model, the amount of support an actor (let's call him/her A) gives to another (let's call her/him B) equals A's resources times the salience of the issue to A times A's utility for B's position.

$$\text{A's support for B} = (\text{A's resources}) \times (\text{salience of issue to A}) \times (\text{A's utility for B's position})$$

To use the model, the amount of support each actor will derive from every other actor is computed and summed. Then the model asks which group's position would win if the policy contest came down to a choice between only two alternatives. In other words, is there an actor or set of actors who support the same position, that can defeat every other actor or coalition in a pairwise contest? In social choice theory the actor or policy that can defeat every other one in pairwise contests is called a Condorcet winner, after a French mathematician, the Marquis de Condorcet. Usually there is a Condorcet winner. If there is none, however, there can be frequent shifts in policy on the issue.

Once the number of actors concerned about an issue exceeds three, forecasting a "winner" becomes too time consuming to do by hand. Computer software has been written to perform the forecast calculation rapidly.

The second model on which FACTIONS and Policon are based is a decision model, also known as an expected utility model. For each actor, this model estimates a hypothetical cost or benefit associated with that actor's attempts to get other actors to accept the policy outcome advocated by the first. The patterns of costs and benefits are the basis of inferences about how groups will

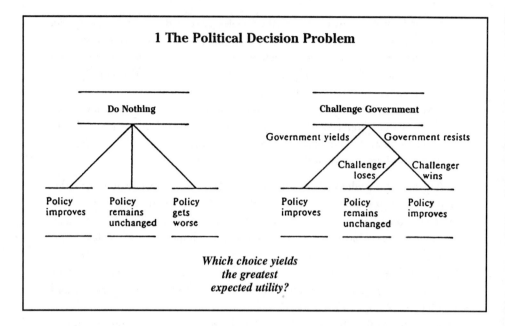

1 The Political Decision Problem

Do Nothing

Policy improves | Policy remains unchanged | Policy gets worse

Challenge Government

Government yields / Government resists

Challenger loses / Challenger wins

Policy improves | Policy remains unchanged | Policy improves

*Which choice yields
the greatest
expected utility?*

react. For example, groups that have a lot to gain by challenging others probably will initiate action. Groups that support different positions and believe they
each have something to gain on an issue are likely to find themselves in conflict
with each other.

With FACTIONS or Policon, the decision problem every actor is assumed to
face is whether to try to influence the other actors to accept the policy preferred by the first. The logic of the cost/benefit analysis is illustrated in Diagram 1. Let's assume that a group (let's call it actor A) wants the government to
change a policy. There are two courses of action open to A: Do nothing or take
actions to pressure or persuade decision makers to change the policy. If A
challenges the government, the latter can react in one of two ways. The government might yield and change its policy to the one that A prefers, or the
government might resist the challenge. If the government resists, A might
muster enough support to get what it wants, or A may lose.

In probability theory the concept of an expected "outcome" is used to
aggregate the values of the outcomes of events or actions. Measures of expected outcome can be used to determine if the action is worth taking. For
example, assume that you are asked to buy a $5 raffle ticket for a new Mercedes
automobile worth $30,000. You know that 10,000 tickets will be sold. If you buy
the ticket, is it likely to be to your benefit? One way to decide is to look at the
expected outcome.

To calculate the expected outcome you have to list the possible outcomes, the value of each to you, and the probability that each will occur.

There are two possible outcomes: you could win or you could lose. The probability of your winning having bought one ticket is one in 10,000. The probability of your losing is 9,999 out of 10,000. If you lose, you are out $5, but if you win you are ahead by $29,995 ($30,000 − $5).

The expected outcome from buying the raffle ticket is the sum of each outcome times the probability of its occurring. Thus your expected outcome would be a loss of $2: ($29,995 × 0.0001) + (−$5 × .9999) = −$2.

With the political decision model a similar calculation can be made, but outcomes are valued in terms of political utility rather than in dollars. Thus we call them political expected utility models.

For analytic purposes, we can think of A as placing some value (utility)—be it positive or negative—on each possible policy outcome. We can also attach a probability to the government's resisting A's attempt to have the policy changed, and to the government's not resisting. Similarly there is a probability that A will win, and a probability that A will lose a potential fight with the government.

In the FACTIONS/Policon approach, A's utility for each possible political outcome can be inferred from the location of alternative outcomes relative to A's position on the issue continuum. The probability that A will win in a political contest with another actor is approximated by A's resources relative to those of the other actor. An estimate of the probability that an actor will resist a challenge is derived from the measure of the importance of the issue to the actor being challenged.

Using these values we can calculate what A is likely to get out of challenging the government. In the jargon of microeconomics, this calculation produces an approximation of A's costs or benefits—its expected utility—in challenging the government on the policy issue.

The value of an approach like FACTIONS or Policon is that it uses country specialists' impressions of groups' relative strengths, positions on an issue, and degree of interest in an issue to generate proxies for the values of probabilities and utilities.

This expected utility calculation describes only A's relationship with the government. In reality, many other actors can be involved. Each of them will make its own political calculations and may either sit back and watch or throw support behind one side or the other if A or anyone else takes action to get the policy changed.

Policon's and FACTIONS' expected utility models take the possible actions of third parties into account and include them in A's simulated cost/benefit perspective. The models also incorporate actors' attitudes toward risk in the calculations.

If the expected utility of challenging a policy is compared to the costs and benefits of not challenging, we can make inferences about what A is likely to do. For example, if A's expected utility of not challenging is greater than that for challenging, A is likely to do nothing. But if A's expected utility of challenging is greater than that for accepting the status quo, A can be expected to take action.

If two actors each perceive that they have something to gain in challenging each other, they can be expected to end up in conflict with each other. When a nation's leader has conflictual relations with many important groups, that country would be considered unstable.

If a national leader has a positive expected utility vis-à-vis another group when the latter has a negative expected utility in relation to the leader, the other group would be expected to accept the leader's position or to try to negotiate a compromise. A group will yield when it believes that less is being asked of it than it believes it could lose. It will resist a political demand when it believes that more is being asked of it than it believes it has to lose. The patterns of behavior deriving from expected utility relationships are summarized in Diagram 2.

The expected utility model also allows analysts to estimate each actor's attitude toward risk. The model assumes that risk-acceptant actors behave as if they overvalue what they have to gain and undervalue what they may lose; risk-

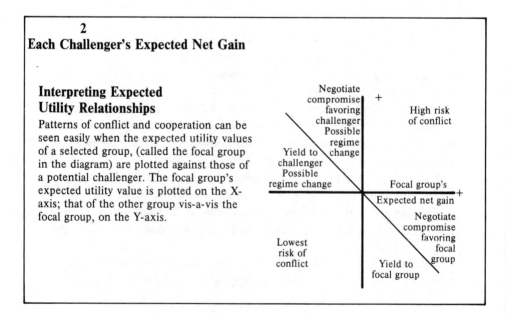

2
Each Challenger's Expected Net Gain

Interpreting Expected Utility Relationships

Patterns of conflict and cooperation can be seen easily when the expected utility values of a selected group, (called the focal group in the diagram) are plotted against those of a potential challenger. The focal group's expected utility value is plotted on the X-axis; that of the other group vis-a-vis the focal group, on the Y-axis.

Table 2 Issues Policon has Addressed in Recent Years

Predicting What Policies Will be Adopted:
- What policy is Egypt likely to adopt toward Israel?
- How fully will France participate in SDI?
- What is the Philippines likely to do about US bases?
- What stand will Pakistan take on the Soviet occupation of Afghanistan?
- How much is Mozambique likely to accommodate with the West?
- What policy will Beijing adopt toward Taiwan's role in the Asian Development Bank?
- How much support is South Yemen likely to give to the insurgency in North Yemen?
- What is the South Korean government likely to do about large-scale demonstrations?
- What will Japan's foreign trade policy look like?
- How much Islamization will the Sudanese government promote?
- What stand will the Mexican government take on official corruption?

Assessing the Potential for Political Change:
- How much austerity can the Egyptian people tolerate?
- When will presidential elections be held in Brazil?
- How much autonomy will be granted to Sudan's southern province?
- What form will cooperation between France's Socialist president and the non-Socialist parliamentary majority take?
- How will a new head of government be chosen in Paraguay?
- How fair are elections likely to be in Panama?
- Can the Italian government be brought down over the wage indexing issue?
- How open will the political system be in Turkey?

---

averse actors, as if they undervalue what they have to gain and overvalue what they have to lose. Using the raffle example, a risk-acceptant person would think that $2 hardly matters in comparison to the car to be won. A risk-averse person would not buy a ticket and feel content to be $2 ahead.

Similarly, by knowing approximate attitudes toward risk, it is possible to make inferences about how actors view the political situations in which they find themselves and to forecast how they will behave. This aspect of the expected utility approach makes it a useful, innovative, and powerful analytic tool.

Drawing inferences from the input data. Once the country analyst has assembled the judgments on which the analysis will be based, the information is typed into the computer. The computer software incorporates a series of mathematical equations based on the spatial voting model and on the expected utility model.

The computer analysis usually can be run in less than a minute, but it generally takes a few hours to interpret the computer results. Findings include a forecast of the policy to be adopted, patterns of conflict and cooperation among the various groups, and insights into the strengths and vulnerabilities of each of the groups.

In many cases, Policon and FACTIONS results will confirm the views of the country analysts. A March 1986 study of the post-Marcos government in the Philippines, for example, bore out the opinion of the intelligence community that President Aquino was unlikely to call for a reduction of US military base rights early in her term. But the analysis also revealed that leftist groups had little real influence on this issue, despite their anti-American activism.

Some Policon and FACTIONS forecasts may run counter to the conventional wisdom. As of October 1986 all unexpected Policon predictions have proven correct. Some examples:

- Policon accurately forecast in May 1983 that after the Peoples' Republic of China claimed the China seat at the Asian Development Bank, Beijing would modify its position to permit some Taiwanese participation in the bank. At the time, even PRC statements that hinted at a "two Chinas" attitude were considered impossible.

- In May 1984 Policon correctly showed that the Italian government under Bettino Craxi was in a strong position on the question of wage indexing, while intelligence community analysts believed this issue would cause the government to fall.

- Almost a year before the January 1985 Brazilian presidential election, Policon correctly predicted the victory of a non-government, consensus candidate and the pressures that then president Figueredo would face during the election process. At the time, community analysts believed a government party candidate would win.

- In October 1985, a Policon study predicted that moderate opposition groups in the Philippines would form an ad hoc coalition that could extract major concessions from the Marcos government. The conventional wisdom held that the moderate opposition groups were too diverse and competitive to cooperate politically. Subsequently, a snap election was called and the unexpected voting strength of the newly unified moderate opposition triggered such extensive government fraud that Marcos fell.

Spotting ad hoc conditions. Politics sometimes makes for strange bedfellows. The Policon/FACTIONS process can help analysts identify emerging coalitions and measure their cohesiveness.

"Ad hoc" coalitions form when groups' similar policy positions result in indirect support for each other during the resolution of an issue. Members of these coalitions may not coordinate their activities, but by working for similar goals they support each other in effect. If the same groups take mutually supportive positions on a number of different issues, a formal or quasi-formal alliance might emerge.

A Policon analysis of the Philippines in October 1985 showed that moderate opposition groups had moved closer together on key issues compared to their positions a year earlier. The tightening of this ad hoc coalition contributed to its increased political influence. These Policon findings helped some analysts anticipate the subsequent decision by opposition groups to field a unified slate of candidates to contest Marcos' reelection.

Estimating risks and opportunities. FACTIONS and Policon provide the analyst with a perspective on how groups see themselves in relation to others. This information about groups' perceptions can tell analysts whether a group is likely to risk intense conflict or yield to others in pursuing policy goals. It also can indicate whether a group is reckless or judicious in choosing its political battles.

Sometimes groups needlessly give up on a policy struggle, underestimating their own strength or the support they can get from others. In a study of Mexico in 1984, for example, modeling showed that the major opposition party was unlikely to win concessions on certain issues because it mistakenly believed that the de la Madrid government held the upper hand.

Other times, groups become risk-takers, thinking they have more of a chance to win on an issue than they actually do. For instance, an October 1985 Policon analysis showed that President Marcos was overconfident, misperceiving the strength of the political opposition. He failed to see that calling an election would be risky, a mistake that subsequently cost him the Philippine presidency.

Testing alternative hypotheses. Once the basic analysis is done, country analysts can next use FACTIONS and Policon to assess the impact of hypothetical political developments. For example, in addition to doing a basic analysis, a country specialist may want to ask:

- Would a leader strength his position if he modified his stand on a contentious issue?
- Would the military gain the upper hand if the current civilian leader were to die?
- What would happen if a foreign country or organization were to throw its weight behind a domestic political group?
- What policies could a country adopt to weaken an insurgency?
- How would the use of repression affect prospects for political reform?
- What would be the political consequences if traditionally apolitical institutions —such as the church and the military—become politicized?

- How would inter-group dynamics and policy forecasts change in a crisis situation?
- How much influence would the political opposition have if all the groups worked together?
- What impact would a change in world oil prices—or other economic conditions, such as foreign aid—have on regime stability?
- What would be the best policy for the United States to adopt toward a country to strengthen that country's government?

To address such questions, data inputs are varied appropriate to the hypothetical political developments and the models are rerun.

Varying resources. Political fortunes change over time and under different circumstances. A group might begin to receive financial support from an external donor, decide to cooperate with a faction of the military, or break up over internal policy disputes. Such changes would alter the influence the group would have on policy matters.

FACTIONS and Polican can simulate changes in clout by adjusting the level of political, economic, or coercive resources a group can bring to bear. An April 1986 study of Panama, for example, analyzed the prospects for a reduction in the influence of the armed forces. The resources of the most powerful military leader—General Noriega—were removed from the model to simulate his death or exile. The analysis showed that Noriega's fall would cause no change in policy forecasts, suggesting that the influence of the military in Panama was independent of Noriega's strong personality.

Varying groups' priorities. To anticipate the impact of a group changing its political program—deciding either to fight harder to get its way on certain issues or to shift its attention to other areas—analysts can adjust the salience values for the group to reflect the hypothetical situation and then rerun the model.

A study of the Philippines done right after Marcos fell in February 1986 assessed the potential impact of both the church and the military reducing their political role in the new government and devoting more time, respectively, to pastoral care and to fighting the insurgents. Under this scenario, Policon analysis indicated that the Aquino team probably would be more vulnerable to extremist pressures and could end up devoting more time to deflecting attacks from the right and the left than to getting on with their reform program. Therefore, according to the Policon study, the continued involvement of the church and the military probably would strengthen the new government, at least over the short term.

Varying policy positions. FACTIONS and Policon allow analysts to evaluate the effects of groups altering their positions on an issue either to respond to changes in the political environment or to ally with other groups to improve their chances of prevailing on an issue.

To anticipate a potentially divisive debate over how long President Sarney should stay in office in Brazil, a January 1986 Policon study exaggerated the groups' positions on the tenure issue to simulate a polarized political environment. Groups in favor of retirement before 1989 were moved toward one end of the issue continuum, while groups in favor of extension in office beyond 1989 were moved toward the other end. Modeling showed that if the debate heated up and groups become strongly divided over this issue, the political balance probably would favor the conservatives who advocated Sarney's extension in office, and the leftists would have to compromise.

A Policon Case Study: Forecasting Aquino's Battles with Enrile

In late February 1986, soon after Corazon Aquino became President of the Philippines, the Political Instability Branch of the Office of Global Issues used Policon to assess the stability of her government. The assessment was based on the analysis of six issues:

- reform of the military command
- policy toward the insurgency
- elimination of crony capitalism
- US military base rights
- legal action against Marcos and his cronies
- legal status/political role of radical leftists.

An Agency analyst with many years of Philippines experience provided the information on which the assessment was based. This information included a list of political groups that the analyst believed would try to influence policy on the six issues, an estimate of the relative strength of those groups, judgments about the policies favored by each group, and an estimate of how important each issue was to each group.

The analysis of the six issues indicated that internal disagreements were not likely to threaten the new, coalition government over the short term. Most disagreements, our analysis showed, probably could be worked out behind the scenes. Among the issues examined, however, the role that radical leftists would be allowed to play in the new government would probably be the most contentious. Attempts to resolve this issue, we wrote, could pit the military against the Aquino/Laurel coalition, contributing to an early end to the honeymoon period.

An analysis of this issue is presented below to illustrate how Policon works

Diagram 3
Legal Status/Political Role of Radical Leftists

Groups to which this issue is:	Very important	Moderately important	Of low importance
	Non-Communist radical left US Government	Communist and Communist- influenced left Church Reform-minded military Middle class/business/ technocrats	Aquino/Laurel group Marcos supporters Old-line military

Issue diagram

◉ Forecast of policy most likely to be adopted.

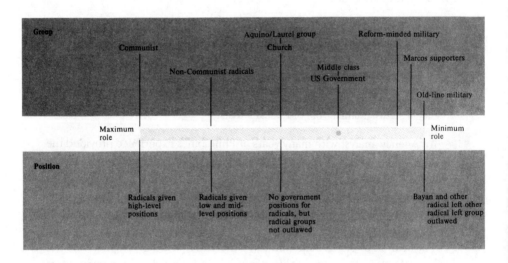

Table 3 Estimated Resources of Groups in the
Philippines°

March 1986

Groups	Resources
Aquino-Laurel group	100
Reform-minded military	100
Church	70
US government	70
Middle class/Business/Technocrats	50
Marcos supporters	50
Old-line military	20
Communist and Communist-influenced left	10
Non-Communist radical left	10

° Many of the political groups in this table represent loose coalitions of like-minded groups/individuals rather than formal political alliances or organizations.

and some of the insights it might provide. The data on which the analysis is based are displayed in Diagram 3 and Table 3.

Under the new government of national reconciliation, the Aquino administration was going to have to decide how far to go in opening up the political process. When Aquino came to power, the Communist Party was illegal. Although the old-line military, Marcos supporters, and the reform-minded military would have liked to see even more leftist groups outlawed, many other political participants would have liked to see all groups invited to participate in open debate as a symbol of the new order. (See Diagram 3.) Communists and non-Communist radical leftists wanted to work their followers into government positions where they could influence policy.

As Diagram 3 indicates, the scope of the debate on this issue among members of the ruling coalition was quite broad; the Reform-minded military and the Aquino/Laurel group were at opposite ends of the political center. The Aquino/Laurel group did not want BAYAN or other Communist-influenced groups to participate in the government but was judged willing to allow them to operate in the political arena. The military, on the other hand, considered Aquino naive and favored continuing to restrict political expression. But at the time, the issue was considered to be not very important to members of the new coalition government.

The Policon analysis indicated that the Aquino/Laurel group and the Reform-minded military might eventually meet each other halfway on this issue, but that the process of compromise was likely to be highly contentious.

Compared to their positions on other issues, the Aquino/Laurel group and the Reform-minded military were far apart. Moreover, as can be seen on the issue diagram, the Aquino/Laurel group, along with the Church, appeared closer to the radical left on this issue than they were to the military. The Reform-minded military, for its part, was much closer to the Old-line military and Marcos supporters in this issue than to the Aquino moderates. These centripetal forces would, we believed, slow the process of compromise.

Tensions were expected to stay under control, Policon's expected utility model indicated, as long as the question of the radical left's political role remained of no more than moderate importance to members of the government coalition. If the Communists, BAYAN, and other radical organizations made enough noise to put this issue near the top of the government's political agenda, however, the centrists should have found themselves in a heated internal political battle.

Thus, although radical leftist groups were unable to influence policy regarding their political inclusion, they could have weakened the government or even brought the honeymoon period to an end by provoking serious conflict between the Aquino allies and the Reform-minded military.

Events during the summer and fall of 1986 were pretty much in line with what was forecast using the Policon approach. This issue did move to the top of Manila's political agenda, and Aquino and Enrile had a major falling-out as a result. True, Policon did not pick up conflicts between Aquino and Laurel, but this was due to our not being concerned about them when the analysis was done in March 1986.

Perhaps more importantly, however, at a time when there was a lot of concern about the stability of the new government and how effective it would be in dealing with the issues facing it, the model enabled us to predict which issues would not be troubling, and which would provoke a confrontation among members of the ruling coalition. The model also enabled us to assess how little influence the far right and far left would have on policy, but how they could influence the political process. In addition, the model enabled us to assess how Filipino groups would react to alternative policies the United States could adopt.

Shortcomings of Policon and FACTIONS. Policon and FACTIONS, like all methods of inquiry, are critically dependent on the quality of information used. The data that go into the voting and expected utility models are the judgments of country specialists, and the models—despite their methodological sophistication—cannot compensate for a lack of expertise.

While these methods provide insights into what developments will occur, they cannot forecast when and how fast events will unfold. The inability of the models to deal with time can be compensated for by analysts estimating the

Table 4   Policon Studies, 1982–86

Countries Studied	Sequence of Studies
Angola: Oct. '82	Oct. '82: Angola, Ghana, Mexico,
Argentina: Nov. '83	South Africa
Asia, Southeast: May '83	Nov. '82: Italy, Pakistan, Turkey
Brazil: Jan. '84, Feb. '86	Dec. '82: Nicaragua
Egypt: Apr. '86	Jan. '83: Italy
France: Nov. '85	May '83: Nigeria, Southeast Asia
Ghana: Oct. '82	June '83: Spain, Yemen
Guatemala: July '85	July '83: Israel
Guinea: Apr. '86	Aug. '83: Mexico
Israel: July '83	Nov. '83: Argentina
Italy: Nov. '82, Jan. '83, May '84	Jan. '84: Brazil, Philippines
Japan: Sept. '84	Apr. '84: Pakistan
Mexico: Oct. '82, Aug. '83, May '84,	May '84: Mexico, Italy
Nov. '85	Sept. '84: Japan, Philippines
Mozambique: Mar. '85	Oct. '84: Pakistan
Nicaragua: Dec. '82, June '86	Jan. '85: Sudan
Nigeria: May '83, Jan. '86	Mar. '85: Mozambique
Pakistan: Nov. '82, Apr. '84, Oct. '84	Apr. '85: South Africa
Panama: Apr. '86	June '85: Paraguay, Saudi Arabia
Paraguay: June '85	July '85: Guatemala
Philippines: Jan. '84, Sept. '84, Aug.	Aug. '85: Philippines
'85, Oct. '85, Feb. '86	Sept. '85: South Korea
Saudi Arabia: June '85	Oct. '85: Philippines
South Africa: Oct. '82, Apr. '85	Nov. '85: France, Mexico
South Korea: Sept. '85	Jan. '86: Nigeria
Spain: June '83	Feb. '86: Brazil, Philippines
Sudan: Jan. '85, Mar. '86	Mar. '86: Sudan
Turkey: Nov. '82	Apr. '86: Egypt, Guinea, Panama
Yemen: June '83	June '86: Nicaragua

The items in this listing have been rearranged for clarity of presentation—HBW.

conditions under which changes might occur and the rates at which groups may become stronger or weaker, alter their political agendas, or modify their positions on issues. Scenarios incorporating a number of possible changes in the political system can be examined to anticipate the changes and assess their implications. However, when a crisis occurs in a country or the political lineup shifts significantly, a new Policon or FACTIONS study needs to be undertaken. But this would be the case with any form of analysis.

In summary, FACTIONS and Policon are methods for structuring political analyses and use mathematical models of political processes. They are analytic tools that enable a country or issue expert to sharpen and expand the depth of his or her analysis. With Policon or FACTIONS, analysts can reliably process their informed impressions of issues, actors, policy preferences, and resources to forecast policy outcomes and processes.

Forecasts and analyses using Policon have proved to be significantly more precise and detailed than traditional analyses. Additionally, a number of predictions based on Policon have contradicted those made by the intelligence community, nearly always represented by the analysts who provided the input data. In every case, the Policon forecasts proved to be correct.

A growing number of analysts are taking advantage of Policon and FACTIONS. Given the increasing demand for analysis that is specific, unambiguous, and forward leaning, continued growth in the use of these methodologies within the Agency seems both justified and inevitable.

Barbara Pace and Anne Rudolph, Office of Global Issues, contributed to this article.

23.

The author, presumably a veteran analyst of scientific and technical (S&T) intelligence, ponders his distinctive craft, emphasizing the need to be multidisciplinary and to use logic, not to become captive to the narrow enthusiasms of specialists. Note that his Postscript, written twenty years ago, already envisaged a shift of attention from military to economic competition, "foreign to much of our past experience." Will this shift ever get beyond "groping" for a role?

Scientific and Technical Intelligence Analysis

ROBERT M. CLARK

In 1939, the British decided to assign a scientist to the Intelligence Branch of the Air Staff. Inasmuch as no scientist had previously worked for an intelligence service, this was a new and revolutionary idea. A tall, solemn physicist named R. V. Jones, then working at the Royal Aircraft Establishment, Farnborough, was picked for the job. Jones's first job was to study "new German weapons" which were believed to be under development. The first of these was a blind bombing system which the Germans called Knickebein. Knickebein, as Jones soon determined, used a pair of radio beams which were about one mile wide at their point of intersection over the city of London. German bombers flew along one beam, and when their radio receivers indicated that they were at the intersection with the second beam, they released their bombs.

At Jones's urging, Winston Churchill ordered up an RAF search aircraft on the night of 21 June 1940, and the aircraft found the Knickebein radio signals in the frequency range which Jones had predicted. With this knowledge, the British were able to build jammers whose effect was to bend the Knickebein beams so that German bombers for months to come scattered their bomb loads over the British countryside. Thus began the famous "battle of the beams" which lasted throughout much of World War II, with the Germans developing new radio navigation systems and the British developing equally effective countermeasures to them.

Jones went on to solve a number of tough Scientific and Technical Intelligence problems during World War II and is generally known today as the

Robert M. Clark, "Scientific and Technical Intelligence Analysis," *Studies in Intelligence*, vol. 19, no. 1 (Spring 1975), pp. 39–48. Originally classified "Secret."

"father of S&T Intelligence." The basic principles of S&T Intelligence analysis which Jones worked out during World War II and which have been previously discussed in *Studies in Intelligence*[1] are just as useful today as they were in the beginning.

Purpose of S&T Intelligence

The primary purpose of S&T Intelligence since Jones's day has been *to identify new enemy weapons and to describe their characteristics.*

Once you know the characteristics of an enemy weapon system, then his tactics and strategy for using the weapon system follow naturally. If, as a result of a heavy research, development, and testing effort, the Soviets manage to squeeze the accuracy of a particular ICBM down below .25 nautical miles CEP, then the primary target of all such ICBMs is almost surely going to be U.S. Minuteman missile silos. If the ICBM has no better than one-half nautical mile accuracy, then it probably will be used against cities, industrial complexes, and other soft targets. As another example, the range of the Soviet BACKFIRE bomber is a critical factor in determining whether BACKFIRE is intended for use against ground targets in Western Europe and for naval use, or whether it is intended for strike missions against the continental United States.

Also, once you know the characteristics of an enemy weapon system, countermeasures against that system become much easier. For instance, we knew a great deal about the SA-2 surface-to-air missile system which was deployed extensively to defend North Vietnam. When the decision was made to launch mass raids against North Vietnam with B-52 aircraft, we were able to tailor our countermeasures against the SA-2 so well that on some raids the North Vietnamese SAM system was almost completely ineffective. On the other hand, we knew very little about the SA-6 SAM system which was deployed in Egypt prior to the Yom Kippur War. Largely as a result of this lack of knowledge, countermeasures against the SA-6 were not effective and the Israelis lost large numbers of their strike aircraft to Egyptian SAM systems.

Cases of S&T Intelligence

Jones found that all the S&T Intelligence problems which he encountered fell into three general cases. Unfortunately, since Jones's time, S&T analysts have had to contend with a fourth case.

---

1. Reginald V. Jones, "Scientific Intelligence," *Studies*, VI/3; and "The Scientific Intelligencer," *ibid.*, VI/4.

S&T CASE #1:

WE DEVELOP WEAPON—

THEY DEVELOP WEAPON

This is the most common problem encountered by S&T Intelligence officers. We develop an ICBM—the Soviets develop an ICBM. We put MIRVs on our ICBMs—they are putting MIRVs on their ICBMs. The Soviets developed an ABM system—we developed an ABM system. Both sides are now developing a laser kill weapon. And so forth. In this case the S&T Intelligence officer's job is not so difficult, because he can turn to his own country's experts on that particular weapon system. Use of your own experts has its own pitfalls, however, as we note later on. A classic example of some of the pitfalls is "The Case of the SS-6."[2] U.S. ICBM experts, insisting on applying U.S. design approaches to Soviet missile designs, managed to hold up an accurate intelligence assessment of the SS-6 for a number of years.

S&T CASE #2:

WE DEVELOP WEAPONS—

THEY DON'T DEVELOP WEAPONS

In this case the intelligence officer runs into a real problem: it is almost impossible to disprove anything in S&T Intelligence. The fact that no intelligence information exists about a particular foreign development cannot be used to show that the development itself doesn't exist. As an Air Force intelligence officer in the early 1960s, I read year after year the USAF estimates that said, "the USSR is probably developing a pulse doppler radar for its interceptor aircraft," and "the USSR is expected to deploy a computerized air defense system similar to the U.S. SAGE system." Years later, the Soviets have still done neither—so far as we can tell. But both estimates are just as difficult to disprove in 1974 as they were in 1964. And the BACKFIRE we mentioned earlier . . . how can anyone conclude that the Soviets do not intend to use it as a strategic bomber against the U.S., no matter how unsuited it may be for such a mission?

2. M. C. Wonus, *Studies in Intelligence*, XIII/1.

S&T CASE #3:

WE DON'T DEVELOP WEAPONS—

THEY DEVELOP WEAPONS

This is the most dangerous case. Here the S&T Intelligence officer has to overcome opposition from skeptics from his own country. Very often these skeptics are scientists who themselves tried a similar approach, failed, and then felt themselves obligated to discourage everyone else from trying the same thing.

One of the most dramatic examples of Case #3 was the Soviet development of the antiship cruise missile. Segments of the U.S. intelligence community sounded a warning in the early 1960s that the Soviet antiship missiles represented a real threat to the U.S. surface fleet. The threat was not taken seriously, however, until the sinking of the Israeli destroyer *Eilat* by an early model Soviet cruise missile in the Six Day War of 1967. Unfortunately, many Defense Department officials then overreacted, and have since repeatedly labeled the U.S. surface navy "a bunch of sitting ducks."

Analysts in the bacteriological warfare and chemical warfare business will become more and more familiar with Case #3 now that the U.S. has stopped all BW/CW weapons research.

S&T CASE #4:

WE DON'T DEVELOP WEAPONS—

THEY DON'T DEVELOP WEAPONS

R. V. Jones never had to contend with this case, since the British were involved in a war and had no resources to waste on academic problems. Case #4 is the most frustrating; it resembles Case #2, but since we haven't developed the weapons system in question, physical restraints can be ignored and *any* of the players can change *any* of the rules of the game at *any* time. Our first real encounter with Case #4 was the SAM upgrade problem, described by Sayre Stevens in "SAM Upgrade Blues."[3]

SAM upgrade—the possibility that the USSR could develop a limited ABM defense using the SA-2 (and later SA-5) SAM systems—made life exciting (and frustrating) for many CIA analysts and senior officials. Anytime an

---

3. *Studies in Intelligence*, XVIII/2.

analyst working on SAM upgrade seemed to be making progress toward a solution, someone would find a new wrinkle in the problem which forced a fresh start. One lesson of SAM upgrade is that we can no longer produce only conventional intelligence assessments. Intelligence analysts will continue to answer questions which read, "What is the capability of weapon system 'X'?"; but more and more analysts will encounter questions which begin "What if . . . ?" These are usually the Case #4 questions.

Last summer, DDS&T intelligence analysts had to address the idea that the Soviets might be developing a space-based laser ABM system. This concept was proposed by a senior official of another government agency (interestingly, most Case #4 problems are proposed by people who are outside the intelligence community but have contact with it; seldom if ever are such cases proposed by intelligence officers). The idea was that the Soviets might be working on a program to put large high-powered ultraviolet lasers into synchronous altitude (25,000-mile-high) orbits. By focusing the laser energy on U.S. ICBM reentry vehicles during their midcourse phase of flight, the Soviets would then be able to destroy any number of the reentry vehicles. The fact that such a program would cost the Soviets more resources than the U.S. put into the Apollo Program seemed to daunt no one—least of all the advocates who insisted that we look for evidence of a Soviet program. After considerable expenditure of analyst time and effort, we concluded that the Soviets were *not* developing a space-based laser ABM system. Unfortunately, this was probably only the initial effort on this particular problem. It seems characteristic of Case #4 problems that they never go away; they simply go through cycles.

Sources of S&T Intelligence

Jones used the analogy of the human head to describe how S&T cases were handled. In his analogy the eyes represented photo intelligence and the ears represented signal intelligence. Both of these intelligence inputs were fed to the brain, which handled the job of collating the intelligence, analyzing what it meant, and making decisions. To complete the analogy, one might consider the mouth to represent the dissemination process.

Despite Jones's comment about the eyes and ears, an S&T analyst normally uses six sources of information in his work. They are:

Photo Intelligence
Signal Intelligence
Human Sources
Foreign Literature
Results of U.S. Work
Basic Physical Laws

Many intelligence analysts refer to the first two of these as "hard" intelligence and the second two as "soft" intelligence. This unfortunate terminology reflects a common bias that photo and signal intelligence information is more reliable than the other kinds. Actually, human and foreign literature sources have provided some of our most valuable insights into foreign scientific and technical developments. Their evaluation, however, requires more judgment and analytical skill than do the photo and signal intelligence sources.

The last two sources—U.S. work and basic physical laws—are not generally considered as sources of intelligence at all. But these sources tell you what *has* been done and what *can* be done. And they take as much analytical time as any of the other sources. In some cases, they may take *more* time; some analysts claim that it is easier to get information on Soviet than on U.S. R&D work.

Intelligence analysis—the brain function in the Jones analogy—is the process of pulling together all the sources of information and drawing conclusions. It is a difficult process, probably no better understood than the functioning of the brain itself. There are a few guidelines, however, the most important of which Jones described as "the cardinal principle of scientific intelligence."

The Cardinal Principle of Scientific Intelligence

Back in the fourteenth century, a philosopher named William of Occam did a great deal of thinking about the best way to draw conclusions from the results of scientific experiments. His conclusion has been used as a guiding principle for scientific researchers in all the centuries since. It also serves as the single most important guiding principle for intelligence analysts. It goes under the name of *Occam's Razor: Use the least number of hypotheses to explain your observations.*

Occam's Razor works this way: Suppose that we discover that the Soviet embassy in Washington has received a copy of a classified briefing which was presented recently in the Headquarters Auditorium. I might then announce to you: "The Soviets must have a bug in the igloo—go find it." After you have finished tearing the igloo apart, you come back and report that no bug is to be found there. My reply is: "Do you *really* expect the Soviets to put the bugs out where you can find them so easily? Call in the sweepers!" So after a very thorough electronic sweep of the wrecked igloo, you come back with a negative report. But I'm ready. "Ah-ha," I say. "It's just as I suspected—the Soviets have developed an unsweepable bug!" As you see, we could carry this game on for quite some time—unless you use Occam's Razor and say, "No! There must be a simpler explanation for our observations."

Now this story may sound a bit farfetched, but it describes the sort of thing that goes on in the intelligence community every day. We recently went through an exercise of this sort with an acquaintance of mine on the Intelligence Community (IC) Staff which ended up with his conclusion that every Soviet satellite had some sort of clandestine mission. And the only reason we hadn't found out about all these clandestine missions was that we hadn't looked hard enough!

Some S&T Intelligence Maxims

In addition to the cardinal principle, there are a number of rules of thumb which most intelligence analysts learn sooner or later through hard knocks or experience. The first of these is: *Suspect all crusaders.*

An intelligence officer should *never* have an ax to grind. The day an analyst says to himself, "I'm going to prove . . . ," he's left the path of reason. Of course you *have* to present proof for any conclusions you draw from analysis. This is quite a different thing than setting out to prove something before you know the facts. The objective of any intelligence analysis effort is the *truth*—not the proof of some preconceived notion. There probably exists no better illustration of this point than the story of the "SS-8 controversy" which David Brandwein described in the Summer 1969 issue of *Studies in Intelligence* (XIII/3).

In 1961, the Soviets began testing a new missile system, the SS-8. Air Force intelligence analysts concluded very quickly that since the Soviets had a large ICBM (the SS-6) and a small ICBM (the SS-7), the SS-8 would be an even larger ICBM than the SS-6. CIA analysts disagreed. By the beginning of 1962, the intelligence community analysts were divided into two camps—a "large SS-8" group and a "small SS-8" group—and the struggle had all the marks of a full-blown crusade. Neither side would concede that its analysis was less than flawless. Each side searched for evidence to "prove" its case. By the middle of 1962, an objective analysis of the SS-8 was no longer possible within the intelligence community. The impasse was not broken until an independent and reasonably impartial committee was formed to assess the problem. The controversy did not end completely until 1964, when the SS-8 was photographed in the Moscow parade and turned out to be a small missile. Unfortunately, much time and money had already been wasted because a few people were more concerned with "proving" their case than [with] finding the truth.

The mark of a true crusader generally is an inability to admit that he might be wrong. The intelligence community seems to have more of its share of crusaders than most government or industrial groups; unfortunately, many of the crusaders are in the S&T Intelligence field—the last place a professional scientist would expect them to be. Professional scientists instinctively distrust crusaders. Crusading is incompatible with the scientific method, which tries only to establish the facts—never to prove something. One of the great scientists of all time, Louis Pasteur, put it concisely: "The greatest derangement of the mind is to believe in something because one wishes it to be so. . . . "

A second rule of thumb in S&T Intelligence is: *Experts can be wrong.*

Of necessity, the intelligence community has to use experts as consultants. It is often argued that the experts are the best people to *do* the analysis, but an expert can develop a closed mind in his own field of expertise more readily than the non-expert. Experts are particularly dangerous in S&T Case #3. When Jones concluded his successful analysis of the Knickebein signal, his proposal to send a search aircraft up after the signal was strongly opposed by Britain's leading expert in radio wave propagation—who contended that the Germans couldn't be using such a signal because it would have to bend around the earth's surface to be received over London. Fortunately, Churchill didn't learn of the expert's opinion until after the search aircraft had obtained the Knickebein signal.

A big problem with experts is that they impress people unnecessarily because they *are* labeled "expert." The expert's opinion may be given more weight than it deserves. Perhaps the mentality of official Washington—which spurns pearls offered by a research assistant for the dross from a research director— has something to do with the problem. Any intelligence analyst foolish enough to propose a major analysis effort on "Possible Soviet Development of a Space-based ABM Laser Weapons System" would have been laughed at. Unfortunately, the idea was proposed by an expert who happened to be influential, and no one laughed (out loud, at least). We did the project.

Experts tend to be most obstinate when they are in the wrong. A few years ago, CIA analysts were trying to assess a particular Soviet ABM radar. Some experts who were consulted came to the conclusion, based on incomplete information, that it was actually two radars—that a large flat structure located next to the main radar antenna was the antenna for the secondary radar. After we had done some additional analysis and had taken a close look at Soviet antenna technology, it became apparent to most intelligence community analysts that the flat structure was an antenna feed structure, not a radar. The experts dismissed this interpretation, and CIA analysts were obliged to search for a signal from the secondary radar. Finally, the Soviets built an operational version of the ABM radar we had been observing. In the operational version of the radar, the flat structure was replaced by a strange-looking flat apparition which no one in his right mind could call a radar antenna. While conceding that the new flat structure was clearly a feed system for the ABM radar antenna, the experts never did admit that their original estimate of the secondary radar had been wrong. They merely avoided all discussions on the subject. Even today, I occasionally ask one of the analysts who were involved in the project if he has found the secondary radar signal yet. Fortunately, our ABM analysts all have a good sense of humor.

When the expert's opinion differs from all the other available sources of intelligence, you have to question the expert's opinion just as you would question any other intelligence source, for reasons which the expert seldom can appreciate. Treat the expert just as you would any other intelligence source; don't worship him. The same could be said for the contractors, who are just another form of expert. Which brings us to our next maxim: *Never trust a contractor.*

This is a bit strong; perhaps I should say, "Don't rely unreservedly on a contractor." There are good contractors and bad ones. Note that I didn't say never *use* a contractor—I said don't trust him. We do and should use contractors in S&T Intelligence analysis to perform jobs which would take too much analyst time, but we tend to depend too much on the contractors. I once asked a good friend of mine, an ABM analyst, about the technical capabilities of a particular ABM radar he was studying. His reply was "I'll have to check with my contractor first." Giving him the benefit of the doubt, I assume that his remark was tongue-in-cheek. But it points to a dangerous trend in CIA as well as much of the rest of the intelligence community.

Remember, a contractor is in the business for the money, much as a professional spy is in the business for the money. Any case officer can tell you how to treat a professional spy. You use them when you have to, but you never trust them. The same is true for contractors.

We once awarded an electronics analysis contract to Company "Z" on the West Coast. Shortly thereafter, the company "Z" project officer visited Headquarters to receive his instructions on how to proceed. After a few formalities and a cup of coffee, we sat down to discuss the contract details. His first question was unforgettable—and typical of many contractors. He said: "OK— What is it that you want us to prove?" We should have canceled the contract on the spot.

Because the contractor wants to earn the money you're paying him, he feels obligated to come up with *something*—whether there's something there or not. A contractor also knows what every good newspaperman knows: *Bad news sells.* So the contractor is particularly vulnerable to the Anak syndrome (a vulnerability which contractors share with new intelligence analysts who are trying to make a name for themselves).

The Anak syndrome goes back to the time when the Israelites found it necessary to spy out the land of Canaan. The spies came back with a completed intelligence analysis which they reported in Numbers 13:32–33.

. . . And they brought up an evil report of the land which they had searched unto the children of Israel, saying, The land, through which we have gone to search it, is a land which eateth up the inhabitants thereof; and all the people that we saw in it are men of a great stature.

And there we saw the giants, the sons of *Anak*, which come of the giants: and we were in our own sight as grasshoppers, and so we were in their sight.

The results of this report were disastrous for the Israelites: 40 more years of wandering in the wilderness.[4]

Based on previous experience with contractors, I will always be convinced that the next day Moses received a letter something like this one:

> Israelite Research Projects Agency
> Kadesh 3
> Wilderness of Paran

Commanding General
Palestine Liberation Army
Kadesh 7
Wilderness of Paran
Unto Moses, Shalom:

1. Recent intelligence reports indicate that Canaanite Army field units have deployed GIANTs. This unprecedented advance in human engineering on the part of a potential enemy puts our forces at a severe tactical disadvantage. IRPA war gaming analys[i]s indicates that PLA units encountering GIANT-equipped Canaanite units one-on-one would incur 76.8% casualties while inflicting only 16.4% casualties on opposing forces.

2. IRPA believes that the magnitude of this challenge to Israelite survival requires a full-scale R&D effort to counter the Canaanite threat. Accordingly, we are pleased to submit our proposal entitled "The Feasibility of Developing GIANTs from Israelite Racial Stock."

3. IRPA is well qualified to conduct this R&D effort. Our related experience includes two prior assessments: "The Biological Impact of Locust Swarms on Egyptian Wheat" (Secret/Israelite Use Only) and "A Tactical Mobility Problem: New Approaches to Crossing the Red Sea" (TS/IUO).

4. We propose to undertake this effort on a cost-plus-fixed-fee basis for a fee of 2,000,000 shekels. The contract effort is expected to be completed in 40 years.

> Signed,
> Ammiel the Son of Gemalli of the
> Tribe of Dan
> Director of Research

Attachments: Proposal

4. For another view of Moses as policy maker and intelligence officer, see "Decision Trees," *Studies in Intelligence*, XVIII/4.

Our final maxim is an obvious one: *Look at the whole picture.*

Or, to put it another way, never ignore sources of intelligence. This rule may be obvious, but it's one of the most difficult things for an S&T analyst to do. The chief problem is one of available intelligence information. NSA, CIA, and Naval Intelligence Command, to name three groups, have many information compartments. An S&T Intelligence analyst on almost any topic will find that the information he needs is scattered across several of these compartments. And sooner or later, in trying to get the information which he needs *out* of these compartments, he has to face up to the *paradox of S&T Intelligence: The more important the subject, the more difficult it is to obtain access to the available intelligence.*

This paradox results not from security regulations, but from human nature. Very few intelligence collectors or analysts are willing to reveal (to other analysts, at least) the most interesting and exciting bits of information which they possess. This is due to a fear—often justified—that the analyst to whom you reveal the information will take it, use it for his own purposes, and get the credit for your work.

Almost all intelligence services over the years have paid a heavy price for this over-compartmentation and professional jealousy. Soon after the British began jamming the Knickebein system, Goering became aware that the British knew in advance when his bomber raids were coming. He put together a team of counterintelligence officers to locate the source of the leak. Goering gave them access to all available information *except* the Knickebein project, which he considered too sensitive to release to them. Of course, Knickebein was the tipoff of the German air raids, so Goering's counterintelligence effort was a failure before it started. As another example, Pearl Harbor resulted in part from too much compartmentation; the people at the top didn't have the whole picture.

Even when the information is available to analysts, we don't always use it intelligently. The bias on "soft" vs. "hard" intelligence mentioned previously is one example. We seem to be training many telemetry analysts, ELINT analysts, photo analysts . . . people who rely primarily on one source of information, and use the others as background. Such people are S&T Intelligence specialists. They are not S&T Intelligence analysts.

An S&T Intelligence analyst has to have a sense of perspective. He must have an instinctive feel for what the foreign R&D groups are like—their biases, preferred approaches, weaknesses and strengths—and the resources that act as constraints on their developments. You can't get perspective from a single intelligence source. You can't get perspective in three months, or even six months, of intensive work in one S&T subject. It takes years of work, with *all* the available intelligence information, to gain the perspective and the insights that a first-line S&T Intelligence analyst must possess.

Postscript

This article has addressed some aspects of S&T Intelligence analysis as it has developed since Jones's day. Its stress has been on weapons intelligence, or the application of science and technology for military purposes. In recent years, as the focus of international competition has shifted somewhat from the military to the economic instrument of national power, a new purpose or objective for S&T Intelligence has begun to evolve: to assess the technical capability of our economic competitors (France, Japan, etc.) in the high technology areas of international trade. The S&T Intelligence community is still groping for a role in this rapidly expanding area of civil technology assessment. It is a job which is foreign to much of our past experience. It would be a very familiar role, however, to the industrial espionage group at General Motors which must keep tabs on the latest developments at Ford and Chrysler. Many of the rules discussed above will apply; some will not. The development of ground rules will be an interesting and exciting task in this new field of S&T Intelligence.

24.

A veteran CIA economic analyst gives an up-beat history of his part of CIA since the 1960s, and the economists' relations with other departments of the government. Fault-finding is here eschewed. The redactions appear to relate to spying on specific friends. The article shows again that the arguments against directly assisting U.S. businesses have been conventional at CIA for at least twenty years. The requests for help will not go away—but predictably neither will CIA's intractability in rejecting them, except possibly in a *counter*intelligence mode.

Economic Intelligence in CIA

MAURICE C. ERNST

Economic intelligence in CIA has reached maturity; it has become accepted as a central function by all major components of the Agency. But, although CIA established a preeminent position in the US Government as a source of analysis and judgment on foreign economies and international economic issues a decade ago, questions as to the necessity and even legitimacy of aspects of economic intelligence have persisted. Why can't State or Treasury or Commerce do it? Is it a legitimate requirement for CIA? Is it really intelligence?

The Agency's discomfort with aspects of economic intelligence reflects some fundamental characteristics of this discipline that differ substantially from those of military or political intelligence. First, the bulk of basic information on economies is in the public domain, and consequently is unclassified. To a large extent, intelligence agencies use much the same information base to assess economic issues as do international institutions, private firms, and government units doing unclassified research. Even in denied areas such as the USSR, the great bulk of economic information is unclassified. Still, classified sources fill important gaps, especially on communist economies and in certain areas of other economies, and provide judgments as to government intentions. Sometimes they make a critical difference to economic assessments. Thus, clandestine collection is essential.

Another unique characteristic of economic intelligence is that it serves a policy community that is of necessity disparate, generally unstructured, and

Maurice C. Ernst, "Economic Intelligence in CIA," *Studies in Intelligence*, vol. 28, no. 4 (Winter 1984), pp. 1–22. Originally classified "Secret" and "Noforn." For definitions, see appendix B.

concerned with both domestic and international issues. International economic issues are important not only to our national security and foreign policy but are also intimately linked with domestic economic policy. For example, any policy decision concerning exports of grain to the USSR must consider not only the impact on Soviet military power and foreign policy and on the interests of other grain exporters, but also the implications for US farmers and consumers. While CIA will focus on the international aspects of a problem, many of its policy customers will try to use CIA's assessments for domestic policy purposes and will angle their questions accordingly. The policy customers of CIA's economic intelligence include not only State, Defense, the National Security Council staff, and Treasury, but also Commerce, Agriculture, the Special Trade Representative, and sometimes Interior and Labor. All of the latter are primarily concerned with the welfare of domestic constituencies, and in some cases are funded by Congress specifically to protect these constituencies.

These characteristics of economic information and policy inevitably create uncertainties and ambiguities for economic intelligence. They require judgment to define the unique contribution of CIA in cases where unique sources are not a factor. They require careful navigation in dealing with the complexities of the economic policy community. But in my view they do not detract from the importance of the role CIA's economic intelligence has played and can continue to play in the US Government.

In what follows, I will try first to sketch the phases of development of economic intelligence in CIA since its inception. Then I will discuss how economic intelligence was produced—with people, methods, products, and sources. Finally, I will touch on a few lessons from the past that I believe have useful implications for the future.

Phases of Development

The history of economic intelligence in CIA through 1972 is exceedingly well covered in a three-volume history of the Office of Research and Reports and the Office of Economic Research in its earlier years by David Coffin, a former ORR/OER analyst and branch chief and a professional historian, who died in January 1982. Like any good history, this study weaves the influences of people, organizations, outside forces, and internal responses into a dynamic picture of how economic intelligence developed. It is on file in the Office of Global Issues. For the period since 1972, I have relied mainly on my personal knowledge, refreshed by a quick review of key documents.

The preliminaries. From the foundation of CIA in 1947 to the creation of ORR in November 1950, economic intelligence was limited to less than a hundred specialists concentrating on key Soviet industries, commodities, and transport; the most important function of this work was to support export control policy. As the cold war intensified and especially during the Korean War, policy officials turned to CIA for answers to questions on Soviet and Chinese economic vulnerabilities to Western economic warfare or military operations. During the early 1950s, the economic intelligence effort became better integrated, bringing together in ORR a growing number of industrial, agricultural, commodity, and transport specialists, a newly hired staff of professional economists, and what had been a separate group of Soviet area specialists who focused on current intelligence and the use of communications intercepts. By 1953, the ORR economic intelligence effort had been expanded to almost four hundred professionals.

The assault on the Soviet Bloc economies. Creation of a single all-source economic intelligence unit and rapid expansion of its personnel enabled CIA to undertake a massive research effort, which at first was focused almost exclusively on the Soviet economy, and by the mid- and late 1950s included a substantial effort on Eastern Europe and China. Although CIA made contributions to current intelligence publications and national estimates, and responded to ad hoc requests from the NSC and other policy-level customers, the great bulk of its work went into basic research. This effort began with what was appropriately called "an inventory of ignorance," in which what little was known about the Soviet economy was put side by side with what needed to be known. The process of building up information was slow, painstaking, and labor-intensive until Moscow in 1957 began publishing annual statistical handbooks and releasing other statistical information. A picture of Soviet economic capabilities—transport system, plant capability, current production, technology—had to be pieced together from odds and ends of information, such as pre-war statistical publications, ambiguous Soviet claims on percentage increases from some pre-war base, and reports by travelers and defectors. Most studies were voluminous and detailed. Although they were of little direct policy relevance, except in the area of export controls, they enabled CIA to develop a unique information base and expertise on the Soviet economy.

Support of export control policy was a major CIA economic intelligence function from the beginning and reached a large scale in the early 1950s as ORR's expertise on the Soviet economy developed. CIA analysts prepared assessments of Soviet industrial and technological capabilities and deficiencies and of the availability of selected products and technologies from other Western countries for use in the implementation of domestic export control legislation and in multilateral negotiations on export controls in COCOM. These functions have continued through the present.

As the flow of officially released economic information expanded, it became possible to spend less time on plant-by-plant studies and more time on analysis of the growth and structure of the Soviet economy and of Soviet economic policy. National estimates on the Soviet economy, which were produced annually beginning in the mid-1950s, became the instruments for integrating the entire economic research effort, since they required contributions on each industry and sector, which were combined into assessments of overall economic growth and the allocation of resources. Policy interest in these studies was enhanced not only by the traditional questions about effectiveness of economic warfare but also by Nikita Khrushchev's declaration of an economic race with the United States and his boast that the USSR would catch up economically by 1985.

On a smaller scale, systematic work was also launched on the East European economies, especially after the Polish and Hungarian crises of 1956. Interest in the Chinese economy surged during the Korean War, especially in assessments of Chinese economic vulnerabilities and of the potential impact of a US blockade. Exploitation in the mid-1950s of what was then relatively good Chinese data established a sound analytical base which made it much easier to assess Chinese developments in what proved to be a long period of information drought during the 1960s and early 1970s.

This was also a period during which CIA was given formal authority for producing economic intelligence on Soviet Bloc countries. NSCID 15 (June 1951) directed CIA to "conduct, as a service of common concern, such foreign economic research and produce such foreign economic intelligence as may be required: (a) to supplement that produced by other agencies . . . ; (b) to fulfill requests of the Intelligence Advisory Committee." Then on 14 September 1954, DCID 15/1 on the production and coordination of economic intelligence assigned "all economic intelligence on the Soviet Bloc" to CIA, with several exceptions. Defense took the main responsibility for military-economic intelligence; State remained primarily responsible for economic doctrines, the political and social aspects of economic institutions, and the relationships between political and economic policies. It was recognized that some overlapping work would be necessary.

Entering the free world. Having established a preeminent position for research on the Soviet Bloc economies, in the early 1960s ORR became involved on a substantial scale in research on free world economies. From the beginning, CIA had done some work on non-communist economies, mostly in response to specific requests from policy levels. During the mid- and late 1950s, ORR closely followed the early phases of Khrushchev's efforts to use Soviet economic aid as an instrument of penetration in less developed countries. In addition, there was a continuing demand for comparative analyses of the size and growth of the Soviet Bloc and Western economies. In the early 1960s world events and bureaucratic changes involving the State Department and CIA gave a major boost to CIA's role on free world economic issues, putting in motion a process of expansion in this area that would continue at least through the 1970s.

US Government concern about the stability of third world countries, and especially about US-Soviet competition in the third world, grew rapidly as the Soviet economic penetration program mushroomed during the late 1950s and early 1960s. It came to a head during the Cuban missile crisis, which helped to trigger an activist approach to the third world by the Kennedy Administration. Policy support requests [to] ORR multiplied, first on Cuba and then on all of Latin America and many other third world countries. In response to these requests, first a Cuba branch and later a Latin America branch were formed.

The critical bureaucratic change which propelled CIA into free world economic research was the decision by the State Department to relinquish to CIA the responsibility for producing the economic sections of the National Intelligence Surveys. In 1961, the Director of the Bureau of Intelligence and Research, Roger Hilsman, decided that producing NISs detracted from what he considered to be INR's principal role, which was to provide research and analysis in support of the Secretary of State and his top aides. Hilsman apparently hoped to compensate for part of the loss of NIS positions by obtaining some new positions from the department which would be used to hire sophisticated professionals to perform the policy support functions. But these hopes were disappointed. INR did not receive new positions. Moreover, because NIS funds represented about half of INR's budget, while the resources used to produce the NISs were far less than half of the total, INR lost not only the NIS function, but also a substantial capability to do other things. Faced with the necessity to cut its personnel from seven hundred to three hundred fifty, INR took the deepest cuts in economic research in order to protect a reasonable capability for political research. Many INR economic units were cut by three-quarters or even more and, as a result, coverage of free world and even Soviet Bloc economies became thin or nonexistent. The NIS functions and a few analysts were initially transferred to CIA's Office of Basic Intelligence, which managed the NIS program. Subsequently, the responsibility for producing the economic and political/social sections was shifted to ORR and the Office of Current Intelligence, respectively, together with a small number of positions.

These shifts in NIS functions had a major impact on ORR, which over the next few years had to develop a research capability on every country in the world, including some forty new African states, in order to fulfill NIS commitments. At the same time, with State's capabilities for economic research and analysis greatly weakened, the Office of National Estimates began relying on ORR as the principal source of economic inputs for National Estimates. Policymakers in the NSC and the various government departments also began to seek research assistance from CIA, especially on third world countries. As experience with NISs and NIEs grew, ORR became bolder, initiating its own research projects on free world economies. Most of the effort was focused on the less developed countries; CIA's role on the industrial economies and on core issues such as economic growth, inflation, finance, and trade remained peripheral, with some notable exceptions mentioned below.

To cope with the growing effort on free world countries an International Division in ORR was established in 1964. This expansion, together with the rapid parallel growth of military and military-economic research, led to the division of ORR into three separate offices. An Office of Geographic Research was broken out in 1965 and the remainder of ORR split in 1967 into an Office of Strategic Research and an Office of Economic Research.

The new CIA economic functions were accepted implicitly but not formally sanctioned. In a letter to the Secretary of State in March 1963, DCI McCone stated that CIA needed to produce economic intelligence on free world countries for both departmental and national purposes. Although State's silence could be taken as implying tacit agreement to what amounted to a major expansion of CIA responsibility, the formal existing authorities under the NSCID of 1951 and the DCID of 1954, which gave State primary responsibility for national intelligence on free world economic issues, were not changed. This apparent conflict between reality and authority proved almost immaterial; it never limited the demands on CIA for work on free world economies and had little effect on CIA's willingness to undertake such work.

The Vietnam War period. Development of the Vietnam problem into a major US war during the mid- and late 1960s placed heavy new demands on OER which temporarily slowed the development of free world economic research and forced a substantial reduction in research on the Soviet economy. The decision to take on detailed analysis in OER (rather than in OSR or OCI) not only of the economic aspects of the war in Indochina, but also of military logistics and, after the Tet offensive, of military manpower and operations, required a major diversion of personnel from other functions, especially from work on Soviet industry and transportation, and on international shipping and communications. At peak, about fifty OER professionals worked on aspects of the Indochina war while only about a dozen new positions were provided for this purpose.

From the early 1960s to the early 1970s, there was a steady erosion of the research effort on the Soviet economy, particularly the coverage of Soviet industries, energy, and agriculture. For example, by the early 1970s, coverage of Soviet energy had been reduced from more than a dozen to three analysts; of Soviet agriculture from ten or so to three or four; of Soviet chemicals from six or seven to two; of Soviet metals from a dozen to four; and of Soviet machinery from perhaps twenty to seven who dealt mostly with high technology sectors and with export control issues. At the same time, the free world effort continued to expand slowly.

Into the mainstream of international economics. Just as growing Soviet-US competition in less developed countries had pulled CIA into free world economic research, so the loss of US predominance in world finance and trade during the late 1960s and the two severe oil shocks of the 1970s drew CIA into the mainstream issues of economic analysis and policy. The fundamental change was the transformation of the US global economic role from one in which economic policy could be largely subordinated to foreign policy and security objectives, to one in which the growing importance of US commercial and financial interests had to be balanced with foreign policy and national security concerns. The forces underlying this fundamental change include: two decades [of more] rapid economic growth in most other industrial countries than in the US; the emergence of Japan as an economic superpower; a large increase in the role of foreign trade (both imports and exports) in the US economy, from less than five percent of GNP in the 1950s to over ten percent by the late 1970s and nearly fifteen percent recently; large-scale penetration of the US market by imports of major products, such as automobiles, steel, textiles, and consumer electronics; a US shift from self-sufficiency in crude oil to a large net import position; and, for almost a decade prior to the abandonment in 1971 of fixed exchange rates based on the US dollar, a growing erosion of the US international competitive position and of the willingness of foreign central banks to increase their dollar holdings. Because of these fundamental trends, the State Department, which had successfully taken the leading role in formulating and managing US and foreign economic policy since the start of the Marshall Plan, found its positions increasingly questioned by Treasury, Commerce, Agriculture, and executive agencies such as the Council of Economic Advisers, which were concerned less with foreign policy than with domestic economic problems and constituencies. For most of the 1970s, attempts to reconcile these often divergent points of view were made through the staff of the Council for International Economic Policy (CIEP) which was headed by a Special Assistant to the President. Inevitably, these diverse economic policy departments and CIEP came to CIA for analysis that did not suffer from a departmental bias, was all-source, and took a broad perspective. By the mid-1970s, CIA had become the most important source of analysis in the government on such key questions as economic growth, inflation, trade, international finance, and energy.

The process of expansion into these core economic areas began in the late 1960s as a result of recurring international financial crises and growing concern about the stability of the international financial system. During the sterling crisis of 1967, which forced the devaluation of that currency and created serious concern that a general assault on the dollar might follow, OER became aware that special intelligence, especially COMINT, could be exceedingly useful in providing advanced warning of possible major transfers or sales of sterling or dollar balances and began to systematically exploit this resource. During 1967–69, various types of special collection provided the raw material for a regular series of reports on gold markets and on South African gold policies and activities, which had become important because of US Government efforts to make a new international agreement on the official price of gold stick, in the face of growing market pressures and South African manipulation. Treasury was the principle customer for this analysis. Other early OER work on core economic issues included assessments of foreign reactions to the US decision to suspend gold convertibility (November 1971), and major studies of US trade relations with Japan, Japanese formal and informal import restrictions, and the Japanese steel industry. At the same time, major briefing books were prepared in 1970–71 for the Secretary of Commerce on US relations with Japan, Western Europe, and Canada. In response to these growing demands for policy support, OER created new branches to better cover Japan and Canada, the European Community, and international energy, fortunately a year or more in advance of the big international crises of 1973 and subsequent years.

The growing CIA role in free world economic intelligence was recognized and strongly supported by the President's Foreign Intelligence Advisory Board in its report to the President on economic intelligence in December 1971. PFIAB noted that State had not carried out its assigned responsibilities for collection and analysis on free world economic activity; noted that OER was the only US Government unit capable of doing the needed production; and recommended that resources be added for production of economic intelligence, that requirements be reexamined, and that the community served by intelligence producers be expanded to include the entire economic policy community. In effect, the concept of economic intelligence was once again broadened to include not only US foreign policy considerations, but also considerations of US economic power and international competitiveness. Even so, it was not until the Executive Order of 1978 that CIA was formally given the responsibility (not exclusive) to produce economic intelligence on the entire world.

By the time of the Arab oil embargo and subsequent tripling of oil prices in 1973, OER had established the organization and some of the expertise needed to respond effectively to demands for intelligence support from the policy levels and had the support of top Agency management, the President, and key economic policy officials. The oil shock created economic problems of a different nature and magnitude from those to which policy officials had become accustomed. During the oil embargo there was of course an enormous demand for information on how much oil was being produced, where it was being shipped, and what was happening in world markets. Although there was only a limited amount of information from special intelligence sources, CIA was the only agency capable of putting all available information together into a coherent, up-to-date picture useful to policy officials at the NSC, State, Treasury, and elsewhere. What became an OER—indeed a CIA—best seller, the weekly *International Oil Developments* (*IOD*), later renamed *International Energy Weekly* (*IEW*), was born in December 1973 in response to a request from the NSC staff. At the same time, OER greatly increased its energy effort, which evolved, as the crisis eased, from monitoring the embargo to assessing the short-term oil market, and then to projecting longer-term energy trends. Before long CIA had become a dominant source of information and analysis in the US Government on international oil issues.

The energy crisis in turn created great uncertainties for the world economy, throwing the US and other industrial countries into a severe economic recession in 1974–75 which appeared for a while as if it would be deep and lasting. There were great uncertainties about how the oil price increases would work themselves through the world economy; about their impact on overall economic activity and inflation; about whether the massive increase in the financial assets of the OPEC countries would be "recycled" by the banks or by the OPEC governments to less developed oil importing countries which were running big deficits as a result of higher oil import costs. Because of the magnitude of the shock and the resulting uncertainties, what had traditionally been the principal sources of routine judgment and projections on the world economy—OECD and the Treasury Department—no longer seemed adequate. In this situation, OER was able to leap into the breach. OER began to produce regular estimates of economic growth, inflation, trade, energy, and economic policies on all the major industrial countries, as well as on key LDCs. Regular reports were also produced on OPEC assets (their size, location, and currency); LDC debt problems; world commodity prices; trends in world trade; and troubled industries such as steel, textiles, and automobiles. By the latter part of the Ford Administration, CIA estimates and forecasts of the principal world macroeconomic trends were being used as a basis for discussion at Cabinet-level meetings, such as the Economic Policy Board. Economic intelligence had indeed come to encompass not only the economic sinews of our enemies' military power but also the economic activities and policies of neutrals and allies which affected US foreign policy and economic interests.

This new, large expansion of OER functions was funded entirely through internal reallocation of OER personnel—in effect, the sixty or so positions (fifty professionals) which had been shifted mainly from Soviet analysis to the Vietnam War were in turn transferred to free world research, especially on energy, trade and finance, and industrial countries as the effort on Vietnam was phased out. There were some small additional cuts in aspects of Soviet economic work. The effort on China remained about constant as CIA continued to piece together information from a wide variety of sources, much as it had done on the Soviet economy in the early 1950s. This painstaking all-source process was necessary because the Chinese released virtually no economic data between the late 1950s and the late 1970s. Indeed, OER studies, many of which could be sanitized and published in unclassified form, became essential inputs into private sector research on China.

As to Soviet work, the period of East-West détente shifted policy demands from economic warfare to trade promotion possibilities. At the same time, the disappearance of US surplus grain stocks left the world grain market and US consumer prices highly vulnerable to big increases in Soviet grain imports in years when Soviet crops were bad, notably 1972 and 1975. There was great interest in CIA crop estimates not only in the NSC staff and State, concerned with foreign policy implications and leverage, but also in the Council of Economic Advisers, Agriculture, and Commerce, concerned with the impact on US farmers and on the US cost of living.

CIA goes public. In April 1977, President Carter at a press conference made reference to an OER report in response to a question on the outlook for the oil market. In effect, he used a CIA estimate to help explain why he considered the energy problem to be "the moral equivalent of war." The President's statement thrust CIA into the public eye and started a period of fairly open CIA participation in public discussion of major economic issues that lasted until 1981. This openness had mixed effects, some good and some bad, on CIA's economic intelligence.

Publication of unclassified studies on economic topics by CIA was far from new. CIA analysts began to prepare articles for publications of the Joint Economic Committee of Congress on the Soviet, Chinese, and East European economies beginning in 1962, and these contributions continue through the present. Although the JEC contributions are reviewed within CIA, they are attributed to the author, not to the Agency. Unclassified publications under CIA imprimatur also began in the 1960s. Most of these dealt with unclassified statistics on communist economies or with technical or methodological topics of interest primarily to academics and other experts—for example, Soviet GNP by sector of origin and use; indexes of Soviet industrial and agricultural production; Chinese foreign trade data. These specialized publications were useful to CIA in establishing contacts and developing dialogue with academics and other private sector specialists; as a means of building CIA's reputation for work of high quality; and as an aid to recruitment of economists. These studies never caused problems because they were not estimative, forward-looking, or politically controversial.

Estimative studies were another matter, especially on politically sensitive topics. Prior to President Carter's press conference, there had been two intentional and one unintentional CIA incursions into unclassified estimates. In April 1958, DCI Allen Dulles publicly presented ORR estimates that Soviet GNP was growing at annual rates of six to seven percent, double that of the US, and might reach fifty percent of the US GNP by 1962. This rapid Soviet growth presented, he said, "the most serious challenge this country has faced in time of peace." This public statement was widely criticized as a blatant attempt to justify increases in US military budgets, even though CIA officials defended their estimates in public testimony before the Joint Economic Committee. CIA then moved out of the limelight on economic issues until January 1964 when DCI John McCone, at the suggestion of the President, gave a press conference on the Soviet economy at which he revealed that Soviet economic growth had slowed to a one and one-half percent rate in 1963, that the USSR faced a difficult hard-currency situation, and that gold stocks had fallen to low levels. The initial CIA plan had been to release this information in an unclassified State Department paper, but the press found out that CIA was the source. The public reaction was mostly negative, focusing on motives rather than facts. Specifically, CIA was accused of trying to justify controls over exports and credits to the USSR and the press gleefully collected adverse reactions of all kinds from real or self-appointed experts. The fact that most outside experts eventually recognized that CIA was correct never received much publicity. This unfortunate experience led to a new, temporary embargo on CIA unclassified publications. A third flare-up over unclassified publications occurred in the spring of 1967 when CIA unintentionally became involved in political controversy in Congress over licensing of US equipment for the Soviet automobile plant for which Fiat was the prime contractor. At that time CIA provided State with some unattributed material for use in congressional testimony and also published an unclassified paper on the Soviet automobile industry. This paper, although basically descriptive and straightforward, was used by Senators and Representatives on both sides of the controversy, and the flap led to another temporary embargo on unclassified CIA publications.

The return of CIA to public controversy on economic issues in 1977 involved some totally new dimensions. CIA did not seek the publicity President Carter had forced on it but, once pushed into the public eye, tried to resolve problems by participating in public debates as much as security considerations permitted. Indeed, DCI Turner generally sought to promote this openness both to enhance the reputation of CIA as a source of high-quality, objective analysis and to divert attention from clandestine operations.

As a result of the President's press conference, two OER papers were released in unclassified form. One of these predicted a decline in Soviet oil production and a potential shift in the USSR's oil trade from a large net export to a net import position. The other paper incorporated the Soviet forecasts into a projection of global oil supply and demand which predicted another massive oil price increase within a very few years. The message that came through clearly to Secretary of Energy Schlesinger and to President Carter was that oil prospects were even worse than they had thought. The new Soviet oil estimates in turn had a major impact on a comprehensive study of the prospects for the Soviet economy, which was also published in unclassified form in 1978. Reduced rates of GNP growth to a range of two to three percent were projected for the 1980s, partly because of a growing energy constraint. The OER estimate on Soviet oil identified some fundamental problems which will probably cause oil production to decline this decade. But it underestimated Moscow's willingness to pour added resources into oil development as a result of which the decline was postponed and a severe crisis was averted.

OER began to back off from its Soviet oil estimate as early as 1978, recognizing that Moscow could not afford to become an oil importer because of its heavy reliance on oil as a source of hard currency earnings. Although the 1977 projection should have been interpreted as a notional gap between demand and supply that would not necessarily be eliminated through foreign trade, the wording was ambiguous. But then, OER discovered another serious cause for pessimism as to prospects for the world oil market. It had become apparent that oil company plans for expanding oil production in the Persian Gulf, especially Saudi Arabia, through the 1980s were pipe dreams. The planned capacity increases were not taking place; indeed, Saudi Arabia and other countries were cutting the investments necessary even to sustain the then current rates of production in the longer term. In 1978, OER predicted another big jump in oil prices at some time during the 1979–81 period (an unclassified version was released in July 1979). OER was right but in part for the wrong reasons. It was of course the Iranian revolution that triggered the price rise although many other forces to set up the rise were in place. The 1979–80 price shock set off a new series of studies on global economic impact—industrial countries, the developing countries, OPEC countries, and communist countries. By 1981, the world economy was again in recession, and energy conservation and substitution of other energy sources for oil was building rapidly. Consequently, the oil market turned soft and it has remained soft.

OER's incursion into controversial economic, especially energy, public estimates on balance probably enhanced CIA's reputation for high-quality analysis. Although the initial public reaction was mainly negative—reflecting both CIA's departure from conventional wisdom and the readiness of the press to attribute political motives—public comments later turned generally favorable, especially in 1979–80 when the new oil crisis CIA had predicted did occur (if partly for different reasons). In the process of explaining their estimates, OER analysts participated in numerous meetings and conferences where they often gave presentations as well as engaged in discussions with experts from the oil industry, academia, state governments, and even foreign countries. In the process, CIA analysts became accepted members of the expert community, especially on energy, macroeconomics, and econometric modeling. Recruitment of well-trained economists became easier and some of the top economists in the country became interested in at least informal consulting. But there were negative effects as well. Participation in public discussion took too much time away from intelligence work. The need to explain and defend estimates in public reinforced the tendency to look harder for corroborating than for contrary evidence. If CIA's Soviet oil production estimates had not been constantly under public attack, they probably would have been changed more promptly than they were. Finally, the fact that classified sources were used in the estimates prevented full documentation, and even several years of partial openness could not eliminate the ambiguities inherent in a public CIA role.

Economic intelligence becomes everybody's business. Throughout the 1950s, 1960s, and much of the 1970s, economic intelligence production in CIA was the almost exclusive domain of the Economic Research Area of ORR and then of OER. OCI produced some current economic intelligence on the free world and the geographic intelligence units worked on some specialized economic topics, such as transportation. As economic issues grew in importance, it was inevitable that they would become of concern to all the main intelligence production units in CIA. The Office of Geographic and Societal Research, working with the Office of Research and Development, developed methodologies for estimating the Soviet grain crop that required specialized expertise (agronomists, photo interpreters, statisticians, and linguists, as well as economists) and inputs of highly specific information on weather and status of crops. Use of this methodology was expensive—requiring several times more people and contract money than the traditional methodology used by OER—but proved substantially more accurate, at least in the years when the main problem was drought. In 1979–80, elaborate methodologies were also developed to estimate likely production in major Soviet oil fields and likely reserves in major oil regions.

These intensive analyses also required inputs of detailed data that were collectible by technical means. Previously, the very thin OER coverage of major Soviet sectors and industries made it necessary to rely heavily on published information and on simpler techniques, since collectors were generally unable to obtain critical unpublished information at a relatively high level of aggregation. By 1981–84, there had been a vast increase in the use of special intelligence sources in the production of economic intelligence. Photography has been a major source of information on oil facility damage during the Iran-Iraq War, as well as on the status of the Soviet grain crop and the construction and expansion of oil and gas facilities in East Siberia. COMINT has been a major source on the LDC debt problem as well as on Soviet oil.

Economic intelligence also expanded into the field of science and technology. In addition to a major increase in the long-standing effort on transfer of technology to the USSR, CIA developed a substantial capability to assess technological developments in free world countries and their impact on industrial trends and competitiveness. Beginning in the late 1960s with what was mainly a series of externally contracted OSI studies on high technology in free world, mainly Japanese, industries, the effort developed into a division-sized unit in the Office of Global Issues doing systematic analysis of free world industries, especially high technology industries. Consequently, what had been a major gap in CIA's coverage of free world economies has been partly filled.

At the same time, economic intelligence has become a more fully integrated part of intelligence analyses and assessments on individual foreign countries. This process began well before the reorganization of the Directorate of Intelligence in 1981, especially with an increasing number of joint OER/Office of Political Analysis studies. With a reorganization primarily along geographic lines, it became inevitable that political analysts would become more aware of economic issues and vice versa.

There have also been some changes in economic intelligence priorities in recent years. With an oil glut taking the place of severe oil shortages, the absence of any major global economic shocks, and the expansion of global macroeconomic analysis in other government agencies and the private sector, the need for independent macroeconomic estimates from CIA has declined. Moreover, the Reagan Administration has given an increased priority to issues of economic structure and efficiency and a smaller one to macroeconomic policy. Most important, East-West détente has given way to a renewed cold war which once again gave prominence to economic warfare issues such as export controls, technology transfer, Soviet dependence on imports from the West, and Western economic leverage on the USSR. The Carter Administration's decision to impose economic sanctions on the USSR in response to its invasion of Afghanistan led to innumerable requests for intelligence support from CIA. The Iranian hostage crisis and the resulting US economic sanctions against Iran had a similar impact. The imposition of martial law in Poland caused a tightening of US restrictions on import of oil and gas equipment to the USSR and led eventually to the Reagan Administration's attempt to prevent construction of the West Siberia to Western Europe pipeline. All of these economic issues involved major demands on CIA's economic intelligence units.

Resources and Processes

The enormous changes over the past thirty-five years in the functions of economic intelligence in CIA have occurred with a fairly constant overall level of staffing but with frequent, often massive shifts in the distribution of effort, in the types of intelligence products, and in analytic methodologies. In turn, these shifts had a major impact on collection requirements for economic intelligence.

People. Personnel costs have always been the predominant part of the economic intelligence budget. External contracting was quite small until the late 1970s and early 1980s when in-depth analysis of oil facilities requiring very specialized methodologies and expertise became both important and feasible. Although precise comparisons are impossible because of changing functions, some of which can be classified in a number of ways, it is clear that the total number of people engaged in economic intelligence reached a peak in the 1950s, reflecting the high labor-intensive requirements of the nuts and bolts approach to the Soviet economy; the number declined slightly during the 1960s to about three hundred professionals, and again the 1970s to about two hundred fifty professionals, and then rose somewhat in the early 1980s as part of the general expansion of the DDI. These ups and downs are far less important than the massive shifts that occurred within the economic intelligence effort: in the 1960s from the USSR to the developing countries and then to Vietnam; in the 1970s from Vietnam to the industrial nations to global economic trends such as energy, economic growth, and trade; and in the 1980s to international finance and to free world high technology industries. During the same time span, State INR's effort in economic intelligence declined precipitously from about one hundred people in the 1950s to fifteen to twenty in the 1970s.

Maintaining even a constant personnel strength required a large, continuous recruitment effort because of a very high rate of professional turnover, which reflected the substantial opportunities available to economists in the private sector. During the 1960s, when government salaries were generally not competitive with the private sector, the professional turnover rate in ORR was between one and one-half and two percent a month, or some twenty percent annually. In the 1970s, with a more competitive salary scale, the turnover rate fell and then stabilized at about one percent a month. Even so, this meant that

OER had to hire at least twenty-five economists each year just to stay even. And, largely because most applicants had other irons in the fire and often could not wait until CIA personnel processing and clearance were completed, we had to put a hundred applicants in process each year to offset anticipated turnover. To reinforce the efforts of the Office of Personnel, ORR, and then OER, sent senior economists to recruit graduate students in universities and took advantage of those trips to develop and strengthen contacts with faculty members and generally to try to enhance the image of CIA as a good place for economists to work. Fortunately, this recruitment effort has been continued since the DDI reorganization.

The majority of new hires had the equivalent of a master's degree in economics or related fields, with perhaps twenty percent in recent years entering with a Ph.D. degree or having completed the course requirements for a Ph.D., and another twenty to twenty-five percent with a bachelor's degree and perhaps a little graduate work. Only a small number came into economic intelligence through the Career Trainee program, although some of these have been among the most successful analysts. Changing functions also changed the mix of skills that was sought. During the 1970s, econometricians, economists with experience in the analysis of international trade and finance, and energy experts were much in demand.

To handle changing functions, it was necessary not only to recruit different kinds of experts, but also to retrain those already on board. The change during the 1950s from specific industrial studies to macroeconomic analysis of the USSR, Eastern Europe, and China required more sophisticated handling of economic issues. Since many of the commodity and industrial analysts and branch chiefs in ORR had received little if any formal training in economics, it became office policy to upgrade all professionals to an equivalent of a master's degree in economics, with the help of in-house courses taught by CIA economists under the auspices of local universities. A broad training program in the use of automated data processing and various analytic methodologies was introduced in the late 1960s and later broadened so that all OER analysts had at least a basic ADP capability.

But the principal means of tackling new functions was to identify individuals who were among the brightest and the most dynamic and creative professionals in the office and to put them in charge of new issues. Although the general thrust of economic intelligence priorities was apparent, the particular development of the effort could not be foreseen. It was necessary to give creative leaders considerable flexibility to take initiatives, react to customer requests, and carve out a role for CIA. Frequently, new functional units were created to tackle new problems—for example, on international trade and finance, energy, and analytic methodologies. Since these units were concerned with issues that were also central to the geographic units (on Japan, Western Europe, Latin America), conflicts of responsibilities often occurred which were sometimes exacerbated by personal conflicts. Although this forced inter-action was wasteful at times, on the whole it was creative in that it caused the major economic issues to be approached from more than one perspective.

Methodologies. In economic intelligence as in other types of intelligence, methodologies have become more and more sophisticated. ORR and OER relied mainly on the traditional tools of economists, which themselves evolved considerably over the years. The simplest tools—national accounting and bal-ance of payments analysis—are of course regularly used to facilitate orderly analysis of economic trends and structure. Use of input-output tables for the USSR and a few other countries began in the mid-1950s and has continued selectively ever since. Advanced statistical analysis was used in the 1950s to estimate production of Soviet equipment and weapons from serial numbers. Some preliminary ADP programs were developed early in the 1960s for special purposes such as calculating an index of Soviet industrial production and ob-taining reports on communist economic and military assistance to LDCs. But it was not until an OER Systems Development Staff was established in 1969 that a systematic effort to provide analysts with high-quality ADP and methodologi-cal support was launched. This effort included training, research and develop-ment, and service—with the emphasis initially on training and research and development. As the service function developed—to include construction of data bases of common concern, methodological problem-solving, and develop-ment of models on issues of central concern to the office, the Systems Develop-ment Staff was expanded into a Development and Analysis center. By the late 1970s, OER had one of the most sophisticated econometric efforts in the world. Beginning with some adaptations of existing econometric models of foreign economies, OER built its own model of the world economy which linked the principal countries through foreign trade flows and which could approximate and simulate the global impact of changes in national economic policies or of major shocks to the world economy. This Link model, as well as the individual country models, proved extremely useful in answering "what if" questions from policymakers throughout the government. For example: What would be the economic impact of a doubling of oil prices on economic growth, inflation, trade? Or what would be the economic impact of a one-percent increase in US government expenditures? As energy problems worsened, the energy sector of the Link model was greatly elaborated to address more com-plex questions on energy, price, and use. The development of econometric models and of related macroeconomic methodologies required both some first-class econometricians and methodologists in OER and access to the talent in academia and elsewhere. OER used a series of annual conferences with some of the best economists and econometricians in the country to help give direction and focus to the development of its methodological effort on macro-economics and energy. These conferences were also helpful in strengthening CIA's reputation and contacts in the top ranks of the economics profession.

By the late 1970s, a large proportion of OER analysts had some familiarity with ADP techniques and were using and manipulating data banks (for example, on trade statistics) and a substantial number were using econometric models as tools of analysis. CIA models were available on the major OECD countries, on several LDCs, and on the USSR. In addition, CIA steadily broadened its access to commercially available data banks and models from IMF, the UN, DRI, Chase Econometrics, and Wharton.

As mentioned earlier, economic intelligence in recent years has used not only the techniques of economic and econometric analysis, but also engineering and agronomic simulations. A model which simulates the phases of plant growth and the impact of shortfalls of moisture and of other weather conditions on plant yields has been the central element of the methodology for estimating Soviet grain crops. Engineering models of major oil fields of a type in general use in the oil industry are being used to estimate oil reserves and production potential. Engineering models also are being used to assess the potential impact of damage to oil facilities in various countries.

This broad expansion of analytical methodologies has required not only larger in-house expertise but also much greater use of external contracts, some of which are quite costly. These expenditures can be justified only on issues that require in-depth analysis.

Sources. As mentioned earlier, the most important sources of economic information are unclassified. They include the official statistical publications of foreign countries and international institutions, newspapers, journal articles, and radio broadcasts. Unclassified sources generally constitute the foundation of any economic analysis, even on the USSR and other communist countries, and provide an essential context to interpret classified material and how it fits into the overall picture. Second in importance is reporting from State and Treasury attachés who provide interpretation and color, as well as up-to-date information. Over the years, information obtained from private US citizens and organizations has probably been the third most important source of economic intelligence. The CIA domestic contact unit (in its various forms) has regularly produced a flow of information on Soviet industrial technology and industrial capabilities, international energy, LDC debt, other financial problems, and innumerable other topics. The domestic contact units have been highly responsive to the needs of economic intelligence analysts who in turn often took the trouble to provide very detailed guidance and requirements because the payoff was evident and quick.

The role of clandestine collection of economic intelligence was quite limited so long as CIA concentrated on the communist countries and covered free world countries only lightly. Clandestine collection on Soviet internal economic issues has generally been weak because of problems of access to high-level information and the limited usefulness of most low-level information. Clandestine sources have been consistently more important on Eastern Europe than on the USSR, and have been of great importance for nearly twenty years on Soviet and East European trade, arms shipments and sales, and financial activities in the third world.

Renewed interest in clandestine economic collection, this time aimed mostly at the free world countries, was stimulated in the early 1970s by the same global trends that had greatly expanded OER functions. A major effort was launched ██████ to collect intelligence on ██████ economic policies and intentions in such areas as trade, finance, and energy. The success of this enterprise, which was supported by the assignment of a senior OER analyst ████████████, led to establishment of similar, although smaller, collection programs ████████████████████████ the critical role of ██████████ as well as of ██████, led to a very important clandestine collection in this area. More recently, clandestine collection has played an important part in assessing management of the debt problem ████████████. By the early 1980s, the clandestine services appeared to have largely overcome their reluctance to collect against economic targets, although some residual resistance persisted, especially in areas like Western Europe, where it is particularly difficult to define a clandestine role because so much information is in the public domain.

COMINT and PHOTINT have become more important as sources of economic intelligence in recent years. Both had long been critical sources on Soviet military deliveries and sales to the third world. The Soviets put out virtually no information on gold. Until recent years, when the Chinese began releasing some data, there was very little information in the public domain on most aspects of the Chinese economy. After the reorganization of the DDI, the combining of the former OER and OGSR effort on energy and agriculture facilitated the exploitation of these sources, especially photography, on a detailed basis.

Products. The change in the mix of economic intelligence products reflected the evolution of ORR and OER from a primary orientation to basic research to a focus on short- to medium-term policy support. During the 1950s and early 1960s, most OER products were large research reports or NISs. Contributions to current intelligence publications were written by a small, specialized staff. There were few papers prepared in a response to direct requests from policymakers. By the early 1970s, as OER developed research capabilities across the entire gamut of international economics, responses to policy requests averaged nearly three per workday and were largely driving the office's work. Indeed, this large expansion of policy support work made it impossible for several years to pursue any sort of coherent production planning; in the late 1960s, annual production planning was abandoned because the majority of planned projects were not done and most projects that were done were not planned.

During the early and late 1970s, the principal mechanism for maintaining some coherence in OER's research and production was the weekly publications. There were two: one on energy (the *International Oil Developments*, later called the *International Energy Weekly*) and one on other economic developments (the *Economic Intelligence Weekly* or *EIW*). Although these publications, especially the *IEW*, covered some current developments, their primary function was to provide relevant background, analysis, and perspective on issues of current policy interest, and on those to which greater policy attention should have been given. Important policy support memorandums were revised and rerun in the publications to reach a wider audience. Articles were planned in anticipation of major international economic policy decisions or meetings. Others were written to warn of potential problems, to explain those that had occurred, or to estimate their impact. The results or partial results of OER basic research that appeared to provide new perspectives on important issues were included. In sum, the publications covered practically all OER had to say that was of interest to the policy levels. And they were a success. Both publications and the combined publication, the *International Economic and Energy Weekly*, that followed them were, and are, regularly read at the top and middle levels of the economic policy community.

Economic inputs to current intelligence publications also increased, especially once the *President's Daily Brief* became established as the principal means of communicating intelligence to the President. Less attention was paid to the *National Intelligence Daily* because OER's own publications were serving the principal economic policymakers.

Longer studies in the form of intelligence memoranda or reports continued to be published if they represented research building blocks or if assessments needed elaboration. Most of the work on the Chinese economy and a substantial part of that on the Soviet economy, for example, continued to take the form of these larger studies which are read mainly by specialists.

A serious attempt was made to distinguish clearly between research studies and other forms of intelligence production. Research projects were planned well in advance and sometimes stretched over several years. For example, a systematic study of the growth and structure of the Soviet economy was planned in the early 1970s and took more than five years to complete, resulting in a number of classified and unclassified publications. Similarly, substantial resources were set aside to do basic research on Mexico—including the growth and structure of the economy; economic policy; illegal migration; agriculture; and labor. This effort, which was launched several years before the surge in policy interest in Mexico, paid off handsomely.

Some of the most elaborate products were never formally published. Briefing books for top-level policymakers had been prepared since the late 1960s. Beginning with the Tokyo economic summit of 1979, CIA has either written most of the background sections of the presidential briefing books or provided substantial inputs in their preparation. Moreover, a senior OER analyst was a key member of a CIA team which provided on-the-spot briefings in all the summits since 1980.[1]

Relations with policymakers. The complexity and diversity of the economic policy community make it necessary for CIA economic intelligence producers to work hard to ascertain the needs of policymakers, the priority of these needs, and the proper role of CIA in meeting these needs. Relations with policy officials were relatively easy in the 1950s when CIA's economic intelligence was largely limited to communist countries. But when this role came to encompass the entire gamut of international economic issues, and requests for intelligence multiplied, it became necessary to gain an understanding of the requester's purpose and his role in the national policy process. Although few high- or medium-level requests were turned down, many were modified to better reflect our interpretation of priorities and the legitimate role and capabilities of CIA. This meant a process of frequent interaction with policymakers rather than a passive acceptance of their tasking. It also meant that economic intelligence producers generally dealt directly with policy officials at the NSC, CEA, State, Treasury, and Commerce. In addition, a senior OER analyst was detailed to Treasury beginning in the early 1970s to prepare daily or weekly briefings for economic officials at the Cabinet, sub-Cabinet and senior staff levels, and to obtain feedback—a function that was eventually incorporated into more formal intelligence liaison units in policy departments. There was relatively little indirect tasking through the Directorate of Intelligence, the National Intelligence Officers (except on national estimates), or the intelligence liaison units in other agencies.

Issues and Lessons

Although economic intelligence has become one of the central areas of concentration for both producers and collectors in CIA, a number of questions

1. For a discussion of CIA's role in economic summitry, see "Castles, Canals, and Colonial Cabins," by Alan R. Paxson, in the Spring 1984 issue of *Studies in Intelligence*, XXVIII/1.

continue to be raised concerning the scope and uses of economic intelligence. In the concluding section of this article, I will raise the most important of these issues and indicate what I believe to be the lessons experience has taught us on each of them.

To what extent is economic intelligence CIA's job? The narrowest view of CIA's economic intelligence function has been that it should be limited to collecting information that cannot be obtained by overt means and to analyses and estimates based to a substantial extent on such information. This definition was always too narrow, even when economic intelligence was limited largely to communist countries. The fact is that CIA provides several ingredients, in addition to special sources, which make for a unique contribution. These ingredients include: the ability to bring a wide variety of skills and perspectives to bear on a problem (economic, technical, political, and military); and, perhaps most important, a mission and organization designed to serve the needs of the national policy community rather than those of a single department. The particular mix of ingredients that yields a unique contribution varies from subject to subject. In assessments of damage to oil facilities during the Iran-Iraq War and its impact, for example, special sources and the ability to use them are critical. In estimates of the future oil market, it is the ability to combine an understanding of the determinants of the demand for oil and of oil market behavior with assessments of political, economic, and military factors which affect oil production in major OPEC countries that constitutes a unique contribution. In the case of briefing papers for the Economic Summit, it is simply CIA's broad scope and organizational ability that justify taking on the work. Moreover, CIA must give some coverage to all major global economic issues and to all foreign countries in order to understand the way events work their way through the world economy. But it is not necessary to give all countries or issues equal treatment. Not only are some more important than others, but some topics are treated much more fully by other government agencies or in the private sector than others. For example, free world agriculture is covered fairly thoroughly by the research unit of the Department of Agriculture, as are world minerals by the Department of the Interior. CIA makes the largest contribution on agriculture and minerals in communist countries, but its coverage on the rest of the world is appropriately thin. CIA also puts in a relatively greater effort on countries which constitute a major security threat to the United States, notably the USSR, than on neutrals and allies. In conclusion, there are no international economic issues that CIA should ignore, but it is appropriate that the degree of coverage by other agencies be taken into account in determining the distribution of the CIA effort.

With regard to clandestine collection of economic information, there should be no issue of principle. At bottom economic intelligence is no different from political intelligence. Indeed, economic issues are the everyday meat of national politics in every country. The reluctance of clandestine collectors to try to obtain material that could be collected by regular State, Treasury, and Commerce officials is understandable, but should not become an excuse for inaction. The important thing is to identify those governments, other institutions, and issues that deserve a systematic clandestine collection effort in the longer term so that well-placed sources can be developed. This approach must be selective, aimed at a few key countries such as the USSR, ██████████████████, and such definable issues as arms sales, nuclear power, or sales of civil aircraft. Development of sources must be based not on detailed requirements, which cannot be projected two or three years ahead, but rather on a judgment that the country or issue is of sufficient importance that requirements for clandestine collection are certain to develop and probably to continue over a period of time. Once sources are in place, the requirements must be as specific as possible and must take into account the capabilities of overt collectors. Assignment of economic intelligence analysts to key stations was designed primarily to help make more sophisticated judgments on the spot on what the stations should collect.

Should there be unclassified CIA publications in the economic area? I believe that building block research which does not reveal classified sources and methods and is of interest to experts in the private sector should be published unclassified. Such publications are important to sustain the generally high reputation CIA economic research has enjoyed in academia and elsewhere in the private sector. These publications help recruitment and make it easier to make effective use of consultants, some of whom do not want to go through clearance procedures. With the exercise of reasonable care and control, the odds on such publications triggering adverse publicity or political flaps are minimal.

I believe that the historical record gives ample reason to *avoid* unclassified publications on estimative, forward-looking topics. There is no doubt that selective CIA attempts to publicize certain research findings have backfired. Selective unclassified publications, especially if publicized at the top levels of the Agency, are bound to be interpreted as attempts to influence policy and public opinion. Unclassified publication of estimative intelligence on a broader scale, such as was attempted in the late 1970s, would make sense only if the DDI were separated from the rest of CIA and became viewed as a kind of research service of common concern to the US Government. This appeared to be the trend in the early years of the Carter Administration, but it never got very far and has obviously been reversed since. Moreover, with the far more intensive use of special sources in the past few years, any separation of the analytical function from the collection function would severely reduce the usefulness of the product. I conclude that any thought of publishing unclassified estimative economic intelligence material by CIA should be abandoned.

Should economic intelligence provide assistance to private US firms? This has been a hot issue for more than a decade. PFIAB recommended in the early 1970s that intelligence try to find ways of providing information and judgment useful to US firms in their international activities without endangering sources and methods. The same issue was taken up again under DCI Turner by an interagency committee chaired by the General Counsel of the Department of Commerce. My position in both of these instances, and it was also the majority position, was that this could be done only informally and that no systematic program should be developed for this purpose. The fact is that American firms do obtain information and judgments from CIA that are basically unclassified but not for attribution, through discussions with DI analysts and through the judicious disguising by State or Commerce officials of intelligence information in briefings of private firms. Any systematic program for providing classified information to private business raises all kinds of problems including: avoiding discrimination among US firms; developing a way for the executives being briefed to use the classified information; avoiding discrimination between business groups and other groups such as labor unions; abiding by the terms of agreements with the Commonwealth countries to share certain kinds of information and not use them for competitive commercial purposes. I believe that any attempt to formalize the process of giving briefings or assistance to private business would do far more harm than good.

Should the organization of economic intelligence be mainly geographic or mainly functional? It should be both geographic and functional. I believe that OER's experience shows clearly the importance of approaching any important issue with more than one perspective. It is extremely dangerous in any bureaucracy, especially a large one like CIA's, to assign the entire responsibility for important issues to a single unit with a particular form of organization. It is too easy for the point of view of an analyst or branch to become the party line for an office, or even for CIA, unless it can be challenged or approached from a different point of view as well. This does not require a formal matrix organization, but it does mean that two or more units will have to share the responsibility for producing intelligence on major issues. In OER's free world work, for example, the basic organization was geographic, but functional units were formed to deal with major issues such as economic growth and development, trade and finance, energy, agriculture and materials, which were also of central concern to each of the geographic units. This is quite different from creating functional units to work in specialized areas, such as international shipping or arms sales, which generally are not of major concern to the country analyst. Joint responsibility creates frictions and conflicts, some of which are time-consuming. But in my opinion it also fosters creativity and makes it far easier to use dynamic people effectively in a bureaucratic environment. The DI reorganization has similar elements both in economic and political areas. For example, responsibility for LDC debt problems is shared by OGI and the regional offices, and I believe that this joint effort on the whole has been productive and creative, with one group stimulating the other to doing better work. I only hope that the process of building functional units not to supplant but rather to interact with geographic units will continue as it has during the past two years. And even in a primarily geographic organization, it is important to sustain a home base for analysts who want to retain their identity as professional economists, rather than develop into area experts. Such economists should be rotated within the DI, and perhaps elsewhere. They should probably keep their home base in a functional economic unit.

The Future of Economic Intelligence in CIA

Economic intelligence in CIA has become too useful to other parts of the US Government and too well established to be vulnerable to drastic cuts in the future, but it is difficult to imagine any major future expansion of its functions, since these already encompass virtually all important international economic topics. To foster high-quality work in the longer term, CIA needs to:

— Anticipate new demands by clearly reading the changing world forces and the changing role of the US Government and take the initiative accordingly to reallocate resources. As ORR and OER history clearly shows, new directions must be taken if possible before policy customers demand them and certainly far in advance of any funding or personnel allocations.

— Continue to develop new ways of using classified information to improve economic estimates.

— Provide an environment conducive to high-quality research and analysis and to attracting and retaining first-class economists by establishing or strengthening functional units dealing with the critical analytic issues in international economics.

— Make certain that important issues are approached from more than one perspective by forcing regional and functional units to share the responsibility for all important economic issues.

— Adapt the bureaucratic system to give particularly energetic and creative people an opportunity to make a mark and to develop new research directions and functions.

VI.

Analysis and Its Consumers

25.

Relations between analysts and their consumers (chiefly the policymakers and implementers) are naturally colored by their respective views of the "successes" and "failures" of previous analyses. Agency self-evaluation teams, operating as part of the ongoing reform in the Directorate of Intelligence in the late 1970s and the 1980s, drew on cognitive psychological experimentation to show that intractable mental processes (not even based in self-interest) make analysts think their predictions better than they have been—and make consumers think analysts' predictions worse than they have been. Clearly this is a recipe for major tension, as this article by an outstanding analyst shows. Can it be ameliorated, by enhanced mutual awareness and by co-determination of achievable standards?

Cognitive Biases: Problems in Hindsight Analysis

RICHARDS J. HEUER, JR.

Psychologists observe that limitations in man's mental machinery (memory, attention span, reasoning capability, etc.) affect his ability to process information to arrive at judgmental decisions. In order to cope with the complexity of our environment, these limitations force us to employ various simplifying strategies for perception, comprehension, inference, and decision. Many psychological experiments demonstrate that our mental processes often lead to erroneous judgments. When such mental errors are not random, but are consistently and predictably in the same direction, they are known as *cognitive biases*.

This article discusses three cognitive biases affecting how we evaluate ourselves and how others evaluate us as intelligence analysts.

- The analyst who thinks back about how good his past judgments have been will normally overestimate their accuracy.
- The intelligence consumer who thinks about how much he learned from our reports will normally underestimate their true value to him.
- The overseer of intelligence production who conducts a postmortem of an intelligence failure to evaluate what we should have concluded from the infor-

Richards J. Heuer, Jr., "Cognitive Biases: Problems in Hindsight Analysis," *Studies in Intelligence*, vol. 22, no. 2 (Summer 1978), pp. 21–28. Originally unclassified.

mation that was available will normally judge that events were more readily foreseeable than was in fact the case.

Evidence supporting the existence of these biases is presented in detail in the second part of this article. None of the biases is surprising. We have all observed these tendencies in others—although probably not in ourselves. What may be unexpected is that these biases are not solely the product of self-interest and lack of objectivity. They are specific examples of a broader phenomenon that seems to be built into our mental processes and that cannot be overcome by the simple admonition to be more objective. In the experimental situations described below, conscious efforts to overcome these biases were ineffective. Experimental subjects with no vested interest in the results were briefed on the biases and encouraged to avoid them or compensate for them, but there was little or no improvement in their estimates. While self-interest and lack of objectivity will doubtless aggravate the situation, bias is also caused by mental processes unrelated to these baser instincts.

The analyst, consumer, and overseer evaluating estimative performance all have one thing in common: they are exercising hindsight. They take their current state of knowledge and compare it with what they or others did or could or should have known before the current knowledge was received. Intelligence estimation, on the other hand, is an exercise in foresight, and it is the difference between these two kinds of thought—hindsight and foresight—that seems to be the source of the bias.

The amount of good information that is available obviously is greater in hindsight than in foresight. There are several possible explanations of how this affects mental processes. One is that the additional information available for hindsight apparently changes our perceptions of a situation so naturally and so immediately that we are largely unaware of the change. When new information is received, it is immediately and unconsciously assimilated into our prior knowledge. If this new information adds significantly to our knowledge—if it tells us the outcome of a situation or the answer to a question about which we were previously uncertain—our mental images are restructured to take the new information into account. With the benefit of hindsight, for example, factors previously considered relevant may become irrelevant, and factors previously thought to have little relevance may be seen as determinative.

Once our view has been restructured to assimilate the new information, there is virtually no way we can accurately reconstruct our prior mental set. We may *recall* our previous estimates if not much time has elapsed and they were precisely articulated, but we apparently cannot *reconstruct* them accurately. The effort to reconstruct what we previously thought about a given situation, or what we would have thought about it, is inevitably influenced by our current thought patterns. Knowing the outcome of a situation makes it harder to imagine other outcomes that we might have considered. Simply understanding that our mind works in this fashion, however, does little to help us overcome the limitation.

The overall message we should learn from an understanding of these biases is that our intelligence judgments are not as good as we think they are, or as bad as others seem to believe. Since the biases generally cannot be overcome, they would appear to be facts of life that need to be taken into account in evaluating our own performance and in determining what evaluations to expect from others. This suggests the need for a more systematic effort to:

- Define what should be expected from intelligence analysis.
- Develop an institutionalized procedure for comparing intelligence judgments and estimates with actual outcomes.
- Measure how well we live up to the defined expectations.

Discussion of Experiments

The experiments that demonstrated the existence of these biases and their resistance to corrective action were conducted as part of a research program in decision analysis funded by the Defense Advanced Research Projects Agency. Before examining these experiments, it is appropriate to consider the nature of experimental evidence *per se,* and the extent to which one can generalize from these experiments to conclude that the same biases are prevalent in the intelligence community.

When we say that psychological experiments demonstrate the existence of a bias, we do not mean the bias will be found in every judgment by every individual. We mean that in any group of people, the bias will exist to a greater or lesser degree in most of the judgments made by a large percentage of the group. On the basis of the kind of experimental evidence discussed here, we can only generalize about the tendencies of groups of people, not make statements about individual analysts, consumers, or overseers.

All the experiments described below used students, not members of the intelligence community, as test subjects. There is, nonetheless, ample reason to believe the results can be generalized to apply to the intelligence community. The experiments deal with basic mental processes common to everyone, and the results do seem consistent with our personal experience. In similar psychological tests using various experts (including intelligence analysts) as test subjects, the experts showed the same pattern of responses as students.

Our own imperfect efforts to repeat one of these experiments using CIA analysts support the validity of the findings. In order to test the assertion that intelligence analysts normally overestimate the accuracy of their past judgments, there are two necessary preconditions. First, analysts must make a series of estimates in quantitative terms—they must say not just that a given occurrence is probable, but that there is, for example, a 75-percent chance of its occurrence. Second, it must be possible to make an unambiguous determination whether the estimated event did or did not occur. When these two preconditions are present, one can then go back and test the analyst's recollection of his or her earlier estimate. Because CIA estimates are rarely stated in terms of quantitative probability, and because the occurrence of an estimated event within a specified time period often cannot be determined unambiguously, these preconditions are rarely met.

We did, however, identify several analysts in CIA's Office of Regional and Political Analysis who on two widely differing subjects had made quantitative estimates of the likelihood of events that we now know either did or did not occur. We went to these analysts and asked them to recall their earlier estimates. The conditions for this miniexperiment were far from ideal, and the results were not clear-cut, but they did tend to support the conclusions drawn from the more extensive and systematic experiments described below.

These reasons lead us to conclude that the three biases are found in intelligence community personnel as well as in the specific test subjects. In fact, one would expect the biases to be even greater in foreign affairs professionals whose careers and self-esteem depend upon the presumed accuracy of their judgments. We can now turn to more detailed discussion of the experimental evidence demonstrating these biases from the perspective of the analyst, consumer, and overseer.

The Analyst's Perspective[1]

Analysts interested in improving their own performance need to evaluate their past estimates in the light of subsequent developments. To do this, an analyst must either recall (or be able to refer to) his past estimates, or he must reconstruct his past estimates on the basis of what he remembers having known about the situation at the time the estimates were made. The effectiveness of

1. This section is based on research reported by Baruch Fischhoff and Ruth Beyth in "'I Knew It Would Happen': Remembered Probabilities of Once-Future Things," *Organizational Behavior and Human Performance,* 13 (1975), pp. 1–16.

the evaluation process, and of the learning process to which it gives impetus, depends in part upon the accuracy of these recalled or reconstructed estimates.

Experimental evidence suggests, however, a systematic tendency toward faulty memory of our past estimates. That is, when events occur, we tend to overestimate the extent to which we had previously expected them to occur. And conversely, when events do not occur, we tend to underestimate the probability we had previously assigned to their occurrence. In short, events generally seem less surprising than they should on the basis of past estimates. This experimental evidence accords with our intuitive experience; analysts, in fact, rarely seem very surprised by the course of events they are following.

In experiments to test the bias in memory of past estimates, 119 subjects were asked to estimate the probability that a number of events would or would not occur during President Nixon's trips to Peking and Moscow in 1972. Fifteen possible outcomes were identified for each trip, and each subject assigned a probability to each of these outcomes. The outcomes were selected to cover the range of possible developments and to elicit a wide range of probability values.

At varying time periods after the trips, the same subjects were asked to recall or reconstruct their predictions as accurately as possible. (No mention was made of the memory task at the time of the original prediction.) Then the subjects were asked to indicate whether they thought each event had or had not occurred during these trips.

When three to six months were allowed to elapse between the subjects' estimates and their recollection of these estimates, 84 percent of the subjects exhibited the bias when dealing with events they believed actually happened. That is, the probabilities they remembered having estimated were higher than their actual estimates of events they believed actually occurred. Similarly, for events they believed did not occur, the probabilities they remembered having estimated were lower than their actual estimates, although here the bias was not as great. For both kinds of events, the bias was more pronounced after three to six months had elapsed than when subjects were asked to recall estimates they had given only two weeks earlier.

In sum, knowledge of the outcomes somehow affected most test subjects' memory of their previous estimates of these outcomes, and the more time was allowed for memories to fade, the greater was the effect of the bias. The developments during the President's trips were perceived as less surprising than they would have been if actual estimates were compared with actual outcomes. For the 84 percent of the subjects who showed the anticipated bias, their retrospective evaluation of their estimative performance was clearly more favorable than was warranted by the facts.

The Consumer's Perspective[2]

When the consumer of intelligence reports evaluates the quality of the intelligence product, he asks himself the question, "How much did I learn from these reports that I did not already know?" In answering this question, there is a consistent tendency for most people to underestimate the contribution made by new information. This kind of "I knew it all along" bias causes consumers to undervalue the intelligence product.

That people do in fact commonly react to new information in this manner was confirmed in a series of experiments involving some 320 people, each of whom answered the same set of 75 factual questions taken from almanacs and encyclopedias. They were then asked to indicate how confident they were in the correctness of each answer by assigning to it a probability percentage ranging from 50 (no confidence) to 100 (absolute certainty).

As a second step in the experiment, subjects were divided into three groups. The first group was given 25 of the previously asked questions and instructed to respond to them exactly as they had previously. This simply tested the subjects' ability to remember their previous answers. The second group was given the same set of 25 questions but with the correct answers circled "for your [the subjects'] general information." They, too, were asked to respond by reproducing their previous answers. This tested the extent to which learning the correct answers distorted the subjects' memory of their previous answers, thus measuring the same bias in recollection of previous estimates that was discussed above from the analyst's perspective.

The third group was given a different set of 25 questions that they had not previously seen, but of similar difficulty so that results would be comparable with the other two groups. The correct answers were indicated, and the subjects were asked to respond to the questions as they would have had they not been told the answer. This tested the subjects' ability to remember accurately how much they had known before they learned the correct answer. The situation is comparable to that of the intelligence consumer who is asked to evaluate how much he learned from a report and who can do this only by trying to reconstruct the extent of his knowledge before he read the report.

The most significant results came from this third group of subjects. The group clearly overestimated what they had known originally and underestimated how much they learned from having been told the answer. For 19 of 25 items in one test and 20 of 25 items in another, this group assigned higher

---

2. The experiments described in this section are reported in Baruch Fischhoff, *The Perceived Informativeness of Factual Information,* Technical Report DDI-1 (Oregon Research Institute, Eugene, Ore., 1976).

probabilities to the correct alternatives than it is reasonable to expect they would have assigned had they not already known the correct answers.

The bias was stronger for deceptive questions than for easier questions. For example, one of the deceptive questions was:

Aladdin's nationality was:
  (a) Persian
  (b) Chinese

The correct answer, which is surprising to most people, is Chinese. The average probabilities assigned to each answer by the three groups varied as follows:

- When subjects recalled their previous response without having been told the correct answer, the average of the probabilities they assigned to the two possible responses was:
  (a) .838
  (b) .134

  As these subjects did not know the correct answer, they had no opportunity to exhibit the bias. Therefore, the above figures are the base against which to compare the answers of the other two groups that were aware of the correct answer.

- When subjects tried to recall their previous response after having been told the correct answer, their average responses were:
  (a) .793
  (b) .247

- When subjects not previously exposed to the question were given the correct answer but asked to respond as they would have responded before being told the answer, their average responses were:
  (a) .542
  (b) .321

In sum, the experiment confirms the results of the previous experiment showing that people exposed to an answer tend to remember having known more than they actually did, and it demonstrates that people tend even more to exaggerate the likelihood that they would have known the correct answer if they had not been informed of it. In other words, *people tend to underestimate how much they learn from new information.* To the extent that this bias affects the judgments of intelligence consumers—and there is every reason to expect that it does—these consumers will tend to underrate the value of intelligence estimates.

The Overseer's Perspective[3]

An overseer, as the term is used here, is one who investigates intelligence performance by conducting a postmortem examination, for example, of why we failed to foresee the 1973 Yom Kippur War. Such investigations are carried out by Congress and by our own management, and independent judgments are also made by the press and others. For those outside the executive branch who do not regularly read the intelligence product, this sort of retrospective evaluation in cases of known intelligence failure is a principal basis for judgments about the quality of our intelligence analysis.

A fundamental question posed in any postmortem investigation of intelligence failure is: Given the information that was available at the time, should we have been able to foresee what was going to happen? Unbiased evaluation of intelligence performance depends upon the ability to provide an unbiased answer to this question.

Once an event has occurred, it is impossible to erase from our mind the knowledge of that event and reconstruct what our thought processes would have been at an earlier point in time. In reconstructing the past, there is a tendency toward determinism, toward thinking that what occurred was inevitable under the circumstances and therefore predictable. In short, there is a tendency to believe we should have foreseen events that were in fact unforeseeable on the basis of the available information.

The experiments reported here tested the hypotheses that knowledge of an outcome increases the perceived probability of that outcome, and that people who are informed of the outcome are largely unaware that this information has changed their perceptions in this manner.

A series of sub-experiments used brief (150-word) summaries of several events for which four possible outcomes were identified. One of these events was the struggle between the British and the Gurkhas in India in 1814. The four possible outcomes for this event were (1) British victory, (2) Gurkha victory, (3) military stalemate with no peace settlement, and (4) military stalemate with a peace settlement. Five groups of 20 subjects each participated in each sub-experiment. One group received the 150-word description of the struggle between the British and the Gurkhas with no indication of the outcome. The other four groups received the identical description but with one sentence added to indicate the outcome of the struggle—a different outcome for each group.

The subjects in all five groups were asked to estimate the likelihood of each

---

3. The experiments described in this section are reported in Baruch Fischhoff, "Hindsight ≠ Foresight: The Effect of Outcome Knowledge on Judgment Under Uncertainty," *Journal of Experimental Psychology: Human Perception and Performance*, I, 3 (1975), pp. 288–299.

of the four possible outcomes and to evaluate the relevance to their judgment of each fact in the description of the event. Those subjects who were informed of an outcome were placed in the same position as our overseer who, although knowing what happened, seeks to estimate the probability of that outcome without the benefit of hindsight. The results are shown in the table below.

Experimental Groups	Average Probabilities Assigned to Outcomes			
	1	2	3	4
Not Told Outcome	33.8	21.3	32.3	12.3
Told Outcome 1	57.2	14.3	15.3	13.4
Told Outcome 2	30.3	38.4	20.4	10.5
Told Outcome 3	25.7	17.0	48.0	0.9
Told Outcome 4	33.0	15.8	24.3	27.0

The group not informed of any outcome judged the probability of Outcome 1 as 33.8 percent, while the group told that Outcome 1 was the actual outcome perceived the probability of this outcome as 57.2 percent. The estimated probability was clearly influenced by knowledge of the actual outcome. Similarly, those informed that Outcome 2 was the actual outcome perceived this outcome as having a 38.4 percent probability, as compared with a judgment of only 21.3 percent for the control group with no outcome knowledge. An average of all estimated outcomes in six sub-experiments (a total of 2,188 estimates by 547 subjects) indicates that the knowledge or belief that an outcome has occurred approximately doubles the perceived probability that that outcome will occur.

The relevance that subjects attributed to any fact was also strongly influenced by which outcome, if any, they had been told was true. As Wohlstetter has indicated, "It is much easier after the fact to sort the relevant from the irrelevant signals. After the event, of course, a signal is always crystal clear. We can now see what disaster it was signaling since the disaster has occurred, but before the event it is obscure and pregnant with conflicting meanings."[4] The fact that knowledge of the outcome automatically restructures our judgments on the relevance of available data is probably one reason it is so difficult to reconstruct what our thought processes were or would have been without this outcome knowledge.

In several variations of this experiment, subjects were asked to respond as

4. Roberta Wohlstetter, *Pearl Harbor: Warning and Decision* (Stanford University Press, Stanford, Calif., 1962), p. 387.

though they did not know the outcome, or as others would respond if they did not know the outcome. The results were little different, indicating that subjects were largely unaware of how knowledge of the outcome affected their own perceptions. The experiment showed that subjects were unable to empathize with how others would judge these situations. Estimates of how others would interpret the data were virtually the same as the subjects' own retrospective interpretations.

These results indicate that overseers conducting postmortem evaluations of what CIA should have been able to foresee in any given situation will tend to perceive the outcome of that situation as having been more predictable than it in fact was. Because they are unable to reconstruct a state of mind that views the situation only with foresight, not hindsight, overseers will tend to be more critical of intelligence performance than is warranted.

Can We Overcome These Biases?

We tend to blame biased evaluations of intelligence performance at best on ignorance, at worst on self-interest and lack of objectivity. These factors may also be at work, but the experiments described above suggest that the nature of our mental processes is a principal culprit. This is a more intractable cause than either ignorance or lack of objectivity.

The self-interest of the experimental subjects was not at stake; yet they showed the same kinds of bias with which we are familiar. Moreover, in these experimental situations the biases were highly resistant to efforts to overcome them. Subjects were instructed to make estimates as if they did not already know the answer, but they were unable to do so. In the experiments using 75 almanac and encyclopedia questions, one set of subjects was specifically briefed on the bias, citing the results of previous experiments; this group was instructed to try to compensate for the bias, but it too was unable to do so. Despite maximum information and the best intentions, the bias persisted.

This intractability suggests that the bias does indeed have its roots in the nature of our mental processes. The analyst who tries to recall his previous estimate after learning the actual outcome of events, the consumer who thinks how much a report has added to his prior knowledge, and the overseer who judges whether our analysts should have been able to avoid an intelligence failure, all have one thing in common. They are engaged in a mental process involving hindsight. They are trying to erase the impact of knowledge, so as to recall, reconstruct, or imagine the uncertainties they had or would have had about a subject prior to receiving more or less definitive information on that subject.

It appears, however, that the receipt of what is accepted as definitive or authoritative information causes an immediate but unconscious restructuring of our mental images to make them consistent with the new information. Once our past perceptions have been restructured, it seems very difficult, at best, to reconstruct accurately what our thought processes were or would have been before this restructuring.

There is one procedure that may help to overcome these biases. It is to pose such questions as the following. The analyst should ask himself, "If the opposite outcome had occurred, would I have been surprised?" The consumer should ask, "If this report had told me the opposite, would I have believed it?" And the overseer should ask, "If the opposite outcome had occurred, would it have been predictable given the information that was available?" These questions may help us to recall the degree of uncertainty we had prior to learning the content of a report or the outcome of a situation. They may help us remember the reasons we had for supporting the opposite answer, which we now know to be wrong.

This method of overcoming the bias can be tested by readers of this article, especially those who believe it failed to tell them much they had not already known. If this article had reported that psychological experiments show no consistent pattern of analysts overestimating the accuracy of their estimates, and of consumers underestimating the value of our product, would you have believed it? (Answer: Probably not.) If it had reported that psychological experiments show these biases to be caused only by self-interest and lack of objectivity, would you have believed this? (Answer: Probably yes.) And would you have believed it if the article had reported that these biases can be overcome by a conscientious effort at objective evaluation? (Answer: Probably yes.)

These questions may lead the reader to recall the state of his knowledge or beliefs before reading this article, and thus to highlight what he has learned from it—namely, that significant biases in the evaluation of intelligence estimates are attributable to the nature of human mental processes, not just to self-interest and lack of objectivity, and that they are, therefore, exceedingly difficult to overcome.

26.

Here is the summa of a veteran reformer-analyst studying analyst-consumer relationships: a case for change, which the resistant traditional culture continues to caricature as "politicization."

Dealing with Intelligence-Policy Disconnects

L. KEITH GARDINER

While serving as Deputy Director of Central Intelligence, Robert Gates wrote that ". . . intelligence collection and assessment are black arts for most presidents and their key advisers, neither adequately understood nor adequately exploited. For intelligence officers, presidential and senior level views of the intelligence they receive and how they use it (or not) are just as unfamiliar. . . ."[1]

There are many possible reasons why this kind of intelligence-policy breakdown occurs. Among the most important are "behavioral" explanations, particularly those that look at questions of personality and temperament. One of the problems that has to be faced when attempting to find behavioral reasons why analysts and policymakers sometimes work at cross-purposes is the lack of real data on how individuals in each community function. We are left primarily with our own anecdotal accounts and those of a few writers whose statements seem to have the ring of truth. We simply do not have broad-based evidence of such common assertions as "policymakers don't like the unknown and the uncertain," even though such statements do make deductive sense and often tally with our personal observations.

Our knowledge of analysts is somewhat better, because some testing data exist, and we benefit from organized introspection. Nonetheless, we do not have much "scientific" evidence about how analysts' minds work that can be used to show differences or similarities with policymakers. Despite these uncertainties, it is impressive how uniform, or at least compatible, the beliefs are of a number of writers who come from widely varied backgrounds about how

L. Keith Gardiner, "Dealing with Intelligence-Policy Disconnects," *Studies in Intelligence,* vol. 33, no. 2 (Summer 1989), pp. 1–9. Originally unclassified.

1. Robert M. Gates, "An Opportunity Unfulfilled: The Use and Perceptions of Intelligence at the White House," in *The Washington Quarterly* (Washington, D.C., Winter 1989), p. 36.

policymakers tend to function, how they differ from analysts, and how these differences lead to tension and imperfect working relations.[2]

Some Crucial Distinctions

On balance, policymakers enjoy possessing and using power. They tend to be decisive and confident. They also are fundamentally comfortable with themselves, and they are not particularly self-critical or willing to accept criticisms. Analysts tend to distrust power and those who enjoy exercising it. They are usually more comfortable with criticism, especially in giving it. Basically, they have questioning personalities.

Whenever possible, policymakers make hard decisions quickly. Though they often are too busy to do everything they need to do, this frequently occurs because they are more comfortable being active rather than being more contemplative. Analysts, however, are given to extensive examination of an issue, in part because they would prefer to avoid making decisions that call for action.

Policymakers dislike ambiguity and complexity because these qualities impede decision-making. Analysts, however, believe that the real world *is* ambiguous and uncertain, and they see their primary role as reflecting it as faithfully as possible. Oversimplification is something to be avoided.

To policymakers, the world is a highly personalized place. Anything that impedes acting out their vision of how things should be amounts to a personal attack, and they do not like to be reminded of the limits of their influence. Analysts are ostensibly more objective and are rewarded for identifying problems and obstacles.

Policymakers feel quite vulnerable. Although they like to be recognized for their accomplishments, they also believe that they run the risk of ridicule, personal attack, or some other negative feedback, such as losing their jobs, if they are perceived too often as wrong or as standing unsuccessfully in the way of some other policymaker's vision of what needs to be done. Analysts have much greater latitude to be perceived as wrong or ineffective without risking their self-esteem or jobs.

The Power Game

From a behavioral viewpoint, the policymaker tends to see himself as a person with power who arrived at and remains in his position because of

---

2. These writers include Professors Richard K. Betts and Richard E. Neustadt, former DIA official G. Murphy Donovan, former State Department official Thomas L. Hughes, and former CIA official Herbert E. Meyer.

personal relationships with other powerful people. His main occupation within the bureaucracy and in the outside world is to use his power to achieve personal goals. Because he has to compete with other policymakers of roughly equal power in trying to win acceptance for his ideas, he spends much of his time negotiating, bargaining, and maneuvering as he attempts to construct or become part of a winning coalition. For him, individuals opposed to his policy views have to be vanquished or co-opted.

In this setting, intelligence analysis is simply one more resource that the policymaker can use either to help decide how to advance toward his goal or to help fend off the attacks of those who would seek to thwart him. Given the action/goal focus inherent in his institutional environment and job function, his attitude toward the intelligence he receives is going to be shaped primarily by how useful it is in describing situations, commenting on options, and forecasting obstacles. Above all, however, he will be searching for information and analysis that help him increase his influence over other individuals, especially those in his own government.

Failed Solutions

Most works on intelligence and policymaking seem not to venture beyond discussions of institutional settings, job functions, and general behavior. While often enlightening as to the kinds of problems that can inhibit the policymaker's use of intelligence, they do not offer much in the way of solutions. The three most widely suggested remedies that these analyses seem to lead to are:

— The analyst has to strive to be policy relevant while not sacrificing professional integrity.
— Policymakers should provide more guidance to intelligence officials concerning what they need and more feedback on the usefulness of what they receive.
— Policymakers have to learn to trust and listen to reputable analysts, usually through extended personal contact, even when they are delivering "bad" news.

These "solutions" do not provide much help. The first prescription does not deal with the central question of what constitutes "policy relevance." There are many cases, such as the Intelligence Community consensus in 1983 that US policy in Lebanon was not working, where the community believed that its work was highly relevant and well presented but where it still did not achieve cognitive acceptance. This latter term is used by former Israeli intelligence chief Major General Shlomo Gazit to mean that the analysis was assimilated and understood in the way the analyst meant for it to be understood.[3] The rub is that, despite what the Intelligence Community believes, the policymaker might argue that the analysis was not relevant because it did not deal adequately with the policy he had already decided upon and was trying to implement.

Regarding the second solution, there have been efforts since the dawn of organized intelligence to persuade decisionmakers to be more forthcoming with guidance and feedback. As others have noted, however, the successes in this area are always temporary. Backsliding inevitably occurs, particularly at moments of rising foreign policy conflict or when policymakers change.

As for the third remedy, there are at least two problems with saying that intelligence-policymaking problems can largely be solved by creating a bond of trust between policymaker and analyst through personal contact. One is that in a government the size of ours no policymaker can have a regular personal relationship with all the analysts who write on subjects of interest and concern to him. The second is that more needs to be known about what exactly blocks the development of that trust and what could stimulate it.

Cognitive Structures

This line of reasoning suggests a need to move to another level of analysis, one that gets at whether good working relations are being impeded by predictable differences or dissimilarities in how analysts and policymakers take in and use information. The differences are predictable because they derive from contrasting personality characteristics that each camp brings to the workplace. In this context "personality" refers to what can be called *structure* of personalities and how that affects communication between two individuals. The critical dimension seems to be the cognitive structures: how their minds tend to "see" the world about them and, most important, how they process that information and come to conclusions about what to do with it.

I have discovered two good examples of approaches that do examine cognitive structures and that cast additional light on the intelligence-policy breakdown problem. The first is contained in a lecture delivered by Professor Richard Neustadt in 1986, in which the focus is on how the thinking of US Presidents seems to differ from that of various expert policy analysts who contribute to presidential decisions.[4] Neustadt is especial-

---

3. Shlomo Gazit, "Intelligence Estimates and the Decisionmaker," in *Studies in Intelligence* (Central Intelligence Agency, Washington, D.C, Fall 1988).

4. Richard E. Neustadt, "Presidents, Politics and Analysis" (Paper presented at the University of Washington, Seattle, Washington, May 1986).

ly interested in understanding how Presidents make choices, particularly among what appear to be incompatible objectives, and how their approach to making choices differs from that of the experts who supply information and analysis relevant to these decisions. Much of what Neustadt says also appears to apply more broadly to policymakers and to their relationships to analysts.

One of Neustadt's most interesting arguments involves the difference in the purposes for which policymakers and analysts "think" and the timeframes they implicitly adopt as they decide when they must make final judgments. In one sense, the policymaker's timeframe is the here-and-now, because he is constantly thinking about or taking action. In another sense, however, he tends to leave his timeframe almost open-ended. He seldom will completely give up a goal, preferring instead to take whatever time is necessary to achieve it, even if faced with what he will interpret as temporary setbacks.

One outcome of this way of thinking is that the policymaker can live much more comfortably and for a much longer time than the analyst with what appear to be incompatible objectives. The policymaker is motivated to keep as many options open as he can for arriving at his vision and for seeing the world in a fashion that supports his belief that his goals are still attainable. Thus, the policymaker avoids as long as possible the notion that he has to trade off one goal for another. If other people are the problem, the policymaker will depend on the belief that he eventually will be able to bend them to his purposes. If inanimate events are the complication, the policymaker often holds to a trust in luck or the unknowability of the future to retain his belief that his objectives are not really inherently incompatible or that one must be sacrificed to attain the other. For Neustadt, the classic case of this was former President Reagan's refusal from 1981 to 1984 to give up on tax cuts, defense spending hikes, and seeking a balanced budget, even though experts were telling him that these goals were absolutely incompatible.

The analyst's view of the world and how he thinks about it are much different. Rather than trying to take action, his task is to order the world mentally so that he can understand it. To support decisionmaking, this involves breaking apart the policymaker's goals into ostensibly achievable parts, assigning mental priorities to what needs to be achieved and in what order, surveying the world to see what actual and potential barriers there are to achievement, and reaching judgments on an action's chances of success. This can be an enormously complicated mental task, particularly if many goals and linkages are involved. To simplify this analytical task, the analyst is strongly motivated to identify incompatibilities as soon as possible and to suggest that some goals be sacrificed for others sooner rather than later.

The MBTI Method

Neustadt's approach is based essentially upon an intuitive grasp of the differences between the ways policymakers and analysts think. The Myers-Briggs Type Indicator (MBTI) is another method for defining personality differences. One of its main values is that it provides detailed categories for predicting how such differences will impact on behavior. The MBTI characterizes human personality in terms of the ways individuals prefer to think and act, thereby creating a useful structure for assessing recurring patterns of behavior and relationships. The MBTI approach helps to distinguish between clusters of personality preferences that tend to characterize analysts and policymakers, respectively. An MBTI technique that converts personality characteristics into temperaments can be used, for example, to demonstrate that policymakers and analysts have significantly different temperaments that may cause them to come into conflict.

How, then, do action-oriented, operational-minded policymakers behave? In MBTI terms, policymakers are intensely duty oriented, and they see their primary duty as deciding on and then implementing policy actions that move toward the achievement of fairly specific goals. They are predisposed to making incremental improvements rather than sweeping changes. They are highly conscious of authority, and they understand how to use bureaucratic procedures to accomplish their plans. When possible, policymakers also like to decide about an issue quickly so that they can move on to other issues and other decisions. They are impatient with or do not understand abstract ideas about the future or about other issues that have no immediate importance. Because of their "realistic" focus, they put highest value on "solid facts," and they can absorb a large amount of detail on any subject that they believe at the moment is important. They dislike complications—in the form, for example, of inconvenient facts, unhelpful analysis, or uncooperative people—that might force them to reconsider decisions they have already made.

In MBTI terms, the contrast with the analytic style that dominates the culture of the Intelligence Community is stark. The latter is primarily inhabited by visionaries who prefer to focus on the big picture, future possibilities, and the abstract patterns and principles that underlie and explain facts. Analysts are fundamentally critics, and their products often disclose the flaws in current policy solutions that the policymakers have worked so hard to achieve.[5]

There is another factor that almost certainly helps establish what appear to

5. The MBTI material is interpreted from research by Otto Kroeger and Janet M. Thusen and by David Keirsey and Marilyn Bates.

be a dominant "operational" personality style in action agencies and a controlling "analytical" personality style on the production side of intelligence agencies. The institutional norms and needs of the two kinds of organizations probably tend to bring out and reward contrasting clusters of personality and cognitive traits in their personnel. In an action agency, for example, even those policymakers whose preferences are non-operational will tend to behave like operators, because they otherwise are not competitive. In essence, institutions attract and are defined by people who prefer to behave in certain ways because of the structure of their personality, and the power of this institutional culture tends to force everyone in it to adapt to the dominant style.

Issue Evolution

There probably are times when policymakers are more open to information and analysis, even if conveyed in a theoretically nonpreferred style. This type of categorization could take many forms. One recent effort focuses on the various stages through which issues often seem to evolve as they are dealt with by a policymaker.[6]

In the first stage, the issue may exist, at least as part of the portfolio of an analyst, but it does not immediately affect the duties, job performance, or power position of the policymaker. Thus, he is indifferent to the issue and largely uninterested in any analysis of it.

In the second stage, the issue—probably because of some action-forcing event—has become very relevant to the policymaker, but he has not yet had time to decide what to do about it. At this stage, the policymaker is likely to be most open to factual intelligence and to analysis that stimulates ideas about how to respond. He also is motivated to reach out and include in his effort to build a winning coalition anyone, including analysts, who he believes can contribute to his ability to perform effectively in his bureaucratic struggle. Because he is eager to make a decision, this stage often does not last long.

In the third stage, the policymaker has developed a strong sense of what should be done. He has decided the issue, even if his decision has not yet been fully accepted by others. At this point, his interest in information and, especially, analysis has sharply narrowed. He wants only that which immediately informs him about the implications of his proposed course of action and the prospects for implementing it. He probably tends to resist analysis that might force him to rethink his decision.

The fourth phase involves implementing a policy designed to resolve an

6. This model is being developed by the CIA and Harvard participants in the John F. Kennedy School project on Intelligence and Policy.

issue. At this juncture, the policymaker, having committed himself to a course of action, generally is only interested in analysis that directly carries forward and supports his plan. The analyst whose product casts any doubt on the probable success of the policy becomes part of the enemy camp.

This situation is understandably painful to analysts. In a sense, the policymaker has moved in an opposite direction from the expert who wants to support him; whatever personality differences exist have become increasingly aggravated. After the initial moment when the policymaker discovers the importance of the issue and is open to contributions from all sources, he becomes more and more closed to the "objective" presentations of the analyst. The latter is trained and predisposed to offer increasingly nuanced, detailed, and critically expressed assessments as his understanding of the policy issue grows.

If the personality and cognitive structures of analysts and policymakers and their respective cultures generally are more different than similar, it is no wonder communication can be so difficult. It is not lack of good will or the desire to cooperate on either side that tends to undermine the utility of the intelligence-policy relationship. Rather, it is that intelligence is often presented in a style that is inherently difficult for policymakers to digest. Moreover, policymakers appear temperamentally incapable of giving the kind of clear, definitive signals the analyst seeks regarding the action goals the policymaker is pursuing, his objective judgment about his situation as it unfolds, and what kind of intelligence support would be most helpful. If he simply tends not to think for himself in those terms about the world and what he is trying to do, why should he do that for the analyst?

Bridging the Gap

In searching for ways to overcome these barriers, monitoring interchanges between policymakers and analysts is probably a good place to begin. If credible ways can be found to demonstrate to both sides that significant structural differences exist in how each views the world and copes with it, the first step toward reducing those differences will have been taken.

Most of the other initiatives that might help probably have to begin with the analyst and his managers. The policymaker has too much information, analysis, and advice available from other, more compatible sources to make a major effort to reorient himself toward intelligence. Even so, the cooperation of policymakers is essential, if the barriers are to be removed.

The analytical community could do at least four things that might reduce the impact of personality differences between policymakers and analysts. The first and second depend upon creating new or strengthened personal links with policymakers. The third involves making intelligence analysis all but indispensable to policymakers in their bureaucratic battles. And the fourth turns on developing new means and forms to convey analysis to policymakers in a way that fits in with their preferred methods of perceiving and thinking.

Role of Leadership

Success or failure in improving the utility of intelligence analysis will be determined largely by the types of people chosen to lead intelligence agencies. More than ever, the analyst and the policymaker depend on intelligence chiefs to understand the different worlds they both live in and to bridge the gap between them. Perhaps more conscious attention needs to be given to selecting people at the top of the intelligence pyramid who can function comfortably in both worlds. In *Real World Intelligence,* Herb Meyer describes that kind of person:

> An intelligence chief must be able to walk comfortably on both sides of the street. To lead the outfit itself, the chief must have those qualities that mark an intelligence officer: a passion for facts, a taste for delving deeply into issues, an insatiable curiosity about what is really going on in far-off places and about arcane subjects. Yet to work effectively with the chief executive—to understand what the chief executive needs from his intelligence outfit [and] to deliver finished intelligence products in a form the executive can absorb—the intelligence chief must also have the qualities that make a successful policymaker: a taste for action, the capacity to make decisions when they need to be made, regardless of whether or not all the facts are available, the ruthlessness to accept small losses in pursuit of larger gains.[7]

There are problems associated with placing in charge of analysis those who are as comfortable with the world of power as they are with the world of thought. The first is that, while we all know individuals in the Intelligence Community who are or probably could be "switch-hitters," there are not many who meet the requirement. More important, however, is the danger that, once in close touch with policymakers and already sharing some of their proclivities for enjoying power, this kind of intelligence chief may move too far from his analytical roots. If that occurs, the gap that earlier separated analysts from policymakers begins to move inside the Intelligence Community to everyone's detriment. In particular, analysts lose faith that their boss can understand and defend their interests and needs, and he loses the ability to motivate them.

Liaison Links

A second change the Intelligence Community could make—probably the most effective one—would be to find ways to put analysts in closer contact with

7. Herbert E. Meyer, *Real World Intelligence* (Weidenfeld & Nicolson, New York, 1987), p. 88.

policymakers. Robert Gates describes certain improvements that have been made in this regard over the last eight years. The *President's Daily Brief,* for example, is delivered in person by a senior analytical officer of the CIA each day to the President's top foreign policy advisers. In addition, the Director of Central Intelligence for several years now has met routinely each week with these same individuals to determine their priority intelligence needs. Gates sees this progress as fragile and highly perishable, however, and calls for something more institutionalized.[8]

In my view, what is probably required is the creation of a cadre of intelligence liaison officers who would sit in the policy agencies rather than visit them periodically from Langley. Under this concept, which is not new, these intelligence "brokers" would act as middlemen between the analysts and the policy people. They would simultaneously interpret the policymaker's needs, guide the analyst in the most effective ways to respond, deliver the product directly, and provide feedback from each to the other. Moreover, these officers also could be provided with the most modern communications capabilities to enable them to query analytical offices directly and to receive analytical contributions immediately.

The key task of an intelligence broker probably would be to decipher the real analytical needs of the policymaker. As Sherman Kent noted in 1949, "Intelligence cannot serve if it does not know the doers' minds; it cannot serve if it has not their confidence; it cannot serve unless it can have the kind of guidance any professional man must have from his client."[9] Gates echoed the same sentiment 40 years later: "Contrary to the view of those who are apprehensive over a close relationship between policymakers and intelligence, it is not close enough. More interaction, feedback, and direction as to strategies, priorities, and requirements are critical to better performance."[10]

Perhaps one reason for this impasse is that too much emphasis has been placed on persuading policymakers that they must do better in this area. Instead of decrying the policymaker's incapacity to provide direction, perhaps it is time to place a surrogate for the analyst—the intelligence broker—in close enough contact with the policymaker that the broker can try to distill appropriate feedback and guidance from what he hears and observes.

Another important task for intelligence brokers would be to persuade policymakers that intelligence analysis is *useful* and then to find or stimulate analysis that fits the need. Most policymakers probably would welcome analysis that helps them to develop a sound picture of the world, to list the possible ways to achieve their action goals, and to influence others to accept their visions. The

8. Gates, *op. cit.,* p. 42.
9. Sherman Kent, *Strategic Intelligence* (Archon Books, Hamden, Conn., 1965), p. 182.
10. Gates, *op. cit.,* p. 40.

last point may be key. Intelligence analysis will adhere and be accepted when policymakers believe that they will be at a competitive disadvantage within the bureaucracy and with foreign challengers if they do not have and understand it. If just a few more policymakers than at present came to be perceived by others as better equipped to negotiate and to get their viewpoint accepted because they have intelligence aides and analytical support, it might not be long before others sought the same resources.

There are risks. Placing analysts in closer contact with policymakers, even if indirectly through liaison officers, increases the danger that analysis will become politicized. Policymakers will become even more intent on finding or generating assessments that prove they are right in their interagency struggles. And the temptation to "join the team," especially for an intelligence officer who "lives" daily in the action agency, would be great.

Much of what would be necessary to defend objectivity when policymaking and analysis are in closer proximity would become clear only when that situation actually develops. One part of the solution probably would take the form of more education for analysts as to what constitutes professional integrity and how to maintain it. Another part might involve slowly expanding the consciousness of policymakers about the risks to their ability to make wise decisions if they routinely try to distort what intelligence analysis has to offer. Most likely, some kinds of institutional measures also would be necessary, both to ensure that the primary loyalty of those in touch with policymakers remains attached to their intelligence home base and to provide an independent "court of appeal" to those analysts—or even policymakers—who believe that crucial analysis is being corrupted. Any such moves would be a welcome sign that intelligence analysis is really beginning to count.

Presenting the Product

The fourth element in increasing the utility of intelligence analysis might be the most wrenching for the analytical community. There probably is a need to change the style of writing and what is produced for top-level policymakers, seeing them as a distinctly different kind of consumer. There is something on which to build. Typescripts, which are usually written for specific individuals, often are better received than most hardcover publications. Intelligence assessments and research papers are crucial to developing a knowledge base, for reaching analytical conclusions, and for communicating with other experts. But, as one analyst knowledgeable of the MBTI approach has pointed out, they are written in the big-picture, dry, analytical style, about as far removed as can be imagined from the way policy operators prefer to take aboard information.

Another analyst makes a similar point. He believes that analysts strongly prefer to transmit knowledge through writing, because only writing can capture the full complexity of what they want to convey. Policy consumers, however, tend to seek what can be called "news" rather than knowledge; they are more comfortable with a mode of communication that more closely resembles speech.[11]

I believe that many of the "improvements" made in presentation and analytical approaches in the last few years have not helped this problem. For example, more "key judgment" sections are written because we understand high-level readers have little time to digest long papers. But these sections, although concise, are often more abstract and dry than the main discussion from which they are drawn. Similarly, the move toward more sophistication in making predictions by use of such devices as alternative scenarios and indicators may be more satisfying and "honest" intellectually, but there is a good chance they do not even marginally help the policymaker use intelligence analysis more effectively. Finally, the extended, hierarchical review process that most intelligence analysis undergoes before dissemination probably removes any vestige of the personal, conversational style that might appeal to a policymaker.

If these observations are valid, the following improvements could be made:

— Circulate *no* hardcover publications to the highest-level policymakers. Instead, recast the intelligence judgments reached in these vehicles into punchy typescripts tailored for them individually. Because much of what we write is of little use to them, we would probably make a net gain by cutting back on the quantity of analysis sent to them.

— Communicate analysis in a more aphoristic, conversational manner. If colorful, anecdotal language gets a better reception, it should be used to help convey analytical information and judgments.

— Use briefing to impart analysis, whenever possible. Human contact is what works best, and it gives analysts their best opportunity to develop trust, obtain feedback, and become sensitive to the needs of particular consumers.

— Overhaul the review process. Although today's disseminated analysis has a corporate imprint, it is of little value if it has minimal impact.

One final thought may be in order on the utility to policymakers of national estimates. It may be useful for the Intelligence Community to go through the extraordinary labor involved in the national estimates process on a given issue. It is, however, about the most unlikely way that can be devised to influence the

---

11. Robert S. Sinclair, *Thinking and Writing: Cognitive Science and the Directorate of Intelligence* (Unclassified monograph published by the Center for the Study of Intelligence, Central Intelligence Agency, Washington, D.C, January 1984), pp. 24–25.

policy process. With a few exceptions, estimates are not issued until all significant negotiations and compromises have taken place among the relevant policymakers. A more useful process almost certainly can be found if the Intelligence Community really believes its collective judgments should influence policy decisions.

27. A veteran both of operations and of analysis, one who is on the reform
side of the analyst/consumer question, gives his update on it. He was
writing just before the Gates nomination blowup (discussed on p. xx).
Gates having now come and gone, the matter remains unresolved.

New Links Between Intelligence and Policy

DAVID D. GRIES

No subject in intelligence has led to more debate and less
agreement than the linkage between the intelligence and policy communities.
Sherman Kent, Ernest R. May, Robert M. Gates[1] and others have explored the
subject in books and articles. Colleges and universities teach courses on it. Yet
some aspects of the linkage remain largely unexplored. What kind of intelligence is transmitted between the two communities? How is it transmitted?
How do policy officers use it?

In the first decade after passage of the National Security Act of 1947, which
laid most of the foundations for an intelligence community, only the most
senior intelligence officers maintained regular contact with policy officers
(deputy assistant secretaries and up or their equivalent). Intelligence officers
were also less numerous in those days, and intelligence agencies were only
partly accepted as players in Washington. The situation changed in the next
three decades. The Intelligence Community grew rapidly, first during the
Korean and Vietnam Wars and again during the Reagan years, and intelligence
agencies gradually became established in national security circles. The result is
that today intelligence and policy officers of all levels spend far more time
together.

An important consequence of increased contact is that the formal and
impersonal linkages of the past have become more informal and personal. Oral
assessments delivered during face-to-face contacts now outnumber written
assessments delivered through classified mail channels. The more senior the

David D. Gries, "New Links Between Intelligence and Policy," *Studies in Intelligence*, vol. 34, no. 2
(Summer 1990), pp. 1–6. Originally unclassified.

1. Sherman Kent, *Strategic Intelligence* (Archon Books, Hamden, Conn., 1965); Ernest R.
May, *"Lessons" of the Past: The Uses and Misuse of History in American Foreign Policy* (Oxford
University Press, 1973); Robert M. Gates, "The CIA and American Foreign Policy," *Foreign Affairs*
(Winter 1987–88), pp. 215–230.

intelligence officer involved, the more likely that oral rather than written assessments will be conveyed. As a result, intelligence officers themselves have become part of the transmission system, and policy officers are using intelligence in somewhat different ways.

Growing Importance of Oral Assessments

Oral assessments are analytical evaluations or judgments as distinguished from current intelligence. They are conveyed during discussions at the countless informal meetings that dot the calendars of senior officers in national security departments and agencies and at the more formal policy-coordinating meetings held at various levels from assistant secretary to the President himself. These meetings offer opportunities for intelligence officers to provide direct policy support, as, for example, when policy officers at a series of meetings in April 1990 solicited assessments of policy options concerning the Lithuanian situation. A senior officer from the mid 1970s—a deputy director, a national intelligence officer, an office director from one of the intelligence agencies—would notice a marked increase in this kind of contact today.

Oral assessments are also transmitted in briefings to a steadily widening audience. On any given working day dozens of intelligence officers give briefings on everything from Soviet agricultural policy to narcotics production in the Andes. On the receiving end are senior members of the Executive Branch, as well as members of Congress. The Intelligence Community is often at its best in these situations, because knowledgeable, working-level analysts usually deliver the briefings themselves. They speak from firsthand exposure to all the available intelligence.

There is another link, perhaps the most important one, that competes with meetings and briefings between intelligence and policy officers. It consists of causal contacts, impromptu discussions, telephone conversations, and conference calls. These channels are much less formal than meetings or briefings, and the oral assessments offered in them are less structured. Arguably, the most important oral assessments are transferred through these least formal mechanisms. They mirror the way the government is doing business in the 1990s: *ad hoc* arrangements, reliance on personal ties, and a high degree of informality. Casual contacts also avoid some of the pitfalls of meetings and briefings, where bureaucratic competition among agencies and principals sometimes diverts attention from issues.

Because people convey oral assessments, the influence of the messenger can overshadow the message. Just as a persuasive officer makes a weak assessment sound good, so a poor briefer destroys a strong brief. When personal relationships also exist between intelligence and policy officers, the dynamics of friendship come into play. Friends are trusted and listened to; strangers may not be. And when a policy officer over time develops confidence in an intelligence officer, that confidence is likely to be transferred to assessments even though they may not be good ones.

Changing Role of Written Assessments

Several kinds of written assessments continue to play a key role in linking intelligence and policy officers. Some policy officers—former Secretary of State George Shultz was a recent example—prefer reading to briefings. Among written products, the *President's Daily Brief* stands out as influential, even critical, in supplying assessments to the President and his inner circle. The *National Intelligence Daily* and INR's *Morning Summary*, which circulate at subcabinet levels, are also influential, and they have a much wider circulation among policy officers.

Four other categories of written intelligence deserve special mention:

— National Intelligence Estimates stretch back to 1950, when CIA's fourth Director, General Walter Bedell Smith, responded to President Truman's request of 10 October 1950 for an assessment of Soviet and Chinese intentions in Korea to take with him to his meeting with General MacArthur on Wake Island. Smith assembled the heads of all the intelligence agencies that afternoon in his conference room and, according to Ludwell Montague's account, insisted that they produce six Estimates on Korea by 8:00 a.m. the next morning.[2] Forty years later, the key judgments of National Intelligence Estimates reach an influential audience in Washington, where they are separately circulated to the President and Vice President and to Cabinet and subcabinet officers. As a result, key judgments of Estimates are among the few written intelligence assessments regularly read at the top of government.

— Unscheduled written assessments—generally short papers in the form of memorandums, discussion papers for meetings, executive briefs and typescripts—also reach high-level policy officers. Such assessments often are prepared at the request of one of these officers to meet a specific need, and they are assured of a small but influential readership. Their key characteristics are brevity and focus. They do not appear on production plans, nor are they supported by extensive research. Yet each year policy officers ask for more of them, thus confirming their value. They are part of the larger

---

2. Ludwell L. Montague, *General Walter Bedell Smith as Director of Central Intelligence, October 1950–1953* (Washington, D.C., CIA History Staff, 1970; declassified version released to National Archives under CIA's Historical Review Program in February 1990), vol. II, pp. 26–30.

trend not only from written to oral assessments, but also from scheduled written assessments to unscheduled ones.

— Written scientific and technical assessments, such as those that evaluate conventional and strategic weapons systems or analyze advanced technologies and economic competitiveness, find a ready audience, especially at the Departments of Defense, Treasury, Commerce, and Energy. The level of detail provided in these assessments is too great to convey in a briefing, and a written record is often needed for future use.

— Unevaluated intelligence—raw reports from clandestine agents, pieces of SIGINT or imagery that have not been subjected to analysis—also flows to policy officers. Occasionally, unevaluated intelligence lands on the desk of a high-level policy officer, even the President, and directly influences decisionmaking. More often, unevaluated intelligence flows at lower levels, where it converges with and is incorporated in written assessments sent to the same customers. The convergence has an unintended byproduct: policy officers and analysts have access to the same unevaluated reports and thus can challenge each other's judgments.

With the foregoing exceptions, scheduled written assessments, formerly the Intelligence Community's chief product, today mainly influence the policy process indirectly. Senior intelligence officers and the staffs that support policy officers are now their principal readers. They rely heavily on them when preparing oral assessments and short papers. Scheduled written assessments thus have assumed a new and vital role, though not the one originally intended: they have become part of the foundation of the intelligence edifice, providing much of the analysis on which other intelligence products are based. Moreover, analysts who prepare scheduled written assessments are doing more than serving the policy process indirectly; they are honing their own analytical skills in preparation for the time when they will be making oral presentations.

Intelligence information conveyed by video cassettes is a special case whose market is growing rapidly. President Reagan was an enthusiastic customer. He recognized that biographic intelligence was more digestible when images and narrative were presented together. The picture of Qadafhi delivering a tirade has more impact than a written assessment alone. Because video intelligence combines the trend towards oral assessment with television's pervasive influence, it seems likely that in the future more intelligence will flow into the policy community in this fashion.

Foreign Policy Decisionmaking

Before exploring how policy officers use intelligence, it is necessary to reflect briefly on how foreign policy is made in today's Washington. Few observers believe that policy formation is an orderly process where facts are lined up, analysis applied, and decisions made. Some would contend that most policy officers avoid making decisions, unless forced by events. Delay is preferable to making a decision that might adversely affect US interests, disadvantage a department, or blemish the record of a policy officer by revealing him or her as wrong. Faced with these possibilities, policy officers slow down the process and seek safety by spreading the responsibility within a wide circle. The larger the number of participants in making a decision, the smaller the risk to any one of them.

Nor are most foreign policy decisions made all at once. Caution marks the process. The pressure of events almost always starts the process; incremental decisionmaking completes it. Of course, not all decisions are made—or avoided—in this way. The recent US action in Panama and the Nicaraguan election are examples of events that forced policy officers to act rapidly and decisively. But they are exceptions.

Usually the events that force policy officers to make incremental decisions are far less dramatic. They include clearing positions for meetings and informal discussions within the Executive Branch; coordination of briefing books, arrival statements, toasts, negotiating positions, and communiqués for policy officers traveling abroad and for foreign visitors; approval of speeches, letters and talking points for senior policy officers; and dealing with Congress and the media. Contacts with the Congress require policy officers to clear briefings and testimony and respond to investigations, new laws, and legislative reports. Dealing with the media requires policy officers to get ready for questions and answers at press conferences, respond to op-ed articles, prepare for discussions with journalists, and try to limit damage from leaks. Although no one of these events is likely to prompt a major policy change, taken together they often nudge policy in new directions or make new policy.

Evolving Uses of Intelligence

Because policy officers rarely make decisions in an orderly fashion, intelligence is usually used inefficiently. The policy process is messy and marked by delay, sharing of risks, and incremental steps. The uses of intelligence are equally messy.

Defending policy. Policy officers spend much of their time shoring up support for decisions already in place or generating support for recent decisions, so the use of intelligence to defend policy is not surprising. Examples of this include defense against congressional criticism and sallies from bureaucratic rivals, as when a policy officer in one department uses an intelligence assessment to weaken the argument of another department. During the 1980s, policy officers dealing with Nicaragua spent most of their energy defending policy.

The policy officer as a defensive player reflects in part the influence of Vietnam, Watergate, and Iran-Contra. Vietnam spawned an aggressive press that today challenges assumptions underlying policy, searches for bureaucratic infighting, and grills policy officers whenever possible. Watergate sharpened skepticism of government institutions and actions. Iran-Contra pulled more foreign policy decisionmaking power away from the Executive and gave it to the Congress. Leaks to the press also play a role. The more open political system that has grown out of Vietnam, Watergate, and Iran-Contra has made it difficult to keep secrets. Against this background, policy officers have become counter-punchers.

Supporting action. Next in importance among the uses of intelligence by policy officers is support of diplomatic or other actions, sometimes to the dismay of the Intelligence Community, which wants to protect its sources and methods. President Reagan used intelligence to put the responsibility on Libya for bombing a disco in Berlin in April 1986 and to hold the Soviets accountable for shooting down KAL 007 in 1983. He used it again to accuse Libya of constructing a factory to produce chemical warfare agents, and the Bush administration repeated the same accusation in March 1990. High-level policy officers frequently use intelligence to confront foreign countries with evidence of unfriendly activities, as when intelligence detected widespread election irregularities in the Phillipines in 1986.[3] Subsequently, the White House issued a series of warnings to President Marcos.

Helping to make new policy decisions. The use of intelligence assessments to assist in making new policy decisions is third in importance. Academicians identify this kind of decisionmaking as the principal use of intelligence assessments. Many would claim there is no other justification for maintaining a large intelligence community. But policy officers, as noted, spend more of their time defending policy and supporting direct action than in making decisions. Even when new policy decisions are being made, intelligence is not always used directly or consistently.

Nonetheless, intelligence assessments can and do help to identify policy options that will work, thus directly supporting decisions on new policies. This was the case in 1980, when President Carter based policy decisions on intelligence about preparations for imposing martial law in Poland.[4] The policy officer may use intelligence to answer important questions underlying portions of a decision, as when intelligence was used to establish Toshiba's violation of

3. Gates, "The CIA and American Foreign Policy," p. 221.
4. *Ibid.*

COCOM regulations. Or, after reaching a decision, policy officers may encourage distribution of a compatible intelligence assessment to unify the Executive Branch behind the decision, as when intelligence was used to demonstrate that the INF Treaty could be adequately monitored. On the other hand, policy officers generally prefer those assessments that buttress their preconceptions. Consequently, they often use intelligence selectively.

Acquiring information. As the traditional foreign policy menu has lengthened to include narcotics, terrorism, and nuclear proliferation, the policy officer's need for information has grown dramatically. Often too busy to read widely in their fields and buffeted by daily events, policy officers draw down their intellectual capital. Intelligence assessments, when they are clear, concise, and timely, provide an efficient way to build capital. To fill specific gaps in their knowledge policy officers can also shape the flow of intelligence, though not its content, by requesting assessments that illuminate policies under review or highlight emerging issues.

Congressmen, and especially their staffs, also use intelligence to acquire information, thus helping to create a common fund of knowledge. This is a new development. In the 1950s and 1960s the Intelligence Community shared few assessments with the Congress, so that there was little commonality in the information base of the Legislative and Executive Branches. The amount of intelligence conveyed to the Congress has picked up steadily since the 1970s, when permanent oversight committees were established. Today, the Intelligence Community supplies similar intelligence to both branches. Policy officers ignore this development at considerable risk.

Users of intelligence have little time for reading lengthy assessments, and they tend to acquire information informally over time as they encounter intelligence counterparts in meetings, briefings, and casual contacts. Thus a general knowledge of the Intelligence Community's conclusions about an issue is slowly accumulated, ready for use when a crisis occurs.

Lost Opportunities

It is no accident that, with the exceptions already noted, oral assessments and short papers have pride of place in the new intelligence-policy linkage, because they most closely match the penchant of today's policy officer for informality and personal transactions. That oral assessments have gained wide acceptance shows the attention intelligence officers are giving to their customers. Yet current practice leaves much to be desired. Too many policy officers fail to understand what intelligence can do for them. Instead of recognizing it as a useful recourse, they view it as unhelpful or as a potentially competing input into the policy process. They also fail to give the Intelligence

Community the guidance and feedback it needs. Some experienced policy officers know better. They identify a point of entry to the Intelligence Community, usually a deputy director, a national intelligence officer or an office director in one of the intelligence agencies. They keep their doors open. When requesting assessments, they frame questions carefully to ensure that the right issues are addressed.

Writing in *"Lessons" of the Past,* Ernest R. May advanced the notion that policy officers should depend more on historians. When historical experience is overlooked, May wrote, mistakes are common.[5] Similarly, when intelligence is overlooked, mistakes can occur. But the press of daily business on policy officers means that the Intelligence Community has to find better and more efficient ways to compete for attention.

Strengthening Intelligence-Policy Linkages

As the transfer of intelligence assessments to policy officers shifts from a predominantly written to a predominantly oral enterprise, the Intelligence Community should pay close attention to the consequences.

— The Intelligence Community should reinforce the trend towards producing oral assessments of all kinds and short papers. A higher standard of performance in oral presentations can and should be achieved through improved training. As short papers become the norm, the temptation to make them longer should be vigorously resisted. Particularly important, annual production plans covering scheduled written assessments should be scrapped; they are not needed in an environment characterized by rapidly changing requirements.

— There are pitfalls in the new game of oral assessments. Intelligence officers making oral presentations often operate alone, separated from the traditional process that subjects analysis to competitive review. Furthermore, a message that is delivered heavy-handedly runs the risk of wearing out the messenger's welcome among policy officers. For example, in 1962 Director John McCone lost much of his direct access to President Kennedy after the Cuban missile crisis. His oral presentations to the President were accurate, but, after missiles were discovered in Cuba, the President told McCone that "you were right all along, but for the wrong reasons."[6]

— The Intelligence Community does not keep adequate records of oral presentations, thus underscoring its failure to recognize their importance. Pro-

5. May, *"Lessons" of the Past,* pp. 172–190.
6. Rhodri Jeffery-Jones, *The CIA and American Democracy* (Yale University Press, 1989), pp. 136–137.

duction records based solely on scheduled written assessments reflect yesterday's reality. They are inadequate for studies of production trends, and they overlook the contribution of oral assessments. A simple records system is needed to keep track of and give appropriate weight to oral assessments and short papers as well as to scheduled written assessments.

— The process through which policy officers task the Intelligence Community is too sporadic, complex, and cumbersome for a world that lives by speed and flexibility. Tasking is most effective when policy officers ask questions over the telephone or in face-to-face discussions, not when questions are submitted in writing. Similarly, most intelligence officers prefer to task their own systems with oral rather than written requests. The long, written tasking documents produced each year with such effort should be shortened and in some cases abandoned.

— Intelligence officers need to understand the policy process better. Too often they know more about how that process works abroad than in Washington. Few intelligence agency schools offer high-quality courses on the American foreign policy process. Rotational tours for intelligence officers in policy agencies offer another way to sharpen understanding of the policy process. Few intelligence officers should reach senior levels without these experiences.

Modern American intelligence is not yet 50 years old. Much has been accomplished to bring intelligence and policy officers together in a productive relationship. In 1965 Sherman Kent concluded in *Strategic Intelligence* that "of the two dangers—that of intelligence being too far from the users and that of being too close—the greater danger is the one of being too far."[7] Today, thanks to the oral assessments and short papers that flow through the informal and personal linkages between intelligence and policy, the danger "of being too far" has been reduced, though not eliminated. As resources tighten, a heavy burden falls on the Intelligence Community to make these new linkages and trends work better.

7. Kent, *Strategic Intelligence,* p. 195.

28.

Here is a detailed case study, by a knowledgeable participant, of how analysts and humint operatives worked as a backup team jointly with American negotiators at an international economic conference. There are many redactions here; but they only slightly close what remains a remarkably open window on kinds of intelligence work that will probably be featured in the post–Cold War world. Notice that the article specifically (p. 375) did not address the problems that arise in utilizing the sensitive "special intelligence" that has particularly restrictive access rules. But one brief mention of NSA sigint contributions to the operation did get declassified (pp. 368–369).

UNCTAD V: Intelligence Support at a Major International Economic Conference

MICHAEL VANDERBROOK

The United Nations Conference on Trade and Development held its fifth session—UNCTAD V—in May–June 1979. Meeting in Manila, representatives of some 150 countries considered proposals to revamp world economic relations in areas of trade, manufacturing, commodities, money and finance, technology, and shipping. Faced by the numerically superior coalition of less developed countries (LDCs) known as the Group of 77, the United States and other industrialized nations had to walk a narrow line between giving in on costly and often ill-conceived LDC proposals on the one hand, or being accused of obstructing the initiatives needed to meet changing world economic conditions on the other—an effort that required the U.S. delegation to be aware of the plans and tactics of the other conference participants.

This article deals with the organization and operation of the intelligence support structure that provided the U.S. delegation with such information.

Early Attention to Intelligence Support

Previous experience with conferences of this sort—primarily UNCTAD IV in Nairobi three years earlier—had indicated the value of intelligence coverage of North-South negotiations ██████████████████████████

Michael VanderBrook, "UNCTAD V: Intelligence Support at a Major International Economic Conference," *Studies in Intelligence*, vol. 24, no. 1 (Spring 1980), pp. 47–56. Originally classified "Secret" and "Noforn." For definitions, see Appendix B.

██████████████████████████████████
█████████████████████████. Intelligence reports █████████████
at the conference were passed to the head of the U.S. delegation and subsequently disseminated. At the Washington end, these reports were immediately passed to high-level policy officials, especially those due to fly to Nairobi for negotiations at the close of the conference.

Postmortems on the Nairobi operation testified both to its basic value and to the need for expanding the base of such intelligence community support.

Developments during 1976–79

After Nairobi, two separate chains of events in Washington worked toward improved intelligence support for policy makers with North-South responsibilities. First, Charles Meissner, an appreciative and long-standing consumer of CIA reports, was appointed Deputy Assistant Secretary of State for International Finance and Development. In the role he called on the Office of Economic Research for analysis of several key North-South issues. The value of these studies is shown by the uses to which they were put:

— At Meissner's prompting, a sanitized version of OER's analysis of LDC debt positions was added to the UNCTAD secretariat paper that served as the baseline for North-South debt discussions.
— Information from an OER paper on the least developed among the developing countries was used to deflect some ill-conceived demarches on that topic.
— An OER paper on trade among the LDCs helped focus OECD preparations for trade discussions at UNCTAD V.

The other chain of events was the steady enrichment of the National Foreign Assessment Center's functional resources on the North-South dialogue. One clear example of this was the creation in July 1976 of an Economic Development Branch in OER. Another was the expansion of interdisciplinary meetings on North-South issues under the aegis of NFAC's Office of Political Analysis. The branches participating in these periodic North-South cluster meetings collaborated on position papers setting forth LDC interests and stances on such issues as debt renegotiation, the Common Fund for commodity price stabilization and development, and the transfer of technology.

Preparations for UNCTAD V

As UNCTAD V drew nearer, Meissner included the Agency in his invitations to interagency preparatory meetings, the first of which took place in

December 1978. From December to May, OER was forthcoming in providing literally hundreds of pages on debt, trade, and other issues. Meanwhile, OPA kept State and the NSC up to date on the dynamics of LDC preparations for the conference. Throughout this period, the DDO was providing copies of internal G-77 documents and reports on LDC deliberations.

Meanwhile, arrangements were made to set up an Agency team to provide support during the conference itself. Negotiations among NFAC, the DDO, and State resulted in agreement to field a team consisting of an NFAC analyst familiar with UNCTAD issues, ██████████████████████████ ████████ and a full-time secretary dispatched from Headquarters. ████████ ██ the NFAC analyst's, briefing U.S. delegation members and generating new requirements as the conference progressed; ██████████████████████████ ████████████████████████████████████. Basic headquarters support was to be provided in the form of a twice-weekly briefing cable summarizing all-source intelligence relating to conference issues. Headquarters also set up a quick-response mechanism to provide the field team with additional analytical support as required.

The Elements of Support

Minimizing Flap Potential: High among both Agency and State Department concerns for this operation was the possibility of exposure. Realizing that the benefits of our effort could be more than negated if Agency activities at the conference became an issue, we instituted the following procedures:

[The first four-fifths of the list of procedures was redacted.—HBW]

— The NFAC briefer's Agency affiliation was ████████ kept concealed. His true affiliation was known with certainty only to the delegation leaders, selected Embassy personnel, and a few delegates with whom he had worked in Washington. To the others, he was known as a member of Meissner's staff, assigned TDY to the Embassy during the conference.
— All classified documents used in briefing the U.S. delegation were kept in concealment devices or safes except when being shown to delegation members. Transportation of classified documents was restricted to official Embassy cars rather than station vehicles or public transportation.

Sources of Information: To ensure that the U.S. delegation was fully informed on events affecting the conference, we drew on any sources considered to have intelligence potential, including: (a) intelligence gathered ██████████████████ (b) similar reports originated by other Agency stations; (c) relevant intercepts picked up by NSA anywhere in the world; and (d) special reports written by NFAC analysts at Headquarters.

Inventory Control: The intelligence reports originating from these several sources were destined not only for the delegation leaders but also for delegation members concerned with specific negotiating points, for the Ambassador and the DCM ██████. Record keeping was critical. It was necessary from the standpoint of support to assure that the 35–40 reports obtained each week were being passed to the right people—not always an easy task in view of the constant flow of delegates to and from caucuses and negotiating sessions. And with so many documents and recipients, it was necessary from the security angle to be able to pinpoint the location of each intelligence report at all times. As a rule, delegates were shown intelligence reports during or just after the morning staff meeting. If schedules prevented such contacts, or if the reports were such that delegates wished to refer to them more than once, the reports were left in the delegation's safe under Marine Corps guard.

The Support Team in Operation

Although the focal point of each day's activities for the support team was the 0830 briefing of the delegation leaders, the workday began much earlier— before dawn for some ██████ personnel—and ended only when the report of the last ██████ meeting had been drafted—often after midnight. Indeed, given the time differential of 12 hours between Manila and Washington, there literally was no hour of the day when the Agency's support effort was shut down.

Commo personnel opened shop at 0500, ████████████ to process the overnight traffic routed to Manila by ██████ messages from the Headquarters support team. At 0700, the NFAC analyst would sound the buzzer on the commo vault door to pick up this material. The next 45 minutes were frantic:

— Multipage cables had to be separated, collated, and logged; their crypts had to be snipped off; then they had to be read and gisted for the rapidly approaching briefing.

— ██
██
██.

— Copies of pertinent incoming traffic would be marked for the Ambassador's bluebook ████████████ and copies of the draft field reports would be put in the reports officer's in-box to be processed for dissemination.

— If, as often happened, commo received additional traffic after the 0700 pickup, someone would run it downstairs to the station for last-minute inclusion in the briefing package.

At about 0745, the briefing materials for the day would be ███████ █████████████ and the motor pool would be called to send an Embassy car around front for the three-mile trip down Roxas Boulevard to delegation head-quarters.

Upon arriving at the hotel where the U.S. delegation was housed, the NFAC analyst would immediately meet with the Headquarters case officer. The two would compare notes on developments at the conference and discuss operational matters and new requirements. Then the NFAC analyst would read, log, and gist the draft reports the case officer had prepared, while the case officer would familiarize himself with the rest of the day's briefing material.

Promptly at 0830, the NFAC analyst would knock on the delegation chief's door; the briefing commenced immediately, running anywhere from 20 to 35 minutes. During this session, the delegation leaders would comment on the reports, give their perceptions of events at the conference, and indicate what they wanted in the way of future reporting and analytical support from Head-quarters.

Next up was the delegation staff meeting. Here the delegation head would brief the delegation on major developments, run through the day's business, and receive progress reports from each of the eight negotiating teams. During or immediately after this meeting, the NFAC analyst would arrange to pass reports to members of the delegation whose specific areas of interest were covered in the day's intelligence take. Any new requirements and informa-tion from these delegates were also noted at this time. Since the NFAC analyst was talking to several delegates individually in this regard, it was a simple matter to use this opportunity to pass any additional requirements ████████ ████████.

This done, the final task at delegation headquarters was to leave copies of any reports that the delegates wished to retain in the safe; to pick up any reports they had finished with; and to get copies of documents such as the head of delegation's schedule for the day, the UNCTAD Secretariat's daily journal of conference proceedings, and the log listing cables sent out by the delegation. A radio call from one of the delegation secretaries would then bring an Embassy car around for the trip back ██████.

Bringing Washington up to date was the next order of business. Returning to the ████████ the NFAC analyst would give copies of the newly obtained intelligence drafts to the reports officer for processing. Working together, the reports officer and the NFAC analyst would edit the drafts, filling in or ver-ifying names from the lists of conference participants, cross-referencing State cables from the delegation log, and adding field comments based on the NFAC analyst's knowledge of the issues. Added to the normal work-load, the UNCTAD reporting put quite a burden on the ██████ single reports officer.

Even with the help of the NFAC analyst and the services of the Headquarters secretary sent out for the conference, the day's final report was often delivered to commo for transmission to Washington as late as 1900.

In between working on reports, the NFAC analyst would meet with the ███████████████ officer to pass along new requirements ███████████ ███████ and to review developments at the conference. Newly arrived cable traffic was read, categorized, and annotated for the next briefing session. Items of general interest were routed to the ████████ branch chiefs, as were copies of all new requirements. As called for, the NFAC analyst would draft information or requirements cables for Headquarters.

The Headquarters Support Effort

Support from Headquarters took three forms: (a) responding to the NFAC analyst's requests for Headquarters analytical support and for operational support from ████████ stations; (b) monitoring worldwide reporting on the conference itself and on other events that could influence its outcome, and summarizing these in a series of update cables sent to the NFAC analyst in Manila; and (c) assuring that policy makers in Washington received the same intelligence reporting that was being passed to the heads of delegations in Manila.

The two principal Headquarters components involved in UNCTAD support were DDO's International Affairs Division (IAD) and OER's Economic Development Branch (D/ED). Both components were actively involved in the task of keeping Washington policy makers informed on the conference and related developments. IAD took responsibility for getting the intel reports issuing from Manila into the hands of the Under Secretary of State for Economic Affairs, while D/ED undertook to do the same with its semiweekly "UNCTAD update" cables.

A total of 11 update cables were put together during the conference. Each Monday and Wednesday, D/ED analysts would complete a cycle that involved collecting and summarizing three or four days' worth of reporting bearing on the conference and drafting an outgoing cable. The basic format of these messages corresponded to the conference's organizational structure, with a section for each of the eight negotiating groups. Other sections of the update covered conference developments not specifically tied to negotiating groups and events elsewhere—such as the concurrent Lome II negotiations—that could impinge on country positions at Manila. The task of gathering the needed materials and drafting and coordinating these cables was a full time job for D/ED's North-South analyst. It was also an effort that would have proved impossible to achieve without support by the Office of Central Reference's Systems Analysis Staff, which surmounted both technical and bureaucratic hurdles to give D/ED access to COLTS, the Agency's computerized system for searching the contents of all incoming cable traffic. By using COLTS to search incoming traffic for any mention of such key words as "UNCTAD," "G-77," and "Lome," D/ED analysts could be sure of seeing *all* pertinent cables and of seeing them promptly. Being able to view "hits" on an electronic screen often cut three to five days from the time required to get hard copies through normal mail distribution channels.

The third support task assigned to the Headquarters team—providing economic analysis in response to the tactical needs of the U.S. delegation— turned out to be more important than anyone had anticipated. During the second week of the conference, rumblings began to emerge within the G-77 over the exclusion of energy issues from the agenda. The threat of a new round of OPEC price hikes had struck a raw nerve among some of the non-oil-producing LDCs. Although they had not planned to raise the energy issue at UNCTAD V themselves, the U.S. delegation leaders quickly recognized the opportunity presented to them. By encouraging those LDCs that had spoken up on this issue, the U.S. delegation sought to put an end to the UNCTAD charade of "analyzing" the world economic and trade situation without reference to one of the major causes of the current economic turmoil.

Even if this goal could not be completely achieved, other U.S. aims, within the setting of the conference itself, could be achieved through exploitation of the LDC split on energy. From the beginning of the conference, radical elements in the G-77 had sought to drum up support for divisive special-interest resolutions. Among these was a resolution sponsored by the Palestine Liberation Organization calling for UNCTAD studies of "occupied territories and peoples under colonial domination." Specific mention was made of Palestine, and by implication the resolution also included Puerto Rico. The emergence of the energy issue gave the U.S. delegation a chance to link the two matters, threatening to include a reference to energy in a resolution on world economic interdependence put forward by Group B (the industrialized nations' caucus), but offering to withdraw the reference if the G-77 would drop the PLO resolution.

Partly to build support among other members of Group B for this linkage, and partly to stimulate the LDCs that had raised the energy issue in the first place to continue pressing their point inside the G-77, the U.S. delegation leaders sought analysis and data outlining the impact of the new OPEC price rises. In response to this requirement, OER quickly provided three energy background papers: "OPEC Countries: Gains in Terms of Trade"; "OPEC Countries: Current Account Surplus to Soar"; and "Implications of Energy Prices for Non-OPEC LDCs in 1979." Armed with this information, the U.S. delegation leaders were able to achieve their tactical aims with Group B—

which agreed to an energy reference in the interdependence resolution—and with the concerned LDCs, which held to their position for another week despite increasing OPEC pressure to drop the subject.

On the whole, the emergence of energy as an issue at the conference was an unforeseen event that was, nonetheless, seized upon with vigor by the U.S. delegation leaders. Their ability to use this occurrence to tactical advantage required, and promptly received, support from the Agency. The ensuing bickering within the G-77 over both the legitimacy of putting energy on the agenda and how to respond to the linkage matter threw the LDCs into such confusion that they were largely unable to focus their energies on other matters. All of this, of course, worked to the advantage of Group B in that it forced the participants to face up to a basic problem for the world economy, it reduced the pressure on Group B to address ill-conceived LDC proposals for costly new institutions and economic reforms, and it lessened the danger that a concerted LDC effort could have split Group B and left the United States isolated on certain issues. That this outcome was achieved is a tribute both to the acumen and flexibility of the U.S. delegation leaders and to the quality and timeliness of their intelligence support.

Lessons for the Future

A review of the results of UNCTAD V from an intelligence perspective shows that: (a) most of the problems involved in such an operation can be overcome by careful advance planning and the exercise of sound judgment during the conference itself; (b) some problems are less susceptible to our control, but good spadework can turn the odds in our favor; and (c) some elements of the operation that we foresaw as highly productive are actually either highly subject to the vagaries of chance or, at worst, are inherently incapable of providing tactically relevant intelligence.

The UNCTAD operation was a success on several counts: the U.S. delegation was helped in achieving its conference goals; policy makers in Washington were kept informed; security was maintained; ███████████████████ ████████████████████████████ These accomplishments were built on the three solid pillars of favorable consumer relations, a well-thought-out organizational structure, and pre-planning for flexibility.

As stated earlier, the relationship between the Agency and the head of the U.S. delegation was one of long-standing mutual respect. This climate made it easy for Agency analysts to keep abreast of diplomatic developments during the months leading up to the conference and prompted an inspired Agency support effort during the preparatory phase. ████████ the NFAC studies ███████ ████████████████████████████ represented a response to high-level State

Department recognition of the value of intelligence and desire for such support. The importance attached to the Agency effort is underlined by the fact that, throughout the four weeks of the conference, the first item on the head of the delegation's daily schedule was his briefing by the NFAC analyst.

The second element underpinning the Agency's effort in Manila—a strong organizational structure—has several facets. The over-all structure of the support effort is shown in the accompanying chart. Particularly noteworthy is the fact that the organization includes both DDO and NFAC components working together at each stage of the support effort. ███████████████████████████. Any initial uneasiness about this arrangement soon gave way to the mutual realization that the professional talents of both directorates were essential to a successful operation.

The third key element in our operational planning was provision for a flexible response to delegation needs in view of the dynamics of the conference. The organizational structure determined what we could do; what we actually did do and how well we did it rested with the personnel chosen to fill the organizational slots. Planning on this point, then, consisted in knowing that on-the-spot adjustments would be called for, and choosing the right people to make them.

The day-to-day reading of delegation needs fell to the NFAC analyst as a consequence of his regular contact with the delegation at the morning briefings and staff meetings. As the delegation leaders discussed conference developments and reacted to the content of the intelligence reports of the day, the NFAC analyst would block out new collection requirements. Given the set of requirements and the relative degree of urgency attached to each, the case officers would then select the assets for tasking. These frequent adjustments in requirements, plus feedback to our assets on their previous reporting, kept our collection efforts homed in on the relevant issues throughout the four weeks of the conference.

We were able to provide substantial coverage in areas of high U.S. delegation interest, including: (a) identification of instances of G-77 splits; (b) political developments (such as the PLO resolution) that threatened to derail the conference; (c) the emergence of energy as a bone of contention within the G-77; (d) G-77 endgame strategy and the turmoil of a threatened African walkout; (e) Philippine government attempts to make (or paint) the conference a success; and (f) detailed coverage of G-77 negotiating strategy on technology issues. We covered just about all the G-77 plenary sessions and many of the African, Asian, and Latin American regional caucuses. ■■■■■■■■■■
■■■.

Problems/Limitations

One of the basic limitations to effective intelligence production stems from lack of ■■■■■■ access to the information sought. In setting up an operation at an international conference, there is no guarantee that all aspects of this problem can be overcome by any amount of pre-planning, since many of the key decisions are out of our hands. [Approximately forty lines of text were redacted here.—HBW]

Some Loose Ends

Despite our efforts, both before and during the conference, two problems remained unsolved. In its own way, each attests to the supremacy of on-site collection efforts *during the conference* over attempts to obtain conference-related intelligence elsewhere. The first of these problems concerns the role of special intelligence, and will not be addressed here.

The second unresolved intelligence problem concerns coverage of the activities of the other members of Group B, the industrialized nations' caucus at the conference. Although common developed-country positions had been worked out during the preparatory phase, as the conference progressed it was essential for the U.S. negotiators facing the LDCs to know exactly where they stood with Group B, where they would be backed up, and how far. While the U.S. delegation had open access to the deliberations of the Group B caucus as a whole, discussions taking place in such smaller groups as the Scandinavian caucus and the European Community caucus were a different matter. When these small groups began changing their stances from the earlier agreements, the United States faced the danger of being isolated on important substantive issues.

This was clearly a matter that had fallen between the slats during the planning of the Manila support ████████ Organizationally, the Agency was ill-prepared to provide coverage of the industrialized nations' maneuvers. In preparation for the conference, nearly all of our North-South resources, on both sides of the house [among analysts and operations officers], had been focused on the LDCs. Basically, this reflected the relative ease with which information on the developed countries' interests could be obtained through normal diplomatic channels. Indeed, what analysis NFAC had done on Group B positions was largely based on State Department cables and memcons. When, in the heat of the conference, normal diplomatic channels began to break down, both the Agency and the State Department were caught some-what off balance. The U.S. delegation was at this point stretched too thin by other conference duties to be able to canvass Group B delegations as well as was needed. Nor did the Agency have ████████ access to the industrialized nations' delegations at the conference. In one instance, Group B splits were headed off by State Department demarches to Group B capitals and some tough tactics by the U.S. delegation leaders. Support from Agency stations in Europe, a backstop that we *had* arranged in advance, proved valuable as well—especially in uncovering the West German fallback position on Common Fund financing. And the disarray in G-77 ranks over energy matters kept them from fully probing Group B's potential weaknesses. ████████████████

██

██.

VII.

Counterespionage

29. CIA's internecine struggle in the 1960s about counterespionage left a cloud over counterintelligence disciplines there. At the core was the chief, James Angleton, and his trusted Soviet defector, Anatoliy Golitsyn; the trigger was the distrusted defection of another Soviet intelligence officer, Yuriy Nosenko. The saga was Homeric. It has been told many times—but never, I think, so well as in this meticulous logical and empirical exercise. The author has been one of CIA's finest intellects. He has published trenchantly in the open literature on theories of deception and counterdeception. Yet one must now acknowledge that cogent exoneration of Nosenko contributed to permanent rejection of Angleton, and eventually to years of reluctance to suspect even Aldrich Ames. So standards for vigilance remain disputable.

Nosenko: Five Paths to Judgment

RICHARDS J. HEUER, JR.

Yuriy Nosenko, a middle-level KGB officer, volunteered his services to the Central Intelligence Agency in Geneva in 1962 and defected to the United States in 1964. His defection initiated a bitter and divisive controversy over his bona fides that lasted at least 10 years, seriously impaired CIA operations against the Soviet Union, and today still simmers beneath the surface of debates about Soviet deception.

This study tells much of this important and fascinating case, but that is not its only purpose. It also explores some of the fundamental yet often unrecognized assumptions that channel our thinking as we analyze the possibility of deception. The Nosenko controversy is used to illustrate five fundamentally different criteria for making judgments about deception. Examination of the controversy shows that the analytical criterion one uses determines what evidence one looks at and possibly the conclusion one reaches. It also shows that one's preferred criterion may be strongly influenced by professional experience and organizational affiliation. It is important for anyone analyzing the possibility of deception to recognize the existence of alternative criteria for making judgments and to understand the strengths and limitations of each.

This report has three parts. Part I is an overview of the Nosenko case and

Richards J. Heuer, Jr., "Nosenko: Five Paths to Judgment," *Studies in Intelligence*, vol. 31, no. 3 (Fall 1987), pp. 71–101. Originally classified "Secret."

the controversy surrounding it. It provides background information needed to understand the more conceptual and analytical parts that follow. Part II presents the five criteria for making judgments about deception and describes how each was applied by different parties to the Nosenko controversy. Part III draws conclusions from the previous discussion.

The report is based on two types of sources. One source is my own memory from the years 1965 to 1969. Although not personally involved in the handling or the analysis of the case, my job at that time did require that I be well informed about it and related counterintelligence cases. More recently, I reviewed files on the case, including the six major studies of Nosenko's bona fides and many lesser reports and memorandums dealing with this issue. This is an extraordinarily rich data base for studying how counterintelligence analysis should and should not be conducted.[1]

I: Overview

Yuriy Nosenko came from a prominent family. His father was the Soviet Minister of Shipbuilding in the 1950s, member of the Communist Party Central Committee, deputy to the Supreme Soviet, and close personal friend of senior Politburo members. He had towns named after him, and his death was commemorated by a plaque on the Kremlin wall.

Son Yuriy joined naval intelligence in 1949 at age 22, then transferred to the KGB in 1953. His initial KGB assignment was in the American Department of the Second Chief Directorate (Internal Counterintelligence) with responsibility for work against American journalists and military attachés assigned to Moscow. In 1955, Nosenko was transferred to the Tourist Department, and in 1958 became deputy chief of the section responsible for work against American and British tourists in the USSR. After spending 1961 and 1962 back in the American Department working against the U.S. Embassy in Moscow, Nosenko returned to the Tourist Department, where he became deputy chief.

In June 1962, Nosenko contacted the CIA Station in Geneva, Switzerland, where he was on temporary assignment as security officer with a Soviet disarmament delegation. In a series of debriefings, he provided information on KGB operations against the United States and Great Britain. Nosenko noted that, with a wife and child in the USSR, he had no desire or intention to defect, but he did agree to work as an agent in place and to meet with CIA officers on

---

1. Information on the Nosenko case is also available in the unclassified literature. Several journalists were able to gain access to sensitive information because the bitterness of the controversy over Nosenko prompted some retired or fired CIA officers to defend their positions in the open press. Owing to the sources used by these journalists, their published accounts focus on grounds for suspicion of Nosenko. Although generally accurate in representing this single point of view, they are inaccurate on many points of detail.

subsequent trips to the West. He rejected contact in Moscow, and, in any event, this seemed unnecessary as he anticipated future travel to the West.

Subsequent evaluation of information provided by Nosenko during the 1962 meetings led to the conclusion that he was acting under KGB control. It was initially believed that the purpose of the KGB-controlled operation was to divert [CIA investigators from pursuing the leads they were given about KGB agents by] another KGB officer, Anatoliy Golitsyn, who had defected to the CIA Station in Helsinki six months before. This thesis is discussed in greater detail below.

When Nosenko returned to Geneva in January 1964, he confronted his CIA handlers with two surprises: he wanted to defect immediately, and he had been the officer responsible for the KGB file on Lee Harvey Oswald. Oswald, a former U.S. Marine who had defected to the Soviet Union and later returned to the United States with a Soviet wife, had assassinated President Kennedy just two months earlier. Given Oswald's background, possible Soviet or Cuban involvement was one of the most burning issues faced by the Warren Commission investigation of the President's assassination.

Nosenko reported that he had personally handled the Oswald case on two occasions—first, when Oswald defected while on a tourist visit to the Soviet Union, and later when he was tasked to review the file on Oswald after the assassination. Nosenko assured the U.S. Government that the KGB had had no involvement whatsoever with Oswald or with the assassination. However, Nosenko's account of the KGB's handling of Oswald differed on several significant points from what were believed to be standard KGB policies and procedures.

These surprises obviously increased suspicion of Nosenko, but they also heightened interest in his full debriefing. If he were bona fide, the value of his information was obvious. If he were operating under Soviet direction, the KGB was clearly trying to conceal some aspect of its relationship with Oswald. A full debriefing of Nosenko in the United States offered an opportunity to break him and learn the true story, or at least to "mirror-read" his account in order to identify Soviet goals on an issue of paramount importance to the Warren Commission and the U.S. Government—possible Soviet involvement in the President's assassination.

Nosenko's defection was accepted, and he was brought to the United States as a parolee under CIA custody in February 1964. The initial debriefing was conducted with care not to reveal to Nosenko any of these suspicions. This debriefing reinforced doubts about his bona fides, so in April 1964, with the approval of the Attorney General, Nosenko was placed in confinement and hostile interrogation began. (Because Nosenko was a parolee rather than a legal immigrant, CIA bore legal responsibility for his actions. Nosenko's own legal rights were ambiguous.) At the end of 1964 Nosenko was transferred to a specially constructed confinement unit at Camp Peary. During hostile interrogation, he was subjected to psychological intimidation and physical hardship, but never to physical abuse.

The hostile interrogation seemed to identify many more gaps and anomalies in Nosenko's story, but it did little to clarify key questions. It was to be argued later that, to the contrary, the way Nosenko was handled during this interrogation simply muddied the waters. Nosenko's handlers were so convinced that he was under KGB control that the interrogation was designed to document guilt, rather than to obtain information or make an objective assessment. The information Nosenko provided was generally ignored, as the objective of the interrogation was to force Nosenko to admit that he did not know what he should have known (according to the assumptions of the interrogators) and, therefore, he had not held the positions in the KGB he claimed. The polygraph examination was manipulated as a means of putting additional pressure on Nosenko, which invalidated its use as a test of veracity.

The conviction that Nosenko was under Soviet control led to this case becoming the touchstone for evaluating other sources on Soviet intelligence. Sources who provided information supporting Nosenko's story were themselves deemed suspect. The theory of a "master plot" developed, subsequently called the "monster plot" by those who rejected this theory, which encompassed about a dozen counterintelligence sources. According to the master plot theory, the KGB had a very high-level penetration of CIA, comparable to the recently exposed penetrations of Kim Philby in the British Secret Intelligence Service (MI6) and Heinz Felfe in the West German Federal Intelligence Service (BND). Therefore, all CIA Soviet operations were at least known to, if not controlled by, the KGB. Nosenko and other defectors and sources in place in Soviet intelligence were being run by the KGB to tie up CIA and FBI counterintelligence assets in unimportant activities, divert the investigation of leads to significant Soviet agents, and protect the security and/or enhance the careers and manipulate the access of Soviet agents within CIA and the FBI—in short, to keep CIA and the FBI fat and happy and unsuspecting of the true state of affairs. The evidence and rationale for this theory are discussed at length below.

This theory led to an extensive search for the KGB penetration. CIA officers with Slavic backgrounds and the most experience in dealing with the Soviets were among the initial suspects; the careers of several innocent officers were permanently damaged. As the magnitude of the information the Soviets were alleged to be sacrificing for this operation became more apparent, the search for the penetration focused at progressively higher levels. At one time or another, the Chief and Deputy Chief of the Soviet Bloc (SB) Division, the

Chief of the Counterintelligence (CI) Staff, and the Director of Central Intelligence all came under suspicion in the minds of some of the principal players.

This atmosphere of suspicion, and the concern that any successful recruitment of a Soviet official might be compromised by the penetration, had a serious, debilitating effect on operations against Soviet targets. It also had a serious adverse impact on morale within SB Division. As time passed, most division operations officers became generally aware of the theory, but were carefully compartmented from any detailed knowledge. A strong resentment and increasingly vocal opposition developed among those who saw or felt the impact of this theory but were not privy to the evidence on which it was based.

As more time passed with no progress toward resolving the case, the "temporary" detention of Nosenko without due process of law became increasingly unacceptable. In August 1966, CIA Director Richard Helms gave SB Division 60 days to conclude its case against Nosenko. In February 1967, Tennant "Pete" Bagley, then Deputy Chief of the Soviet Bloc Division, submitted a report whose bulk caused it to become known as the "Thousand Pager," although it was "only" 835 pages long. The report presented reasons for believing Nosenko to be under [KGB] control and described hundreds of unexplained gaps or discrepancies in his story. The Soviet Bloc Division had been given three years to prove its case. It developed substantial circumstantial evidence but no hard proof in the form of a confession from Nosenko or identification of a KGB penetration of CIA. Operations against Soviet targets had been adversely affected, dissension and morale problems were growing, and the continued detention of Nosenko was untenable.

Now it was the critics' turn, and the pendulum began its swing. Helms assigned his newly appointed deputy, Rufus Taylor, to oversee the case and to develop a plan for the final disposition of Nosenko's case. DDCI Taylor asked Gordon Stewart, who was shortly to become Inspector General, to review the case and develop a recommendation for future action. Stewart was critical of Bagley's Thousand Pager. He said it read like a prosecutor's brief, assuming guilt and interpreting every discrepancy as evidence of this guilt. Stewart granted that SB Division had shown many of Nosenko's assertions to be blatantly false. However, the gaps and contradictions could possibly be explained by personal motives, faulty memory, and coincidence, and did not necessarily compel a conclusion of KGB control. Stewart concluded that SB Division had not proved its case against Nosenko, that certain proof might never be available, and that the time had come for CIA to start to "distance" itself from the matter. Whether Nosenko was a Soviet agent or not, he had to be removed from solitary confinement, gradually rehabilitated, and eventually given his freedom to settle in the United States.

Meanwhile, CI Staff had also objected to the Bagley report. The Staff strongly supported the master plot theory, but took exception to one major element of the SB Division analysis. With the help of CI Staff comments, Bagley's Thousand Pager was edited down to 407 pages. This report was known as the "Green Book" and became the official SB Division position on Nosenko. By the time of its completion in February 1968, however, the case had already been taken out of SB Division and CI Staff hands, and the report was a dead letter before it even went to press.

In September 1967, DCI Helms had transferred responsibility for the Nosenko case from the SB Division to the Office of Security. In October 1967 a security officer, Bruce Solie, began a nine-month, friendly reinterrogation of Nosenko. Rather than trying to trap Nosenko into inconsistencies, the goal of this debriefing was to obtain as much information as possible and to give Nosenko an opportunity to develop a single coherent story.

Nosenko "passed" a polygraph examination in August 1968. In October 1968, Solie submitted his report, the third of an eventual total of six major studies of this case. It concluded that Nosenko was a bona fide defector, not under Soviet control. Solie based this judgment primarily on the value of information provided by Nosenko, plus benign explanations for many of the anomalies and inconsistencies identified by SB Division interrogation.

By this time, the SB Division leadership that had propounded the master plot theory had been reassigned and replaced by officers who would take a fresh look at the issue. The new leadership gave three experienced SB Division officers carte blanche to examine the original debriefing reports, reassess the evidence, and recommend whether or not SB Division should change its position on Nosenko's bona fides. The three-man SB Division team, which represented different backgrounds and points of view, agreed to focus on the anomalies in Nosenko's story. The ground rule was that if any member of the team stipulated an anomaly as important, it had to be addressed by the other two members. Each officer could prepare his own analysis, but they would all address the same issues. Their report, which was finished in January 1969, became known as the three "Wise Men" report.

There was easy agreement that most of the inconsistencies listed in Bagley's original Thousand Pager were really insignificant. Attention eventually narrowed to the 14 "stipulated anomalies" that any one of the three officers had designated as important. When these were examined from the perspective of searching for the truth, rather than proving guilt, the case against Nosenko began to unravel. By this time, it was not difficult to develop nonsinister explanations. Some of the anomalies and how they were resolved are discussed later.

The SB Division team split 2 to 1 in favor of Nosenko's bona fides. The analysis moved the thinking of all three officers significantly in the direction of accepting Nosenko. One officer who had always felt that Nosenko might be bona fide felt he could now prove the case. One who started out believing Nosenko was dispatched by the KGB changed his mind as a result of the new information that was developed. The officer who continued to vote for KGB control had been one of the principal analysts and advocates of the master plot theory; he became substantially less confident of this conclusion than he had been.

In a meeting convened by Inspector Gordon Stewart, the Solie report was accepted by DCI Helms, DDCI Taylor, and the new SB Division leadership, over the strong objection of the CI Staff. Nosenko was subsequently released from confinement and, in March 1969, put on the payroll as a CIA consultant. Although Helms still had doubts about Nosenko, he awarded Solie an intelligence medal for his work in rehabilitating him. (About four years earlier, Helms had awarded Tennant Bagley an intelligence medal for his work in unmasking Nosenko as a KGB plant.)

James Angleton, longtime Chief of the CI Staff, remained convinced of the master plot theory and considered himself the last remaining obstacle to KGB manipulation of CIA. In December 1974, DCI William Colby's offer of another assignment precipitated the resignation of Angleton and three other senior CI Staff officers. CI Staff—which was reorganized under new management—was now convinced that the master plot was actually a monster plot that existed only in the minds of its believers.

Dismissal of the top CI Staff leadership encouraged those pushing for Nosenko's total exoneration and his recognition as an important and valuable source. In 1976, John Hart was recalled from retirement to spend six months investigating the Nosenko case and its effects on CIA. Hart became incensed by what he perceived as an inhuman approach to handling Nosenko and the prosecutorial approach to assessing his bona fides. At DCI Stansfield Turner's request, Hart gave CIA senior officers a series of lectures on lessons learned from the case, and he testified on the subject before Congress.

Hart's study, entitled "The Monster Plot," concluded that doubts about Nosenko's bona fides were of our own making. Much of his study was devoted to demonstrating that those who handled the case were "not objective, dispassionate seekers of truth," and that the case was mishandled because the goal from its inception was to obtain proof that Nosenko was guilty, not to determine whether he was or not. Hart effectively documented much of what went wrong—errors in the transcripts of the initial meetings with Nosenko, faulty assumptions about the KGB, and the preconceptions that made it virtually impossible at that time for any source on Soviet intelligence to establish his bona fides in the eyes of SB Division or the CI Staff. But Hart did not really answer the arguments of those who claimed Nosenko was dispatched by the

KGB. Hart believed that those initially responsible for the Nosenko case were so thoroughly discredited by the way they handled it that it was unnecessary to answer their arguments in any detail.

The election of President Reagan and the subsequent appointment of William Casey as DCI led to the sixth full-scale study of the Nosenko case— 17 years after his defection. Tennant Bagley, who had retired nine years earlier, sought to use the opportunity of a new administration with a harder line on the Soviet Union to reopen the case. In March 1981 he sent the new DCI a lengthy study entitled "Why Nosenko Is a Plant—and Why It Matters." He argued that acceptance of Nosenko indicated continued high-level penetration and manip- ulation of CIA by the KGB. Director Casey named Jack Fieldhouse to investi- gate Bagley's allegations.

In August 1981, Fieldhouse produced a study entitled "An Examination of the Bagley Case Against Yuriy Nosenko." Whereas previous analysts had fo- cused exclusively on Nosenko's statements and his handling, Fieldhouse recog- nized the importance of the historical context in which the case transpired. He noted at the outset, for example, that the foundation of the problem was laid before Nosenko ever arrived, as this was at a time when fear of the power of the KGB was perhaps at an all-time high. This historical context, and the reasons for the fear, are discussed in detail below. Fieldhouse's report refutes Bagley's arguments point by point; identifies what went wrong and how it was possible for so many capable CIA officers to be so wrong for so long; and describes the serious adverse impact the master plot theory had on the handling of many other Soviet cases.

Until now, we have paid little attention to the reasons why various analysts concluded Nosenko was or was not under Soviet control. We have limited the presentation to background information for those not previously initiated into the mysteries of the secret war between the CIA and the KGB, or the secret war within the CIA itself on this subject. We turn now to the purpose of this study, an analysis of how the analysis was done.

II: Strategies

The intelligence or counterintelligence analyst seeks to determine the truth. But let's go back a step and ask, how do we know the truth? What criterion, or measuring rod, do we use for determining that something is or is not true, that something probably is or is not deception? In this section, we identify five criteria that might be used for making this judgment, and we examine which ones were employed by different analysts, at different times, to judge that Nosenko was or was not a Soviet agent.

For convenience, we have labeled the five criteria according to some salient characteristic—the motive approach, anomalies and inconsistencies approach, litmus test approach, cost accounting approach, and predictive test approach. These approaches are not mutually exclusive; any concrete case of deception analysis usually contains elements of several approaches, but one or at most two will generally be dominant and serve as the main basis for judgment. A principal point is that different criteria have different strengths and weaknesses, lead one to focus on different sorts of evidence, and may lead to quite different conclusions about the presence of deception. A second important point is that these criteria are complementary, and that a complete analysis requires all five approaches.

In this section, we take arguments used in the Nosenko case and group them under the five strategies for analyzing deception. The purpose is to gain a better understanding of the different approaches, to document conclusions about their strengths and weaknesses, and to seek a better understanding of how intelligence officers looking at the same case could arrive at opposite judgments. By comparing and contrasting each approach, we see what each magnifies and reveals, as well as what it blurs or ignores. Discussion of each approach begins by describing its basic characteristics:

Motive Approach.

Some attention to motive must be part of any deception analysis. What distinguishes this approach is a matter of emphasis. The identification of a motive for deception, and of the opportunity and the means to engage in it, becomes a driving force behind a judgment that deception is in fact present. This is similar to the approach taken by a prosecuting attorney; if the prosecutor establishes motive, opportunity, and means, then circumstantial evidence may be sufficient to prove the defendant guilty. The deception analyst taking this approach starts with a motive, then tries to view the situation as it appears to the adversary. Given the motive, how would the adversary view the opportunities, costs, risks, and means available to accomplish the task? The analyst seeks to reconstruct details of the deception plan through inference from fragmentary evidence.

The weakness of this approach is that motive, opportunity, and means alone are not sufficient for a valid inference of deception. They show only what could have happened, not what actually did happen. Most people have motive, opportunity, and means to commit many crimes—for example, cheating the government on taxes—yet they don't do it. To develop a stronger inference of deception, it is also necessary to evaluate past deception practices to show not only that the adversary could have done it, but also that the adversary makes a habit of that type of activity.

We first present, uncritically, arguments used pursuant to the motive approach to demonstrate that Nosenko was a KGB plant. This is followed by counterarguments subsequently used in refuting this view.

The origins of the master plot theory cannot be understood without an appreciation of the historical circumstances at the time. This was the era of the construction of the Berlin Wall and the Cuban missile crisis. More important, it was a period of extreme and justifiable concern about Soviet penetration of Western intelligence services, as well as a time when CIA was just beginning to receive reports on increased KGB emphasis on disinformation.

In January 1963, Kim Philby had finally been confronted with evidence of his KGB service, and had responded by fleeing to Moscow. He had been a KGB agent since 1933, and during those years had seen lengthy service in the British Intelligence Service (MI6). At one time, while a KGB agent, he had been chief of MI6's counterintelligence operations against the Soviet Union. As chief of MI6's Washington liaison with CIA during postwar years, he had served as a mentor to CIA in developing organization and policy during its formative years. Philby's stature was such that his colleagues had anticipated he would eventually become Chief of MI6.

Another British Intelligence officer, George Blake, had been arrested in the spring of 1961. As part of his MI6 duties, he had taken the minutes of joint CIA-MI6 meetings to plan the Berlin tunnel operation to tap Soviet military phone lines. Before Blake's arrest, the Berlin tunnel had been regarded as one of the most successful operations against the Soviet target during the decade of the 1950s. Blake's arrest suggested strongly that the KGB had known about the tunnel from its inception, but had let the operation run for 11 months to protect the penetration source who had reported it. This fueled suspicions about when and how other major operations of that era had been compromised.

Anatoliy Golitsyn, a KGB officer who defected in 1961, reported high-level Soviet penetration of the French intelligence and security services. The agents had not yet been identified, quite possibly because the agents were themselves in a position to block effective investigation. In [West] Germany, Heinz Felfe had been arrested in November 1961. With KGB assistance, he had maneuvered himself into the ideal position of chief of counterintelligence operations against the Soviet Union for the West German BND.

It seemed unlikely that CIA could have been fortunate enough to avoid completely the disasters that other services had suffered as a result of high-level KGB penetration. Indeed, there were specific indications that CIA had not been spared. Golitsyn reported that the KGB had placed an agent within the highest echelons of American intelligence, but he could provide no details. Three years earlier Colonel Michal Goleniewski, a CIA penetration of Polish intelligence, who defected in December 1960, had reported a KGB penetration of CIA Soviet operations. Goleniewski knew the codename for this penetration but had little identifying data. Although a Pole, Goleniewski was knowledgeable of KGB operations because he had served as a KGB agent within the Polish service and had close personal contact with KGB officers. He confirmed his credibility by providing accurate information leading to the arrest of George Blake as a KGB penetration of British MI6 and Heinz Felfe as a KGB penetration of West German intelligence.

Another major source of concern about penetration was the arrest of two important CIA penetrations of Soviet Military Intelligence, the GRU. Pyotr Popov had been arrested in 1959 and Colonel Oleg Penkovskiy in 1962. CIA counterintelligence analysts were still trying to determine if the two men had been compromised through Soviet penetration or by operational accident or error. Given the remarkable record of successful KGB penetration of Allied services, to say nothing of specific reports of penetration of CIA from our most recent defectors, Golitsyn and Goleniewski, Soviet penetration of CIA seemed a likely explanation.

Concern about KGB penetration of CIA was one pillar of the master plot theory. If the KGB had such a penetration, this would provide both motive and opportunity for deception. Moreover, if the KGB had a penetration in a position to compromise Popov and Penkovskiy, that same penetration probably would have been in position to report to the KGB on the 1962 meetings with Nosenko; by this reasoning, Nosenko's reappearance in the West in 1964 was itself evidence of KGB control.

The second pillar of the master plot theory was concern about KGB disinformation. Department D, the KGB's disinformation department, had been formed in 1959. Goleniewski was the first CIA source to report in detail on its anticipated functions and significance. He stated that one of the many objectives of KGB disinformation was the protection of Soviet agents by means of actions designed to mislead Western security services. He listed among specific objectives and types of disinformation operations those designed to discredit accurate information of significance received by the opposition through sources not under Soviet control, such as defectors, thus casting doubt on the veracity of the source of this true information. Goleniewski stated further that, in extreme cases, the KGB would be willing to sacrifice some of its own agent assets to enhance the reputation of an agent penetration of a Western intelligence service.

Golitsyn confirmed Goleniewski's reporting on Department D and added that a KGB or GRU defector's file would be sent to this new unit. Department D would review the areas of information compromised to the opposition by the defector and search for opportunities to exploit the situation. Golitsyn elaborated on this report with his own speculation, which played a major role in development of the master plot theory. (It should be noted at this point that Golitsyn was a highly egocentric individual with an extremely conspiratorial turn of mind; after his defection, he became certifiably paranoid.) Golitsyn felt that his information was so important and damaging to the KGB that the Soviets would feel compelled to send out another source to discredit him or his information. In short, Golitsyn predicted the appearance of someone like Nosenko as a KGB plant. Golitsyn also predicted that a KGB penetration of American intelligence would be assisted by other KGB agents— false defectors and double agents—who would provide information designed to bolster the penetration's position and access in the service. The penetration, in turn, would be in a position to help authenticate the other agents.

Golitsyn's speculation became the core of the master plot theory. Circumstantial confirmation of this speculation came from an analysis of how the KGB had exploited Heinz Felfe in the West German service. They had exploited Felfe in exactly the manner Golitsyn had predicted they would exploit a penetration of CIA—with assistance from a series of double agents and false defectors.

Felfe himself had been running an East German journalist, codename LENA, as a double agent against the KGB. The KGB was ostensibly running LENA as a principal agent for operations against West Germany, but was actually running him to support its operation with Felfe. The LENA case, among others, established Felfe as a Soviet specialist and successful operations officer. It provided Felfe with cover for monthly trips from Munich to Berlin, where he met with his Soviet handlers as well as with LENA. More important, the case provided cover for Felfe to investigate any person or subject of interest to the Soviets. When LENA reported the KGB had targeted him against a West German official, for example, Felfe organized the resources of the West German Government to investigate that official to uncover the reason for Soviet interest and determine if that person might actually be susceptible to Soviet recruitment. When the KGB asked LENA to obtain specific political or technical information, Felfe would investigate the subject himself to determine what could be released to the Soviets and what was so sensitive that it had to be protected. In short, the KGB used LENA to provide cover for Felfe to make inquiries on virtually any subject of interest to the KGB. Was the KGB using the Nosenko case in some similar manner to support a penetration of CIA, as predicted by Golitsyn?

All these details of recent counterintelligence history were deeply etched in the minds of senior counterintelligence officers in the SB Division and the CI Staff. Much of this information was unknown to other Agency personnel. The differences in available information created fundamentally different viewpoints concerning Soviet operations and the security of CIA. Were the counterintelligence officers paranoid, or were the others simply uninformed, and perhaps somewhat naive, about the true nature of the secret war between CIA and the KGB?

Into this atmosphere of concern and suspicion came KGB officer Yuriy Nosenko. At the initial series of meetings in 1962, Nosenko provided information on about 10 of the same KGB operations on which Golitsyn had reported six months earlier. The overlapping information was especially noteworthy because Golitsyn and Nosenko had served in different Chief Directorates of the KGB, Golitsyn in Foreign Intelligence and Nosenko in Internal Counterintelligence. Was it pure coincidence that they should both have information on the same KGB operations? It appeared that Golitsyn's prediction might have come true, that Nosenko was providing information intended to divert the investigation of agents partially identified by Golitsyn.

From the KGB's point of view in planning such a deception, the overlap of information between Golitsyn and Nosenko would confirm Nosenko's bona fides, reduce the amount of new information the KGB would have to sacrifice, and provide an opportunity to deflect American investigation of those agents the KGB considered most important.

At the 1962 meetings, Nosenko also reported that Colonel Popov, CIA's first important penetration of the GRU, who had been arrested in 1959, had been compromised by postal surveillance. A maid, working for an American Embassy officer in Moscow who had been co-opted to assist CIA, treated his clothes with a so-called thief powder to facilitate postal surveillance. The KGB picked up three operational letters mailed by this officer [on behalf of] CIA when the powder activated a sensor in the Soviet postal system. This "innocent" explanation for Popov's compromise indicated that CIA Soviet operations were not penetrated after all. To those who already believed in the existence of penetration, this was clear evidence of deception. The KGB's motive was to protect the penetration who had actually compromised Popov, and to do this it had to provide CIA with an alternative explanation for Popov's arrest. Another Golitsyn prediction appeared to have come true—that the KGB would support its penetration of CIA by use of false defectors and double agents.

Thus was born the initial conviction that Nosenko was under KGB control. This conclusion, in turn, seemed to confirm that CIA must be penetrated. KGB control of Nosenko made little sense except as part of a high-stakes game involving penetration of CIA. If the KGB had a well-placed penetration of CIA Soviet operations, it followed that all of CIA's Soviet sources were at least known to, if not controlled by, the KGB, as had been the case in British and West German intelligence. With this reasoning, the Nosenko case grew into the master plot—or monster plot—that eventually encompassed about a dozen sources on Soviet intelligence. Any source who claimed ability to report on

Soviet intelligence matters, but could not reveal either the assumed KGB deception program or the penetration of American intelligence on which it was based, was automatically assumed to be part of the deception effort. Nosenko was but the first of many to suffer the consequences of this thinking.

As critics have accurately noted, deception was taken as a premise; it was not a finding arrived at after careful investigation of Nosenko's story. Fieldhouse concluded ". . . there was never an honest effort to establish Nosenko's bona fides. There was only a determined effort to prove Nosenko was mala fide and part of a KGB deception meant to mislead CIA into believing it was not penetrated—thereby covering up the 'real' reason for the compromise of Popov and Penkovskiy." Hart observed that ". . . at no time from June 1962 to October 1967 was Nosenko afforded the kind of systematic, objective, non-hostile interrogation . . . which otherwise had been standard operating 'procedure' in dealing with similar sources."

It is noteworthy that none of the background on assumed penetration of CIA or the Soviet disinformation program is included in the formal SB Division assessments of Nosenko's bona fides. It is documented in limited distribution memorandums of that period, but those who doubted Nosenko believed they could and should prove their case only on the basis of anomalies and inconsistencies in Nosenko's own statements, without reference to penetration of CIA or to all the other Soviet operations that were considered part of the master plot. Except for Jack Fieldhouse, those who subsequently defended Nosenko adopted these same ground rules, so systematic refutation of many master plot arguments is lacking in their analysis.

The principal counterargument was the simple assertion that the KGB would never mount such a deception because of the cost to itself in information given away (to be discussed later) and the risk that a KGB defector, penetration, or disaffected provocateur might compromise the entire enterprise at any time. It was also noted that, to obtain Politburo approval to place one of its own staff personnel in contact with the enemy as a false defector, the KGB would have to be able to demonstrate that this was the best and least costly, perhaps the only, way to achieve its objectives. This too seemed quite implausible. No objectives were ever suggested that could not be achieved by less costly or less risky means.

This counterargument has passed the test of time. It seems impossible that the KGB could have concealed such an extensive and all-inclusive deception for so many years, given the steady flow of new KGB defectors and sources in a position to reveal such a conspiracy had it actually existed. One may, of course, argue that many of these subsequent sources up to the present day are also part of the plot. This would imply, however, that the entire KGB as we have known it for 25 years is, unbeknownst to most of its officers, little more than a cover organization for deception, with the truly secret work being done elsewhere.

Concern about high-level penetration of CIA Soviet operations has been alleviated with time. Although the exact basis for the Golitsyn and Goleniewski reports has not been clarified, several nonstaff (contract agent) penetrations have been identified. In any case, it appears that whatever source the KGB may have had was not in a position to compromise CIA penetrations of Soviet intelligence. Subsequent KGB defectors and penetration sources have reported no indications of the type of high-level penetration of CIA that had been suspected. The argument that compartmentation would prevent all but a very few KGB officers from being aware of such an important case is weakened by our experience with the Philby, Blake, and Felfe cases. Knowledge of the existence of these penetrations, although not the specific identity of the agents, was more widespread in the KGB than one might expect. The more important and productive the sources, the more difficult it is to prevent the gradual expansion of knowledge about [them].

One initial basis for suspicion of Nosenko in 1962, the overlap between his reporting on KGB agents and information previously received from Golitsyn, was clearly resolved in Nosenko's favor. One suspected duplication turned out to be a separate case, more important than the one Golitsyn had reported on. In three of the most important cases of overlapping information, it was the more detailed and better sourced information from Nosenko that served as a basis for effective counterintelligence action to terminate the KGB operations. Rather than providing disinformation to discredit Golitsyn or divert investigation of his leads, as had been hypothesized as the KGB goal, Nosenko's reporting confirmed and supplemented Golitsyn's information and permitted effective action to be taken. Nosenko never said a bad word about Golitsyn. Golitsyn's prediction that the KGB would try to discredit him never materialized.

Golitsyn's claim that a penetration of CIA would be assisted by false defectors and double agents is also open to question. The basis for his speculation is not clear; it could have developed from seeds planted by [James Angleton as] Chief, CI staff, in discussions with Golitsyn. There is no evidence that the KGB exploited Philby or Blake in this manner. They did manipulate Felfe this way, but Felfe was an imaginative and aggressive officer who very likely masterminded his own case. The LENA operation, and the way it was used to enhance Felfe's reputation and expand his access, may well have been Felfe's own idea rather than a typical element of KGB modus operandi. Moreover, the double agents used to support the Felfe operation had little access to sensitive information, so there was little cost to the KGB; this was no precedent for KGB use of its own staff officers as double agents or false defectors. To the contrary, the

Felfe case clearly indicated that the KGB could support and manipulate an important penetration of an opposition service without having to sacrifice valid information about itself. In any event, there does not appear to have been a penetration of CIA to be manipulated in this manner, so there was neither motive nor opportunity for the hypothetical deception.

Anomalies and Inconsistencies Approach.

The most common approach to counterintelligence analysis is to focus on anomalies and inconsistencies, then infer a motive or other explanation for these unusual circumstances. Counterintelligence analysis often bases judgments on "deviation from an assumed standard of what is normal," for example, security practices would normally prevent the source from obtaining access to the reported information, or, conversely, the source disclaims access to information he is expected to have.

This approach underrates the frequency of accident, coincidence, inaccurate translation, inadequate debriefing, and misunderstanding. It overrates an analyst's ability to judge what is normal or abnormal in the adversary's organization or society. Events that accompany the accidental exposure of sensitive information or the defection of a trusted official are, by definition, never normal and, therefore, invariably provide a basis for suspicion. This approach to analysis, which is characteristic of the counterintelligence officer, is very difficult to implement correctly; conclusions are frequently wrong.

The three Soviet Bloc Division studies of Nosenko's bona fides—the Thousand Pager and the Green Book that judged him a plant, and the Wise Men report that later saw him as bona fide—all used the same explicit criteria for testing bona fides. The criteria are cited here, as they are a clear statement of the anomalies and inconsistencies approach as it applies to human sources. To be judged bona fide,

> . . . the information Nosenko provides about his life and related persons and events must be coherent and his accounts of important events must be consistent. Allowing for personal vagaries, such as lapses of memory and so forth, as well as for factors of accident and coincidence, the information he relates must conform within reasonable limits with that which is known from independent and reliable sources to the United States Government about Soviet realities and about the events, topics, and individuals Nosenko describes.

In short, the appropriate test of bona fides was seen as plausibility, coherence, consistency, and compatibility with known facts. Note the absence of any mention of value of information supplied to the U.S. Government or damage to Soviet interests. Also note the absence of any mention of putting oneself in Soviet shoes to evaluate motives, opportunities, and problems that might be encountered in mounting a deception operation. We have already seen that this was done in practice by the SB Division analysts, but that this discussion was largely excluded from the bona fides assessments.

Following the established criteria, Nosenko's handlers concentrated on identifying inconsistencies and implausibilities in Nosenko's story, gaps in his knowledge, conflicts with known information, and suspicious coincidences. In fact, identification of such anomalies became the principal goal of interrogation, at the cost of failure to learn all the information Nosenko had to offer on KGB operations. So many anomalies were found that Bagley required 835 pages to document them all.

The interrogators had ample grist for their mill, as Nosenko did lie, exaggerate, err, and change his story, and he admitted this under interrogation. His motive was to conceal embarrassing elements of his personal background and to exaggerate his importance. Rather than accepting Nosenko's admissions as resolving some of the anomalies, however, the interrogators interpreted the admissions as further "proof" of the conclusion that he was dispatched by the KGB. The admissions were viewed as an attempt to cover up the holes the interrogators had found in his story.

We shall cite here only a few of the more significant anomalies in the Nosenko case. Again, we first present, uncritically, some of the arguments used to build the case against Nosenko, then show how these anomalies were subsequently resolved by more objective analysis and investigation.

Two months after the assassination of President John Kennedy by Lee Harvey Oswald, Nosenko arrived in Geneva and advised CIA that he, personally, was the KGB officer responsible for Oswald's file at the time Oswald defected to the Soviet Union. The KGB had never heard of Oswald, he said, until Oswald told his Intourist guide that he wanted to renounce his American citizenship and stay in the USSR. Without ever talking to Oswald or having anyone else talk with him, Nosenko, as the responsible KGB officer, judged that Oswald was of no interest. The KGB did not even want to accept Oswald's request for asylum, and relented only after he tried to commit suicide after being advised of his rejection. The KGB never debriefed Oswald on his experience as a U.S. marine radar operator as he was of "little importance," and never conducted an investigation to ascertain he was not an American agent before allowing him to stay in the Soviet Union. The KGB did not object to Oswald marrying a Soviet woman, Marina, or to Marina's subsequent departure with him to the United States, as Marina was "stupid, uneducated, and possessed anti-Soviet characteristics." In brief, the KGB had never had any contact whatsoever with either Oswald or his wife and was happy to be rid of them both. Within hours of Oswald's identification as the presidential assassin, Nosenko personally was ordered to review the KGB's Oswald file to assess Soviet liability. At this time, Nosenko was already an American agent with incentive to collect and remember as much information as possible on this vitally important subject. Nosenko expressed absolute certainty that he had the complete and accurate story of KGB contact with Oswald.

At a time when the Warren Commission was just opening its investigation, the fact that CIA found itself in clandestine contact with the one KGB officer who on two occasions had been personally responsible for Oswald's file seemed to be an unbelievable stroke of good fortune. Nosenko's account of the Oswald case appeared equally incredible. The following elements of Nosenko's story seemed contrary to Soviet practice: that the KGB would turn down an American defector before even talking with him to assess his knowledgeability; that after accepting him for residence in the USSR, he was not debriefed on his prior military service; that he would be granted residence in the USSR with no KGB investigation of his bona fides to determine he was not an American agent; and that no obstacles were placed in the path of his wife Marina's emigration when Oswald decided to leave the Soviet Union.

Another group of anomalies identified by the interrogators related to Nosenko's personal background and KGB career. At different times, he gave three different dates for his entry into the KGB and two different stories concerning how he came to be hired. He could not describe the normal personnel procedures a new KGB employee would go through. He admitted lying about his KGB rank. The pattern of transfers from one department to another and back again and lengthy overseas TDYs appeared unusual. He could not describe any operational activity for which he had been personally responsible that would justify his claimed promotions and awards. He admitted that, at one time, he was probably the only officer in the KGB who was neither a Komsomol nor a party member. In short, his description of his KGB career simply did not ring true.

There were also gaps in Nosenko's knowledge of KGB operations. The positions a source has held imply he should be knowledgeable of certain events. That Nosenko was uninformed on things he should have known was viewed as evidence he did not really hold the claimed positions. The most serious gaps in Nosenko's knowledge concerned the 1960–61 period, when he claimed to be deputy chief of the KGB Second Chief Directorate's section responsible for all operations against the American Embassy in Moscow. He claimed specific responsibility for supervising the case officers working against American code clerks in Moscow during this period. This is a subject about which CIA had a great deal of collateral information against which to check Nosenko's reporting. Nosenko did provide credible detail to establish his knowledge of significant aspects of at least six cases, but he was unaware of significant developments or events he should have known if he were really the supervisor of the case officers handling these cases. And he lacked any information at all on some operations he should have known about if he were really the deputy chief of the section.

One item concerning Nosenko's work against the American Embassy in 1961 was of particular interest, as it related to how Penkovskiy was compromised. Nosenko consistently maintained that he was the case officer responsible for covering the activities of an American Embassy officer who was observed in December 1961 visiting the location of what the KGB believed to be a deaddrop site in Pushkin Street. He also claimed to have received surveillance reports on this site for three months thereafter. The site is significant, as it is the place where a CIA officer was subsequently arrested while picking up a deaddrop from Penkovskiy. The problem with Nosenko's account is that at the time the American Embassy officer visited this site, Nosenko had already been transferred from the American Embassy Department to the Tourist Department. His story was interpreted as showing he did not really serve in the American Department during the dates he claimed, and that the purpose of his false account was to make CIA think Penkovskiy was discovered by surveillance rather than by penetration.

A series of gaps and conflicts of this type led interrogators to conclude that Nosenko had not actually served in the positions he claimed. In fact, Bagley's original Thousand Pager concluded that Nosenko had probably not been a KGB officer at all, that he was just an empty receptacle into which the KGB had poured a very detailed legend. This despite the fact that Golitsyn, whose bona fides were not in question, had confirmed knowing of Nosenko as a KGB officer.

Any single conflict, gap, or coincidence might be explainable, but the massive compendium of anomalies compiled by SB Division seemed difficult to reconcile with any hypothesis other than KGB control. In fact, however, this analysis of Nosenko's bona fides was a prime example of Murphy's law—that everything that can go wrong will go wrong. Most of the problems with Nosenko's story have been resolved. In many cases, the explanation amounted to a clear refutation of the basis for suspicion. In many others, it was simply a plausible alternative hypothesis.

The sources of analytical error may be grouped into six main categories: biased analysis, inaccurate record of Nosenko's reporting, misunderstanding of Nosenko as a person, invalid assumptions about the KGB, honest mistakes by Nosenko, and genuine coincidences.

Biased Analysis

There was no effort to seek out alternative explanations for seemingly suspicious events. For example, one case officer who met with Nosenko in

Geneva in 1964 wrote that he suspected him from the very first meeting on the basis of Nosenko's emotionless and mechanical delivery of his statement announcing his intention to defect. The statement appeared to have been rehearsed. At the time, Chief, SB Division, attributed considerable weight to this further indication of opposition control. But there are many reasons why Nosenko might have delivered the statement in this manner. Rather than being emotionless, his emotions may have been so strong that he forced himself, consciously or subconsciously, to repress them to avoid an emotional scene. Most intelligence officer defectors, under similar circumstances, probably prepare with great care what they want to tell us about their reasons for defection. In other words, the evidence used against Nosenko was also quite consistent with the alternative hypothesis—that he was bona fide.

Similarly, after hostile questioning began, it was noted that Nosenko "became quite erratic, contradicted himself many times, and became upset physically. . . . As a result of this session, we know that Subject can be thrown off balance by aggressive questioning in those areas which we know to be important parts of the entire KGB operation." No consideration was given to the fact that a bona fide defector whose entire future depends upon acceptance in his new homeland might react the same way when falsely accused of being a KGB plant.

Some of the most important inconsistencies and gaps in knowledge that were held against Nosenko can also be interpreted as actually supporting his bona fides. The three different dates for the start of his KGB service are a case in point; surely, if it were all a KGB legend, this would have been one of the most important dates and one could expect him to remember it accurately. That he was far from consistent on this date certainly appears at least as explainable in terms of some personal idiosyncrasies as in terms of the deception theory.

Another example was Nosenko's inability to report on some KGB operations against American Embassy personnel during 1960–61. This did invalidate his claim to be knowledgeable of all such operations, but it did not necessarily support the deception theory. If the KGB wanted us to believe that Nosenko had the complete knowledge he claimed to have during this period, surely it would have researched how much CIA already knew or could be presumed to know, and it would have had Nosenko tell us about all of these operations. His failure to report on any single operation CIA knew about would discredit his claim to total knowledge. Thus, his false claim does not fit the deception hypothesis. More credible is the thesis that he was exaggerating, that he didn't have an accurate picture of the limitations of his own knowledge, or that we made false assumptions about how much a person in his position should know or remember.

A great many of the anomalies and inconsistencies cited in Bagley's Thousand pager and in the subsequent Green Book were of this type. That is, they were consistent with the deception hypothesis, but they were also consistent with the hypothesis that Nosenko was not under control. Therefore, they had little analytical value.

Inaccurate Record of Nosenko's Reporting

During four of the five clandestine meetings with Nosenko in Geneva in 1962, two CIA case officers were present. The more senior officer, who took notes and wrote reports to Headquarters, spoke mediocre Russian and made many errors in his written record of the meetings. The second officer, who handled much of the discussion with Nosenko, was a native Russian speaker. After the series of meetings was completed, the tape recordings of the meetings were "transcribed" by the native speaker. The tapes were of poor quality and were difficult to follow. Therefore, the native speaker, who had little patience for detailed work, dictated from the Russian-language tapes directly into English, generally following the faulty notes that the other officer had prepared. Thus, the many errors of translation and understanding were carried over from the meeting notes to the "transcripts." For example, an Army sergeant at the American Embassy who Nosenko reported was recruited by the KGB was described by Nosenko as a code machine repairman. This was translated as a mechanic and generally assumed to refer to garage mechanic. When Nosenko corrected this misunderstanding in 1964, he was criticized for "changing his story."

These reports and transcripts formed the basis for the original judgment that Nosenko was a dispatched agent, but they were so flawed as to make any analysis subject to considerable error. These inadequacies were not discovered until 1965, when a faithful Russian-language transcript was finally prepared. The full impact of the inaccuracies was not realized until 1968–69, when the Russian was translated into English and a 35-page report was prepared on the major errors and the effects these errors had had in supporting the charge that Nosenko was a false defector.

Misunderstanding of Nosenko as a Person

CIA initially failed to understand Nosenko's background and how it affected his life and career. This failure was caused, in part, by questioning that was designed from the beginning to trap Nosenko rather than to understand him and by errors in the tape transcripts. It was, however, largely due to the fact that Nosenko himself was an anomaly within the KGB, so it is no wonder that his career seemed anomalous. Nosenko was the spoiled-brat son of a top leader and, in the mid-1960s, CIA had no experience with that type of Soviet official.

A story that came to light much later, from an independent source, is illustrative of Nosenko's background. In Naval Preparatory School in 1943, Nosenko was caught stealing and was beaten up by a number of his classmates. Nosenko's mother complained to Stalin, and the whole school was subjected to strict disciplinary punishment, with some of the students being sent to the front.

Nosenko lied to CIA about his date of entry into the KGB to conceal the fact that his graduation from the Institute of International Relations had been delayed a year because he flunked the exam in Marxism-Leninism. He entered the KGB through the influence of a high-ranking family friend, bypassing the normal personnel procedures. The first few years he received a poor performance evaluation and was recommended for dismissal, his job being saved only by parental intervention. He contracted a venereal disease, concealed this by using false KGB documents to receive treatment under an alias, was caught, served 15 days in prison, and was dismissed from his position as Komsomol secretary. Nosenko's father refused to intercede yet again for his wayward son, but his mother intervened with high-level friends and saved his KGB job.

After several years in the KGB, Nosenko seems to have matured and settled down to an adequate performance. His frequent transfers and lengthy trips abroad may have been because his superiors considered him a hot potato—a mediocre officer and a troublemaker with political connections that could destroy his boss's career; it is understandable that his supervisors were happy to transfer him, send him abroad, or award him undeserved honors.

Nosenko lied to conceal his personal weaknesses, his professional limitations, and the fact that his entire career depended upon his parents' influence and intervention. A need to enhance his own self-esteem and to ensure acceptance by CIA led Nosenko to exaggerate his responsibilities and knowledge of KGB operations.

Interrogators under instructions to obtain evidence against Nosenko, rather than to evaluate him, persisted in judging his story by inappropriate standards. They failed to recognize, or to accept, that because of his family's status and privilege, Nosenko's life and to some extent his career had developed outside many of the rules, regulations, and restrictions imposed on the average KGB officer. They also failed to recognize that a person with Nosenko's family background and poor performance record is certainly not the type the KGB would select for the extremely important and difficult mission of going over to the enemy as a false defector.

Invalid Assumptions About the KGB

Before Nosenko's defection, CIA had very little information on the KGB's Second Chief Directorate (Internal Counterintelligence), where Nosenko served. To evaluate the plausibility of Nosenko's reporting, his interrogators formed a stereotype of the Second Chief Directorate against which to compare Nosenko's information. That stereotype contained assumptions regarding the Second Chief Directorate's authority in the USSR, its relations with the KGB First Chief Directorate (Foreign Intelligence), the relative weight the Second Chief Directorate placed on the recruitment of foreign embassy officials as compared with controlling or monitoring their activities, how much the Second Chief Directorate ought to know about certain events, and how much a specific officer, such as Nosenko, should have known and recalled.

Some of these assumptions were erroneous—based on an exaggerated view of overall KGB capabilities. This made possible a series of discoveries of "duplicity" by Nosenko and other counterintelligence sources who could rarely measure up to CIA's expectations of what they *ought* to have known, accomplished, or said.

An important example concerns the gaps in Nosenko's knowledge of operations against the American Embassy in 1960 and 1961, while he was deputy chief of the responsible section. The interrogators developed their own job description for a deputy chief of a section, then used this as a criterion for judging what Nosenko should have known. The job description was faulty, as it was based on the American concept of a deputy who is fully informed, has authority paralleling the chief, and who automatically fills in for the chief when he is absent.

The Russian word that Nosenko applied to himself was *zamestitel*. When the meaning of this term was researched in 1968, it was found to be broader than the American concept of deputy. It is perhaps most accurately rendered in English as assistant. This different concept of Nosenko's position, his at best mediocre performance as an officer and supervisor, a tendency to exaggerate his importance, and a perhaps unconscious self-delusion as to the extent of his own knowledge all combine to explain the gaps in Nosenko's knowledge during the 1960–61 period.

Honest Mistakes by Nosenko

There are other possible explanations for the previously noted anomaly in Nosenko's reporting on surveillance of the Penkovskiy deaddrop site on Pushkin Street. One is that Nosenko confused the Embassy officer's visit to the Pushkin Street drop with an earlier visit by this same officer to a different deaddrop site on Gorkiy Street, which did occur about the time Nosenko described, and while he was responsible for covering this officer's activity. The subsequent notoriety given to the arrest of a CIA officer at the Pushkin Street site provides ample explanation for how Nosenko may have learned that his former target visited this site as well. After the publicity surrounding the arrest, it is normal that Nosenko would have discussed the background with his former colleagues. Nosenko apparently erred by confusing the two deaddrop sites, and by failing to recall when and how he learned of the Pushkin Street site. In any bona fides assessment, allowance must be made for this sort of faulty memory.

Legitimate Coincidence

The amount of overlap between Nosenko's and Golitsyn's reporting on KGB operations was, indeed, unusual. So was our good fortune in learning that the one Second Chief Directorate officer with whom CIA was in contact just happened to have been the KGB case officer for Lee Harvey Oswald and to report this to CIA just as the Warren Commission was beginning its investigation of President Kennedy's assassination. There were quite a few other equally fortuitous—and, therefore, suspicious—coincidences in other cases associated with the master plot. Coincidence is a normal part of life, but to a counterintelligence officer it is like waving a red flag in front of a bull. Nosenko's interrogators made no allowance whatsoever for the fact that coincidences are not always sinister.

Although most of the discrepancies that generated suspicion have been resolved, there are still some unexplained anomalies. This is probably inevitable given the complexity of Nosenko's personality, the limits of our understanding of the Soviet system, and the confusion generated by the hostile manner in which Nosenko was initially questioned.

Nosenko's reporting on Lee Harvey Oswald is the most significant remaining mystery. As late as 1978, long after Nosenko's bona fides had been established, John Hart, in testimony to Congress, defended Nosenko as a reliable source but described his reporting on Oswald as "incredible" and suggested that it be ignored. Hart attributed the problem to compartmentation within the KGB, that Nosenko was uninformed even though he genuinely thought otherwise. Such a possibility is understandable in principle, but is hard to accept in this case because Nosenko plausibly claimed to have been inside the relevant "compartment" that would give him full knowledge. Nosenko's demonstrated tendency to exaggerate his importance and access may have played a role, but it may also be that we greatly exaggerate out own understanding of how the KGB might react to a low-level defector like Oswald.

At the start of this section, we noted that the anomalies and inconsistencies approach is difficult to implement well. It underrates the frequency of coincidence, inaccurate translation, inadequate debriefing, and misunderstanding. It overrates an analyst's ability to judge what is normal or abnormal in an adversary's organization or society. That assessment is certainly borne out in the Nosenko case.

Many of the problems were of our own making. Because of the *a priori* assumption of guilt, no attempt was made to resolve the many discrepancies; instead, the discrepancies were cherished as proof that Nosenko was dispatched by the KGB. Even under more normal circumstances, this case would have presented difficulties for the anomalies and inconsistencies approach because of Nosenko's personality and unusual background, our limited knowledge of the KGB's Second Chief Directorate, some noteworthy coincidences, and the historical time period in which it occurred.

Litmus Test Approach.

The information or source to be evaluated is compared with other information or another source of known reliability and accuracy. The known information or source serves as a litmus test for evaluating the new or suspect information or source. This approach is similar to that of the finished intelligence analyst who asks: Is the information consistent with the facts as we know them from other sources? For example, a statement by a Soviet leader or an article in a military journal may be compared with information from a classified source of certain reliability. If the open source differs from the reliable classified information, it may be judged deceptive.

Use of this approach presupposes that one can be certain of the reliability and accuracy of the information or source used for comparison. Unfortunately, such certainly is seldom available. When this degree of certainty is present, and is justified, the approach yields strong inferences about deception.

This litmus test strategy played an important role in extending the master plot theory. The conviction that Nosenko was under KGB control led to his case being used as a touchstone for evaluating other sources of information on Soviet intelligence. If another source supplied information supporting questionable elements of Nosenko's story, or supporting the line that Popov and Penkovskiy were detected by surveillance rather than penetration, or supporting any other aspect of the theme that CIA was not penetrated, then that source automatically became suspect as part of the master plot. (Recall that belief in a well-placed penetration of CIA led to the further assumption that all CIA Soviet sources were probably known to, if not controlled by, the KGB. Knowledge of which additional sources were being actively manipulated by the KGB would, it was believed, lead to better understanding of Soviet goals and possibly offer clues to identification of the penetration.)

Nosenko was only one of about a dozen sources on Soviet intelligence who eventually came to be considered part of the master—or monster—plot. To illustrate the application of the litmus test approach in this case, we discuss only two of these other sources—both of whom may have lost their lives as a result of U.S. preoccupation with Soviet deception, one through no fault of CIA, the other as a direct consequence of the master plot theory.

Cherepanov was a former officer of the American Department of the KGB Second Chief Directorate, the same department in which Nosenko had served for a time. He was known to CIA from an abortive attempt to contact the American Embassy in Yugoslavia. After his return to Moscow, he was assigned to the Second Chief Directorate. He was subsequently dismissed from the KGB and went to work for *Mezhkniga*, the book distribution enterprise. In October 1963, Cherepanov gave a packet of documents to an American couple visiting Moscow to purchase books and asked that it be delivered to the American Embassy. The package, which contained KGB reports dealing mainly with surveillance techniques and operations against the American Embassy, was opened by the political counselor of the Embassy. He concluded this was a Soviet provocation and, after copying the documents for CIA, insisted they be returned to the Soviets.

Nosenko reported that when the documents were returned the KGB immediately identified Cherepanov as their source. A quick check revealed that Cherepanov had disappeared. Nosenko himself then became part of a team of KGB officers hastily organized to find and arrest him.

The legitimacy of the Cherepanov documents was questioned at the time they were first received and analyzed at CIA Headquarters, but no firm conclusion was reached. In 1962, Nosenko had reported that CIA's first penetration of the GRU, Colonel Popov, had been arrested in 1959 as a result of surveillance of an American diplomat in Moscow. This comfortable explanation deflected suspicion of a KGB penetration of CIA as the cause of Popov's demise. One of the Cherepanov documents, plus a note from Cherepanov that accompanied the documents, confirmed Nosenko's earlier report and provided additional plausible details.

A different Cherepanov document concerned another area of concern relating to Popov's compromise. It was a detailed KGB analysis of movements by FBI surveillance teams in New York City. It showed KGB awareness of a special FBI surveillance at precisely the time an illegal agent dispatched by Popov had arrived in New York City. CIA had given the FBI information on this illegal's arrival. A compromised FBI surveillance would have drawn suspicion to Popov, and there was speculation that it was a possible cause of Popov's compromise. The Cherepanov document could have been planted to exacerbate the already difficult relationship between CIA and the FBI.

The information from Nosenko and Cherepanov was mutually reinforcing. The documents Cherepanov delivered in 1963 confirmed Nosenko's earlier report that Popov had not been compromised through penetration of CIA. Then, when the Cherepanov documents were questioned at CIA Headquarters, Nosenko came out in 1964 to confirm their authenticity. If a KGB team had been sent out to apprehend Cherepanov, then obviously the documents he provided were genuine rather than a KGB provocation. When Nosenko was judged to be under KGB control, it seemed clear that Cherepanov must have been under control as well, and that both were confirming each other's bona fides while pushing the view that Colonel Popov had not been compromised through penetration of CIA.

Yuriy Loginov was a KGB illegal who volunteered his services to CIA in May 1961 while abroad on an illegal's training mission. He came to the West again in 1962 and for a third time in 1964, shortly after Nosenko's defection. The purpose of his 1964 trip was to cultivate and prepare for recruitment an American military communicator stationed in Cairo. Loginov brought with him several items of interest, including a copy of a Top Secret KGB training manual presenting KGB doctrine on the recruitment of Americans. After 15 months in the West, Loginov returned to Moscow to report that he had developed a good personal relationship with an American, but that the target did not appear recruitable and was being reassigned to the United States.

The Loginov case baffled SB Division from the start. Although the information he provided, particularly in the counterintelligence field, appeared to check out, this very fact gave rise to consternation, as Loginov did not conform to SB Division's conception of the type of man the KGB would select to train and dispatch as an illegal. Nor did the instructions Loginov received from the KGB while in the West conform to SB Division ideas of how the KGB would handle such an agent (anomalies and inconsistencies approach).

The decisive evidence that condemned Loginov, however, was his reporting that supported the bona fides of both Cherepanov and Nosenko. Loginov's father had a dacha next door to Cherepanov, and Loginov reported that, in the fall of 1963, he witnessed the KGB search of Cherepanov's dacha. Nosenko had reported participating in this search. Loginov's story seemed to confirm the reality of Cherepanov's flight and capture, but the coincidence of the neighboring dacha that justified his knowledge seemed extraordinary. Loginov also reported on KGB reactions to Nosenko's defection, and said that, because of the defection, his own dispatch to Canada on a new mission had been canceled. (Unbeknownst to Loginov, Nosenko knew about another illegal also being readied for dispatch to Canada, which undoubtedly persuaded the KGB it would be prudent to delay sending Loginov.)

As a result of these two reports, Loginov was immediately labeled part of the master deception plot, with the role of supporting the bona fides of Cherepanov and Nosenko. The document on KGB operational doctrine for recruitment of Americans was judged authentic and was exploited extensively to improve the security of American installations and businesses abroad. This was considered the price the KGB was prepared to pay to support Loginov's bona fides and, thus, make him more effective in his role as a deception agent.

When Loginov traveled West again, on a Canadian passport with a mission to legalize himself in South Africa before moving permanently to Canada, CIA arranged for him to be arrested in South Africa. Under questioning by the South Africans, he admitted to being a KGB illegal doubled by the Americans. After Loginov spent six months in solitary confinement, two CIA officers interrogated him for over three months in an effort to force an admission that he had been directed by the KGB to contact CIA and pass disinformation. Despite optimal interrogation conditions, Loginov refused to change his story, so the South Africans were left with the same problem that CIA originally had with Nosenko—what to do with a Soviet who was not trusted but against whom one had no juridical evidence.

A fortuitous solution to this problem appeared when East Germany claimed Loginov as an East German citizen (a common ploy in such cases) and suggested he be included in an East-West German prisoner exchange. CIA encouraged the idea despite Loginov's pleas not to be exchanged. At the exchange point, in July 1969, Loginov resisted repatriation for four hours until he was forcibly turned over to the waiting KGB officers. Subsequent reporting indicates he may have been executed.

There is every reason to believe that both Cherepanov and Loginov were bona fide sources, not under KGB control. They produced valuable intelligence consistent with their access, but they failed the master plot litmus test. Consideration of other anomalies in these cases or the value of information supplied were all subordinated to the overwhelming importance attributed to the fact that both sources supported themes considered to be part of the master deception plot.

These clear examples of the litmus test strategy illustrate the major weakness of this strategy for analyzing deception. The strategy presupposes certainty about the information or source used as a basis for the test. In this instance, the analysts were certain about Nosenko being under control, but their certainty was unjustified and led to wrong conclusions in about a dozen cases, with immense consequences for CIA in lost operational opportunities, and often with adverse personal consequences for the Soviets involved.

Cost Accounting Approach.
An analyst employing this strategy focuses on the cost incurred by the adversary to conduct a deception. If the cost is higher than any potential gain, the decep-

tion hypothesis is rejected. Most frequently considered is the cost of providing valid and valuable information to establish and maintain the credibility of a deception channel. This approach judges a source on the basis of its production. This is the strategy generally used by the Directorate of Operations (DO) reports officer, as distinct from the DO operations officer, who is more likely to focus on anomalies or inconsistencies in the circumstances under which the source obtained the information or passed it on to us.

The cost accounting approach assumes an accurate understanding of how much an adversary is willing to sacrifice to achieve his goals. This is difficult because, in principle, there always can be a goal that is important enough to justify any cost. Such analysis, therefore, may be correct in routine cases that follow the established pattern, but wrong in the rare, exceptionally high-stakes situation when it counts the most. Traditional theory holds that deception is most likely when the stakes are highest—for example, when an adversary would be willing to pay the greatest price to achieve his goals.

The three previous approaches—motive, anomalies and inconsistencies, and litmus test—are best used to show the presence of deception. One cannot do that with the cost accounting strategy. This strategy can be used only to prove the absence of deception, not its presence. This is because high cost may (or may not) imply the absence of deception, but low cost does not necessarily imply its presence.

ᴄ

Cost accounting was the primary strategy employed by those who believed Nosenko was a bona fide defector. Briefly, it was argued that information provided by Nosenko was so valuable to CIA and so damaging to the USSR that it was inconceivable the KGB would willingly give it away. The KGB would never deliberately place one of its own officers into the hands of its principal adversary.

Bruce Solie, the Office of Security officer who handled Nosenko's rehabilitation, believed a source should be judged on the quality of information received. He felt that too much attention had been paid to challenging Nosenko's story, and not enough to finding out everything he could tell us about KGB operations. Accordingly, Solie's debriefing concentrated on obtaining more information. Since the value of Nosenko's information created a presumption of bona fides, Solie's approach to anomalies and inconsistencies was to seek some plausible explanation and to recognize that, given the nature of the case, some anomalies may never be explained. Subsequently, the FBI reported that a minimum of nine new counterintelligence cases were developed as a result of Solie's reexamination, and that new information of considerable importance was developed on old cases; additional detailed information was also obtained on KGB operations in other countries, and on KGB organization, modus operandi, and personnel. Altogether, the information pointed to a valuable, bona fide source.

Nosenko provided identification of, or leads to, some 238 Americans and about 200 foreign nationals in whom the KGB had displayed varying degrees of interest, and against whom they had enjoyed varying degrees of success. He provided information on about 2,000 KGB staff officers and 300 Soviet national agents or contacts of the KGB. His information on the methods and scope of Second Chief Directorate operations against foreign diplomats and journalists in Moscow and visitors to the Soviet Union filled a large gap in our knowledge and had an enormous impact on the raising of CIA's consciousness of these operations; the result was important improvements in the physical security of U.S. installations and in the personal security of U.S. officials and visitors to the USSR. The Soviet Union suffered additional costs through the adverse publicity and deterrent effect of Nosenko's defection and the arrest of several agents he identified.

The master plot theorists also assessed the value of Nosenko's information, not as the overriding criterion for evaluating his bona fides, but certainly as a relevant consideration. They came to the opposite conclusion. They argued that KGB operations reported by Nosenko had been previously reported by Golitsyn or other sources, involved agents who had lost their access, who the KGB had reason to believe had been compromised, who were unimportant, or where the information could not be confirmed. At times, this argument was made with a stacked deck, and Nosenko always came out the loser. If Nosenko reported on a KGB operation previously reported by another defector, this was not counted as a plus for Nosenko, because the KGB already knew the operation had been compromised. If he reported an operation not previously known, the information was judged doubtful because it could not be confirmed.

The argument that Nosenko's information was unimportant was always difficult to sustain, as it kept being contradicted by reality. For a time, various rationalizations were possible, but eventually Solie's supplemental debriefing of Nosenko, a more objective interpretation of his information, and successful investigation of the leads developed a clear record to Nosenko's credit.

For example, Bagley argued that Nosenko's information on microphones in the American Embassy in Moscow was a KGB giveaway, as Golitsyn had already reported on this subject. Golitsyn's report, however, was only a general statement that the Embassy was bugged. Nosenko identified which offices, where in these offices the mikes were located, and what conversations had been monitored. It was only Nosenko's more detailed, first-hand information that persuaded the State Department to incur the significant cost and disruption involved in tearing out walls to find and neutralize the installation. They found 52 mikes, 47 of them still active, covering many of the most interesting offices in the Embassy.

Nosenko's supporters and detractors largely ignored each other's arguments, as they approached the analysis of Nosenko's bona fides from entirely different paths and used different criteria for judging the truth. In the context of the master plot, the value of information provided by Nosenko measured only the magnitude of the deception to come. To believers in Nosenko, on the other hand, the list of espionage cases the FBI had developed from his information and the many leads to KGB agents in other countries were ample proof of his bona fides. As the KGB would not willingly sacrifice this information, there must be some other explanation for the conflicts in his story.

Ironically, one of the strongest points in favor of Nosenko was not made in any of the studies of his bona fides. This is because of the tacit agreement by Nosenko's detractors and supporters alike that he should be considered on his own merits, without reference to the master plot as a whole. This was an artificial limitation, as almost everyone on both sides of the issue recognized that, if Nosenko were bona fide, the master plot theory would collapse. Conversely, if the master plot theory could be disproved, the case against Nosenko would be difficult to sustain.

The point is that Nosenko's information was only a small part of the total information on Soviet intelligence being received at that time from multiple sources believed to be part of the master plot. If all the valuable information from all the supposedly controlled sources had been collected in one massive compendium to show the incredible magnitude of what was allegedly being sacrificed, it would have made a most powerful argument against the master plot theory and, therefore, against the argument that Nosenko was under control.

To the few who were informed of all these other cases and saw events from the master plot perspective, it began to appear as though the entire KGB might have become a sacrificial lamb on the altar of deception and diversion. The diehards—some would call them paranoids—rationalized this by concluding that the deception must be even bigger and more important than previously believed; as the KGB sacrifices mounted, the level and importance of the assumed penetration went higher and higher. Others, however, who initially had accepted the inherent plausibility of the master plot, began to have doubts. There had to be some limit on how much the KGB would give away.

A former Chief of the CI Group in SB Division told me, for example, that he first began to doubt the master plot theory when he learned about a senior East European military officer who had been supplying CIA with very important Warsaw Pact documents for many years. Giving away counterintelligence leads to divert opposition security services was one thing, but the wholesale sacrifice of military secrets was quite another. Continuation of this operation seemed to belie the existence of a well-placed KGB penetration of CIA, which was an essential part of the master plot theory.

In 1976, John Hart visited Tennant Bagley, who had retired four years earlier, to inquire whether, after so much time, he still rejected Nosenko's bona fides. Bagley asked if there had been any new evidence confirming Nosenko's story, to which Hart replied there had not. I believe that Hart was wrong; there was much additional evidence to refute the master plot theory. During the intervening years, old sources continued and new counterintelligence sources were developed that produced a continuous flow of very valuable information, thereby greatly increasing the total cost to the Soviets if the master plot theory were valid. The most knowledgeable new sources would have failed the master plot litmus test, for they confirmed genuine KGB distress at Nosenko's defection, reported that the KGB would be unwilling to use a KGB staff officer as a double agent or false defector, and failed to report any massive counterintelligence deception program or penetration of CIA at the level that had been feared.

In summary, this cost accounting strategy led to an accurate judgment of Nosenko's bona fides. Our discussion does, however, illustrate the principal weakness of this approach, namely, how to determine what the adversary might regard as an acceptable cost. Analysts on both sides of the issue recognized that a source's production is a useful criterion for judging bona fides, but they had radically different views on how much information and the kinds of information the KGB would be willing to sacrifice in the interest of deception.

Predictive Test Approach.

This approach is not normally used in intelligence analysis, but it could and should be used under select circumstances. It might also be called the scientific approach, for it addresses a problem the way a scientist does. The scientist develops a tentative hypothesis to explain the phenomenon under study, then devises tests to prove or disprove the hypothesis. The same approach can be used in deception analysis.

A tentative hypothesis about deception can often be tested by using the presumption of deception to make a series of predictions. If the deception theory generates predictions that are borne out by subsequent experience, this suggests that the hypothesis is true. If expectations are contradicted by experience, this suggests that the hypothesis may be wrong.

The principal value of testing views in this manner is that it makes it more difficult to rationalize contradictory evidence. There is a human tendency to interpret new information in ways that do not require us to change our minds. By using a hypothesis about deception to make explicit predictions, one specifies the circumstances under which one could be proved wrong. The predictions are either confirmed or they are not. The latter outcome points to possible flaws in one's understanding of the subject and provokes thought as to where reasoning went astray. If one has not made explicit predictions, one may not concede or even recognize that the reasoning was ill founded.

The weakness of this strategy is that it presupposes some form of ongoing activity, so that one can make short-term predictions and see if they come true. Another weakness is that it requires more self-conscious introspection and willingness to question one's own assumptions than most intelligence analysts are comfortable with, and therefore is seldom used.

This strategy was not used explicitly in any of the analyses of the Nosenko case. This form of reasoning did, however, implicitly affect the thinking of some persons involved in the case. The master plot theory did lead to certain expectations, or implied predictions, and when they were not borne out in practice this did engender doubts about the theory.

The most obvious expectation was that it might be possible to break Nosenko. Of course, one could never be certain Nosenko would break even if he were under KGB control, but the interrogators had important psychological advantages. They had total control over Nosenko, were "certain" he was a KGB-dispatched agent, and even "knew" the purpose of the KGB operations. Yet Nosenko did not confess to anything more than a few self-serving lies. Similar advantages existed in the CIA interrogation of Loginov in South Africa; again, the interrogation was unsuccessful.

The master plot theory assumed the existence of a well-placed KGB penetration of CIA. It predicted that KGB agents, such as Nosenko, were either being directed with guidance from the penetration, or were being used to build up or protect the penetration. This limited the suspects to a finite number of CIA officers. It was estimated that astute counterintelligence analysis and security investigation would identify the penetration, but no such penetration was discovered despite extensive investigation. Again, the theory was contradicted by events. This might logically have led the proponents of the theory to question their assumptions, but it did not.

Additional expectations concerned the KGB operations on which Nosenko reported. One would expect the KGB to try to achieve its deception goals with the minimum necessary cost to itself. This led to the view that Nosenko's revelations about KGB operations were probably less important than they appeared to be. Specifically, if was anticipated that investigation of Nosenko's leads to seemingly well-placed KGB agents would show that these agents had recently lost their access or were, for some other reason, expendable to the KGB. Further, it was expected that investigation of tantalizing leads to agents who could not be fully identified by Nosenko would lead to dead ends, so the KGB would really have sacrificed nothing at all. In some cases, these expectations were accurate, but in a significant number of cases investigations did identify valuable KGB agents.

These beliefs and expectations were, in effect, logical deductions or predictions based on the master plot hypothesis. If they had been set forth explicitly as predictions, and recognized as valid if partial and imperfect tests of the hypothesis, it would have been far more difficult to ignore the implications of their being contradicted by events. Unfortunately, the advocates of the master plot theory were seeking to prove it, not to test it. They regarded the master plot as a fact, not as a hypothesis to be subjected to critical examination, so developments that seemed to contradict this view were ignored, rationalized, or misinterpreted.

III: Conclusions

Heretofore, I have tried to present an objective account of the diverse arguments used, or in some cases not used, by those on both sides of the Nosenko issue. What follows is personal opinion. The reader is cautioned that opinions on this case are as numerous and varied as the many CIA and FBI officers who were personally involved in one or another phase of it. The opinions expressed here are certainly not the final word.

I will start by making my personal bias clear. I became a believer in the master plot theory in 1965 when first exposed to the reasoning described above under the motive approach. Although initially a believer, I never put much stock in Bagley's Thousand Pager, as I had learned from experience to be skeptical of conclusions based on the anomalies and inconsistencies approach to counterintelligence analysis. My first doubts arose when, one by one, various expectations failed to materialize, which is the reasoning described above under the predictive test approach. Subsequently, for reasons discussed under the cost accounting approach—the high volume of significant intelligence being received through multiple sources—I rejected the master plot theory and concluded that Nosenko was not acting under KGB control. This conclusion was recently reinforced when, in doing research for this study, I learned how the many anomalies and contradictions were eventually explained.

I remain firmly opposed to the view that the master plot was an irresponsible, paranoid fantasy. Given the information available at the time, as described under the motive approach, it would have been irresponsible not to have seriously considered this possibility. The mistake was not in pursuing the master plot theory, but in getting so locked into a position that one was unable to question basic assumptions or to note the gradual accumulation of contrary evidence. This type of analytical error is not uncommon, and all of us are susceptible to it. It can lead one to overlook deception as well as to perceive deception when it isn't there, as happened in the Nosenko case.

Gordon Stewart was correct in criticizing Bagley's analysis for assuming guilt and then interpreting every discrepancy as evidence of this guilt. After serious doubts began to be raised about this analysis, the Soviet Bloc Division should have assigned an officer in a devil's advocate role to do an analysis that assumed innocence, then examined how the evidence could be interpreted as being consistent with this view. By failing to give a fair shake to the opposing view, SB Division lost control of the case to another component that approached the analysis from a totally different perspective. This lesson should be taken to heart by any component involved in a serious controversy over deception.

Most important for this study is not what we learn about the Nosenko case, but what can be learned about deception analysis in general. There seem to be five quite separate and distinct paths to reaching judgments about deception. Which path one chooses is strongly influenced by one's past experience and the patterns of thought associated with one's functional responsibilities or organizational affiliation. The path one take determines, in turn, the evidence one seeks and, in large measure, the conclusion one reaches.

Generally, analysts in the Nosenko case gave greatest weight to the kinds of evidence they were most familiar and most comfortable with, and this in turn determined which approach they took. Some counterintelligence personnel were very familiar with and influenced by the concern about penetration of CIA. Speaking for myself, for example, I had been the Headquarters desk officer on the Goleniewski case at the time we received both of his reports, the one on the penetration of CIA and the one that led to identification of Felfe as a KGB penetration of West German intelligence. I had also seen first hand how much damage a well-placed penetration, such as Goleniewski, could do to an opposition service. This personal experience made the master plot seem very real and very plausible. Other counterintelligence specialists, more directly involved in the Nosenko case than I, had personal experience with the seeming contradictions and extraordinary coincidences in his story, so this is what most influenced them.

One's professional experience and organizational affiliation play important roles in determining the strategy one employs to analyze deception. Counterintelligence officers, DO reports officers, and DI intelligence analysts look at deception through different conceptual lenses. The strategy employed, in turn, largely determines what evidence one seeks and the conclusion one reaches. Examination of Soviet motives led Bagley to review the entire history of CIA and KGB counterintelligence operations. Anomalies and inconsistencies perceived by counterintelligence personnel in the initial debriefing of Nosenko led to hostile interrogation to develop still more anomalies and inconsistencies. Solie's cost accounting approach led to friendly interrogation designed to produce as much information as possible, while playing down the anomalies. The litmus test approach focused attention on how other sources' information related to the Nosenko case, while overlooking the total value of these sources' information.

The Nosenko case vividly illustrates the weaknesses inherent in each of the five strategies for analyzing deception. Bagley identified a plausible motive for Soviet deception and supported it with voluminous circumstantial evidence, yet Nosenko was not under Soviet control. There was an enormous number of anomalies and inconsistencies in Nosenko's story, yet they were all produced by sloppy translation and inadequate debriefing, the unique aspects of Nosenko's background and personality, genuine accident and coincidence, and the circumstances of his handling; they were not truly indicative of hostile control.

Comparing the value of information received from a source against some criterion of the cost the adversary would be willing to incur also leads to strong inferences about deception, but only if the putative threshold of acceptable cost is correct; in the Nosenko analysis, that threshold was itself a major point of disagreement. Comparing suspect information against some objective criterion of truth can lead to strong inferences about deception, but only if the criterion does indeed represent the truth; in the Nosenko case, it did not. Making test predictions can prompt reconsideration of one's views if they fail the test of experience, but, typically, this was not done in the Nosenko case; analysts were too busy trying to prove they were right, rather than testing their assumptions.

If there is a single lesson to be learned from this, it is that all five approaches are useful for complete analysis. Exclusive reliance on any one strategy is dangerous. The cost accounting approach led to a correct conclusion in the Nosenko case, but it, too, has inherent vulnerabilities, and there is no guarantee it will be correct in all future cases. This places a heavy burden on the deception analyst. To do a thorough analysis of all the possibilities, one must examine the diverse bodies of evidence relevant to each of these strategies. This will often require investment of substantial time to gain understanding of previously unfamiliar fields.

30.

This article is an extraordinarily detailed, tough-minded manual on how to resist counterintelligence interrogation. Implicitly it is also a manual on tactics and strategies available to interrogators themselves in many countries. Explicitly it is Cold War focused, but readers remain free to extrapolate. (One way, still Cold War but inverted, would be to put oneself in Nosenko's place or that of his American interrogators.)

Defense Against Communist Interrogation Organizations

GEORGE STANTON

The suggestions offered herein for practical defense against Communist interrogation organizations are designed to be used *very selectively* and with caution in the briefing of anti-Communist secret agents running the danger of Communist imprisonment.[1] Because some of the tactics outlined could be of use to other categories of persons, such as prisoners of war, political prisoners, and noncombatants, this study is offered with the reservation that it is not to be construed either as a modification of official U.S. Government doctrine or an exhaustive treatment of the Communist system of prisoner management and exploitation.

The Importance and Techniques of Preparation

Most of the available guidance on this subject is too much concerned with the tactics of the conflict between the prisoner and his interrogator after arrest, and not enough with the *preparations* that the endangered agent can and should make in advance. His preparations are very often decisive in determining the outcome of his resistance effort. The agent must be prepared physically, organizationally, and mentally.

Among the most important physical preparations is to separate oneself as far as possible from incriminating materials such as commo plans, one-time pads, radios, secret inks, weapons, special cameras, documents, and money in bulk. Linkage to incriminating persons must be adequately covered, and all the

George Stanton, "Defense Against Communist Interrogation Organizations," *Studies in Intelligence,* vol. 13, no. 4 (Fall 1969), pp. 49–74. Originally classified "Confidential."

1. Briefers should bear in mind that some agents, getting the full briefing, might decamp rather than take the risks.

standard procedures of operational security and conspiratorial discipline must be understood and maintained. Plans for emergencies must be worked out in advance and *rehearsed.* These plans should be set up for use under unfavorable conditions, when one is under surveillance or suspicion.

Organizationally speaking, the agent should have made all possible arrangements for the support and safety, rescue or warning of his family and others dependent upon him. He should have set up some system whereby his sponsors will learn of his arrest—if it occurs—at an early date, so that they can begin to help him. He should have arranged a simple code for concealing information in any letters or messages he might be able to send to his family, if the family is witting of his secret activities or affiliations.

This is a grim subject, and part of the mental preparation—a most important part—consists in accepting and living with these possibilities. An agent conditioned to face them honestly is likely to be far more capable and careful than the chance-taker who hopes somehow to get by without self-discipline and without the intensive preparation that is the only way to success in any clandestine operation. The agent should have studied the security service and interrogation systems operating in his area and should have prepared himself against surprise. The agent must prepare and thoroughly rehearse his cover story and his fall-back cover story for his status, action, and associations, and backstop them as far as possible. He will usually be able to get help with this work from his sponsors. There is an inward, or psychological, aspect of imprisonment for which the prisoner must be fortified. Prisoners with a high ideological motivation are able to defend themselves and to continue to struggle against the opposition longer than others, even under conditions of extreme hardship. Persons who have strong religious beliefs are able to resist much more effectively than those with a weak faith or none. A person undertaking the dangerous work of the secret agent should in any case develop an ideological basis. If not religiously inclined, he should review in his mind the great cause of human freedom and the price that others have willingly paid to defend and advance it. Patriotism, the welfare of families and friends, and concern for his own future self-respect, all help to reinforce the will to resist. Very few persons are aware of how much hidden strength they actually have. The medical profession, which has the opportunity to observe persons fighting for their lives—often against incurable ailments—can testify to the fact that, when a person makes up his mind to resist, he can accomplish miracles.

The Arrest

It is, of course, essential that the agent, as a standard procedure, maintain a level of preparation for arrest. However, since he has to take chances in order to accomplish anything, it becomes important to know something of the signs of impending arrest. History is replete with accounts of agents arrested with incriminating evidence in their possession *long after they themselves had good reason to expect arrest.*

Any change, however subtle, in the attitude of persons with whom one is in everyday contact must be fully reviewed as to possible causes. From the point of view of preparation, the agent should carefully study people with whom he has casual contact, such as an apartment house janitor, a storekeeper, a barber, for example. In a totalitarian country, people of this sort are keenly alert. If they have been approached under some cover by a local security officer to provide information about the agent, they will have received a tremendous shock and their attitude toward the agent is bound to change. He may observe signs of fear, sudden prying curiosity, avoidance, or even unusual pleasantness on the part of such persons. He may have nothing but a feeling that their attitude has changed. Such warning signs should never be ignored.

If the agent is carrying out proper countersurveillance procedures he may detect signs that he is under observation. Although one would think that an agent detecting such signs would take strict measures to remove evidence, in many cases he has simply continued on his way—often with unfortunate results.

From time to time the agent may detect that his quarters, or his place of work, have been tampered with. He may discover articles out of place or missing, or signs of the rumpling of clothing in drawers, and the like. There are simple methods of so arranging various objects that their movement can be detected. Very frequently, the secret search of one's premises is an important warning that one is suspected. However, inquisitive persons and thieves also engage in this kind of activity.

The arrest or disappearance of confederates or accomplices is, of course, a warning that no one could misunderstand.

It is often possible for the sponsor of a secret agent to warn him through some prearranged system of communication that he should suspend operations, flee immediately, or the like. *The most careful preparation and planning are essential to assure that the agent will be able to verify the authenticity of a warning, as well as to understand it correctly.* From time to time persons have been trapped by "warnings" fabricated by the local security service and intended to stampede them into some unwise action. Persons who should have known better have fallen for such simple tricks as an anonymous telephone call from "a friend," an anonymous letter dropped into the mailbox or shoved under the door, even a visit by an unknown well-wisher. Of course, in the areas where resistance to Communism is high there will be a person here and there who, out of the goodness of his heart, will assist an enemy agent. But in the vast majority of cases, in a totalitarian country, fear of the consequences and general suspicion of everybody effectively prevent people from helping each other secretly—which is one of the main reasons why totalitarian governments survive.

Arrest occurs in two basic forms: overt and secret. In overt arrest actions, the Communist services tend to use a good deal of manpower to bar escape and to crash into the rooms of the suspect with the minimum loss of time. Occasionally they will have access to the keys to the suspect's lodging and use them for even swifter invasion of the premises. Sometimes these services deliberately create a great fuss during the arrest action, presumably in order to intimidate and impress the population. Arrest in this form indicates the intent of the authorities to liquidate the operation and formally charge and sentence the persons apprehended. The agent is advised to plan his resistance toward minimizing the offense, trying to get the charges changed to criminal charges and in general to aim at leading the arresting authorities to conclude that common crime is in fact the principal activity of the arrested persons.

In case of overt arrest, the prisoner in Communist hands in a civilized area can expect standard criminal processing, including photographing and fingerprinting, body search, replacement of belongings with a prison uniform, medical check, a hot shower bath, and assignment to a cell under close guard. In the case of espionage suspects, these procedures will be very thoroughly carried out. The arrestee can expect to confront one or more interrogators for a long time to come.

In the case of secret arrest, quite a few of these procedures may be omitted. The prisoner may find himself in a safehouse, and the physical search may concentrate on depriving him of the means of suicide. The search for evidence may thus be a good deal less thorough than it might otherwise be. There may be evidence of concern for his state of mind in many cases; but in others the sternest and most thorough processing will occur. The prisoner should keep alert to every nuance of the processing, as he can often gain clues as to how much is known and what is intended. He should be particularly alert if he is left in the company of talkative guards or "fellow prisoners" for long periods of time, as these persons will in all probability be plants trying to elicit information from him and influence his attitudes.

In secret arrest operations, the person detained is usually accosted on the street by a number of men who "escort" him to prison or a safehouse as inconspicuously as possible. *Secret arrest as a rule means that the arresting service has plans which require that the fact of the suspect's arrest be concealed as long as possible.* This does not necessarily mean he is to be turned loose to be used as an informer, for the intent may only be to gain time and avoid scaring others before arrests can be made. It may mean that the arrestee is expected to provide evidence leading to the identification and arrest of persons not yet known to the security service. Occasionally a person is arrested on trumped-up charges in the hope of getting him to provide evidence against himself by surprise and under high pressure. The possibility also exists that the arrest has been undertaken secretly in order to avoid embarrassment if the prisoner has to be released for lack of evidence later—that is to say, the arrest is a bluff. But in a good percentage of the cases there is a substantial prospect that the person detained may be let loose to function as a doubled agent, and the arrested person should take comfort from this circumstance and plan his defense accordingly.

Interrogation

While the prisoner is being processed into his cell, last minute preparations for his interrogation will be under way. The interrogators who are to deal with the prisoner will be putting the finishing touches on their interrogation plan and examining the materials recovered during arrest and body search. Frequently, the prisoner will not be interrogated for some time after entering his cell. During the interval the prisoner should review the main points of his cover story and of his fall-back story and decide what his attitude toward the interrogators will be. He may be fed, briefed on the rules, and allowed to go to sleep, only to be suddenly awakened and hurried off to an interrogation cell.

If the prisoner has been *secretly* arrested, his handling can vary widely. He may not be searched. He may be brought to a safehouse. He may be given a very friendly reception. On the other hand, he may be subjected to very harsh and violent treatment, in an effort to force or frighten a confession out of him. Harsh or violent treatment and hasty interrogation are indications that the arresting authorities are on a "fishing expedition" and do not really have sufficient information and evidence in hand.

In the initial stages of any interrogation it is best for the prisoner to play the role of a well-intentioned but confused and innocent victim. The jails are full of prisoners who made the mistake of being clear and precise in their replies to seemingly harmless questions. The first thing every interrogator has to determine is whether his prisoner can tell a straight story about anything, or whether he is in a state of confusion. Prisoners are under no obligation to collaborate with their captors by exhibiting good memories and making coherent statements. This is the time to forget as much as possible.

In *all* interrogation sessions, the prisoner should try to discover the following:

    a. What is known about him; more specifically, what evidence does the interrogator have? Even Communist interrogators have to have evidence to convict suspects, and they seldom have as much as they pretend to have. Nothing should ever be admitted unless the evidence that the interrogator exhibits is overwhelming. In such cases the admission should be framed in such a way as to mislead the interrogator as to the true nature of the evidence. *One should never assume that the case is hopeless and that one might as well tell all.*

b. Where did the interrogator get his information? The prisoner often overlooks the fact that the interrogator may let slip information which will indicate who betrayed the operation. By feigning stupidity and confusion and pretending not to understand questions, the prisoner may maneuver the interrogator into making further disclosures which may indicate the source of the betrayal.

c. What are the intentions of the authorities? By the time the prisoner is in his cell, he will have many clues to analyze: The arrest procedure, the search procedure, the remarks which the arresting authorities may have made within his hearing, and other circumstances preceding the arrest which he may call to mind. Thinking these things over as calmly and as thoroughly as possible can help the prisoner to plan his defense.

d. How much importance do the authorities attach to the prisoner? When the prisoner faces his interrogators, he can gain valuable clues as to how much effort the opponent intends to make in his case. He may find himself confronted with an expert interrogator who knows the prisoner's language and background very thoroughly, or he may find a relatively inexperienced and ignorant interrogator working against him. The type of custodial handling, such things as the number of persons making the arrest, the speed and efficiency of his handling, the level of rank of officers dealing with him, all provide clues in this direction.

In the period before arrest—and certainly before interrogation—the prisoner should have made up his mind as to what facts he must conceal at all costs. Such facts would include: the identity or hiding places of other agents, the hiding places of items of evidence, the true objectives of the operation, and important information concerning his superior officers and his sponsoring organization.

Some General Rules

The rules which will help a prisoner to deal with his persecutors fall into two general categories: rules concerning attitudes and psychological defenses, and rules covering practical actions and defenses.

The first psychological rule is never to give up hope, no matter how desperate the situation appears to be. One must always bear in mind that the opponent is not only human but in all likelihood under heavy pressures of doubt and handicapped by fragmentary information. In espionage matters so much is cloudy and confused in even the clearest cases, that prisoners who know the game can frustrate their opponents—if they persist.

The second psychological rule is to view oneself in custody *as continuing the fight with other weapons and on another basis.*

The third rule is to view oneself as a patriotic hero fighting to free his people. After all, the soldier fights in groups, from which he draws courage. The secret agent generally spends most of his time fighting singlehanded without this type of strong support. His fight is waged against great odds; hence he deserves extra credit for heroism—not condemnation as a "cowardly spy." One's own evaluation of oneself tends to get across to associates—and guards and interrogators are *de facto* associates of a sort, who may come to respect the prisoner who respects himself in spite of themselves. The safest pose is the pose of calm equality: "We are both doing our duty according to our principles."

Rule four is in many ways the most important: Care must be taken not to slip insensibly into the attitude that there is no world except the prison, no future, and that the time scale of the prison is all that counts. It must consciously be remembered that there is another world and that one day the prisoner will have to face that world and its rewards or punishment. Liberation may be very sudden and soon—then what?

Rule five is to remember one's own importance. The agent, confronted with the vastness of the prison and the clandestine activity, tends in any case to come to consider himself and what he does as unimportant. This is both a harmful attitude and an error: the agent is often very important and never unimportant. He can within limits continue to have an effect upon the world even while tied hand and foot, possibly even a greater effect than when he was at large. He cannot know what is going on behind the scenes of the opponent's organization. His case may be a *cause célèbre,* or even the subject of international negotiations. The prison administration, however, will make every effort to make him appear to himself as the forgotten man.

Combatting Environmental Influences

The tactics of most Communist services are designed to weaken the prisoner through relatively simple but highly effective methods. "Brainwashing" as commonly understood is an inexact notion. The prisoner can expect to be confined in a bleak and uncomfortable cell illuminated with a very bright light 24 hours a day. He will be under constant observation but unable to communicate with anyone. He will be required to obey minute, irritating, and senseless restrictions. His food supply will be inadequate and particularly deficient in vitamins. He will be deprived of sleep, required to sleep in a certain position when he does get a chance to lie down, and may have to stand for many hours on end. Interrogators and others will suggest that he is guilty of all sorts of things and may alternate their treatment with sudden, unexpected interludes of kindness and even friendliness. The alternation of this treatment, especially when one is not prepared for it, can induce a state of mind gravely weakening the power to resist. Many former prisoners have stated that they were most weakened by friendly approaches after a long period of hardship. They found themselves forgetting that the interrogator was their enemy. They found themselves accepting the idea that they had to exonerate themselves and rehabilitate themselves, succumbing to intense feelings of guilt.

The interrogators, while they have a great deal of latitude and authority over the prisoner's situation, nevertheless would get into trouble, possibly quite serious, if the prisoner died or became demented or crippled as a result of the treatment he had been subjected to. The interrogator is not all-powerful. Prisoners should eat whatever food is placed before them to sustain their strength. With a little practice, however, some persons can vomit at will, and it could be effective if the prisoner suddenly did so upon the interrogator or in his presence. No interrogator enjoys close and continued contact with a prisoner who has lost control of his bowel movements. Fainting is sometimes an effective gambit. This interrupts the interrogation and creates time-wasting interludes while the prisoner is revived. The prison administration takes care to forestall attempts by prisoners to commit suicide. However, people have committed suicide in prison through dashing their heads against the walls, through biting their wrist arteries open, through inhaling items of food causing strangulation, and through other ingenious methods. There is nothing to prevent the prisoner from experimenting with suicide attempts in such fashion as to alarm the interrogator, and it takes a pretty determined interrogator to avoid making the prisoner's lot easier when this threat becomes evident.

Immediately upon imprisonment the prisoner should devise some method of keeping track of time. This is most difficult if there is no daylight in the prison cell. The prison schedules and routines are often deliberately varied in order to distort the prisoner's sense of time. The prisoner can pass the time he records very profitably by engraving upon his memory, through the process of repeated recall, important details about his opponents which will be valuable later on. Unless the prisoner makes a conscious effort to memorize these details, when he gets out of prison he will usually be unable to recall important facts, dates, and the like. The prisoner should memorize the features and mannerisms of the interrogators, particularly unusual items such as an accent, a deformity, or some striking habit. He should attempt to find out as much as he can about the building in which he is housed, particularly its location. He should attempt to become familiar with the guards, who in a sense are also prisoners. The "friendly" guard, of course, is usually a provocateur, so he should be told nothing of significance except what the prisoner wants to reach the ears of his interrogators. However, cultivation of the guard can be used to elicit interesting details from him and may enable the prisoner to ease his own lot a little. Now and then the guard will be found who is in fact sympathetic to the prisoner. The prisoner should attempt to identify the vulnerabilities of interrogators and, of course, always look for clues as to their identity. The intelligence services of the free world are very well informed as to the identities of interrogators and can match the information the prisoner supplies with the information they already have to identify the interrogator fully later.

People captured by Chinese or other Asian Communists may find themselves imprisoned with a group of "reformed" prisoners, rather than isolated. The other prisoners are under heavy pressure to "reform" the victim. They will endlessly argue with him, plead with him, and abuse him, exerting moral pressure, and surrounding him with an ideological environment that will cause him to feel deserted, guilty, and hopeless. A person caught in such a situation can play for time, as this process takes days and often weeks to be effective. He can also use the situation to create confusion. For example, he can tell different individuals "in confidence" very different stories, and if he is good at dealing with people, he can create feuds amongst the people seeking to "reform" him, playing one off against another.

The effects of isolation and inactivity quickly weaken all—especially persons who are congenial and like human company. We all depend to a great extent on our associates for moral support and for a feeling of reality. When held in a dark cell, all alone, day after day, the desire for human contact, which can be satisfied only by the interrogator, grows very strong in many persons. Worry becomes an incessant companion. The tendency to see the interrogator more and more in a heroic light and as a friend also develops. Most prisoners expect to find the enemy to be vile and revolting, and their resistance is greatly weakened when they discover that the interrogator can be a fine, clean-cut, idealistic, and quite charming person. The best defense against this approach is to keep telling oneself this is just another trick. If one can develop insight into one's own human weakness, much of the effect of this trick will be lost. The prisoner should realize that it is normal for a person in isolation to feel that he is losing his mind, to feel extremely guilty, to feel terribly lonely and anxious. The prisoner's fear that he is losing his mind is the best guarantee that he will not lose it.

The personal equation in the relationship with the interrogator must be borne in mind. Most people do not have dominant personalities or great powers of leadership and persuasion. Some interrogators have a great deal of such power. They are persons who exercise natural authority over others, and the prisoner will find himself emotionally affected by the demands of such commanding persons. Here again, insight into one's own weakness is the best defense.

It is also particularly hard to resist the blandishments of an interrogator who is obviously convinced of the justice of his own cause and sincerely attempts to "reform" the prisoner. It is well to remember that some of the most sincere persons in history have been the most vicious, such as, for example, Adolf Hitler. Sincerity is no guarantee of the justice of a cause, but unless one is on one's guard against it, one can become persuaded.

As long as possible, and certainly until the pressure becomes intolerable, the prisoner should stick to his cover story. If he has worked up a plausible story, and has learned it reasonably well, and has lived his cover, he may be able to make the interrogator believe it. This happens more frequently than most people think. The interrogator is just another human being. In any case, as the interrogation proceeds, the prisoner can elaborate and develop the legend or cover story, especially if he has had the foresight to appear to be very confused and mixed up in the beginning. If gaps in the cover story become apparent, the prisoner can think up lies to insert. As the interrogation proceeds, he can rehearse these lies with the interrogator until the prisoner himself begins to believe the story. If, after a long time, the prisoner is forced to make a false confession he can use his fall-back cover story and go through the same routine as he did with the first story. Finally, if and when the prisoner is brought to admit that the fall-back cover story was a lie, *he should go back to the original cover story,* telling the interrogator that he had told the truth the first time and then had been forced to lie and now can think of nothing but to tell the truth. It should be noted, and remembered, that the truth would quite possibly not be believed in any case. It has been the experience of many prisoners who, at an early stage, made a truthful confession, *that they received the same treatment as if they had lied.* The reason is that the opponent expects the prisoner to lie and very often has no way of telling how much of his story is true and how much is false, most cover stories being a mixture of truth and falsehood.

During interrogation it is well to try to distract the attention of the interrogator from sensitive items of information. This can be done by pretending to conceal information of secondary importance in such a way as to get the interrogator interested in prying it out of the suspect. For example, a prisoner who has no confederates can tell his story in such a way that the interrogator will conclude the prisoner must have had help. Eventually the prisoner can involve innocent persons—preferably persons loyal to the regime—thus causing the investigative apparatus to waste a great deal of energy and quite possibly to arrest and interrogate persons who cannot possibly provide assistance.

Combatting Arguments

The prisoner can expect to be assailed with many arguments, all intended to persuade him to cooperate. One argument that is frequently effective is the statement: "We know all about your activities anyway. What I am doing is giving you a chance to explain and justify yourself." While this argument seems silly to a man who is not in prison, it has been extremely effective with many prisoners. Threats and promises are often made in a linked fashion. For example, the prisoner may be told he will be executed as a war criminal unless he cooperates, in which case he may be redeemed and even allowed to go free. Particularly effective is the trick of minimization. The interrogator takes the position that the prisoner was a dupe, really did not intend to commit a terrible crime, was victimized by his superiors, did not understand what he was doing, and so forth. The interrogator says that he fully understands the prisoner's activities and reasoning and might do the same if he were in the prisoner's shoes. This technique is quite effective in inducing a prisoner to make small admissions. Once such small admissions have been made, they are used to pry more and more information out of the victim.

Another argument which is very effective when several persons in the same network have been arrested is based upon the natural distrust people have for each other. The interrogator will say or imply that the other persons arrested have long since confessed, putting the blame on the victim now being interrogated. The prisoner is then asked what he has to say in his defense, and if he believes he has been betrayed, he may easily fall into the trap of trying to put the blame on his accomplices. The only safe rule, no matter how overwhelming the evidence may be that others have confessed, is to stick to the story, and under no circumstances to attack one's associates.

Political arguments are often effective, especially against prisoners who do not know the inside story of Communist activities. People will be confused by long quotations from political authorities attacking their beliefs. It should be remembered that the devil himself can quote Scripture to his purpose. Often quotations from very great men, such as Abraham Lincoln, are twisted and edited to suit such purposes. Very effective is the "inevitable victory of Communism" approach. The prisoner is told that soon his homeland will be occupied by Communist forces and that he will be personally responsible for what happens to his family and friends if he does not cooperate. He will be told that Communist success is only a matter of time, and that he is wasting himself trying to prevent it. He will be told that he is pulling the chestnuts of other countries out of the fire, that he is a dupe of the capitalists, that his superiors are quislings and that the only way out is for him to help his enemies.

A particularly dangerous interrogator is a convert to Communism who was formerly on the prisoner's side of the fence. He can say, "I used to believe the same way that you do. I changed my mind for such and such reasons, and you can do the same." The convert can persuade the prisoner to hope that he too can be redeemed by conversion. After a long and miserable time in prison, this temptation becomes very strong. The best defense for the prisoner is to remember that conversion under duress is always suspect, and that, if the man interrogating him is a genuine convert, the circumstances of his conversion could not have involved duress.

A prisoner can sometimes waste a great deal of the interrogator's time by long and involved descriptions of trivial affairs and matters. This is particularly effective if, *from the beginning,* the prisoner has used complicated constructions and confusing non sequiturs in his explanations. When stopped in a rambling discourse, the clever prisoner flounders and gets mixed up, loses the thread of what he was saying and then winds up starting at the beginning once more. Most interrogators tend to let the prisoner talk in the hope that he will say something of value. In most Communist prisons the interrogator is required to report the prisoner's statements in writing. The more confused and rambling the information is, the more time-consuming and repulsive the task of transcription becomes.

In some circumstances it may be profitable for the prisoner to tell the interrogator that the day may come when the interrogator—like a number of the Nazi Gestapo—may find himself on trial as a war criminal. Some interrogators fear this ultimate fate. A prisoner can sometimes profitably attempt to involve the interrogator in an ideological discussion. Most Communists render lip service to Marxist ideology, but know as little about Marx as the average religious person knows about the Bible, the Torah, or the Koran. It does no harm to ask for Marxist literature. Anything which will delay or sidetrack the interrogation can be useful. Sometimes such literature will be supplied on demand, and the ingenious prisoner can contrive to waste the interrogator's time and energy in fruitless ideological discussions. The prisoner who knows the laws pertinent to his case can often quote [them] to help himself. Communist law is usually a farce, but it is a farce that Communists are expected to maintain.

Warning

In all cases, whether or not the prisoner undertakes to arouse the curiosity or the fears of the interrogator, great care must be taken not to arouse personal hostility. One of the most foolish and dangerous things a prisoner can do is to incur the personal hatred of the guards or the interrogators.

It is customary in most Communist prisons for the prisoner to be required to sign the written protocol of each day's interrogation. If the prisoner has had the foresight not to carry specimens of his own handwriting with him, he can sign the protocol in a distorted handwriting (which he should have memorized). However he signs, he should always first write, "I have read this document," and then cross his signature over this line of writing. This is legal in most Communist prisons and hinders the use of the signed protocol as if it were a signed confession. To the limits of his ability, the prisoner should refuse to countersign documents written in a language he does not understand.

Coping with Interrogator Tricks

In addition to environmental influences, direct accusation, and moral pressure, the prisoner will have to deal with a great many tricks of the interrogation trade. There are so many of these that a full catalogue is impossible. Most of the tricks, however, are relatively simple, and once one has studied the pattern of trickery and types of common tricks outlined below, one should readily be able to spot most of them. It should be noted that these tricks are not confined to Communist interrogators, but are used by police and other interrogators all over the world. The defense suggested will be discussed in connection with the individual approaches.

A most obvious trick which is still surprisingly effective is to ask the prisoner why he thinks he has been arrested. The trick is very simple and very often provokes the prisoner into making disclosures which the interrogator had never suspected. The best defense is some statement which fits into the cover arrangement. If, for example, the prisoner is posing as a national of some other country, he may [imply] that he has been arrested because it is the policy of the local government to persecute citizens of his country. Whatever explanation the prisoner volunteers should be along the line of imputing persecution, or error, or blackmail, or some other discreditable motive to the arresting authority. This is part of the basic posture of the prisoner of rejecting any implication that he could be guilty of an offense. As always, the reply should not be conspicuously clear. It is always safe to say one has no idea, but this reply is negative, and attacking is usually a better defense.

Sometimes the prisoner will find himself accused or suspected of activities in which he has never engaged. This can be a trap, for it is quite possible that the prisoner, in his haste to establish an alibi by proving where he really was at a given time, will provide the arresting authorities with information of great importance which they did not have and may not even have suspected to exist.

Sometimes elaborate scenarios are set up to induce the prisoner to believe that he is not, or not yet, under interrogation. For example, he may find himself awaiting processing in a cell with two or three other "prisoners," one or more of whom are actually informers. These persons will seek to involve him in a harmless conversation. The wise prisoner never forgets that *there is no harmless conversation in prisons.* The prisoner may be asked to fill out some simple form concerning his belongings, and involving notification of relatives, employer, or friends. By filling out such a form the prisoner may provide the interrogator with a specimen of his handwriting and often a great deal of useful information. If forced to fill out any forms, the prisoner is well advised to use a distorted handwriting and to put in false or misleading information. Occasionally an interrogator will pose as a technical specialist. That is to say, a "guest" of the interrogation staff will be left alone with the prisoner on the pretense that the interrogation has been interrupted to "talk shop." Depending on the cover story that the person under interrogation is supporting, he should or should not go along with this trick.

A particularly devastating trick is to compel the prisoner to tell his cover story or legend backwards. It is, therefore, a good idea, when memorizing a cover story, literally to learn it forwards and backwards.

When a question of alibi arises, that is to say, a determination of where the prisoner was at a certain time, the prisoner who has not lived his cover is especially vulnerable. For example, the prisoner may state that at a certain time he was at a certain hotel in a certain city. The interrogator makes a note of this and then, after some hours or days have passed, calls the prisoner in and says that he has investigated the alibi and asks the prisoner whether he noticed any unusual event during his alleged stay at the hotel. Conversely, the interrogator may tell the prisoner that at the time he was supposedly at the hotel, there was a hold-up or some other spectacular event. This he will do in the course of a "conversation" and the prisoner, in his effort to sustain his alibi, may go along with the interrogator's fabrication and so trap himself. The interrogator, of course, may not let the prisoner know that he has been trapped. The best defense of a prisoner who has not been at the place he claims to have been is to plan in advance to claim a place where he could have been sleeping at the time something unusual occurred. He could, for example, in the hotel situation, easily have missed even a fire in some other part of the hotel through being asleep.

The interrogator may have an enormous file on his desk and look into it from time to time as if reading about the prisoner. He may speak as if he knows a great deal, dropping names, mentioning addresses, even telephone numbers. This type of technique can be exploited to the prisoner's advantage, for the interrogator, in his efforts to impress the prisoner, may let slip many valuable items of information, including the extent of his own ignorance.

Some interrogators have success with very simple tricks such as staring silently at the bridge of the suspect's nose. This gives the suspect the feeling that the interrogator is looking through him. Most persons cannot stand a sustained silence. The wise prisoner will simply sit and stare back.

Sometimes interrogators resort to very persistent and detailed questioning about matters about which the prisoner has no knowledge, with the result that, when a question is slipped in to which the prisoner can provide a satisfactory answer, he will feel relieved and let fall information he should keep to himself.

Sometimes a prisoner is plied with questions which make no sense. Most persons worry about losing their minds or at least self-control in such situations and naturally assume that they themselves are slipping, when in fact the interrogators are deliberately talking nonsense. It is a good idea to play around with this trick to keep the interrogator talking nonsense as long as possible, as this gains one time.

On occasion prisoners are stripped naked and made to stand before one or more interrogators for long periods of time. Sensitive individuals find this extremely trying. We all rely upon our clothing to sustain our image and our status. One good defense against this kind of thing is to begin to cough and sneeze and tremble and to show preoccupation with the physical rather than the mental result of such indignity.

A common expedient is to upgrade the prisoner's living conditions as he becomes more cooperative. He may begin prison life in a dank or mosquito infested cell and advance to a cell which may even have a carpet and a private toilet. He may be confined with other prisoners who pretend to have a dreaded disease, such as tuberculosis, a venereal disease, or a skin disease, or even leprosy.[2]

A prisoner of importance may find himself in the hands of a "medical" specialist who gives him psychological examinations and may tell him he is on the verge of insanity and suggest that he take some injection. Everyone has heard rumors of the use of truth serums and other debilitating drugs, "brainwashing" drugs, and the like, and many persons are disposed to feel that no one could blame them for confessing when confronted with or injected with drugs.

As a matter of fact, a determined person can successfully resist truth serums and other chemical gadgets. It is obviously very frightening to be visited by a *soi-disant* medical specialist suggesting shock treatments, nerve resection, frontal lobotomy, or castration as a means of "helping" the prisoner to become "normal." These expedients lose their effectiveness, however, if the prisoner realizes they are tricks, and that a prison administration will not usually countenance any such activities.

The Cuban interrogators have used a particularly devastating expedient to

2. Persons who have visible leprosy are no longer infectious. Tuberculosis bacteria exist everywhere in prisons anyway. Venereal disease cannot generally be communicated without the cooperation of the victim.

break the will of prisoners who resist: the false firing squad. A common variation of this trick is to have the prisoner brought out to witness the execution of some other prisoner. Sometimes the execution is real and sometimes it is staged. He then is told his turn is next, he is blindfolded and led to the stake, a volley of blank cartridges is fired. The effect of this is naturally overwhelming and is heightened when the prisoner is told, after he discovers he is still alive, that the next time he may not be so lucky and then he is given one more chance to tell his story. One defense against this trick is the knowledge that *he will not be executed as long as he has not provided the information the regime seeks.* As a matter of fact, prisoners nowadays are seldom executed without some form of trial, even in Communist areas, because of the effect upon the prison administration of allowing too much arbitrary mistreatment of prisoners. As far as is known, Communist services make little use of electromechanical "lie detectors" or polygraphs, apparently because the general hypocrisy and paranoia of Communist societies make it impossible to get reliable results. On occasion some trickery employing a machine represented to be a "lie detector" may be employed. The person interrogated is best advised to deny any imputations by the machine that he is lying.

A variant of interrogation trickery that is as old as the hills but still traps many persons is the "good guy," "bad guy" trick. This is worked as follows: One interrogator consistently harasses, insults and badgers the suspect, accusing him of lying, threatens him with violence, pushes him around and in general behaves very badly. The other interrogator is a friendly and rather well-intentioned man who plays the role of the friend of the prisoner, attempting to restrain the "bad guy" and protect the prisoner. Eventually the prisoner is left alone with the "good guy" who then attempts to win the prisoner's confidence by condemning his colleague. Strange as it seems, many a prisoner falls for this trick. Most persons are now aware of the existence of mirror windows or two-way mirrors and realize that someone may be watching them. Ordinary mirrors, however, are occasionally used so that the interrogator can watch the prisoner and his reactions while appearing to look elsewhere. The interrogator may go to some other part of the room to fumble with a drawer or some other object and casually make a remark to the prisoner which contains frightening implications, and observe how the prisoner reacts when he does not believe he is under observation.

Interrogators often seek to aggravate a prisoner by pointing out such signs of guilt as sweating, crossing and uncrossing of legs, nail biting, blushing, or aversion of the eyes. Persons not guilty of anything become exceedingly nervous and uncomfortable when under interrogation. In point of fact, only hardened criminals and aberrant personalities of certain types behave calmly in such a situation. The best defense is to say one is always nervous and ill-at-ease when interrogated or questioned or even in conversations. The display of horrible photographs of bombing victims, murder victims, or other atrocities occurs occasionally. The interrogator calls to the prisoner's attention that he is responsible for atrocities. This provocation has two objectives. It can make a person feel guilty, or it can provoke him into attempting to justify the acts of the power he supports. The best defense is to deplore these misfortunes and to take no stand whatsoever with regard to them.

The prisoner finds himself in a particularly hazardous situation when he makes some small admission and the interrogator tries to use this to pry more information out of him. Of course, "the longest journey beings with a single step," but there is no law that says that a person, having made one step, necessarily has to take further steps. An admission or a slip of the tongue can be used by the resolute prisoner to lure the interrogator up a false trail.

Some interrogators will provide the prisoner with pencil and paper and demand that he write his life history. This is a very tiring and time-consuming activity. If the prisoner has maintained his posture of confusion effectively, there is nothing to prevent him from preparing a most confused biography. A great deal of time can be gained in this way, as well as much peace and quiet for recovery of equilibrium and review of the situation.

The prisoner should conceal all knowledge of foreign languages, as far as possible. The interrogator will be very interested to identify the foreign languages spoken by the prisoner and may use a number of tricks, such as suddenly addressing the prisoner in a language he is suspected to know, or speaking to a third person in this language, while observing the prisoner. He may say something uncomplimentary or startling about the prisoner, seeking to cause a visible reaction. If a strange language is spoken in his presence, the prisoner should always make the appearance of trying to hear and understand what is said. Many prisoners who know a foreign language act ostentatiously uninterested in such a situation, but the normal behavior of a man who does not know a language is to listen attentively in the effort to catch a word here and there, finally to give up and lose interest.

Prison informers are not usually brought forward while there is intensive interrogation, but may be after the prisoner has been interrogated or if he is held indefinitely in detention pending investigation. The prison informer can be exceedingly dangerous or useful depending upon the skill of the intended victim. It is wise to regard all fellow prisoners as informers. Especially suspect, however, should be persons who warn the prisoner against other inmates of the jail, persons who are quite healthy in spite of the miserable prison conditions. The informer often has the task of discouraging a resistant prisoner. The prisoner should never lose sight of the fact that contact with an informer or other provocateur gives him an opportunity to supply deception information to the interrogation staff, while pretending to be telling the truth in confidence.

The interrogator will tell the prisoner, "we are alone and can talk completely privately." A tape recorder may be ostentatiously displayed and turned off so the prisoner can talk "off the record." Many fall for this although common sense should tell them that no prisoner is ever alone with any interrogator. Even if several people are not listening in on concealed microphones and recording on concealed machines, what the prisoner tells the interrogator will be told to everyone needing to know and often enough to the world-at-large. In fact, no prisoner can ever be sure he is truly alone anywhere. Not only are peepholes and audio devices easily employable, and closed circuit TV a possibility, but the prisoner may find himself quartered in a cell with a person he has every right to trust and who *is* in fact trustworthy, in order that concealed devices can pick up their conversation. Stool pigeons confined in a cell with a prisoner may point out a "hidden" microphone and involve him in a discussion outside its range, where another microphone is known to them to be hidden.

Propaganda Exploitation

One of the most painful ordeals the agent-prisoner has to undergo is the attempt of the apprehending service to exploit him for propaganda purposes. Efforts may be made to get him to denounce his sponsors and the regime he has been serving in favor of the Communist system, both on paper and in public before cameras. Depending on the intentions of the Communists, the prisoner may have to undergo a show trial or some other legal farce. Show trials usually require that the prisoner rehearse his part in the show until it is letter perfect. Commonly, he will be rehearsed in a story which displays him as pleading for mercy and as the victim and/or accomplice of a capitalist machination.

One gambit used with success in many cases is to invite or allow the prisoner to write one or more letters to his loved ones. These letters must conform in many parts to a prescribed text. If the agent has prepared for this contingency in advance by arranging a simple open code with his loved ones, he can use this opportunity to convey useful information. The code must be simple and cannot convey complicated ideas. Provision in such a code should be made to send at least the following messages:

a. What is stated about my situation is (is not) true.
b. I am (am not) being severely maltreated.
c. I suspect (know) I was betrayed by _____.
d. The enemy knows (does not know) who my accomplices were.
e. The enemy has a source in _____.

In some show trials, prisoners have had the courage to denounce their rehearsed pleas. In the case of a prominent prisoner this action may have some value, as the foreign press may be represented or hear of it. However, in the average show trial no reporters other than Communist sympathizers will be in the courtroom. The most heroic conduct on the part of a prisoner ordinarily will not be mentioned by such persons. As a rule, therefore, the prisoner should aim to make himself as uninteresting and useless for propaganda purposes as possible. The propagandists do not like to put on a show with unreliable persons—or persons who show symptoms of crippling mental or physical mistreatment which might arouse the sympathy of an audience. All trials end with a predetermined verdict on which courtroom conduct, unless it is bitterly hostile to the Communists, will have no effect.

The thing to bear in mind in refusing cooperation in propaganda exercises is that *in the long run* it will have no effect on the fate of the prisoner whether he complies or not. On balance he will probably be better off if he does not comply. For some reason, the Communists tend to inflict more suffering and demands on the weak than on the strong.

At times the prisoner may be trapped by technical devices used without his knowledge. He may be asked to review some propaganda statement out loud and then state what he thinks of it. A secret tape recorder will be set up to record his voice apparently saying what in fact is merely being read. It is, therefore, advisable for anyone given anything to read to read it in silence. Sometimes statements of the prisoner are taken out of context and merged with something he said elsewhere to make a damaging statement. There is little the prisoner can do to guard himself against an effort of this kind unless he says nothing at all, which is always a method to be tried but can seldom be sustained long if the interrogator chooses to employ drastic measures.

Penitentiary, Escape, Release

Once the prisoner has passed through the sentencing procedure, the interest of the authorities in his case declines very sharply, although attempts may later be made to recruit him as an informer. The prisoner should bear in mind that entry into a penitentiary with a long sentence does not necessarily mean that he will serve this sentence. Important captured Communist agents are from time to time exchanged for agents of the West. From time to time there are diplomatic negotiations, as in the case of the Cuban and the East German prisoners, resulting in the release of thousands of individuals who had resigned themselves to many years in prison. There is the possibility of escape. There is the possibility of the overthrow of a Communist regime. This is a danger that the regime is constantly preoccupied with. In the recent case of Czechoslovakia, an explosion of the entire Communist system in Europe was thought to be imminent. This can and will happen again and again, possibly with increasing frequency. The prisoner should bear these consoling factors in mind.

In the penitentiary or concentration camp the prisoner will again find human association. Among the prisoners he meets there will be persons with whom he can cooperate, but there will also be secret informers against whom he must defend himself and whom he can also exploit by telling them whatever it is he wants the authorities to believe. The prisoner should always beware of special officers in the prison who have a stature higher than the guard personnel, especially "welfare officers" or "morale officers," or "political indoctrination officers." These are very often state security service men responsible not only for keeping an eye on the prisoners, but for watching the guards. Some of the guards will be extremely venal and others will hate the regime.

The prisoner should look upon himself in the penitentiary as continuing the fight in a special situation, not simply as a man who is out of action until release. His conspiratorial skills and training can be used to good advantage in the prison. He can learn a great deal more about conspiracy in the prison. This is, after all, the school of conspiracy in which the Communists learned their trade. A prison is, in a very real sense, a typical Communist country in miniature. Skillful and determined prisoners have effectively operated within such penitentiaries safely and for long periods of time to create great difficulties for the prison administration, organize escapes, subvert guard personnel, and sabotage the installation.

In considering escape plans and confederates, the prisoner must never forget that the prison administration from time to time may induce provocateurs to suggest escape, and thus dupe the prisoners, later visiting heavy additional punishment on them. A provocation of this kind generally destroys escape ideas for quite a long time.

A provocation which is elaborate, but sometimes is used, is to allow the prisoner to escape in company with another prisoner who is actually a member of the security service. Usually the escape is "miraculous" and the prime mover is the provocateur. The intent is to win the confidence of the prisoner. In a variant of this trick, the prisoners escape and meet the confederates of the provocateur, who profess to distrust the prisoner, consider him a stool, become very angry, and threaten to kill him unless he can prove his loyalty by proving that he has been operating against the regime. The temptation to betray operations and contacts under such conditions is strong. The best defense is to say nothing on the grounds that one can never trust anyone and take one's chances, for it is after all by no means unusual for one prisoner to help another escape without ulterior motives.

The prospects and conditions governing physical escape and subsequent evasion of controls vary so widely that only very general rules can be given here:

a. Be careful whom you trust (see above on types of provocations).
b. Be realistic as to the prospects of success: it is one thing to get out of a prison; it is quite another to get out of the country, and it may be foolish to try physical escape if other factors are tending to promote the chances of early release. Prison guards may be lax because there are other obstacles to escape beyond the perimeter.
c. Do not aggravate your situation by committing serious crimes in the escape effort; for example, murdering a guard will usually result in a death sentence. Of course, there may be occasions of active warfare in which the prisoner in his escape action is in effect undertaking guerrilla warfare. This is not commonly the case, however, for a secret agent arrested in alien territory.
d. Beware of becoming involved in escape plots from which you may later want to withdraw. The other plotters may decide you know too much.
e. Above all, never become involved with persons who are sincere but indiscreet.

Release from prison can come about, as already mentioned, through a number of factors over which the prisoner has no control. One of the ways to get out of enemy custody most easily is to get oneself recruited as a double agent, that is to say, to let oneself be "turned." The hostile service, of course, is aware of this, but sometimes has no choice but to try to recruit agents from among its captives. It is well for the agent to memorize the factors which can make him a desirable "turn around" for his captors:

a. Special access or other capability to accomplish something for them.
b. Lack of publicity in his case.
c. Fundamental "job loyalty." If a man conveys the impression that he has desperately and loyally defended the interests of his sponsor so long as he thought the sponsor was in the right, only turning his coat when he came to see how wrong his sponsor was, he will win a great deal more trust than if he gives the impression of merely yielding to pressure.
d. "Unpacking." In general, before a person will be considered really "doubled," he will have had to make a full confession of his activities. It is possible to display the appearance of this provided the planning has been thorough, even while concealing vital information. The agent can best plan his ultimate "confession" (really a third cover story) at his leisure in his cell after he has had many sessions with his interrogators and has discovered what they actually know. He can devise a story which explains the known factors and makes

him look attractive from the point of view of *potential* to do things the opponent wants him to do. Woven into the story should be factors which induce the opponent to think he can *control* the potential "double agent" through blackmail. For example, the prisoner in the course of "unburdening his soul" can confess to serious but not easily checkable misdeeds, such as embezzlement or fraud. Confession to crimes such as murder is fine, provided investigation by the opponent will confirm that such a crime was in fact committed, the guilty person not apprehended, and the prisoner could have committed it. The prisoner may "betray" an ambition to become a figure of power in his homeland which can only be realized by collaboration with the enemy. The prisoner must be very careful in pretending to become "converted" to the opponent's faith. Protesting too much is usually suspect, but true believers seeking converts are often quite vulnerable to being deceived by the pretense of belief on the part of others. Easy capitulation is, of course, fatal to any hopes of emerging as a double agent.

Most prisoners in jail for clandestine operations find themselves free as a result of one or another event unexpectedly and suddenly. A word of caution is in order: There is a tremendous temptation to share one's joy and information with all one encounters in the first wild elation of release. This should be rigorously suppressed, for only harm can come from spontaneous disclosures, even when fully true, to unauthorized persons before coordination with the original sponsor has been effected. Publicity may for example alert the person who betrayed the prisoner, so that he may escape or destroy evidence. Whatever is said will be twisted by certain publications to the detriment of sponsors, friends, and relatives and thus may endanger innocent persons. Public recriminations against the Communists for treatment received in prison can hinder the release of other prisoners, and possibly damage secret operations which are under way. For maximum effect, release stories have to be enriched with information not known to the released or escaped person, and publicized at the right time and place. It may be desirable to avoid any publicity, as this may be just what the opposition hoped to achieve.

Above all, the prisoner should never forget that one can turn almost any situation to one's advantage with a little luck and careful planning.

31.

"Double agent" operations are counterespionage's bread and butter or at least the frosting on its cake. They are the animator of intelligence fiction. They can also be expounded soberly and systematically, as in this article, by an experienced operations officer.

Observations on the Double Agent

JOHN P. DIMMER, JR.

The double agent operation is one of the most demanding and complex counterintelligence activities in which an intelligence service can engage. Directing even one double agent is a time-consuming and tricky undertaking that should be attempted only by a service having both competence and sophistication. Competence may suffice for a service that can place legal controls upon its doubles, but services functioning abroad—and particularly those operating in areas where the police powers are in neutral or hostile hands—need professional subtlety as well.

Other requisites are that the case officer directing a double agent have a thorough knowledge of the area and language, a high order of ability in complex analytic reasoning, a thorough grounding in local laws governing espionage, enough time from other duties to run the operation well and report it well, a detailed understanding of the adversary service or services (and of any liaison service that may be involved), adequate control of the agent's communications, including those with the adversary, a full knowledge of his past (and especially of any prior intelligence associations), a solid grasp of his behavior pattern (both as an individual and as a member of a national grouping), and rapport in the relationship with him.

Like all other intelligence operations, double agent cases are run to protect and enhance the national security. They serve this purpose principally by providing current counterintelligence about hostile intelligence and security services and about clandestine subversive activities. The service and officer considering a double agent possibility must weigh net national advantage thoughtfully, never forgetting that a double agent is, in effect, a condoned channel of communication with the enemy.

John P. Dimmer, Jr., "Observations on the Double Agent," *Studies in Intelligence*, vol. 6, no. 1 (Winter 1962), pp. 57–72. Originally classified "Secret."

Some Western services have become highly skilled through long experience with double agent cases and other counterespionage operations. Of the Communist Bloc services, the Soviets manifest patience and a conceptual pattern both intricate and inherently consistent; to create or enhance confidence in an important double agent they are willing to sacrifice through him information of sufficient value to mislead the reacting service into accepting his bona fides. They make extensive use of provocateurs to establish double agents, especially among émigrés. Not much is known about Chinese Communist capabilities in this specialty; available indications suggest mediocrity. The remainder of the Bloc is spotty: the North Koreans are amateurish, the Hungarians and Czechs have demonstrated competence, and the Poles, maintaining an old tradition, show a level of skill (but not of resources) approaching that of the Soviets. We Americans have acquired a broad range of experience since our entry into World War II, but twenty years is not enough time for mastering such an art. We are especially unversed in active and passive provocation.

His Nature and Origins

A double agent is a person who engages in clandestine activity for two intelligence or security services (or more in joint operations), who provides information about one or about each to the other, and who wittingly withholds significant information from one on the instructions of the other or is unwittingly manipulated by one so that significant facts are withheld from the adversary. Peddlers, fabricators, and others who work for themselves rather than a service are not double agents because they are not agents. The fact that doubles have an agent relationship with both sides distinguishes them from penetrations, who normally are placed with the target service in a staff or officer capacity.

The unwitting double agent is an extremely rare bird. The manipulative skill required to deceive an agent into thinking that he is serving the adversary when in fact he is damaging its interests is plainly of the highest order.

The way a double agent case starts deeply affects the operation throughout its life. Almost all of them begin in one of the three ways following:

The Walk-In or Talk-In. This agent appears in person, sends an intermediary, makes a telephone call, writes a letter, or even establishes radio contact to declare that he works for a hostile service and to make an offer to turn against it. Although the danger of provocation is always present, some walk-ins and talk-ins have proved not only reliable but also very valuable.

The Agent Detected and Doubled. A service discovering an adversary agent may offer him employment as a double. His agreement, obtained under open or implied duress, is unlikely, however, to be accompanied by a genuine switch of loyalties. The so-called redoubled agent—one whose duplicity in doubling for another service has been detected by his original sponsor and who has been persuaded to reverse his affections again—also belongs to this dubious class. Many detected and doubled agents degenerate into what are sometimes called "piston agents" or "mailmen," who change their attitudes with their visas as they shunt from side to side. Operations based on them are little more than unauthorized liaison with the enemy, and usually time-wasting exercises in futility. A notable exception is the detected and unwillingly doubled agent who is relieved to be found out in his enforced service to the adversary.

The Provocation Agent. The active provocateur is sent by Service A to Service B to tell B that he works for A but wants to switch sides. Or he may be a talk-in rather than a walk-in. In any event, the significant information that he is withholding, in compliance with A's orders, is the fact that his offer is being made at A's instigation. He is also very likely to conceal one channel of communication with A—for example, a second secret writing system. Such "side-commo" enables A to keep in full touch while sending through the divulged communications channel only messages meant for adversary eyes. The provocateur may also conceal his true sponsor, claiming for example (and truthfully) to represent a Satellite military services whereas his actual control is the KGB—a fact which the Soviets conceal from the Satellite as carefully as from us.

The passive provocation, or "stake-out," is a subtler member of the tribe. In Country C, Service A surveys the intelligence terrain through the eyes of Service B (a species of mirror-reading) and selects those citizens whose access to sources and other qualifications make them most attractive to B. Service A then recruits from these and waits for B to follow suit. The stake-out has a far better chance of success in areas like Africa, where intelligence exploitation of local resources is far less intensive, than in Europe, where persons with valuable access are likely to have been approached repeatedly by recruiting services during the postwar years.

Sometimes a double agent operation is turned over by a liaison service to a U.S. service or by one U.S. service to another. When such a transfer is to be made, the inheriting service ought to delve into the true origins of the case and acquire as much information as possible about its earlier history.

For predictive purposes the most important clue imbedded in the origins of an operation is the agent's original or primary affiliation, whether it was formed voluntarily or not, the length of its duration, and its intensity. In extreme cases the agent may have volunteered or willingly agreed to work for a hostile service before the U.S. case officer who is now weighing the merits of doubling him was even born. The effects of years of clandestine association with the adversary are deep and subtle; the American case officer working with a double agent of Russian origin against, say, the KGB should never forget that the agent and his Soviet case officer share deep bonds of language and culture, even if the agent is profoundly anti-Communist.

Another result of lengthy prior clandestine service is that the agent may be hard to control. In most operations the case officer's superior training and experience give him so decided an edge over the agent that recognition of this superiority makes the agent more tractable. But add to the fact that the experienced double agent may have been in the business longer than his U.S. control his further advantage in having gained a first-hand comparative knowledge of the workings of at least two disparate services, and it is obvious that the case officer's margin of superiority diminishes, vanishes, or even is reversed.

The Value of His Services

The nature and value of the double agent's functions depend greatly on his personal ability as well as on his mission for the other service. He can always report on the objectives and conduct of this mission and possibly more broadly on the positive and counterintelligence targets of the other service or on its plans. If he is skillful and well trained, he can do valuable work by exploiting the weaknesses of others: all intelligence officers of any service, despite their training, have some weaknesses. Some are loose-mouthed, some like to drink, others tend to brag.

The case officer may find his agent to be a wonderful fellow and confide in him, putting him in a good position to elicit specific information and making him the recipient of all manner of unsolicited information. The agent may be able to learn the operational techniques, the security practices, the training methods, and the identity of other members of the service. Possibly, if at a high enough level, he may even be able to report the policies and intentions of the government. Although such a double agent is extraordinary, there are on record some whose reports have been of major national importance. Normally, however, the double agent does not have access to such information.

Often a double agent, after a period of time, is able to report on the capabilities of the other service, if not directly at least by giving information on his own handling from which specific capabilities can be inferred. For example, he can report on the type of support given him in servicing dead drops, providing accommodation addresses, arranging transportation, and supplying technical equipment. If he has been issued some modern technical device, say an automatic transmitter, it can logically be concluded that the service has a good support capability.

The double agent often has access through his travels for the other service to positive intelligence on that country, or on third countries of interest to the controlling service. But even when his mission does not afford such opportunities, he is always able to report his observations of the other service. These bits of information can be accumulated until they give a picture of the other service's administrative practices, its personnel, and possibly its liaison with other intelligence and security services. Debriefing for this purpose in minute detail is time-consuming, however, and it is a real problem to strike the right balance in the agent's time between extensive debriefing and running him back into the other service.

The double agent serves also as a controlled channel through which information can be passed to the other service, either to build up the agent in its estimation or for purposes of deception. Often operational build-up material is passed first to establish a better reception for the deception material: obviously the greater the stature of the agent in the eyes of the other service, the better the reception of the reports he provides. In the complex matter of deception we may distinguish here between operational deception, that concerning the service's own capabilities, intentions, and control of the agent, and national deception, that concerning the intentions of the controlling government or other components of it. National deception operations are usually very delicate, frequently involving the highest levels of the government, and therefore require prior coordination and approval at the national headquarters level.

The double agent channel can be used by the controlling service to insert data into the mechanisms of the other service with a number of possible objectives—for example, to detect its activities in some field. The inserted material is designed to induce certain actions on the part of the other service, which are then observed through another operation or group of operations. The material has to be designed very skillfully if it is to deceive the other service and produce the desired reactions. A sophisticated operation of this type is most likely to be used when the stakes are high or the case complicated. Such a situation might arise if a case officer handling several operations wanted to set up still another and needed to find out in advance what the pertinent operational pattern was. The passing of data through the double agent channel for the consumption of the other service for whatever purpose requires a great deal of knowledge about the other service.

A double agent may serve as a means through which a provocation can be mounted against a person, an organization, an intelligence or security service, or any affiliated group to induce action to its own disadvantage. The provocation might be aimed at identifying members of the other service, at diverting it to less important objectives, at tying up or wasting its assets and facilities, at sowing dissension within its ranks, at inserting false data into its files to mislead it, at building up in it a tainted file for a specific purpose, at forcing it to surface an activity it wanted to keep hidden, or at bringing public discredit on it, making it look like an organization of idiots. The Soviets and some of the Satellite services, the Poles in particular, are extremely adept in the art of conspiratorial provocation. All kinds of mechanisms have been used to mount provocation operations; the double agent is only one of them.

There is still another important function the double agent can perform. He can provide a channel for a recruitment or defection operation against the other service. If he is shrewd and personable enough to have succeeded in establishing a psychological ascendancy over his case officer in the other service, he may be able to recruit him or persuade him to defect. If the attempt fails, of course, the whole operation has to be terminated. In a double agent operation that is valuable only for a certain span of time or one that for any reason is about to collapse, there may be an opportunity at the point of termination to use the agent to make a recruitment or defection approach. The agent can be instructed to make his last job a pitch to the other service's case officer, revealing that he has been under the control of the opposing service for x number of years, pointing out that the case officer's name will be mud when he returns to his headquarters, and suggesting that he may as well save his skin and make a switch. In this attempt the agent might be limited to planting the seed, or he might carry through the complete recruitment or defection.

Occasionally a service runs a double agent whom it knows to be under the control of the other service and therefore has little ability to manipulate or even one who it knows has been successfully redoubled. The question why a service sometimes does this is a valid one. One reason for us is humanitarian: when the other service has gained physical control of the agent by apprehending him in a denied area, we often continue the operation even though we know that he has been doubled back because we want to keep him alive if we can. Another reason might be a desire to determine how the other service conducts its double agent operations or what it uses for operational build-up or deception material and from what level it is disseminated. There might be other advantages, such as deceiving the opposition as to the service's own capabilities, skills, intentions, etc. Perhaps the service might want to continue running the known redoubled agent in order to conceal other operations. It might want to tie up the facilities of the opposition. It might use the redoubled agent as an adjunct in a provocation being run against the opposition elsewhere.

Running a known redoubled agent is like playing poker against a professional who has marked the cards but who presumably is unaware that you can read the backs as well as he can.

Sometimes, although infrequently, double agent operations are started for propaganda purposes. A Soviet-controlled provocateur works for a Western service for a year or two and is then pulled back home, where he is surfaced on the radio and in press interviews to denounce his former Western spy masters. More frequently the Soviets use this trick to get added mileage from an operation that is dying anyway.

Finally, liaison services running a double agent jointly against an adversary quite naturally use this opportunity to assay each other's capabilities. There is nothing perfidious in this practice as long as it is kept within bounds. Unless the U.S. service operating from a friendly country, for example, can realistically gauge its host's capabilities in such vital matters as physical surveillance, phone taps, and hostile interrogation, the operation is likely to go awry.

Controlling Him

Since a good deal of nonsense about control sometimes crops up in our thinking about double agents, a definition is first in order. Control is the capacity of a case officer (and his service) to generate, alter, or halt agent behavior by using or indicating his capacity to use physical or psychological means of leverage. A case officer does not control an agent the way he controls an automobile. And a case officer working overseas does not control a double agent the way a policeman controls an informer. The intelligence officer who thinks of control in absolutes of black and white does his operation a disservice; the areas of gray predominate.

First, the U.S. case officer running an operation abroad usually lacks executive powers. Second, the very fact that the double has contact with the opposition affects control. For example, pressure exerted bluntly or blindly, without insight into the agent's motivation and personality, may cause him to tell the truth to the adversary as a means of escaping from a painful situation. Before the case officer pushes a button on the agent's control panel he should know what is likely to happen next. Finally, the target service inevitably exercises some control over the double agent, if only in his performance of the tasks that it assigns to him. In fact, it is a primary principle of the counterintelligence service not to disrupt hostile control of the positive half of the operation and thus tip its CI hand. Even if the positive side is being run so poorly that the misguided agent is in danger of coming to the attention of local authorities whose intervention would spoil the CI aspect too, the case officer must restrain his natural impulse to button up the adversary's operation for him. At the very most , he can suggest that the agent complain to the hostile case officer about insecure practices, and then only if the agent's sophistication and relationship with that case officer make such a complaint seem normal.

Complete physical control of the double agent is rare in peacetime situations. Normally it is achieved only over the agent captured in war. Limited physical control, however, may be exercised in varying degrees: an agent may have his home in an area where he is subject to complete surveillance or he may live in an uncontrolled area but work in a controlled installation.

The degree to which an agent's communications can be controlled runs closely parallel with the degree to which he is physically controlled. Communications control, at least partial, is essential: the agent himself is controlled to a considerable extent if his communications are controlled. But even when his communications are completely controlled, a well-trained agent doubled against his will can appear to be cooperating but manage at an opportune moment to send a signal to his own service indicating that he is under duress. A number of captured wartime Soviet, British, and German agents did manage to get off such signals.

With only partial control, if the agent is in communication with the opposition service through a courier, dead drop, or live drop, some control or surveillance has to be established over these meetings or servicings. The double agent who makes trips in and out of the area where he can be physically controlled presents a multiplicity of problems.

Assessing His Potential

Acquisition of a double agent may be the result of a deliberate follow-up of leads, or it may be opportunistic. The counterintelligence screening process that forms part of security programs produces many leads. Others may arise in the course of positive operations. Opportunistic acquisition, as of a walk-in, has the disadvantage of being unexpected and therefore unplanned for: the decision to run a double agent should be made only after a great deal of thought, assessment, and evaluation, and if the candidate comes as a volunteer, the service may have to act without sufficient time for reflection. In this situation the necessity of assessing the candidate conflicts also with the preservation of security, particularly if the officer approached is in covert status. Volunteers and walk-ins are tricky customers, and the possibility of provocation is always present. On the other hand, some of our best operations have been made possible by volunteers. The test of the professional skill of an intelligence organization is its ability to handle situations of this type.

When a double agent candidate appears, judgments are needed on four essential questions in order to decide whether a potential operation exists, whether to run the candidate, and whether the service has the capability to do so.

Has he told you everything? Enough information can ordinarily be obtained in one or two sessions with the candidate to permit testing by polygraph, investigation of leads, and file checks. These steps must be taken very quickly because it is not possible to un-recruit a man. The two areas of possible concealment which are especially dangerous are prior intelligence ties and side-commo.

Does he have stayability? This term combines two concepts—his ability to maintain access to the counterintelligence target for the foreseeable future, and his psychological stamina under the constant (and sometimes steadily increasing) pressure of the double agent's role. If he lacks stayability he may still be useful, but the operation must then be planned for short range.

Does the adversary trust him? Indications of adversary trust can be found in the level of the communications system given him, his length of service, the seniority of the adversary case officer, the nature and level of requirements, and the kind and extent of training provided. If the opposition keeps the agent at arm's length, there is little prospect that doubling him will yield significant returns.

Can you control his commo both ways? Control of communications on your own side can be difficult enough, especially if the agent lives in hostile territory. But control of adversary channels is hard under even the best of circumstances. It requires a great deal of time, technical skill, and—as a rule—manpower.

Negative answers on one or even two of these questions are not ground for immediate rejection of the possible operation. But they are ground for requiring some unusually high entries on the credit side of the ledger.

The initial assessment is made essentially through interrogation, used in a broad sense to include friendly debriefing or interview. The interviewing officer may be relaxed and casual, but underneath the surface his attitude is one of deliberate purpose: he is trying to find out enough to make an initial judgment of the man. A human being in a stress situation is a complicated personality, and the interviewing officer must penetrate below the surface, sensing the man's emotions and mental processes. For instance, if an agent walks in, says he is a member of another service, and reveals information so sensitive that the other service would presumably not give it away just to establish the informant's bona fides, there are two possibilities: either the agent is telling the truth or he is attempting a provocation. Sometimes the manner in which the man conducts himself will suggest which of the two it is.

In addition to establishing the individual's true identity and examining his documents, the officer should get as many details as possible on the service he belongs to and his position in it. His job may be such that it is necessary to make a fast initial judgment: for example, he may be one of the two or three intelligence officers in a small office where a prolonged absence would cause suspicion.

It may be more difficult to determine the reason why the agent presented himself than to establish who he is and what service he represents, because motivation is a complex of mental and emotional drives. The question of the double agent's motivation is approached by the interviewing officer from two angles—the agent's professed reasons and the officer's own inferences from his story and behavior. The agent may profess a love for democracy, but the officer cannot elicit any convincing evidence of such a love. Some of the agent's reasons may not ring true. To decide between what the officer thinks the motive is and what the agent says it is is not easy, because double agents act out of a wide variety of motivations, sometimes psychopathic ones like a masochistic desire for punishment by both services. Others have financial, religious, political, or vindictive motives. The last are often the best double agents: they get pleasure out of deceiving their comrades by their every act day after day.

Making the judgment about the agent's psychological and physical suitability is also difficult. Sometimes a physician or psychiatrist can be called in under some pretext. For the most part, however, professional assistance is not available, and the interviewing officer must rely upon his own skill in assessing human beings and understanding what makes them tick. Such skill can be acquired only by experience.

Experience suggests that some people who take to the double agent role— perhaps a majority of willing ones, in fact—have a number of traits in common with the con man. Psychiatrists describe such persons as sociopaths. From the point of view of the double agent operation, here are their key traits:

— They are unusually calm and stable under stress but cannot tolerate routine or boredom.
— They do not form lasting and adult emotional relationships with other people because their attitude toward others is exploitative.
— They have above-average intelligence. They are good verbalizers— sometimes in two or more languages.
— They are skeptical and even cynical about the motives and abilities of others but have exaggerated notions about their own competence.
— Their reliability as agents is largely determined by the extent to which the case officer's instructions coincide with what they consider their own best interests.
— They are ambitious only in a short range sense: they want much and they want it now. They do not have the patience to plod toward a distant reward.
— They are naturally clandestine and enjoy secrecy and deception for its own sake.

In brief, the candidate must be considered as a person and the operation as a potential. Possibilities which would otherwise be rejected out of hand can be accepted if the counterintelligence service is or will be in a position to obtain and maintain an independent view of both the double agent and the case.

Perhaps such independent collateral can be acquired from another operation, in being or in the offing.

The officer's estimate of the potential value of the operation must take into consideration whether his service has the requisite personnel, facilities, and technical support; whether running the operation will prejudice other activities of his government; whether it will be necessary or desirable, at the outset or later, to share the case with foreign liaison; and whether the case has political implications.

Running the Operation: Do's and Don'ts

The following principles apply to the handling of all double agent operations in varying degrees. In composite they form a checklist against which going operations might be periodically reviewed—and given special examination with the appearance of danger signals.

1. Remember that testing is a continuous process. Use the polygraph early and run later tests as well. Be alert for changes in agent motivation. When you can do so securely, employ such additional means as further records investigation, checking out of operational leads, technical analysis of documents and equipment, surveillance and countersurveillance, mail and telephone taps, and substantive analysis of reporting. Although name traces cannot be run on every person mentioned by the agent, do not be stingy with them on persons who have familial, emotional, or business ties with him.

2. Train the agent, but only as a double. Give him training as needed in security of the doubled part of the operation, CI reporting, cover as a double, the handling of technical equipment used for CI purposes, etc. But do not poach on enemy territory by teaching him the skills he needs for adversary purposes. An "inexplicable" improvement in his work would draw suspicion.

3. Be careful about awakening in the hostile service an appetite which cannot later be satisfied without giving away too much. Do not furnish build-up material that transcends the agent's access or that will rouse adversary interest in sensitive areas. In general, let the agent carry out his adversary assignments on his own instead of spoon-feeding him, although there are exceptions to this rule.

4. Require the agent to report and, as security permits, turn over to you everything he gets from the other side—money, gifts, equipment, documents, etc. If he is permitted to hold out anything he may grow confused about which side he is working for. But do not be too rigid in following this rule. It may be better, for example, instead of confiscating his payments from the adversary, to put them into a third-country bank account and promise him the lump sum upon successful termination.

5. Avoid interference. Oblige the other service to solve any problems that arise from the agent's activity on its behalf. For example, if the agent is arrested or threatened with arrest by local authorities, the counterintelligence officer should not rush to his aid. The threatened agent should take his problem to the adversary, who may be forced to surface a new asset in order to help him. It should be explained to the agent that you are not indifferent but on the contrary too concerned about his security to blow him by meddling.

6. Be constantly alert for hostile provocation. The opposition may create a security crisis for the agent, or he may at their instigation report such a crisis. If he does, examine the claim thoroughly and test it.

7. If the adversary appears to be a Satellite service, do not lose sight of the possibility that the agent is being manipulated behind the scenes by the Soviets, probably without the Satellite's knowledge.

8. Keep analyzing the agent as well as the case. Do not be satisfied to fix a label (such as "anti-Communist") to him instead of learning to understand him.

9. If the agent is to pass classified U.S. information to the adversary, keep precise records of what was passed, which department or agency cleared the release, and the dates.

10. Do not plan a deception operation or pass deception material without prior headquarters approval.

11. Do not reveal your service's assets or CI knowledge to a double. It is vital that double agents be run within the framework of their own materials—the information which they themselves supply. Junior CI officers, especially, may be tempted to impress double agents with the omniscience of their service. The more you keep from an experienced double the information he should not have, the more he will be reassured that his own safety is in good hands.

12. Prepare all briefings carefully. Have the agent rehearse his instructions. If you think it advisable, brief him on resistance to interrogation; but be cautious, if you do, about revealing to him the specifics and scope of your knowledge of the adversary.

13. Mirror-read. Look at the operation from the viewpoint of the hostile service. But be careful not to impute to it the motives, ideas, methods, or other characteristics of your own service. Do not put the adversary in your place; put yourself in his, a task which requires both knowledge and understanding of him.

14. Do not run the operation in a vacuum. Be aware of any political implications that it may have, locally or internationally.

15. Do not hesitate to ask for help.

16. Review the case file periodically. Restudy of the operation sometimes throws into relief facts previously ignored, misinterpreted, or improperly

linked to one another. As new information develops, it will throw a new light on the old facts. And review cover now and then—for your service, yourself, the agent, and your meetings with him. Consider whether new developments require any changes.

17. Decide early in the operation how it will be terminated if the need arises. Do not merely drop it without further steps, leaving an unsupervised hostile agent in place. If he is to be turned over to a local security service, try to make the transfer while there is still some equity in it for them.

18. If the operation is joint, weigh its probable effect upon the liaison relationship.

19. Keep a full record, including dates, of all adversary assignments given the agent.

20. Report the case frequently, quickly, and in detail. The hostile services are centralized. Pitting against them the limited resources of one U.S. officer or field installation means giving them needlessly favorable odds. Only timely and full reporting to your headquarters will permit it to help you effectively.

32.

Even if "double agent" is loosely defined, rarely does one survive who is competent enough and is trusted enough by the final protectors to get away with composing a personal memoir of the experience, for publication and without a ghost writer. One such is the CIA veteran who wrote this article about performing as a double in his early career.

The Case of Major X

HANS MOSES

"Now it can be told: the biggest spy story since the Alger Hiss Case. It concerns the Russian spies who were . . . TRAPPED AT THE WASHINGTON MONUMENT."

That is how Jack Anderson and Fred Blumenthal, then known as the principal associates of the late Drew Pearson, captioned a feature story published in *Parade Magazine* on 6 January 1957. Theirs was probably the most interesting of the various stories on the same topic that had begun to appear in the press some three years earlier. In January 1953, two American residents of Vienna, Austria, Kurt Ponger and Otto Verber, had been arrested on espionage charges, and Yuriy Novikov, a Soviet diplomat accredited to Washington and linked to them in the indictment, had been declared *persona non grata*. Six months after their arrest, Ponger and Verber had pleaded guilty and had been sentenced to jail. Thus there had been no need for a trial, and most of the events leading to the legal climax were never disclosed.

Anderson and Blumenthal had set out to provide part of the missing background, and, perhaps, to dispel some of the mystery. For introductory purposes, their account is worth summarizing here. They related how Ponger, once an inmate of Nazi jails, had fled in 1939 to America, where two years later he met two fellow refugees, Otto Verber and his attractive sister Vera. In World War II, both men had enlisted in the U.S. Army, where Verber rose to the rank of Second Lieutenant and Ponger to Staff Sergeant. Both had maneuvered themselves into Army intelligence assignments, and later wangled jobs as interpreters at the Nuremberg war crimes trials, where they made contact with a professional spy. In 1948, Ponger married Vera Verber, who had meanwhile worked for a red spy ring in England. Ponger opened a press agency in Vienna,

Hans Moses, "The Case of Major X," *Studies in Intelligence,* vol. 18, no. 1 (Spring 1974), pp. 1–24. Originally classified "secret" and "No foreign dissem[ination]."

and [Otto] Verber helped by carrying the photographer's bag. In 1949, as *Parade* put it, Verber made one mistake: he solicited information from a U.S. Air Force officer—"Major X"—who happened to be a counter-intelligence officer.

The major's superiors instructed him to play along. This, the authors noted, was a delicate assignment: both spies had been trained by our own Army intelligence; both had served as interrogators at the war crimes trials; both had started by learning to parry questions in concentration camps. But "Major X" turned out to be their match. Ponger and Verber, masterminded by the scheming Vera, were duped into thinking he was an easy mark, and paid him in old, untraceable $20 bills for carefully phonied "secret" defense documents. "Major X," meanwhile, watching the spy ring over a period of four years, discovered that Ponger and Verber were only links in a spy network that reached all the way across the Atlantic into the Soviet Embassy in the United States. He thereupon doctored some seemingly vital documents which Verber and Ponger found so exciting that they arranged for "Major X" to carry them personally to their contact in Washington.

Thus, on a balmy April evening in 1951,[1] "Major X" passed his doctored data at the Washington Monument to a mysterious Russian who turned out to be a Soviet diplomat. The scene might have been staged in Hollywood, the authors observed; but the only cameras aimed at the meeting were operated by FBI agents hidden in the vicinity. Surveillance continued for two more years. Finally, when counter-intelligence had learned enough about the spy ring, they arrested Verber and Ponger and sent the Soviet diplomat packing.

I had a far more than ordinary interest in the Anderson-Blumenthal version of the events for, unbeknownst to the authors, I was the man they had dubbed "Major X." Thus I venture to call my own reminiscences of the operation "The Case of Major X," even though I do have a name, and I have never been a major. Like Ponger and Verber, I had left Europe in the late 1930s, and during and after World War II served in the infantry and in U.S. Army intelligence. In 1949, when the story began, I was a civilian employee of an air intelligence unit of the U.S. Army, not an Air Force officer.

The *Parade* story needs correction and elaboration in many other respects, if we are to view the case as intelligence officers rather than as magazine readers. Firstly, it was *not* a matter of one man's exploits against the Soviet spy system; it was a story of teamwork on one side against teamwork on the other.

Secondly, it was not a sequence of romantic adventures. Even though it had its share of excitement for the participants, it was mainly a grim and tedious

---

1. *Parade* evidently overlooked the fact that this date would not have allowed the aforementioned "four years" of observation.

operation, with more than a fair share of disappointment and frustration, which brought me as close to a breakdown as I would ever want to come. Thirdly, it was not a story of superior planning crowned by success; it was rather a tale of trial and error, with only partial successes.

Finally, it was not an operation run under perfect conditions, thoroughly supported by all security organs, to the undimmed benefit of the nation's security interests; it was a matter of give and take, of risk and compromise, and, I think, of well-suited as well as misapplied security considerations.

This raises a number of questions, among them the following:

1. Were American personnel, including myself, properly prepared for the method of approach used by Soviet agents?
2. Was the U.S. Government sufficiently well equipped and organized for this type of operation?
3. How, if at all, could we have gained more than we did?

These and related matters have long been debated by participants in the "Major X" case, and by others who have studied and analyzed it. It has been and continues to be a useful debate. My contribution to it can be made most informatively, I believe, in the form of an abbreviated chronological review. My account of these experiences is being offered here in print for the first time. Although I have provided some comments, it is my hope that the story for the most part will speak for itself.

Background

Of the two individuals mentioned, I came to know Verber much better, but I actually met Ponger first. In November 1946, when I was aboard ship headed for Europe, Ponger was one of my co-passengers. Like myself, he had been hired as a civilian government employee. I heard from others aboard the ship that he had a distinguished combat record with the Office of Strategic Services. Only once did I have any occasion to talk to him alone. At that time, he asked me if I intended ever to return to the United States. When I expressed my surprise at such a question, he informed me that he himself would never go back. What little he owed to the United States, he said, he had paid back a hundred times. The only ties he had anywhere bound him to Austria, where his family had once owned property which he would try to recover.

This was the last talk I had with Ponger for a number of years. Should it have given me a clue as to his real state of mind? Perhaps it should have. The fact remains that it did not. It appeared to indicate no more than an odd sort of attitude.

I saw both Ponger and Verber in 1947, when I was assigned to the war crimes trials in Nuremberg, where both of them worked as interrogators. Here I had no private contact with either of them, and the only observation I made was that Verber wrote good concise interrogation reports, whereas Ponger produced practically none at all. It is indeed possible, as *Parade* says, that they made contact with a professional spy there. If so, the fact is that no one seemed to know, or take notice.

My first more personal contact with Verber was made some time in 1948 in Vienna, where I had taken a civilian job with an air intelligence unit of the U.S. Army. Verber, originally a Viennese, had arrived in his old hometown as a student under the G.I. Bill and, I heard, also intended to go into the news business with Ponger, his brother-in-law. Verber occupied a house in the American sector in Vienna; Ponger lived in the Soviet sector.

In the months that followed, Ponger kept very much in the background. Verber I met at first casually. After I invited him, equally casually, to look me up some time, I was surprised when late in 1948 he paid me an unscheduled visit at the office, getting past the Austrian receptionist's desk by introducing himself as an old friend of mine. I found him extremely curious about two escaped Soviet fliers who had landed in Austria. Inasmuch as the story had just been published in the Austrian press, however, his curiosity seemed explainable.

There followed a period of social contact with Verber and his wife. Nothing remarkable seemed to happen during those days. The Verbers did their level best to teach us how to play bridge, but never quite succeeded. It may be significant that he maintained this kind of contact for several months without asking for information.

First Phase: The Approach

He made a different approach, however, in June 1949, when my family and I had returned to Austria from home leave. We were sitting in Verber's garden in the beautiful Viennese sunshine, sipping cool drinks and thinking everything was all right in the world, when Verber asked to talk to me privately. Broaching the subject of anti-Semitism in general, he charged that the U.S. Government was actually engaged in furthering anti-Semitic and pro-Nazi purposes. As examples, he mentioned former Nazi technicians and scientists, who normally would have been considered war criminals, and who now were being sent under secret contracts to the United States. Informants of American intelligence agencies in many cases were also former Nazis, he said. I could help the cause of anti-Nazism if I could give him the names of such people as they might become available to me in the course of my duties.

When I asked him how someone like myself could separate Nazis from non-Nazis, he told me I could leave that to him; as long as I gave him the names, he could find the criminals. When I wanted to know what he proposed to do about them once he knew their names, Verber said he could get the Israeli government to launch official protests. He had the necessary contacts, he said.

I would like to point out here how carefully Verber adjusted his approach to what he thought were my points of vulnerability. He did not try to persuade me to work for the Soviet Union or for Communism; that evidently would not have worked. Instead, he tried to take advantage of the fact that I was a Jew, an anti-Hitlerite, and a former employee of the war crimes trials. In effect, by implying that if there was any government involved it was Israel, he was using the classic recruitment tactic of the "false flag approach."

Launching the Operation

As it happened, his judgment was not very sound. I left him with the impression that I was going to think about his proposition, and I did think about it. In fact, on the very next working day, I invited my entire office staff to help me think. At least one of them had the idea that Verber might, consciously or unconsciously, be working for the Soviet Union. Accordingly, we checked his file at the counter-subversive section that same morning. There was, we found, no information on him, but quite a bit on his brother-in-law Ponger. There was enough reason for me to make a written report of the incident. I did this with mixed feelings, and requested that I be allowed to stay away from Verber in the future.

If my request had been granted, there would be no story to tell. But after an interval of a few days, I was asked through the local CIC office to stay in touch with Verber, and report on possible subversive activities. I agreed to do what I could, especially since such an investigation seemed to have its intriguing possibilities. I then made my next appointment with Verber.

(At this point, the 1949 Cold War atmosphere in Vienna is portrayed by a senior CIA operating officer who at the time was the senior U.S. civilian air intelligence officer in Vienna, and the author's direct superior.)

The visitor to contemporary Vienna will see little tangible record beyond the Soviet Memorial in Schwarzenberg Platz of the city's most recent military occupation, nor sense anything of the atmosphere of sometimes lethal clandestine combat of the first few years following the end of military hostilities in 1945. Viewers of "The Third Man" may dismiss mention of the hazards of the "Soviet Era" of Vienna as fanciful melodramatics. But the Soviet troops, moving freely throughout the city, and in control of Europe from the Enns River far to the west, all the way to Siberia, were an inescapable reality to the Viennese. During this 1940s period in Vienna, people simply disappeared—a high police official, for example, or a government economics expert, one of the few who eventually returned after years in Soviet prisons. In those years Soviet intelligence even succeeded in recruiting two American military policemen to abduct a Western agent (although this mystery was unsolved when the case of "Major X" began— all that was known was that another Austrian has disappeared totally, without trace). "Siberia" could be a present reality in the Vienna of 1949.

Or murder. Irving Ross, for instance, who was found brutally battered to death with the jack handle of his car, late at night, in the Soviet sector of Vienna on 1 November 1948. And there were to be others.

In such an atmosphere, the risks which might be involved in embarking upon a double agent operation against Soviet intelligence were clear to all concerned, most especially to the central figure, "Major X."

I count it my good fortune to have been one of those in the author's office staff. I recall the discussion vividly still, and remember distinctly my immediate visceral feeling that Verber's pitch had the ring of authenticity. Here was no amateur proposal, but a real attempt, by what I (and all others privy to the case) assumed from the outset was Soviet intelligence, to recruit a member of the American intelligence staff in Vienna.

We had long realized, from Soviet defectors and from information gleaned through Army counter-intelligence informants, that the Soviets were actively seeking to penetrate the U.S. Headquarters in Vienna. Moreover, we were forced privately to concede the possibility that the Soviets had already managed to recruit operatives within our ranks. The wartime assignments of Lt. Verber to Army intelligence and Sgt. Ponger to OSS were in themselves examples. The decision to undertake the case took into account from the outset the consideration that the Soviets might possess a formidable cross-check capability.

Prospects for a successful double agent play were poor for other reasons, too. "Major X" was a member of the air intelligence staff, and therefore separated physically from the main Army intelligence components, G-2 and CIC, which were located in other buildings at some distance from the air staff. That air staff, however, as was well known in G-2 and CIC, was de facto a section of G-2, responsible for evaluating specialized air intelligence information and serving requirements in its particular area upon all Army field collection units in Austria. That air intelligence staff comprised only four persons in 1949, when the case began. We thus faced the dilemma of persuading the Soviets, via Verber, that "Major X" had only limited access to intelligence information, all the while knowing that many members of G-2 knew or would assume that this was not in fact so.

Nor was our problem made any easier by the presence in Austria of literally scores of former civilian employees of the Nuremberg war crimes trials staff. Hired by G-2 in Austria as interrogators of the Austrian prisoners of war returning from the USSR and Yugoslavia, many of these interrogators knew Verber, Ponger, and/or "Major X," and we had no idea what the Soviets might be able to construe from even elicited remarks made innocently by former colleagues about "Major X" and his activities.

Of course, not all these hazards were clearly perceived at the outset, but they quickly became evident. Yet the decision to engage in the double agent gambit, despite all, was not unsound viewed in the perspective of the times. A vague awareness that American intelligence in Austria was a Soviet target was transformed, that April day in 1949, into a highly personal, direct, and tangible reality. One of ours had been approached by the Soviets, and was ready to use the opportunity to frustrate and negate the Soviet effort.

Throughout the overseas phase, those of us engaged in the case were constantly cognizant of the psychological stress imposed upon "Major X." The difficulties we experienced in obtaining clearance for build-up material moved some of the officers with responsibility for the case to a pessimistic estimate of its viability. Some even reached the flat conclusion that the Soviets had perceived the double play and were laying a trap. (One of the lessons I derived from this case was provided after his arrest by Verber, who stated he never had been suspicious of "Major X." What a help it was to us, at times, to have Verber actively looking for plausible excuses to explain his agent's failure to produce!)

In this atmosphere of uncertainty about the real state of the case, we countered what we regarded as a threat [by making a fairly sudden transfer of "Major X"'s unit to U.S.-occupied Salzburg. Also we] fended off with what we hoped were plausible arguments the importunings to meet "the General" in the Soviet Zone, and finally felt compelled to adopt the precipitous transfer device once again, and sent our man back to the United States in early January 1951 to avoid the physical risk to him which we felt was real.

All of this, of course, was most clearly evident to "Major X" himself. Still vivid in my memory is a telephone call I got from his wife on New Year's Day, 1951, asking me to meet her. "Major X" was even then, as our surveillance had confirmed, meeting with Ponger. She handed me the gun we had provided him, and explained that he had told her, in essence, that he was not afraid to meet Verber or Ponger, but was afraid to carry the gun, lest one of them somehow notice it and draw the proper inference.

To me, thus, the point is clear. This was a successful counter-espionage case, which achieved the goals of exposing its Soviet intelligence backing and neutralizing the Soviet agents directly involved. There were many, many people involved in the support and, at times, non-support of the operation, but its success was the work of one man: "Major X."

Early Stages

After having gotten my apparent agreement to work with him, Verber expressed great interest in having a "fundamental talk" with me, which would show him what kind of information I could get, and would enable him to ask me "more intelligent" questions. When the first meeting in my house was in prospect, I decided, rather than to depend on my own eyes and ears alone, to ask for the installation of listening devices. My quarters were not exactly designed for that sort of thing; we lived on the top floor of a six-family house, and had only Austrian neighbors, among them a very curious housekeeper. The maid happened to be on vacation, however, and her room could be used. In it we locked a CIC agent, a secretary, and an enlisted man who ran a huge tape recorder. I maneuvered Verber onto a sofa with a microphone taped behind it, and he talked quite freely about what he wanted me to do. His requirements this time included one for names of employees of American intelligence agencies. The meeting lasted for several hours. Verber was so absorbed that he did not notice the noise when the microphone fell to the floor, and he paid no attention to my badly disguised attempts to enunciate my words carefully. That effort was to no avail, anyhow, because the recorder failed to operate.

After that, Verber and I had frequent meetings, most of them with a social flavor. We usually just separated from our wives, and conducted our business in a "private" room in one of our houses. At my home, listening devices were used regularly. On some occasions a photographer was placed on the back porch, where he could take pictures of Verber and myself. There was even a proposal to install a two-way mirror in the wall—something to which I objected, as I did not know how I could explain the hole in the wall to outsiders. As time went on, my wife became quite unhappy at the interference with her privacy, and the need to keep the children and the maid out of the way at specified times. Finally, when we were asked to transform our maid's room into a permanently equipped observation post, she put her foot down, and government affairs had to move outside.

Security

During the first phase of the case, security precautions were somewhat problematic. As I noted earlier, a fairly large number of people, including my entire office staff, knew of the beginning of the operation. With a great deal of enthusiasm and, for my part, all the blessings and afflictions of inexperience, we made arrangements and decisions. A special problem was created for me by the people who knew both Verber and myself, as I had to ask myself in every case whether or not they could be trusted, whether they were in a position to know anything that would give me away, and to what extent I should treat each of them as a friend or a potential enemy. I sometimes compromised by warning people to be careful with Verber and Ponger, without telling them about the operation. Fortunately, not too many people knew both sides well enough to cause real difficulty.

Objectives and Methods

As for the objectives in the case, they were largely self-conceived in the early stages. I determined my approach to Verber before each meeting, and displayed the attitude which I thought would be best suited to gain his confidence and at the same time attain results. We wanted to prove, first, that Verber actually was a foreign agent, find out which country he was working for, and discover the contacts he had and the operating methods he used. In order to break his story of Israeli connections, I pretended to be just as dissatisfied with the state of the world as he was, but indicated that Israel, to me, just was not the right solution. I thus displayed an ideological vacuum which I asked Verber to help me fill. In general, when he offered opinions or made requests, I tried to appear receptive but not too bright, and usually willing but not always able. Above all, I did my best to display a consistent attitude and have an explanation for everything I did, just in case it was observed.

Information to be passed to Verber was cleared for me through the CIC. As weeks turned into months, Verber wanted to know more and more. I had to help myself by pretending to get information from outside the office where I [would not be able to] follow it up, and by describing my activities in the office as very limited, which made it impossible for me to observe too much. One of the subjects of his inquisitiveness was the Central Intelligence Agency. He tried to find out who was representing it in Vienna, and what it did. I am afraid that I was not of much help to him there.

Considering how little guidance we had during this first phase, our efforts seemed to have splendid results. Verber appeared to believe that he was leading me on, and came somewhat closer to admitting his Soviet sympathies. I even induced him to admit, to the benefit of a secret tape recording, that in case of a war he would prefer to fight for the Soviet Union.

Second Phase: Commitment

Our own plans now became somewhat more ambitious. I was asked through intelligence channels whether I would consent to become a long-range double agent, or whether—in view of the danger to my family and myself—I wished to be excused. If I would go along, I was told, this would mean that the operation would become the foremost thing in my life, and that in effect I would have to eat, drink, and sleep with it. In return for this service, I was informed, I could virtually set my own conditions. What followed was very simple: I accepted, and made no conditions whatsoever.

The working set-up now became more systematic, and security restrictions were tightened considerably. I could no longer discuss the progress of the case with just anyone in my office which, at times, was a bit uncomfortable. I also received more direct guidance on what I was supposed to accomplish, and how this was supposed to be done. The operation was divided into prospective phases: I was supposed to establish myself progressively more firmly in a spy system which by now we all assumed to be Soviet; eventually, the operation was supposed to be transferred to Washington; and in the hoped-for final stage, was to be used to feed the Soviets false information.

Initiatives and Problems

One of the first requests I had to make under the new program was this: I had to ask Verber for money—a $5,000 bank account. When Verber declined, the request was changed to one for a monthly salary of $50. After some apparent hesitation, Verber seemed happy to comply. Altogether I collected about $300 from him in Vienna. He now needed a code name for me for use on his vouchers, so he called me, of all things, "Lindbergh"—probably because I had once reported to him having met Charles Lindbergh at an air base in Bavaria. Verber continually admonished me not to take the money too lightly, because it not only was a token of appreciation, but also represented the earnings of working people. (For the time being, however, he still refused to tell me who his actual sponsors were.)

While Verber's pressure for information was still remarkably light after the first payment, it soon grew much more intense. We often did our talking in one of our cars, and I quite often carried listening devices in the car or on my person. My meetings sometimes led me into the Soviet sector, and once or twice to Ponger's home. In order to realize how uncomfortable that was, one must know that Ponger's place was practically surrounded by Soviet intelligence installations. Several times Verber came to my house before breakfast, offered to drive me to work, and talked business on the way.

How to remain in good standing with him without jeopardizing valuable information now became a major problem. I was thinking practically night and day of what information I could give him, how I could present it without inviting further questions which I would be unable to answer, how to explain things about which I could not tell him the real story, and how to keep myself from withholding information which he might know I had. The passing of some genuine intelligence data could not be avoided. While he never received any information which was really valuable, he was given enough to keep him interested. I preferred to provide him with data which looked more significant than they were. I also now told him, upon the advice of my superiors, that I hoped eventually to get an intelligence job in Washington. This, as much as anything else, probably served to keep his interest alive.

The Lighter Side

This period was not without its amusing incidents. Verber once invited my wife and me to a masquerade party in the Soviet sector. We shared a table with the Verbers, the Pongers, and various other people. Naturally, the CIC showed up in force; this was a splendid chance to observe, protect, and have fun all at the same time, especially since one could wear a mask and avoid being recognized. Ponger had his camera, and I, not wearing a mask, was one of his very favored focal objects. Occasionally strangers came to the table, seemingly reporting to Ponger, who reminded me of Napoleon talking to his troops. One of the CIC men—now a senior CIA official—later told me that he once came close enough to hear me whistle "The Battle Hymn of the Republic," thought I might be giving him a signal, and wondered whether he should call a general alarm. Luckily he decided against it; far from giving him a signal, I did not even recognize him.

When Verber took us back in his car, I told him it had been a very nice affair. "It must have been," he said. "Half the CIC was there."

I can chuckle now about another incident which at the time didn't seem funny at all. When we were about to move from our apartment to a different place in the neighborhood, I removed the hidden listening devices and wiring, put them in a briefcase, and took a cab to a safehouse, expecting to turn the equipment over to a CIC officer. On my way upstairs, I suddenly realized that I had left the briefcase in the cab. I ran back down again and after some jogging through the streets, ran my cab down at a nearby stand. When the driver saw me coming, he recovered the briefcase from the rear seat. "You didn't have to worry," he said soothingly as he handed it to me. "I would merely have turned it over to the police." I think my heart skipped a beat.

Pressure

We soon reached the stage where, in order to make progress, I was supposed to attempt to establish a new contact in hopes of uncovering another link in Verber's network. I told Verber that I had found some derogatory information on him and his brother-in-law in the CIC files and could no longer afford to be seen with him. Taken aback, Verber promised a new contact, but apparently was induced later to change his mind. Inasmuch as I refused to give him any more information under the prevailing circumstances, but he continued to try to see me, we had an increasing number of arguments. In one instance, I reached the point of offering to return the money he had given me, which caused Verber to hint darkly that I could never extricate myself from my alliance with him.

While I tried to give Verber the impression that I was getting quite impatient with him, he himself displayed signs of growing impatience. My wife now often heard the telephone ring, but heard no voice when she tried to answer. As the pressure was so obviously increasing, our authorities became apprehensive that it might lead to a kidnapping attempt against me or a member of my family.

Exit from Vienna; Operating in Salzburg

It was though best, therefore, that we move to Salzburg in the American Zone of Austria. In order to cover the real purpose of the move, it was decided to transfer my entire unit. A somewhat comical note was injected into the proceedings when one of my unit chiefs tried to exclude my particular branch from the unit transfer because he thought my branch could operate more efficiently in Vienna. He was overruled.

The move to Salzburg was apparently accomplished without making Verber unduly suspicious. He continued to visit me, and I continued to refuse to tell him anything, although I offered to accept his requirements for the day that a new contact would appear. Verber obliged by asking me questions. The greatest headache for our side was caused by his query regarding American evacuation plans from Austria, especially as parts of such a plan were then being developed in my office.

The plan was TOP SECRET, and I never told Verber about it, although I had the remarkable experience, before I left Europe, of seeing it published in an English-language newspaper. Indirectly, however, the request for evacuation plans was responsible for making me wish to leave the scene. All married American personnel had received a pamphlet, classified RESTRICTED, telling them what to do and where to report if evacuation became necessary. The fact that these instructions had been distributed to all personnel involved was stated in the pamphlet, and so I could see no safe way of maintaining to Verber that I did not have them. Someone in the local American headquarters, however, decided that we could not afford to disclose such information, intentionally or otherwise, and refused to clear it for passage. My reaction was that in that case, security considerations made it impossible for me to carry on a successful operation overseas. My superiors agreed, and as it was just about time to take another step anyhow, we prepared my transfer to Washington.

Climactic Meetings

When I notified Verber in writing that the Washington goal was in sight, it took him a while to answer. When he did, it was with an urgent plea for me to come to Vienna and talk to "the boss." I was half-tempted to go, but my superiors concluded that I had a poor chance of returning from such a trip, and did not let me undertake it. Eventually, Verber contacted me in Salzburg, apparently after spending the night outside my house in order not to miss me, and proposed that I cross the zonal border with him at an illegal crossing point. He said he wanted to introduce me to "the boss," a Soviet general who had arrived in response to a telegram Verber had sent to Moscow. I had to refuse. Similarly I refused to see Ponger, which he proposed as an alternative.

On our side, the significance of that meeting was debated practically all night. It was the first time that Verber had literally admitted Soviet connections. The prevailing opinion seemed to be that there was neither a Soviet general nor a case, that we had been compromised, and that my proposed trip was intended to be a one-way affair. It was proposed that I meet Verber the next day, hand him some documents, and help in arresting him. I successfully resisted that solution. I felt that the Soviets had ample reason for wanting to test me, but I did not believe that they were ready to give up on me just yet.

As it turned out, the next day Verber agreed to prepare me for my future career in the United States without the benefit of a trip across the border. In response, I gave him some information, notably personnel and organizational data which had been specially cleared for the occasion—the first information he had received in months. Verber questioned me in detail on some of the people I mentioned, especially on their susceptibility to drink and women, and on possible homosexual tendencies. Finally, he asked me to give him a handwritten list of groceries. If someone should present that list to me in the United States, I would know that person would be my contact.

This, however, did not stand up. On New Year's Day in 1951, Verber returned, cancelled his arrangements, and insisted I see Ponger, who alone was entitled to prepare me for stateside operations. (He asked me not to mention his own previous provisions to his brother-in-law.) This time I agreed to meet Ponger.

He had his own plan all prepared. He gave me $300 "to help with resettlement" in the United States, and told me that I was now a "comrade" working for the people of the Soviet Union. He made me write a letter to the "general" who would be my future contact, and whom I had offended by not coming to Vienna—a ploy undoubtedly designed to compromise me should I ever try to escape from my "comradeship." He admonished me to act like a patriotic American, and to avoid criticizing the United States.

Again I had to write a note, this time purporting to introduce a "Mr. Williams" as "Lindbergh's" friend, which my future contact would use to identify himself. At 8 p.m. on the second Tuesday in April 1951, I was supposed to wait for "Mr. Williams" at the Washington Monument, wearing, among several items, a piece of adhesive tape around one finger of one hand, and carrying a red-covered book under the other arm. I had to memorize several code questions and answers, which had to precede any further discussion with my contact. Ponger also made a series of alternative arrangements, leaving nothing to chance.

I had just one more short meeting with Verber, during which he told me that he hoped we would see each other again in a "more decent" United States. This was the last time I saw either him or Ponger before they were sentenced to jail.

Homeward Bound

A few days after my last meeting with Verber, my family and I were homeward bound. All of us were extremely happy, even if our feelings were not based on identical reasons. We were all looking forward to a more normal life, of course. While the children did not realize the danger that had threatened us for more than 18 months, they seemed to feel as much relief at the change in atmosphere as their parents did. I myself, however, was thinking primarily of a resumption of the case. True, there had been frustrations, arguments, and disappointments, and I had not always had the weapons I thought were needed for a successful fight. It seemed to me, for example, that there was rarely as much information provided and cleared for passage to Verber as I would have liked to ease the task of establishing my "usefulness" to the Soviets. It is probably true that in these cases the agent is under psychological pressure to give the appearance of "producing," while his handlers are primarily under similar counter-pressures to see to it that nothing of any great value is passed. Be that as it may, in retrospect I recall that frequently during the overseas phase, and even more often stateside, I felt I was not being given enough material to grease the wheels of the operation in a satisfactory manner.

Yet I proudly told myself that the fight, after all, had been successful up to this point. The cover had been removed from some of our hidden enemies; the finger had been pointed at others, who might in time be identified; and countless clues had been provided for those who studied the methods of enemy penetration. Above all, I had met the challenge to "eat, drink, and sleep" with the case, and had become a long-range double agent, ready for further assignments. The generally splendid support I had received overseas from so many individuals left me no doubt that I had embarked on the most important venture of my life. The continued success of the operation had become an intensely personal matter; I had given it all I had, felt it was more worthwhile than anything else I would ever want to do, and was anxious to pursue it in the

United States. Paradoxically, perhaps, I also felt relief when I thought that I would first have some time to catch my breath—at least until the second Tuesday in April.

Stateside Reception

Two days after our arrival in New York, I reported to an office in the Pentagon which, I was told overseas, would give me further instructions. Here I met a number of G-2 personnel who, I was informed, had been directing the operation from the Washington end. I also meet some people with whom I had been associated overseas, in one case a tearful reunion.

The schedule for that day included a discussion of certain facets of the overseas operation and a clarification of my own future. I was told that I now was a free agent, but that the way would be cleared for me if I was willing to resume my double agent's role. In the latter case, I would be introduced to an agent of the FBI, which was prepared to take charge of the operation, and to the Air Force general in whose division I was supposed to work. I reaffirmed my willingness to pursue the case further.

I was also offered reimbursement for any expenses I might have incurred while returning to the United States, but I had no reason to accept and did not.

The FBI agent arrived in the afternoon. I pointed out to him and to the G-2 representatives that I had felt the overseas operation in its later stages had been hamstrung by lack of information available for passing to my contact, and asked for assurances that I would not have to work under a similar handicap in the United States. I was informed—it may have been in a subsequent meeting, and it is possible that the assurance came from the G-2 side—that the difficulty would be largely eliminated with the compilation of a backlog of information to which the interested agencies were expected to contribute. It was also indicated that once in a while, in addition to this backlog, enough current information could be cleared for release, even if the interested organs should have to apply some pressure on the clearing board. I was satisfied, and made an appointment with the FBI agent for further discussion a few days later.

In the late afternoon, I met my prospective Air Force employers. My assignment was about what I had been led to expect, but my rating was somewhat below expectation. The G-2 officer who had introduced me to the Air Force officials agreed that it was disappointing, but advised me to take up such problems with the FBI.

First Operational Talks

I met my FBI contact, in accordance with his instructions, in front of a Washington drug store. After a few maneuvers designed to make sure that I had not been followed, we drove through the Virginia countryside and had our first conference. Among other things, I wanted to know how I could settle future questions about inconvenience and costs arising from operational requirements, and pointed out that I had been advised to discuss such matters with the FBI. The answer was straightforward enough. At the present time, I was told, the Bureau could do very little for me, because we were not as yet engaged in an operation. The overseas case was a thing of the past; and a new operation, in which the FBI would be interested, would begin only if and when I would meet a Soviet contact in the United States. In that case, I would have information to offer, and I could get paid for it; before that, the Bureau could not very well be responsible for a case which it did not have.

I objected vigorously. I simply wanted to be protected against mishap or disadvantage. Right now, I pointed out, I was expected to stake my entire future on a case in which the FBI at this point refused to have much of a stake and which, if the Bureau's contention was correct, did not even exist.

The FBI man was unimpressed. It was up to me, he stated, whether or not I wanted to do the job. He reminded me, however, that I had certain responsibilities as a citizen of the United States, a fact which he thought might influence my decision.

My own feeling was, of course, that I had made my decision, and I wasn't about to change it. It seemed strange, however, that after my work overseas I should once again be reminded of *my* responsibilities, but that corresponding responsibilities on anyone else's part were hard for me to detect at that precise moment.

Getting Ready

I had accumulated quite a bit of leave overseas, so now I spent some time with my family. I fitted practically everything I did, however, into the framework of my counter-espionage operation. As Verber had been told that the deteriorating health of an aging relative was the reason for our going home, I thought it best to spend some time with the relative in Philadelphia. Whenever I went to Washington to talk to the FBI agent, I made sure to visit the Pentagon as well, in order to have a logical explanation for each trip for the benefit of possible Soviet observers. I never talked to a stranger without adapting my words to the possibility that he might be a Soviet agent or might later be contacted by the Soviets.

When talking to Verber and Ponger overseas, I had presented my assignment to Washington as a certainty. It seemed logical for me to settle in the Washington area before I had the first appointment with the new Soviet contact, even if I had not actually started working. We moved to Falls Church in

March 1951. I had agreed with the office that I would be on the job by the middle of April, and had later been asked to come in on 20 April. At least I had a definite date I could mention to my prospective Soviet contact who, it will be remembered, was to meet me at the Washington Monument on 12 April.

At the Washington Monument

I was a few minutes late for my 8 p.m. meeting on 12 April. Carefully following all the instructions I had received from Ponger, I came equipped with adhesive-taped finger and red-covered book, and had memorized the pre-scribed questions and answers. I knew, of course, that FBI agents were cover-ing the meeting, but I had been told that they would stay at a respectable distance.

It was getting fairly dark when I approached the Monument, and I couldn't help thinking how silly it was to carry a book at a time like that. Soon I distinguished the figure of a man in a dark suit, who appeared to be the only other visitor. After I had walked around the Monument, he stopped me and asked me the questions I had been expecting: Was the National Gallery still open? Did I know the way to the White House? I gave my own prepared answers, and then waited for him to produce a piece of paper. Even in the uncertain light, I could recognize my own handwriting. "I am Mr. Williams," the man said in a guttural accent, quite superfluously.

"Mr. Williams" turned out to be extremely friendly, and obviously very happy to have met me. In guiding me away from the Monument, which he characterized as a "very bad meeting place," he patted me on the back and managed to touch various parts of my rearward anatomy, until I was sure he had inconspicuously frisked every inch down to the waistline. After that, he seemed interested in making the meeting as short as possible. I managed to tell him what my job situation was, and he found time for a few reassuring words. After that, he made arrangements for the next meeting, which was, as I recall, to take place in nearby Maryland a week or so later. At that time, he indicated, we could settle some of my "problems." Then he left after making sure that I did not go in the same direction.

Walking back to my car, I was somewhat excited, but not surprised at what had just taken place. I had assumed that the operation would follow me to the United States, and it had.

Identification

Later that evening I met a number of FBI agents who now, of course, were willing to drop some of their earlier reservations. My description of the new contact—about 30 years old, weighing about 200 pounds, with dark hair, round face, horn-rimmed glasses, and speaking with a guttural accent—seemed to fit someone they knew, although they could not be sure. At the FBI Field Office, I examined picture after picture. Finally I pointed to one showing a man walking in front of a building. This time there was no doubt. The man with whom Ponger had placed me in contact was Yuriy V. Novikov, Second Secretary of the Soviet Embassy in Washington, D.C.

The FBI agent in charge of the case took me home after midnight. The case had indeed begun, he said; the Bureau valued my services and was willing to pay for them. I declined. Although the FBI would undoubtedly not have seen it in the same light, it still would have given me the feeling that my services were for sale. The information I obtained as the by-product of a penetration attempt directed against the enemies of the United States was not a commercial item, to be paid for upon delivery.

Job Problem

If my contact with a Soviet official in Washington was, as it seemed to me, a tremendous thing, I failed to feel its effect in my relationship with the Air Force. As agreed, I started to work on about 20 April, although I was not scheduled to go on the payroll until 1 May. Just prior to 1 May, moreover, I received word that I had not been properly processed, had not been cleared, and could not be allowed to work in the designated office until my papers had properly gone through channels. This was supposed to take a maximum of three weeks—and it took exactly that. In the meantime, my available cash had dwindled to almost nothing, and all my earthly possessions were tied up in what I had come to regard as the "Washington venture." At that time, I entertained serious doubts that the Air Force would honor its commitment to employ me, or that I had enough time to wait for the decision. I attempted and failed to find suitable short-term employment outside the government, and wondered how I would have explained an outside job to my Soviet contact without making him lose interest in me.

For the second and third weeks of May, fortunately, my anticipated Air Force salary was paid by the FBI. On 20 May, the Air Force finally opened its doors. I still had not been cleared, and my rating had been cut yet another notch, but it was a starting point.

Next Meetings

My next meetings with my Soviet contact were quite different from anything I had experienced overseas. He seemed to be interested mainly in avoiding possible surveillance. He never talked to me at the location where we met, and refused to talk in the car. Usually he drove me around for as long as an hour, going through a park, crossing main streets, suddenly stopping and reversing himself, and all the time watching for other vehicles. When he seemed to be satisfied that no one had followed him, he parked in a spot quite distant from our meeting place, and we both got out of the car and discussed our business while walking or standing out in the open. Afterward, he sometimes drove me to the vicinity of my own car, but more often told me to take a cab. He always gave me the time and location of the next meeting before we started on the return trip, and also made careful arrangements for alternative meetings if we should happen to miss each other. I usually wrote the details down, but could never induce him to give me a sample of his handwriting.

Subjects of Meetings

Novikov was as systematic in his approach toward my exploitation as he was in his anti-surveillance precautions. Right at the beginning, he informed me that he wanted to proceed "scientifically." First, he questioned me on my personal history and background, then on my associates in the office, and finally on my capability to provide information.

One of the first things I got cleared for him was my job description, which stated, truthfully, that I was working on general interrogation requirements as well as specific requirements on installations in the Soviet Union. Novikov immediately pounced on the latter and asked for as many details as possible. Unfortunately, it was subsequently decided that I could not give him such information, and I had to figure out a very intricate retreat, involving a change in my job description and a rearrangement of the functions attributed to other office personnel.

Otherwise I had hardly any information for him at first. The fact that I had not been cleared served as a temporary explanation, although it was somewhat difficult getting through a meeting with the pretense that I knew absolutely nothing. Novikov, however, was surprisingly patient, and even counseled me to be patient too. He provided me with several hundred dollars, which, as always, I immediately turned over to the FBI, and told me to be careful, as the time element was less important than the necessity for me to gain the confidence of my associates.

I thus helped myself over the dismal present by making implied promises for a more productive future. At the same time, I tried to get Novikov to give some requirements, and to reveal something about himself and his superiors; I thought it would be in character for me to be curious about those things. Novikov, however, would only tell me that I was working for the benefit of the

Soviet Union, and that information of interest to the USSR was more important to him than data pertaining to satellite countries. He advised me to use my own intelligence in determining what information would be of interest to the USSR. Beyond that, he never revealed anything—not even his own identity.

Clearance Procedures

In the early days, my official contact regarding all phases of the operation was confined to the FBI. After I had stalled Novikov for a while, I kept asking for the backlog of information which I thought I was supposed to receive. I was told that there was some delay, and that in the meantime I should collect the information myself and hand it to the FBI agent, who would hand it to the clearing body, which would pass it back to the FBI agent, who could then return the cleared items to me.

For some time, that was actually the way it worked. As I had not yet received my clearance papers, however, I did not have a chance to do much collecting. I could merely use some items which I had accidentally seen or overheard, and I hated myself for handing them in. More to the point, that type of information was neither voluminous nor significant enough to satisfy my contact, especially because a fairly high percentage usually failed to get cleared.

It was, I felt, an impossible situation. At one time, I asked the FBI whether it would not be better to have me transferred to a different agency, preferably G-2, where better working arrangements might be obtained. (I actually prepared Novikov for a potential change to a "different intelligence agency," whereupon he solicitously asked if, perhaps, I meant the Central Intelligence Agency.)

Finally, after some additional pressure, the Air Force came through with my full clearance for the job, which helped the case as well as my morale. I had to continue to collect my own information, however, and have it cleared by the somewhat cumbersome procedure I outlined earlier. Usually I got my items back so shortly before I was scheduled to meet Novikov that there seemed to me to be too little time to clear up debatable points, weave the items into a fitting cover story, and make my way to the meeting place. In addition, items once cleared were occasionally withdrawn later. I was also told to volunteer nothing and to give as little as possible, but instead to get Novikov to tell me what *he* wanted.

My FBI contacts in those days gave me the impression that they appreciated my difficulties, but could do little about them. After all, the FBI also had to wait for the items to be cleared. I was encouraged to do the best I could with what I had. In retrospect, I can appreciate that my view of the goals of the operation at that time may not have coincided with the concepts of those who were setting the policy. At any rate, eventually I wrote a memorandum, pointing out what I thought were the flaws in the working set-up, expressing my conviction that they were endangering the operation, and making several concrete proposals, including one for direct contact between me and the responsible organs of the Air Force. The memorandum was directed to, and evidently vigorously supported by, the FBI. A short time later, I was called into a joint conference of Air Force and FBI representatives. From then on, I had my own Air Force case officers, two senior colonels, whose efforts in my behalf and in behalf of the operation I came to appreciate, especially when it became evident to me that they were working with very limited resources.

Policy

To me, the purpose of the operation had seemed quite clear overseas, but it was less clear in the United States. I knew, of course, that Novikov's identification had been useful to the FBI, and that the operation could help them to identify some of his associates. I received no explicit guidance, however, as to the type of information I was supposed to provide, or what I was supposed to accomplish with it. Later, I heard that there was a policy to keep the case going with a minimum of information. (This would be in keeping, of course, with a goal of simply keeping the fish in play for further identification purposes, but would hardly achieve what I had understood to be the ultimate aim: deception. This may well explain the discrepancy between how much information I got, and how much I felt was needed.) Otherwise, I knew only that I was supposed to collect evidence, and get as much money from Novikov as possible. I tried my best to do what I was asked, but did not derive much inspiration from it, and at times found it difficult to maintain a strong sense of direction.

Relaxation

Novikov, in the meantime, seemed to lose some of his extreme apprehensiveness. My FBI associates told me that he sometimes no longer investigated the meeting place prior to my arrival, although that had been a regular habit of his. His trips through the countryside with me before settling down for our conferences became shorter and more relaxed, and the FBI was occasionally able to keep up with us. We often had our talks in restaurants or other public places, rather than in the open, and Novikov invariably ordered a sumptuous meal for both of us and tipped generously. If the information I gave him was less than adequate, I never ceased to impress him with my anxiety to do "better work" in the future; and if I once again used my battle-tested story of being wary of security regulations, Novikov at that time agreed that it was wise to be careful.

Novikov's relaxation was a great help in the FBI's efforts to gather evidence. It now was possible for me to steer him past designated points where he could be easily identified. Often I drove him around in my car, where he left a generous supply of fingerprints. Inasmuch as my car was equipped with listening devices, it was sometimes possible for the FBI to hear his voice, although he still did not do much talking during the ride. Once, he even made an appointment with me in front of a theater in broad daylight, where he, one of his associates, and I could be filmed meeting each other. My elation over this accomplishment, however, was dimmed by the inability of the FBI agent in charge to get permission for me to see the film. At the beginning of the case, I had felt like a participant in the investigative machinery; now, I thought at the time, I was accepted as no more than an informant.

Information and Requirements

Most meetings started out simply with Novikov asking me what I had for him. I would then tell him what I had allegedly heard or observed, and, if required, how I had heard or observed it. I often took my cue from handwritten notes, undecipherable to anyone save myself, in which I had connected isolated scraps of information, often in order to give them an artificial significance. I could not make my information more important than it was; but I tried my best to make it appear important to the man in front of me. For some time, I apparently succeeded.

As was inevitable, Novikov one day asked me to tell him exactly what I did in the office, to what information I had access, what my associates did, and how documents were routed and processed. Luckily, he gave me a few weeks in which to provide the answer. I drew up a semi-fictitious paper, replete with non-existent compartmentation and security restrictions, and handed it in for clearance. It was cleared without change, including a statement that I had access to certain Army, Air Force, and CIA reports. Characteristically, Novikov immediately seized on the subject of CIA reports in preference to everything else, and asked me to pay special attention to subject matter and sources of information. Later I was informed that information on CIA reports was not clearable after all, and that I would have to extricate myself from the statement I had made to Novikov. This situation created one of the severest headaches I had yet experienced. I finally did figure out a solution which, I thought, might be both feasible and in character, but which is too complicated to be set down here. I was, however, beginning to feel that my main task in the case was that of devising excuses for Novikov.

Among Novikov's requirements, of which I finally got a few, was one for information on Western countries, which, of course, I denied having or being able to get. I also remember that he asked for a Justice Department telephone book, but was not interested in the Pentagon directory. In some instances, he tried to follow up scraps of information which I had given him. Notably, he did this in the case of a vague statement of mine to the effect that it was planned to use Soviet emigrés for intelligence purposes overseas. More surprisingly, he also tried to follow up an item on a proposed change in the U.S. air attaché staff in Argentina. In almost all instances, I pretended to have obtained the information in such a way that further news on the same subject was uncertain. My item-by-item clearance procedure made it impossible for me to use a more systematic approach.

Novikov still seemed to be convinced of my good faith. At least he kept on paying money in multiples of $100. One day, he even asked me to recommend other personnel who might be susceptible to a Soviet approach, saying that I myself would not be required to do the approaching. We never got to the point, however, of taking advantage of the offer.

Pressure

Signs of pressure on Novikov's part began to appear when the stateside operation was nearly a year old and—as far as benefit to the USSR was concerned—had produced absolutely nothing. He pointed this out to me one day. Conceding that the shortcomings might be at least partly his fault, because he might have omitted some of the things I had reported, he nevertheless pointed out that the results were not satisfactory. While he appreciated my desire to remain uncompromised, he had to make me realize that our meetings entailed considerable risk for both of us—a risk which did not seem justified by the present product of our arrangement. My reaction was one of feigned indignation. I told him that our relationship was meant to be profitable for him, not for me, and that I was ready to break it off if he did not properly appreciate it. Novikov, somewhat flustered, agreed that everything would work out.

He tried by various means to increase my "productivity." Once he told me that I could earn "a lot of money" with the right kind of work, and asked me to think of a good way to camouflage large earnings. His interim solution, as it eventually developed, provided for fewer personal meetings and a sort of mail-drop system. I was instructed to buy a typewriter, for which he furnished the money. Such items as he would be interested in were to be typed in my home, enclosed in a tin can, and dropped in a designated place, where they would be picked up at specified times. Novikov contended that the system was practically foolproof, as no one could be caught giving or taking classified information, and indicated that tin cans had been used before.

After some hesitation, I agreed to try his "system." We actually had a dry run. I placed a folded piece of newspaper in a tin can, flattened the can, and deposited it under a designated shack in Glencarlyn Park in Virginia. Although no one was observed removing the can as far as I know, it was gone several days later, and during our next meeting Novikov ironically thanked me for the newspaper.

Interruption

I had informed the FBI and the Air Force, of course, that Novikov was apparently under pressure to make the operation more productive and less risky. It was decided that I would have to go along with the mail-drop proposition for the time being. My request for more impressive information was answered with the clearance of a larger number of items than I normally had, but they were hardly more impressive.

The next meeting with Novikov took place around March 1952. After I had given him the information and told him I was willing to work with typewriter and tin cans, he surprised me by saying that the new program would have to be postponed. He would be out of town at the time when we would normally have our next face-to-face meeting, and that too would have to be postponed for more than a month. He did, however, set a definite date for the next meeting, and gave me exact instructions for alternative arrangements. Provisions previously made for an emergency meeting, which I was to call if I had something particularly important to report, were reaffirmed. Novikov assured me, however, that he saw no reason why the intended meeting should not take place as scheduled. In his customary surreptitious way, he put $400 into the pocket of my overcoat, which was hanging on a rack. It was the largest single sum I had ever received from him, and brought the total up to about $2,000.

My first feeling after that meeting was one of relief. For some time, I had felt that the preparation for my meetings, climaxed by the meetings themselves, was more of a strain on my nerves than I could continually impose upon myself. Not only had my family started to suffer under my badly frayed disposition, but I was beginning to suspect that I was reaching a point where I could not go on trying to fashion successful meetings out of the morsels I had to dig up under the "minimum of information" policy. In addition to that, I had begun to wonder what would happen to my family and myself if the emotional strain should result in an impairment of my health. On that point, I had no reassurances whatever from anybody. I was happy, therefore, that Novikov intended to stay away from me for a while.

Last Meeting

I knew that Novikov's "out-of-town" trip had taken him all the way back to his own country. He had not yet returned when we were supposed to get together again; in fact, he failed to appear at several alternative meetings. Although he had never failed to show up before, we remained hopeful.

Our "permanent" meeting place was in Anacostia at the corner of 30th and R Streets SE, and the schedule called for me to be there every second Tuesday if other appointments had failed to materialize. One Tuesday—I believe it was early in June—I saw Novikov again. He shook my hand, and I had time to tell him that I was very anxious to talk to him. He told me to drive slowly along the street while he walked beside the car. As I drove around a corner and he dropped back slightly, I saw a car stop behind mine, then pull slowly ahead. I recognized it as Novikov's car and believed he had gotten in, so I followed it as I had done countless times before. As usual, we circled slowly around the area. Finally, the car stopped at a street corner on Pennsylvania Avenue. Only then did I see that Novikov was not in the car, but that I had followed a stranger, accompanied by a woman whom I later identified as Mrs. Novikov.

I returned hurriedly to the meeting place and waited, but I had no more company that night, nor did I ever see Novikov again.

The End—Last Attempts

All of us, I believe, were reluctant to concede defeat. One solution appeared to be to call an emergency meeting. When the Air Force could not come up with an item of information urgent enough to justify such a call, I went ahead anyway, and gave the required signal, consisting of white chalk marks on a designated stone wall in the city. In the first few instances, Novikov was out of town, and we persuaded each other that the case had merely become unimportant to him, and that he would meet me again when his schedule permitted it. Eventually, however, he failed to answer the call even though he was in Washington. It became clear that I could discontinue my trips to 30th and R Streets.

After overcoming the initial letdown, I felt rather happy at the conclusion of what I now considered to have been an impossible assignment. I decided that the future ought to be devoted to my family, where I had sadly neglected my obligations in favor of those I had accepted for the pursuit of the case.

In December 1952, I had the first indication that the case might wind up with arrests and trial, and that I would be required to testify. Although I knew that the guilt of Ponger and Verber could easily be established, I was opposed to another experience which might result in violent attacks on our emotions as well as our reputation. Anyhow, I testified before a Grand Jury and geared myself for the main trial, realizing that it might bring not only tension, but also recognition. This never happened, however; the two suspects confessed and were sentenced to jail terms without my having to testify.[2]

Comments

In August 1953, when I had become a CIA employee, I expressed my feelings about the entire matter in an in-house memorandum as follows.

> The case is over, and my comments will be short. Ponger and Verber are in jail; Novikov has been expelled; countless others have been questioned; and personnel and case files have been filled with reams of paper. With only a few odds and ends remaining to be settled, my own work is done. I probably should be proud and happy at what I helped to accomplish.
>
> Instead, however, I have to confess, I feel more bitterness than elation, and more disillusionment than pride.
>
> The way the operation was conducted overseas has nothing to do with this. There were shortcomings, of course; but there were also men who lent their understanding, their courage, and their support. Personally I felt, without being told, that my family and I were protected to the best of the government's ability. When it was over, I rode home on what I thought was the crest of a wave of success.
>
> In the United States, I suddenly found a different attitude. I found that an appeal to patriotism could be used as a matter of operational routine, to disguise an arrangement under which an agent trying to penetrate foreign intelligence appeared to be treated according to the same rules as an informer reporting on his neighbor. . . . I found that an informer, like a racehorse, was retained mainly for his usefulness. . . . [Ellipses in original article.—HBW] I found that I had many obligations toward the government, and was often reminded of a combat soldier's sacrifices; but I did not have the protection that soldiers and their dependents are entitled to receive. My own obligations included risking my life, my health, and my ability to work; the government's obligations included no consideration of such possibilities. I also found, finally, that the more efforts and sacrifices I offered, the more were taken for granted.
>
> The case itself has probably been concluded with some degree of success. I shall never stop believing, however, that it could have been immeasurably successful if, at some decisive stages, it had been given the benefit of more support, more vision, and more wisdom. For a long time, I had the feeling that I was pursuing the case on my own, supported by nothing but my own personal obsession. I have even asked myself if my fight for recognition and support of

---

2. Ponger was sentenced to 5 to 15 years, Verber to 3 to 10. Both men were paroled after serving part of their sentences and returned to Vienna, where they now live as Austrian citizens.

the case was not more exhausting and frustrating than my face-to-face encounter with Soviet agents. . . .

The case was finally thrown open for the sake of taking legal and diplomatic action against the suspects; only my own identification was refused in the name of security. And that is where the case now stands, after it has been concluded.

Perhaps everything is exactly the way it should be. I realize that I have not yet gained the emotional distance from the operation that would produce a more factual appraisal and a well-balanced judgment. I hope to have shown, however, that in its various phases the case could have been conducted differently; that it neither had to carry me to the limits of my emotional endurance, nor needed to end short of a more complete accomplishment. Perhaps my experiences can be useful even where they portray failure. I sincerely hope that there is a chance for that, and that someone else may be spared my disappointment.

More than 20 years have passed since I wrote that, and bitterness and passion have indeed given way to reflection and analysis. I now can recognize that my angle of vision could not have been, and cannot now be, all-encompassing, and that my views, even after they have become dispassionate, remain personal. With this understanding, a brief examination of the questions I raised in the introduction now is in order.

First, I do not think that I, any more than many others, was sufficiently prepared for the Soviet approach, or sufficiently suspicious. International intrigue of this type appeared to belong to a different world, and to fiction more than to reality; one certainly did not connect one's colleagues and acquaintances with it. This view was surely naive, but hardly exceptional. In the last analysis, it took a rather crude initiative by Verber to jolt me into the realization that he might be part of a conspiracy. Most of us have matured since that early post–World War II period, but I doubt that we have reached a point where we can relax.

Second, It seems to me that at that time our policy in running this operation and others like it suffered from a fragmentation of interests, procedures, and terms of reference. This is no reflection whatsoever on the competence, integrity, and efforts of the several investigative elements; within their own frames of reference, they all worked superbly. For someone attempting to work clandestinely, as a matter of civic responsibility and challenge, to further the interests of the U.S. Government, however, it can be disconcerting to receive the impression that he is dealing less with a government than with a variety of components, each of which may have a different understanding of what, specifically, U.S. interests are, how they should be supported, how he should be put to work, and even how he should be treated. Conversely, it is clear that there has to be room in our society both for police informers, who can help us in preparing for legal battles, and for intelligence operators, who can support us in our struggles for international position and insight; but the two are *not* automatically interchangeable, and confusion of the two concepts can be disillusioning and morale-shattering for those affected. The evidence, as I read it, indicates that at the time of the "Major X Affair" we were not in a good position to maintain a consistent and fully coordinated program—for better or for worse—for operations of the kind that mine was—or might have been.

Third, How, if at all, could we have gained more than we did? What would have happened if we had taken more risks, compromised more information, and played for higher stakes? I cannot answer that categorically. No one can. Our additional sacrifices might have brought us no gain. We might have been defeated, with even less success than the operation produced as it ran. On the other hand, if successful, we might have established a functioning penetration of the Soviet espionage system; we might have used it to learn their secrets; we might have led the Soviets to rely on the information furnished by us sufficiently to make deception operations possible.

Which way lay the national interest? The answer is never simple. Other cases may be even more complicated, and the decision more difficult. One thing I know is this: the protection of our security through penetration efforts, in its highest sense, is a tremendously important task, and a tremendously complex one. If properly executed, it demands a sense of discrimination embodying caution and care as well as vision and courage. Those are the ingredients of wisdom. No one, least of all I, can lay down the rules for wisdom. I can only hope that our government will be wise enough for any task at hand, and that in helping to build a secure nation, it can use cement made from experiences like mine.

The Next Most Valuable Articles

These are the titles of the articles that survived all but the final cut in my selection for this volume (see introduction, pp. xvi–xvii). They are accessible at the National Archives and are well worth attention.

Bimmerle, George. "'Truth' Drugs in Interrogation." *Studies in Intelligence,* vol. 5, no. 2 (Spring 1961), pp. A1–A19.

Bolfrone, Kenneth E. "Intelligence Photography." *Studies in Intelligence,* vol. 5, no. 2 (Spring 1961), pp. 9–16. Even amateurs may sometimes find themselves in places where opportunity arises to photograph a scene that may be useful to intelligence. Here is how to do it, with ordinary equipment.

Brugioni, Dino. "Spotting Photo Fakery." *Studies in Intelligence,* vol. 13, no. 1 (Winter 1969), pp. 57–67. A guide for the layman.

Brugioni, Dino, and Robert Poirier. "The Holocaust Revisited: A Retrospective Analysis of the Auschwitz-Birkenau Extermination Complex." *Studies in Intelligence,* vol. 22, no. 4 (Winter 1978), pp. 11–29. Two of CIA's best imagery analysts reexamine with up-to-date methods all the surviving declassified U.S. wartime aerial photographs of the Auschwitz region for contemporary evidence of the Holocaust. They find much that contemporary photointerpretation probably could not, and they show it to us.

Carey, Warren, and Myles Maxfield, "Intelligence Implications of Disease." *Studies in Intelligence,* vol. 16, no. 1 (Spring 1972), pp. 71–78. How to track internationally communicable and dangerous diseases spreading in "denied areas" countries.

Cote, Maureen. "Translation Error and Political Misinterpretation." *Studies in Intelligence,* vol. 27, no. 4 (Winter 1983), pp. 11–19.

Davis, Jack. "The Kent-Kendall Debate of 1949." *Studies in Intelligence,* vol. 35, no. 2 (Summer 1991), pp. 37–50. An early installment of the perennial debate among analysts over "objectivity versus usefulness," here revisited by a veteran apostle of usefulness.

Friedman, Richard. "A Stone for Willy Fisher." *Studies in Intelligence,* vol. 30, no. 4 (Winter 1986), pp. 19–30. The story of Willy Fisher, who became famous as the nonofficial-cover Soviet agent Rudolf Abel.

Gries, David. "Intelligence in the 1990s." *Studies in Intelligence,* vol. 35, no. 1 (Spring 1991), pp. 5–11.

Harris, William. "March Crisis 1948, Act I." *Studies in Intelligence,* vol. 10, no. 4 (Fall 1966), pp. 1–22. "March Crisis 1948, Act II." *Studies in Intelligence,* vol. 11, no. 2 (Spring 1967), pp. 9–36. Intelligence history of a climactic escalation of the early Cold War: simultaneous crisis in Germany, Italy, and Czechoslovakia.

Haus, Lance. "The Predicament of the Terrorism Analyst." *Studies in Intelligence,* vol. 29, no. 4 (Winter 1985), pp. 13–23.

Johnson, William R. "Ethics and Clandestine Collection." *Studies in Intelligence,* vol. 27, no. 1 (Spring 1983), pp. 1–8.

Kent, Sherman. "A Crucial Estimate Relived." *Studies in Intelligence,* vol. 8, no. 2 (Spring 1964), pp. 1–18. Kent's account of his greatest mistake: the predictions three weeks before the Cuba missile crisis that Moscow would be unlikely to station missiles in Cuba that could reach much of the United States.

Knobelspiesse, A. V. "Captain Stephan Kalman: A Classic Write-In Case." *Studies in Intelligence,* vol. 6, no. 4 (Fall 1962), pp. A1–A13. What to do about a "write-in" who never becomes a "walk-in"? That is, what to do about a person who sends apparently valuable information but never appears or identifies himself or herself?

Langan, John, S. J. "Moral Damage and the Justification of Intelligence Collection from Human Sources." *Studies in Intelligence,* vol. 25, no. 2 (Summer 1981), pp. 57–64.

Lowenhaupt, Henry S. "Mission to Birch Woods, via Seven Tents and New Siberia." *Studies in Intelligence,* vol. 12, no. 4 (Fall 1968), pp. 1–12. How CIA set targets for the first U-2 flights over Soviet nuclear production and testing facilities in 1957.

———. "Ravelling Russia's Reactors." *Studies in Intelligence,* vol. 16, no. 3 (Fall 1972), pp. 65–79. Multidisciplinary intelligence analysis in the late 1950s of how a major nuclear production facility in central Siberia worked.

McCreary, John F. "Warning Cycles." *Studies in Intelligence,* vol. 27, no. 3 (Fall 1983), pp. 71–79. Prescribing steps for a warning process and for judging whether it has been a success or failure.

Oliver, Kay. "Analyzing Economic Espionage." *Studies in Intelligence,* vol. 36, no. 1 (Spring 1992), pp. 23–27.

Stockinger, Edwin. "Five Weeks at Phalane." *Studies in Intelligence,* vol. 17, no. 1 (Spring 1973), pp. 11–19. A 1971 siege in CIA's secret war in Laos.

Taylor, Jack H. "Wohlstetter, Soviet Strategic Forces, and National Intelligence Estimates." *Studies in Intelligence,* vol. 19, no. 1 (Spring 1975), pp. 1–8. Here is evidence that CIA, in house, very quickly agreed that Wohlstetter's breakthrough claim (1974) was essentially correct, namely, that the United States had for years been underestimating the pace of Soviet arms racing.

Welzenbach, Donald E. "Observation Balloons and Reconnaissance Satellites." *Studies in Intelligence,* vol. 30, no. 1 (Spring 1986), pp. 21–28. The effort by the United States in the 1950s to send reconnaissance balloons across the Soviet Union.

———. "Science and Technology: Origins of a [CIA] Directorate." *Studies in Intelligence,* vol. 30, no. 2 (Summer 1986), pp. 13–26.

Welzenbach, Donald E., and Nancy Galyean. "Those Daring Young Men and Their Ultra-High-Flying Machines." *Studies in Intelligence,* vol. 31, no. 3 (Fall 1987), pp. 103–115. The first U-2 flights over Murmansk, 1957.

Williams, Robert. "Commanders and Surprise." *Studies in Intelligence,* vol. 26, no. 3 (Fall 1982), pp. 9–19. How commanders should handle intelligence.

Abbreviations, Acronyms, and Definitions

AFTAC: Air Force Technical Applications Center

CEA: Council of Economic Advisers (at the White House)

CEP: Circular error probability (for calculating the probability that a warhead will impact within a certain radius of its target)

CIC: Counterintelligence Corps (U.S. Army)

CS: Clandestine Service(s) (CIA's Directorate for Plans/Operations)

COCOM: Coordinating Committee on Multilateral Export Controls

COMINT: Communications intelligence (a component of signals intelligence)

Commo: CIA's apparatus for its communications

Confidential: The level of classification designated by Executive Order 12356 for "information, the unauthorized disclosure of which reasonably could be expected to cause damage to the national security." The defined difference between this standard and "Secret" (see below) is that "Secret" applies when the expected damage would be "serious."

Crypts: Cryptonyms

DCI: Director of Central Intelligence

DCID 1/2: Directive No. 1/2 of the Director of Central Intelligence

DDO: CIA's Deputy Director for Operations; or CIA's Directorate for Operations, also called DO

Direction finder: A device to determine the direction from which electronic emissions are coming and to locate their source by triangulation

Dissems: Disseminable reports

ERIR: Economic Research Intelligence Report

FBIS: Foreign Broadcast Information Service (CIA)

FORMAT: Intelligence specialization in the acquisition and exploitation of foreign material supplies

FSO: Foreign Service Officer (State Department)

G-77: The caucus of the less developed countries (originally seventy-seven governments) in the series of sessions of the United Nations Conference on Trade and Development (UNCTAD)

GVN: Government of (South) Vietnam

IAM: Intelligence Analytical Memorandum

ICBM: Intercontinental ballistic missile

INR: Bureau of Intelligence and Research (State Department)

LDC: Less-developed country

Lome II: Negotiations of the European Community and associated countries of Africa, the Caribbean, and the Pacific. The series began at Lomé, Togo.

MBO: Management by objective

NFAC: National Foreign Assessment Center (CIA's Directorate for Intelligence during the Carter administration)

NIAM: National Intelligence Analytical Memorandum, coordinated among the agencies somewhat less elaborately than the National Intelligence Estimates (see NIE and NIC below)

NIC: National Intelligence Council (successor to the Board of National Estimates). The Council is a senior analysis arm of the DCI, comprising the National Intelligence Officers (NIOs) and their staff.

NID: *National Intelligence Daily*

NIE: National Intelligence Estimate, coordinated among agencies largely by the NIOs (see NIC above)

NIO: See NIC above

Noforn: The official definition is "classified intelligence that may not be released in any form to foreign governments, foreign nationals, or non-U.S. citizens without permission of the originator."

NPIC: National Photographic Interpretation Center (interagency, based in CIA). "Photographic" now comprises imagery in general.

NSCID: Intelligence Directive of the National Security Council (NSC)

OCI: Office of Current Intelligence (in CIA's Directorate for Intelligence)

OGSR: Office of Geographic and Societal Research (in CIA's Directorate for Intelligence)

OPC: Office of Policy Coordination (the covert action and paramilitary operations corps that was merged into CIA's Directorate for Plans/Operations in the early 1950s)

ORR: Office of Research and Reports (precursor to the Office of Geographic Research, the Office of Strategic Research, and the Office of Economic Research, all in CIA's Directorate for Intelligence)

OSI: Office of Scientific Intelligence (a component of the Directorate for Intelligence, which was merged in 1963 with other units to form the Directorate for Science and Technology)

OSR: Office of Strategic Research (in CIA's Directorate for Intelligence)

OTR: CIA's Office of Training

PHOTINT: Photographic intelligence (now part of imagery intelligence)

R & R: Rest and recreation

Secret: The level of classification designated by Executive Order 12356 for "information, the unauthorized disclosure of which reasonably could be expected to cause serious damage to the national security." The defined difference between this standard and "Confidential" (see above) is that "Secret" applies when the expected damage would be "serious."

Sihanoukville: A Cambodian port through which many more supplies moved to the Viet Cong than Americans recognized

Sitrep: Situation report

SNIE: Special National Intelligence Estimate (see NIE above)

SOVMAT: Intelligence specialization in the acquisition and exploitation of Soviet material supplies

TDY: Temporary duty assignment

T/O: Table of Organization

Acknowledgments

Disclosure of the mysteries of intelligence activities while they are still in practice requires some cooperation from the practitioners themselves, at least from the veterans. Their writings, their symposia, and especially their conversations—as clues to what to believe and whom to believe—deserve premier acknowledgment from me. Over a score of years I have, though an outsider, found myself warily trusted, enough to acquire the pieces to many puzzles about intelligence activities. For this openness I am very grateful, particularly to the veterans who have shared the most and who therefore know who they are.

The culminating opportunity has been to construct this book myself, selecting and editing a massive set of new disclosures from the Central Intelligence Agency. Initiating the project and continuously helpful, while always respectful of my autonomy, has been CIA's Center for the Study of Intelligence, especially David D. Gries, its innovative, "glasnost"-minded director during most of this enterprise; Jennifer Waring, whose dedicated efficiency repeatedly solved the recondite problems I encountered; and the Historical Review Group, which expeditiously declassified nearly everything I asked for.

I am grateful, too, to the individual authors, who all consented to have articles they had written originally for in-house consumption only—sometimes rather long ago—now be published to the world because they are still fresh and revealing.

At Yale University Press, the inspiration for the project came from Charles Grench, and Richard Miller was the principal editor; both were continuously helpful, perceptive, and sensitive to its unfamiliar complexities. Barbara O'Neill Phillips improved my prose and helped give the book its final integrated form. Marnie Wiss was painstaking and alert in her proofreading; remaining errors are surely my responsibility.

To teach is to learn from one's students and colleagues—in this instance especially from Mark R. Shulman and Carl E. Lackstrom at the beginning of the article selection process and from Professor Ernest R. May, of Harvard University, who gave valuable advice and encouragement.

For help in the final stage, the indexing, and in everything else I do professionally, I am deeply indebted to my fine secretary, Ruth Muessig, whose patient cheer and loyal aid make it all feasible.

My family, especially my dear wife Carolyn, have endured my roving researches longer than I like to remember. Her periodic nudging me to produce is probably good for me. The lifelong love and support certainly is—and gladly I reciprocate as best I can, always.

Index

Afghanistan, 239–40, 241, 253–54
Agency for International Development (AID), 161, 177–78, 180, 192–93
Agriculture Department, 161, 177–78, 326
Air Force, ix–x, 450–77 *passim. See also* Military attachés
Aliens in United States: targeted to be CIA contacts, 52, 60–62
Analysis function, 137n; in OSS/CIA history, viii, ix, x, xi, 123–24; collectors' reporting as preliminary analysis, xix, 99–107, 108–17, 137, 140, 141, 147, 194–96; politicization, xx, 352–54; and covert action, 120; relation between amount of information and accuracy of estimate, 218–26, 338–39; importance of models utilized, 224–27, 230–31; retrospective evaluation of analyses, 229–30, 333–43; failures, 238–54; forms of presentation of analysis, 354–60, 363–65; and counterespionage/deception, 379–414
—methodology, 238–92; and social science, xx, 255–92, 321–22; probabilistic vs. single-outcome predictions, 238–54; Bayesian approach, 255–73; social choice theories, 274–92
—personal and organizational relationships: among CIA analysts, 232–37; between CIA analysts and policymakers, 325, 344–56, 357–65; with Congress, 363
—*See also* Directorate for Intelligence (DI); Directorate for Operations (DO), reports of humint collectors, evaluated; Economic intelligence; Scientific and technological intelligence, analysis
Analysts. *See* Analysis function
Andersson, Ernst Hilding: Youth and recruitment as Soviet agent, 84–86; performance and handling, 86–92
Angleton, James J., ix, x, xxi. *See also* Directorate for Operations (DO), Counterintelligence (CI) Staff
Anissimov, Viktor, 85–87, 89, 91
Army Department, 123, 125, 126, 134
Assessing prospective agents and contacts, 56, 70–82, 444–47, 452–55, 458, 470

Bagley, Tennant ("Pete"), 383–414
Basic intelligence, 207–17, 309, 323
Blake, George, 388, 393
Board of National Estimates (BNE). *See* National Intelligence Council (NIC)
Britain, 168, 293, 300, 303
Bureau of Intelligence and Research (INR). *See* State Department
Bush, George H. W., xi, xx
Business people, American: targeted to be CIA contacts, 52–58

Casey, William, x–xi
Center for the Study of Intelligence: at CIA, xi, 118
Central Intelligence Agency (CIA). *See specific directorates and offices*
Cherepanov, Aleksandr, 404–406
Cherne, Leo, 152–58
China, 15–20, 22–26, 154, 240–46 *passim,* 264–73, 307, 308, 314
Church Committee, 157, 161, 183–84
Clandestine Service. *See* Directorate for Operations (DO)
Classification for security, xiv–xvii, xx–xxii
Cline, Ray S., 121, 124, 160
Commerce Department, 177–78, 180, 327, 329
Commission on the Organization of the Government for the Conduct of Foreign Policy. *See* Murphy Commission
Communications intelligence (comint). *See* Signals intelligence (sigint)

Compartmentation. *See* Security
Compensation, in humint: 58, 61–62, 87, 89, 447, 459–68 *passim*, 472, 473
Congress, U.S., xviii, 363
Counterespionage: and FBI, vii, viii, 53, 54, 61, 123, 404, 407–408, 464–77; in CIA history, ix, x, xi, xv, xvi, xviii, 131–34, 379–414; as defined by William R. Johnson, 13, 182–83; analysis in, 379–414; tradecraft, 438–49; and U.S. military, 450–77. *See also* Directorate for Operations (DO), Counterintelligence (CI) Staff; Interrogation
Counterintelligence. *See* Counterespionage
Cover, 150, 186–92 *passim*, 424–28 *passim;* as foreign-language interpreter, 29–34
Covert action, 120–21, 184; in CIA history, viii–xviii *passim*, 157–58
Cuba, 12–15, 240, 259–60, 262
Cutouts. *See* Intermediaries, humint

Data banks. *See* Basic intelligence
Deception analysis, 379–414
Defectors, 70–82, 379–414, 445–56
Defense Department, 138, 180; Defense Intelligence Agency (DIA), 197
Directorate for Administration (DA), 157–58
Directorate for Intelligence (DI): origins and history, viii, ix, x, xi, 123–24, 127, 129, 181; and *Studies in Intelligence,* xvi; Office of Reports and Estimates (ORE) and Office of Research and Reports (ORR), 127, 129, 134, 142, 306–10 *passim*, 315–20 *passim*, 323, 329; and intelligence watch officers and Operations Center, 144–48; Office of Economic Research (OER), 145, 306, 310–25 *passim*, 328–29, 367–72 *passim*
—Office of Current Intelligence (OCI), 121, 137, 175–84 *passim*, 251; origins, 126–43 *passim*, 151, 181, 309, 310, 317
—*See also* Analysis function; Directorate for Operations (DO), origins and history, reports of humint collectors; Economic intelligence; Human-source collection (humint), as CIA journalism
Directorate for Operations (DO), origins and history, viii, ix, x, xi, 127–40, 142–43, 151, 178; and *Studies in Intelligence,* xvi; Counterintelligence (CI) Staff, 131–34, 383–414; affected by Intelligence Watch Officers Group (IWOG), 144–48; career incentives, 148–50, 158, 171, 181; in Saigon during Vietnam War, 148–50, 171–72; "can do" spirit, 157, 163–67, 179, 188
—collection of economic intelligence, 116, 322, 326–27; on Japan and Western Europe, 116, 152–59, 311–12, 318–19, 323,
326–27, 375–76; for diplomatic negotiations, 200, 366–76
—reports of humint collectors, 99–117, 140, 141, 147, 175–76, 180, 183, 370; evaluated, 152–56, 158–62, 168, 171–72, 194–203
—and State Department, xix, 140, 150, 156–57, 177–80, 185–93; for economic reporting, xix, 152–59, 175–76, 200, 322, 326–27, 375–76; for political reporting, xix, 159–72, 175
—*See also* Analysis function, retrospective evaluation of analyses; Counterespionage; Directorate for Intelligence (DI), Office of Current Intelligence (OCI); Espionage; Human-source collection (humint)
Directorate for Plans (DDP). *See* Directorate for Operations (DO)
Directorate for Science and Technology (DS&T), and *Studies in Intelligence,* xvi
Domestic acquisition of foreign intelligence: U.S. citizens targeted as contacts, 51–60; contact officers, 51–62
Donovan, William J., 121–26
Double agents, xxi, 74–75, 131n; and Cold War suspects, 389–94, 397–98, 403–14; problems of handling, 437, 439–40, 443–49 *passim*, 456–77; defined, 438; recruitment, 438–40, 444–47, 452–54; problems of objectives, 440–43, 458–59, 464–77 *passim;* and case of counterespionage penetration, 450–77
Dulles, Allen W., xii, 134

Economic intelligence: overt humint collection, 41–48, 305, 322; for private U.S. firms, 293, 304, 305, 328; sigint collection, 312, 318, 323, 366, 368–69, 375; imint collection, 318, 323
—CIA analysis, 305–29, 354–56, 359–60, 369–76; governmental consumers of, 306, 311, 325
—*See also* Agency for International Development (AID); Agriculture Department; Commerce Department; Directorate for Operations (DO), collection of economic intelligence; Oil; Scientific and technological intelligence; Soviet Union, economy; State Department
Elicitation, humint, xix, 63–69, 154–55, 158
Espionage: in CIA's history, viii, ix, x, xi, xvi; tradecraft, xii, 63–71, 75, 83–96, 116, 118–84, 368–76 *passim;* and covert action, 120–21; contingent positioning of agents, 128–29, 132–33, 139, 170–71, 177–84; as defined by William R. Johnson, 131, 183–84. *See also* Double agents

Estimates. *See* Analysis function; National Intelligence Council (NIC)
Ethiopia, 239–40, 249–53

Federal Bureau of Investigation (FBI), vii, viii, 53, 54, 61, 123, 404, 407–408, 464–77
Felfe, Heinz, 382, 388, 390, 393, 413
Fieldhouse, Jack, 386, 392
Foreign Broadcast Information Service (FBIS), 180, 181
Foreign Service. *See* State Department
Friendly countries: their nationals as targets of CIA recruitment, 63–69; as targets for U.S. collection, 115, 116, 304, 311–12, 318–19, 323, 326, 375–76

Gates, Robert M., xx, 353
Germany, West, 63–69
Goleniewski, Michal, 388, 389, 393, 413
Golitsyn, Anatoliy, 379–414 *passim*

Handling of agents and contacts: humint, 56–58, 61–62, 86–92, 437, 439–40, 443–49 *passim*, 456–77
Hart, John, 385, 386, 410
Helms, Richard M., 383, 384, 385
Human-source collection (humint), x, xv, xviii, xix, xxi, 297; clandestine, xviii, xix; overt, xviii–xix, 29–48; as CIA journalism, xix, xx, 118–19, 140–43, 145–51, 159, 171–74, 179; domestic semi-clandestine, 51–62, 180, 194–200, 322. *See also* Directorate for Operations (DO), reports of humint collectors; Espionage; *President's Daily Brief*

Imagery intelligence (imint), ix–x, xi, xvi, xviii, xix, 3–26, 245–46, 297, 318, 323, 360
Intelligence cycle, xvii–xviii, 175
Interior Department, 326
Intermediaries, humint, 58
Interpreters as agents, 29–34
Interrogation, xxi, 381–86, 392, 394–414
—and resistance to it: 406, 410–11, 448; in prison, 92, 418–35; preparing for possible arrest, 415–17; confronting actual arrest, 416–20, 427; getting out, 433–36
Iran, 241
Italy: *1983* budget issue, 277–78

Jones, Reginald V., 293–94

Kennedy, John F., 260
Kent, Sherman, xii–xiv, xxii, 129, 173–74, 194, 203, 353
KGB (Komitet Gosudarstvennoy Bezopastnosti), 379–414 *passim*

Labor Department, 161
Liaison with foreign intelligence services, xvi, xix, 168–71, 443, 449
Libraries. *See* Basic intelligence
Libya, 239–40, 241
Loginov, Yuriy, 405–406, 411
Lonsdale, Gordon A., 83
Loyalty: and defectors' childhood, 76–78

Mail interception, 65
Material acquisition and exploitation, 6–7
Meissner, Charles, 367–68, 370, 373–74
Military attachés, 35–40, 161, 165, 172, 177–78
Moses, Hans, 450–77
Murphy Commission, 158, 160, 162, 179, 192

National Intelligence Council (NIC, formerly Board of National Estimates), xii, 124, 239–54 *passim*, 309, 355–56, 360
National Intelligence Estimate (NIE). *See* National Intelligence Council (NIC)
National Intelligence Officers (NIOs). *See* National Intelligence Council (NIC)
National Intelligence Survey (NIS). *See* Basic intelligence
National Reconnaissance Office (NRO). *See* Imagery intelligence (imint)
National Security Agency (NSA). *See* Signals intelligence (sigint)
Navy Department, 123, 126
Nicaragua, 239–40
North, Oliver, x–xi
Nosenko, Yuriy, xxi, 379–414; history of case, 380–86, 388–92, 400–402, 408–10, 413–14; official reviews of case, 383–86; application of criteria for determining suspected deception, 386–414
Novikov, Yuriy, 467–74

Office of Current Intelligence (OCI). *See* Directorate for Intelligence (DI), Office of Current Intelligence (OCI)
Office of National Estimates (ONE). *See* National Intelligence Council (NIC)
Office of Policy Coordination (OPC). *See* Directorate for Operations (DO), origins and history
Office of Reports and Estimates (ORE). *See* Directorate for Intelligence (DI), Office of Reports and Estimates (ORE) and Office of Research and Reports (ORR)
Office of Research and Reports (ORR). *See* Directorate for Intelligence (DI), Office of Reports and Estimates (ORE) and Office of Research and Reports (ORR)

Office of Special Operations (OSO). *See* Directorate for Operations (DO), origins and history

Office of Strategic Services (OSS), viii, x, xii, 121–26

Office of Training (OTR), 132n

Oil, 241, 247–49, 312–13, 316–17, 326, 372, 373, 375

Open-source documents collection, xviii, xx. *See also* Basic intelligence

Organization of Petroleum Exporting Countries (OPEC). *See* Oil

Orlov, Nicolai, 91–92

Oswald, Lee Harvey, 381, 395–96, 402

Overhead reconnaissance. *See* Imagery intelligence (imint)

Paramilitary operations, 120; in CIA's history, viii, ix–xi, xvi

Penkovskiy, Oleg, 389, 397, 403

Philby, Harold Adrian Russell ("Kim"), 382, 388, 393

Philippines, 284–91 *passim*

Photo-interpretation. *See* Imagery intelligence (imint)

Photo-reconnaissance. *See* Imagery intelligence (imint)

Political intelligence. *See* State Department; Directorate for Operations (DO)

Polygraph, 430

Ponger, Kurt, 450–60, 474–75

Popov, Pyotr, 389, 403, 404

President's Daily Brief, 121–26, 134–35, 148, 353, 359

President's Foreign Intelligence Advisory Board (PFIAB), 152, 328

Professionalism at CIA, xi–xiv

Psychological profiles, humint, 70–82, 445–46

Reagan, Ronald, x–xi, 360

Reconnaissance, overhead. *See* Imagery intelligence (imint)

Recruitment of agents and contacts, 56, 74–75, 85–86, 444–47, 452–54

Reference services. *See* Basic intelligence

Relinquishment. *See* Directorate for Operations (DO), and State Department

Roosevelt, Franklin D., 122–25

Satellite reconnaissance. *See* Imagery intelligence (imint)

Scientific and technological intelligence: multi-source collection, 3–7; humint collection, 63–69

—analysis, 293–304; quality of U.S. analysts, 247; kinds of Cold War problem cases,

294–97; sources, 297–98, 303–304; maxims of, 299–304; contractors, 301–302; compartmentation, 303; civil technology of friendly countries, 304

Scoville, Herbert, Jr., 172–83

Security, xxi, 86–96 *passim,* 128–35 *passim,* 190, 444–49 *passim,* 455–57, 461–68 *passim,* 470–76 *passim;* and usability of intelligence, 113–14, 303, 369, 373. *See also* Classification for security; Federal Bureau of Investigation (FBI); Soviet Union, obstacles to foreign military attachés

Senate Select Committee to Study Governmental Operations with Respect to Intelligence Activities (*1975–76*). *See* Church Committee

Signals intelligence (sigint), viii, x, xv, xviii, xix, 297, 312, 318, 323, 360

Solie, Bruce, 384, 385, 407, 408, 413–14

Soviet Union, 154; nuclear weapons, 3–7, 241, 246–47, 299; obstacles to foreign military attachés, 35–40; economy, CIA exploration of, 41–48, 307–308, 314–19 *passim,* 324–25; and Cuba, 259–60, 262; split from China, 264–73; intelligence services of, 379–414 *passim,* 438, 450–77; interrogation methods, 415–33

Spotting prospective agents and contacts, 52–56, 63–69, 140

State Department, xix, 123, 126, 134–35, 138, 140; Bureau of Intelligence and Research (INR), 134, 166, 168, 170, 175, 184, 189–90, 197, 309; attitudes of Foreign Service Officers, 162–67, 179, 181, 184, 185–93. *See also* Directorate for Operations (DO), and State Department

Statesman's Yearbook, 209

Stewart, Gordon, 383, 385, 413

Studies in Intelligence, xii–xvii, xix–xxii, 41, 207

Sweden, 83–92

Tasking: of analysts, 325, 365, 370

—humint, xix, 56, 111–12, 181; a Soviet case, 83, 86, 87, 89, 92; a U.S. case, 93–94, 95; and consumers of humint, 114–16, 141, 172–73, 176, 201–202, 370, 371, 374–75; a double-agent case, 456, 458–60, 468–72, 476–77

Taylor, Rufus, 383, 385

Technical-source intelligence (techint). *See* Imagery intelligence (imint); Signals intelligence (sigint)

Treasury Department, 123, 158, 161, 177–78, 180, 322, 327

Truman, Harry S, 125, 126

Truth drugs, xxi

U-2 reconnaissance planes. *See* Imagery intelligence (imint)

United Nations Conference on Trade and Development (UNCTAD), 366–76

United States Information Agency (USIA), 161, 177–78, 180, 192–93

University personnel, American: targeted to be CIA contacts, 52, 58–60

Verber, Otto, 450–60, 474–75

Vietnam, 148–51, 171, 240

Vinogradov, Konstantin, 85

Walk-ins: humint, 70–82, 438–39, 444–47

War Department. *See* Army Department

Warning, 144–48, 257–59, 264

Watch officers: impact on Directorate for Operations (DO), 144–48